MISTRESSES:
A HISTORY OF THE OTHER WOMAN

A History of Celibacy

Sugar

A History of Marriage

Haiti

ELIZABETH ABBOTT

Mistresses: A History of the Other Woman

Duckworth Overlook

LONDON & NEW YORK

This edition first published in the United States
and the United Kingdom in 2010 by Overlook Duckworth

NEW YORK:
The Overlook Press
Peter Mayer Publishers, Inc.
141 Wooster Street
New York, NY 10012
www.overlookpress.com
For bulk and special sales, please contact sales@overlookny.com

LONDON:
Gerald Duckworth Publishers Ltd.
90-93 Cowcross Street
London EC1M 6BF
www.ducknet.co.uk
info@duckworth-publishers.co.uk

First published by HarperFlamingo Canada,
an imprint of HarperCollins Publishers Ltd

© 2003, 2010 by Elizabeth Abbott

Excerpts from *The Concubine's Children:*
The Story of a Chinese Family Living on Two Sides of the Globe
by Denise Chong, Copyright © 1994 by Denise Chong.
Reprinted by permission of Penguin Books Canada Limited

Cataloging-in-Publication Data is available from the Library of Congress
A catalogue record for this book is available from the British Library

Manufactured in the United States of America

2 4 6 8 10 9 7 5 3 1

ISBN 978-1-59020-443-6 US
ISBN 978-0-7156-3946-7 UK

To the memory of my aunt
Margaret Abbott Cameron,
Canada's first female race car driver

Contents

AUTHOR'S NOTE   xiv

INTRODUCTION

Meeting Mistresses   1

CHAPTER 1

Love out of Wedlock
in the Ancient World   10

Hagar 11 · Aspasia 13
Corinna 19 · Dolorosa 28

CHAPTER 2

Eastern Concubines and Harems 34

CONCUBINES IN CHINA 34 · Yu-fang 38 · May-ying 39
CONCUBINES IN JAPAN 44 · Lady Nijo 46
GEISHA MISTRESSES 48
HAREM CONCUBINES 53 · Roxelana 53 · Tz'u-hsi 59

CHAPTER 3

Whose Whore? Europe's Royal Mistresses 71

Nell Gwynne 72 · Jeanne-Antoinette de Pompadour 77
Jeanne du Barry 83 · Lola Montez 88 · Katharina Schratt 91
Alice Keppel 96 · Elena Lupescu 99
Camilla Parker-Bowles 106

CHAPTER 4

Marital Arrangements in Aristocratic Circles 115

Lady Bess Foster and Georgiana, Duchess of Devonshire 115
Lady Caroline Lamb 123 · Claire Clairmont 130
Countess Teresa Guiccioli 135

CHAPTER 5

The Clandestine Consorts
of (Un)Celibate Clerics 144

THE PRIEST'S "HOUSEKEEPER" 147
PAPAL MISTRESSES 153 · Theodora and Marozia Theophylact 153
Vanozza d'Arignano and Giulia Farnese 156
THE MODERN CLERICAL MISTRESS 161
Annie Murphy 164 · Louise Iusewicz 169
Pamela Shoop 172

CHAPTER 6

Conquerors
and Their Mistresses 176

SPANISH CONQUISTADORS AND NATIVE WOMEN 176 · Malinche 176
"COUNTRY WIVES" IN COLONIAL AMERICA 183
Sally Fidler, Betsey Sinclair and Margaret Taylor 187
MISTRESSES IN CONQUERED ASIA 190
Le Ly Hayslip and Dao Thi Mui 191

CHAPTER 7

Interracial Sexual Unions
Within the "Peculiar Institution" 195

Phibbah 197 · Julia Chinn 202 · Sally Hemings 204
Julia Frances Lewis Dickson 208
Harriet Jacobs 215

CHAPTER 8

Sexual Unions and the Jewish Question 225

CONCENTRATION CAMP LIFE BEFORE DEATH 227
Eleanore Hodys 234
"PARTISAN" FOREST CAMPS 236
EVA BRAUN: MISTRESS TO THE AUTHOR OF THE SHOAH 238
JEW AND GENTILE, BEYOND THE CAMPS 249
Hannah Arendt 249

CHAPTER 9

Mistresses as Muses 258

Héloise 259 · Émilie du Châtelet 264 · Jeanne Hébuterne 271
George Eliot 275 · Lillian Hellman 284 · Catherine Walston 293
Joyce Maynard 304

CHAPTER 10

Mistresses of Men Above the Law 313

MOBSTER MOLLS 313 · Virginia Hill 313 · Arlyne Brickman 320
Sandy Sadowsky, Georgia Durante and Shirley Ryce 323
KREMLIN DOLLS 326
CASTRO'S COMRADES 327
Naty Revuelta 328 · Celia Sanchez 339

CHAPTER 11

Mistresses as Trophy Dolls 344

Marion Davies 344 · Gloria Swanson 359 · Maria Callas 366
Marilyn Monroe 377 · Judith Campbell 388 · Vicki Morgan 393

CHAPTER 12

Fallen Women:
Mistresses in Literature 401

Jane Eyre 401 · Hester Prynne 404 · Emma Bovary 408
Anna Karenina 413 · Mildred Rogers 415 · Ellen Olenska 419
Lara 423 · Sarah Miles 427 · Merrion Palmer 429

CHAPTER 13

The 1960s Transform Marriage
and Mistressdom 433

Pamela Digby Churchill Hayward Harriman 435 · Lillian Ross 439
Simone de Beauvoir 442 · Paula 448 · Rachel 451 · Michaela 454

CONCLUSION

Mistresses Met 458

ENDNOTES 465
ACKNOWLEDGMENTS 495
INDEX 497

AUTHOR'S NOTE

IN my Introduction, I refer to Kati and Ghislaine, two mistresses of my own acquaintance. To avoid possible embarrassment to these women, I have changed their names and those of their partners. These aliases, however, in no way detract from the authenticity of their stories.

In chapters 3, 8 and 13, I have used the word *Shoah* rather than *Holocaust*. The term *Shoah* is preferred by many Jewish scholars, because it refers specifically to the Jewish experience during World War II, while *holocaust* is a more generic word describing any "great destruction or loss of life."

I have provided bibliography-style endnotes that include the main sources for each section. After that, only direct quotations or concepts are referenced. This endnote style eliminates the need for a formal bibliography, and makes it much easier to locate source material by subject.

Introduction:
Meeting Mistresses

I GREW up knowing about mistresses because my great-grandfather Stephen Adelbert Griggs, an affluent Detroit brewer and municipal politician, maintained what my mother scornfully referred to as a "love nest" occupied by a series of "fancy" women. Great-grandmother Minnie Langley had to tolerate this, but she exacted a price: for every diamond Stephen bought his latest mistress, he had to buy one for her. This was how his love nest hatched a glittering nest egg of rings, earrings, brooches and uncut gems, which Minnie bequeathed to her female descendants.

Great-grandfather Stephen walked a well-trodden path. I realized this as I matured and met real mistresses and their lovers. The first, whom I encountered during the summer after my freshman year in university, was a young woman who shared her sometimes exciting but mostly wretched experiences with me. Katerina was an exotic, sloe-eyed East German who fled to West Berlin two weeks before her high school graduation, forfeiting her diploma in exchange for freedom. Kati was a governess—actually, an exalted babysitter—for the same family that employed me during summer vacation at their resort hotel in Quebec's Eastern Townships. Despite (perhaps because of) my parents' objections, she and I developed a curious sort of intimacy. What they frowned on as fast and cheap, I admired as sophisticated—Kati's lean, tanned and flat-chested body proudly exposed by her signature strapless tops; the hennaed rope of hair that swung nearly to her knees; the guttural, heavy accent that transformed me into "Elisabess," or "Bess" for short.

That first summer, Kati was not yet a mistress. In fact, she longed to be a wife and was actually engaged to marry Charles, an RCMP officer who came calling in a long, white Cadillac convertible. But after Charles abruptly called off their wedding, Kati's never very stable life fell precipitously apart. Not long after that, I returned to Montreal for my second year of university.

A History of Mistresses

A few months later, Kati resurfaced in my life when she phoned and practically begged me to bring her a bag of groceries. She had money, she explained, but was temporarily bedridden and could not go out shopping. Kati had become the kept woman of a married lawyer who grudgingly supported her in a cramped room sublet from the unfriendly tenant of a shabby apartment. Unexpectedly, she had become pregnant.

I bought Kati the food she requested. My modest gift, it turned out, was all that she had for post-abortion sustenance. She had endured an illegal abortion alone, the abortionist having prudently banned anyone but his "clients" from his premises. I tried to ease her through the bout of severe depression that followed; shortly thereafter we resumed our very different lives.

Over the years, I saw Kati less and less. The last time was on a lake in Quebec's Laurentian Mountains. She was perched on the bow of a powerboat, her stunning mane loose and whipped by the wind. I called out and waved, and the man at the helm of her boat slowed down and steered over to my smaller craft. Kati seemed startled to see me, and she immediately put her forefinger to her lips as if to forestall my embarrassing her in front of her glamorous companions. I understood, greeted her briefly, then smiled goodbye. I never saw her again, but I heard that she had married and then divorced. For a long time afterward, when anybody spoke about mistresses, an image of Kati came into my mind.

I was living in Haiti when I met Ghislaine Jeudi, the mistress of a man who had returned there after decades in the United States. In New York City, Jerome Constant had made a fortune in the numbers racket. In Port-au-Prince, he reinvented himself as a respectable businessman. Constant had closets full of white linen suits and a locked chest full of gold jewelry, but his finest acquisition, the one that made him happiest, was Ghislaine, his light-skinned, blondish, swaggering and middle-aged mistress. Ghislaine was certainly attractive, and in hungry Haiti her portly girth seemed provocative and sexy. She was also a recent convert to evangelical Christianity, and spouted scriptural aphorisms on every occasion except, of course, when challenged about the morality of her position as the mistress of a married man.

The fact was, Jerome Constant had no intention of divorcing his wife, no matter what reprisals his mistress threatened. Ghislaine's tenure was secure only as long as his love for her lasted. Knowing this, she made sure that his investment in her compensated for her insecurity. Besides providing clothes, jewelry and overseas trips, Constant built her a house, contributed heavily to one for her adult daughter and provided bountiful spending money. Though he complained about how much she cost him, the truth was that he adored Ghislaine and was immensely proud of her.

One of her principal attractions was her much-talked-about sexual history. In the early 1960s, Ghislaine had been one of the first of Haiti's privileged mulatto women to ally herself with one of dictator "Papa Doc" Duvalier's Tonton Macoutes, armed thugs who constituted the civilian militia Duvalier had created to protect himself against his own army and other potential enemies. Ghislaine felt no shame, and never apologized for consorting with the savage men who persecuted other mulattos (and anyone else they suspected of opposing their leader-for-life). But no matter how contemptuously others referred to Ghislaine, Constant admired her for her bravado, her notoriety, her beauty and her steadfast (though admittedly far from disinterested) loyalty to him. Even when his health deteriorated and he was robbed of his sexual potency, his union with Ghislaine was too precious to contemplate ending. "Her senses flow with my senses" was how he explained the bond with his mistress.

I was never close to Ghislaine, but even after I returned to North America, I sometimes thought about her and recalled how shrewdly she parlayed her emotional command of her lover into tangible collateral. Yet it was neither Ghislaine nor my long-ago friend Kati who inspired me to write about mistresses. It was while writing my book A History of Celibacy that I came to realize that mistressdom, like celibacy, is a crucial lens through which to explore how women relate to men other than in marriage; mistressdom is, in fact, an institution parallel and complementary to marriage. Even before I finished writing A History of Celibacy, I was already beginning the research for what has become A History of Mistresses.

There were sources in abundance, including in the daily news; mistresses, it seemed, were everywhere. In 1997, for example, when prominent journalist Charles Kuralt died, Patricia Shannon, his mistress of twenty-nine years, launched a successful claim to part of his estate. In 2000, Toronto mayor Mel Lastman's former mistress, Grace Louie, announced that he had sired her (Mel look-alike) sons, Kim and Todd. In 2001, the Reverend Jesse Jackson's mistress, lawyer Karin Stanford, sued for child support for their two-year-old daughter, Ashley, already in utero as Jackson advised and prayed for President Bill Clinton, under attack for his relationship with intern Monica Lewinsky. (Simultaneously with prosecuting Clinton, the self-righteous Newt Gingrich was secretly pursuing a passionate relationship with Callista Bisek, whom he married after divorcing his wife, Marianne.) I began to make lists and take notes, trying to understand the nature of these relationships, the modern as well as the historic.

As in the past, today's presidents and princes also succumb to their desires and take mistresses, though they, too, risk exposure by scandal sheets and mainstream media (unless, like French president Francois Mitterand, they were impervious to criticism and enabled by a docile press; Mitterand lived with his primary mistress, museum curator Anne Pingeot and their daughter, Mazarine, while his wife, Danielle, remained in the family home. At Mitterand's 1996 funeral, the three mourning women stood side by side, as he would have expected.) President Dwight D. Eisenhower had a very special "friend," the Englishwoman Kay Sommersby. JFK dallied with many women, including film idol Marilyn Monroe. Though rivaled in prominence by the story of President Bill Clinton and unforgettable White House intern Monica Lewinsky, the longest-running scandal belongs to England's Prince Charles. When I began my book, he was in disgrace. Years later, widowed and remarried to hislongtime mistress, Camilla Parker-Bowles, his image and hers have been largely rehabilitated.

Legions of other provocative unions are replacing Charles' and Camilla's in the spotlight. Champion golfer Tiger Woods' multitudinous sexual partners included only one, Rachel Uchitel, whom he treated as a mistress rather than a casual fling. But politicians in a steady and adulterous stream have mistresses, and often media "scoops" are the first inkling their wives have that their husbands have been betrayuing them.

US presidential hopeful and former Senator John Edwards ignored his fear that "Falling in love with you could really fuck up my plans for becoming President" and capitulated to his passion for Rielle Hunter, who likened it to a "magnetic force." Edwards was prescient: their affair destroyed his career and shattered his marriage to his cancer-stricken wife Elizabeth Edwards. It also produced a daughter, Quinn.

So did New York Congressman Vito Fossella Jr.'s affair with Laura Fay, a retired Air Force Lieutenant Colonel; Natalie was three years old when Fossella incurred a DUI charge while on his way to visit his mistress and their daughter.

Congressman Mark Souder, an evangelical Christian, resigned in 2010, repentant (he said) for having "sinned against God, my wife and my family by having a mutual relationship with a part-time member of my staff." Ironically, he and his married mistress, Tracy Meadows Jackson recorded a web video urging youth to abstain from sex "until in a committed, faithful relationship."

Governor Mark Sanford, caught out in adultery, admitted his infidelity to wife Jenny with his Argentinean mistress and "soul mate," Maria Belen Chapur. But he could not give her up. The scandal escalated, he resigned and Jenny divorced him. Afterward, Sanford continued to pursue his relationship with Chapur.

California State Assemblyman Mike Duvall, winner of an Ethics in America award, was a more cavalier lover forced to resign after an open microphone broadcast him bragging that "I've been getting into spanking her [one of his two mistresses]. I like it."

British radio and television presenter Jonathan Dimbleby's brief affair with his dying mistress was the most dramatic and obsessive, and it destroyed his until-then happy marriage of thirty-five years. In May 2003, Dimbleby interviewed the magnificent soprano Susan Chilcott, found her enchanting and began to sleep with her. Days later, Susan was diagnosed with terminal metastasized breast cancer. Against her anguished pleas that her very new lover consider his own well-being and not ruin his life for her, Dimbleby vowed to care for her until she died, and moved in with her and her little son. "I still do not adequately understand the intensity of passion and pity that animated my decision," he said later.

It felt like an unstoppable force. I knew what I was doing but I didn't know what the outcome would be. It was odd, but I didn't want to be away from Bel either – I felt absolutely torn. But I was entranced; and then of course we didn't know how long she had – it might have been a few weeks or months or it might have been a few years. It was a very powerful, overwhelming experience and also a kind of test.

Part of that test was watching Susan's last public performance, playing Desdemona and, garbed in white linen, singing sorrowfully, her voice rising to a crescendo, "Ch'io viva ancor, ch'io viva ancor!" (Let me live longer, let me live longer!)

Less than three months later, Susan died and Bel Mooney, Jonathan's wife, waited for her husband to return home to her and say, "That madness is over, let us pick up the threads of our life again." He did not, Bel moved out and on, and their tattered marriage unravelled into divorce. Susan Chilcott and Jonathan Dimbleby's love affair was fleeting and fuelled as much by her impending death as by passion. Push back its timing to an earlier century or set it on the stage of a romantic tragedy and it looks exactly as it did at the end of the 20th century, in cosmopolitan England.

After years of research, what interested me was the structure and common denominators of the relationships between men and their mistresses, especially how mistressdom reflects the nature of marriage and male-female relations in different eras and cultures. After much deliberation, I decided to frame my exploration of mistressdom through the perspective of individual mistresses whose experiences tell the story of men and women's relationships in their society. By grouping these women into categories that reflect different cultures and historical periods, I could present their unique circumstances while also drawing conclusions about their society's versions of what a mistress was and how its men and women lived together. The result of this approach to my material was that I titled my book *A History of Mistresses*.

From the outset, as I researched, reflected and contemplated how to interpret my material, I struggled with the question of definition. Classic dictionary definitions were only marginally helpful, especially as it became clearer to me that Eastern concubines belonged in this book every bit as much as Western mistresses. In The New Shorter Oxford English Dictionary, a mistress is "a woman other than a wife with whom a man has a long-standing sexual relationship," while a concubine is "a woman who cohabits with a man without being his wife." These definitions are too vague to be very useful, and the latter does not distinguish between a concubine and a common-law wife, nor does it clearly describe the Eastern concubine, who frequently but by no means always lives with her lover-master and his family. Another problem is that in the Western world, the words mistress and concubine are often used synonymously. In *A History of Mistresses*, I decided to use a working definition of mistress as a woman voluntarily or forcibly engaged in a relatively long-term sexual relationship with a man who is usually married to another woman. This definition applies to concubines as well, whose particularities are further discussed in the chapters devoted to their cultures.

Mistressdom is inextricably linked with marriage, human society's most fundamental institution, and almost automatically implies marital infidelity, sometimes by the husband, sometimes by the wife. Indeed, marriage is a key element in determining who is a mistress and who is not. Though many people assume that adultery undermines marriage, many others believe that, paradoxically, it shores marriage up. Frenchmen, for example, can justify the cinq à sept, the after-office-hours rendezvous a man enjoys with his mistress, by quoting French writer Alexandre Dumas's pithy observation: "The chains of marriage are so heavy that it often takes two people to carry them, and sometimes three."

This association between marriage and mistressdom, and also Eastern concubinage, extends through time and place, and is deeply ingrained in almost every major culture. British multibillionaire Sir Jimmy Goldsmith, who died surrounded by wife, ex-wives and mistresses, commented famously that "when a man marries his mistress, he creates an automatic job vacancy." Not surprisingly, Western models are more familiar to North Americans than those of the Eastern world, with their different and more elaborate versions, notably institutionalized concubinage and harems.

In all societies and at all times, the custom of arranged marriages has been most likely to produce mistressdom and concubinage because parents or other relatives selected their children's spouses for economic reasons or to cement family, business or political alliances and usually dismissed romantic love as an irrelevant, self-indulgent and sometimes even treacherous foundation for a marital relationship. Husbands and wives were expected to cohabit and operate as an economic unit, and to produce and raise children. They were not expected to quiver at each other's touch, to adore one another or to fulfil each other's emotional needs.

Sometimes romantic love developed after the fact but more often, regard, tolerance and resignation were as much as anyone could hope for, and many marriages were desperately unhappy. All but the most puritanical societies permitted men unwilling to suppress or sublimate their romantic and lustful urges to satisfy them extramaritally by taking mistresses or concubines. Women, however, were almost always discouraged from straying and punished severely if they were caught. Many went ahead and took the risk.

The unbreachable chasms of class and caste have also created mistresses who might otherwise have been wives. Saint Augustine, the 4th-century bishop of Hippo, subscribed to his North African society's proscription against marrying below one's class, and so he lived with the lower-ranked woman he loved as his concubine. When he decided to marry, his mother found a suitably well-born girl.

Caste determined by nationality, race or religion can also relegate women to the lower status of mistress. Xenophobic ancient Greece, for instance, forbade its citizens to marry foreigners, so the Athenian leader Pericles could never marry Aspasia, his beloved Miletian concubine and the mother of his son.

In many Eastern cultures, concubinage was integral rather than peripheral or parallel to marriage, and concubines' duties and rights were spelled out in the law or in social custom. Concubines frequently lived in their master's house, under the same roof with his wife and other concubines. In modest homes, a concubine or two assisted the wife in her daily chores. Concubines were bound by wife-like sexual obligations, including fidelity, and confined to the same domestic sphere. There were excellent reasons for this. In sharp contrast to Western mistresses, one of the principal duties of most Eastern concubines was to bear their masters' heirs.

In a few countries, notably imperial China and Turkey, some royals, aristocrats and men of privilege displayed their wealth and power by maintaining harems of concubines, often captured or purchased. Their crowded, eunuch-run harems were turbulent communities where intrigue, competition and conflict—to say nothing of children—proliferated. Older and less-favored harem concubines were drudges consigned to household labor. Their still hopeful younger colleagues filled their empty days with meticulous grooming and plotting, with and against eunuchs, wives, relatives, children, servants and each other. Their goal was to spend a night with their harem's owner and, if they were extraordinarily lucky, to conceive the child who could catapult his mother from obscurity into a life of privilege and perhaps even power.

In stark contrast, the laws of Western societies have almost always reinforced the primacy of marriage by bastardizing the offspring of mistresses, from the lowest-born slave to the highest-ranked duchess. Legally and culturally, fathers had no obligation to accept responsibility for their natural children and couldcondemn them to the ignominy and perils of illegitimacy. Indeed, the law often made it difficult, even for men so inclined, to recognize and provide for their "outside" children.

Yet some men defied their society's strictures against supporting their illegitimate children. Royals such as England's Charles II, who elevated so many of his mistresses' sons to dukedoms that five of today's twenty-six dukes are their descendants, assumed that their bloodlines were exalted enough to outweigh such niceties as legitimacy. Commoners driven by personal passions also flouted their society's values. A few slave owners, for example, risked serious reprisals from their profoundly racist compatriots by acknowledging paternity of a slave mistress's children. In the Western world, however, acknowledging bastards has always been the exception to the rule.

Today's mistress rightly expects better treatment for any child she might have with a lover. Like her precursors, she is the bellwether for female-male relations, and her status reflects how these relations have developed. The improving condition of women, the liberalization of the laws governing families and personal relationships, and the growing acceptance of DNA tests have greatly increased the likelihood that her lover will recognize, or at least contribute to the support of, her child. (John Edwards is an egregious example of this. After requesting an aide to pinch one of Frances Quinn's diapers for a secret DNA test to determine whether or not he was her father, he systemically denied that he could be or was the father until, irreparably tarnished by a public trail of falsehoods, he admitted paternity and sought forgiveness, especially from Elizabeth, his furious wife.) At the same time, the advent of accessible and reliable birth control and of legalized abortion has substantially diminished the number of those children a mistress is likely to have.

And yet, like Rielle Hunter, mistresses do have children with their lovers. Some, like Karin Stanford, have to do battle for their children's rights. Others, like François Mitterand and Vito Fossella, Jr. offer secret financial support. But even these cooperative fathers cannot guarantee that their legitimate children will take kindly to their "outside" siblings. Ashley Stanford-Jackson's mother complains publicly that her daughter's siblings have no interest in her. And Mitterrand's son, Jean-Christophe, snubbed Mazarine in the hospital where both were visiting their father. "As long as my father doesn't speak of this young woman, for me she doesn't exist," he told friends. When she was thirty-four years old, Mazarine assumed the legal surname of Pingeot-Mitterrand, explaining "For nineteen years I was nobody's daughter, but I've finally decided to add my father's name to my identity papers."

An even more extraordinary case was that of African-American Essie Mae Washington-Williams, daughter of sixteen-year-old domestic Carrie Butler and her employer's twenty-two-year-old son, Strom Thurmond, a politician who died, still in public office, aged one hundred, and was notorious for his relentless advocacy of racial segregation. "There's not enough troops in the army to force the Southern people to break down segregation and admit the nigra race into our theaters, into our swimming pools, into our homes, and into our churches," he thundered. "He became an outright racist, cloaked in the ancient doctrine of states' rights," Essie Mae recalled. He sounded "like the ghost of Adolph Hitler."

But in private, Thurmond offered financial support and was keenly interested in and proud of his bi-racial daughter. They first met when Essie Mae was a teenager, when she and her mother visited his office. "He never called my mother by her first name. He didn't verbally acknowledge that I was his child. He didn't ask when I was leaving and didn't invite me to come back. It was like an audience with an important man, a job interview, but not a reunion with a father," Williams wrote. Yet she left it convinced that her mother's relationship with Thurmond was ongoing and that they cared for each other.

At Thurmond's recommendation, Essie Mae attended an all-black college now known as South Carolina State University. He paid her tuition and arranged occasional visits in the privacy of the office of the college President, who must have guessed at or known the nature of their relationship. So did Thurmond's sister, Mary Tompkins, whom he delegated at least once to bring money to Essie Mae.

Yet Essie Mae never revealed her father's identity. "It's not that Strom Thurmond ever swore me to secrecy. He never swore me to anything. He trusted me, and I respected him, and we loved each other in our deeply repressed ways, and that was our social contract," she wrote.

Thurmond died in 2003 and only then, in Dear Senator: A Memoir by the Daughter of Strom Thurmond, did Essie Mae disclose what Thurmond's colleagues and friends had long suspected. The Thurmond family publicly confirmed her paternity and spoke of her right to know her heritage. (It helped that she had no interest in suing for a share of her father's estate – her moral and legal right.) Her half-brother, Strom Thurmond Jr., added that he was eager to get to know her. In 2004, South Carolina's Governor Mark Sanford added her name to the list of children engraved on a public monument commemorating Thurmond. Times were changing, even in South Carolina.

But in those societies where time stands still, mistresses and concubines closely resemble their forbears. One such realm is the Roman Catholic Church, which steadfastly nurtures its deep-rooted mistrust of women, notably in its refusal to ordain them, and which rejects abolishing the compulsory celibacy that is an insuperable obstacle to clerical marriage. Women intimately involved with priests today tread the same path as they would have in past centuries: they are passed off as housekeepers and forced to hide their true relationship behind aprons and floor mops. The Church still views these women as temptresses and vehicles of sin and, just as with the sexual abuse of children by its religious, is concerned primarily with damage control and concealing the situation from the outside world.

Feminism, expanded women's rights and effective and accessible birth control have altered mistressdom, its parameters and its possibilities. As sexual mores surrounding pre-marital sex have relaxed and common-law living arrangements become increasingly the norm, the line between mistress and girlfriend has blurred. In many cases today, the answer must lie in the partners' perception of their status and, to a certain extent, in society's. Modern mistresses are less likely than their forbears to be married or to depend financially on their lovers. Today's mistresses fall in love, usually with married men unwilling to divorce and regularize the relationship. The only alternative to breaking up is to reconcile themselves to an illicit relationship. But often these mistresses are reluctant to accept the status quo, and they hope that somehow, someday, their liaison will be legitimized through marriage, as Camilla Parker Bowles' was.

Introduction: Meeting Mistresses

Just as often, the love affair itself—the romance and the passion, the arousal of desire and its delirious fulfillment—is what matters. Even if guilt coexists with the excitement of sexual adventure and the challenge of defying social norms, that does not negate the bonding force of shared secrecy and the mutual trust underlying it. The relationship's forbidden dimension also affects its balance of power, which is in part controlled by the unmarried mistress's restraint and discretion. Though it forces on her considerable free time, especially during traditional holidays, it also liberates her from wifely domesticity into the mode and mystique of showing only her best face and her best behavior. The relationship may also feel or actually be egalitarian, with both partners bringing to it what they can and taking from it what they want.

So many mistresses, and concubines too, with so many stories! Slowly, I chose the women in each category who would best illustrate the various themes and subtexts I had begun to discern in the mass of research material. The triage was difficult as I excised woman after woman, at first gingerly and then more ruthlessly. Slowly, an entire bookcase filled up with my often fascinating rejects—Lady Emma Hamilton! Diane de Poitiers! George Sand! Coco Chanel!—victims of redundancy and space, and of my decision to focus on individuals. But what a cast of survivors, each with a story that is unique yet at the same time links her with so many other women. They come from all times and places, and from every class, caste, color and condition. They are aristocrats and slaves, wives, mothers and spinsters, and they are lodged in huts and harems, houses and mansions. Some are famous, usually because of their relationships, while others can only be coaxed back to life through the reminiscences of their lovers and others or from official documents. What all these women have in common is that they have been either mistresses or concubines. This book is about their experiences and their special stories. What makes each woman important in this book is the unique way in which her life story reflects and sheds light on the multifaceted institution of mistressdom.

CHAPTER 1

Love out of Wedlock
in the Ancient World[1]

FROM its origins, the institution of marriage has been associated with various forms of concubinage, systems that permitted and to some extent defined parallel and intimate relationships between men and women other than their wives. The Bible, which provides the underpinning of much of Western culture and literature, introduces us to scores of concubines. King Solomon had three hundred in addition to his seven hundred wives, and other biblical kings and patriarchs enjoyed the prestige of scores or hundreds of concubines. A concubine was used for sexual purposes and for what the Japanese called "borrowed wombs." If a man's wife was barren and he needed heirs, he might impregnate a concubine, then acknowledge and raise her child as his own. Concubines had the status of secondary wives, without a wife's security or rights. Concubines were often slaves. The law stipulated that even if a wife's slave was designated her husband's concubine, that concubine remained her owner's property.

Over the centuries, changing circumstances and mores altered concubinage. By late antiquity, Roman law extended some protection to concubines, notably by allowing their children a small share of their natural father's estate, a claim made even stronger if he died intestate or without legitimate heirs. The early-4th-century Christian emperor Constantine, who died in 337, sought to discourage concubinage by granting men the right to marry their concubines and thereby legitimize their children. But no law could eradicate concubinage when Greco-Roman culture generally accepted male infidelity in marriage. Saint Augustine, who for over a decade lived with his beloved concubine and their son, explained that men justified concubinage on the grounds that they would otherwise be driven to seduce other men's wives or to resort to prostitutes. The concomitant of the notion that males were innately incapable of monogamy was that concubinage was an essential adjunct to marriage.

Hagar

The first concubine to be named in recorded history may well be Hagar, an Egyptian slave woman who might have been black. Hagar was the bondwoman of the matriarch Sarah, the wife of the patriarch Abraham (c. 2000–1720 B.C.). We know nothing about Hagar's circumstances, or how and when she came into Sarah's possession. Her biblical biographer, who clearly considered her a minor character and would no doubt be astounded by the fascination she continues to provoke four millennia later, introduced her as a subtext in the ongoing tragedy of Sarah's infertility and devoted only seven tiny biblical chapters to her.

Sarah and Abraham had many adventures, including a dangerous sojourn in Egypt, where the lovely Sarah unwittingly attracted the attention of Pharaoh, who wanted to induct her into his harem. Abraham saved the situation by claiming her as his "sister," after which Pharaoh showered them both with gifts of sheep, oxen, donkeys, camels and slaves, both male and female, and likely black.

When Pharaoh learned that Abraham and Sarah had duped him, he ordered Abraham to take his wife and get out of Egypt. Considerately, he permitted them to keep all their livestock and slaves.

Abraham had become a man rich in everything but progeny, for Sarah was barren. This was not likely to change because she was by then seventy-six (or so the author of Genesis reports). No wonder Abraham despaired and prayed about his childlessness. Sarah blamed herself for her barrenness, which the ancient world considered such a curse that it was even grounds for divorce. But her society had a solution to infertility—a fertile concubine.

Which is where we first meet Hagar. "You see that the Lord has prevented me from bearing children," Sarah said to her husband; "go in to my slave-girl; it may be that I shall obtain children by her."

Abraham was agreeable, and Hagar had no say in the matter. Soon, despite being eighty-six, Abraham managed to impregnate her. But Hagar's swelling belly transformed her. To Sarah's astonishment, her docile and companionable slave woman metamorphosed into a self-confident, even arrogant, woman who looked down at Sarah with "contempt." And why not? Hagar might be enslaved, but her womb was good enough to provide her owner's husband with a legitimate heir.

Sarah was confused and vexed by Hagar's attitude. She complained bitterly to Abraham, but he merely reminded her that as Hagar's rightful owner, she could chastise her bondwoman however she wished. We do not know what Sarah did—one prescribed remedy for insolence was to scour the offender's mouth with a quart of salt—but she acted so harshly that Hagar decided to run away.

Fortunately, an angel of the Lord found Hagar as she wandered in the wilderness: "Hagar, slave-girl of Sarai ['Sarah' is a variation of 'Sarai'], where have you come from and where are you going?" Hagar explained her predicament. "Return to your mistress, and submit to her," the angel ordered, but he softened this admonition by promising her children too numerous to count. "Now you have conceived and shall bear a son; you shall call him Ishmael [meaning 'God hears'], for the Lord has given heed to your affliction."

After this encounter, Hagar returned and gave birth to Abraham's son, who was duly named Ishmael. Quite likely she delivered him squatting between Sarah's legs, assisted by a midwife, in the customary "bearing on one's knees" of a child destined to become the heir of its "social" mother rather than of the mother of its flesh and blood.

Hagar remained with Abraham and Sarah for thirteen more years, suckling and caring for Ishmael. Then came a miracle. God made a complicated covenant with Abraham that ended Sarah's infertility. At first, Sarah laughed at so preposterous a notion. She was too old. How could she have sex, much less a child? But the Lord reproached her for laughing and asked her, "Is anything too wonderful for the Lord?"

Apparently nothing was, and Sarah conceived her son, Isaac. By then she was ninety, and Abraham one hundred. "Who would ever have said to Abraham that Sarah would nurse children? Yet I have borne him a son in his old age," Sarah rejoiced.

Isaac grew into a robust child and Sarah weaned him. But one day, as she watched her little boy playing with his older half brother, Ishmael, she felt intense resentment. As Abraham's first son, Ishmael would share his father's inheritance. "Cast out this slave woman with her son!" Sarah cried to Abraham, "for this son of a slave woman shall not inherit along with my son Isaac."

Abraham was deeply disturbed, though only on Ishmael's account, not

Hagar's. He prayed for guidance, and God instructed him to do as Sarah demanded, for both Isaac and Ishmael would found great nations. The next morning, Abraham got up early, fetched a loaf of bread and a goatskin container of water, and called Hagar. Then this exceptionally wealthy man gave her these meager provisions and told her to take Ishmael, their adolescent son, and go away.

Bewildered, Hagar and Ishmael roamed about in the wilderness. Before long, they had eaten and drunk the last of their puny rations. In despair, Hagar led Ishmael to a bush, then walked away and sunk to the ground. "Do not let me look on the death of the child," she wept.

But God was watching over her and again sent an angel. God will not let Ishmael die, the angel said, because he plans to build a great nation from his descendants. Hagar opened her eyes in amazement and saw that God had provided a well. She filled her goatskin and gave her thirsty son a drink.

For years Hagar and Ishmael lived out in the wasteland. They had contact with other people, and enough financial resources for Hagar to arrange Ishmael's marriage to an Egyptian girl. Though the Hebrews had enslaved her, Hagar remembered and reclaimed her Egyptian heritage.

This is the end of Hagar's story, though presumably not of her life. Biblical references to Ishmael tell us that God kept his promise to Hagar, because Ishmael had twelve sons, the princely founders of the Ishmaelite tribes. Ishmael himself survived until he was 137, the long-lived son of a long-lived father. (Abraham died at 175 years old, and Ishmael and Isaac together buried him in the cave of Machpelah.)

Hagar's tenure as a concubine was short, but her plight resonates through the ages, in an extensive and growing literature. Millennia after she lived, her existence recorded in a few brief sentences, Hagar has become a symbol for the dispossessed and persecuted of the earth, a woman sexually and economically exploited, deprived of rights, cast out without succor. But unlike other women to whom these terrible things also happen, Hagar was saved from misery and doom by God himself.

Aspasia [2]

In the mid-5th century B.C., the city-state of Athens eclipsed the rest of Greece; the democracy that prevailed there epitomized the finest of ancient Greek achievement. But Athens's golden age did not gild Athenian women, who spent most of their lifetimes confined to their quarters. Foreign women were doubly damned, by their gender and their caste. One of them, Aspasia, an immigrant from Miletus in Asia Minor, attempted to overcome her disadvantaged status through her relationship with Athens's leading statesman, Pericles.

Aspasia arrived in Athens after the debilitating Persian Wars had ended and the Five-Year Truce of 451 had halted hostilities between the Greek states. She came with her relatives, whom unspecified circumstances had forced out of Miletus. Despite the presence of her family members, her aristocratic birth and her good connections, she had no financial resources and was forced to seek paid employment.

Unfortunately for Aspasia, her arrival in Athens coincided with a glut of postwar immigration, which had driven Pericles to enact draconian measures to ensure the social superiority of the Athenian citizenry. He restricted citizenship to Athenians with two Athenian parents and drastically limited the rights of *metics*, foreigners such as Aspasia and her family. Anyone caught impersonating an Athenian citizen could be enslaved. Thanks to Pericles' legislation, Aspasia could never marry an Athenian or enjoy even the meager rights of Athenian women.

These rights were few. Unlike their brothers, Athenian women were not potential warriors, so infant girls were often left exposed on hillsides for wild beasts to maul or devour. Those permitted to survive were indifferently educated, kept cloistered at home and taught only household skills. At the onset of sexual maturation, usually about age fourteen, their parents would marry them off to much older men who had completed their military obligations and were at last free to marry.

Married life was no liberation for Greek wives ensconced in their new homes. Athenian homes, like Greek houses generally, reflected the superior status of men. They were small, because men spent many of their days elsewhere, with other males. Most rooms opened onto a central courtyard. The dining room, or *andron*, was the largest and best-furnished room in the house, because men entertained there. But they excluded their wives, daughters and other female dependents from these events. They often invited *hetaerae*—top-drawer courtesans—or, if they were poorer, prostitutes to entertain them.

Women in ancient Athens had minimal rights and could only divorce their husbands if the latter consented. Their dowries alone provided some financial protection. In a society that praised decent, submissive and hardworking matrons, the most a woman could aspire to was a good reputation.

What, then, was the young *metic* to do in this macho city? Aspasia was not merely beautiful. She was also unusually intelligent, and unlike most Athenian women, she had managed to acquire an education, though she never revealed how. She began to teach rhetoric and philosophy, and soon earned such a reputation that Socrates himself claimed her as his teacher, or so Plato tells us in his *Menexenus*.[3]

Quite likely, Aspasia had initially supported herself by joining the nebulous world of the *hetaerae*, foreign-born women who traded sex, companionship and friendship for valuable gifts and money. Unlike prostitutes (and most wives), *hetaerae* were educated and cultured, elegant and sophisticated. Their wit, knowledge and ease of discourse distinguished them from other Greek women, and they conversed and debated on terms of intellectual equality with their male companions. Vase paintings depict them as slender, small breasted and ornately dressed, easily differentiated from heavier, unadorned Greek matrons.

Aspasia was about twenty-five when she met Pericles and inspired the passionate love that lasted until his death. But Pericles' own laws of citizenship condemned her to life as his concubine and never his wife. Because he felt he could not live without her, Pericles moved Aspasia into his house. When Aspasia gave birth to baby Pericles, his illegitimacy and *metic* status did not trouble his father, who already had two legitimate sons.

Pericles was far from being the only admirer of Aspasia's compelling intellectual and erotic presence. When she established a salon, Athens's leading intellectuals, scholars and statesmen flocked there to debate politics and philosophy, and to maintain their social and political networks.

Aspasia did not confine her analyses to affairs of state. She also turned rigorous Socratic reasoning to the issue of spousal relationships, a subject that her own status must have spurred her to contemplate. Later writers Cicero and Quintilian reported a dialogue witnessed by the philosopher Xenophon, which Aspasia conducted with Xenophon's wife. "Tell me," Aspasia asked,

> "if your neighbor's gold jewelry was finer than yours, would you rather have hers or yours?"
>
> "Hers."
>
> "So if her gown or accessories were more costly than yours, which would you prefer?"
>
> "Hers, of course."
>
> "Well then, if her husband were better than yours, would you want hers or yours?"[4]

Xenophon's wife reddened. Aspasia broke the embarrassed silence. To satisfy a longing for excellence in a partner, she explained, one must perforce *be* the best partner. Though eroticism is the dimension through which men and women express their devotion to each other, the key element in the attraction is virtue.

Fabricated or real, this argument suggests to us Aspasia's views on relationships between men and women—that they enter them on the same terms and must be equally committed to seeking the path of virtue. In other words, Pericles' mistress seems to have been an advocate of an egalitarianism monumentally at odds with the rigid stratification and codified inequality of her time and place.

Meanwhile, Pericles spent much of his time at home so he could be with Aspasia, but nonetheless devoted himself to the business of government and directing the restoration of the Athenian temples that were damaged or destroyed during the Persian Wars. Athenians by and large supported Pericles' public policies, but the same could not be said for his not-so-private life. Citizens accused him of having ejected his wife from their home so he could install Aspasia in her place, ignoring the fact that he and his wife had divorced more than a decade before he ever met Aspasia. They also muttered that he should keep his concubine discreetly in the background as other men did—advice that Pericles disregarded. A groundswell of opposition to Aspasia mounted, and she, rather than Pericles, bore the brunt of it. She was slandered mercilessly in public forums and political broadsides. Comic poets outdid themselves with bawdy ripostes, likening Aspasia to Thargelia, the powerful Ionian courtesan and wife—of fourteen husbands!—who had used her immense influence to aid the enemy during the Persian Wars.

In 440 B.C., after the important city-state of Samos revolted against Athens, this campaign against Aspasia intensified. Though Pericles eventually quashed the revolt, his sneering opponents charged that his whore Aspasia had, for personal reasons stemming from her Miletian origins, convinced him to wage the ensuing Samian War. In *Cheirones*, the satiric writer Cratinus ridiculed both Pericles and Aspasia, whom he cursed as the Dog-Eyed Whore.

This label stuck, and more and more Athenians condemned Aspasia as a filthy and despicable harlot. Her reputation as a *hetaera* evoked other images, the crudely sexual ones on Greek vases and drinking cups that depict *hetaerae* naked, or lifting their robes to display their genitalia to potential clients. These clay-fired *hetaerae* engage in group sex, take a variety of positions and even obligingly bend over, bracing their hands against the floor to permit anal intercourse. Sometimes clients beat them on their bare buttocks with a shoe or other object to force them into unwelcome or painful sexual acts. Likening her to these caricatured women was the gutter level of the crusade against Aspasia, the refined intellectual, devoted mother and Pericles' beloved companion.

The real reason for the backlash of bitterness and hatred against Aspasia was that she threatened the social fabric of Athens's slave-based, male-run society, which expected its women to live as domestic drones or, if they were *metics*, forced them into even grimmer existences. Aspasia, female and foreign, should have borne the legislated burden of her dual disability. But she had escaped and somehow bamboozled their foolish old leader into disregarding both her gender and her status. Clearly, Aspasia was a danger to the established order, a revolutionary disguised as a seductress.

For a decade after the Samian debacle, Aspasia's life continued to be domestically harmonious and intellectually enriching, but publicly nightmarish. In 431 B.C., at the onset of the Peloponnesian War, the verbal assaults intensified. The comic poet Hermippus launched a new attack, accusing her both of impious behavior and of pimping free-born Athenian women for Pericles. He succeeded in whipping up such public outrage that charges of immorality and treason were laid against Aspasia. Pericles notwithstanding, the popular will would prevail.

As a foreigner, Aspasia could not appear in court to defend herself. Instead, Pericles pleaded on her behalf. He wept as he spoke, his voice shaking with emotion, and communicated with such eloquence and conviction that the jury accepted his argument that Aspasia had been slandered, and it acquitted her of all charges.

This victory over malice and vilification bound Aspasia and Pericles even closer together. Soon after, she was publicly acknowledged as Pericles' mate. But the loving couple was not destined to enjoy a comfortable old age together. Pericles' military strategy of defending the Athenian empire by safeguarding its citizens and army within the city's walls led to severe overcrowding and rampant disease. In 430 B.C., a terrifying plague killed one out of every three soldiers and one out of four civilians.

Pericles himself lost his first two sons, his sister and most of his relatives and friends. But most other Athenians also suffered terrible losses and in their frantic grief looked for someone to blame. Pericles was the obvious scapegoat, and he was ousted from office, charged and convicted of accepting bribes.

Pericles was now disgraced and dishonored, and without any heirs. Bad as this was, it provided Aspasia an unexpected benefit—her son Pericles Junior's status had suddenly improved. Pericles, desperate for an heir, had to plead before Athenian officials that Pericles Junior, bastardized by his own xenophobic legislation, be legitimized. Athenians at last took pity on the ruined old man and granted young Pericles—but not Aspasia—citizenship. Nonetheless, her son's success must have provided Aspasia with a good deal of satisfaction.

Pericles and Aspasia enjoyed a brief respite from persecution, during which he was rehabilitated and restored to office. But the pestilence in Athens raged on and soon carried him off as well, leaving his concubine alone and unprotected in the hostile, plague-stricken city.

Without Pericles—or should we say after Pericles?—Aspasia turned to another man, a sheep-dealer who was also a rising general. Her haste in establishing this relationship may seem to reflect badly on the sincerity of her affection for Pericles. She was probably not destitute; her son had inherited Pericles' estate. Perhaps she felt she needed protection against a citizenry that hated her. Perhaps, too, she was attracted to Lysicles, who was dynamic, ambitious, wealthy and much closer to her age than Pericles had been. And after all, she must have concluded, given that Athenian laws stigmatized her as a foreigner and the Athenian citizens tormented her, her wisest course would be to replicate her relationship with Pericles and become the concubine of another powerful man capable of fending off her legions of enemies.

Aspasia had almost certainly become acquainted with Lysicles through Pericles. Perhaps Lysicles had been among those impressed by her intelligence and good looks. Her position as Pericles' concubine might have appealed to him as well; after all, Pericles had defied his people in order to live with and honor this woman.

Whatever had motivated it, Aspasia's union with Lysicles was brief. She had just borne him a son when Lysicles died in battle, and she was once again left to fend for herself, this time with an illegitimate baby.

But the Athenians could not leave her alone. When Aspasia was forty-five, Aristophanes launched a new and breathtaking attack. In his play *Acharnians*, he accused her of nothing less than causing the Peloponnesian War. The character Dikaeopolis details the events that triggered the war. According to the story, some young drunks sneaked into Megara and stole a whore called Simaitha. Furious, the Megarians retaliated—and stole two whores from Aspasia, whom they called a female pimp. Enraged by the theft of her whores, Aspasia hounded Pericles into launching the Peloponnesian War.

We do not know what happened to Aspasia after Lysicles' death, though to this day her story generates scholarly debate and analysis. What is certain is that Aspasia was astute enough to assess her personal situation in middle age just as she had in her youth. She was aging and unprotected, a foreign woman in a society that feared and despised her. She had certain assets: fading good looks, a reputation for scintillating wit and formidable powers of reason, and a son who was Pericles' legitimate heir. And she had a reputation as a whore, something that would certainly appeal to some men.

The likelihood is that Aspasia sought refuge in the protection of another man, just as she had very soon after Pericles died. A less likely scenario is that her eldest son, Pericles, assumed the role of her protector. Had that happened, we would expect some literary allusion, sardonic or otherwise, to mother and son. But Aspasia's playwright tormentors were silent, and we may reasonably conclude that Aspasia allied herself with a man too insignificant to mention, moved away from Athens or died in obscurity.

Judging from the available traces of her teachings and beliefs, Aspasia was the champion of justice and virtuous living, and of balance in an unbalanced world. But as a perpetual alien and a woman governed by harsh Athenian laws and mores, she had to rely on her relationship with Pericles to achieve a measure of power and financial security.

Corinna [5]

One of the most enigmatic and sensational of mistresses was "Corinna," whom the great poet Ovid celebrated and immortalized in his collection of poems, *Amores*, though he never divulged her real identity. Corinna and Ovid conducted their tumultuous relationship in a Rome whose decadence was the target of imperial moral-reform legislation that hedonistic citizens observed mostly in the breach.

Two decades before the rise of Christianity, the Rome of Ovid and Corinna was a city both magnificent and terrible. It was crowded with fine villas and teeming slums, mighty aqueducts and public baths. It boasted sophisticated theaters but, at the same time, reveled in circuses where citizens cheered or jeered as trained lions eviscerated bound criminals (and later Christians), and archers slaughtered herds of terrified wild elephants and panthers. Roman markets were emporiums of produce from all over the empire, crammed with foodstuffs, silks and woolens, wine and fermented fish sauce.

Up on the Palatine Hill, the urbane and autocratic genius Caesar Augustus surveyed his empire and was dismayed by what he saw. Before the end of his reign in A.D. 14, he would recast his beloved but decaying Rome into marble buildings—the Marcellus Theater, Circus Maximus and eighty temples—as durable as his Pax Romana. He would also try to reform its citizens' jaded morals with the Leges Juliae, laws that governed marriage, sexual relations and inheritance.

Decades of anarchy, insurrection and military campaigns had corroded Roman social values. Augustus, nostalgic for the old days, was especially concerned that Roman women were no longer like their virtuous foremothers, unassuming and devoted drudges. But why would they be? By conscripting men, war also transformed women.

When their husbands were away soldiering, most wives ran their households on their own, with wealthy women even administering large estates. With the sense of entitlement and contact with the outside world that this brought, inevitably, some women took lovers.

In peacetime, Romans did not revert to the mores of yesteryear. They delayed marriage but not sex, and higher-ranked men took concubines they could repudiate when it came time to wed a suitable bride. Many marriageable but unmarried women were left without any expectation that a suitable man would ever marry them. In this state of uncertainty, some women experimented with erotic if forbidden pleasures.

Rome's collective self-indulgence at this time has never been rivaled. The citizenry was obsessed with amusements, and flocked to parties, theaters, sports events and circuses. Wealthy Romans gorged and vomited in a kind of socially sanctioned bulimia. When respectable women had retired for the night, their husbands often caroused with courtesans or prostitutes. Even the righteous Augustus, who made a fetish out of revering Livia Drusilla, his wife, had a well-deserved reputation as a philanderer.

In Augustus's Rome, two standards coexisted, the legal and the actual. Like Greece, Rome was a slave-owning democracy whose free men—but nobody else—had rights and power. Free and freed women were substantially better off than slaves, but no woman, no matter how rich and powerful her family, had even a fraction of the rights that her brother was raised to expect or that her father already held.

The *paterfamilias* was a legal regime breathtaking in its subjugation of women. A father's legal authority—*patria potestas*—was rooted in his own interests, not his wife's or his children's, even when the latter were adults. It began when the newborn was deposited at his sandaled feet so he could exercise his right of mortal triage. If Papa picked up the mewling boy or ordered that the girl be fed, he granted life. Otherwise, the little ones were smothered, starved or left on hillsides or riverbanks to be killed by wild animals. Not surprisingly, far fewer sons than daughters suffered this fate.

Most exposed baby girls died. A few were rescued by kindly well-wishers. Others were sought out and, after miserable childhoods in domestic servitude, sold into slavery or—much more commonly—raised to be prostitutes.

Even children not condemned at birth were far from safe. At any given moment, a father could sell them into a form of bondage, *causa mancipii*—slavery by another name. Angering Papa was a life-risking enterprise, and many fathers willfully destroyed vexatious offspring.

Marriage brought a daughter no relief. Her husband, chosen for her, replaced her father, often when she was still a child. If she dared to commit adultery, her husband could kill her. He could also beat her, even to death, for drinking wine. Wine testing (as opposed to wine tasting) developed into investigatory kissing, the *ius osculi*, which males exercised if they suspected their female relatives of imbibing anything alcoholic. Such was the condition of free women, and freed and slave women were still more degraded.

A Roman *concubina* had even less status than a wife. She was a free or freed woman who cohabited with a man who was not her husband. Men were not supposed to have both wife and concubine, at least not simultaneously. It made sense, then, for a man to take a concubine of inferior social status. That way, he could kick her out if she bore his illegitimate children or if he decided he was ready to marry.

Widowers also preferred to take a concubine rather than remarry. There was no commitment, and no threat to the inheritance of legitimate offspring should the concubine produce a bastard. Conveniently, neither she nor her child would have any legal claim on her lover or, after his death, on his estate.

Concubinage had a few benefits. It was a legal practice, and concubines were exempt from prosecution for adultery, though not from the charge of fornication. Occasionally, a lover managed to circumvent Rome's oppressive laws and legally adopt his concubine's child. Even less frequently, he would marry his concubine.

But privileged Romans acted as if none of the unforgiving laws existed. Unlike Livia Drusilla, Augustus's wife, who wore determinedly simple and unflattering garments, the new Roman woman was neither unpretentious nor absorbed by her children. In fact, the birth rate had plunged because of the lead poisoning from the otherwise admirable aqueducts, as well as the effects of primitive forms of birth control and abortion.

Privileged women from good families no longer began the day with prayers then settled down to relentless domestic tasks. Now, a privileged woman awoke taut-faced and ghostly under the dried milk-and-flour mask she had applied before bedtime. After a slave girl brought water, the woman would rinse off the paste, then soak in her bath until the masseur, or *unctor*, appeared with his unguents to knead her limbs into suppleness. Immaculate and fragrant with scented oils, this lady dressed and had her hair combed, pinned, ironed or coaxed into a wreath of curls or prettily trailing plaits. Afterward came whitening face powder, reddening cheek and lip rouge, and blackening ash or kohl eyeliner. The final touch was jewelry, fine stones from the vast empire, set in silver or gold and fashioned into rings, bracelets, necklaces, brooches and anklets.

For women attracted to this new and indulgent way of life, the rigorous beauty routine was a prelude to sexual adventure. Some women even modeled themselves on the Greek *hetaerae*. Augustus, horrified and disgusted to learn that females were just as interested in extramarital dalliance as he was, acted decisively against them.

This was the background to Augustus's Leges Juliae (18–17 B.C.), famous for their repression of adultery, which was transformed into a criminal act and severely punished. But adultery applied only to wives who cheated on their husbands and to men who slept with other men's wives, not to husbands who indulged with unmarried women. Widows and unmarried free women who dared to be sexually active risked being charged with the lesser crime of fornication. These new laws were designed to force women—in particular those of the elite class—to marry or remarry, and remain virtuous, submissive and housebound.

But as so often happens when penalties are too severe—convicted adulteresses lost half their dowry and one-third of their property, adulterers half their property, and all were exiled to faraway islands where enforcement was virtually impossible—the laws were rendered almost meaningless. Augustus did have one spectacular victory: the successful prosecution of his own daughter, Julia, one of Rome's most notorious adulteresses.

The great Roman poet Ovid, an aristocratic, wealthy and supremely talented young man obsessed with women, love and sex, fit perfectly into this permissive world. At sixteen, Ovid married the first of his three wives, a teenaged bride he never ceased to belittle. At twenty-three, in his *Amores*, he introduced Corinna, his willful, sensual and unfaithful mistress. Romans responded with fiery enthusiasm, and a few ardent fans scribbled his verses on public walls. Quite possibly the content and great success of the *Amores* helped push Augustus to enact his puritanical legislation.

To this day, scholars still speculate about the identity of the pseudonymous Corinna. The most tantalizing suggestion is that she was actually Julia, Augustus's defiant daughter, but the evidence for this hypothesis is shaky. Whoever she was, Corinna rises up from the couplets of Ovid's searing poetry. With imagination, sympathy and shrewdness, we can come to know her.

Facts easily extrapolated from the *Amores*: Corinna was slightly older than Ovid and married to a much older man (a senile dodderer, in Ovid's unkind words), and she cheated on both of them. Before she was twenty, she became the mistress of the man with whom she had her first orgasm. Afterward, she pouted and complained if a lover did not make her writhe during intercourse.

Corinna was as vain as she was lovely, and adept at applying cosmetics. She was self-possessed, tempestuous and passionate. She liked to tease Ovid and inflame his jealousy.

Corinna was also addicted to luxurious living. She shunned men who lacked the means to help her, and expected expensive gifts. Under the guise of being a fan of horse racing, she flirted with jockeys. She took risks, and she co-opted her servants, notably her maid Nape, into her amorous intrigues. She loved her poetic young lover, and he loved her even more.

Or perhaps Ovid was really in love with love, because in the midst of begging Corinna to love him forever, he admitted that

> . . . when you give me yourself, what you'll be providing
> Is creative material. My art will rise to the theme
> And immortalize *you*. . . .
> Through poems, of course.
> So you and I, love, will enjoy the same world-wide publicity,
> And our names will be linked, for ever, with the gods.[6]

Ovid was right. Their lengthy affair provided him with material galore, a veritable soap opera of misery, ecstasy, miscommunication, intrigue, danger, threats, lies and comic surprise. The *Amores* is a brilliant depiction of the intimate workings of an elite Roman relationship.

Visualize this bitter exchange between the lovers as they discuss an upcoming formal banquet. Ovid fantasizes about the fun they will have together, until Corinna cautions him: I won't be alone. My husband is also coming.

Ovid, clearly not expecting this, responds with sullen fury, "I hope he drops down dead before dessert!"[7]

Ovid then reverts to suggesting coded gestures that only they will share: pretend to be the Respectable Wife, he urges Corinna, "but nudge my foot as you're passing by." During the general chatter, he would send her secret messages by raising his eyebrows or by tracing his words in wine. Corinna should touch her cheek whenever she thought about the last time they made love, or pinch her earlobe to signal that she was cross with him. At other parties, he reminds her, he sneaked his hand under her garment and masturbated her to climax, all sight unseen!

Ovid's reflections prompt a gush of jealousy: don't drink from a wineglass your husband's lips have touched; spurn his embraces, especially those fingers roving under your dress to squeeze or caress "those responsive nipples."

> . . . Above all, don't you dare
> Kiss him, not once. If you do, I'll proclaim myself your lover,
> Lay hand upon you, claim those kisses as mine. . . .

Ovid cannot bear the thought of Corinna's husband making love to her. Pretend you're frigid! Make sex a dead issue, he orders her, and, in parentheses, implores the goddess Venus to grant his prayer that neither his mistress nor her husband should enjoy sex together, "*and certainly not her!*"

Ovid reveled in Corinna's physical beauty, and unhesitatingly described its intimate details: her lustrous long auburn hair as fine as a spider's web, her soft white throat, her suggestive way of dressing, reminiscent (to him) of either an Eastern queen or a courtesan of the highest rank. When he stripped off these shimmering clothes and Corinna stood before him utterly exposed, Ovid catalogued the wonders of her nakedness: smooth shoulders, seductive nipples that invited fondling, flat belly beneath magnificent breasts, sweetly curvaceous rump and long lean thighs, and then. . . . At the genitals, even the uninhibited Ovid stopped his recital and simply described his own surrender to his mistress's sensual perfections.

But when the lovers quarreled, Ovid could be cruel in his mockery, employing his sharp wit and critical eye to detail Corinna's flaws. Once she dyed her masses of hair one time too many with a harsh compound made of leeches and vinegar, and also used hot irons to curl it into ringlets. Then her hair fell out in clumps, and she wept as she looked sadly into her mirror. Until it grew back, she would have to content herself with the false glory of a wig made from the hair of conquered German maidens. Ovid reproved her: And it's all your very own fault!

Ovid also recorded his own reactions when Corinna got pregnant and, without telling him, had an abortion that nearly killed her. I should be furious but I'm only frightened, he noted with self-absorbed righteousness. Please, never again, he finishes.

Ovid felt sorely tried when Corinna "nagged" him for gifts. Weren't his brilliant verses the most wonderful offering any woman could desire? But when Corinna, who loved silk gowns and gold jewelry, expected more tangible tokens, Ovid found her repellent. Stop making demands, he advised her coldly. I'll give, but only when I feel like it.

When vexed, the impetuous Ovid succumbed to rages so fierce he later admitted he would have been capable of horsewhipping his own father or even the gods. Once, he yanked Corinna's hair and raked her face with his fingernails, then watched, appalled, as she shrank in bewildered terror from him. But his self-recriminations lasted only seconds, and he could not refrain from chiding her: "At least remove the signs of my misdemeanor / Just rearrange your hair as it was before!"[8]

The mechanics of conducting the relationship also preoccupied Ovid. He and Corinna were excellent strategists, but they were helpless without the cooperation of Nape, Corinna's personal maid. Nape was the perennial go-between, carrying notes and arranging meetings, often persuading a reluctant Corinna to slip out to Ovid's house.

Despite their mutual passion, Corinna and Ovid deceived each other with different lovers. There was an awful night when Corinna barred Ovid from her home, then made love in her bedroom while he stalked her house like a specter. When his exhausted rival staggered out the next morning, he caught Ovid in the humiliating act of watching him. Whenever Corinna and Ovid quarreled and broke up, she would sit on his lap, stroke and sweet talk him into taking her back, and she was so beautiful that Ovid always melted. Please, he pleaded in his poetry, just don't flaunt your infidelities. You're far too lovely to be virtuous, because beauty and virtue are incompatible. But at least hide the hickeys, smooth your hair and make your bed before you receive me.

After several years as Ovid's mistress, Corinna ended the relationship. Why? The *Amores* suggests she left him for a soldier, a virile brute with illicitly obtained financial resources. Did she catch Ovid *in flagrante* with her own hairstylist, whom he seduced, or with another dissatisfied wife? Or was it because Ovid, despite boasting that Corinna had once driven him to reach nine climaxes in a single night, suffered from more than occasional bouts of impotence, likely caused by lead poisoning from Rome's famous aqueducts? As he confessed in wry verse in his *Amores*,

> When I held her I was limp as yesterday's lettuce
> a useless burden on an idle bed.
> Although I wanted to do it, and she was more than willing,
> I couldn't get my pleasure-part to work.
> . . . A sorry sight!
> I lay there like a rotten log, a dead weight.
> I even thought that I might be a ghost."[9]

Whatever her reasons, Corinna disappeared forever from Ovid's life, but not from the speculation of historians, who have tried and failed to identify her. What was her experience as Ovid's mistress? How did she feel when she read her ex-lover's new work, *Ars Amatoria*—a didactic poem that offered specific advice on love affairs?

Picture the middle-aged Corinna, a still-lovely widow whose ailing old husband has recently passed away. The *Ars Amatoria* is the season's literary sensation. Her friends are all exclaiming over it, and her intimates know how much it owes to the tumultuous years Corinna spent as Ovid's mistress. Surely she was struck by Ovid's cynicism, the barefaced effrontery of his calculated and analytical approach to mistressdom, when he had spoken with such heartfelt conviction of loving her forever! Now, he had sunk so low as to write an actual manual, with Book One advising how to find and win a mistress's heart, Book Two how to keep her affections and Book Three, for mistresses, how to do the same with men.

How would the jaded Corinna react? Not with outrage or even surprise, for she had always known that Ovid's art reflected his life, and that with every kiss, every lyrical sentiment, every provocative touch and every volcanic orgasm, he was taking mental notes. And Corinna had assumed the role of mistress knowing at least the outlines of the game. As the much younger wife of a man her parents had probably pressed her to marry, she had no interest in the old Roman wifely values of fidelity and child rearing. Instead, she had chosen to dissipate the long hours of her childless days in frenetic partying and entertainment, particularly at the racecourse, where the riders were as sleek and conditioned as their steeds.

Ars Amatoria must have seemed liked déjà vu, a replay of her early years as

Ovid's mistress. Technique is everything, Ovid began, and Corinna must have nodded knowingly. First, where to look for a mistress? Theaters, racecourses, circuses, banquets, even temples have excellent possibilities. (We met at a dinner party. I was wearing my purple silk dress, and my hair was coiled atop my head. You sat nearby and would not stop staring at me.) And remember, women are lustier than men and cannot resist a really skilled and persistent suitor. (How true, at least about the lustiness. But skill and persistence pay off only so far and, as you yourself discovered with me, can become annoying.)

Win over and bribe her servant to act as go-between and spy. (Ah, Nape, do you remember those days?) Make extravagant promises, spend little money. Seduce her with eloquent words, and indulge in marathon letter writing. (Cheap as ever, are you? I'll take solid gold and emeralds any day.) Dress neatly, keep fit and clean. Feign drunkenness and declare your undying love. (So I was right to call you a liar! But I didn't realize you weren't really drunk.) Flatter her mercilessly, weep supplicating tears. If she barricades her door, climb onto the roof and slip down through a skylight or a window. Then, should she hesitate, take her by force, for women adore rough treatment and are disappointed if you allow them to fight you off. (So in the end, you learned nothing. You scorned soldiers, but you assaulted me so violently I was too terrified even to tell you to leave.)

If you cannot avoid quarreling, patch it up in bed. (We spent our time doing both.) If you need to, kiss her feet. When you make love, it's essential that she, too, reach—or dramatically fake—orgasm. (Oh, so you hate it unless both lovers reach a climax? But what about all those nights when no matter how hard I tried, you stayed as limp as yesterday's lettuce?)

Book Three must have put into stark perspective just how cavalier and condescending Ovid's view of women must always have been. Don't neglect your looks, for few of you are natural beauties. (But *I* was, and even now I am far from unattractive.) Hair is especially important. Style it elegantly, keep gray at bay with dyes or wigs. (I have to rely on a wig—my fine hair still can't bear the harshness of dye.) Guard against stinking armpits and pluck away leg hairs. Use cosmetics: rouge, powder, eyebrow pencil. Keep teeth white and breath pure, or else a chuckle might cost you a lover. Learn music, poetry, dancing and games. Play hard, but not too hard, to get. During the act of love, adopt a sexy position, whisper forbidden words, moan with delirious pleasure and don't open windows—your naked body is best left in semidarkness. (But not mine, O Poet—mine was perfection itself.)

Even when their mutual passion was at its steamiest, Ovid had not worried about Corinna's possible reactions to his poetry. He had, however, feared a much more dangerous critic: Augustus himself. In 2 B.C., after having charged his daughter, Julia, with, adultery and exiling her, and a decade later banishing Julia's daughter Vipsania Julia as well, Augustus turned on Ovid. He accused the great poet of encouraging adultery and exiled him to a far-off port city in present-day Romania. Ovid spent the remaining ten years of his life pleading, lobbying and groveling to return, but Augustus was adamant, and Ovid died in unhappy exile.

If she was still alive, Corinna must have been shocked. She, like most of her social circle, had been equally guilty. Ovid, however, had called attention to himself by becoming the Latin world's supreme chronicler of illicit love, the world of mistressdom. She, Corinna, had merely indulged in it.

In choosing the pleasures of child-free mistressdom, Corinna rebelled against her arranged marriage and fashioned her own kind of life. She made choices: to reject Old Rome for the New, to seek out constant pleasure, to exact precious tributes to her loveliness, to decline motherhood. By her daring and cavalier disregard for the rituals of yesteryear, Corinna had dignified and made sense of her womanhood, if only in her own eyes.

Dolorosa [10]

In the historical record, Dolorosa—my imagined name for this sorrowful concubine—fares worst of all, for despite all his *Confessions*,[11] the man who became Saint Augustine never once identified this woman who shared his life for fifteen years and bore his only son, Adeodatus.

This omission is not evidence of Augustine's indifference. Indeed, he named Monica, his beloved mother, only once in his writings, though his best friends, Alypius and Nebridius, figure often, as do other males. In Augustine's society, men mattered, but women, in all ways subordinate and lesser beings, did not. Nonetheless, Augustine shared the first half of his life with Monica and Dolorosa, and the depth and fervor of his attachment to them both was crucial in his development as a Christian, a teacher, a theologian and a careerist.

Of Dolorosa's childhood and adolescence we know nothing. Her documented existence begins in A.D. 370, in Carthage, where she met the eighteen-year-old student Augustine, who loved her profoundly for far longer than the fifteen years they lived together. Alas, we can only extrapolate from Augustine's childhood something of what Dolorosa encountered.

Augustine's father, Patricius, was a pagan member of the civic aristocracy of Thagaste in what is now Tunisia. His was a prestigious but impecunious livelihood, so he and Monica worried constantly about how to finance the education of their son Augustine, an academic star in his village school and much brighter than Navigius, his brother, or Perpetua, his sister.

In 371, after one year at a provincial university and another spent restlessly waiting for Patricius to save up more money, Augustine arrived in Carthage to complete his education. For the young student and his fellows who converged on the great city from all over Africa, Carthage was a boiling cauldron of cosmopolitanism, licentiousness, danger and freedom. Augustine took up with a so-called demonic fraternity called Eversors—"shit-disturbers" would be an apt modern translation—who tormented newcomers and teachers by playing vicious pranks. He haunted theaters, seeking out tragedies so with his tears he could express and exorcise his personal sadness.

Augustine was tormented by lust as well, for at seventeen he was "in love with love" and driven by "a hidden hunger." He sought out sexual adventure, later recalling how he had "raced headfirst into love, eager to be snared."[12] He was also jealous, suspicious and fearful, which led to angry outbursts and quarrels between Augustine and his companions. A few months into this libertine life, however, he met the submissive young Dolorosa.

At about the same time, Patricius died, leaving Monica alone to finance her son's education. Augustine was by then acknowledged as the best student of rhetoric, and like other impoverished academic stars, he began to focus on a career—in his case, a lucrative position in imperial legal administration—and on honing the talents and social connections that could make it a reality.

Dolorosa fit perfectly into this scenario. Even in the Christianizing 4th century, students routinely kept concubines they later abandoned when they found suitable women to marry. Neither centuries nor Christianity had altered this institution. Concubinage was a long-term union and, for the woman, monogamous. Concubines were either slaves or social inferiors whom their lovers would not marry, an elitist perspective that the Christian Church Fathers supported. In fact, these men taught that sending a concubine (and her children) away was a moral improvement.

Concubines did, however, merit the honorific "Matron," and though disempowered in their relationships, they were by no means social pariahs. Dolorosa was so devout and upright that the widowed Monica had no hesitation moving in with her and Augustine.

Later, Augustine described his years with Dolorosa: "In those years I had a woman. She was not my partner in what is called lawful marriage. I had found her in my state of wandering desire and lack of prudence."[13] Dolorosa understood and accepted her situation, and made a lifelong commitment to Augustine.

Augustine and Dolorosa had their frictions. Though both were intensely spiritual, they had crucial religious differences. Like Monica, Dolorosa was an orthodox Christian, and Augustine's conversion to Manichaeism, a sect the Church later decreed heretical, must have deeply troubled her. Just as serious was Augustine's perpetual struggle with the conviction that he was sinfully lustful, and that each surrender to his urges was a testimony to her overpowering sexual allure and a betrayal of his moral purity.

Postcoitally, Augustine berated himself for his insatiable lust, the "disease of the flesh" that afflicted him. His very vocal anguish must have pained and frightened Dolorosa, who believed that monogamous sexuality should be enjoyed as a God-given gift. Augustine insisted that concubinage was a mutual pact to indulge in physical lust, and so should not produce children, whereas Dolorosa disapproved of and, at least at the beginning, apparently resisted using birth control. The consequence was that when Augustine was nineteen, Dolorosa gave birth to their son, Adeodatus—"Given by God," a popular name among Carthage's Christians. Adeodatus was unplanned and unwanted (Augustine later said), but as soon as he was born, he became a much-beloved little boy.

For the next thirteen years, Augustine, Dolorosa and Adeodatus lived together happily. Unlike Patricius, who did not hide his extramarital love affairs, Augustine was monogamous, a considerable achievement in an age of flagrant male infidelities. He had, he said, taken up with Dolorosa in a period of raw emotion and reckless sexual appetite, yet "she was the only one, and I remained faithful to her."

Like Monica, Dolorosa was probably an uneducated but intelligent woman who had much to contend with: Augustine's soaring intellect; the intense male friendships he valued over his union with her; his complaints that her sensuality wrought havoc with his attempts to focus on studying philosophy; his Manichaeism; his internal turmoil as he debated his future; their shared parenting of little Adeodatus; and the news that Monica was moving in.

At the same time, much else about Dolorosa's situation was good. Augustine excelled as a rhetoric teacher and earned them a decent living, though he complained about the unruliness of Carthaginian students. He never betrayed her with other women, and he doted on Adeodatus, a gifted and obedient child. When Monica arrived, she proved to be very friendly, sharing Dolorosa's religious convictions and her uneasiness at Augustine's erroneous views. Above all, Monica adored her brilliant grandson.

Nonetheless, Dolorosa's life with Augustine and his mother was often troubled. Manichaeism preached that childlessness was the least sinful form of concubinage, and so after Adeodatus was born, Augustine insisted on birth control. And though he loved his son, Augustine was tormented by guilt that he had created Adeodatus in sin, a thought he voiced openly and repeatedly. He never referred to Dolorosa as a mother, only as his concubine. He also debated, with his friends and his mother, sometimes presumably in Dolorosa's presence, the advisability of marriage—not to Dolorosa—as a career move.

Monica's love was obsessive—this most pious of mothers pursued her son over land and sea so she could live with him, Augustine recalled—and also became burdensome. Though he rationalized and accepted it, he also craved independence, or at least a brief respite from his mother's overbearing presence. In 383, more than a decade into his union with Dolorosa, Augustine took action. He fled in the night, secretly, with Dolorosa and Adeodatus, and sailed away to Rome. For Dolorosa, his accomplice, their joint getaway must have been fraught with nuances, most of them unpleasant.

Rome proved disappointing. Augustine attracted an abundance of followers, but quickly learned that Roman students, too, were no angels: they learned as much as they could from one teacher, then transferred en masse to a new one.

Frustrated and in financial difficulty, Augustine prevailed on his Roman Manichaean contacts to obtain for him the position of public orator in Milan, where he had previously traveled and heard the great Ambrose (who was later to become Saint Ambrose). Ambrose had not encouraged the young rhetorician with the awkward African accent; nonetheless, Ambrose's impressive oratory had convinced Augustine that his own future lay in Milan. Soon, Augustine converted from Manichaeism to mainstream Christianity. Then Monica arrived from Carthage and settled down in their new home. Dolorosa undoubtedly rejoiced with Monica at Augustine's newfound religious conviction, the bedrock of her own spirituality, but the next stage of his personal development could only have grieved her.

First came relentless discussions about how marriage to an heiress would catapult the talented but unwealthy Augustine into a splendid career. Augustine wavered, torn between the argument of his best friend, Alypius—that marriage would quash their project of forming a monastic community devoted to the pursuit of wisdom—and his own conviction that marriage was the very thing to stoke his professional success. Monica assured him that marriage would ready him for the baptism that would wash away his sins, and she flung herself into the project of finding a candidate.

Did Dolorosa voice any objections, or did she—with sinking heart—agree with Monica? Augustine later portrayed her as a woman who subjected her will to his and accepted his decisions without objection. But she must have suffered; after fifteen years and a son together, she must have mourned and regretted and wept, even in silence, at this unraveling of her life.

Augustine and Monica, meanwhile, aggressively sought a suitable wife. They found a girl, still a child, whom Augustine met and "liked well enough" to demand in marriage. Her parents agreed, and the pair was betrothed, though her age required a waiting period of almost two years. But the continued presence of Dolorosa under Augustine's roof, in Augustine's bed—and, had they only known it, indelibly etched in his heart—distressed his future parents-in-law. Dolorosa, suddenly, was the proverbial fly in the ointment, and she had to be plucked out. Augustine, or perhaps Monica, gave her the bad news.

Meekly, without causing a scene, Dolorosa said she understood. For the sake of Augustine's material and spiritual well-being, she would voluntarily remove her no-longer-welcome self from the premises. What did she feel besides racking grief as she said her final farewells to her beloved Augustine and her only child? Unlike almost all other men who sent away their concubines, Augustine had decided to keep his (illegitimate) son with him. What words of comfort did Dolorosa wrench out of her bursting heart for Adeodatus as he watched his mother pack her trunks?

Dolorosa set sail again for her African homeland, alone, pledging never to give herself to another man. Her departure broke Augustine's heart, crushed it into a bleeding organ of pain (he said), and though the sharpness of his lust drove him to take up with another concubine while waiting for marital sex with his child bride, he never recovered from the blow of losing Dolorosa. Then God spoke to him, commanding him to refrain from sexual intercourse with a concubine and to rethink his plan to marry. Augustine responded instantly and became celibate.

We can assume that the aftermath of the ruptured love affair was at least as painful for Dolorosa as for Augustine, who never really recovered. He reneged on his betrothal and devoted himself to advancing in the Church, where he was becoming a major figure. But he continued to mourn his lost sweetheart.

Their relationship might well have endured for a lifetime had not Augustine's disgust at his powerful sexuality, reinforced by his personal ambitions, driven him to renounce his lower-caste concubine.

Dolorosa's solitary life continued, for her death was an event Augustine would have noted. Yet he wrote only about his own agony, his own regrets, his own suffering. If he ever inquired about her, sent her money or notified her when sixteen-year-old Adeodatus died, he did not mention it. She must have known, however, that in 389 Augustine returned to Africa, that two years later he was ordained as a priest, and that in 396 he became bishop of Hippo. She must have felt great satisfaction that he had been ordained in her form of Christianity, and that he had soared in the Church hierarchy.

Centuries later, Augustine's conversion to orthodox Christianity is still unfairly credited to Ambrose instead of to the woman who had urged it on him for fifteen years. Instead of being honored for her enormous contributions to her lover's spiritual development, Dolorosa has passed into history unnoticed and unnamed, apart from her legal and sexual status as Augustine's concubine.

CHAPTER 2

Eastern Concubines
and Harems

IN the eastern world, concubinage was the handmaiden of marriage, recognized by law and accepted by society. It developed in response to men's disinclination to accept one sexual partner, and accommodated their desire to vaunt their virility and underscore their wealth through possession of women other than their wives. Such institutionalized infidelity could operate only in thoroughly male-dominated societies. Even then, making it workable on the individual level, as husbands introduced new women into their marriages, required at least minimal accommodation to the needs of both wife and concubine. Specifically, the laws governing concubinage attempted to protect wives from their husband's emotional defection, and concubines from retaliation by those same insecure wives. The most striking difference between concubinage and mistressdom was that the laws acknowledged the concubine's children as legitimate.

CONCUBINES IN CHINA[1]
"How sad it is to be a woman! Nothing on earth is held so cheap," lamented the 3rd-century Chinese poet Fu Xuan.[2]

In ancient China, a system of overweening patriarchy dictated the tiniest detail of a woman's life, discouraging individualism and prohibiting choice. From antiquity to modern times, the subjugation of women remained a constant feature of dynasty after dynasty. The condition of Chinese women

34

underwent drastic changes only when the old order disintegrated in the face of 20th-century revolutionary movements.

Confucianism, the way of life founded by the sage Confucius (551–479 B.C.), dominated the thought and political structure of the Chinese people for over two millennia. In the Han period (206 B.C.–A.D. 220), it was adopted as the official ideology. Confucianism taught that the family was the basis of all society, and it disdained women as intellectually wanting. Confucian-influenced laws decreed that wives should be subject to their husbands, daughters to their fathers, widows to their sons, and women in general to men.

Buddhism, which originated in India in the 6th century B.C., traveled to China, where it struggled against Confucianism. Buddhism did not succeed in replacing the traditional Chinese Confucian way of life but, by the 4th century, it coexisted with and influenced it. Chinese Buddhism, too, denigrated women, characterizing them as lustier and weaker willed than men. The tenets of both Confucianism and Buddhism reinforced a way of life that subjugated women and repressed their wayward natures.

Like the Greeks and Romans, the Chinese greeted the birth of daughters without joy, often with displeasure. A baby girl was another gaping mouth her family would never profit from. She would either become a wife who would labor for her husband or be sold as a concubine or a *mui tung*, a slave, likely fetching a smaller sum than her parents had spent to rear her. So why should she live, a losing proposition from the instant she slithered out of the birth canal? And if she survived this neonatal triage, why bother giving her a name, when she was only a temporary family member destined for life elsewhere, under another man's roof? And so, for centuries, many girls were numbered rather than named: Daughter Number 1, Daughter Number 2. We know from psychological studies of prisoners how such a system demoralizes its subjects. In China, this contemptuous disregard for the individuality spilled over onto named women, who in most other ways shared their numbered sisters' status.

Concubinage in China was integrated into the all-important family structure. Concubines had a clearly defined role and duties. They supplemented wives and had a certain status, lowly but distinct. They were less likely to be despised as whores than were the accomplished Aspasia or the devout Dolorosa or their Greek and Roman counterparts, though Chinese men often recruited their concubines from brothels.

Some lucky concubines were maintained in separate residences, but most shared their master's household with his wife, children, servants and often other concubines. This provided a certain security, but it also led to complex and difficult relationships between the household's various inmates. A concubine's well-being and happiness usually depended on her skill at domestic intrigue and, literally, sexual politics.

Possessing concubines was highly prestigious. The more a man could accumulate, the better. Concubines were given as gifts to officials or bridegrooms. At the same time, everyone knew that a decent woman did not become a concubine, "married off in shame without wedding or ceremony."[3]

A concubine accompanied her master on business trips when the wife could not shuck off her domestic responsibilities. More importantly, she provided heirs when a wife could not. Producing a son bestowed limited tenure on even the humblest concubine. If she was a slave, she would not now be at risk of being sold off at the slightest whim of any senior household member.

Though a Chinese concubine had a legal status, she had few rights but many obligations. If she slept with another man, she was adulterous, and if her master caught her in the act, he could kill her and her lover. Other punishments might be seventy-seven and eighty-seven strokes respectively with a bamboo cane, or being drowned together in the sort of basket used to transport pigs to market. In sharp contrast to murdering a wife, murdering a concubine brought a light punishment.

Masters could divest themselves of their concubines in a sort of divorce, and in theory at least, concubines could divest themselves of their masters. The master could invoke seven traditional "outs," or grounds for his action, including wanton conduct and garrulousness. A concubine could claim only three, including having no home to return to, often a euphemism for her master's poverty.

Concubines came from backgrounds as various as their masters'. Some had respectable families whose fathers benefited from the arrangement. Many had been *mooi-jais*, slave girls abandoned or sold by destitute parents and often recruited into brothels or street prostitution before being trained and sold (for handsome, even extortionate, profits) as concubines.[4]

The criteria for choosing a wife and a concubine were quite different. Unlike a wife, a concubine's status and behavior did not carry great weight, but she had to have either skills or potential in the erotic arts, and—if a man was making the selection—physical charms. When a jealous or cautious wife or an influential concubine had a say in the matter, she preferred a homely *mooi-jai*, unlikely ever to threaten her own position.

Mooi-jais sold as concubines were displayed like merchandise, and in accordance with the ritual of *shou-ma*. This required the girl to parade in front of potential buyers, to speak, to show her face, hands and arms, and above all her unbound feet. In foot-obsessed China, feet mattered greatly, especially their size. The girl's unique body scent was also explored, first teeth and breath, then armpits, which buyers sniffed, and sometimes vaginal odor. A date might be slipped into the vagina, then removed so clients could smell or lick it.

Fragrance, in fact, made one concubine a legendary heroine. To this day, Xiang Fei, the "fragrant concubine" of the 18th-century Manchu (Qing) dynasty, is the revered heroine of fictional romances and Chinese opera. Xiang Fei's fabled fragrance emanated from her very essence, and she had no need of perfumes or powders. The Manchu emperor was so intrigued that he had her spirited away from her husband and brought back to him at the royal court. On the journey, he organized daily butter massages and camel's-milk baths to keep her sweet-smelling.

Xiang Fei did not reciprocate the emperor's adoration. Instead, she hid tiny daggers in her flowing sleeves and confided to her serving women that she intended to use them to avenge her abduction from her beloved husband and her country.

The empress dowager, fearing for her son's safety, intervened and granted Xiang Fei "the favor of death" by strangulation. The emperor, in agonies of grief, embraced her lifeless body. Even then, a pure scent enveloped her corpse.

For real (and gamier) women, concubinage was neither tragically romantic nor heroic. Usually, a concubine's life was tantamount to house arrest, cooped up with rivalrous inmates: a wife, other concubines, even servants, all embroiled in the household's endless squabbling and intrigue. At issue was security—or rather, the lack of it. Because everything depended on their husband or master, all these women vied for his attention and favor in a grim jockeying for position that forced each one to undermine her competitors. The best way a concubine could achieve this was to bear a boy child.

In a lowlier household, a concubine might spend her days in domestic drudgery, made wretched by a watchful, jealous wife or rival concubines. In a wealthier home, she might find the days interminable, dribbled away in household chores, grooming routines, gossip and marathon games of mah-jongg. To stave off boredom, concubines often smoked opium. Their mates encouraged this practice because opium-addicted women were less discontented and more docile.

Centuries of Chinese concubinage spawned millions of concubines, but as is so often the case with ordinary people, very few left any records of their lives. Some, such as the 18th-century's "fragrant concubine," live on in legend. Others, from the 19th and early 20th centuries, survive in the memories of their children and grandchildren. Of these, a few have passed on whatever they can document and remember to researchers and writers. Two such remembered concubines are Yu-fang, who lived in China, and May-ying, who began her life as a concubine in China but soon after emigrated to Canada.

Yu-fang

Yu-fang was born on the fifth day of the fifth moon in the early summer of 1909, in the turbulence of southwest Manchuria, 250 miles northeast of Peking. She was a beautiful girl with an oval face and glowing skin that set off her rosy cheeks. Her shiny black hair was twisted into a thick braid so long it brushed her waist.

Yu-fang also had bound feet, a sign of gentility, a guarantee of subservience and a mark of beauty. On top of that, she was demure and well behaved. As a concubine, she was worth enough money for her father to fulfill his lifelong ambition of acquiring concubines of his own. He negotiated with General Xue, a warlord and police chief, and soon Yu-fang was transferred to the general's custody.

Yu-fang was lucky in that General Xue did not move her into the house he shared with his wife and other concubines. Perhaps because she was so young and lovely, he installed her in her own home, with servants and a companionable cat. The general visited and made love to her, and provided an allowance. He urged but did not force her to smoke opium. When she was alone, Yu-fang passed her time reading novels and poetry, tending her roses and her garden, and playing with her cat. General Xue permitted her to attend the opera and, though he did so reluctantly, to visit her parents. When she poured out her litany of fears about her precarious hold on her lover, her father was unsympathetic.

One day Yu-fang's fears came true: General Xue stopped visiting. For six years, Yu-fang lived alone. Sometimes he wrote, and he always sent money, but Yu-fang was restless and miserable. She mourned his inexplicable withdrawal and continually reviewed their time together, trying to understand. One day he reappeared and, as if he had not absented himself for six years, made love to her.

A month later, Yu-fang was overjoyed to discover she was pregnant. When their daughter was born, the general instructed her to name the child Bao Qin. A year later, he summoned her and Bao Qin to the mansion he shared with his wife and other concubines. Sick at heart, Yu-fang complied.

In her new home, Yu-fang's worst fears were realized. Upon her arrival, a servant snatched Bao Qin from her arms and handed her over to Madame Xue, who had decided to raise the child as her own daughter. Bao Qin would no longer call Yu-fang "Mama"; she would reserve that endearment for Madame Xue. Furthermore, Yu-fang would kowtow to Bao Qin just as she did to Madame Xue.

Overnight, Yu-fang became a secondary concubine with a status much like a servant's. Madame Xue resented her bitterly. Even more distressing was the realization that the elderly General Xue was dying. Now Yu-fang understood clearly the reason behind General Xue's sudden reappearance in her life. Childless and in failing health, he and his wife had decided that Yu-fang's womb would be the vessel to give life to his last child.

Soon Yu-fang's fate would be in Madame Xue's unsympathetic hands. To rid herself of Bao Qin's natural mother, Madame Xue would likely sell Yu-fang, perhaps to a wealthy man, even to a brothel.

General Xue saved Yu-fang. With his dying breath he implored his wife to free his concubine. Madame Xue honored his request and Yu-fang fled home to her parents, where she entered a minefield. Her mother had lost her power struggle with the two concubines purchased with General Xue's money, whom her husband vastly preferred to her. The concubines functioned as a team, terrorizing the household, including the newly returned Yu-fang. Yu-fang's story has an atypically happy ending. A liberal family friend was overwhelmed at her beauty and married her, thus liberating her from her desolate existence.

May-ying [5]

In 1907, two years before Yu-fang's birth, Leong May-ying was born in south China, in the province of Kwangtung, and she died nearly sixty years later in the Canadian province of British Columbia. Thanks to her granddaughter Denise Chong, author of the moving and meticulous memoir *The Concubine's Children: The Story of a Chinese Family Living on Two Sides of the Globe*, May-ying's sad story has not been lost.

May-ying's family was not quite poor enough to drown or otherwise dispose of their unfortunately female infant. At four, she was already so headstrong that she resisted her mother's efforts to bind her feet, a custom that might have qualified her as a child bride. Instead, she was sold as a servant. At a marriageable seventeen, her owner resold her as a concubine to Chan Sam, a married peasant who wanted a companion in Canada, where he was laboring to earn money to improve his wife and daughter's lot back in China.

May-ying was horrified. She believed that no decent girl became a concubine, but her only alternative was suicide. May-ying chose life, and first met Chan Sam at the Vancouver wharf. After a welcoming lunch, he told her that she had to wait tables in a teahouse for two years to work off the money he had borrowed for her passage. May-ying was shocked and angry; Chinese culture considered waitresses little better than prostitutes. Her new relationship was off to a bitter start.

But May-ying proved a popular waitress who earned good tips. She was a doll-like woman, well under five feet tall and as slender as a stalk of bamboo, with white-powdered skin, plucked eyebrows, delicate features and thick hair becomingly dressed.

When May-ying was nineteen, she and Chan Sam had a daughter, Ping, followed a year later by Nan, whose gender upset May-ying just as her own had upset her mother. Soon after, the little family returned to China for an extended visit because Chan Sam wanted to reassure his wife, Huangbo, who had just learned that he had a concubine, that they would all live happily together under one roof.

Right away the two women quarreled, with the domineering May-ying bullying the meeker Huangbo and refusing to do her own share of the chores. To keep the peace, Chan Sam sent May-ying to school and decided to take a second concubine to help with the housework. At this news, May-ying and Huangbo united in protest, forcing Chan Sam to cancel his plans. Though he usually slept with Huangbo, he also impregnated May-ying, who persuaded Chan Sam that her first son should be born in Canada to enjoy the benefits of Canadian citizenship. He agreed, but Ping and Nan remained in China with Huangbo. As Chan Sam's wife, she was considered their mother.

Back in Canada, May-ying was devastated to deliver another daughter, Denise Chong's mother, Hing, later known as Winnie. The relationship between Hing's parents quickly deteriorated. The Depression had smashed British Columbia's economy, and its Chinatowns were even harder hit. While May-ying waitressed to support both the Canadian and the Chinese branches of the family, Chan Sam searched in vain for work. One day, May-ying simply ran away without a word and left him with the baby.

May-ying did not go far. Chan Sam located her at a teahouse and reminded her of her obligations, and May-ying returned home. But she was not reconciled to her concubine status, which demanded much yet rewarded her with so little, and she took to drinking liquor and gambling with appreciative teahouse customers. Partly to free herself of Chan Sam's vigilance and constant moralizing, May-ying encouraged him to visit China, hoping he would father the son they all longed for. He agreed, and she paid his passage with an advance against her salary.

Back in the village, Chan Sam and Huangbo began to build a house with remittances from May-ying, who met their constant demands by borrowing from her employer and selling lottery tickets on commission. Nobody thanked her—these sacrifices were expected.

But May-ying was not the sacrificing kind, especially not with the tedious Chan Sam safely in China. She began to indulge herself with more borrowed money, buying smart clothes, gambling, taking short trips to Victoria.

Gambling, however, became more than a casual pastime, and soon May-ying was a serious addict, unable to stop herself from wagering future wages, which she often lost. Finally, seriously indebted, she began to trade sex with teahouse clients who paid off a gambling debt for her or gave her money.

Worse was to come. In 1937, Chan Sam decided to return to Canada, leaving Huangbo, Ping, Nan and his new son, Yuen, in China. The family had grieved rather than rejoiced at this long-awaited child's birth because little Yuen's feet were grotesquely deformed, pointing directly behind him as if his torso were walking forward and his feet backward. (In Canada, May-ying so longed for a son that she tried to transform Hing into one, dressing her in pants and cropping her hair.)

Despite the financial pressures on her and her descent into the hell of gambling addiction and paid sex, May-ying had greatly enjoyed her personal freedom during Chan Sam's extended stay in China. Their reunion quickly degenerated into bitterness. He criticized her gambling, smoking, excessive drinking and spendthrift ways, and "held an ever higher regard for his moral authority over her."

May-ying was contemptuous of his thriftiness (a meal of rice smeared with ketchup or jam, for instance), and enraged by his authoritarianism, the Confucian sayings he spouted and his attempts to control her.

On the day Chan Sam found May-ying in another man's lodgings, she left him for good, took Hing and moved to Nanaimo, British Columbia. Chan Sam took this calmly: "she was still his concubine; the only difference was that they were living apart." His heart, joined in love with Huangbo's, was untouched by May-ying's defection. Besides, he knew she would continue to hand over money for the family in China.

May-ying served meals, gambled and succumbed to such alcoholic excesses that she constantly vomited. She channeled her rage at what had become of her life into systematically beating Hing and tormenting her in other ways. "Why don't you just go and die?" she repeatedly taunted her daughter.

Eventually, May-ying found a man she respected. Chow Guen was a clever man, undefeated by the Depression, and they began a relationship that lasted for years. Guen, with a wife and children in China, did not support May-ying, and, indeed, kept meticulous accounts of money he loaned her. But he helped her acquire what she most wanted, a son to care for her in her old age. Adoptable Chinese boys were like rare gems, worth ten times the price of a girl, and May-ying had to pay three hundred dollars for baby Gok-leng, later Leonard.

May-ying's changed circumstances—lower Depression-era wages, two children, Guen—reinforced both her resentment of Chan Sam and her feeling of independence. If she saw Chan Sam on the street, she cut him dead, and she forbade Hing to call him *Baba* because "He's not your father." She no longer gave him money, and it was Chan Sam who paid Hing's school fees.

In 1939, May-ying moved to Vancouver, where Guen lived, boarded Gok-leng with an elderly couple and took Hing to live with her in one room. Guen was her lover, but he spelled out the conditions of their relationship: she must rent her own lodgings and pay all her own expenses.

Chan Sam, longing for Huangbo and humiliated by May-ying's bad reputation in the Chinese community, decided that his self-respect required him to "divorce" her. "I'm the one who brought you from China. And by right, [Chow Guen] should be asking me for permission to have anything to do with you."

May-ying was furious. "I don't have a wedding ring on my finger," she retorted. But Chan Sam did, because unlike his concubine, he was married. Chan Sam was determined to sell his disobedient and disreputable concubine. Chow Guen, he told May-ying, had to pay him three thousand dollars for the right to her.

"I am not for sale," she spat. Chow Guen would never pay Chan Sam one cent, and she herself would do precisely what she wished with her life. What she did with it was to continue drinking and gambling, pawning then reclaiming her jewelry, mistreating her daughter, whose greatest sin was her despised gender, and loving Guen.

One day Chan Sam brought May-ying the terrible news that their daughter

Nan had died. May-ying sent her condolences to Huangbo and also wrote Ping, her oldest daughter: "Do not write to me anymore. I am too heartbroken." With that she cut off her links to the Chinese family that had bound her and Chan Sam together for so many years.

May-ying's life established a pattern. She moved from room to room, chasing ever cheaper rents. She boarded out, then took back, the children. Once, she tried to fix up their home. She bought furniture, including a used easy chair for Hing. Later, Chan Sam reappeared in their lives as a casual acquaintance, the passage of time having dissipated the animosity between him and his concubine.

Hing, however, was distressed by her mother's indebted and unstable life as Guen's unkept mistress. May-ying cared so much for Guen that she sacrificed Hing to chase after him, sometimes from city to city. Yet late at night, she still had to creep back from his room to hers. Where, Hing asked herself, was her mother's honor in all this? Finally, to relieve her little family's perpetual poverty, Hing enrolled in nursing school and endured the relentless slights and discrimination directed against her as an Asian. Every month, she sent May-ying her $105 paycheck. May-ying cashed it and sent Hing five dollars for spending money.

When Hing, who now called herself Winnie, became engaged, May-ying demanded a five-hundred-dollar bride price and Winnie's promise to raise Gok-leng, now Leonard, in exchange for her parental blessing. She got the bride price, but Winnie's fiancé refused to take Leonard. May-ying accepted this, and gave Winnie the traditional wedding gift of a down comforter and two pillows, plus a cedar chest she bought in instalments.

May-ying continued to drink, quarrel and neglect herself, her son, her home and even her beloved Guen. She contacted Winnie again only when she was desperate. Guen had abandoned her, saying that even if she were penniless, he would not give her a cent.

May-ying moved in with Winnie, but her insatiable need for alcohol and the money to buy it created impossible tensions. Once, when she urged Winnie to die, Winnie lashed out bitterly, "You almost spanked me to death; why didn't you just tie me to a telephone pole, whip me until I died? Then I wouldn't have to live through such misery!"

After May-ying refused to move out, Winnie's husband carried her to his car and drove her to Chan Sam's room in Chinatown. In a rare truce, she and Chan Sam united against Winnie. Then they resumed their separate lives; he died of cancer in 1957.

May-ying's life was a downward spiral of alcohol, loathsome rooming houses and seasonal work picking fruit and vegetables. She and Winnie had brief reconciliations and reunions until 1967, when May-ying was killed in a car accident.

The coroner's report noted that at the time of her death, May-ying was four feet nine inches tall and weighed about ninety pounds. Her estate was equally tiny: $40.94, a pawnshop receipt for her jade jewelry, bottles of dried herbs and a cashmere sweater Winnie had given her. Guen, dry-eyed, contributed fifty dollars toward the funeral he did not attend. May-ying, doomed from birth by poverty and gender, was buried several rows from Chan Sam, estranged from him in death as in life.

CONCUBINES IN JAPAN[6]

Unlike China, ancient, agrarian Japan valued its women, though not to the extent of according them equality with Japanese men. The goddesses in the pantheon of its animist Shinto religion were revered, and when the sun goddess, Amaterasu O-mikami, the Heaven-Shining-Great Deity, sent her grandson down from heaven to rule Japan, she founded the sanctioned Japanese imperial family.

The Japanese people also worshipped Shinto goddesses whom oral legends portrayed cavorting freely and indulging in serial love affairs.[7] These lascivious goddesses were divine proof that sex was a joyous activity and that females could initiate and enjoy it as much as males. The result was that in Shinto-inspired Japan, women as well as men could express their sexuality quite freely. The warrior samurai class alone was sexually reserved. Even today, the Japanese reverence for sex is at the core of the national culture.

Japan's early woman-friendly culture welcomed female rulers. From legendary, unrecorded times until the 12th century, women held positions of authority and power. The era from A.D. 522 until 784, for instance, is memorable because queens ruled as often as kings. Ironically, it was some of these supremely influential women who introduced foreign belief systems into Japan that would deeply influence and often replace Shintoism. Empress Suiko (592–628) succeeded in implanting Korean Buddhism, initially introduced at least fifty years earlier, into Japan, and she patronized Buddhist arts. Two other notable empresses, Ko-myo (729–49) and her daughter and successor Ko-ken (749–58), were also devout and proselytizing Buddhists.

Over time, the misogyny at Buddhism's core permeated Japanese society. New double-standard codes of conduct emerged. Women's rights were eroded in all areas. Empress Jito (687–97) oversaw the codifying of Japan's fundamental laws into the Taiho Code of 701. The Taiho Code overhauled tax and land laws, and specified that women could receive only two-thirds as much as men when land was distributed. In the 15th century, so-called landowners generated "house laws" that regulated women's legal and social inferiority. Other legal and social codes of behavior demanded virginity in brides, but sexual experience in grooms.

An influential 17th-century textbook outlining women's roles urged girls to be virtuous, chaste, obedient and quiet. A woman "must look to her husband as her lord, and must serve him with all worship and reverence, not despising or thinking lightly of him. The great life-long duty of a woman is obedience."[8]

Wives were not, however, enjoined to love and adore the husbands their parents had arranged for them to marry. Centuries later, Japanese marriage is still characterized by pragmatic considerations, which make extramarital affairs far more palatable than they would be in societies that expect spouses to love each other.

Docile but emotionally unengaged wives from prosperous households often had to share their homes, or at least their husbands, with one or more concubines. By the 17th century, concubinage modeled on the systems in Buddhist China and Korea was well developed in Japan, and it was governed by comprehensive rules.

Neither wives nor concubines were necessarily antagonistic. Concubinage was common, and many wives had been raised in households that included concubines. Concubines themselves were often concubines' daughters. Both wife and concubine knew the rules and the consequences of disobeying them.

Concubines had the status of servants and could never attain wifely status. Even widowers or bachelors who wished to marry them could not do so. If the concubine was brought to live in her master's home, she was subject to his wife's authority and could never infringe on her position. In theory, wives approved their husbands' choice of concubine. Wives with personalities strong enough to implement their authority coexisted harmoniously with concubines. Despite the guarantees of their marital status, weaker women often found themselves in internecine struggles with willful or contemptuous concubines.

Men who took concubines did so for myriad reasons: prestige, sex, romantic love and, most importantly, to provide an heir in a hitherto childless marriage. A wife's failure to conceive a child gave her husband legal grounds to divorce her, but she could be saved from such an extreme measure if her husband's concubine could do the job. For this reason, many wives gladly welcomed fertile young concubines into their household.

One of the most common words for a concubine, *mékaké*, means "borrowed womb." A *mékaké*'s son by her master would not really be hers. His father's wife would raise the infant as his official mother, and his father would acknowledge him as an heir. His concubine birth mother would remain their servant, and now also her son's. The first time she would see her baby after delivering him would be on the thirtieth day after his birth, when she accompanied the other servants on a formal visit to pay her respects to her new little master.

Many men who were the fathers of families took concubines for purely erotic reasons. A man might even fall in love with a lovely young woman and maintain her in separate lodgings to spare her his wife's stern discipline or to avoid the unpleasantness of rivalries with other previously favored concubines. There was another reason, too. If his wife accused him of placing his concubine above her, her family could intervene and demand the return of her dowry. Separating potential rivals made good economic sense. In most households, however, the master assumed that the rules of concubinage were sufficient to guarantee the sort of harmonious coexistence that would reflect well on his authority and make his life a comfortable one.

Lady Nijo [9]

As is so often the case, most Japanese concubines lived and died undocumented. But one rather exceptional woman has left copious records of her experience as a Japanese court concubine. Lady Nijo does not speak for millions of her less-favored sisters, but her autobiographical book, *The Confessions of Lady Nijo*, is compelling because she was so observant and transparent and, at the same time, so self-absorbed that her autobiography has unintended elements of self-satire.

Lady Nijo entered the 13th-century court of ex-emperor GoFukakusa when she was four years old, just after the death of her teenaged mother, Sukedai. GoFukakusa, a frail and timid young man lamed by a deformed hip and overshadowed by his handsome and charismatic younger brother, Kameyama, had at one time adored Sukedai. He transferred his unrequited love onto her pert and pretty little daughter, and in 1271, with her father's consent, he took the girl as his concubine. Lady Nijo was then twelve or thirteen years old, a typical age for maidens to graduate into the adult world of marriage and concubinage. GoFukakusa was thirteen years her senior.

46

Lady Nijo expressed little grief at her mother's death, and no resentment that her childhood was abruptly curtailed. What she truly cared about was clothing—everyone's, including her own. Despite this obsession, Lady Nijo was cultured, well read, musical, artistic and swaggeringly proud of her (mostly indifferent) poetry.

As GoFukakusa's concubine, Lady Nijo proved to be a savvy contender in a competitive court devoted to *sake*, love, music and poetry. She was vivacious and talented, and bore a son whom GoFukakusa formally acknowledged even though he was well aware that she had a string of other lovers. He actually encouraged Lady Nijo to seduce the high priest, Ariake, despite (or perhaps because of) his sworn celibacy.

But the young concubine had several setbacks that counterbalanced her successes. After her father died, leaving her bereft of champion and counselor, GoFukakusa did not bother to establish her as an official concubine.

Lady Nijo also overestimated her irresistibility. Because GoFukakusa tolerated her affairs with other men, she attempted—recklessly—to pawn off as his the three babies she conceived with other men. (One lover had seduced her with "words [that] would have reduced a Korean tiger to tears," she recalled tenderly.) At the same time, Lady Nijo was visibly uninterested in GoFukakusa. It did not help that their infant son died or that her arrogance incurred the hostility of Higashi-Nijo, GoFukakusa's empress. Even the self-absorbed Lady Nijo noticed that Higashi-Nijo did not seem as friendly to her as she had formerly been.

Lady Nijo's final miscalculation was to involve herself romantically with Kameyama, the younger sibling GoFukakusa was so intensely envious of. After twelve years, GoFukakusa abruptly expelled his concubine. During their last, bitter encounter, Lady Nijo wore a delicate and shimmering silk gown with a red hood and blue embroidered designs of arrowroot and pampas grass. After he dismissed her, GoFukakusa went off humming, "How I hate arrowroot."

Lady Nijo finally acknowledged that she had lost her imperial lover's affection and respect. "How could he be so unfeeling?" she wondered. Despite her long tenure as his (unfaithful) concubine, GoFukakusa cut his financial support. Lady Nijo avoided destitution—narrowly—by reciting her poetry, advising on interior decor and generally living by her wits. She also became a Buddhist nun, but one of unusual ilk, traveling widely and meeting people of every social level.

After eight years on the road, Lady Nijo unexpectedly encountered

GoFukakusa at a shrine. (At this juncture, he, too, had taken holy vows.) She was wearing a soiled nun's habit, dusty, mossy and disheveled, and her traveling companion was a hunchbacked dwarf. GoFukakusa recognized her anyway, and they spent an entire night in nostalgic reminiscing. "Love affairs have not the charm nowadays that they used to have," he sighed—or at least that was how Lady Nijo remembered his sentiments."

Despite the penurious finale to her life story, the never-modest Lady Nijo assumed it was interesting enough to record. It was. Her memoirs are one of the rare testimonials to a concubine's loves, thoughts and reflections, and to her worlds, at first the 13th-century royal court and, later, the scrambling bustle of ordinary Japan.

Lady Nijo mirrored the Japanese aristocracy's libertine sexuality, frank materialism, social snobbery and intricate rituals. She shared the conventional view of love as an intimate game in which romance and poetry mattered, and fidelity did not. Whether in the imperial court or in a prosperous merchant's home, concubines lacked the security and status of wives, but they often commanded intense emotional and erotic love. As for maternal love, Lady Nijo was a typical court concubine mother, detached from the children their father controlled and his servants raised.

But Lady Nijo was unique in other ways, notably in the very fact of her extensive and self-serving memoirs, and in her extraordinary resilience in the face of adversity. Astonishingly, she made the transition from concubine to vagabond cadger without self-pity or despair. This was undoubtedly a function of her admirable coping skills. But perhaps Lady Nijo also felt relief that she had finally escaped the constrictions and artificiality of life as a court concubine, and escaped having to pretend to love the unattractive, even repellent GoFukakusa.

GEISHA MISTRESSES

Concubinage and the family structure that supported it were not the only reflections of Japan's double standard. As in so many other societies, that double standard also flourished in extensive prostitution. Prostitutes were poor girls, usually sold into the trade by their parents. The Kamakura shogunate (1185–1333) undertook supervision of prostitutes, and the Ashikaga shogunate (1338–1573) set up a Harlots' Bureau to tax them. The Tokugawa shogunate (17th to 19th century) went further and established Japan's famed Pleasure Quarters, the licensed, zoolike ghettos for prostitutes that so profoundly shocked—and titillated—hordes of foreign visitors.

But many 19th-century Japanese men in sterile arranged marriages wanted much less than the permanent responsibility of a concubine and much more than the fleeting attention of a prostitute. They wanted a Western-type mistress, Japanese style.

One source of mistresses was the teahouse world of the geisha. The first geisha (the word means "people who entertain") were men, but by 1800, most were women. The appearance of a typical geisha distinguished her from all other women. Her chalk-white face was a startling backdrop to dark-rimmed eyes and rosebud lips, and her whitened neck strained under a heavy, stiff black wig. In her gorgeous and outrageously expensive kimono with an *obi* girdling her slender waist, the geisha was not so much a woman as an ethereal creature with immense erotic appeal. By the 19th century, geisha defined *iki*, which translates loosely as "cool chic."

Geisha were usually drawn from the poorer classes, and they entered the profession as apprentices at about ten or twelve years old. Becoming a geisha was by far the best way a disadvantaged girl could upgrade her social status. She would be educated. She would help her parents, who received a sum of money when they signed the contract binding the new apprentice geisha to a term of service.

The geisha's training program was rigorous and lengthy. It included singing and music, knowledge of the immensely complicated tea ceremony, and flower arranging. Elegant ritual dancing was the most elevated level of performance and the most essential to acquire a wealthy patron, or *danna-san*. Inordinate amounts of time and money were spent on makeup and clothing. Painting the whitened geisha face mask and dressing the elaborate oiled (and smelly, dandruffy) hair were daily chores that consumed tedious and self-absorbed hours in front of mirrors.

The geisha was overworked, underfed and undervalued—subjected to, in other words, the typically unsentimental and harsh treatment considered appropriate for girls. At the geisha school, etiquette dictated that newcomers be introduced as "girl of very little talent," though they were in fact exceptional to have gotten into the school in the first place.

Geisha were also sexually initiated in an ancient ritual, the *mizu-age*. An older, experienced man would spend seven nights with the virgin geisha, massaging egg whites into her inner thighs, higher each night, until the night he penetrated her genitals with his probing fingers.[10]

Geisha learned that they had to observe the utmost personal discretion so patrons could be absolutely certain that no matter what a geisha heard or overheard, she would rather cut out her tongue than reveal it. In the 19th century, samurai conspired in teahouses to overthrow the shogun government, and geisha said nothing. Japanese politicians held top-secret meetings in teahouse *zashikis* (or drawing rooms) staffed by their favorite geisha.

A geisha apprentice became a "Younger Sister" to a more experienced geisha "Older Sister," who instructed her in everything from the mysteries of makeup ingredients to conversational ploys designed to enchant clients. The payoff for the Older Sister was a share of the geisha fees that a successful Younger Sister would eventually earn. For the Younger Sister, the ultimate geisha goal was to become a rich man's mistress.

The apprentice became a full-fledged geisha only after she passed an exam presided over by the madam of her teahouse, by her teachers and by officials from the geisha headquarters. For two or three years afterward, she worked for room, board and clothing, the latter a major expense. Later, she pocketed her tips while the teahouse kept the high fees it charged for her services. In fact, the geisha was locked into financial bondage to her teahouse, and only those with a patron, or *danna-san*, could pay off their crushing debt. Usually, the geisha became her *danna-san*'s mistress.

A geisha's potential *danna-san* would introduce himself to the teahouse owner, who investigated him carefully, particularly his finances, before deciding. If he was accepted, he would contract to help pay off his geisha's debts, underwrite her living and perhaps medical expenses and still pay her hourly fee whenever he spent time with her. A few leading geisha would have no more than a couple of *danna-sans* in a lifetime, but all the others could expect a *danna-san* to tire of them after six months or a year.

A geisha did not expect to love her *danna-san*, though she was trained to flatter, charm and kowtow to him as if she did. Their relationship was a ritualized and controlled arrangement. She was an expert mistress, he an appreciative client. If, as sometimes happened, they fell in love with each other, it was an unexpected bonus. If, as also sometimes happened, she fell in love with another man, she did so at the peril of losing her *danna-san*, incurring the wrath of her teahouse owner and ruining her reputation.

There were some advantages to geisha life in Japan, where even today women who complain of sexual harassment are ostracized and only the bravest feminists dare challenge the status quo and demand gender equality. Geisha were usually very pretty little girls discovered in very poor neighborhoods, and their new milieu elevated them to heights unimaginable and unobtainable by those they left behind. Geisha were thoroughly educated and artistically trained. They were exempted from most domestic labor, indeed had no time and little inclination for it. As part of a complex and comfortable world that incorporated traditionalism, elitism and eroticism, they were catapulted to the higher ranks of society.

Like all mistresses, geisha had little security and no tenure. Once *danna-sans* fulfilled their initial obligations, they were free to dismiss the geisha, and most did so, trading in the old for a newer model. However, the promise of being accepted back into the teahouse took the sting off a *danna-san's* dismissal, though it meant the geisha had to resume the daily grind of procuring clients and entertaining them. Some geisha managed to put aside money for such contingencies, but most suffered financially when a *danna-san* withdrew his support.

On balance, a geisha could be said to have improved her lot in life only because women were otherwise such undervalued members of Japanese society, and poor girls even more so. But the cost of this improvement was high; for every benefit granted the geisha—education, training, introduction to high society, financial reward—a price was exacted. She was contractually bound to her sponsors, and required to incur a huge debt she then spent her lifetime repaying. But the principal price was imprisonment in the rarified and reified exotica of her own body. Without the mask, the hairstyle, the kimono, *obi* and scores of accoutrements, the geisha was a mere woman, with a mere woman's worth.

A diminished number of geisha still function today. Unlike 98 percent of Japanese women, geisha never marry, but live in women's communities called *hana-machi*. Though unmarried, they often have children, some with a *danna-san* who does not force them to have an abortion, or with a secret lover who provides this child that brings such joy to the lonely geisha's life. Tellingly, only in these *hana-machi* and geisha-run teahouses is the birth of a baby girl celebrated more joyously than a boy's. In many ways, geisha are profoundly traditional, but in others they display a surprisingly feminist sensibility.

Today, geisha mistresses still have *danna-sans* who provide a steady source of income and companionship. Even so, most geisha continue working. They live lavishly and need the money. Those who leave their teahouse when a patron sets them up independently are always welcome to return to work should a *danna-san* drop his geisha or die without providing for her in his will.

Geisha report, however, that the most trying aspect of their jobs is the emotional anguish of knowing that a beloved *danna-san*—for some geisha truly love their patrons—goes home at night to his wife. (Wives are less likely to worry about geisha, who pose little threat of destroying their marriage by divorce.)

Another grief common to mistresses around the world, is their backroom status—their lovers will seldom openly acknowledge them. One geisha's *danna-san* was a high-ranking political figure who kept her hidden from his wife and the public, though not from his secretary and friends. When he died, mere hours after she had spoken to him on the telephone, nobody notified her, and she learned of his death on a newscast. She requested permission to attend his funeral, and his secretary and friends agreed on condition that she wear inconspicuous "civilian" clothes rather than her telltale kimono. "I understand," the geisha said, and she did. But upon reflection, she changed her mind and wore her kimono to bid farewell to her lover.

Soon after, her monthly allowance was cut off. She believed it was because she had worn her kimono. In fact, it was because her *danna-san* had made no provisions for her in the event of his death. Fortunately, she was a financially adroit woman who operated her own teahouse, so her *danna-san*'s death did not ruin her.

Geisha mistresses have recently scandalized Japan after news media abandoned their traditional policy of preserving the privacy of public figures' personal lives. In 1989, Prime Minister Sosuke "Mister Clean" Uno was one of the first high-level politicians to be exposed, and he resigned in disgrace. In fact, his sins were only retroactively sinful: generations of politicians, including their opponents, were also teahouse politickers who took geisha mistresses, and everyone in Japan knew it. But then a couple of geisha formerly involved with Uno broke with tradition and talked. "You bought my body with 300,000 yen a month," raged Mitsuko Nakanishi, Uno's former geisha mistress. The reporters whom the angry women spoke to published rather than ignored their stories.

Subsequently, a female legislator, Manae Kubota, disregarded the parliament's traditional veil of silence over personal matters. She questioned the prime minister, explaining that she was distressed that he had "treated women like merchandise." Mitsuko Nakanishi added, "a person like him who treats a weak woman badly should not become prime minister."

The principal culprit in the Uno debacle was the fundamental inequality between Japanese men and women. In an era when slight chinks appeared in the wall of male privilege, a previously silent witness did the unprecedented if not the unthinkable: she told the world what the world already secretly knew.

HAREM CONCUBINES

Imperial harems conjure up images of sensuous concubines at the mercy of bitter and effeminate eunuchs and of sexually insatiable emperors and princes. The reality of the Ottoman and Chinese imperial harems, however, had less to do with sex and more with power.

The Arabic word *haram*—"harem" in English—means the condition of living isolated from the outside world, and it describes an oxymoronic sanctuary for women that also imprisons them within its unbreachable walls. The last Turkish harems died out in 1909. Of all the tens of thousands of concubines they swallowed up over the centuries, the most famous—Turks might prefer "infamous"—was the 16th-century woman known as Roxelana, "the Russian woman."

Roxelana [11]

Roxelana was a clever and ambitious beauty, petite and energetic, with a small upturned nose and flashing eyes. A Polish story identifies her as Alexandra Lisowska, daughter of an impoverished Orthodox priest from Rohatyn, in Ruthenia, in the Carpathian mountains. In this account, raiding Tartars captured her, then sold her to Grand Vizier Ibrahim Pasha, who gave her to Suleiman, probably the greatest sultan of the Turkish Ottoman Empire. Nothing more is known of her origins, her family, her childhood or her education. Roxelana's life as a historical figure began only in 1526, when she emerged scratched and bloodied from a fistfight with Suleiman's number one concubine.

Losing that fistfight—on purpose—was one of Roxelana's most brilliant strategies. She was already the second *qadin*, or royal concubine, but the Tartar woman Gulbahar, the first *qadin* and mother of Prince Mustafa, heir to the throne, was an insuperable obstacle blocking her from becoming Suleiman's principal concubine. During a quarrel, Roxelana provoked Gulbahar to attack. Gulbahar fell into the trap. She yanked Roxelana's hair and raked her face with her fingernails, temporarily disfiguring the other woman's lovely face.

But Gulbahar's victory was Pyrrhic. Though Roxelana had invited an attack, she knew that the harem's rigid protocol prohibited her from counterattacking, which could lead to her expulsion from the harem. So as her adversary lashed out in rage, Roxelana simply absorbed the blows.

Later, she took her revenge. For days afterward, she rejected Suleiman's summons on the grounds that she was mutilated. Suleiman was so shocked and angry that he evicted Gulbahar. Almost immediately, Roxelana replaced her as first *qadin*.

Beautiful though she was, Roxelana's swift rise to the apex of Suleiman's harem was astonishing, and underscored her intelligence, zeal and physical presence. His harem was three hundred women strong, so the competition was as ferocious as the stakes were high. The concubines were by no means equal. Most spent dreary lifetimes scrubbing the floors and performing other menial labor. Black women fared the worst; the heaviest, dirtiest work was relegated to them. White women such as Roxelana performed a wide range of other tasks, anything from account-keeping to coffee-making.

The harem, located in the old palace, had a rigid hierarchy and complex protocol. At the very top, reflecting the Turkish view that wives were disposable but mothers were permanent, was the sultan's mother, Hafsa Hatun, the Valide Sultan ("Queen Mother"). She was second only to her son in imperial power, and in the old palace she ruled supreme. But her relationship with her son's concubines was neither cozy nor intimate. She communicated with these women, who envied, resented and plotted against her, through the intermediary of her second in command, the Kizlar Agha, meaning "the girls' general," chief of the black eunuchs. Between them, the older woman and the emasculated Nubian man governed the women of the harem.

The Kizlar Agha, however, was too involved in imperial administration to spend much time dealing with harem business, which he delegated to other eunuchs. These men worked with the concubines who were the harem's real supervisors. The controller, the treasurer, the jewel keeper and the Koran reader were usually ambitious older women with little or no chance of attracting the sultan, and they welcomed the chance to exercise their power and to accumulate the wealth their positions entitled them to.

The harem was a complex, dangerous and closed society, isolated from the realities of the outside world and even from the sultan and his entourage, who lived apart in the grand seraglio. The harem's female and eunuch inmates were of diverse ethnic and racial origins: Russian, Circassian, Tartar, Greek, Serbian, Italian, Nubian and Ethiopian. Many were Christian. None were Muslims, whose enslavement the law forbade. All were powerless, captives of the labyrinth institution designed, at enormous human and monetary cost, to accommodate the sultan's libido and pride, and they learned quickly the roles they were supposed to play.

But knowing did not reconcile the concubines to their condition. They quarreled bitterly and vied for the attention of the harem's authorities, the

Kizlar Agha, the Valide Sultan and the heads of each department. The concubines had been snatched away from their large families and poor farming villages. There, they would have married and raised children. Here, in the harem, surrounded by women and eunuchs, their only (permissible) sexual outlet was the sultan. But he fancied only the most delectable of them, and so sexual tension was acute and never-ending. The concubines were supposed to suppress or sublimate their longings until the sultan should call for them.

Some of these trapped women did just that. Others turned to each other for sexual gratification, knowingly or otherwise, in the guise of fragrant oily massages, hair brushing and styling, and a host of other grooming and beautification procedures.

Concubines unable to endure the absence of men sometimes risked their lives and, if they could, bribed eunuchs to smuggle unneutered and discreet males into their quarters. It was not unheard of for eunuchs to attempt to service the women themselves. Though castrated, they still felt sexual urges. With these familiar women, who alone in the world would not mock them, a few eunuchs engaged in sex play as best they could, desperate lovers making desperate love.

Besides sexual frustration, one important byproduct of harem life was the concubines' collective menstrual misery. For one week out of four, their pheromones called out and responded to each others', establishing a shared cycle. Then the harem groaned with hundreds of women sadder and testier than usual.

But unwanted concubines feared more than celibacy. They repeated stories about the women the Kizlar Agha and his cronies took stealthily to the Bosphorus in the dark of night, thrust into sacks weighted down with stones, then rowed out to sea to be heaved overboard and drowned. In one ghastly version, a diver hoping to salvage treasure from a sunken vessel found instead scores of rhythmically swaying sacks, the funeral shrouds of dead women held down by rocks.

Harem eunuchs could also be dangerous if a concubine crossed, insulted or disobeyed them. Kidnapped in childhood and mutilated before puberty, these men had endured unspeakable trauma, including the brutal surgery that killed over 90 percent of those subjected to it. Though their intense training for harem duty had dulled the eunuchs' memories of family and culture, they were at best ambivalent about their situation. On the one hand, their prospects for advancement and property were good. On the other, they were embittered by the nature of their mutilation, and by the fact that mainstream society dreaded and shunned them as *mujbubs*, men without penises, and scorned them because they were black.

For the most alluring and nubile of the concubines, the obvious strategy was to catch the sultan's eye. Then he would toss the lucky woman a richly embroidered handkerchief, a sign of his favor that could change her life.

When this happened, the lucky woman was separated from the other concubines, moved into her own apartment and assigned personal slaves. Then various harem officers bathed, massaged, anointed, perfumed and shaved her. They dressed her hair and painted her nails. They draped her with exquisite lingerie and gorgeous gowns. Afterward came the waiting. Would the sultan invite her to his chamber? If he did, could she conjure up the magic to captivate him? Melt his heart so she became his favorite? Or, best of all, conceive a son who could, one day, raise her to the highest possible rank, Valide Sultan?

Sometimes the sultan forgot he had ever seen her. Then the forsaken woman would be stripped of her finery, evicted from her private quarters and returned to the crowded cubicle she had so triumphantly left. As she aged and hope withered, she conceived a single new ambition—a transfer to the old seraglio, where she might be permitted to marry and leave the premises.

But a few concubines triumphed: the sultan remembered and desired them. Each experienced a variation on this theme: at night, a black eunuch would escort her to the royal chamber in the woman's quarters, a room always ready for the sultan's assignations. Silence prevailed there. Nobody was supposed to know the identity of the chosen woman or when the sultan seduced her (or, if she learned her lessons well, when she seduced him).

The concubine approached the sultan from the foot of his bed, where he lay waiting. With every show of submissiveness, she lifted the foot of the bedspread. Then, according to prescribed custom, she insinuated herself into the bed, crawling slowly up to the sultan, rump upward, sidling forward propelled by soft elbows and knees.

Even then the concubine and the sultan were neither alone nor in darkness; two elderly black women spelled each other guarding the door and fueling two torches. In their presence, the night passed in lovemaking, with the novice concubine doing her utmost to enchant her master. She was usually a virgin, but her harem sisters and their eunuch tutors had coached her in the erotic arts. Above all else, she was primed to please. The morning after, the sultan in effect graded her performance by leaving her his clothes with money secreted in the pockets. Later, he might send additional gifts to express his appreciation.

If a pregnancy resulted, the woman became a sultana, and her future was assured. If the child was a son designated as heir to the throne, she dreamed of the day she would rule as Valide Sultan.

This was the curious and challenging world into which the spritely young Roxelana was sold. Unlike many other concubines, she was not depressed by her fate. Within the seraglio she was known as Hurrem, the laughing woman, whose tinkling laughter rang out even in the sultan's presence. Swiftly, she sized up the seraglio and harem. From the outset, she dazzled young Suleiman, though not enough to dislodge Gulbahar, his first *qadin* and mother of the heir apparent, Prince Mustafa.

Suleiman was in his thirtieth year and Roxelana much younger when she emerged victorious from her contest with Gulbahar, whom Suleiman banished from the harem. At the same time, he committed himself exclusively to Roxelana, an unheard-of decision for an emperor with hundreds of women at his personal sexual disposal. He went so far as to arrange marriages for the loveliest women in his harem, to ward off temptation and to allay Roxelana's jealousy. Years later, a foreign observer marveled that "he bears her such love and keeps such faith to her that all of his subjects ... say that she has bewitched him, and they call her ... the witch."[12] Indeed, Suleiman's fidelity to one woman was unique among Ottoman emperors.

Roxelana disregarded the growing resentment toward her. Millions of Turks might hate her, but the only one who mattered, the sultan Suleiman, adored her. Yet Roxelana could not alter one fact: that Mustafa, the son of the disgraced Gulbahar, remained Suleiman's heir.

What terrified Roxelana was that when Mustafa became sultan, the Code of Laws would require him to kill his three half brothers, her sons. This "fratricide law" stemmed from a skewed interpretation of a Koranic verse—"What is a prince's death compared to losing a province?"—and was designed to prevent paralyzing royal power struggles. Mustafa's eventual assumption of power would be a death warrant for Cihangir, Selim and Bayezid, Roxelana's sons. As Mustafa neared the age of majority, Roxelana grew desperate and persuaded Suleiman to move him to various remote locations. Gulbahar, who had lived with Mustafa since her expulsion, usually followed him to these dreary outposts, another potential threat removed. At the very least, Roxelana had diluted Mustafa's influence on his father.

Roxelana's next target was the ostentatious and arrogant grand vizier Ibrahim Pasha, Suleiman's trusted confidant, administrator and brother-in-law.[13] Suleiman and Pasha were inseparable, and even had adjacent bedrooms. Pasha was as loyal to Suleiman as Suleiman was to Roxelana, and he was also protected by Hafsa Hatun, the Valide Sultan. But in 1535, when Hafsa Hatun died, Ibrahim lost his most important ally. Roxelana relentlessly pressed her advantage and poisoned Suleiman against his old friend.

Her success was lethal. On the night of March 14, 1536, the sultan summoned the seraglio goons, mutes who could never betray him, and ordered them to strangle Ibrahim. The grand vizier fought for his life against his silent assassins. The next day, servants discovered his corpse. His clothing was ripped, and the walls of his bedroom were bloodstained. Though Pasha had been a Christian, Suleiman buried him in a dervish monastery, without a marker, like a vagabond rather than the second most powerful man in the Ottoman Empire. Long ago, Roxelana had eliminated her sexual rivals. Now, out of the same blind jealousy, she had eliminated Suleiman's most trusted, loyal and able confidant.

Several years later, in 1540, a raging fire gutted the old palace, leaving hundreds of concubines, eunuchs and slave attendants homeless. Roxelana immediately convinced Suleiman to lodge her in the grand seraglio, though women never lived there. Here, she lived at the heart of imperial power and politics. A decade later, when the new palace replaced its burned-out predecessor, Roxelana simply stayed where she was. By then, she had become such a forceful presence in government that historians credit her with initiating the Ottoman Empire's Reign of Women, which ended only in 1687.

Soon after she joined Suleiman in the grand seraglio, Roxelana may have persuaded him to marry her, though this is impossible to confirm. Most Turks denied that Suleiman could ever have married a Christian (albeit a forced convert to Islam), a foreigner and a concubine. But a certain week of public festivities was interpreted by non-Turkish diplomats and visitors as a gala celebration of Suleiman's nuptials with Roxelana. If so, Roxelana had managed to trade concubinage for wedlock.

As empress or first concubine, Roxelana was Suleiman's confidante and adviser, but her most important focus was on saving her sons from Prince Mustafa, who would be forced to kill them after his father's death. In 1553, she used a forged letter to implicate Mustafa in an insurrection against his father. Suleiman, knowing nothing about her nefarious hand in the affair, reportedly agonized over how to respond, and vacillated between mercy and reprisal. But Roxelana urged Suleiman to condemn Mustafa to the traditional execution by strangulation.

At last Suleiman made his decision, and summoned Mustafa to meet him.

The prince, forewarned, strode courageously toward his father, declaring proudly that if he had to die, he would gladly do so at the hands of the man who had given him life. Like Grand Vizier Pasha, he was strangled by mute seraglio thugs.

Roxelana had triumphed. Her son Selim would now succeed his father. As for the fratricide law, she believed—correctly, it turned out—that the chosen prince would never do away with his brothers. (She did not foresee, however, that her cruel son Bayezid would plot to overthrow his father, and that Suleiman would execute him.) Roxelana did not live to enjoy her son's accession to power. Five years after Mustafa's murder, she died, mourned by Suleiman but by few of his subjects.

Roxelana was one of the most powerful concubines in any imperial harem. She has been criticized for her cruel and self-serving behavior, and demonized for influencing policies that contributed to the decline and fall of the Ottoman Empire. Even if all this were true, what else can one expect from a woman confined to harems crammed with degraded women? By ignoring their basic needs and desires, harem culture gave birth to poisonous politics.

Tz'u-hsi [14]

China's Forbidden City was a vast complex of orange-roofed, rose-walled palaces and of humbler dwellings that housed the entire imperial court, including the imperial concubines. The court was the seat of Chinese imperial power during the Ming and Qing dynasties, from 1368 to 1911. As a physical plant it was a fortified maze—walls within walls within walls. The Great Wall of China kept out foreigners, forty-foot-high and fifty-foot-thick walls protected the city of Peking (now Beijing), and the soaring purple walls around the Forbidden City opened to admit only court associates.

Inside, the Son of Heaven—the name reflecting the emperor's supposedly divine origins—lived and ruled with his enormous coterie of consorts, up to 3 wives, 9 secondary wives, 27 lesser-ranked wives, 81 concubines: a potential total of 121 women for one single man. In addition, hundreds of children and thousands of relatives, eunuchs, servants, bureaucrats, astrologers and other functionaries cohabited and worked alongside the vast imperial family.

Imperial concubines, like those belonging to lower-ranked men, were tenured members of the emperor's household. They had to be Manchu or Mongol, have unbound feet and proper clan membership. Once chosen, they were forced into intense competition to attract the favor of the emperor or the empress or, in the case of Emperor Hsien-feng, of the empress dowager, his stepmother. The few who succeeded were rewarded with a luxurious life free of any domestic labor, and the hope of conceiving the emperor's baby. Bearing an imperial son would even promote a concubine mother to the status of one of the emperor's full wives.

A millennium earlier, two imperial concubines had achieved enormous power. The exquisite Yang Kuei-fei used Emperor Hsuan Tsung's passion for her to enrich her relatives, and was strangled to death during a subsequent rebellion. Empress Wu began as a concubine to Emperor Taizong, and after his death so fascinated his son Emperor Gaozong that he made her his chief concubine. After his death, she managed to be named empress, and ruled until she was deposed at eighty years of age.

In the next millennium, the most memorable court concubine was a Manchu girl, Lady Yehenara, born on November 29, 1835, to a minor mandarin family headed by Kuei Hsiang, about whom almost nothing is known. Unlike thousands of other concubines immured in the imperial court, there is a wealth of information about Lady Yehenara, known to history as Tz'u-hsi, Empress of the West, from both Chinese and foreign sources. Unfortunately, much of this information was fabricated by expatriates in China and by the empress dowager's political enemies. One reliable source is Sir Robert Hart, the foreigner who overcame Tz'u-hsi's loathing of "foreign devils" and was appointed China's Inspector General of Customs. (For ten years he also had a concubine, Ayaou, with whom he had three children, whom he acknowledged and supported but never saw after they reached adulthood.) Other sources are foreign women who met and spoke with Tz'u-hsi; physicians who examined her; Chinese courtiers and one lady-in-waiting, Princess Derling; and foreign diplomats interested in reporting accurately to their home countries.

Tz'u-hsi was five feet tall, slender and beautifully built. She had dainty hands and, on her third and little fingers, four-inch fingernails sheathed in jade nail guards. She had wide, lustrous eyes, a high nose and higher cheekbones, shapely lips and a rounded chin. Her smile was enchanting. Like most Manchu girls, she had unbound feet that photos show in tiny slippers.

In keeping with her destiny as either wife or concubine, Tz'u-hsi kept her rather sallow skin soft, pale and fragrant with creams, ointments and oils. She used traditional Manchu makeup: face whitened with leaded powder, cheeks glowing with two red spots of rouge, her lower lip's paleness broken by a startling red cherry-shaped splotch. Her glossy black hair, never cut, was brushed back and caught up into an elaborate confection of jeweled barrettes, pins in the form of insects and flowers, and pearl tassels. "A lot of people were jealous of me, because I was considered to be a beautiful woman at that time," she recalled.[15]

Tz'u-hsi's character, however, was far from traditional. Acquaintances remarked on how serious and pensive she was, a quiet, brooding girl who kept her thoughts to herself, though later in life she expressed her lifelong resentment that her parents had always favored her siblings. She was close to illiterate, as all girls were, but spoke some Chinese as well as her Manchu mother tongue, and was a skilled painter.

In 1851, when she sixteen, the Chinese emperor Wen Tsung died and Hsien-feng, his nineteen-year-old heir, succeeded him as Son of Heaven. Now, because of her father's clan membership, Tz'u-hsi and her sisters could audition for the new imperial harem. Many eligible Manchu families were reluctant to expose an eligible daughter to the competition. Once in the harem, their daughter was lost to her family. If the emperor ignored her, even if he died, she was no longer theirs to marry off to a suitable husband. She would remain forever in the bleakness of the Hall of Forgotten Favorites, in a cubicle that looked out onto gnarled pine trees. She might in her loneliness and frustration enter a passionate love affair with another forgotten concubine. Tz'u-hsi's struggling family, however, had no such qualms, and eagerly prepared Tz'u-hsi and her sister for their ordeal.

The selection process began. Tz'u-hsi, already chaperoned by palace eunuchs, advanced to the second round. It was intense and invasive. The girls were examined for blemishes, illnesses and virginity. Their all-important horoscope was studied. They were also tested for everything from their social graces to their grasp of Manchu and Chinese—Manchu girls like Tz'u-hsi often knew little Chinese. A very few succeeded to round three, tea with the empress dowager, Hsien-feng's stepmother. Tz'u-hsi acquitted herself well, and was one of the tiny number chosen as concubines-in-training.

While Tz'u-hsi trained for her life as an imperial concubine, Emperor Hsien-feng married his deceased first wife's sister. The new empress joined his harem along with the novice concubines, including Tz'u-hsi, now a concubine of the fourth rank.

Emperor Hsien-feng's harem was modest. It included one empress, two consorts and only eleven concubines, a fourteen-woman contingent that reflected revenue issues and not creeping puritanism. (China was plagued by corrupt and incompetent leadership, wars, floods, crop failures and famine.)

Theoretically, all fourteen women were sexually available. In fact, some never even met the emperor and were nothing more than servants to the empress dowager. Tz'u-hsi was determined not to fall into their ranks.

Tz'u-hsi's apartment in the magnificent, marble-floored palace was private though close to the other concubines, and large enough for her eunuchs and maids to properly care for her. The emperor had given her jewelry and gowns, court robes and footwear, and her father had done even better, receiving bolts of costly silk, gold and silver, horses, saddles and bridles, and an elegant tea set.

The serious and observant Tz'u-hsi quickly learned how the palace operated. The eunuchs were the real powermongers. It was wise to befriend them, and dangerous to defy them. They were also the concubines' only male company, and so their flattery was welcome, their conversation instructive and their gossip enlightening. Tz'u-hsi offered the eunuchs her deep and enduring friendship. She reached out as well to Niuhuru, the empress, developing a complicated relationship with her that lasted over two decades. In her isolation in the harem, Tz'u-hsi also surrounded herself with dogs, Pekinese bred only at—and for—the palace. Tz'u-hsi remained a virginal concubine, and the regal pups were her *enfants manqués*.

Tz'u-hsi's lack of contact with the emperor deeply disturbed her. But in his frenzy for sexual experimentation, the Son of Heaven preferred to exhaust his energies in brothels, and ignored his anxious concubines. To rectify this, Hsien-feng's stepmother and the palace officials pressured him into turning to his harem instead of his favorite bordellos. He did so, and impregnated one of his concubines, the gentle and lovely Li Fei.

Li Fei's pregnancy gave Tz'u-hsi her big chance. Protocol forced pregnant concubines into total celibacy, and even the Son of Heaven could not countermand this. That was why, driven by lust one day in 1855, Hsien-feng inscribed the chaste Tz'u-hsi's name on the traditional jade tablet that denoted his nightly wish list, and handed it to the chief eunuch.

Tz'u-hsi had been waiting for this moment. When the chief eunuch arrived at her rooms, he stripped her, swaddled her in a scarlet rug and carried her, on his back, to the emperor's bedchamber. (This tradition originated in the days of the Ming dynasty, whose concubines had bound feet and could not walk.) There he deposited her at the foot of the bed and removed the rug. Tz'u-hsi, no doubt trembling and fearful, nonetheless knew what to do. Submissively, she crawled up to where the emperor sprawled, watching her. She confided her little body trustingly and hopefully, allowing the exalted but callow young emperor to glimpse only her modesty, and not her dread.

The encounter was successful. Nine months later, in a pavilion called the Library of the Topaz Wu-t'ung Tree, in the majestic Round Bright Garden Summer Palace, Tz'u-hsi delivered Tung Chih, the longed-for imperial son. This was especially gratifying because Li Fei had earlier produced the princess Jung An, a dynastically worthless daughter. Tz'u-hsi had guaranteed the imperial succession, and as the vessel that had carried the seed, she was promoted to concubine of the first rank, or consort, a status only the empress surpassed.

It is difficult to suppose that Tz'u-hsi or Li Fei, or even the empress, felt romantic love for the dissolute and ungainly man they belonged to. On the other hand, they were intimate only with eunuchs, and were seldom alone with other courtiers, such as the emperor's jealous half brothers. So Tz'u-hsi's longing for the love of the Son of Heaven was sensible and strategic, and perhaps tinged with pride. In later life she remembered wistfully the brief period when "the late Emperor became very much attached to me and would hardly glance at any of the other ladies."[16]

But the emperor had little taste for this concubine whose attempts to emulate Buddha's tranquil mien earned her the nickname "Little Buddha." Night after night, he inscribed the name of the delightfully unserious Li Fei on the jade tablet. At the same time, however, Hsien-feng began to respond positively to Tz'u-hsi's enthusiastic questions and comments about current events, about which she was woefully ignorant, and palace affairs, about which she was well informed and shrewd. As a result, he gave her access to some of his documents, thereby tacitly ushering her into the darkly echoing corridors of power. But she often wept in despair because he did not love her.

Until 1860, this was Tz'u-hsi's life. She was obsessively attentive to appearances and never deviated from her lengthy ritual of daily ablutions, grooming and hair styling, scenting herself with musk. (Eunuchs helped all concubines with these rituals.) She walked compulsively, even in the rain, to the annoyance of the court ladies who had to accompany her. She ate sparingly, selecting from 150 tiny dishes of delectable foodstuffs, many of them sugared fruits and sweets. She seldom saw her imperial son, who was breast-fed by wet nurses and cared for by eunuchs, though she and the empress often discussed his upbringing.

The mother of the prince whiled away the hours reading and studying, now that palace tutors had taught her how to read and write. She created origami rabbits and birds. She played with her pack of black Pekinese, lodged in their own pavilion. And, because her appetite for flowers was insatiable, she decorated each of her apartments with floral bouquets, wove flowers into her hair, even entwined them in the fur of Shadza, meaning "Fool," at that time her favorite dog. At night, she slept on a little pillow stuffed with tea leaves, thought to be good for the eyes.

Tz'u-hsi's life as a respected concubine and mother of the future emperor was as meaningful as her strong will, energy and resources could make it. Yet despite her mastery of palace life, she and most of her circle knew literally nothing about the maddened world outside the Forbidden City. That world, the real China, was in turmoil, maladministered, bled dry by corruption, under attack from dissident citizens and under seige from greedy and manipulative European nations, the "foreign devils" Tz'u-hsi so rightly mistrusted.

The right to dump vast quantities of Indian opium into China—an immoral stance assumed by Britain and its allies—provided the immediate context for a foreign onslaught. Desperate to control addiction, the Manchu government had established a monopoly that taxed the drug so heavily that the rich alone could afford it. British traders, however, smuggled opium into China, fueling widespread enslavement to the drug, a disintegration of family life and widespread impoverishment.

Ten years after the first Opium War, Britain hounded the Son of Heaven with new demands, including legalization of the opium trade. After more bullying, the British invaded Canton (Guangzhou). In 1860, they stormed Peking and, with barbaric ferocity, sacked the Summer Palace. Hsien-feng, the empress, Tz'u-hsi and most of the imperial court, including three thousand eunuchs, had already fled in a ludicrously lavish procession of sedan chairs and mule-drawn carts that extended for five miles.

After a year in luxurious exile in the safety of an imperial hunting lodge 110 miles away from Peking, the twenty-nine-year-old emperor sickened and died, anguished at the chaos and humiliated by defeat. As he grew weaker and weaker, the court officials discovered he had not appointed a successor. Tz'u-hsi was galvanized into action. "As has always been the case in emergencies," she later recalled, "I was equal to the occasion, and I said to him: 'Here is your son,' on hearing which he immediately opened his eyes and said: 'Of course he will succeed to the throne.'"[17] Minutes later, Hsien-feng died.

This was Tz'u-hsi's first political intervention, and it shaped her life and China's. Just twenty-five, she came into her own. She had no intention of retreating into meek, widowed retirement. Instead, she successfully pressed for recognition as empress dowager and as coregent for her son, Tung Chih, with Niuhuru. She was named Concubine of Feminine Virtue, and would henceforth be known as Empress Dowager Tz'u-hsi, Empress of the West.

(Niuhuru became Tz'u-an, Empress of the East.) Tz'u-hsi immediately allied herself with her brother-in-law, Prince Kung, and the empress dowager, and the trio became China's true rulers. Their first act was to consolidate their position by eliminating the so-called Gang of Eight, who conspired against them. The Gang's leader was beheaded, two others permitted to commit suicide and the rest exiled.

Tz'u-hsi enjoyed her power, but she was careful not to demonstrate too much intelligence, and in her biographer Sterling Seagrave's assessment, she "appreciated that her job at court was to be a mediator and arbiter on all issues. . . . In the early years she avoided pressing a view of her own. . . . She provided the stable point on which all state policy was to be weighed."[18]

In 1864, the government ended the long-running Taiping Rebellion in the south, in 1868, the Nien Rebellion in the north. In the peaceful aftermath, Tz'u-hsi and Tz'u-an's government implemented promising reforms and focused on eliminating corruption and attracting capable men into China's government service.

The two empresses were still in their mid-twenties, inexperienced, ignorant of administrative protocol and only passably literate. They had never seen or been seen by foreigners. They sat behind screens as they consulted with their male advisers. Tz'u-hsi's subsequent reputation as a vicious and arrogant tyrant could not have been more undeserved.

Unfortunately, the two empresses, the Son of Heaven's two mothers, fared rather worse at mothering. Tung Chih was a problem child, lazy, cruel and, in adolescence, sex-crazed. He sneaked out of the Forbidden City to forbidden pleasures in brothels, and he also experimented with his eunuchs. "Women, girls, men and boys—as fast as he could, one after the other," noted Robert Hart in his diary.[19] When Tung Chih was fourteen, his doctors were treating him for syphilis.

Tz'u-hsi and Tz'u-an fought back by finding Tung Chih a bride and some concubines as incentive for him to seek his pleasures at home. Six months after his marriage, Tung Chih renewed his sexual forays into Peking. He also neglected his duties, stymied the efforts of his officials, demoted and degraded senior administrators and fired cabinet ministers. The process of government was effectively halted.

The two empresses intervened and restored officials to their positions. Government resumed. China limped on. Three months later, Tung Chih was diagnosed with the smallpox that plagued Peking. From his sickbed, he issued a decree assigning his powers to the empresses until he recovered. In January

1875, Robert Hart confided to his diary that a foreign physician "says it is syphilis and not smallpox that the Emperor is ill of."[20]

Whichever it was, it killed Tung Chih on January 12. Tz'u-hsi wept for the son who had made her empress but had himself grown into an ogre, a spectacularly arrogant and vicious boy who many people felt had redeemed himself only by dying before he totally destroyed the government. Many others gossiped about murder.

Tung Chih had not named a successor, so the empresses continued to rule until one was found. The Forbidden City became truly forbidding as the partisans and relatives of the various eligible princes lobbied for their candidates. But the princes were either too impetuous or tainted by sexual forays into brothels, and Tz'u-hsi found a more suitable prince, her three-year-old nephew, her sister's son, a choice Tz'u-an approved. As she had with Tung Chih's succession, Tz'u-hsi confronted the court with a surprise announcement. "I'll adopt a child, the son of the Seventh Prince," she announced. Soon after she left them, she reappeared with her new "son" and declared, "this is your Emperor!"[21]

The baby emperor, renamed Kuang Hsu, "Glorious Succession," was not a happy child. His empress aunt was not merely using him to keep China out of the hands of princes like her dead son, she was also rescuing him from his abusive home. His neurotic mother and drunken father had abused and nearly starved the boy and his siblings, several of whom died.

Two months later, Tung Chih's pregnant wife, Alute, died. Official reports of her suicide notwithstanding, she was probably murdered to avert the arrival of a rival baby who would be seen as the true heir of Tung Chih. Tz'u-hsi was among those suspected, and her reputation was subsequently tarnished by doubts about Alute's death.

Sterling Seagrave adduces evidence that exonerates Tz'u-hsi. She had chosen Alute as her daughter-in-law and had never shown signs of regretting it. She had nothing to fear from Alute's baby, who as her grandchild would guarantee her own position. Lastly, Tz'u-hsi was herself poisoned at the same time Alute died. Tz'u-hsi was so ill with what was diagnosed as liver disease that until 1883 she was chronically ill. She was often absent from court, and several times reportedly on her deathbed.

Robert Hart believed that of the two empresses, Tz'u-hsi was the more influential and clever, Tz'u-an the nicer. Tz'u-hsi, he noted in his diary, "has temper—but she has also ability."[22] That ability was often undermined, however, by her lifelong craving for affection and her susceptibility to flattery.

66

"Our Hart," Tz'u-hsi's nickname for her dedicated and capable foreign official, spent the next twenty-three years as the only expatriate who portrayed her "consistently as a woman and not a monster."[23]

The emperor of China was now a traumatized and stammering child, and his maternal aunt was too sick herself to assume a leading role in his upbringing. Despite his tormented infancy and the misguidedly severe palace upbringing by eunuchs instructed not to spoil him as Tung Chih had been spoiled, Kuang Hsu developed into a committed emperor, albeit a melancholy and reclusive one.

In 1881, Tz'u-an sickened and died, leaving the ailing Tz'u-hsi China's true ruler. In 1887, at the behest of several court officials, her regency was extended for an additional two years, though at fifteen Kuang Hsu was supposedly old enough to assume power. The extension gave Tz'u-hsi time to select a wife and two concubines for her adopted son.

The new empress was Tz'u-hsi's niece, Lung Yu, a slender, bucktoothed girl she was very fond of. The concubines were attractive sisters recommended by an influential eunuch. Tz'u-hsi hoped that Kuang Hsu would produce heirs and assume his full role as emperor. Then she could leave the heat and turmoil of the Forbidden City and retire to the splendor of the rebuilt Summer Palace.

But Kuang Hsu suffered medical conditions that led to involuntary ejaculation and, with women, impotence. To make matters worse, Lung Yu was a reluctant bride whose parents had forced her into the arrangement. Nonetheless, the sullen teenagers married, and Tz'u-hsi, now fifty-four, relaxed into retirement. The foreign legation was optimistic about Kuang Hsu, and Charles Denby, the American diplomat, predicted that "railroads, the electric light, physical science, a new navy, an improved army, a general banking system, a mint, all in the bud now, will soon be in full flower."[24]

Instead, the willing but indecisive Kuang Hsu confronted the devastating Sino-Japanese War of 1894–5. Japan, modernized and bellicose, sought to forestall Russian expansion into Korea and northern China. China and Korea both wanted to preserve the relationship in which China protected Korea, its dependent. But Korean public opinion was divided, and in 1894 a rebellion ensued. China sent troops to assist the Korean government while Japan sent soldiers to support the opposition, and they seized the palace. Fierce fighting preceded the official declaration of war on August 1, 1894.

The Sino-Japanese War was in many ways the beginning of the end of dynastic China. The Japanese easily defeated the Chinese on land and sea, and destroyed the Chinese navy. They pushed on into Manchuria, and China was forced to sue for peace. The Treaty of Shimonoseki humiliated and cannibalized China, which lost its control of Korea and had to cede Taiwan and two other territories, open four treaty ports to external trade and pay the enormous sum of two hundred million *taels* in tribute. Russia, France and Germany intervened and forced Japan to return one territory to China, but China had to pay an additional thirty million *taels*. (One *tael* in Chinese currency usually contained forty grams of silver.)

China's crushing defeat in the Sino-Japanese War was proof incarnate that the Qing dynasty was degenerate and ineffective. Angry reformers, noting how modernization had empowered Japan, intensified their campaign to modernize China, and the countryside pulsated with revolution. Tz'u-hsi's critics and rivals seized on China's military disgrace to accuse her of misappropriating funds destined for the navy to beautify the Summer Palace. This charge was false. She did not direct the restoration project, though she appreciated its results, and she would have had no way to funnel money from the navy, something only the Admiralty Board could have done.

The tension and urgency in imperial politics skyrocketed. Tz'u-hsi was galvanized by fear when Japanese agents orchestrated a coup in Korea against the ruling Queen Min, who was stabbed repeatedly then burned alive. Meanwhile, Kuang Hsu decided to fire everyone who had so much as questioned his decisions—his version of reform. Conservatives appalled at his apparent cavalier disregard for Manchu tradition, and at his intended introduction of a Japanese statesman into a senior position in China's government, urged Tz'u-hsi to come out of retirement. After hearing all the evidence of her nephew's missteps, she reluctantly agreed. She resumed her previous position as ruler, working with Kuang Hsu at her side.

Some of Kuang Hsu's reforms were retained. But some reformers deemed traitors were punished or executed. Despite the obvious personal harmony between the emperor and his old aunt, rumors flew that she and co-conspirators had placed him under house arrest in the palace. One man forced to flee China titillated people with his stories about the evil woman at China's helm. One of his more elaborate fabrications was that the sixty-three-year-old Tz'u-hsi sneaked false eunuchs into the palace and had sex with them. This same expatriate also plotted to assassinate Tz'u-hsi.

In certain ways, Roxelana would have understood the imperial court. For instance, Tz'u-hsi was pressured into granting two princes the Shangfang swords and hence the literal right to decapitate anyone they wished to. Her more moderate colleagues now had reason to watch what they said and did.

In 1898, in an attempt to counter her enemies' campaign of vilification, Tz'u-hsi broke all tradition and invited foreign diplomats' wives to the palace for tea. Her guests found her friendly and curious, with no hint of the cruel nature they had heard about. To their surprise, the emperor was also there, though he seemed indifferent to them and sat there chain-smoking cigarettes.

In that same year, the anti-foreign Boxer movement began to spread through China. Harassment of often arrogant Christian missionaries and Chinese converts escalated into outright terrorization. Then, after a young Englishman shot dead a Chinese man who shouted at him, a furious crowd of Chinese burned the Peking Racecourse so popular with foreigners. Churches and foreign residences were also destroyed.

Back in the palace, Tz'u-hsi was torn between supporting and suppressing the Boxers. She later recalled that the government decree ordering all foreigners killed had been issued against her wishes by pro-Boxer ministers. At the time, foreigners accused her of encouraging the Boxers and of sending troops to foil foreign military attempts to defeat them.

From June 13 to 16, 1900, the Boxers and their followers destroyed and looted foreign quarters. They targeted Chinese merchants who sold to foreigners as well. Foreigners and Chinese Christians sought refuge in cathedrals. Chinese servants fled foreign employers. In the countryside, Boxers slaughtered thousands of Chinese Christians.

In this tense situation, the German minister to China, Clemens Freiherr, Baron von Ketteler, provoked German marines to shoot and kill a group of Boxers. Tz'u-hsi and Kuang Hsu issued decrees against the Boxers, against killing foreigners, against inciting people to kill foreigners. Nonetheless, foreigners began to die. In one massacre, forty-five missionaries, including women and children, were beheaded. For days, several heads were displayed in cages atop a wall.

By August 14, 1900, an army of international soldiers reached Peking, rescued the foreigners, looted the city, then began a slow and savage march through the countryside to the Summer Palace, where Tz'u-hsi and the emperor and court had fled. These soldiers killed tens of thousands of Chinese, destroyed and looted thousands of homes and then laid waste the Summer Palace and Buddhist temples and statues.

From a new palatial refuge, Tz'u-hsi ordered that officials and nobles who had instigated the Boxers be punished. Two were executed. Then she, the emperor and their court returned to the Forbidden City. The Europeans demanded reparations and dictated a peace treaty. Tz'u-hsi was restored to power and resumed governing, her emperor-nephew at her side. She also resumed her tea parties with foreign women.

At seventy, Tz'u-hsi suffered a stroke, but still managed to work. On November 14, 1908, the always ailing emperor Kuang Hsu died. The day after, so did Tz'u-hsi, overworked, exhausted and ill with influenza. The Manchu dynasty survived her by only three years.

History has judged Tz'u-hsi harshly, and many of her contemporaries reviled her as a murderous despot. In fact, as an empress, Tz'u-hsi was the victim of her personal inadequacies—her lack of education and her uncertain grasp of administrative protocol and procedure. She was equally the victim of a system that imprisoned her in the Forbidden City, utterly ignorant of the catastrophic conditions outside it. She also had personal qualities that sabotaged her ability to govern effectively and wisely. Her incessant need to be liked put her at the mercy of flatterers. She was sometimes fearful and indecisive.

Yet Tz'u-hsi is noteworthy for impressive achievements. From the perspective of her blinkered life, her determined rise to power was remarkable. In China's dangerous and corrupt imperial court, she parlayed her intelligence and her focused ambition into a position of enormous power. For an unbeguiling concubine, she was a paragon of success.

Neither Tz'u-hsi nor Roxelana should be evaluated out of their own contexts. A balanced historical perspective about them would recognize how extraordinarily well both these women adapted to their concubinage and mastered harem rules, etiquette and traditions and then established relationships that catapulted them into power and kept them there for decades. They transformed coerced concubinage into supreme power, and even succeeded in dying naturally in their beds.

CHAPTER 3

Whose Whore?
Europe's Royal Mistresses

"KINGS are justly called gods," England's King James I wrote in 1609, and "they exercise a manner . . . of divine power upon earth." Like God, "Kings have power of . . . life and death . . . over all their subjects . . . and yet [are] accountable to none but God only. . . . Kings are also compared to fathers of families: for a king is truly *parens patriae*, the politique father of his people."[1]

The concept of the divine right of kings was at the core of monarchy; it legitimized the powers of Europe's royal rulers. These rulers had vast powers and, until the reforms that began in the 18th century, little accountability. Their courts were models of extravagance and protocol. They were also breeding grounds for intrigue and danger, as courtiers competed to gain the monarch's favor and influence his decisions.

Royal marriage was close to the top of the list of important decisions. Its object was to perpetuate the monarch's divinely sanctioned bloodline and to strengthen his country with strategic economic relations or military alliances. Royal marriages were the stuff of high diplomacy, as experienced officials and courtiers sought the most suitable candidate for their sovereign. As in most arranged marriages, romantic love did not play a role though it sometimes developed. What mattered was that the royal couple produce legitimate royal children—an heir and a spare, and other little nobles as pawns and future kings and queens in Europe's eternal marital chess game.

The inevitable consequence of these marriages, and of the sense of entitlement a king was encouraged to feel, was extramarital liaisons fueled by desire, romantic love, pride of possession and convenience. As a result, royal mistresses were a common feature of most European courts.

Many royal mistresses came from the nobility or aristocracy, but others, such as actresses encountered onstage in theaters, introduced a distinctly common element into the court's rarified atmosphere. Often a king would eliminate the social embarrassment this created by elevating favorite non-noble mistresses to the nobility.

But royal or not, even the most powerful royal mistress could not shed the ignominy of her status: the king's whore. James II's former mistress, the countess of Dorchester, stated it concisely when she unexpectedly encountered the duchess of Portsmouth and the countess of Orkney, Charles II's and William III's respective mistresses, and alluded without embarrassment to "we three whores." This inelegant label applied in Europe not only to prostitutes but also to the titled "kept women" whose bailiwick was blue bloods writhing on tousled bedsheets.

Competition for the attention of a divinely appointed king could be vicious. Nell Gwynne, mistress of Charles II, king of England from 1660 to 1685, once invited her rival, Moll Davis, to share a plate of delicacies Nell had laced with a laxative. That night, as Moll lay pinioned in Charles II's amorous embrace, nature called—suddenly and imperiously. Poor Moll! Poor Nell, too, to be placed in a position so precarious that she had to resort to such gutter tactics. Royal mistressdom could catapult women to enviable social heights, yet it was at best a risky business.

Nell Gwynne [2]

Nell Gwynne was the pertest and perkiest of royal mistresses, a gamine with an uptilted nose, lustrous chestnut hair, hazel eyes that regarded you with all the directness and honesty she was famous for, and firm and full breasts. Nell was so utterly delightful that Charles commissioned a series of nude portraits of her, then dropped in at her modeling sessions to ogle her.

But it was Nell's uninhibited and generous nature that won Charles over; he could not resist the quick wit and giggly good humor that made her seem like a "licensed court jester presiding over his stag parties."[3] And as he would learn with the passage of time, Nell was fiercely loving and—despite his remorseless roving—faithful to him. She was also an unpretentious woman who could write little more than her own scrawled initials, and an energetic sport who could party all night then greet the dawn as boisterously as she had midnight.

Nell met the king when she was seventeen and he was twenty years older. It was 1667, eighteen years after the execution of his father, Charles I, and seven years since his own restoration to the throne after a period of exile that had resulted from the monarchy's defeat in the English Civil War. The English, disillusioned after decades of Cromwellian austerities, had welcomed Charles ecstatically, though the nation he returned to rule was bitterly divided, politically, socially and religiously.

European exile had marked Charles deeply. For one thing, he so strongly favored ending England's severe discrimination against Roman Catholics that people suspected him of being a secret Catholic. For another, he was appalled at the dismal state of English theater. He hastened to revive it and to grant women the right to perform on stage, to give depth and accuracy to dramatic representations. Not coincidentally, he had a keen eye for actresses, notably leading ladies Moll Davis and Nell Gwynne.

Just before he met Nell, Charles had confronted three major crises: the bubonic plague of 1664–6, which killed about one hundred thousand Londoners; the Great Fire of London in 1665, which razed thirteen thousand houses, ninety-seven parish churches and the magnificent Saint Paul's Cathedral; and the second Anglo-Dutch War of 1665–7, which England provoked then lost after humiliating defeats.

But neither these calamities nor his wife, Catherine of Braganza, prevented Charles from attending the theater and from indulging in erotic adventures. "God will never damn a man for allowing himself a little pleasure," he liked to jest, while his enemies labeled him the "great enemy of chastity and marriage." The teenaged Nell, for her part, had overcome her lowly origins as the daughter of a soldier who died in an Oxford debtors' prison and a mother who sold beer in a brothel off Drury Lane and then drowned in a ditch after passing out in a drunken stupor. Nell had progressed from peddling oysters to selling oranges at the King's Theatre, and by age fourteen had debuted on stage and become the mistress of Shakespeare's great-nephew, Charles Hart. When King Charles met her in 1667, Nell had a new lover and was an acclaimed actress, the stage rival of his current favorite mistress, Moll Davis.

Charles had often watched Nell perform, but when he met her in person at the theater, he was smitten by her saucy wit and her lack of airs. She did not kowtow to him as king or rein in her bawdy humor. Their first outing together, at an eating place, included her current lover and ended in a comedy of errors. Charles dug into his pocket to pay for their dinner and came up short, so while Nell merrily mocked his temporary poverty, her lover was forced to foot the bill for all three of them.

Soon afterward, Nell became one of Charles's mistresses. In a certain way, theirs was a love affair, though they were both more pragmatic than romantic. They indulged in no passionate outbursts or frantic exchange of love letters. Instead, Charles relegated Nell to his stable of mistresses while she chose fidelity and explained, "I am but one man's whore." She urged Charles to follow her example—"One whore at a time is enough for you, sire," she assured him as she declined to invite a rival mistress to his birthday party.[4]

Nell and Charles agreed broadly on what being his mistress entailed. A house, living allowance and generous gifts were *de rigueur*. Charles customarily gave his mistresses titles and his "outside" sons dukedoms, and she expected the same. Nell gave birth in 1670 to Charles Stuart and, a year later, on Christmas Day, to James. Because the king's wife, Queen Catherine, had suffered miscarriages and was unable to give Charles any legitimate heirs, Nell and Charles's other mistresses expected him to be generous with his illegitimate children. Indeed he was, and five of today's twenty-six dukes are their descendants.

When Charles tried to economize by proposing a rented house for her, Nell not only rejected this move, she protested by resuming her career as an actress. Just as she had given, not leased, Charles her heart, she said, she should have a freehold, not rental accommodation. A suitably contrite Charles relocated her to an excellent Pall Mall house whose garden backed onto his, so from the convenience of home they could chat back and forth in relative privacy.

These conversations meant a great deal to Nell, who confided in Charles as a wiser, more experienced friend and also as her lover. "He was my friend and allowed me to tell him all my griefs and did like a friend advise me and told me who was my friend and who was not," she recalled sadly after his death.[5]

The lovers also often discussed money. Like Moll Davis but unlike Charles's other mistresses, Nell seemed to be a woman who wanted only her due, and she asked for a modest annuity of £500. Although Charles rejected this request, Nell managed in one four-year period to extract an extra £60,000 from the royal purse. She needed it! How else could she pay for her smart coach with its six horses, her eight servants, her mother's medicines, her charitable donations and her ornately engraved silver bedstead? Sometimes Nell sent her bills (for such items as white satin petticoats, red satin nightgowns and scarlet satin shoes embroidered with silver) to the Office of the Exchequer, the financial department of the royal government—which paid them—probably as advances on money she claimed the king owed her.

Extravagant as these expenses seem, they were a pittance compared to the amounts received by some of Charles's other mistresses. Barbara Palmer, later Lady Castlemaine, enjoyed £19,600 yearly from national revenues and enormous sums from other sources. Louise de Kéroualle, Nell's sophisticated French rival, had £10,000 yearly from the revenue from English wine licenses as her basic income, and in a single year was given another £136,668 for construction of her new palace. Records from 1676 testify to Louise's dominant position with Charles: she received £36,073 to Nell's £7,938.

The issue of titles irked Nell far more than money. Charles granted duchies to his other important mistresses, but refused to do the same for Nell, evidently because of her humble origins. Nell was understandably resentful. When Charles saw her in a new gown and exclaimed that she looked fine enough to be a queen, Nell quipped, "And whore enough to be a duchess!"[6] Though Nell remained plain Nell, she was determined that Charles should ennoble her sons, and to underscore the urgency of the matter, she referred to them as "little bastards." When Charles reproached her for this, Nell retorted that she had nothing else to call them. Her strategy succeeded. Charles relented slightly and gave them the aristocratic (though non-ducal) title Beauclerk or Beauclaire. Four years after their younger son died in 1680, a grievous loss to Nell, Charles conferred a dukehood on their surviving son, Charles, who became duke of St. Albans.

Throughout her seventeen-year relationship with the king, Nell was never Charles's only mistress. She easily outshone the rival actress, Moll Davis, but in her battles with aristocrats such as Louise de Kéroualle, Nell's origins proved difficult to surmount. Louise was Nell's opposite in all but beauty. Regal, educated, cultured, snobbish and ambitious, Louise determinedly set out to win Charles's heart. By 1671, she was spending as many nights with him as Nell was. She also maligned the illiterate Nell as often as she could, proclaiming her rival to be as common and vulgar as she had been as a youthful orange seller.

Nell retaliated in every way she could. She teased, mocked, insulted and stuck out her tongue at Louise. She referred to her as Squintabella, because one of Louise's eyes had a slight cast. And why, Nell demanded, would someone who boasted endlessly about her noble antecedents degrade herself by becoming a mistress? When Louise appeared in mourning for deceased foreign royals she claimed were relatives, Nell waited until a foreign king died, then draped herself in equally dramatic weeds. "Let us divide the world," she proposed sardonically to Louise. "You shall have all the kings of the north, but leave me the kings of the south."[7] When a lovely Italian, Hortense Mancini, duchesse de Mazarin, replaced Louise in Charles's favor, Nell was relieved to have a more pliable rival.

Nell's decision to refrain from meddling in politics was also a clever strategy. Though she understood the crucial issues of her day, Nell never attempted to influence events, policies or politicians. Charles greatly appreciated her restraint, and so did the public, who recited this popular ditty: "She hath got a trick to handle his prick, / but never lays hands upon his sceptre."

Nell's sole foray into politics came at the height of the parliamentary crisis of March 1681, in which Charles battled with Parliament over the intertwined issues of royal succession and the legitimacy of Roman Catholicism in England. Feelings were at fever pitch, and anti-Catholic gangs terrorized the streets, shouting "No Popery! No Slavery!" Charles himself, thought by some to be a secret Catholic, was suspect, and public outrage erupted against his prancing Catholic mistress, Louise de Kéroualle. One afternoon, the swarming troublemakers noticed a coach driving toward the king's quarters. The king's Catholic woman! they roared, and blocked its way so they could attack its occupant. But it was Nell Gwynne, not Louise, who leaned out the window shouting, "Pray, good people, be civil. I am the *Protestant* whore."[8] This sally defused the crowd's anger, and ever since, history has cheered Nell's spunk, perspicacity and frankness. Charles, too, must have complimented her on her sagacity. The incident also highlighted how his restless subjects saw Nell: she was, at heart, one of them, and they loved her for it.

Nell managed, as well, to ingratiate herself with Queen Catherine. Given the reality that royal mistresses were a kingly prerogative, Catherine had little choice but to tolerate them. However, she did not have to like them, and she did not hesitate to show her displeasure. But she was quite fond of Nell, who never tried to upstage her. Nell's very earthiness and raucous humor no doubt reassured Catherine that she was simply a strumpet who lacked the pretentions of the philandering king's other mistresses. (Another English queen, King George II's wife, Caroline, detested Lady Henrietta Suffolk, her husband's mistress of twenty years, but objected when George dismissed Henrietta as an "old, dull, deaf, peevish beast." Caroline interceded, fearing the advent of younger, more dangerous rivals.)

In 1685, on Nell's birthday, Charles had a stroke; he died a few days later. Nell had given him seventeen years and two children, and had abandoned a brilliant acting career to become his mistress. Nevertheless, Charles's only provision for her future was a feeble deathbed request: "Don't let poor Nell starve." Despite Charles's cavalier attitude to her welfare, Nell died fairly well off, but only because she survived the king by a mere two years. Had she lived to fifty-five as he had, she would certainly have died in penury.

Charles's death also brought home the fact that her seventeen years as Charles's mistress had not given her any status at court or, two children notwithstanding, in his family. But Nell had loved the king, and wished to mourn him befittingly. She ordered black drapery for her coach and her house, and planned other formal observances. A court official intervened and forbade Nell to usurp rituals restricted to the royal family, though she longed for this display of both her grief and her intimate attachment to her lover. Her tenure had been at that lover's pleasure, and his death brought her world crashing down about her.

Jeanne-Antoinette de Pompadour [9]

Vive la différence! France's royalty, too, indulged in mistresses. After all, royal marriages were affairs of state, arranged for diplomatic or political reasons. But the rulers's hearts—and loins—also cried out for recognition. Indeed, French kings gloried in extramarital sexual conquest, and at the royal residence at Fontainebleau, mementos of kings and their mistresses were carved into stones: Henri II (1519–59) and Diane de Poitiers, Henri IV (1553–1610) and Gabrielle d'Estrées.

Then in 1643, Louis XIV ascended the throne, a handsome, forceful man later known as the Sun King, who epitomized absolute rule, who dominated Europe and unified France. Among his other accomplishments, Louis subdued his restive nobles by engrossing them in elaborate court ceremonies, and altered conventional court etiquette to suit his own tangled love life.

For his rank and era, Louis had remained virginal remarkably long, until his eighteenth year, when Madame de Beauvais, one of his mother's ladies-in-waiting, seduced him as he returned from his bath. From then on, Louis treated Madame de Beauvais with unfailing respect. He developed a kingly appetite for sex, and though he loved his adoring wife, Maria Theresa, he exercised his royal prerogative and took a series of mistresses from among the pretty young court women.

However, Louis made one significant change. He legitimized his favorites as *maîtresses en titre*, official mistresses, moved them into apartments in the palace and acknowledged the children they bore him. This gave his mistresses power that far exceeded that of their sisters in other courts, for Louis's women were integral members of the court, often in the service of the queen. The king's mistresses supped with him, had access to the nation's powerbrokers and foreign diplomats and, if they so wished, could be powerbrokers themselves.

There was, however, a ritual formality involved in making the transition from mere mistress to *maîtresse en titre*. The potential *maîtresse en titre* needed a court lady to sponsor and present her at court. Louise de La Vallière, Louis's first candidate for the position, was already his long-term mistress, but their two children were officially bastards. Louis, setting out for the battlefield and aware that he might not survive it, reevaluated his life and made some changes. He named Louise Duchess of Vaujours and acknowledged his surviving daughter, Marie-Anne de Bourbon. Marie-Anne was then brought up as a royal family member, though she and two siblings born later had no succession rights to the throne.

Not long after he had accorded her the position of *maîtresse en titre*, Louis's attention strayed from Louise to her friend, Athénaïs, Madame de Montespan. Louise could not even grieve in privacy. She had to continue living at court, sad witness to her beloved Louis's growing passion for Athénaïs. Louise's religious devotion deepened. She fasted, slipped a hairshirt under her fancy court gowns, slept on the bare floor. Twice she ran away to a convent, and each time Louis fetched her back. In 1674, she implored him to release her so she could take holy vows. Her melancholy and faded looks touched him so deeply that he assented. Louise dropped to the floor in front of the queen and publicly repented her adulterous relationship. Soon after, she kissed her children goodbye. Then, as Sister Louise de la Miséricorde, she disappeared forever into the Carmelite convent in Paris.

Louis's next *maîtresse en titre*, Athénaïs de Montespan, introduced a new dimension to her position: her marital status. Not only was Louis committing adultery with her, she was committing adultery with Louis. Only Louis's queen agonized over his adultery—he had promised to give up his mistresses when he turned thirty, but his birthday came and went, and his mistresses stayed. Athénaïs's adultery was another story. Even the Sun King found it difficult to refute critics outraged that a woman would commit adultery, which was both a sin and a crime. Clearly Athénaïs needed a legal separation, which the reluctant French parliament granted only after five years of Louis's nagging.

Athénaïs's husband added a bizarre note to the proceedings. Though Monsieur de Montespan did not much like his wife, he was insulted that the king could simply snatch her up. He raged into Paris and created scenes. He broke into Athénaïs's bedroom and slapped her. He ostentatiously entered his own castle through the main doorway because, he said piteously, "My horns are too high to pass through the small door."[10] At one point, Louis had him thrown into prison. Montespan was not cowed. On his release, he staged a mock funeral for his wife and declared her the victim of her own philandering and ambition. Fortunately for Louis, his mistress's inconvenient husband soon tired of this game. Nonetheless, Montespan had the weight of religion and morality on his side. Kings might be the law, but their mistresses were not. Marriages might be unwillingly contracted, but for all that, they were sacred.

Montespan notwithstanding, it was obvious that on balance, married mistresses were easier to integrate into court life than unattached maidens, who could undermine the dignity of the queen's position in a way that a married woman did not. A mistress's marriage might be a cynical sham, but for the cuckolded queen, it served to save face, a tiny comfort in the midst of the relentless scrutiny and savage gossip of the palace. As it was, that poor royal could not spend a day in the palace without seeing and hearing the latest *maîtresse en titre*, whose apartments connected with the king's, whose belly swelled with his offspring, whose extremities glittered with gems from the royal purse.

Louis XIV was an intelligent man who had thought long and hard about the business of incorporating mistresses into his—and therefore France's—life. To instruct his son Louis, he composed a memoir about mistresses and how to avoid the pitfalls they caused for their lovers.

First, Louis warned, do not neglect affairs of state for your mistress. Second, and more difficult, though you surrender your heart, you must remain master of your mind. Do not allow women to speak of anything serious, for they will embroil themselves in plots and schemes, and cause havoc in the running of the country. History's examples abound, he warned his son: dynasties have died out, kings have been overthrown, provinces ravaged, empires destroyed through the machinations of scheming women.

Louis's great-grandson, the ineffectual Louis XV, disregarded much of his great-grandfather's advice and allowed his *maîtresses en titre* to become influential and powerful court figures. He also violated the tradition that royal mistresses should be of noble birth, and took the commoner Jeanne-Antoinette Poisson—later Madame de Pompadour—into his heart and bed.

Jeanne-Antoinette had an unusual background. Her father, a steward for Parisian financial officials, had been wrongly indicted for embezzlement and had fled to Germany to escape prison. Jeanne-Antoinette, nicknamed

Reinette, or "Little Queen," and her brother, Abel, were left behind with their mother. To provide for them, Madame Poisson took wealthy lovers. She also gave her delicate daughter an excellent education and training in the skills an upwardly mobile woman needed to attract a suitable husband or lover.

Reinette appreciated her mother's efforts, especially after a clairvoyant gazed into her nine-year-old eyes and intoned, "You will be the King's mistress." Reinette grew up to be a polished and cultured young woman known for her generous nature, acting ability and, despite (or perhaps because of) recurrent throat and chest problems, an entrancingly gravelly voice. She also had a dream—to make the fortune-teller's prophecy come true.

Reinette matured into an enchantress. She was slender and shapely, an oval-faced brunette with a glowing complexion and a regal elegance. When she was nearly twenty, her mother arranged her marriage to Charles-Guillaume Le Normant d'Étoiles, a government official. Reinette and Guillaume had children, and their daughter, Alexandrine, survived. Unexpectedly, the groom fell deeply in love with his bride, who laughingly reassured him that she would stay with him forever, except, of course, if the king wanted her.

In time, the king did. Louis XV knew Reinette by reputation, and he had remarked on her beauty when they had crossed paths. She was increasingly known in society, and Voltaire and other great intellectuals admired her and treasured her friendship. But the king's energies were monopolized by his mistress, Madame de Châteauroux, the third of a trio of sisters he had fallen in love with.

In 1744, however, this headstrong woman, afraid to let the king out of her sight, traipsed after him onto the battlefield during the War of the Austrian Succession. This flouting of propriety backfired on her when Louis XV fell gravely ill, and a bishop was summoned to give him last rites. But the cleric refused to absolve him unless Louis publicly confessed and repented of his sins. Terrified of hellfire, Louis confessed his adultery with Madame de Châteauroux, begged for repentance and ordered the offending woman away.

The matter did not end there, because the confession was widely publicized. Louis was forgiven, but his mistress was not. People threw stones and emptied chamber pots at her carriage as she passed, and mocked and humiliated her. The horror of her experience was so debilitating that she developed pneumonia. Meanwhile, the king recovered and, no longer anticipating death, recalled her to Versailles. Madame de Châteauroux, however, died soon after.

Two months later, in 1745, at his son the dauphin's wedding celebration,

Louis, dressed as a yew tree, turned his attention to Reinette, glamorous and elegant as the goddess Diana, and hovered around her for the entire evening. Soon after, she became his mistress.

The advent of a new royal mistress caused a stir in the French court. How long would she last? the courtiers wondered. Who were her allies? her enemies? What were her strategies, her likes and dislikes, her goals? In a hierarchical system rooted in the notions of divine right and blue blood, the potential power of a new mistress to influence affairs of state and, more importantly, the royal household and its legion of hangers-on was truly terrifying. Worse, how could one even guess what a trashy parvenue like Madame d'Étoiles, one of the hated bourgeois class, the intimate of such atheists as Voltaire, might be like?

But Louis was fixated on his new woman, and was visibly disagreeable to anyone betraying the slightest disapproval of her. Reinette reciprocated his love, with a passion inspired by the fantasies she had nurtured about him since childhood. Despite her sincerity, gossip about her, much of it malicious, engrossed the court.

Meanwhile, Reinette and Louis were busy. She asked him to clarify her role, and he did so—he wanted her as his *maîtresse en titre*. Reinette acquiesced, joyfully. She insisted, however, that Louis arrange a formal separation from her husband. The devoted Charles-Guillaume took the news badly, weeping and fainting. Only after he understood that her decision was irrevocable did he accept the rupture with his beloved wife.

Yet despite her passion for the king, mistressdom was not easy for Reinette. She had been a fragile child, and her throat and lungs had always bothered her. In adulthood, as the problem worsened, she hid her deteriorating condition from all but her closest friends. But the hawkeyed courtiers, noticing how thin and tired she looked and how she spat blood, spread spiteful reports. Her physician prescribed rest, fresh air and exercise. How can I? she lamented. Court life was rigorously regimented and exhausting, the elaborate toilettes and grooming rituals interminable, the overheated air stifling. As for exercise, she was too fatigued to attempt it.

Her eroding health also affected Reinette's lovemaking, and she was terrified that what she bitterly called her frigid nature would drive Louis into another woman's arms. One night, calling her "cold as a fish," he stomped out of her bed and slept on the sofa. Reinette tried to stave off losing him by following a diet designed to heat up cold blood: hot chocolate laced with vanilla and amber, truffles, celery soup. Another time, she drank asses' milk. "I would sacrifice my life to please him," she confided to a friend.[11]

Though her body was failing, Reinette somehow managed to make herself indispensable to the king. In 1745, he named her the Marquise de Pompadour, which, as Voltaire noted, rhymed with *l'amour*—the love Reinette offered in such abundance to her lover. As Louis's *maîtresse en titre*, she managed as well to mollify the queen, though Marie-Leczynska sometimes humiliated her in public. Reinette devoted her life to the king, compensating for her lack of sexual prowess by charming him in time-honored ways. She enthusiastically took up his interests. She joined him in card games, though she hated them. She hunted, though the sport sapped the little strength she had. She edited the racy, gamy reports that arrived weekly from Louis's spy network. She held daily briefings with the ministers of state. She counseled the king and became his dearest friend as well as his mistress.

Reinette also insinuated herself into the affairs of state, exactly what Louis XIV's memoir had warned against. She convinced Louis to fire and exile his minister Maurepas, the alleged mastermind of a verse that mocked her leukorrhea, a gynecological condition characterized by thick white vaginal discharges. She arranged to appoint her brother, Abel, Intendant General of the King's Buildings, an important position he fulfilled efficiently and honestly. She distributed royal patronage to literature and the arts, about which she was knowledgeable and sensitive. She cofounded the military school to train officers, and the now famous porcelain factory at Sèvres.

In 1751, after much deliberation, Reinette renounced sexual relations with the king, and made this known. This enabled both of them to take Holy Communion, because neither was committing adultery with the other. For Reinette, the renunciation had a double benefit: it assuaged her religious conscience and it released her from a chore she simply could not perform well. However, the great danger was that Louis would replace her with a new mistress. In 1752, when Louis made Reinette a duchess, gossipmongers interpreted his gesture as a golden handshake of dismissal.

To maintain her hold on Louis, Reinette endeavored—or so people said—to find unthreatening young women for him. Contemporaries accused her of whoremongering, of arranging the brothel that was established in the palace's Parc aux Cerfs ("Deer Park") district. There, adolescents recruited from poor Parisian families were lodged and prepared for Louis's erotic consumption, often in groups of two or three together. These girls were well fed and nicely clothed, taught the social graces and checked medically. The turnover rate was high, probably because the youthful "retirees" received pensions and often married wealthy men eager to benefit from their training. Girls who gave birth to Louis's offspring were told that their babies had died. Then these infants, *princes et princesses manqués*, were given annuities and adopted out to suitable parents.

Two years after Louis's Parc aux Cerfs whorehouse was set up, Reinette's ten-year-old daughter, Alexandrine, died. Reinette was inconsolable. "All happiness for me died with my daughter," she told a friend.[12] Her critics, stooping to gutter level, swore that Reinette's tears were shed for herself, because now Alexandrine would never become her surrogate in Louis's bed.

Reinette pieced her shattered life together. For another decade, she immersed herself in state affairs and in the court's internal politics, gambling that her allies would be strong enough to vanquish her growing number of enemies, including partisans of other beautiful women they hoped might replace her. She pressed Louis to fire ministers who disliked her. She survived the internecine warfare of the court, and her new chastity made her feel so virtuous that she supported the Church in its various struggles against the French parliament. She worked closely with her protégé, the duke of Choiseul, whose diplomatic ventures ultimately led to the Seven Years' War that set France, Austria, Russia, Saxony, Sweden and Spain against Prussia, Great Britain and Hanover, a catastrophe that nearly bankrupted France. She spent extravagantly from her impoverished nation's coffers on splendid artworks and architecture; the style she imposed on France was so unerringly brilliant that she defines an aesthetic era. She indulged the indolent king, while outside the palace a restless populace verged on starvation.

Soon after the 1763 Treaty of Paris ended the war, Reinette succumbed to what was probably lung cancer. Her friend Voltaire regretted the passing of a sincere woman who loved the king for himself. However, a popular ditty that slyly vilified her expressed how the majority of her contemporaries saw her: "Here lies one for twenty years a virgin / Eight years a whore, / And ten years a pimp."[13]

Jeanne du Barry [14]

Louis's next *maîtresse en titre*, Jeanne Bécu, later the countess du Barry, came from even lowlier stock than Reinette de Pompadour. Jeanne was the illegitimate daughter of Anne Bécu, a beautiful and enterprising cook, and Frère Ange, a monk, who could not marry her. Jeanne was introduced to mistressdom in early childhood after Anne took a live-in job with a Parisian official and Francesca, his exciting Italian mistress. Francesca made a pet of the adorable blond tot, and arranged for her to be educated at a convent school.

There Jeanne studied literature and the arts, and developed the passion for Shakespeare and the refined diction that would later delight Louis XV. By the time she graduated at fifteen, Jeanne was so stunning that Francesca suddenly saw her former protégée as a rival for her lover's affections, and abandoned her to her own resources.

Jeanne found work at a wig shop, and at eighteen, for a brief period, became mistress of her employer's son. After that, she combined work with mistress-dom, climbing upward socially and financially as she consorted with important officials and intellectuals. Her reputation spread. She was heartstoppingly lovely, tall and slender with masses of blond hair, wide blue eyes and an elegant aquiline nose. Her beautiful breasts, often displayed by tasteful décolletage, overwhelmed even jaded observers, and she enhanced her natural charm with understated makeup and dresses of gossamer pastel that highlighted her pale perfection.

Jeanne was also renowned for her lovemaking skills. In contrast to the fragile and frigid Madame de Pompadour, Jeanne was a robust and rollickingly sensual woman whose sexual partners crowed about her agility and repertoire. She was neither shy nor reserved, and traded erotic sessions for large sums of money and gifts of jewelry. Her primary lover, the count Jean-Baptiste du Barry, was also her agent or pimp, and he guided her career ever upward until she achieved the ultimate conquest, Louis XV.

An apocryphal story describes Jeanne's first meeting with Louis XV at the Versailles palace. She curtseyed thrice, as protocol demanded, then walked over and kissed him full on the lips. This certainly never happened, but it conveys the contemporary opinion about Jeanne's bursting sexuality. In fact, du Barry probably steered her in the king's direction, knowing that Louis could not fail to notice such an enchantress. Du Barry was right. For the first time since his great passion for Reinette, Louis lost his heart to a woman, the only one, he confided, who could make him feel like a young man again.

But du Barry's court contacts had lied to Louis about Jeanne's antecedents, presenting her as a respectable married woman of aristocratic birth. In fact, Jeanne was an illegitimate, unmarried courtesan of peasant stock, documented in police records as du Barry's whore. What to do? Louis's worried courtiers were forced to tell him the truth. Louis was too lovesick to spurn the captivating young imposter. Get her married, he ordered.

Count du Barry was frantic. He was himself of noble stock and would gladly have married Jeanne to formalize her position at court. Alas, he already had a wife, an unloved woman he had abandoned after dissipating her fortune. But the count had an older brother, so impoverished that no suitable woman had ever consented to marry him. For a sizeable fee, Guillaume du Barry consented to become Jeanne's husband.

Money changed hands again, and suddenly Jeanne had a "revised" birth certificate that elevated her ancestors to the status of nobility and subtracted three years from her age. After a brief ceremony held at 5 A.M. to avoid gawking onlookers, Jeanne emerged from Paris's Saint-Laurent Church as the Countess du Barry. Her wedding, allegedly performed by Frère Ange, her birth father, was the first and only time she met her husband. This arrangement suited him. He settled down with the young mistress he would marry after Jeanne's death, and lived happily ever after on his new pension.

Jeanne was now a married countess, eligible for presentation at court. Louis dealt with his nobles' hostility toward her by bribing an indebted countess to sponsor her. Jeanne arrived at court, unapologetically tardy and dazzling in a diamond-studded white gown, and proceeded through the ceremonious presentation with dignity and aplomb. On that day, April 22, 1769, she became Louis's *maîtresse en titre*.

For six years Jeanne dominated Louis's social and sexual life. The aging king was overjoyed, because like Reinette de Pompadour, his new mistress loved him for his personal qualities (such as they were) as much as for his power and wealth. Though Jeanne was present at most of the suppers and events at which state policy was discussed, she never interfered or even showed much interest. Her great loves were literature and the arts, and expanding her enormous collection of precious jewels, which ultimately cost the French treasury over 2,500,000 *livres*. Jeanne also spent vast sums on dresses by designer Rose Bertin, on refurbishing the houses Louis gave her, on a retinue of servants and on thousands of books bound in hand-tooled leather.

Jeanne's life at court was consumed by prescribed etiquette, elaborate grooming, hairdressing and endless changing of outfits; sitting through audiences, performances, suppers, musicals and other gatherings; riding and hunting with the king. She, more than anyone else, had to be available to him at all times and could not escape on restorative vacations. She dealt daily with people determined to undermine her, including Marie-Antoinette, the bratty teenaged wife of the king's grandson (who would later become Louis XVI). Marie-Antoinette considered Jeanne stupid and impertinent, and Louis's fascination with her contemptible.

Court etiquette also dictated that Jeanne have no privacy, from her perfumed morning bath to her nighttime ablutions. Court ladies were always present, and often outsiders were, too: supplicants and petitioners, in endless lines, hopeful that the woman they vilified in public would extricate them from their various personal plights. They begged Jeanne for money and jobs. They urged her to intercede on their behalf with harsh officials, to sponsor their children, to patronize their charities. Only when she was actually making love to the king could Jeanne escape public scrutiny.

Despite these constraints, Jeanne was a cheerful and indefatigable woman, kindhearted and forgiving. But she was reviled in pre-revolutionary France for her extravagances and (unlike Nell Gwynne in England) condemned as a traitor to her modest origins. Rather than turning against the once loved old king, the public blamed "the royal whore" for all their woes—hunger, bread shortages, unemployment. When Jeanne ventured out, rioters attacked her carriage.

In 1774, after six years of enjoying sexual and emotional rejuvenation with his lovely *maîtresse en titre*, Louis fell ill with a lethal form of smallpox. He understood that he was dying and his thoughts turned toward Judgment Day. He told Jeanne that for the sake of his eternal salvation she must leave the court. "I owe myself to God and my people," he said.[15] Jeanne fainted but, as soon as she revived, went directly to her coach and left the palace. No tears or reproaches—she too understood. She was morally polluting, an insurmountable obstacle to Louis's redemption.

Louis shed a few tears of grief at losing his mistress's constant companionship and care, her soothing words and gentle touch. Then he called for priests to absolve him of his sins, in particular his lustful relationship with her. He kissed a crucifix with the same lips that had so often kissed Jeanne. A few days later, serene and peaceful in the certainty that his last-minute repentance had guaranteed his eternal salvation, Louis died.

Almost immediately, the new king, Louis XVI, and queen, Marie-Antoinette, exiled Jeanne du Barry to a convent and ordered her held there in isolation. Torn from her world and her few friends but hounded by creditors, Jeanne adapted to penurious imprisonment as gracefully as she had to courtly splendor. She transformed the abbess, Mother Gabrielle de La Roche-Fontenille, into a staunch friend who convinced Louis and Marie-Antoinette to permit Jeanne the solace of visitors. One of these, Jeanne's notary, arranged the sale of some jewelry so she could pay off her most insistent creditors.

Eleven months later, Louis and Marie-Antoinette released Jeanne from the convent, but banned her from entering a ten-league radius around Paris and Versailles. For sixteen years she lived quietly, taking lovers, making love, eating bountifully, growing fatter, enjoying life. She also received the lump sum pension of 2,812,500 *livres,* as Louis had promised before his death.

Jeanne's idyllic life ended in 1791, when thieves broke into her château and stole jewelry worth millions. A month later, when she learned that London police had recovered the jewelry, she rushed across the English Channel to recover the gems. This was unwise, however: the old regime was crumbling, a desperate Louis XVI had just appealed to Prussia for a military coalition and Marie-Antoinette was secretly pleading for the Spanish king to help the royal family to flee. Instead of retreating into anonymity and hiding her assets, as other aristocrats and wealthy people did, Jeanne, through her actions, called attention to herself and her property. In London, she failed to recover her gems from the English authorities. She also failed to notice that French police agents had trailed her to England and spied on her as she met with antirevolutionary *émigrés.*

Politically and socially compromised, condemned as a royalist and a whore who had robbed France of millions, the former royal mistress was again catapulted into public notoriety. Though the revolutionary politician Mirabeau himself once remarked that her only sin was that the gods had made her so beautiful, the revolutionary government arrested her. The first indictment charged that "even after her supposed disgrace . . . she was acquainted with those people who are today our most cruel enemies."[16] Jeanne was also accused of misusing state funds and making antirevolutionary remarks.

In prison, Jeanne evaluated her situation and believed that she would be spared. In the months before her trial, she enjoyed the camaraderie of her fellow prisoners, a mélange of aristocrats she had known and prostitutes she had not. When she was condemned to death, Jeanne howled with horror. Yet still she hoped she could trade her life for her remaining treasures. When this desperate measure proved fruitless, she was paralyzed by fear and understood that she was doomed. On the bitterly cold afternoon of her death, she had to be dragged to the guillotine. At one point she tried to escape, crying out, "You are going to hurt me, please don't hurt me." Her impatient executioners grabbed and tied her down. The blade bit deeply into the back of her now fleshy neck, and she shrieked in agony. "Long live the Republic!" shouted the ghoulish onlookers as she was decapitated.[17]

Jeanne du Barry was the last of the *maîtresses en titre,* and the embodiment of royal mistressdom. She enjoyed enormous material rewards, which Louis raided France's treasury to pay for: vast sums of money, an abundance of magnificent real estate dazzlingly furnished and decorated, a jewelry collection historians still marvel at, exquisite clothing. But her insatiable consumerism and relentless ostentation fueled the public's rage, and she was ultimately forced to pay with her life. Ironically, even as she was dragged to her bloody execution, Jeanne du Barry could not fathom how her six years as Louis's mistress had condemned her to death.

Lola Montez [18]

A half century after Jeanne du Barry died, another royal mistress briefly captivated a king and cost him his crown. Lola Montez, who inspired the slogan "Whatever Lola wants, Lola gets," wanted much what Jeanne du Barry had— fame, fortune and the undiluted adoration of wealthy and powerful men. Lola's wealthiest and most powerful conquest was the king of Bavaria, Ludwig I, whom she met in 1846. Fortunately for her, consorting with kings was by then a much safer enterprise than it had been in revolutionary France.

Lola Montez, whose real name was Eliza Gilbert, was born in India, in 1820, to a hastily married English soldier and his fourteen-year-old wife. Her father died, her mother remarried and Eliza was sent to England for schooling. She eloped at seventeen with Thomas James, a lieutenant thirteen years her senior, but soon left him. After her embittered husband sued for divorce, Eliza fled to Spain, where she studied dancing. She reinvented herself and returned to England as Maria Dolores de Porris y Montez—"but call me Lola"—the dancing daughter of an impoverished Spanish nobleman. She had also become a fledgling courtesan with a constantly changing clientele. She even married one of her admirers, despite the fact that she was not legally divorced.

Lola was a blue-eyed, black-haired woman with, as one biographer put it, "fiery eyes ... beautifully formed nose ... beautifully arched eyebrows."[19] "Her beauty, of rare, voluptuous fullness, is beyond any criticism. Her dancing, however, was no dancing at all but a physical invitation ... she writes Casanova's Memoirs with her whole body," one reviewer remarked.[20]

Lola traded on much more than beauty. She was intelligent and adventurous, a complex and erratic woman who lied chronically (or pathologically) yet occasionally showed flashes of noble high-mindedness. She spent a man's money, then moved on to a new, still affluent conquest. In her frenetic travels through Europe, she became intimate with composer Franz Liszt, the son of British statesman Robert Peel and a string of other admirers, including several journalists. Lola's biggest coup was conquering the heart of the aging King Ludwig of Bavaria.

In 1846, Ludwig was sixty years old and had ruled Bavaria for twenty-one years. He was a stern and disciplined administrator who began work before dawn and had transformed Bavaria into a financial success story, Munich into a cultural and artistic haven, and its university into a great European center of learning.

But Ludwig had unfinished personal business. His devoted wife, Therese, mother of his eight children, had recently embraced celibacy. Therese had always accepted Ludwig's extramarital trysts as necessary outlets for his lust. But suddenly, on the cusp of old age, homely and pockmarked though he was, this king who was also a poet and an intellectual desired more than casual encounters with discreet courtesans. Instead, he longed for a woman who would reciprocate his passion and love him just for himself.

Ludwig had another unexpected passion: for Spain and the Spanish language, which he had taught himself. Enter the predatory and supposedly Spanish Lola Montez, clad in a smashing black gown and her most seductive manner. And whatever Lola wanted, Lola got, so when she secured a personal interview with Ludwig, she used her few minutes with him to mesmerize the deaf, mistrustful and choleric king.

From that day on, Ludwig, who could erupt in fury if he felt slighted, cheated or betrayed, believed Lola's every lie. Despite others' hints to the contrary, she convinced him that she was an aristocrat whose family was reeling from the loss of its ancestral wealth. Lola was also an amusing polyglot whose ripe lips Ludwig read with joy as they conversed in her "native" Spanish. ("Yo te quiero con mi vida," he rhapsodized.) True, Lola could be impulsive and self-indulgent—she refused to go anywhere without her lapdog, Zampa—but Ludwig attributed this to her femininity. Like a dozen men before him, Ludwig had fallen hopelessly in love with her.

"I can compare myself to Vesuvius, which seemed burned out until it suddenly erupted again," he confided to an old friend. "I'm in the grip of passion like never before. . . . My life has a new vitality, I'm young again, the world smiles at me."[21]

Lola became Ludwig's official mistress, with an annuity of ten thousand florins and twenty thousand more to redecorate her palatial new home. Though cabinet ministers had to make do with six thousand florins annually, and dancers a mere two hundred, Lola's fortune was not enough—she needed silver services, crystal, jewels, luxurious house fittings, spending money. After a business manager failed to rein in her expenditures, Ludwig, tut-tutting avuncularly, simply doubled her annuity.

Ludwig was perplexed and hurt that a small band of admiring male students always congregated around his Lola, but he drew no conclusions about her choice of friends. Even when Lola scandalized Munich by pounding on a young lieutenant's apartment door at night, later demanding that Ludwig transfer the lieutenant out of the city and subsequently pleading for the order to be rescinded, Ludwig steadfastly denied the rumors that she was cuckolding him. "Lolita (that's what I call her) is slandered terribly," he complained to a friend.[22]

Before long, Lola's reputation as a gold digger put her in danger of physical assault by citizens infuriated at how she had bewitched their king. Lola responded with outraged bravado, stalking the hostile streets of Munich with Turk, a huge black dog. A new danger surfaced when published reports identified her as Eliza Gilbert James. Lola, as Maria Dolores de Porris y Montez, defended herself vociferously. She also launched an attack on the Jesuits, who she believed were behind these attempts to unmask her.

Ludwig, meanwhile, had been privileged to make love to his Lolita only twice, though she frequently permitted him to kiss her parted lips and suck her dancer's toes. Entranced, he agreed to raise her to the nobility. In 1847, Lola became Countess of Landsfeldt. "I can do without the sun above," he confided to her, "but not without Lolita shining in my soul."[23] He also assured his confidants that Lola was deeply in love with him.

As the countess of Landsfeldt, Lola grew more imperious and defiant. Her only friends were the alienated students who responded to her anti-Jesuit tirades, but her enemies included most of Munich, if not all of Bavaria. She was so hated that Ludwig, the formerly beloved king, was in danger of losing his grip on the throne. Soon Munich rioted, smashing Lola's house and the buildings her enemies suspected she might be hiding in. Lola fled to Frankfurt, and Ludwig was forced to revoke her citizenship. The people would murder you if you came back here, he wrote to her. For her sake, he added, he was contemplating abdicating the throne.

Countess Lola shrugged, then moved to Switzerland with a new lover she supported on Ludwig's money, even after Ludwig abdicated the throne in favor of his son Maximilian and had his income slashed. Yet the former king could still not join his beloved Lola in exile because in Bavaria, relentless public rage against her drove his family to forbid him to so much as visit her. Even a visit, the new king told his father, would endanger the very institution of the monarchy.

Lola, with new lovers, spared little thought for Ludwig, but her infrequent letters melted him with their sentiments, and he complied with her urgent requests for more money and for her jewelry. Then one of her ex-husbands resurfaced, and for once, Lola could not talk herself out of the situation and refute his revelations. Ludwig, stunned and despairing, finally grasped that he had been duped. Lola confirmed this by blackmailing him, threatening to sell his passionate (and ridiculous, he now saw) letters to newspapers.

Ludwig could not afford to echo Lord Nelson's defiant "Publish and be damned!" He wheedled and negotiated until, unexpectedly and without explanation, Lola returned all his letters. Ludwig sent her a final payment, then slunk away to lick his wounds.

Lola remembered Ludwig fondly, and publicly, for he loomed large in her hugely successful memoirs, published in North America, where she switched from dancing to lecturing. In her *Lectures of Lola Montez*, published in 1858, she boasted about her annuity, swollen in the telling to seventy thousand florins, and about her immense influence on European history.

More to the point, Lola also justified her own brand of mistressdom as "one woman going forth in independence and power of self-reliant strength to assert her own individuality, and to defend, with whatever means God has given her, her right to a just portion of the earth's privileges"—including, evidently, Ludwig's. In many ways, Lola's *Lectures* could be read as a mistress's vindication of the rights of women:

> Genius has no sex! . . . Great men have passed measurably unscathed because, I suppose, the world had no right to expect any degree of morality in the life of a great man. But woman—ah! she must be a saint . . . well, so she should be, and thus leave to man the entire monopoly of all the sin of the world![24]

As she matured and faded, Lola no longer sought fame and fortune. She embraced religion and good works. She lived with the simplicity demanded by her increasing poverty. When she was forty, she died of pneumonia and the complications of a stroke, in Brooklyn, New York. She was buried as Eliza Gilbert, the commoner who won a king's heart, ended his monarchy and earned her living by recounting the details—fabricated and real—of her amorous conquests.

Katharina Schratt [25]

Two decades after a Bavarian mob chased Lola Montez away from their king, another Germanic ruler met an entertainer who would become the great love of his life. In 1873, Austrian emperor Franz Josef was forty-three years old when he first saw the twenty-year-old Katharina Schratt on a Viennese stage, a pretty blond sensation in *The Taming of the Shrew*. But the emperor was too preoccupied by Austria's recent stock market crash to really notice her. Indeed, he devoted most of his life to duty, rising before five to work until late at night on national issues. Despite several notable international debacles, he considered foreign policy his special domain. He was also deeply interested in the civil service, which under his supervision became highly efficient.

Franz Josef's personal life was less successful, if happiness and fulfillment are measures of success. In many ways, the emperor lived a spartan life in the midst of Vienna's luxury. He slept on an iron bedstead and neglected creature comforts such as a new bathrobe or a bedside rug to cushion his feet on cold mornings. His rigid self-discipline and sense of dynastic duty extended to his family, whom he expected to behave according to his exacting code. He forced his unstable son, Rudolf, into an arranged marriage, ignoring Rudolph's pleas for understanding. Franz Josef was equally insensitive to other relatives' needs and desires, and he treated those who challenged him with cold opprobrium.

Franz Josef's marriage to the glamorous and sadly erratic Bavarian princess Elisabeth was full of sorrows. For a brief time after they married in 1854 they had been very happy. Then Elisabeth felt that the monotony and oppression of court life were crushing her soul, and she longed to be "as free as a seagull." She escaped through travel and, in about 1867, fled the marital bed as well, and never again allowed her husband to make love to her. Franz Josef continued to love her, and her long absences and acute unhappiness tormented him.

Katharina, or Kathi, Schratt was in many ways Elisabeth's opposite. She was an ambitious and accomplished actress. She had been forced into self-reliance after her husband had accumulated enormous debts then cravenly abandoned her and their son. She managed to extricate herself after her admirers set up a fund for her. Despite her experience of financial insecurity, Kathi was a reckless spendthrift and gambler. In other respects, she was methodical and orderly, hardworking and domestically inclined, a caring mother and an excellent cook, deeply superstitious and just as deeply religious. Her friends thought her generous and kind, gossipy and adventurous, but as Franz Josef soon discovered, she hated not getting her own way and was a chronic complainer.

It was Empress Elisabeth who sparked the famous affair between Kathi and Franz Josef. She was as smitten with the blond actress as the rest of Vienna and, in 1885, concocted the idea of introducing her to Franz Josef as a way of alleviating his loneliness.

Elisabeth's wishes came true. Within months, Kathi had become the emperor's mistress in all ways except sexually. Franz Josef showered her with magnificent jewels and large sums of money. In return, she offered him four-leaf clovers and other trinkets, and attended early morning mass so he could see her up in the gallery, after which she breakfasted with him. She lived a double rather than a duplicitous life, performing on the stage twice daily and spending time with her friends but reserving the rest of her time for Franz Josef, for breakfasts, long walks, outings to the theater, and reading and writing the letters they exchanged almost daily.

In 1888, one of Kathi's letters transcended her usual banalities and touched Franz Josef to the core. Please, he had requested her in a letter enclosing money, calculate how much more you will need for your various expenses, including ballgowns and dresses, so I may send it to you. This missive struck such a nerve that Kathi replied with an impulsive "letter of thoughts," in which she offered herself as Franz Josef's mistress. (We can only guess at the text of the letter from Franz Josef's responses to it. Before he died, he destroyed the letter itself.)

The emperor would reread this letter countless times. He responded gently that Kathi could not have failed to notice that he adored—indeed, worshipped—her. But he loved his wife and would never "abuse her confidence and friendship" for Kathi. He hoped Kathi's heart would always have a place for him, though their relationship could never transgress the line they had already drawn.

Kathi was contrite, and worried that the emperor would see her as "a scheming seductress." She need not have. Franz Josef was entranced by her every word, every deed, every worry, even her "quiet week," the menstruation that drove her monthly to her sickbed. But his letter had spelled out clearly that if Elisabeth should turn against Kathi, he would, on principle, feel compelled to end their relationship. It also clarified his belief that consummating his deep love for Kathi through sex would dishonor Elisabeth and betray his marriage vows.

Ironically, the handsome emperor had enjoyed many sexual adventures, but until he met Kathi his heart had not been engaged and he had felt no guilt. Because he loved her, Kathi Schratt had to settle for being a mistress without sexual duties. Instead, she had to provide other services, including early morning availability for her crack-of-dawn lover, an onerous task given her grueling afternoon-to-night schedule as a professional actress. Kathi summed up her new life as "seemingly not quite real." She was the intimate companion of the emperor. She owned a palatial Vienna home and a large summer residence. She was wealthy and indulged, influential in the theater. Her worries were trivial: a weight problem she described as "galloping fatulence," the stress of pressuring reluctant directors to cast her in leading roles. She refused to worry about her compulsive gambling, reveling in her wins and letting Franz Josef cover her losses. She never resented Empress Elisabeth, who at any moment could—but never did—smash her life to smithereens.

Kathi and Franz Josef had especially tender times during crises. The most agonizing was Rudolf's death in 1889, which was the fulfillment of a suicide pact with a seventeen-year-old girl he felt he could not live without. Franz Josef was horrified and disgusted at what he perceived as his son's disgraceful disregard of his obligations and noble rank. Kathi, however, eventually led him to sense something of Rudolf's pain and suffering so he could remember and speak of his dead son with compassion rather than shame.

Such emotional events deepened Franz Josef's reliance on Kathi. But they also inflamed his latent jealousy—each onstage embrace between her and other actors tortured him and pushed him to be more demanding. The crux of the problem (as he saw it) was Kathi's acting, and the independence and publicity it afforded her. He longed for her to curtail or end her career. Kathi, however, was determined to preserve the independence he so resented, and absolutely refused to retire.

Despite this impasse, their affair flourished, staid and circumspect. They met for breakfast, and sometimes Kathi received him in bed, in her negligee. Afterward they walked in the royal gardens and the palace's private zoo, where they fed the animals with scraps of food. They also squabbled and fought—because she pestered him to arrange a well-paid job for her estranged husband; because she loved mountain climbing, and once took a balloon ride he considered dangerous and frivolous; because she was hungry from dieting; because he was irritable from stress—and they resolved nothing.

Unspoken because unacknowledged must have been the tremendous frustration of two attractive people who expressed their love in every way but sexually. Years into their union, Franz Josef relaxed his stiff propriety and invited Kathi to dine with him as well, then fussed happily over each detail of the menu. If he could have, he would have swallowed her up entirely, so possessive had he grown.

In 1897, the unthinkable happened. In Geneva, an alienated young Italian assassinated Empress Elisabeth. Franz Josef's grief over her death consumed him for the rest of his life. Kathi, too, mourned Elisabeth, despite the ambiguity of their friendship and Kathi's always precarious position.

Almost any other woman would have wondered, at least in the quiet of her own heart, if the death of her lover's wife would change or even legitimize her position. If Kathi harbored such thoughts, she was sorely disappointed. Franz Josef, who had forbidden his son and other family members to marry beneath them, would never have contemplated marrying a commoner, even the woman he loved.

In fact, Elisabeth's death drove the lovers apart rather than together. Kathi comforted him during his initial shock, but soon his daughter Marie Valerie, who had always found Kathi's presence awkward, turned against her. After a while, Kathi simply left. The emperor was devastated. Finally, friends intervened, and in 1902, Kathi returned to Vienna on her own terms. For one thing, she outlawed those dreadful 7 A.M. breakfasts—she was not civilized until nine, she said. When someone discovered that her frayed nerves resulted from frightening debts—her (undivorced) husband's and her son's—the emperor hastened to settle them all. Kathi also borrowed a page from Elisabeth's book, perhaps feeling the same sense of suffocation, and began to travel extensively—to the Canary Islands, the Mediterranean, Malta, Tunisia, Algeria and Egypt. At home, she spent her time with the emperor and doing volunteer work.

After Kathi's feckless husband finally died, rumors flew that she and the emperor had contracted a morganatic (highborn–commoner) marriage. No evidence but wishful thinking suggests this, and Franz Josef's temperament seems proof absolute it never happened. They may, however, have slept together. Why not? She was a widow, he a widower, they loved each other, he had the means and he could count on her absolute discretion. Despite a decade or more of celibacy, theirs was an erotic love, and only iron duty—Franz Josef's—had kept them chaste.

The final years of their love affair ended with Franz Josef's death on November 21, 1916. Unlike most other mistresses, Kathi was ushered into the family's presence, where the formerly vindictive Marie Valerie wept and embraced her. The emperor's mistress folded two white roses into Franz Josef's stiffened hands and bid him a final farewell.

As in all other areas of his life, Franz Josef fulfilled his obligations and provided munificently for Kathi Schratt. She outlived him by almost twenty-four years, and when the stock market crashed in 1929 and banks failed, she and her son, whom Franz Josef had ennobled as Baron Hirsch, continued to live well.

Alice Keppel [26]

In 1898, Alice Keppel, a married Englishwoman, met Queen Victoria's son Albert and almost overnight became his mistress. Unlike her Austrian contemporary Katharina Schratt, Alice had no profession other than mistress. Perhaps for that reason, she approached her role as a mistress with confidence and dedication.

Born Alice Edmonstone, Alice Keppel was the ninth and youngest child of a minor Scottish noble. After an idyllic childhood spent in a castle, Alice emerged into adulthood a witty and generous-spirited young woman. She was strikingly pretty, with reddish brown hair, flashing dark eyes, strong sculpted features and a radiant expression that reflected an inner serenity. She was buxom and shapely, and very proud of the small feet and dainty hands that won her so many compliments.

Alice's happy marriage to the tall and handsome Honorable George Keppel, an earl's son and a lieutenant in the Gordon Highlanders, was marred by only one thing: too little money. The Keppels had fewer servants than their friends, and they worried about keeping up appearances. After analyzing their situation, Alice announced that she would have to take a wealthy lover, and her agreeable husband acquiesced. By the time Alice met Albert, the Prince of Wales, afterward Edward VII, she had already been mistress to two men, and her affairs were no secret.

For his part, Albert—"Bertie" to his intimates—had been doing military service in Ireland as a young man when his parents heard about his indiscreet affair with an actress. His father, Prince Albert, rushed to Ireland to intervene, contracted typhoid and subsequently died. Queen Victoria was devastated, and always blamed her son for her husband's death. At the age of twenty, young Bertie had lost both his father and his mother's love.

By the time Bertie met Alice, he was fifty-six years old and a confirmed womanizer whose best-known mistresses were the actress Lillie Langtry and the socialite Daisy Warwick. Bertie was a dutiful man and respectful of convention. As Prince of Wales he performed his official duties diligently and astutely. With Germany becoming increasingly sinister, his role in creating the Entente Cordiale between France and England earned him the nickname "Uncle of Europe." Europeans applauded him, and in England he was wildly popular.

On a personal level, however, Bertie was incapable of self-discipline. He was a serious overeater who consumed five copious meals a day, and ended them with brandy and a cigar. (Another of his nicknames was "Tum-Tum," and his waist measured forty-eight inches.) Bertie was a bridge fanatic who bid high and hated losing. He also had a ferocious temper that cowed everyone in his inner circle—everyone, that is, except Alice.

From their very first meeting, Alice mesmerized Bertie. For the remainder of his life he would stare fixedly at her whenever they were together, and would be visibly agitated whenever she spoke to another man. Despite his obsessive fascination with Alice, he was not faithful to her. Alice understood that jealousy and threats were ill-advised and simply ignored his philandering. But to prevent the possibility that Bertie would dump her as he had Lillie and Daisy, she set out to bind him inextricably to her.

In this, Alice's husband, George, was the perfect ally. Bertie had arranged an excellent job for George with Lipton Tea. This gave George both an income and an excuse to absent himself from the house before Bertie arrived—at 12:15 P.M. sharp—for his lingering daily visit.

Thanks to George's job and Bertie's gifts, Alice could now dress and entertain regally. She dedicated her life to pleasing, soothing, amusing and loving her lover. She was his enthusiastic companion at country shooting parties, at London galas and at intimate dinners capped by the inevitable bridge game. Though she was witty, clever and bold, she seemed incapable of meanness. "She never utilized her knowledge to her own advantage, or to that of her friends," recalled an acquaintance, Lord Hardinge of Penshurst, "and I never heard her repeat an unkind word of anybody."[27] Alone, Alice and Bertie made love in her luxurious bedroom with its heaped cushions, velvet drapes and fragrant lilies in cut-glass vases. Downstairs, she entertained him in her thickly carpeted, gray-walled rooms made vibrant by red lacquered cabinets and stately oil portraits.

When Bertie took his annual vacation in Biarritz, Alice and her daughters, Viola and Sonia—whom Bertie adored—joined him, though he lodged in a hotel and they at a friend's villa. During the day, the couple spent every minute together, strolling on the boardwalk and picnicking English-style, with servants waiting on them as they feasted.

Alice's position was official insofar as Bertie acknowledged her as his mistress, and their fellow British aristocrats referred to her as La Favorita. But when Bertie's mother died in 1901 and he ascended the throne as Edward VII, Bertie could offer Alice no revenue from the national coffers as Charles II had Nell Gwynne and as Louis XV had Madame de Pompadour and Madame du Barry. And when he traveled to Austria on diplomatic business, Bertie left Alice behind. He knew that Austrian emperor Franz Josef always kept his mistress,

Kathi Schratt, behind the scenes, and understood that the Austrian imperial family would be scandalized if Alice were to appear at his side.

More disturbing for Alice was that Bertie's wife, Queen Alexandra, disliked her. Years earlier, Alexandra had confronted Bertie about Daisy Warwick, which generated terrifying talk of divorce. After that, Alexandra understood that she must swallow her pain and her pride, and tolerate her husband's mistresses. When Bertie became king, the new queen forced herself to be civil to Alice. But Bertie's health crises brought home the fact that she, Alexandra, was still his wife, and Alice only his mistress. Accordingly, when Bertie suffered an attack of appendicitis, Alice extracted a letter from him, urging his family to admit her to his bedside any time he was seriously ill.

On May 6, 1910, when she heard the horrifying news that Bertie was truly on his deathbed, Alice retrieved her precious letter from safekeeping and rushed with it to the palace. With majestic reluctance, Alexandra allowed the hysterical woman into the sickroom, where Bertie instructed his wife, "You must kiss Alice." Alexandra submitted to Alice's embrace, then hissed at the attending physician to get rid of the intruder. But Alice was no longer urbane and levelheaded. The king's death throes had transformed her into a shrieking, demented banshee whose ranting—"I never did any harm, there was nothing wrong between us, what's to become of me?"—could be heard for hours throughout the palace.[28] When she recovered, Alice discovered that the new king, George V, had already taken measures to guarantee her exclusion from royal life. And Alexandra pointedly returned to her Bertie's Fabergé cigarette case, Alice's cherished gift to him. She was invited to Bertie's funeral, but was forced to enter the church through a side door, an embarrassment to everyone.

Alice recovered rapidly from her loss, and she and George resumed a privileged and monied life of travel and society. They purchased a villa in France and made it their principal residence. In 1932, when Alice was in her sixties, Virginia Woolf lunched with her and described her as "a swarthy thick-set raddled . . . old grasper . . . the extensive, jolly, brazen surface of the old courtezan, who has lost all bloom . . . no sensibilities . . . nor snobberies."[29]

Alice's personal assessment of her life belied Woolf's indictment: Alice lamented only that her love affair with the king had not gone on longer. She survived another ten years and died in Florence at the age of seventy-eight, a confident old lady who never doubted the rightness of having been the last official royal mistress. In 1936, when Edward VIII abdicated so he could marry Wallis Simpson, Alice sniffed, "Things were done better in my day."[30]

Elena Lupescu [31]

Germany spawned the Shoah, but by the 1920s, anti-Semitism already resonated throughout Eastern Europe. It was particularly virulent in Romania, though Jews constituted less than 5 percent of Romania's total population and were denied many of the rights enjoyed by Romanian gentiles. Some ambitious Jews traded their religious affiliation for public conversion to Christianity, which enabled them to escape the most egregious restrictions that hobbled their more uncompromising co-religionists. Nothing they did, however, could entirely eradicate the official "memory" of their Jewish origins.

One such convert was the Jewish-born Nicolae Grünberg, who changed his name first to Wolff and then to Lupescu, its Romanized version. To claim Romanian citizenship and advance in business, Lupescu also joined the Romanian Orthodox Church. His wife, Elizei, also a Jew, converted to Roman Catholicism. In 1899, their daughter, Elena, was born, and she and her brother, Costica, were raised as Christians. As an adolescent, Elena even boarded at a finishing school run by German nuns, who coached her in the social graces and taught her the rudiments of French and German.

The "finished" Elena was a charming, intelligent and flirtatious young woman with striking good looks, a flawless ivory complexion and green eyes that highlighted her red hair. She had a seductive figure, a sashaying gait and—despite her convent training—a reputation for promiscuity. After a brief marriage to a military officer, who quickly divorced her on the grounds of adultery, Elena resumed the carousing she so enjoyed.

A male friend desperate to establish a friendly connection with the crown prince, whom he believed could aid in his career, orchestrated Elena's first meeting with him. The friend was gambling on the likelihood that her sensual good looks would attract the prince, who was known to cheat on his Greek wife, Princess Helen. The ploy worked. Carol, enchanted by Elena's handsomeness and *joie de vivre*, was soon as madly in love with her as he had once been with the commoner Ioana "Zizi" Lambrino, his first wife, whom his family had forced him to divorce so he could marry the suitably royal Helen.

Carol and Helen had a strained, often vitriolic marriage that, in 1921, produced Michael, their only child. By 1924, when Michael was three years old, Carol and "Duduia," his pet name for Elena, were deeply committed to each other both sexually and emotionally. Before long, Carol bought Elena a house that, for reasons of discretion and caution, he had registered in her brother's name. From then on, the crown prince could meet his mistress in perfect safety at her home on Bucharest's Mihail Ghica Street.

Crown princes routinely kept mistresses, but a crown prince as lovestruck as Carol—and with a woman tainted by both divorce and Jewish blood—was decidedly peculiar. Carol's father, King Ferdinand, was so infuriated by his son's obsession that he even contemplated exiling Elena.

In 1925, the situation reached crisis proportions when Carol traveled to London to represent his family at the funeral of their English cousin, Queen Alexandra, Edward VII's widow. Afterward, he went directly to Paris, where Elena waited. In an attempt to avert the relentless publicity that marked his London sojourn, he and Elena slept in (or at least registered for) separate hotel rooms.

But Parisians were too curious, and Paris too close to London. The lovers fled by car to Italy, where, from Venice, Carol complained in a bitter note to his mother that he could not bear his life and had decided, at the risk of causing his family "great sorrow," not to return to Romania. "I'm young enough," he argued. "I've never been frightened of work, and I'll manage to make a life for myself."[32] In other words, the crown prince preferred to live in peaceful exile with his mistress rather than do battle with his family, his wife (who later divorced him) and his political enemies. It helped, of course, that he could draw on substantial trust funds to support his comfortable lifestyle, and that he never really equated his impetuous rebellion with abdication.

After his declaration of independence, Carol and his beloved Duduia returned to France. In Neuilly, they rented a modest house together and Carol immersed himself in cars, cards, music, his beloved stamp collection and Elena. Elena, for her part, occupied herself with grooming, entertaining, making love to Carol—and preventing him from spending time alone with other women.

For Elena, keeping the man who had just renounced his royal birthright for her sake was a full-time job. An essential part of her strategy was to ensure that Carol did not stray far from the seductive power of her love. Above all, he must not be drawn back into the orbit of his poisonous family, especially his mother, Queen Marie, who loathed the woman she described as "an attractive, redheaded, little Jewess of the most scandalous reputation."[33]

The happy equilibrium of Carol and Elena's life together was broken after less than two years by King Ferdinand's death. Within hours, Carol and Helen's six-year-old son ascended the throne. Before dying, Ferdinand had ensured that Michael's succession would proceed smoothly. "Let my son Carol respect scrupulously the legal conditions made by his renunciation of the throne and the sacred duty of a Roumanian son and a father to respect the undertaking that he has given of his own free will," Ferdinand cautioned in an official letter.[34]

Carol, however, regretting his dramatic sacrifice-for-love, began to vilify those who held him to it, and charged publicly that he had abdicated under force. Back in politically unstable Romania, opposition leaders supported his restoration as monarch as a way of ousting the repressive men who governed on Michael's behalf. Yet even his partisans demanded that Carol "renounce a certain liaison" with the detested Elena Lupescu.[35] They also bombarded Romania with flyers denying that he had left his homeland because of Elena.

Carol had to choose between a kingship and his mistress. Elena intervened and declared that she would be "the happiest person alive" if Carol returned to Romania as its king.[36] And so on June 8, 1930, with constitutional contortions and coercion, Carol took the royal oath and dethroned his young son.

Back in France, Elena was wretched. Would Carol succumb to his mother's plea that he remarry Helen? Would political pressures force him to abandon his divorced Jewish mistress? Would he continue to love her? Distraught and terrified of losing him, Elena lost seventeen pounds and suffered migraines. She vowed to enter a convent. She threatened suicide. "If you still loved me you would not act like this. Be good. Don't cheat!" she pleaded.[37]

After two agonizing months, Elena sneaked back into Romania. Carol was annoyed—until he saw her again and was as enchanted as ever. At first he kept Elena in a hotel, later inside his palace in Bucharest. In 1932, he bought her a two-story red brick house on Avenue Vulpache in a fine Bucharest neighborhood.

Interestingly, though Carol was besotted with her, the house he gave her was, in the words of an acerbic observer, dingy and "crammed with indifferent furniture and bric-a-brac. . . . [It] proved only one thing—that sin did not pay. Madame Pompadour would have turned in her grave could she see what her profession had come to."[38] Apart from a fine green marble bidet, Sears, Roebuck, and Company could have furnished her bathroom. However, Carol footed the bill for the exquisite, usually black, Parisian designer clothes that set off Elena's porcelain complexion and fiery hair. He also made sure she was suitably bejeweled.

Besides the respectability of her house and her designer wardrobe and precious gems, Elena had an abundance of what she wanted: Carol's love and devotion, and the freedom to wield influence among leading Romanians who gathered at her house, where they might also meet the king. In fact, her clique ran Romania, just as Queen Marie's had during Ferdinand's regime. (Marie's lover, Prince Barbu Stirbey, who Carol believed was his sister Ileana's real father, had essentially run King Ferdinand's clique.) Elena's power over Carol was such that "the key to understanding . . . his reign is his relationship with his mistress," one historian concludes.[39]

Elena was also an astute businesswoman, and with freedom to control cartels, even to profit from Romanian armaments orders, she created her own fortune. The only thing Carol refused her was the security and recognition of marriage. "A King must have a dual life, one royal, one personal," he said.[40] In any case, because of the intensification of institutionalized anti-Semitism in Romania and in Nazi Germany, Carol's monarchy could not have survived marriage to his Jewish mistress.

Corneliu Zelea Codreanu, the young zealot who founded the virulently anti-Semitic, paramilitary Iron Guard, forged important political ties, notably with the Interior Ministry. Together, the Guard and the Ministry inspired pogroms, the destruction of synagogues and a nationwide spate of anti-Semitic violence.

In 1933, Ion Duca, the prime minister whose National Liberal Party was instrumental in transforming Romania into a constitutional monarchy, outlawed the Iron Guard. The Guard retaliated swiftly: Codreanu ordered Duca assassinated. Afterward, the Guard resurfaced so powerfully that Carol had to act. He attempted to undermine the Guard's influence by supporting other political groups, including the Romanian Front, though the Front, too, condemned international Jewry and the alleged Judaization of the press and national literature.

In fact, most Romanian political parties targeted Jews, which enabled Parliament to persecute them through repressive legislation. Jewish lawyers were dropped from the legal register. Jewish students faced entry quotas—sometimes as low as zero—at universities. Jewish businesses were denied import quotas for raw materials and goods. Banks refused to lend money to Jewish industries. At the same time, these industries were subjected to crushing taxes intended to ruin them.

As the German Goliath swallowed its European neighbors—the Anschluss of Austria (1938), the annexation of Czechoslovakia (1939), the occupation of western Poland—many Romanian politicians leapt at the opportunity to accept directorships in joint German-Romanian enterprises, and these arrangements invariably involved firing any Jewish associates. In 1940, when Romania traded its autonomy for the relative safety of becoming a satellite of Nazi Germany, its Jews became even worse off. Yet until he fled on September 6, 1940, the titular head of this Nazifying, anti-Semitic nation was the king whose mistress and chief adviser was Jewish.

It would be inspiring to learn that Carol and Elena were heroic foes of anti-Semitism. The truth is otherwise. Neither seemed profoundly troubled by the erosion of Romanian Jews' liberties and rights, including the right to earn a living. Elena's circle of intimates included an unlikely mélange of Jews and anti-Semites, who apparently tolerated each other, or at least suspended their animosity in the presence of the woman deemed by many historians "probably the most powerful mistress of the twentieth century."[41] Only her unassailable position as Carol's mistress protected her from the indignities inflicted on other Jews.

Elena was well aware of this. She spoke out bitterly against Hitler and plotted against Codreanu, all the while denying her Jewish roots. In a memoir published in the London *Sunday News,* she wrote that "My father was a Rumanian. My mother was Russian. We are not Jews although it has been said that we are. . . . I have some well-loved Jewish friends and would be proud to say I was Jewish if I were."[42] In safer company, however, she admitted to (the genetically impossible) one-tenth Jewish blood. But despite her dissembling, Romanians and others, including Hitler, identified her as a Jew.

The Iron Guard's charismatic Corneliu Zelea Codreanu declared that he had not killed Elena only because he feared that Carol would break down without her. When Carol finally grasped how dangerous the Guard was, he had Codreanu murdered. No tangible evidence implicates Elena in the killing, but her immense behind-the-scenes influence suggests that, at the very least, she must have urged Carol to rid Romania of one of its most popular and vicious anti-Semites.

But Codreanu was only one of countless enemies, and other anti-Semites hounded Elena. Rallies of university students demanded her death. The chauffeur who delivered her to the palace for nightly sex with King Carol was fired when his wife tattled about his references to "that dirty Jewess." Dr. Neubacher, who headed Germany's economic commission in Bucharest, told Elena how difficult it was for Germany to ally itself with a king whose mistress was Jewish. He tried to convince her to leave Romania for neutral Switzerland, but Elena refused.

Life as Romania's most powerful woman was neither easy nor simple. Despite her iron grip on the ruling clique, Elena was *persona non grata* at the royal palace. Bucharest gossips knew that she went there only at night, and they were both titillated and horrified to hear improbable stories about how Michael, the young prince, had once woken to discover his father running naked down a palace corridor while Elena, pistol in hand and clad only in a flimsy negligee, pursued him. Another shocking rumor was probably true. It linked Elena sexually with her new chauffeur, who had become a trusted confidant.

If Elena occasionally slept with other men, her interest in them was purely erotic and fleeting. The glue between her and Carol was their deep and vibrant love. It stood the test of time, the trial by fire of Romania's Byzantine politics and anti-Semitism, and, ultimately, of the European conflagration. A dedicated telephone line linked Elena's bedroom to Carol's palace. "She brings me everlasting joy," Carol confided to his diary. Again, "I feel an absolute need for her. She is an integral part of my very being." A year later, "My love for her is as deep as ever. I cannot imagine life without her."[43]

Carol wanted Elena to share every aspect of his private life, including his relationship with his son. Deeply concerned that Helen might turn Michael against Elena, he fought to have Helen virtually exiled. At the same time, he encouraged Michael to accept Elena. Elena did all she could to work her magic on the son as on the father, and referred to him and Carol as "my boys."

As Elena consolidated her domestic position at the palace, her bitter enemies consolidated theirs. After its leader's murder, the Iron Guard's appeal intensified, and in death Codreanu soared, Christlike, in popular esteem. Carol responded with what he styled a revolution from above. He disallowed existing political parties, imposed his own National Rebirth Front and declared himself dictator. His Front so slavishly aped the Mussolini-Hitler model that it included a fascist salute. Even anti-Semitic Romanians began to charge that Carol was colluding with Hitler, though they agreed that because of her Jewish blood, Elena was not party to such treason.

By the spring of 1939, as the Nazi juggernaut rolled across Europe, Germany's Russian ally moved against Romania, annexing Bessarabia and Bukovina. Carol turned frantically to the Nazis to protect Romania from the communists. Instead, Germany helped Hungary gobble up Transylvania. Carol, now desperate, attempted to rally the Iron Guard to his assistance. Instead, the Guard staged a coup and led street mobs that howled for Elena Lupescu's blood. Elena fled to the palace, which she set about dismantling. She crated all its treasures and, in a two-day bonfire, burned incriminating documents. Soon she and Carol were ready to flee, but where could such a couple go? Carol ordered a trusted associate to ask Hitler for asylum. "I'll take him, but I won't take the woman," replied the author of the Shoah.[44]

On September 6, Carol grimly signed what was effectively an instrument of abdication, leaving the throne of the rebellious and dismembered country to his nineteen-year-old son, Michael, though Michael wept and begged not to be forced to shoulder such herculean responsibilities. Carol ignored his pleas. He and Elena boarded the royal train that stood at the ready, crammed with tons of their belongings, including cars, two Pekinese and three poodles.

But flight was not that easy. Iron Guardists who wanted Elena's head had mounted an attack farther up the railroad line. After paralyzing indecision, Carol accepted the recommendation of Elena's chauffeur to simply ram the train right through the ambushed station. As the surprised Iron Guards fired at the train, Elena lay flat in a bathtub that Carol shielded with his own body.

The fugitives reached neutral Spain, but relentless surveillance there drove them to sneak into Portugal, Carol squashed into a car trunk as they passed through the border. All Europe seemed unsafe. They decided to cross the Atlantic, but their first choice, the United States, condemned Carol for his collaboration with the Nazis and for his moral turpitude in committing adultery with Elena. Cuba was less judgmental and accepted them, but Elena found Havana too hot. They moved again, first to Mexico and, in 1944, to Brazil, where they remained.

In 1947, Elena fell gravely ill with pernicious anemia. Her physician told Carol that her condition was incurable, and that Elena was close to death. "Sweet and lovely friend," her friend Barbara Hutton, the American heiress, telegraphed her, "am so distressed to learn of your illness and want you to know that all my heart, thoughts and prayers are with you."[45]

Carol was devastated. Believing that he was losing her forever, he gave her the one thing he had always refused her: marriage. On July 5, 1947, in a hotel bedroom, he made his mistress Her Royal Highness Princess Elena of Romania.

Miraculously, Her Royal Highness made a spectacular recovery. Elena may have exaggerated the severity of her illness in the hopes that Carol would marry her. His aversion to doing so must have been rooted in his convictions about the nobility of his royal blood and the ignominy of Elena's.

Soon after their marriage, the royal couple settled in Portugal, where Carol remarried his nearly fifty-year-old wife in a ceremony conducted by a prelate of the Romanian Orthodox Church. Their marriage lasted until April 3, 1953, when Carol succumbed to cancer. Few members of his family attended his elaborate funeral, at which a haggard Elena wept and murmured brokenly, "I want to die."

Carol's estate, or apparent lack of it, generated much more interest among his relatives, who sued for a share in it and argued that the ex-king had secretly stashed away a fortune. Elena's very different version was that Carol had left her only fourteen thousand dollars, with their house already registered in her name. Whatever the truth, Elena enjoyed a comfortable widowhood with servants to care for her and her home. In fact, her money might well have been her own, accumulated in Romania during her tenure as the king's influential mistress.

Without Carol at her side, Elena lost much of her social élan and respectability. Perhaps in reaction, she reminisced incessantly about her royal relatives, real and imagined. She no longer denied her Jewish roots and invented stories about how much she had done to help "her people" during the Shoah. By then she was aware of the extent of the carnage: 43 percent, 264,900, of Romania's Jews had perished in pogroms, mass murders, deportations and extermination camps, or were victims of disease, starvation or exposure.[46] Though Elena probably could not have alleviated Jewish suffering even if she had attempted to, she took false credit for imaginary acts of kindness. She died on June 28, 1977, her legacy that she had once been one of the world's most powerful mistresses.

Camilla Shand Parker Bowles and Prince Charles[47]

Without question, Camilla Parker Bowles is this century's most celebrated royal mistress. Despite her disregard for most of the conventions and paraphernalia traditionally associated with such women, Camilla managed to conquer the stately heart of Britain's heir-to-the-throne, Prince Charles. She also transformed the once-hostile national psyche, and with public acquiescence, if not support, eventually married her prince.

Alice Keppel, Camilla's great grandmother and the mistress of Charles's great great grandfather, would not necessarily have approved – she had been famously irked when Edward VIII abdicated the throne so that he could marry Wallis Simpson. In *her* day, she sniffed, things had been better done. In her day, kings had had wives, and kings had had mistresses, and there was an end to it. Today, the times are different, and Prince Charles's needs and his way of doing things are quite different from his great-great-grandfather's.

The story of Camilla and Charles is well known. Their first meeting, at a rain-lashed polo field, was unexceptional – she was still Camilla Shand, a fun-loving young aristocrat who, though dripping wet and garbed in unflattering stable gear, introduced herself to Charles as he smoothed down his damp polo pony. They chatted for over an hour, and at some point, Camilla reminded him that her great-grandmother had been his great-great-grandfather's mistress.[48]

It was 1970, and Camilla was then twenty-three years old, Charles twenty-two. Though not fabulously rich, she and her family were very much Charles's social peers. Camilla had been raised and educated to be the wife of a rich and important man. Her school, Queen's Gate School in South Kensington, educated the future wives of half the diplomatic corps and even more of the nobility. "Milla," as Camilla was then known, was "just a good, solid, dependable type, lots of fun and popular," one schoolmate reminisced. Another commented that despite her lack of beauty, "she had a certain aura. What she lacked in looks, she made up for in confidence." And, said Carolyn Benson, Camilla's lifelong friend, she was "funny and bright; boys loved her... She could talk to boys about things which interested them. She was ... always a boy's girl."[49] Camilla never bothered primping to attract boys and, later, men – with ordinary clothes, bitten and grimy nails, tousled hair and little or no makeup, she still exuded sex appeal, and was a magnet for male attention.

When she met Prince Charles, Camilla was sharing a flat with a friend who tolerated her dirty and clothes-strewn room because "she was so sweet, it was impossible to be angry with her. She was like a big, boisterous pup."[50] Camilla was also seriously involved with Andrew Parker Bowles, a military officer and one of Charles's friends. Andrew was charming, sexually experienced and generous, but his infidelities wounded Camilla deeply.

At first, Camilla encouraged Charles as a way of getting even with Andrew. The Prince was smitten with her, and soon everyone in their circle knew that they had become a couple. Charles loved Camilla's wry wit, her good nature and her lack of pretension. They shared a deep love of horses and the rural life as the English upper classes live it. And like Camilla's other lovers, Charles responded wholeheartedly to Camilla's exuberant sexuality.

Charles encountered no official opposition to his affair with Camilla. But his mentor and confidant, his uncle Lord Louis Mountbatten, considered her to be mistress rather than wife material. He even noted approvingly that Camilla's physical likeness and her mannerisms were "extraordinarily" close to Alice Keppel's.[51] Unlike her formidably focused forebear, however, Camilla's heart was so divided that she asked a friend if it was possible to love two men simultaneously.

In 1971, Charles enrolled at Dartmouth Naval College and sailed away, leaving a trail of long, romantic shipboard letters in his wake. Andrew was impressed that Camilla had taken up with the Prince of Wales and showed renewed interested in her. Before long, Camilla succumbed to her passion for him.

She did not, however, make a clean break with Charles until, during a visit, he proposed to her. Camilla refused him gently. She loved him, she said, but she could not marry him. Not long after, aboard the naval ship *Minerva*, Charles learned that Camilla and Andrew Parker Bowles were engaged. He retreated alone to his cabin. Later, his shipmates noticed that his eyes were red-rimmed.

Once he was land-bound again and had recovered from his grief, Charles dated many eligible young women. He also resumed his friendships with the now-married Camilla and her husband.

Camilla and Andrew, by then, had what their friends described as an open marriage. Camilla spent her weeks alone at Bolehyde, their country estate, while Andrew lived in London and returned home mainly on weekends. Camilla seemed happy in the country, tending her household, gardening, riding and caring for her babies and her dogs. When her son, Thomas Henry Charles, was born, her ex-lover and dear friend Prince Charles stood as godfather.

In 1979, a year after Camilla's daughter, Laura Rose, was born, an IRA assassin killed Lord Mountbatten. Charles was devastated and sought consolation from Camilla. Before long they had become inseparable. In the press of emotion, Charles urged Camilla to divorce Andrew and marry him. Once again she demurred, this time out of concern that such an imprudent act would destroy his chances of ever ascending the throne. Charles accepted her decision, but afterward seemed incapable of concealing the intensity of his feelings for her. At a polo ball, after Charles spent the evening dancing closely pressed against Camilla, his official date finally borrowed the host's BMW and raced away in a rage.

But the future king still needed a bride, a virgin who would provide heirs to his throne. Camilla, his trusted confidant, began to evaluate suitable women. She and the Queen Mother, independently of each other, both settled on the "quiet as a mouse" Lady Diana Spencer, a tall, leggy and demurely attractive teenager from the right sort of family, and with the right sort of past – that is, none at all.

According to some accounts, Charles and Diana's fairytale wedding was preceded by a pre-nuptial night of lovemaking – between Charles and Camilla,[52] as they took a sad, fond and erotic farewell of one another. Diana entered her marriage with foreboding about Camilla. "I asked Charles if he was still in love with Camilla Parker Bowles and he didn't give me a clear answer," she confided to Charles's assistants. "What am I to do?"[53] What indeed? Her confidants could only sympathize, not reassure. Charles approached his nuptials in a "confused and anxious state of mind" made more difficult by the fact that he still loved Camilla. Yet he expected that somehow, once he married Diana, he could learn to love her as well.

Just before the wedding, Diana discovered an engraved gift that Charles had ordered for Camilla – a sort of going-away present, he told her. But Diana was jealous and frightened. She did not believe Charles's explanations, and wept and raged that he was emotionally committed to the other woman.

The royal marriage was doomed from the start by a chasm of incompatibility, by Diana's immaturity and instability, by Charles's sarcasm and icy criticism and by their mutual self-absorption and self-centeredness. Their lovemaking, too, was marred by Diana's dislike of sex, and by the terrible struggle with bulimia that debilitated and preoccupied her. As if all these negatives were not enough, Diana's suspicions that Charles was sleeping with Camilla further poisoned their relationship.

Early on, Charles responded to Diana's outpourings of anger and sadness by withdrawing into himself and by confiding his growing wretchedness to his friends, especially Camilla, whom he styled his best friend in the world. Diana's supporters believe that Charles and Camilla were intimately involved almost from the beginning of his marriage; Charles and Camilla's partisans insist that for years their relationship was non-sexual though loving, and that Charles truly invested time and effort in his difficult and unsatisfying marriage. What seems incontrovertible is that, after five years, his marriage had disintegrated. In *The Prince of Wales*, the definitive biography that Charles perused line by line before its publication, Jonathan Dimbleby writes that no one incident ended it, but that the marriage "collapsed gradually."[54] As it did so, Camilla was always available to hear Charles's version of his domestic tribulations. In 1986, she and Charles resumed sexual relations.

Very early on in his marriage, Charles had taken over Highgrove, a country estate eleven miles from Camilla's home. Highgrove, a handsome neo-classical mansion set on 340 acres of scenic farmland, suited Charles, but disappointed Diana. Charles's cousin, Prince Michael, believed that Diana was such a "catastrophe" that Charles had bought Highgrove to be near his former girlfriends, notably Camilla.

Diana's developing problems – amongst them her bulimia and recurrent depression – repelled and irritated Charles. Diana commented despairingly on her inability to move him, and even his sympathetic biographer admitted that "the Prince was not always solicitous."[55] When Charles confided in Camilla, however, or when their mutual friends related Diana's latest escapade, Camilla loyally dismissed Diana as "that ridiculous woman," and exonerated Charles from any blame in having contributed to his wife's instability.

Indeed, Diana's frantic efforts to reclaim her husband reinforced the union between Charles and Camilla. A lovemaking session did more than fulfill an urgent need; it became a victory over Diana. The more degraded the royal marriage became, the more Charles depended on Camilla's love and support.

Camilla, too, was unhappy in her marriage. For years she tolerated Andrew's womanizing and his extended absences. But after her dear old friend Charles made it clear that he loved her with a slow-burning passion that would endure forever, Camilla responded. Sympathetic friends facilitated the affair. They lent the couple their homes, invited them over for safe rendezvous and legitimized their relationship by permitting it to flourish in discreet and welcoming company.

When Diana discovered that supposed friends were helping Charles and Camilla behind her back she felt betrayed and powerless to win out over her hated rival. One of Diana's great frustrations was that, despite her beauty and her carefully cultivated taste, she could not compete with her husband's older, plainer and less fashionable mistress. Countless snide columnists and correspondents shared this view. A favorite journalistic cliché was to juxtapose photos of the two women – Diana smartly turned out, Camilla verging on dowdiness. Often editors chose photos that had captured Camilla grimacing or frowning. In real life, Camilla was a pretty woman, trim and nicely rounded, and blessed with luxuriant hair that she chose to style in the same way for decades.

Though Diana cut a spectacular figure, Charles was not merely immune to her charms, he was shocked at her extravagance. And despite increasing evidence that she, too, was unfaithful, Charles was incurious to the point of indifference; his intimates concluded that he welcomed anything, even infidelity, that would keep Diana away from him. All of this must have reassured Camilla, who risked seeing images of or stories about Diana every time she picked up a newspaper or turned on the television.

By 1986, Diana had all but moved out of Highgrove, which she referred to as a "prison," and Camilla had all but moved in with Tosca and Freddy, her Jack Russells, and Molly, her favorite chestnut hunter, who boarded in Charles's stable. Camilla greeted Charles's guests and hosted dinners. Afterward, she and Charles retired together to bed.

Once, Camilla crossed paths with Diana, who arrived for a rare visit. Diana later told a friend how she had screamed at Charles "for sleeping with that woman in my bed... I kept asking him why he was bonking her. ... I knew for sure he was sleeping with that bitch. ... I knew there was no chance. I knew he loved her and not me – and always had done."[56] Diana, by then a media queen, made sure that the public shared her loathing of Camilla.

As the public attacks against his mistress mounted, Charles defended her and, to his friends, described her as the only love of his life. Camilla reciprocated. From the detritus of two unhappy marriages, a great love affair had arisen – or so Charles and Camilla's suggested and perhaps came to believe.

If they needed moral or even social justification for their adulteries, both Camilla and Charles could invoke their spouses' extramarital affairs. "That ridiculous woman," Camilla repeated. "The Rottweiller," Diana countered to her friends about the woman who would not let go of her husband.

By 1988, though she had already had several love affairs herself, Diana's obsession with Camilla intensified. She talked about her to friends and staff, and, in early 1989, consulted her astrologer Debbie Frank about how to deal with "the presence of Camilla." In February, at a birthday party for Camilla's sister Annabel, she decided to confront her husband's mistress.

Well into the evening, Charles and Camilla slipped away and Diana found them chatting with a few other guests. She asked to speak privately with Camilla. Everyone retreated, Charles reluctantly. Diana was, she recalled, "calm, deathly calm." In one version of the confrontation, she asked Camilla humbly, "What am I doing wrong? What is wrong with me? What makes him want to be with you and not me?"[57] In another version, she said to a noticeably uneasy Camilla, "I would just like you to know that I know exactly what is going on between you and Charles; I wasn't born yesterday." At this point another guest intervened, but Diana continued, "I'm sorry I'm in the way. I obviously am in the way, and it must be hell for both of you but I do know what is going on. Don't great me like an idiot."[58] A partygoer's version was that Diana had demanded publicly, "Why don't you just leave my husband alone?"[59] Diana told Charles, however, that she had simply told Camilla that she loved him. Whatever the truth, Camilla never spoke to Diana again.

In the great sniping war of the Windsors, Diana was clearly the winner. Her most brilliant coup was to convince a palace security adviser to secretly tape a cell phone call between Charles and Camilla. In the recording, they openly express their physical longing for each other, and Charles groans, "Oh God, I'd just live inside your trousers or something," then jokes that he could achieve this if he were transformed into a Tampax.[60]

Three years later, in 1992, this tape was aired publicly. It was instantly labeled "Camillagate," and people outdid each other parodying Charles's unfortunate comment about Tampax. Few mentioned how supportive and comfortable the tape showed the relationship to be. Camilla, for example, was eager to read a speech Charles was delivering. Charles responded to Camilla's plaint that she had not achieved much in life by praising her for loving him, "your great achievement." "Oh darling, easier than falling off a chair," Camilla replied.[61]

After "Camillagate," and the 1997 publication of Andrew Morton's sensational *Diana: Her True Story – In Her Own Words*, the tell-all book about Diana's life and love-gone-wrong, Camilla could no longer go anywhere unnoticed. She, and her life, became public property. She lost over fifteen pounds, began to chain smoke, and agonized about the damage the unsought publicity would do to Charles, to her husband and to her family.

Then the pain of public shame and condemnation rebounded onto Diana, as various journalists challenged her stance as aggrieved wife. *The Sun* newspaper, for instance, decided to publish what became known as the "Squidgey" tape. In this embarrassing testament to eavesdropping, used-car salesman James Gilbey professes his love for Diana, asks her if she has recently masturbated, discusses her fear of becoming pregnant, and sympathizes as she complains about "that fucking [royal] family."[62]

The publicity surrounding Charles and Diana, and by extension Camilla and Diana's several lovers, was sustained and mostly negative; it damaged the royal family as nothing had since 1936, when Edward VIII abdicated the throne to marry Wallis Simpson, the twice-divorced American he loved. Charles withdrew into tearful, angry despair and, Byronically, contemplated fleeing England for Italy. The Queen and Prince Philip were outraged at the bad press – "Now the whole bloody country knows who you're bonking!" the Prince shouted at his son.[67]

Camilla's father, Major Bruce Shand, was even more furious. "My daughter's life has been ruined, her children are the subject of ridicule and contempt," he told Charles. "You have brought disgrace on my whole family. ... You must sever all links with Camilla – and you must do it now!"[64]

On December 9, 1992, Buckingham Palace announced that Charles and Diana would separate. On Christmas Day, 1993, Charles phoned Camilla and told her that though he loved her, he had to end their relationship. Gracefully, Camilla accepted his "irrevocable" decision. But after three months, Charles could not bear living without her. By February 1994, Camilla was once again his mistress.

In June 1994, in a television documentary, Charles admitted that after five years with Diana, by which time their marriage was beyond hope or repair, he and "Mrs. Parker Bowles" had become lovers. "She's been a friend for a very long time and will continue to be for a very long time," he said.[65] Camilla had urged him to make a clean breast of their relationship, believing that full disclosure alone would end the media frenzy about it.

Public reaction to the documentary vindicated her opinion. Charles came to seem like countless other men in failed marriages who had taken a mistress. The documentary put Camilla, "the other woman," firmly back in public view. She acquitted herself with admirable forbearance, and finally won the approval of the palace, her father and her husband, who remarked that he could not understand what everyone was fussing about. The *Daily Mail* inquired rhetorically of its readers, "Isn't it time we stopped hating this dignified woman?"[66]

Diana did not think so. After the press exposed her apparently unending amorous escapades, she attacked again. In 1995, during a rehearsed television interview on *Panorama*, Diana confided to millions of television viewers that "there were three of us in this marriage, so it was a bit crowded."[67]

Charles' friend Nicholas Soames, the Minister of Defense, styled Diana's interview as "toe-curlingly dreadful." Her journalistic confidant Richard Kay wrote that "everywhere was the stench of revenge. She laid waste her husband and her love rival with the skill of a woman betrayed." *The Daily Telegraph*, however, cautioned that "some part of her performance appeared to confirm ... her reputation for being unstable."[68]

Camilla was not laid to waste. She and Charles quietly flourished. She and Andrew finally divorced, truly amicably; neither he nor any of Camilla's friends ever express negative or disloyal comments about her. Charles provided her with a car, and they began to spend several days a week together. Camilla was not yet royalty, but Charles ensured that she enjoyed some of royalty's perquisites.

When Camilla turned fifty, Charles threw a birthday party for her at Highgrove, which with his approval she had divested of Diana's pretty pastel décor and redecorated to suit Charles's taste. Camilla was radiant, and she and Charles danced cheek to cheek to ABBA songs. The party, observers said, was Charles's public endorsement of their relationship. Media interest in their love affair continued, but it was not unkind. Then in 1997, Diana was killed in a Paris car crash, and once again, the spotlight fell on the survivors. One headline captured the gist of these stories: "Can Camilla Compete with a Deceased Diana?"[69]

Apparently, she can.

Camilla's media image has steadily improved. In 2000, at a party for Constantine, former King of Greece, Queen Elizabeth publicly acknowledged Camilla; she had previously refused to be in the same room with her. In June 2001, Camilla attended her first dinner at Buckingham Palace. A month later, Charles fondly kissed her in public. In 2002, she was invited to attend his grandmother's funeral. In February 2005, Charles obtained legal and constitutional consent to marry Camilla and, at a party at Windsor Castle, he and Camilla announced their engagement. Camilla, resplendent in a scarlet gown, sported the heirloom diamond ring that Charles's parents had agreed she should have. The wedding, civil rather than religious because Camilla was a divorcée with a living husband and could not, therefore, marry in the Church of England, was set for April 8th.

On April 9th, after a twenty-four hour postponement to allow Charles to represent the Queen at the funeral of Pope John Paul II, the fifty-six-year-old groom and his fifty-seven-year-old bride were married at Guildhall, Windsor. All the senior royals except Charles's parents were present because the Queen, as Supreme Governor of the Church of England, could not endorse a civil wedding by attending it. As the wedding party emerged from the building, they were greeted by a cheering crowd of twenty thousand, a few booing protesters and placard carriers – Queen Diana forever! King Charles and Camilla never – and one streaker, quickly cornered and clothed by police. Camilla, now the most senior female royal after the Queen, was radiant as she and her smiling husband thanked their well-wishers.

Hours later, Rowan Williams, Archbishop of Canterbury and leader of the Church of England, blessed the marriage in a televised service at St. George's Chapel. An ebullient Queen Elizabeth and Prince Philip attended along with eight hundred other notables. Afterward, at the reception she hosted in Windsor Castle, the Queen toasted Charles and Camilla in metaphors of Grand National horseracing. "[D]espite ... all kinds of terrible obstacles, my son is home and dry with the woman he loves. Welcome to the winner's enclosure,"[70] she declared.

Charles's sons, Harry and William, the latter a smiling witness to the wedding, sprayed "C+C" and "Just Married" onto the windshield of the newlyweds' Bentley, and decorated it with bunches of red, white and yellow metallic balloons. They also embraced Camilla and kissed her, the first time they had been photographed with her.

The princes' public affection and the Queen's evident joy were harbingers of Camilla's changed status. But far from ending the controversy, her marriage has ignited new challenges. Critics now question the constitutionality (but not legality) of Charles's civil wedding, and hence his right to succeed his mother on the throne.

The issue of Camilla's queenly future also vexes her opponents. To avert sad and bitter reminders that the beloved Diana was also once Charles's Princess of Wales, Camilla is known by her secondary title of Duchess of Cornwall. An official Palace statement referring to her as "the Princess Consort" implies as well that, though she would become queen when Charles became king, her title would be Princess Consort. Meanwhile, in real life, Camilla gamely performs royal duties, patronizes scores of worthy organizations and belies gossipy carping by living happily ever after with her former lover.

As a younger woman, Camilla loved to joke that her great grandmother had taught her to "curtsy first and later jump into bed." Her family's lore about Alice Keppel taught Camilla that becoming a royal mistress was entirely acceptable, indeed commendable. But Charles is a sentimental and idealistic man, and despite his wretched experience of it, treasures marriage. He refused to rest until his beloved mistress became his wife. If Alice Keppel were alive, she might be mystified; legions of other royal mistresses, whose contemporaries disdained them as whores, would likely applaud.

CHAPTER 4

Marital Arrangements
in Aristocratic Circles

Ngland in the last quarter of the 18th century was in the midst of fundamental transformation. The Industrial Revolution was transforming it from an agrarian to an industrialized society with a flourishing merchant class and a grindingly poor and growing working class. The revolution in the far-off American colonies and the subsequent involvement of France gave England a military cast and an unpleasant taste of defeat. But it was the French Revolution, with its murderous attacks on the aristocracy, that made England's outrageously profligate upper classes shudder and take stock of their own changing world.

In the vanishing world of privilege, marriage remained a practical arrangement, and daughters were their parents' pawns. Happiness was an elusive ideal, and it had nothing to do with marriage.

Lady Bess Foster and Georgiana, Duchess of Devonshire [1]
Happiness was not an expectation of Lady Julia Stanley, the fictional heroine of *The Sylph*, a novel published anonymously in 1778, written by Georgiana, Duchess of Devonshire. At least, she did not expect it from her marriage, which offered her a title and rank—and little else. Lady Julia and Lord Stanley seldom even met. Both understood that marriages were contracted as either commercial arrangements or family alliances—"The heart is not consulted." In fact, since their wedding day, Lord Stanley had had a mistress.

"What law," Lady Julia asked plaintively, "excludes a woman from doing the same?"

An outrageous question, of course, with an implacable answer: the law of the double standard, the law that tolerates adultery in husbands but condemns it in wives, the law of England, indeed, the law of most lands.

It was also a rhetorical question, as *The Sylph*'s twenty-one-year-old author knew full well. Even as a giddy sixteen-year-old debutante whose parents had just accepted the young duke of Devonshire's request to marry her, Lady Georgiana Spencer had known the rules of marriage, at least for aristocratic women. The wife, selected as an appropriate vessel for her husband's illustrious seed, was expected to produce an heir. Until then, she must remain faithful. Afterward, she should be exceedingly discreet and ensure—somehow—that she did not conceive another man's child. Reputation was crucial and, once lost, could never be recovered. The husband, for his part, was to protect and provide for her and the family they would establish.

Georgiana Spencer tried very hard to play by the rules, and whenever she seemed likely to stray, her controlling mother, Lady Margaret Spencer, reminded her forcefully of her duties. These were not easy to fulfil: Georgiana's husband William, fifth Duke of Devonshire, was at best indifferent and usually sullenly disapproving or antagonistic. Besides, he had cheated on her from the beginning of their marriage, celebrated two days before her seventeenth birthday, with his mistress, Charlotte Spencer.

Charlotte Spencer (no relation to the exalted Georgiana) was the well-bred and sweet-mannered daughter of a poor clergyman whose death left her destitute. Charlotte could not earn a living in her rural parish, so she set out for London to pursue a career as a seamstress or a hatmaker. At the coach terminal there, she encountered that ubiquitous villain, the pimp posing as a friend to new arrivals. Almost at once she was seduced and abandoned. Desperate, she became the mistress of an old playboy who died shortly after but willed her enough money to open her own hat shop.

It was in this establishment that William saw her and was smitten by her charm, deferential manner and sensibilities, so much so that he fell in love with her. Charlotte became his mistress, moved to a house he rented for her and made this sluggish man very happy. Just before he married Georgiana, Charlotte bore him a daughter, another Charlotte.

Though their mismatched social ranks made a legal union inconceivable, Charlotte had conquered William's heart, and he had no intention of allowing his marriage to interfere with his affair. Consequently, Georgiana was competing for the affection of a man already committed to his gentle mistress.

Charlotte, however, died soon after 1778 and left few traces of her life. Until she met William, she epitomized the classically betrayed woman forced into mistresshood: penniless, vulnerable, defiled. In many ways she was luckier than most; her second lover had financed her little business, and her third, the duke of Devonshire, supported her and cared for their daughter.

In his own minimalist way, William discharged his fatherly obligations. After Charlotte's death, he summoned little Charlotte and her nurse, Mrs. Gardner, to Devonshire House, where he informed Georgiana that he had fathered the girl. Georgiana, whom he had already reproached for her failure to produce an heir, greeted the child joyfully and helped her husband concoct a surname—Williams, as close to William as they dared come. (Illegitimate children were often given surnames that hinted at their paternity.) The Devonshires also invented a background for the little girl—she became Georgiana's distant and orphaned relative. Young Charlotte's future was secure, and her father's next mistress would play an important role in it.

Meanwhile, William needed a woman who would adore him as Charlotte Spencer had, and he found her in Lady Elizabeth "Bess" Hervey Foster. Like Charlotte Spencer, Bess was the daughter of a cleric, but her father was the bishop of Derry, later earl of Bristol. However, the Hervey family was socially and financially far inferior to the Devonshires. More seriously, the Herveys had a reputation for libertine living.

Bess endured a brief and bitter marriage to John Foster, a respectable family friend. But John's outward geniality did not extend to his wife, at least after she learned that he was sleeping with her maid and he learned that she had another "attraction." No documents tell us the fate of John's servant-mistress—she was too insignificant to mention. We do know, however, that John was furious over Bess's infidelity. He rejected her pleas for a reconciliation and forced her to accept a total separation, which, according to 18th-century English law, gave him exclusive custody of their toddler and even the child Bess was carrying. As soon as the infant was weaned, she was to relinquish him or her to John, who had denied her visitation rights. He also refused to give her a penny of support. John's behavior was monstrous but perfectly legal, so Bess was doubly victimized.

Bess's father was as cruel and parsimonious as her husband. He grudgingly gave Bess a skimpy allowance, often neglected to pay it and expected her to survive. He treated her long-suffering mother just as callously, stripping her of the means to help her daughter.

Bess's predicament was worsened by the ironic fact that her father's earldom made her a lady, a title that made it more difficult for her to earn a living as a governess or paid companion, the traditional occupations for distressed gentlewomen. Nor could she hope for redemptive remarriage—divorce required an act of Parliament, and divorcées were seldom permitted to remarry. For the despairing young woman, mistressdom became overwhelmingly attractive. In later years, Bess described herself as a wife without a husband, and a mother without children, "by myself alone to steer through every peril that surrounds a young woman so situated."[2]

Fortunately for Bess, her assets outnumbered her liabilities. She was petite, luminously beautiful and exquisitely groomed. She was well bred and spoke fluent French and Italian. She was an interesting conversationalist who excelled at anecdotes. She chose tasteful and flattering clothes that enhanced her charm. She was an extrovert given to dramatic expressions of the maudlin sentiment her century reveled in. She was capable of sustained emotional attachments and was devoted to her friends and, *in absentia*, to her lost children. And to an unusual degree, Bess understood herself and analyzed and recorded her emotions and strategies in a self-serving journal intended for posthumous publication.

Georgiana's mother introduced this woman to the unhappy Devonshires. Georgiana responded to Bess with unreserved sympathy and an affection that swiftly deepened into lifelong love. Bess had been disgracefully treated— Georgiana would make it up to her. Bess was poor and alone—Georgiana would provide for and solace her. And surprisingly, when Bess appeared, the aloof and uncommunicative William thawed and opened up, and even treated Georgiana more considerately.

Bess and the Devonshires became a self-contained threesome, with pet names that highlighted their intimacy: he was "Canis," named for his love of dogs; Bess was "Racky" because of her chronic cough; and for reasons unknown, Georgiana was the "Rat." Georgiana was enchanted with her new best friend and found the perfect way to cement their relationship. Bess would become young Charlotte Williams's governess, a very nice arrangement for Charlotte, and financial and social salvation for Bess.

Georgiana's was an unusual personality. As a newlywed she set up a little geology and chemistry lab, and she delighted in undertaking experiments. William considered this unseemly and shut it down, so Georgiana threw her energy into other activities. One, which William applauded, was politics. Both his family and hers were committed Whigs, and she became a determined campaigner. She hosted an endless round of enormous dinners to reward party loyalists or seduce potential allies. She engaged in street electioneering and, oblivious to filth and danger, went into the seediest neighborhoods to knock on doors for the Whig cause.

Politics consumed a good deal of her time, but Georgiana needed other outlets for her abundant energy. She found them in fashion and gambling. As a fashion leader, she introduced hats so high they swept low ceilings, and so feather-laden they must have denuded flocks of peacocks. As a gambler at cards, she lost staggering sums but never confessed the true amounts to her husband. She spent much of her lifetime evading or lying to creditors, but agonizing about what she acknowledged as her most serious personal flaw.

Georgiana's gambling further alienated William, and provided Bess with one of her most effective weapons. So did Georgiana's unrestrained non-judgmental affection, which "hurried me down the precipice," Bess confided to her journal.[3] The women's friendship was based on immense trust, and they confided deeply in each other, Georgiana unreservedly, Bess selectively. Each time Georgiana's indebtedness threatened to overwhelm her, she deluged Bess with the sordid details and entreated her to intercede with William on her behalf, so he would—once again—produce the money.

It is unclear how soon after meeting the Devonshires Bess began to sleep with William. Given his personality, it is likely that he first fell deeply in love with her, then waited a while before hinting at his erotic interest. But before too long, they were sexually involved, which further confounded Bess's already tangled life. Her financial and social survival was totally dependent on the Devonshires, and she knew only too well that her reputation was a crucial factor in her continued success. Georgiana was such an undisputed social leader that she held Bess's fate in her two bejeweled hands. At the same time, Bess could be fairly certain that Georgiana would not turn against her, if only because she would be loath to have Bess reveal what she knew about Georgiana's life, from her gambling to her agony as "the Prince" (their name for menstruation) regularly dashed her hopes that she had conceived a child.

In her situation, with her needs and her goals, what could Bess do? If she withheld her body, William might withdraw his money or, worse, find another mistress. If she worked up the courage to tell Georgiana the truth, she would almost certainly lose her closest, most important friend. As it was, tongues wagged, and the most virulent belonged to Lady Spencer.

So Bess accepted a life of ongoing deception and betrayal, and she became a master liar and hypocrite. Time and again she convinced William to rescue

Georgiana from debt, then graciously accepted her friend's gratitude. She despaired with Georgiana about her infertility, rejoiced when Georgiana produced little Georgiana and all the while suppressed her jealousy that Georgiana was also sleeping with William. She swore eternal devotion to Georgiana, then struggled with her own envy as (it seemed) the entire aristocratic world melted at the other woman's charm and natural warmth. And, on the rare occasions Georgiana seemed suspicious of her, Bess died the thousand deaths of the proverbial coward, nearly paralyzed at the thought of returning to her grim former life.

At one point, the Devonshires sent Bess abroad, ostensibly for Charlotte's cultural improvement but actually to squelch rumors about her relationship with the duke. These rumors distressed Georgiana and alarmed the Spencers. From Europe, Bess sent effusive letters to maintain her hold over both William and Georgiana. She also tried to make them jealous by describing a brilliant social life at the French court, which was totally fabricated.

While Bess struggled in France, she received news that underscored the precariousness of her position, and also its unfairness. At approximately the same time as Georgiana wrote with the joyful news that she was again pregnant, Bess discovered that she was, too. This meant that the duke must have slept with her days or even hours before or after he slept with Georgiana, Bess calculated, and she was riddled with jealousy.

Even more galling was the contrast between the pregnancies and the births. Georgiana gloried in pampered luxury. Bess, on the other hand, had to hide her swelling belly, then when she reached term, creep away to a wretched apartment owned by the doctor who would deliver her baby. She shared her humiliation with her servant, Louis, who posed as her husband. Baby Caroline was born and immediately secreted with a poor family. Bess resumed her life, breasts still tender from surging milk and heart heavy from the weight of her deception, while Caroline was hidden away, a dirty secret.

But despite her jolly letters to Georgiana, Bess knew that having William's baby had radically altered the once happy trio's easiness with each other. William sensed her anxiety and sought to allay it: even if Georgiana knew about them, he reassured her, she wouldn't really mind. Bess was unsure and, in any case, knew how harshly everyone else would judge her.

Back in England, Georgiana's family was censorious and displeased at Bess's reappearance into William and Georgiana's life. Georgiana herself noticed nothing. She was obsessed by her most terrible gambling debt yet, a sum too large to even contemplate repaying. When she finally confessed it to

William, he demanded a separation. Bess was torn between secretly gloating at Georgiana's despair and fear and her own terror that if he sent Georgiana away, propriety would demand that she, too, decamp from Devonshire House. Then, instead of the frenetic social life she adored, she could at best expect a Charlotte Spencer–like arrangement, a modest, isolated house, her world shrunk to William's visits, her future precarious and dependent on his whims.

For complex reasons topped by an unquenchable vanity, Bess began an affair with the duke of Richmond. All the while, she swore her undying love for and fidelity to Georgiana's husband, and also Georgiana.

For her part, Georgiana (supported by her ferociously loyal and involved mother, sister, Harriet, and brother, George) was opposed to any arrangement that would kill all chances for reconciliation with her husband. She and her family correctly assumed that ostracizing Bess would have precisely that effect.

William was also loath to divorce: Georgiana's debts had seriously drained his resources and her lies infuriated him, but legally, only she could provide his longed-for heir. Besides, he missed having the two women compete for his attention. As a result, he, Georgiana and Bess engaged in interminable negotiations. Georgiana unwittingly turned the tide by describing to Bess her regret at squandering the Devonshire money. Bess was taken aback, utterly unprepared for kindness and decency from the woman whose husband she had stolen. At that point, her surging affection for her friend outweighed her envy.

Astonishingly, Canis, Rat and Racky resumed their *ménage à trois* almost as if they had never been estranged. "What a happiness it is to me that my dearest loveliest friend and the man whom I love so much and to whom I owe everything, are united like brother and sister, that they will ensure one another's happiness till I hope a very great age," wrote Georgiana.[4] Georgiana continued to hide the gambling fever that consumed her. She also had an affair with the duke of Dorset. Bess became pregnant again, and Georgiana arranged for a French hideaway that proved to be more suitable than the previous one. But William was never sure that the child was his, nor, in fact, was Bess, for either he or the duke of Richmond could have fathered young Augustus.

Meanwhile, William had impregnated Georgiana as well, and in 1790, she triumphantly delivered William Hartington "Hart" Spencer, the heir her husband had so eagerly awaited. Georgiana regarded Hart's birth as liberation from her wifely obligations. She began a passionate love affair with the much younger Charles Grey, who would in the 1830s shepherd the Reform Laws through Parliament. Like Bess, whom she continued to confide in, Georgiana had become a mistress.

In 1791, Georgiana became pregnant—by Grey. Furious, William sent her to France, though it was seething with revolution, and her close connections to Marie-Antoinette and leading members of the nobility made her situation precarious. He gave her a choice: Grey or the children, whom he would never allow her to see if she continued her liaison. Georgiana's capitulation was immediate. Grey was devastated and accusatory, but nothing he could say persuaded her to choose him over her three children.

Eliza Courtney was born in 1792 and sent to Grey's parents. "Unhappy child of indiscretion, / poor slumberer on a breast forlorn / pledge of reproof of past transgression / Dear tho' unfortunate to be born," Georgiana mused afterward in a poem.[5] Now Georgiana, like Bess, had a lost child. She could not acknowledge Eliza and, on her few clandestine visits to her, saw for herself that Grey's parents treated the child unlovingly, like a burdensome embarrassment. Like oxen that can only pull their burden together, William Devonshire's wife and mistress were yoked in an indissoluble union.

In 1796, Bess had a stroke of luck. Her husband died, and she could at last take custody of her two children. A decade later, Georgiana also passed away, her body ravaged by the nervous strain provoked by her relentless gambling and her creditors' persecution. Bess mourned her friend, then devoted herself to convincing William to marry her. Georgiana's unexpected and premature death had opened up what Bess saw as the opportunity of a lifetime—to cease living on the Devonshire sidelines and to actually become the new duchess of Devonshire.

William resisted. He missed Georgiana and worried about what people would say if he remarried precipitously, at least if Bess was his bride. But in 1809 he relented and made his mistress his wife. For two years, Bess was the duchess of Devonshire. It was an embittering experience. Most of those whose society she craved shunned her. Worse, William quickly developed another attachment and began to spend his nights with his new mistress. In 1811, when he died, his legitimate children unleashed the resentment they had previously kept in check. They forced Bess to return the Devonshire family jewels William had given her, and effectively kicked her out of Devonshire House. She spent five more years in relative isolation, then left England for Italy.

Toward the end, Bess's life was secure and fulfilling. Georgiana's son, Hart, the new duke of Devonshire, granted her a secure pension. She never lost her beauty, and used it to attract new lovers, including an Italian cardinal. She read widely and interested herself in excavating ancient Roman sites. Most of all (or so Bess believed), Hart's kindness redeemed her lacerated social pride in the eyes of at least a few of the Devonshires' social circle.

Bess's critics—contemporary and current—have been harsh judges, but in blaming her they have misidentified the principal villain: the double standard. Bess was unquestionably devious, but portraying her as evil is to hold her up to a standard of independence she did not possess. In fact, until she met the Devonshires, Bess was utterly dependent on two cruel men, her husband and her father.

Lady Caroline Lamb [6]

The sexual elasticity of the Devonshires outlived William and Georgiana through her sister Harriet's daughter, Lady Caroline Lamb, one of England's most famous mistresses. Caroline was born into the savagely unhappy marriage of Harriet (Henrietta Frances Spencer) and Frederick Ponsonby, third earl of Bessborough. Harriet was too focused on her own personal crises to provide the structure and discipline Caroline needed. The sad result was a self-absorbed and wildly disruptive child who dominated her little world through her rude manners, fearful tantrums and outrageous lies.

When Caroline was nine, her parents engaged in a particularly brutal marital skirmish, which her mother assuaged with an intense love affair with the much younger Lord Granville Leveson-Gower. Caroline was sent to live with her aunt, Georgiana Devonshire. At Devonshire House, the atmosphere was scarcely better than at home, and Caroline tyrannized the household with her rages and screaming, and kicked and bit anyone who attempted to restrain her.

What to do? The Devonshires decided to send Caroline to school, a genteel seminary for young ladies. But Caroline was made of tougher stuff than the headmistress. The academic solution, too, was a spectacular failure.

Caroline's powerful grandmother, Lady Spencer, called in the family doctor, who examined his recalcitrant patient and diagnosed her as a gifted but nervous child whose delicate brain should not be subjected to the strain and stimulation of education. What Caroline needed was to play, not study, in an ambiance free of stress and care.

She played, therefore, "preferred washing a dog . . . or breaking in a horse, to any accomplishment in the world,"[7] and entered adolescence as spoiled and headstrong as ever. She developed fervent religious beliefs and, as best she could, given her near-illiteracy, sought answers in her Bible. At thirteen, she was confirmed at Westminster Abbey, and she took her vows with heartfelt sincerity.

Physically, Caroline matured into a pixy-like siren whose eccentric behavior aroused male admiration as much as her fair good looks. She wrote poetry and rode horses bareback. She was merry, unselfconscious and graceful. She alternated between dressing in boy's clothes and wearing floating, transparent gowns that emphasized her femininity. She won many hearts, including her cousin Hart's, and was the darling of the aristocratic world, which nicknamed her "Sprite," "Ariel" and, perhaps tellingly, "Savage," for her lack of inhibitions.

At twenty, Caroline married William Lamb, the much older natural son of Lady Melbourne and the earl of Egremont (though Lord Melbourne acknowledged him). William had known Caroline since she was a child. The marriage began as a family-sanctioned love match, the groom kindly and doting, the bride innocent and steeped in romantic notions. But the surreal Devonshire world of manic gambling and spending, parties and sports, romantic love and sexual relationships, had not prepared Caroline for marriage.

At the actual ceremony, Caroline was excessively nervous, and even more so as she lay trembling with fear in her nuptial bed. William loved her dearly, and made gentle love to the nymphet who had just become his wife. Nonetheless, Caroline's sexual initiation sickened her, and for days afterward she refused to see even her closest relatives. Months later, friends thought she looked pale and ill, and her mother worried that she seemed more schoolgirlish than wifely.

But young Caroline was pregnant. Before she reached full term, she delivered a stillborn child. She suffered profound postpartum depression and tried to dull the pain with hot baths, laudanum and frenzied partying. At the same time she noticed that William was less attentive, and she confided to a friend her great sadness about the difference between William the devoted lover and William the neglectful husband. Later, she gave birth again and was devastated when it became apparent that her baby boy was mentally retarded and unresponsive. A third pregnancy, her last, ended in miscarriage.

Caroline's unhappiness and emotional frustration intensified. She tried to renew William's interest by threatening to have affairs. William laughed and asked, mockingly, what man would want such a frigid, sexually unresponsive woman? "William cared nothing for my morals. I might flirt and go about with whom I pleased," Caroline said later.[8]

Caroline was crushed but not defeated. She fussed over a lapdog given her by a would-be lover, until it bit her son. Then she vowed that if her child recovered, she would rededicate her life to her husband. Little Augustus survived and Caroline gratefully sought to keep her promise. She returned to wooing William, but could not transform him back into the ardent lover who had disappeared after marrying her. By this time they had been married nearly seven years.

At precisely this juncture, a friend selected Caroline to evaluate a manuscript for publication. Socializing and flirting had not been enough to counter the loneliness of her marriage. Caroline had also decided to educate herself, and had become an autodidact who had painstakingly acquired a liberal arts education. She was mesmerized by *Childe Harold's Pilgrimage*, and after reading it she set out to meet its author, the fascinating George Gordon, Lord Byron. After their first encounter Caroline wrote prophetically, "Mad, bad and dangerous to know. . . . That beautiful pale face is my fate."

So began one of their century's most scandalous love affairs. At first the two self-absorbed lovers were ecstatically happy. They met frequently, and Byron coaxed from her slender and restrained body the erotic responses William had never awakened. When they were apart, they poured out their talented hearts in letters and poems. Caroline adored her Byron and abandoned herself to celebrating her love.

Briefly, Byron reciprocated, though from the first he had reservations. He preferred voluptuous, fleshy women, and he abhorred clinging, unstable attention seekers. What he truly loved were Caroline's social connections, her lively mind and her profound appreciation of his artistic brilliance. He tried hard to stay in love with her, and whipped up his senses with ardent love letters. Even when he was impatient with her, he demanded that she abandon her family life (such as it was) and lock herself away with him, reading and discussing. He insisted she stop waltzing because he loathed seeing her in another man's arms and because the clubfoot that tormented him prevented him from dancing. Caroline complied, though she was an enthusiastic dancer.

For several months they consumed each other. William Lamb seemed uninterested and put no obstacles in Caroline's way, so the lovers felt free to appear together in public. Some hostesses even invited them as a couple. But Caroline's disregard for propriety horrified Byron, and they quarreled almost from the start. Byron called her volcanic and urged her to observe a modicum of discretion. But she could not and would not, and the more he withdrew from her, the more she pursued him. If they attended the same event, she always left with him, in his carriage. Much worse, when he went somewhere without her, she would hover outside, indifferent to onlookers, waiting for him.

More and more, Caroline's behavior disgusted her lover. Her reverence for his genius struck Byron as abject, while her independent spirit was irritating and unfeminine. He never appreciated her fragile beauty, which he associated with hysteria and ill health. He tormented her by flirting with other women. This was particularly painful as Caroline was well aware that he was young, increasingly eligible as his poetic reputation soared, and so handsome that he was routinely likened to a Greek god. Once, when Byron spoke with flirtatious tenderness to another woman, Caroline bit down so hard on her drinking glass that she shattered it.

Less than four months after they met, Byron was tiring of both Caroline and the delirium of their few months together. He referred to their relationship as "thralldom" and proposed a month's separation to cool emotions and regain focus. Later, he attributed his failure to simply end the affair to his own indolence as much as to Caroline's hold over him.

Caroline sensed his growing indifference and irritation, and shared her misery with her astonishingly understanding husband. William, realizing that Byron would soon drop her, comforted her as best he could. But Caroline was inconsolable and began to act more and more irrationally. She decided Byron must elope with her. She disguised herself as a boy and sneaked into his lodgings, then pleaded with him to run off with her. When he refused, she tried to stab herself.

Byron was by then seriously alarmed, yet still could not bring himself to make a clean break. Instead, he sent her ambivalent notes that left her both sad and hopeful. Caroline launched a raging campaign to keep him. She sent him a ringlet of her pubic hair, a bizarre gift he kept until his death. "I cut the hair too close and bled more than you need," she wrote, as if she expected him to reciprocate in kind.[9]

Next, she ran away, pawning an opal ring and other jewels to pay for her passage to Portsmouth, where she planned to board the first vessel she found, no matter where it was heading. Her frantic family tracked her down and brought her back home. The rescue was complicated by Caroline's suggestion—soon proved untrue—that she was pregnant with William's child. She also threatened to run away again, either to be with Byron or to escape from him.

But lava still flowed in the veins of Byron's "little volcano," his pet name for Caroline, and he continued to madden her with vague promises and faint hopes. At one point, he confided to a friend that if absolutely forced into it, he would marry Caroline, wretched though this would make him.

Marital Arrangements in Aristocratic Circles

Caroline's family managed to send her off to Ireland to recover both her sanity and her physical health, which was deteriorating. She was by then bone thin, haggard with grief and tormented by wild mood swings. In this turbulent emotional state, she received Byron's last letter, eloquent and passionate, full of protestations of love interspersed with his uneasiness that she was actually mad, yet still holding out hope that they would end up together forever. Meanwhile, he was courting Annabella Milbanke, partly because he believed that only a speedy marriage with any suitable woman who "does not look as if she would spit in my face" could save him from Caroline.[10] He was also sleeping with Lady Jane Oxford, an amorous older woman who alleviated her boredom with her distinguished but dull husband by seeking out—and boasting about—sexual conquests, particularly her affair with the prestigious young poet.

Byron's complicated love life became more so after Annabella rejected his proposal of marriage. He comforted himself with Lady Oxford, and with a married Italian singer he enjoyed in bed but whose robust appetite for food disgusted him. He also hinted to Caroline that he might like to see her.

Then, perversely, he sent her a letter Lady Oxford had maliciously concocted. "Lady Caroline," Byron wrote, "I love another . . . I am no longer yr lover."[11] Caroline read it and was so stricken that she became a feverish, incoherent and bedridden skeleton. William, under pressure from his family to separate from his mad wife, made a last-ditch attempt to help her by moving her to the country home she loved. But Caroline was incapable of understanding that she was destroying her marriage. She could think only about Byron and avenging her wrongs by self-mutilation.

Caroline began to ride recklessly. She slashed her throat with a razor. She demanded that Byron return her gifts, even trinkets. She enlisted local village girls, dressed them all in white and, one wintry night, staged a grotesque *pièce de theâtre* in which she burned Byron in effigy and tossed duplicates of his letters and various mementos into the fire while the all-girl chorus chanted a vitriolic poem likening Caroline's private traitor, Byron, to the public traitor Guy Fawkes. She had originally intended, like an Indian *sati*, to immolate herself in the flames. Back home, she sent Byron a description of the evening's proceedings. He was unmoved and wrote spitefully that she was possessed by "the foul fiend *Flibbertigibbet*." He never again wrote to her.

Caroline's mad melodrama had not healed her. She deluged Byron with letters and announced that she would ruin him. She regretted burning his picture and intercepted a new one intended for Lady Oxford. Byron, furious, cursed her as a maniac possessed by devils, and swore that he would hate her until his dying day.

Finally, wearily and angrily, he agreed to meet her, something he had resisted for months. It was an emotional reunion. Byron wept and implored her to forgive him, while Caroline was stonily impassive. Afterward, she was overjoyed, and told him that he had raised her from despair to heavenly happiness. They met repeatedly, until the madness struck again.

The ex-lovers met at a party, and Byron tauntingly dared Caroline to waltz. She and a partner danced. Then she fled the ballroom, grabbed a knife and slashed herself. Later, she insisted that she had cut herself by mistake. Her mother-in-law described her as a barrel of gunpowder that the tiniest spark could ignite.

Caroline continued to stalk her former lover. She managed to get inside his home, and left him a scribbled note imploring, Remember me. Byron was so angry that he produced a hateful poem, "Remember thee!" cursing her as a false wife and a fiendish mistress. He also succeeded in convincing Annabella Milbanke to marry him.

Caroline, often suicidal, struggled to live. Life, she lamented, was not brief, as people so often complained, but very long. Hyperactive and sleepless, she had endless time on her hands. She survived Byron's marriage, but when it soon foundered because of his frequent abuse, Caroline intervened on Annabella's behalf. She stated in writing that she had factual knowledge of Byron's homosexual affairs and of his incestuous relations with his half sister, Augusta Leigh. Her revelations were in fact unsubstantiated, but they precipitated and sustained a frenzy of gossip so vicious that Byron's and Augusta's reputations were ruined, and he realized that he would never again be welcomed into the elite world Lady Caroline Lamb had once opened for him. In 1816, he went into self-imposed exile in Italy and never again returned to England.

Byron fled just before Caroline launched a new and unexpected attack in the form of a novel. In the two years since she and Byron had separated, Caroline had secretly written the melodramatic *Glenvarvon, or The Fatal Passion,* a three-volume *roman à clef* about their affair. In it she pilloried Byron and many of their acquaintances, and reproduced some of his letters nearly unaltered. She appeared as Calantha, the beguiling and impulsive heroine betrayed by the monstrous Glenvarvon. *Glenvarvon* was trashy and poorly written, but the buying public rushed out to discover its secrets. William Lamb was appalled. Caroline had betrayed his private habits and his family and friends. Though he had tolerated her adultery and public pursuit of her scornful lover, *Glenarvon* crushed William. At one point, he wished he were dead.

Caroline, oblivious to her husband's pain, mourned her former lover as never before. Then, truly alone in her wretchedness, racked by what was probably manic depression, she tried to flesh out the years of life that remained to her. She wrote a manual on household management that was not published. She campaigned for the Whigs. She set up a quasi-religious memorial in her bedroom that included an image of Byron. Always, she followed his progress as his poetic fame and personal deterioration increased.

In 1824, in a terse letter, William informed her that Byron had died, and instructed her to behave well. "I am very sorry I ever said one unkind word against him," Caroline wrote piteously.[12]

The shock of Byron's death was followed by the publication of *Recollections of Lord Byron* by his friend Thomas Medwin. Caroline was devastated to read that Byron had dismissed her as a skinny and heartless eccentric who had never loved her husband and as a sexual conquest that his friends envied. Even more painful was the news that on his deathbed Byron had not even mentioned her.

At a certain point, William could no longer bear to live with his wife and instituted a legal separation. Caroline smashed dishes, created terrible scenes, embarrassed everyone and exhausted her family. She begged William to reconsider and promised to be obedient and gentle. It was too late. For months afterward she wandered aimlessly in Paris and London. At last William relented and permitted her to return home, but he never again slept under the same roof with her. She was diagnosed as insane, and assuaged her anguish with too much wine and with laudanum. She wrote another novel, about that soothing drug's mind-bending effects, and was desolate when publishers rejected it. She wrote and self-published a third novel, anonymously. It, too, sank and died.

Caroline's life continued to be desperate. Society abandoned her. However, she still attracted important lovers. She permitted them to wear a ring from Byron that had escaped her burning ceremony. As soon as she tired of them or they of her, she took back her ring.

In 1828, at the age of only forty-two, Caroline died, reconciled to William but never to her own anguished life. William allegedly scripted her obituary, which was gentle and forgiving: poets' mistresses are judged leniently, because their passion stems from the imagination rather than depravity. William noted, as well, that despite Caroline's failure to live responsibly and wisely, she was a gifted and warmhearted woman who had died painlessly. In the manner of her death, Caroline Lamb had at last achieved peace.

It is difficult not to see Caroline Lamb's as a wasted life, consumed by her mental instability, her self-absorption and the brittle and unproductive world she was born into, the high society that dazzled and also gorged itself on the flesh of its own errant or mediocre members. History remembers her only as Byron's mistress. Sadly, Caroline concurred in this version of her life. Her brief affair, with all its tumult defined for Caroline the meaning of her life, and made sense of its emptiness. She came to believe that loving and being loved by Byron summed up her life's achievements.

Claire Clairmont [13]

Byron was still involved with Caroline Lamb when eighteen-year-old Claire Clairmont begged him for an introduction. Claire was a very pretty and well-read freethinker and atheist. She was also the illegitimate stepsister of Mary Shelley, Mary Wollstonecraft's daughter, the future author of *Frankenstein* and wife of the great poet Percy Shelley. Claire's situation contrasted bleakly with Caroline Lamb's. Socially, she was on the outer fringes. Financially, she was dependent on the Shelleys, and she knew that she would have to earn her own living.

But Claire did not see herself as pitiable. She assessed her talents, a spectacular singing voice and literary flair, and believed she could parlay them into a career on stage. She had, as well, a profound admiration for poetic genius and, according to her own testimony, had loved Byron for years before she appealed to him for help.

This appeal came in the form of a letter, long-winded, girlish and bold, enclosing one of her literary pieces and pleading for a meeting so Byron could assist her in planning how to establish herself in the theater world. Claire described herself as a woman whose reputation was still "unstained," and with "beating heart" confessed her love for him. But she was only one of scores of delectably available young women, and Byron was still shocked and deeply wounded by the (to him inexplicable) failure of his marriage. "I feel as if an Elephant has trodden on . . . my heart," he grieved. "I breathe lead."[14] Claire, importuning and romantic, did not interest him. Nonetheless, she persisted. They met, and she regaled him with her story of life with Mary and Percy Shelley, whose literary partnership she yearned to replicate with Byron himself.

Claire had calculated correctly that her association with the Shelleys would interest Byron, though he remained indifferent to her. She proposed an overnight rendezvous. Byron shrugged and accepted. "I was young and vain and poor," Claire said much later. Their amorous night together, during which Byron initiated her sexually and made love to her several times, fired Claire's adoration. "I do not expect you to love me; I am not worthy of your love," she wrote. "I feel you are superior."

So did Byron, who was so reluctant to see her again that he almost declined a meeting with Shelley because Claire, the go-between, would be there, too. Claire knew this. "Though I love you you do not feel even interest for me," she wrote sadly. "Were I to float by your window drowned all you would say would be 'Ah voilà!'"[15] But she was too deeply in love to stop hounding him.

Claire had insinuated herself in Byron's life precisely when he decided to exile himself. Coincidentally, Mary and Percy Shelley also decided to flee England to avoid the scandalous repercussions of their elopement after Percy abandoned his wife. Claire saw this as providential and (at their expense) accompanied them to Geneva so she could see Byron again.

As he had in England, Byron succumbed to her pleas for a rendezvous. Their lovemaking fueled Claire's ardor but not his. "I never loved nor pretended to love her, but a man is a man, and if a girl of eighteen comes prancing to you at all hours, there is but one way," he confided to a friend.[16] Cynically, Byron also set Claire to work copying his manuscripts. Despite his coldness toward her, she fell eagerly into her new role as unpaid amanuensis and sexual partner.

Within two months, Claire realized she was pregnant. Shelley attempted to broker an arrangement with Byron about the child, but Byron simply stopped speaking to Claire, who finally returned to England. In January, without any financial or emotional assistance from Byron, she gave birth to their daughter. "Is the brat mine?" Byron wondered.[17]

Now came a great struggle of wills between Claire and Byron. Claire adored the baby and wanted to raise her. Byron, who had settled in Venice, wanted her sent to his half sister, Augusta. When Claire refused, Byron decided to "dispose of this new production" himself. Appalled at the idea that Claire might inculcate the child with atheistic views, he proposed entrusting the child to a Venetian convent, where she would become a good Catholic, perhaps even a nun.

Claire grasped how her atheism frightened Byron, and compromised her principles by having her baby baptized. At Byron's insistence, she even renamed her Allegra, after months of calling her Alba. By this time, Claire's situation had become untenable. Without child support, she was forced to rely on the Shelleys' charity. But Mary worried constantly that Claire was trying to seduce Percy, who was in his turn distressed by rumors that Allegra was his. Claire decided to relinquish her toddler to Byron, on condition that he grant her visitation rights.

Claire and the Shelleys brought Allegra to Italy, Claire fantasizing that the child might soften Byron's heart and provide a link between her parents. Byron, however, refused even to see Claire. However, he loaned a rural villa to the Shelley contingent so Claire could spend two more months with her daughter. Then he separated Allegra from her mother to send her into temporary lodgings with the English consul and his wife. At the same time, he hinted that Claire would never again see the girl.

Claire began a marathon of misery. For two years, she begged and wheedled for permission to visit Allegra. Byron was immovable. He treated Allegra like one of the pets in his unwieldy and growing menagerie, referred to her as "my bastard," boasted about her Byronic beauty and ruefully admitted that she had inherited his own headstrong nature. Then he had her shunted back and forth between various temporary caretakers and his own household.

In despair, Claire assaulted Byron with accusatory letters. He was breaking every promise he had made to her. He was depriving Allegra of her mother. He was forcing her into Catholicism, an unenlightened religion. She suspected, as well, that he was neglecting Allegra's physical well-being. "I think Madame Clare [sic] is a damned bitch," Byron complained to a friend.[18] In fact, he felt himself aggrieved. He had taken the unusual (and in his view, generous) step of caring for his bastard daughter, and this was his reward.

Byron also glimpsed Claire in his daughter, whom he described as difficult and willful. When she was four, he deposited her in the Capuchin convent of San Giovanni, where his prestige and a double payment persuaded the nuns to waive the rule against accepting children under seven. He reasoned that because English society would never accept her, he would raise Allegra as a convent-educated Catholic girl who could either become a nun or marry well in Italy. Perhaps he also wanted to be rid of her demanding and irritating presence.

At this point, Shelley went to the convent and was permitted to visit Allegra. He found her taller and slighter and paler, probably from inadequate nutrition, but more beautiful than ever. The nuns, whom the imperious Allegra had initially mistaken for servants, pampered her. Claire, who had finally stopped loving Byron, was not reassured. She concocted but did not execute a desperate plan to kidnap her daughter and hide her somewhere. Shortly afterward, Allegra died, following a fever.

Claire was plunged into sorrow made bitterer by her regret that she had delivered Allegra into Byron's hands. He had "wantonly, willfully, destroyed my Allegra" and "were the fairest Paradise offered to me upon the condition of his sharing it," she wrote decades later, "I would refuse it."[19]

Byron, too, suffered—in his own way. The terrible news of Allegra's death "chilled my blood with sorrow," he told a friend. "It was perhaps the most lively sorrow I have ever felt."[20] He also felt some regret, but maintained his composure and, in the end, easily forgave himself. Claire never did.

During the funeral preparations, Byron granted Claire's three piteous requests: to see the coffin and to be given Allegra's image and a lock of her hair. Otherwise, he was pitiless. He delegated his current mistress, Teresa Guiccioli, to arrange for shipping the body back to England. He claimed that he had been overcharged for Allegra's embalming, coffin and undertaker, and refused to pay the bills.

Later, despite intercessions from several well-intentioned friends and a promise to Mary Shelley, Byron reneged on his pledge to assist Claire financially. Childless, her reputation ruined, close to destitution and chronically ill, Claire accepted that she had to earn her living as a governess, the profession she had once recoiled from as a "living death."

Claire spent the next half century as a governess and a lady's companion, in Vienna, Russia, Paris and London. She was often lonely and depressed, and frightened that she would succumb to the fevers and diseases that had sapped her strength since childhood. Though she found governessing a torment and a drudgery, she dared not request time off for fear of being turned out to starve. Yet she took pride in her work, and when her pupils were difficult, even hateful, she empathized with them and attributed their cheekiness and violent behavior to the parental constraints that deprived them of necessary exercise and self-expression.

Claire always worried that an employer would discover that she had borne an illegitimate child and fire her. As it was, one family cancelled their offer of employment after learning that she had been raised an atheist and freethinker. "I feel a secret agitation which consumes me the more for being repressed," she confided to a friend in 1826.[21]

Though Claire was still young and attractive, she refused to contemplate falling in love again. "A happy passion like death has *finis* written in such large characters in its face," she believed. Her own passion had lasted a mere ten minutes, "but these ten minutes have discomposed the rest of my life; the passion God knows for what cause, from no fault of mine however disappeared leaving no trace whatever behind it except my heart wasted and ruined as if it had been scorched by a thousand lightnings."[22]

In 1841, nineteen years after Percy Shelley's death, his estate settled twelve thousand pounds on Claire, her first taste of financial security in a lifetime of precarious existence. She invested her windfall in an opera box at Her Majesty's Theatre in London, but the returns from renting it were so disappointing that she was forced to sell it. She never had enough money, and she moved from one rude lodging to the next, to seek a living and to preserve her fragile health.

Throughout her unsettled lifetime, Claire sought the intellectual stimulation she had so enjoyed with Mary and Percy Shelley. She attempted to earn money writing, and two of her stories were published but—at her own request—under Mary Shelley's name. She enjoyed rich friendships that endured and deepened despite her sharp tongue and propensity to quarrel.

In later years, Claire moved back to Italy and, surprisingly, embraced Roman Catholicism. When she was nearly eighty, a visitor described her as "a lovely old lady: the eyes were still bright and sparkled with irony and fun; the complexion clear as at eighteen, the lovely white hair, the slender willowy figure remained unaltered . . . a very silvery laugh."[23] Claire had at last banished "that stupid Melancholy" by reflecting on how many "distinguished and virtuous" friends she had known, and she regretted only one thing: that she "had trodden life alone without a guide and without a companion."[24]

Claire died in 1879, in her sleep, a month short of her eightieth birthday. The epitaph she chose for her tombstone reads:

> She passed her life in sufferings,
> expiating not only her faults
> but also her virtues.[25]

Claire Clairmont had the distinction of being the only mistress Byron never loved. She never understood Byron's essentially conservative and elitist social values. She failed, as well, to realize that her relentless demands for his time (and attention, and love), coupled with her coy attempts to reform him—eat properly, drink moderately—and her bitingly sarcastic comments about his friends, irritated Byron almost to a frenzy. Even the most sympathetic reader must cringe at the nagging, proprietorial tone of her letters. No wonder that some of them are crushed, as if Byron strangled these missives in lieu of Claire herself.

Too late, as a bereaved mother, Claire saw Byron clearly. But she never saw how both he and she were products of their overlapping worlds, his privileged and arrogant, hers fragile and dangerous. Claire (and later Allegra) were trapped in the maw of harsh laws that deprived illegitimate children of most rights and reinforced society's condemnation of them as bastards, the very laws Byron used to coerce her into surrendering their daughter.

Countess Teresa Guiccioli [26]

Teresa Guiccioli was Byron's last and greatest love, though before his premature death he had already cooled and hardened toward her. And, from the first, he had been unfaithful. The cynical and restless Byron met the eighteen-year-old Teresa Gamba Ghiselli the year after she married the very wealthy, sixty-year-old count Alessandro Guiccioli.

Teresa was extremely pretty, with the plump hips, narrow waist and full breasts that Byron so appreciated. Her thick blond hair was styled in massed ringlets brushed back from her high forehead. Her eyes were enormous, her brows arched, her nose slender and aquiline, her mouth an agreeably smiling and plump bow. Only the proportions of her limbs were wrong, with her short legs making the rest of her body seem top-heavy.

Socially, Teresa was pleasing, a convent-educated aristocrat whose father had arranged her marriage. She read widely, was (in Byron's estimation) "clever enough" and loved literature. She was also hopelessly romantic, steeped in the tradition of seduction and intrigue. After one year in a dutiful and loveless though sexually satisfying marriage, she was as irrevocably attracted to Byron as he was to her. She described their mutual fascination as "mysterious," soul-shaking and deliciously frightening.

Teresa succumbed easily, after a single private rendezvous, during which love—or so they named it—flowered. The next day, they slept together. Erotically, they were perfectly matched, with Teresa as uninhibited as Byron. Love erupted into lustful passion, and Byron was as smitten with Teresa as she was with him. Almost. If he were to discover any trickery or falseness on her part, he told friends, he had sufficient self-love to dump her.

For four straight days, the lovers met and explored each other's bodies. Yet Byron could not confine himself to one woman. He continued to court another eighteen-year-old aristocrat so assiduously that moments after declaring his undying love for Teresa, he tumbled into the Grand Canal and arrived dripping wet to see his other lady. Teresa, blissfully unaware of her lover's extracurricular trysts and too innocent to be nervous about his occasional bouts of depression, was utterly happy.

Byron remained lovestruck, but began to worry about Teresa's tactlessness, her public demonstrativeness and her evident pride in having caught the celebrated English poet—"mio Byron" she called him. Yet though he hated social impropriety, and the least whiff of hysteria *à la* Caroline Lamb chilled his blood, Byron, too, spoke far and wide about his new love.

The lovers had confederates: Teresa's servant Fanny Silvestrini, and a priest who passed along the impassioned letters they showered on each other. As always for Byron, these missives were a crucial part of the relationship, though he had to compose his in Italian. From the beginning, he was fatalistic about the permanence of their love, warning Teresa that "Sentiment is not in control, but is what is most beautiful and fragile in our existence."[27] Nonetheless, he declared his devotion to her and swore that, for once, no other woman could appeal to him.

And yet he continued to pursue the Venetian teenager, and to implore his half sister, Augusta, to rekindle her love for him. Teresa had no inkling of this. She had her own problems. She was in the fourth month of pregnancy, her second. The year before, she had given birth to an infant son who had died. After ten intense days of lovemaking with Byron, so violent that it may have affected her health, she was obliged to follow her husband to Ravenna.

In Ravenna, Teresa developed a lingering illness that she hinted was consumption but that was really the consequence of a miscarriage. Byron's inflamed letters to her railed against their separation and begged her to love him. At the same time, he warned her that in England, at least, his love had been fatal to those he loved. To a friend, on the other hand, he wrote sardonically that "I was not the father of the foetus . . . whether the Count was the parent or not I can't imagine; perhaps he might."[28]

Meanwhile, Teresa was complaining to him that jealous women had spread poisonous stories about her. Byron was worried and, in an impulsive moment, set out for Ravenna. But Teresa kept him at bay, and he grew increasingly restless. Then she saw him once, briefly. Afterward, he proposed that they run off together—an echo of his crazed relationship with Caroline Lamb. But Teresa refused, because she knew what Byron still had to learn—that in Italy, a woman may have both a husband and a *cavalier servente*, an eternally faithful and devoted lover who followed her wherever she wished him to. Teresa did not need to run off. She could have Byron and Guiccioli together.

The institution of *cavalier servente* was integrally linked to marriage. Marriage was still a parental arrangement, and dissatisfied husbands simply took mistresses. It seldom mattered whether their wives knew or if they objected. A husband's wishes and needs were paramount.

But the wives in these arranged marriages also had wishes and needs, and the unusual institution of *cavalier servente*, with its elaborate rules and notions of decorum, accommodated them. A *cavalier servente* usually appeared after the wife had produced her husband's heir and, preferably, a spare child or two. Then she was free to cavort with an *amico*, a so-called friend who entered this supposedly chaste affair on the understanding that he would be hers forever. His mistress's husband accepted him, indeed sometimes even selected him. Priests were a favorite choice, for their vows of celibacy, even if they breached them, precluded marriage.

The *amico* had many obligations, notably fidelity to his mistress and a promise never to marry or to leave Italy. Toward her husband he had to show the greatest cordiality and respect, as if they were fast friends.

The system of *cavalier servente*, however, protected the cooperative husband: should the latter die, his merry widow could never marry her *amico*. Murder or suspicious accidents, in other words, could not change the *amico*'s status, a fact that must have comforted many hated (and hateful) husbands. The premise behind this was that the *amico* and his mistress enjoyed a platonic relationship, *agape* love of the purest order. Marriage implied sex, unthinkable (or so people pretended) between the *amico* and his lover while she was still married. Clearly this had not happened, ergo, it must and could not happen merely because the husband had died.

The wife's conduct was also regulated. She could see her *amico* in her own home, but not in his. She could invite him to theatrical productions in her family's box, but dare not even think of joining him in his. She was, in fact, bound forever to her husband and could never think of eloping. She had to display admiration and affection for her husband, and never shame or dishonor him or his family's name, or, for that matter, her father's.

For the first year of her marriage, Teresa had tried to fall in love with her elderly husband, to give him a son and to disregard the stories about his despicable treatment of her two predecessors. (Guiccioli exiled his first wife to the countryside after she complained that he seduced several of her maids. Then he summoned her home and convinced her to change her will in his favor. Soon after, she died in suspicious circumstances. Guiccioli next married one of the maids, who gave him seven children. The night she died, he went to the theater.)

But Guiccioli was unlovable and, with his sardonic eyes and heavy, menacing features, singularly unappealing. In addition, he had no interest in Teresa's feelings or in her company. If she wished to amuse herself with a *cavalier servente*, albeit this limping, balding, chubby and reputedly very rich English poet, why not?

Byron shared Guiccioli's unflattering assessment of his physical charms. At thirty, he was thickening and graying, losing his hair and worrying that his teeth remained affixed to his gums as a mere courtesy. He attempted to banish his fatness through rigorous and unhealthy dieting, laxatives and excessive exercise and sweating. He greased his hair to camouflage the gray, and he tried to draw attention away from his awkward gait. Fortunately for Byron, Teresa adored him anyway, which made her husband's disdain all the more convenient.

Indeed, Guiccioli fostered the affair, inviting Byron to take up residence in his palace. Guiccioli also "borrowed" a large sum of money from Byron and requested that Byron arrange for his appointment as honorary British consul at Ravenna, a position he had long wanted. (The consulship would have conferred limited privileges, notably the right to travel freely within Italy. Guiccioli was active in opposition politics and vulnerable to losing the right to visit his various estates whenever he wished.) Byron tried, and failed, to obtain the consulship for him.

Meanwhile, living apart under the same roof did not facilitate the lovers' lovemaking, and they had to fight to sneak away, alone, for increasingly rare intimate encounters. As well, Byron had sent for Allegra, by then a serious and willful child traumatized after being shifted from one unloving caretaker to another.

Teresa was happier than Byron, who complained—disloyally—that a man should not be hobbled to a woman, and that his "existence [as a *cavalier servente*] is to be condemned."[29] But he did nothing to alter it, and Teresa did not fathom the extent of his angst. How could she? His letters, lyrical and passionate, described unending love and his jealousy when (he thought) she stared at another man, or much worse, when Guiccioli exercised his husbandly right to have sex with her.

Byron concealed the growing restlessness he complained about to his friends. The nights pass more quickly with a mistress than a wife, he said sarcastically, but the evenings are just as interminable. In *Don Juan*, he immortalized this cruel thought:

> Think you, if Laura had been Petrarch's wife,
> He would have written sonnets all his life?[30]

At the same time, Byron considered his sexual liaisons as crucial to his art. How, he demanded of a friend, could he have created such powerful poetry without "tooling" ("screwing" is the modern equivalent)—in coaches and gondolas, against walls, atop and under tables? He would have been more explicit, he admitted, except the public outrage at *Don Juan* inhibited him: "the *Cant* is so much stronger than *Cunt*," he wrote.[31]

Byron continued to writhe silently, exasperated by Teresa's unrelieved adoration and her earnest postulations about the meaning of his poetry, especially its references to his former lovers. He endured, as well, the homesickness that afflicts expatriates. Teresa, self-absorbed and self-confident, refused to analyze the clues Byron dropped everywhere about his unhappiness.

Meanwhile, the countess had problems she could not ignore, namely, the count. She and Byron had flouted Italian decorum so egregiously that shocked observers had informed her husband and her father. Teresa was forced to grasp that she was in serious trouble.

Guiccioli certainly thought so. He presented her with a list of "Indispensable Rules" dictating the details of her existence: when she must get up ("not late"), listen to music or read ("after midday"); how she should behave ("without conceit or impatience"), speak ("sweetly, modestly"), even appear ("absolutely docile"); above all, that she must break off relations with anyone who deflected her single-minded focus from her husband. Unexpectedly, at least to Guiccioli, Teresa refused, and dashed off her own list of demands: the right to rise whenever she cared to, a fully equipped horse and, most importantly, the right to receive any visitor she wished to—in other words, the right to continue to see Byron. In a dramatic confrontation, Guiccioli demanded that she choose between husband and lover. "I choose my *amico*!" Teresa exclaimed.

At one point, Guiccioli begged Byron to help him tame his wayward wife. Byron offered to leave Italy, if that would ease the situation. Teresa was frantic, while Byron was torn by his desire to see Augusta at home in England and his equally strong desire to remain with Teresa. He equivocated, packed his bags, summoned the gondola and then at the very last second decided to stay. Teresa had a most convenient relapse of her previous illness, swore hysterically (and falsely) that she had not slept with Byron, and convinced her father and husband that she must not be prevented from seeing him. Finally, they agreed. On Christmas Eve, 1819, Byron and Teresa were reunited.

Guiccioli again offered Byron rooms in his home, and he accepted. Guiccioli then ordered at least eighteen servants to spy on his wife and her *amico*. He also pressured Teresa to ask Byron for another "loan." But Byron was notoriously stingy, and more than anything else, Guiccioli's financial demands corroded Byron's relationship with Teresa.

Guiccioli then raised the stakes. He presented evidence gleaned by his household spies that Teresa had betrayed him sexually, and he demanded a divorce. Teresa's well-connected family rallied and managed to stave off the divorce, with its shame and unacceptable financial consequences, and pressed for a legal separation instead. Byron intervened as well, urging Teresa to remain with her husband. She refused, unless she could have her *amico*, Byron, always by her side.

The affair now deteriorated badly. Byron was unwilling to wrest her away from her husband, family, country, and so Teresa wept and questioned his love. Guiccioli, hoping to avert a separation, public humiliation and, above all, alimony, implored Byron to convince Teresa to love him, her husband.

With love and duty stalemated, a reconciliation between the count and his countess was impossible. Byron, his back to the wall, agreed to stand by his mistress. Teresa was triumphant. "Promise!!!! to be my Husband!!" she afterward labeled the letter in which he announced this decision. Even in retrospect, she refused to acknowledge Byron's reluctance, his fatalism, his weariness with the whole entangled enterprise.

Byron's capitulation ushered in the most tranquil period of their love affair. Teresa won a separation based on her husband's bad behavior, and kept her dowry and possessions. She sneaked out of his home and fled to her father's, where for the entire winter season she and Byron saw each other regularly. By this time, Byron was devoting less and less time to her. He read and wrote throughout the night, woke late and worked again. Then he rode with Teresa's brother, ate supper and spent only what remained of the evening with her.

Before long, Byron had completed a new volume of poetry, his payoff for enduring their relationship. Teresa was thrilled and, despite her shaky English, pored over every poem, trying to understand the images and also the experiences and sensations that had inspired her lover. Teresa believed she had finally succeeded in guaranteeing herself a lifetime at Byron's side. Byron, too, accepted this as his destiny, though unlike Teresa he was no longer "furiously in love." (It was during this period of fertile creativity that Byron deposited Allegra in the convent he had chosen because Teresa's grandparents were patrons. Afterward, he was too engrossed in his poetry to visit her, even when she was gravely ill.)

About this time, Teresa left her father's home and moved into Byron's, a flagrant violation of the terms of her separation agreement and of the rules of *cavalier servente*. She did not enjoy it. The heat was so ferocious it caused a drought, and Byron spent little time with her. More seriously, she did not get away with it: the pope ordered her alimony suspended.

During this period, volatile Italian politics and her family's (and Byron's) active support of the Carboneri—revolutionary secret societies advocating political freedom—forced the Gambas to move to Genoa. There Teresa and Byron again shared a house where Byron effectively shut her out of his life, banning her from his quarters and communicating with her only in writing. When her beloved sister, Carolina, died, Byron scribbled Teresa a brief note of condolence but waited four days before bothering to visit her.

Teresa's life was in shambles. Where was her great love? More and more frequently she erupted in the jealous outbursts Byron referred to as her *éclats*. Byron's alienation from his bewildered mistress was so profound that he seemed bent on escape. Abruptly, he announced that he was leaving for Greece, then in revolt against Turkish subjugation. Teresa took the news badly and declared that she, too, would go to Greece. "Absurd womanhood," Byron called her, and worried that she would cause a scene. She did not, but she suffered, and mourned his defection, sometimes weeping and clinging to him, at other times speaking in grandiose terms of his nobility and sacrifice.

Before leaving, Byron revised his will and left Teresa the five thousand pounds he had intended for Allegra. Teresa received the news of her legacy with tearful indignation, just as she had always refused any gifts of monetary value except a gold ring she adored for sentimental reasons. Her love was utterly pure, she declared, and she wanted nothing from him but the same devotion. Byron confided to his friends that unlike most women, Teresa was utterly disinterested. Of course, he quipped, it helped that she was an heiress.

Teresa grieved over their separation. The rules of *cavalier servente* forbade an *amico* from parting from his mistress, yet Byron had done so, breaking her heart and humiliating her in the eyes of her society.

Teresa had practical problems as well, notably the papal suspension of her alimony. She and her family had rejected Byron's offer of financial assistance, and in consequence, she was now penniless. In Rome, where the pope had stipulated she must live, she had to lodge in the attic of Paolo Costa, an old friend and teacher. (Teresa's poverty was relative. A maid went with her.) Her father could not help because his revolutionary activities had landed him in jail.

Byron was no consolation. He sent only the occasional brief note, promising to visit or send for her, which never happened. His last note to her, a year after he left for Greece, was a scribbled appendage to a lengthy and tender letter from her brother, who had accompanied him.

Even during his frenetic and exciting year on a quixotic mission, Byron had developed another emotional attachment, perhaps even fallen in love, with Loukas, a fifteen-year-old Greek boy he indulged so ludicrously that at one point, he put thirty soldiers under the boy's command. Loukas, however, did not reciprocate Byron's affection.

In 1824, when he was only thirty-six, Byron died. His deathbed exhortations, recorded by several witnesses, repeatedly mentioned Ada, his daughter with Annabella, and Augusta, his half sister. He made no mention of Teresa, Claire, Caroline or other mistresses.

Teresa's great love affair was over. She had gambled on a lifetime with her beloved *amico*, whose death left her bereft at the tender age of twenty-three. All she had were stacks of letters between Byron and herself, and between Byron and scores of other correspondents, including flirtatious women. She also had a brooch that Byron's half sister, Augusta, forwarded to her. Teresa had once refused to accept it, telling Byron it was too expensive.

How to live out the rest of her life? Briefly, Teresa returned to her husband. After a mere five months that arrangement failed yet again. This time, the Guicciolis separated amicably, and corresponded like old friends until the now blind and elderly count died.

Teresa had once rashly vowed to wait for Byron in a convent. Now that he was dead, she transformed her life into a shrine to him. In middle age, Teresa married the French marquis de Boissy, who was as proud as she was that she had been Byron's mistress. In a revisionist personal history, Teresa claimed that Byron had gone to Greece to die rather than face life without being married to her.

In 1856, the French poet Lamartine published a book that—to Teresa—distorted and mocked her sublime love affair, and denigrated Byron as a spiteful cripple. Teresa responded to this travesty by writing her own memoir, *Lord Byron jugé par les témoins de sa vie* (*Lord Byron Judged by Witnesses to His Life*). She published it anonymously, and it was universally dismissed as dull and unenlightening.

Teresa wrote a second, more revealing account of her liaison with Byron, *La Vie de Lord Byron en Italie* (*The Life of Lord Byron in Italy*). She did not publish it, considering such revelations indecent during her lifetime, but her biographers have used it and learned—among other things—how she bowdlerized

Byron's letters so she could present herself as a blameless, almost angelic companion to the great poet.

In many ways, she was. Byron had recognized her impenetrably romantic nature, and romantic Teresa remained. Even as an old lady, she treasured scraps from her long-ago love: an acorn, her letters to Byron and Byron's letters to her, slightly corrected where necessary to show the world what he really meant rather than what he said. There were miniatures of him as well. In one, a pudgy Byron gazes longingly at Teresa. But her face has been scratched out in another bowdlerization, as if she felt the artist had not captured her image as she would have wished.

Teresa fed on altered memories and dismissed anything that conflicted with her version. For two years she had been Byron's mistress, lying to her father, deceiving her husband, flouting social conventions, caring only for Byron. Those two years dominated the remaining five decades of her life. Even her second marriage was rooted in her Byronic experience. It was as if Byron were a mission rather than a spellbinding and melancholy man who had briefly loved and desired her. Byron had given Teresa's life meaning, and—she fervently believed—added immensely to its value.

Caroline Lamb and Teresa Guiccioli were both privileged aristocrats whose cultures acknowledged and accommodated the romantic and erotic needs of women in arranged marriages with incompatible husbands. Conventions defined what was acceptable: wifely fidelity until enough legitimate heirs arrived; respectful relations with the cuckolded husband; avoidance of scandal (no mating with the coachman, though husbands and sons routinely seduced and impregnated chambermaids); no running off to cohabit with a lover; no unseemly behavior.

On the other hand, society condemned Claire Clairmont for her illegitimacy and poverty, and for becoming a mistress. When she, too, was overwhelmed by "true love," she pitted herself against the rules. Yet on balance, Claire risked little by gambling on happiness as a mistress. Eighteenth-century society was so structured that she faced a wretched and lonely life anyway. At the same time, because Byron was an unresponsive partner, the disastrous results of her foray into mistressdom were entirely predictable.[32]

CHAPTER 5

The Clandestine Consorts
of (Un)Celibate Clerics[1]

W<small>HO</small> could ever imagine that the women who cast their lot with
God's servants would find themselves vilified by Saint Jerome as
"one-man harlots"? And this was the same Jerome who, as a neo-
phyte monk in the latter part of the 4th century, had struggled so furiously to
conquer his own lust. Many clerics succumbed, sometimes easily, to the
temptations that bedeviled Jerome, and because they could not or would not
live without a woman, they either married or took mistresses.

In the earliest days of Christianity, priests and monks loved and lived with
women just as laymen did. But by the 4th century, the doctrine of clerical
celibacy began to take root. Theology, asceticism and practical and property
considerations dominated the Church Fathers' campaign to impose clerical
celibacy. The attack was multipronged and persistent. The theologians
invoked doctrines about the seductive and immoral nature of Eve's daughters, the sinfulness of sexual intercourse with them and the valor of Christian
ascetics whose deprivations included sex. At the same time, these Church
officials accused sexually active clerics of lacking the moral superiority they
needed to minister to others. They added that sexual relationships distracted
priests, who should focus exclusively on their ministry and spirituality.

Quite apart from theology, the most compelling argument for clerical celibacy
was the Church's growing wealth. Married or not, priests with family obligations
consumed resources that would otherwise accumulate in the Church's coffers—

unlike celibates, they spent money to support wives, mistresses and children, and bequeathed property to them rather than to the Church.

The Church's Synod of Elvira, held in Spain in 305, imposed celibacy on all married bishops, priests and deacons. The Synod assumed that celibacy would raise clergymen's moral standards and justify their higher social status. It also decreed that those who continued to have sex would be defrocked. In 325, the more influential Council of Nicaea banned clerical marriage and forbade bishops, priests, deacons and all other ecclesiastics from cohabiting with a woman "unless perhaps a mother, a sister, an aunt, or such person only as be above suspicion."[2] This pronouncement effectively defined and condemned the ecclesiastical concubine, who would afterward be scorned and persecuted throughout Roman Catholic Christendom.

From 370 onward, papal dicta tightened the noose, banning sexual relations and not just marriage. The ideal of clerical celibacy was becoming widespread, though the practice was not; most married priests continued to have sex with their wives, though a stream of edicts persuaded bachelor clerics that they should not marry after they were ordained. Ambitious priests, however, recognized that celibacy was a good career move.

Despite the ban, some clerics married, joined in holy matrimony by priests either unaware of their status or willing to overlook it. Others, whether single or married, took mistresses. Pope Agapitus I, elected in 535, was the bastard son of Gordianus, one such priest. Pope John XIII (965–72) was murdered by a husband he had cuckolded. The ironically named Pope Innocent VIII (1484–92) acknowledged his brood of "bastards." And from the 9th century to halfway through the 11th century, papal mistresses Theodora Theophylact, her daughter Marozia and their descendants were so influential that the papacy of their era is known as a "pornocracy."

Papal mistresses, of course, were pampered and protected, but the humbler parish priest's female partners were not. Stern 10th-century German bishops branded and humiliated women they suspected of sexual intimacy with priests by ordering their heads shorn. Spanish bishops excommunicated priests' mistresses and, upon their deaths, had them buried without ceremony or monument.

By the 11th century, canon law was beginning to define priests' wives as "concubines," and it bastardized their children. In 1018, the Synod of Pavia enslaved the children of ecclesiastics and made them Church property. In 1089, the Synod of Amalfi extended this servitude to clerical wives and concubines, and those whose partners were subdeacons or higher-ranked clerics could be seized as slaves by feudal lords.

Many priests opposed these decrees. Some pleaded that they would be forced to choose between their wives and their vocations. Others predicted, correctly as it turned out, that the abolition of open marriage would lead to clandestine affairs and widescale concubinage. Secular rulers and parishioners also intervened against concubinaries—the official term for priests who kept mistresses—and the result was turmoil and chaos. In the late 11th century, German princes punished married bishops by confiscating their property, and mobs of irate parishioners hounded unpopular priests on the flimsiest pretexts. On the opposing side, concubinaries assaulted agents of Pope Gregory VII, a reformer dedicated to abolishing ecclesiastical marriage. Gregory's reforms led to such persecution of priests' mistresses that some of these women committed suicide.

The battle raged throughout Europe. In 1215, lawyer-pope Innocent III convened the Fourth Lateran Council, which proclaimed all clerics legally celibate, even those who had been married before their ordination. Ironically, this implied that Catholic marriage was less sacred than ordination. It also suggested to some theologians that concubinage would now become an unavoidable adjunct to the priesthood. The frequency with which solitary priests seduced—or were seduced by—women seeking spiritual and practical counseling prompted congregations to demand priests who already had a resident concubine. The rationale was that priests were driven as much by loneliness as by lust to prey on parish women; it followed that a mistress's daily presence would curtail these sexual assaults.

Furthermore, as David Lederer and Otto Feldbauer point out in *The Concubine: Women, Priests and the Council of Trent*, "long-term relationships increased internal social and economic stability, bonded the clergy to their community through semi-formalized kinship ties and, as responsible fathers and husbands, presumably rendered parish priests more dependable in their discharge of their office. Minor secular officials also viewed this as an opportunity to better integrate the clergy into the ranks of the local elite."[3] It was often argued that the laity, who were such an important element of the Church, had little to gain and much to lose from clerical celibacy.

From the early 16th to the mid-17th century, the Protestant Reformation again focused attention on celibacy, and reformers were scathing in condemning it. Martin Luther himself appealed for acceptance of human weakness in matters of the flesh. His subsequent marriage to former nun Katerina von Bora spoke volumes. Many reformers cynically accused the Church of outlawing concubinage so Rome could collect vast amounts in fines from offending priests. One German bishop fined only those diocesan priests who fathered bastards, but another, to save himself the bother of identifying actual offenders, taxed all his priests. When babies arrived, they were often passed off as nieces and nephews whom the priest would be raising.

THE PRIEST'S "HOUSEKEEPER"

The usual priestly ploy, which survives to this day, was to pretend that his mistress was just the housekeeper. The custom of lodging Christian virgins and widows in suitable homes—and what home could be more suitable than a priest's?—provided sanctuary and a livelihood for these women. It also provoked scandal, as closeness made so many hearts grow fonder. In later years, a priest's mistress was known as a *focaria,* a term that had evolved from its original meanings of housewife, kitchen maid or soldier's concubine, and the character of the *focaria* became a literary staple.

The life of a real *focaria* could be treacherous. The (unchristian) Christian Church continued to persecute these women relentlessly. To ferret out offenders, its officials would descend on a parish and, detective-like, interview the local priest and his parishioners. They conducted their interrogations in pairs, asking: What was known about the priest? Had he a mistress? Did he consider himself married? Had he fathered children? Did he and a woman dance with each other at weddings? Did they frequent public baths together? Some innocent parishioners, who considered their priest effective and reliable in part because he had proved himself to be a good husband and father, willingly supplied this information. But their answers had a different result from what they intended.

At first such "visitations" were sporadic, but by the 16th and 17th centuries they were a regular feature of a cleric's life. It is impossible to evaluate the accuracy of the information gleaned from them, but the reports, which varied widely in their findings, suggest both that celibacy was becoming more common and that priests and their congregations were becoming adept at hiding what they did not want visiting church officials to know. In 1516, for example, visitations indicated that in southeast Germany, only 15 percent of priests had concubines, but in 1560, the records of another visitation pointed to markedly different conclusions. The 1560 visitation involved 418 clerics, of whom 165 refused to cooperate and 76 claimed they had never had sexual relations with their domestics. However, 154 priests acknowledged that they were in long-term sexual relationships with women, and 128 admitted to fathering between one and nine children.

The ideas of the Reformation, in particular the challenge to compulsory clerical celibacy, profoundly influenced even clergymen who remained Roman Catholic. There was a notable increase in the number of clerics openly engaged in committed relationships with women; the clerics risked the Church's wrath, their mistresses public censure as concubines.

But anti-Reformation forces strove to quash these instances of defiance. In 16th-century Bavaria, for example, Duke Albert V and his son and successor, William the Pious, launched a crusade against clerical concubinage and marriage. William authorized his officials to hunt down offenders. The Church also granted him the right to conduct secular visitations, to search parish houses and to arrest both priests and their concubines.

In 1583 and again in 1584, at William's instigation, Bavarian parishes were subjected to visitations. One can only imagine William's grim satisfaction when his eager agents confirmed his suspicions. In one instance, a noblewoman had denounced a priest and his mistress-cook. Their relationship was one of such marriage-like commitment that the cook had provided a dowry just as she would have in a sanctioned marriage, and they had also exchanged rings. They lived together so openly that they thought nothing of remaining together in bed as they received people on official business. The cook's friends testified, as well, that she had told them she had become pregnant, though it is unclear from the records whether or not she gave birth. She also defended her priestly lover from those who disparaged his virility; she insisted he was "a full-blooded man who needed a woman [and] was enough of a man for any woman." The priest who loved her went further. If the authorities forced his mistress to leave him, he declared, he would "have his way with the other local women like the village steer."[4]

The details of other relationships also emerged from the testimony of priests and their parishioners, but few mistresses were available to answer questions; they had been prudently spirited away. Yet the cautious clerics saw no reason to conceal that they were as good as married and had fathered children whom they proudly acknowledged. They even revealed that they held property jointly with their mistresses, and older priests described financial arrangements they had made to care for the women they had once slept with and loved.

After diligently recording all these details of affection and sex, procreation and domesticity, the officials involved in the 1584 visitations concluded that in some parishes, the rate of concubinage was as high as 70 percent. High as that estimate seems, the reality was almost certainly higher: the accuracy of the visitations was fundamentally flawed. First, the lay population generally tolerated and often approved these priestly unions, and so were not necessarily cooperative witnesses. More significantly, the priests had often been forewarned by an unidentified government official who had seen an excellent way to generate money. His warning and the willing collusion of local officials gave the priests enough time to either relocate their mistresses in safe houses or send them out of Bavaria.

When William learned how his mission had been sabotaged, he vowed to impose severe fines on anyone who ever again leaked confidential information. What he could not do was try priests as concubinaries under secular law. That remained the province of ecclesiastical law. The mistresses themselves, however, had no such protection, and so William declared open season on them.

A priest condemned as a fornicator by the ecclesiastical authorities typically paid a fine, ate only bread and water for three days and did a penance, often a pilgrimage. His mistress—his accomplice, in legal terminology—was also fined and subjected to rituals of public humiliation, and often received the "social death sentence," that is, she was forced into exile.

William's son Maximilian I, who succeeded when William abdicated to join a monastery, went even further than his grandfather and father. The result was what some historians call "a religious police state" so repressive that priestly concubinage went underground and in many cases ended. But priestly sexuality did not, and the unintended consequence of Maximilian's vengeful crusade was an outbreak of scandal as frustrated priests without mistresses ventured into surreptitious affairs with parish wives or unmarried domestic servants. Instead of being the cherished offspring of a loving union, children conceived as a result of these hidden and dangerous liaisons were seen as incontrovertible proof of sexual transgression. Sometimes desperate parents, a priestly father or a concubine mother, abandoned or even killed their children. Priests frequently abandoned pregnant lovers to endure alone the shame and penury of unmarried motherhood.

Many priests simply hid their private lives. Under tremendous pressure from an ecclesiastical court, one elderly priest confessed that he had fathered ten children with his now-ailing sixty-year-old mistress. Another cleric, clearly beyond sexual relations, admitted that he still loved his former concubine. Some priests were unable to choose between their vocations and their families. Often they emigrated to Protestant territories, where they could serve God with the benefit of a loved helpmeet.

The relentless pressure of being spied on damaged other relationships, often irreparably. Mistresses were particularly vulnerable. The civil authorities, frustrated because they could not directly touch errant clerics, tormented their female partners. These unprotected women were subjected to interrogation with the ever-present threat of "judicial torture," to say nothing of normal indictment, condemnation and punishment.

By the Reformation, torture was a well-established feature of legal procedure in criminal cases. It was, in the words of Ulpian, an eminent jurist, "the torment and suffering [inflicted on] the body in order to elicit the truth."[5] Torture was seen not as sadistic violence but as a calculated procedure designed to assist in the administration of justice. The torture should neither kill nor mutilate (though it frequently did). A medical expert had to be in attendance, and a notary had to record everything that transpired. A confession made under torture had to be repeated a day later, though an accused who recanted was simply tortured anew. Even confession did not necessarily end the torment; post-confession torture was the norm because it encouraged the guilty to supply the names of their accomplices.

Women and children were generally exempt from the most excruciating and crippling tortures. Instead, their hands would be tightly tied, cutting circulation, untied and retied. They were deprived of sleep for forty-hour stretches. Sometimes their soles were coated with flammable liquids and set afire. Occasionally, women, too, were stretched on the rack, burned or otherwise mutilated as men were. Women guilty only of loving a priest were justly terrified at the prospect of torture. Relationships eroded under the strain and stress of the visitations and the subsequent repression of uncelibate priests and their partners in love.

Increasingly, priests unwilling to abide by their vows of chastity satisfied themselves with women they could take to bed without consequences. Married parishioners were obvious candidates. They were accessible, either had or could invent reasons to be in the priest's company, were quite unlikely to incur their husbands' wrath by confessing their adultery and did not have to explain how they became pregnant.

One priest had so refined his strategies of seduction that he used the church as a love nest. He had a secret door installed and at night sneaked his married lovers through it. Then, under the altar, he had sex with them. Father Adam Sachreuter, a German priest, had a different *modus operandi*. While gambling with a would-be lover's husband, he would ply him with alcohol until the man was dead drunk. Sachreuter then kindly helped his parishioner home and, after seeing him safely to bed, had sexual intercourse with the man's wife.

Father Georg Scherer was another egregious offender; his convictions for concubinage began in 1622 and continued until 1650. Scherer slept with at least four servants, each of whom he would send away to another city when he took up with a new woman. Father Scherer's former mistresses, who had each borne one of his children, two of whom died in questionable circumstances, were charged with the crime of fornication and incarcerated in Munich's notorious Falcon's Tower, the site of infamous interrogation by judicial torture. Before the women were interrogated, they were warned that if they refused to cooperate they would be tortured, and they were shown the tools that would be used to do the job. At this point the women broke down and confessed. Three were found guilty and were punished: they were either publicly shamed by being forced to don penitential garb and to stand for an entire day in the stocks in full public view in front of the church, or were permanently exiled. Scherer, held in a much less disagreeable ecclesiastical jail, was fined a paltry sum.

Clara Strauss was the fourth of Scherer's convicted mistresses and the mother of one of his sons. Scherer testified that Clara had been the aggressor in their affair, seducing him when he was drunk and exacting thirty florins from him for her services, which made her a whore. Indeed, he had called her so, but she had laughed and made disparaging comments about his manhood. Their coupling had been a purely mercenary transaction, Scherer declared, a single incident of whoring. Alas, his son had been conceived that very night. Like Scherer's other women, Clara was punished.

Four years later, Scherer again stood accused of impregnating Clara. Despite evidence indicating that he had urged another priest to baptize the infant, Scherer denied the charge, and the court released him without punishment. Another four years passed, and Scherer resurfaced in ecclesiastical court, pleading guilty to having a sexual relationship with another domestic and begging for mercy. Again the court was lenient. Instead of being removed from his parish, Scherer was given a stern warning, restricted to bread and water for three days and fined.

Twenty years later, the now aging Scherer faced new charges relating to his cook, Maria, who was also his mistress and his daughter-in-law. His son with Clara had married Maria, likely to cover up her relationship with his father. The priest who officiated testified that Scherer had threatened to kill him if he did not perform the ceremony. Other evidence pointed to Scherer's having assisted Maria in obtaining an abortion, perhaps not her only one. Both the death threats and the procurement of an abortion were extremely serious crimes, and Scherer was sentenced to life imprisonment in a monastery. Maria was executed, probably burned at the stake unless she was one of the lucky prisoners who managed to arrange for a quicker, easier death by garroting. Unlike Scherer, who faced ecclesiastic judges, Maria confronted less merciful secular jurors who equated abortion with infanticide and condemned her.

By the end of the 16th century, celibacy had replaced concubinage as the standard for the Roman Catholic clergy. The Reformation, the third session of the Council of Trent in 1562 to 1563, decades of repression and changing methods of training priests had forced it to take root. In time, the medieval ambivalence about clerical celibacy that had so profoundly influenced parishioners' expectations about their local priest evaporated. Now parishioners expected their priest to be celibate, an ideal that coincided exactly with what he had learned during his time in the seminary. He was expected to dress in distinctive clothing that distinguished him from laymen and to refrain from overindulgence in the secular vices of gambling, boozing and whoring. The reality, of course, was rather different. Though most priests no longer dared to live openly in a sexual relationship, many still lost their perpetual struggle to maintain the celibacy to which they had pledged themselves. Paradoxically, the story of clerical celibacy is also the story of clerical concubinage: where marriage is forbidden, even the most committed unions are illicit.

The intervening centuries have not seen great changes. Clerical celibacy remains largely unenforceable, and as scholarly research now reveals, about half of all priests are—as they have always been—uncelibate. But the Church and its congregations have radically different stakes in the issue. Not surprisingly, they have never found a common ground.

The Church's public justification for hounding priests stemmed from its traditional theological commitment to celibacy, and from its conviction that celibacy would free priests from distractions and obligations so they could devote themselves exclusively to their duties. A third unspoken but equally compelling motive was that single priests were much cheaper to maintain and, unlike married men, would not use Church property to support families, underwrite sons' careers and endow marriageable daughters. Clerical mistresses and their children were seen as deadly rivals both for priests' loyalty and for the Church's operating expenses.

On the other hand, as historian Henry Lea points out, these risks to the

Church's corporate body "rendered matrimony more objectionable than concubinage or licentiousness."[6] When all was said and done, concubinage and licentiousness created few obligations; marriage and legitimate children, on the other hand, could drain the Church's resources. A priest involved in a clandestine relationship threatened the Church far less than one who married.

The consequence was that amid all the confusion and the controversy, clerical mistresses proliferated. And despite regulations that prohibited priests from engaging housekeeping women under the age of thirty or even forty, the mistress as housekeeper flourished. The very clandestineness of these relationships, and the women's usually low social ranking, meant that until the 20th century changed attitudes and loosened tongues, few traces of individual mistresses survived.

The exception is that underutilized source: the reports of the official visitations that so thoroughly documented both personal and domestic details about clerical mistresses and their lovers. Lederer and Feldbauer's pioneering work in this field takes the first step toward remedying this. Meanwhile, like so many historical women, these mistresses' stories must be imagined and suggested by hypotheses based on what we know they faced: the fear of detection and its consequences; resentment at their reviled status; the promises they extracted from their priestly lovers to protect them and provide for their children. We also know that many of these women felt love, desire and pride at being chosen by these special men who held the key to divine mysteries, even to salvation.

Another key factor in these love affairs was that until celibacy was firmly entrenched as the clerical *modus vivendi*, women viewed priests as eligible bachelors, men with a vocation not unlike a teacher's or a physician's. But over the centuries, as the ideal of celibacy spread, priests developed a mystique as untouchables of a higher order. This fundamental change did not affect the majority of priest-mistress relationships until well into the medieval period. In the liberated second half of the 20th century, when reform-minded Catholics began a sustained attack on clerical celibacy, some freethinking and adventurous women again saw male religious as fair game for their erotic desires and also their romantic love.

PAPAL MISTRESSES
Theodora and Marozia Theophylact[7]

Theodora and Marozia Theophylact were a mother-and-daughter team of mistresses who had papal lovers. These women became so politically powerful that, unlike millions of anonymous "Marthas," contemporary accounts, mostly venomous, describe them in some detail. In 890, Theodora and her husband, Theophylact, moved from the charming old Etruscan city of Tusculum to Rome, fifteen miles away. Theophylact was a courageous and capable man who became a senator, a judge and lastly a duke responsible for the papal finances and the Roman militia. Theodora, too, was named a senator.

But Theodora aspired to more than fluttering around the papal flame in a state where the pope was the paramount leader. Her dream was to establish a family dynasty she could manipulate so she herself could rule Rome. Apparently, Theophylact shared her vision. Together, the Theophylacts maneuvered the man known to history as Sergius III, whom they had supported when his party was in exile, into the papacy.

The deal between Sergius and the Theophylacts included giving Sergius their fifteen-year-old daughter, Marozia, as his concubine. Marozia was already ripening into a woman of legendary beauty, and she and Sergius began a steamy sexual relationship. Soon, she bore him a son.

After ushering her nubile daughter into Sergius's bed, Theodora consolidated her position and soon controlled the papal court. In 911, when Sergius died after only seven years in office, Theodora cleverly averted the usual bloody wars of succession by arranging for her nominee, Anastasius III, to take office. When Anastasius died, in 913, she promptly undertook to have Lando installed, and he survived until 914.

It happened that Theodora had fallen rapturously in love with a younger man, Bishop John of Ravenna. Lando's death inspired her to catapult John into the papacy. He would move permanently to Rome, and not only satisfy her erotic needs but allow her to continue as the *éminence grise* behind the papal throne. For this "monstrous crime" of forcing her lover to become Pope John X, the much-quoted historian Liudprant condemned Theodora as a "harlot."[8]

With John, Theodora became well and truly ensconced in the papal power structure. He proved much longer-lasting and more industrious than her previous puppets. He also worked harmoniously with Theophylact, her cooperative husband, to create a coalition of Italian rulers under the papacy.

Shortly after John's installation, Theodora turned her attention to her widowed daughter. Marozia was still a highly marketable commodity, and Theodora gave her in marriage to Alberic, Marquis of Camerino. As she had been with Pope Sergius, Marozia was her parents' reward for services rendered. Alberic was a German soldier of fortune whose band of veterans had been vital to the newly united Italian allies. As their son-in-law, Alberic joined Theodora and Theophylact in the family palace on the Aventine Hill, and he continued to provide essential military protection.

Sometime before 924, Theodora and her husband died; how, where or when we are not certain. By their society's standards, they had carved out extraordinary lives, Theodora especially. The Theophylact dynasty thrived, and together, Theodora's husband and her lover and accomplice, Pope John X, facilitated her mission of governance. As a mistress and a wife, Theodora succeeded in doing what few women can, uniting and dominating the two men closest to her, and doing so openly, impervious to the consternation of her compatriots. Her men were intelligent, capable and brave. They shared her dreams and treated her with respect; indeed, they honored her with their personal and professional trust.

But all was not well between Marozia and Pope John. After her parents' death, Marozia headed the powerful Theophylact dynasty. Unlike them, she was not interested in sharing power with Pope John, their ally. Instead, she pitted herself against him in bitter rivalry. In 924, when Alberic was instrumental in repelling a Saracen attack, Marozia took the credit. At the same time, she seemed to dislike Alberic as a husband, and cheated on him with a series of lovers. But these men satisfied only her erotic desires, not her personal ambitions. To achieve those ambitions, Marozia cast her lot with John, her bastard son by Pope Sergius.

Just as Theodora had envisaged a political dynasty, Marozia contemplated a hereditary papacy, with John as its first pope. But this required getting rid of the incumbent pope, her mother's former lover. Marozia accomplished this by divesting herself of Alberic and marrying the brother of Pope John's military ally. Then, urged on by enthusiastic Romans, she and her new husband's army orchestrated a siege of the gateway to the Vatican. At last Pope John capitulated, and was thrust into a dungeon, where he died, either starved to death or strangled.

Theodora, the mistress who had loved him, would have been appalled and grieved, but Marozia had no regrets. Instead, she placed two acolytes on the throne of Saint Peter until her son John turned twenty. Then she arranged his installation as Pope John XI, and continued to administer Rome in both its temporal and spiritual dimensions.

With her son ensconced as pope, Marozia no longer needed her new husband and had him murdered. Then, for militarily strategic reasons, she proposed marriage to his brother, a married man notorious for his court's brothel-like ambiance. He quickly accepted her offer and "arranged" to become a widower. The pope, Marozia's dissolute and docile son, officiated at their wedding. But during the wedding feast, Alberic, Marozia's legitimate son, an astute and resourceful teenager, publicly denounced his treacherous, unloving mother and her consort. "The majesty of Rome has sunk to such depths that now she obeys the orders of harlots. Could there be anything viler than that the city of Rome should be brought to ruin by the impurities of one woman?" he bellowed.[9]

Rome heeded Alberic's warnings, and mobs of citizens stormed the castle. Marozia's bridegroom scrambled down a rope over the walls, and fled. Marozia was not so fortunate. Her rebellious people captured her, and though Alberic shrank from killing her, she was too dangerous to release. Instead, he imprisoned her in the bowels of the castle and kept her there until she died months later, unregretted and unmourned.

Marozia's fate was horrible: entombed by her own child in dank darkness, untouched by the hot sun or fresh breezes and guarded by incorruptible men she could neither seduce, coerce nor persuade to free her. As she languished there, she must have rained curses onto Alberic's head—all in vain. For above ground, the popular young man reclaimed the temporal power from his unfit brother, leaving him only ceremonial papal duties to attend to.

On his deathbed, Alberic begged his noblemen to elect his son, Octavian, to the papacy. They did so, and thereby ensured Marozia's extraordinary legacy as the woman who, as mistress to a pope, spawned an entire line of popes, an irony she would likely have appreciated.

Marozia's life was not easy. Her parents had valued her only as a tradable asset, and impounded her into mistressdom. After Sergius died, they imposed Alberic on her. After their deaths finally freed her from their control, Marozia flouted convention and sold herself as she had been sold.

But Marozia went much further than her ambitious mother. She killed and she kept faith with no one, including her husbands or the younger son who was to be her nemesis. And as mistress and mother to popes, Marozia seemed devoid of spiritual conviction, piety or belief in anything other than her own venal world.

Vanozza d'Arignano and Giulia Farnese[10]

Five centuries later, the powerful Borgia pope Alexander VI made his two mistresses famous. Rodrigo Lenzuoli was born in 1431 to the mighty Borgia clan. Like his brother Luis and his maternal uncle Alonzo, Pope Calixtus III,

once a Spanish law professor, Rodrigo joined the Church. He was an imposing man, intelligent and learned, an industrious and skillful administrator
and elegant in speech, manner and person. He was tall and strapping, reputedly able to hack off a bull's head with a single stroke. He was also a graceful
and fine equestrian. He was tremendously handsome and he drew women to
him "as a magnet attracts iron."

But Rodrigo had a less appealing side, especially for a cleric (though not yet
a priest—in that chaotic era, unordained men could still hold Church offices,
and Rodrigo was ordained only in 1468). His incurable womanizing had produced several children whom he acknowledged and provided for generously,
drawing on his enormous income from the Church, several Italian and Spanish cloisters and cathedrals, his salary as vice-chancellor (1457) and money
from an inheritance. Rodrigo lived extravagantly, like a prince. The one
exception was his table, so frugally supplied that his friends avoided dining
with him, though no doubt his abstemious diet was in large part responsible
for his strength and his stamina. But Rodrigo was not a prince, he was a cleric,
and his contemporaries criticized his conduct as unclerical and unseemly.

When Rodrigo met Vanozza, the daughter of a widow he was helping with
legal matters (he also practiced law) and sleeping with as well, his uncle Calixtus III had already named him a cardinal. When the widow later died, Rodrigo
made the eighteen-year-old Vanozza his mistress and sent her homelier sister
into a convent. But first, the ambitious cardinal took the precaution of paying
Domenico d'Arignano, an elderly lawyer, to marry Vanozza and give her—
and more to the point, her future brood of papal bastards—his name. After
d'Arignano and a subsequent husband (Giorgio di Croce) died, Borgia found
replacements. He needed them—a year after her first marriage, Vanozza
delivered the first of her four children with him.

Vanozza was beautiful and undemanding; she asked nothing more than to
entertain Rodrigo and to raise their children in her home. She never forgot to
maintain a facade of formality with him, even in her letters, and she never
referred to their intimacy. Rodrigo, a stickler for etiquette and hungry to follow his uncle on the throne of Saint Peter, appreciated her discretion. Surprisingly for such an apparently unassuming woman, Vanozza also had a serious
sideline: amassing a personal fortune through real estate deals and the management of inns and a pawn-broking business.

Eventually, Rodrigo had to relocate to Rome. Though for reasons that are
today unknown he had ceased having sex with Vanozza, he missed her companionship so badly that he established her and the children in a house near

Saint Peter's, where they lived ostensibly with her current husband. But quietly, almost every night, Vanozza welcomed her beloved Rodrigo into her home, where they chatted companionably.

Then in 1483, without any explanation, Rodrigo broke off their decades-long affair and sent their children to live with his widowed cousin, Madonna Adriana da Mila. The only plausible reason for this abrupt termination of their relationship is that Vanozza's relations with her husbands-of-convenience were not always strictly platonic. Gossipy contemporaries suggested as much, and Vanozza's fifth child, Ottaviano, was known to be the son of Carlo Canale, her fifth and last husband. Rodrigo sometimes also denied—publicly and angrily—that he had sired Joffre, her fourth son.

We can only guess at how Vanozza responded to these accusations, but her anguish at losing her children, especially Lucrezia, her beloved only daughter, endured to the end of her life. Perhaps because she acquiesced in Rodrigo's decision, however cruel, he made no attempt to excise her completely from their family's life. His few dealings with her were friendly, and he continued to assist her financially. He granted her and Carlo the right to the Borgia coat of arms with its built-in tax exemptions. He arranged for Carlo's appointment as warden of the Torre Nona prison, a post much coveted for its potentially enormous bribes from high-ranked prisoners. Most importantly, he permitted Vanozza to see her children, though his cousin Adriana effectively dislodged her as their mother. Vanozza endured and concentrated on her business ventures. But her signature to Lucrezia, "Your happy and unhappy mother, Vanozza Borgia," evokes the melancholy that haunted her for the rest of her long life.

After his breakup with Vanozza, Rodrigo soon found a woman—a very young one—to assuage his longings. Giulia Farnese was sixteen, a spectacular beauty known as "Giulia la Bella." She was blessed with inordinately long and golden hair, and a sunny and uncomplicated nature.

Though she was forty years his junior, Giulia clearly enjoyed Rodrigo's obsessive love for her. As he had done with Vanozza, he negotiated a marriage for Giulia with the obliging Adriana's young son, Orsino Orsini, who after the wedding was packed off to his family's country estate at Bassenello. Giulia continued to live with Adriana and the Borgia children, and became Cardinal Borgia's acknowledged mistress.

Giulia respected and liked her ecclesiastical lover, and was delighted by his gifts of shimmering jewels and splendid clothing. She sparkled at the parties and entertainments they attended, where the well-preserved Rodrigo danced as enthusiastically as his youthful mistress did. His good health and spartan regimen must have spared him, as well, the indignities of sexual impotence that plague so many older men.

Giulia particularly enjoyed her elevation from the modestly dowered daughter of an insignificant family to the mistress of a famous cardinal, and her family appreciated her new powers of patronage and pressured Giulia to request that Rodrigo grant positions and other favors to the Farnese clan. Fortunately, Rodrigo was sympathetic to their desire to consolidate the family fortunes, and he gladly acceded to Giulia's embarrassed solicitations.

Rodrigo and Giulia's affair was far from the staid and stable arrangement that had kept him with Vanozza for twenty-five years. Despite the apparent domesticity—his mistress was the close friend of his daughter, Lucrezia, and both of these young women were kept under the watchful eye of Adriana—Rodrigo suffered from raging sexual jealousy. Worse, the prime suspect was Giulia's husband, Orsino, whom she refused to abandon and who was mesmerized by his wife's charms.

Meanwhile, Rodrigo had a public professional life, and he was also a cardinal eagerly anticipating the death of the current pope. In the daytime, he ostentatiously performed good works, assumed a pious mien and vigorously lobbied other cardinals for their vote when the time came. In his spare time, he visited his mistress.

On July 25, 1492, Innocent VIII, the first pope to openly acknowledge his children, breathed his last. Seventeen days later, during the night of August 10–11, the cardinals voted for his successor. When the votes were counted, Rodrigo cried excitedly, "I'm Pope! I'm Pope!" Giulia Farnese was now mistress to Pope Alexander VI.

And like his uncelibate predecessor, Pope Alexander openly identified Giulia as his escort—wags dubbed her "Christ's Bride"—and Vanozza as his children's mother. One of Rodrigo's first papal actions was to name Giulia's brother Alessandro a cardinal, which earned the young man, later Pope Paul III, the nickname of "the Petticoat Cardinal." A year later, Giulia delivered Laura, her only child, whom Rodrigo joyfully acknowledged. And when the thirteen-year-old Lucrezia was married in the Vatican, Giulia was a prominent member of the wedding party. It is unlikely that Vanozza, the bride's mother, was allowed to attend.

Despite Giulia's affability and delight in the excitement of splendid balls and other entertainments, she was capable of defiance, and she balked at ignoring her husband. Whenever she visited him at Bassenello, Rodrigo was racked by jealousy. Two years into his popedom, he wrote his "thankless and treacherous Giulia" a bitter letter. He excoriated her for "the evil of your soul," which had led her "to break your solemn oath not to go near Orsino . . . [and] surrender yourself once more to that stallion." Return to me at once, he ordered, "under pain of excommunication and eternal damnation."[11]

To avert Rodrigo's wrath, Orsino sent Giulia back with his mother. By the worst sort of luck, hostile French soldiers waylaid them, and the commander notified Rodrigo that if he wished to see Giulia again, he would have to pay a ransom. Rodrigo was devastated. He paid up, then waited for his mistress at the gate to the city. As she rode in, the four hundred Frenchmen who escorted her jeered as the old pope, draped in sword and dagger, ushered home the lovely blond woman he had just redeemed from captivity.

That a pope threatened his mistress with spiritual penalties because she visited her husband is ludicrous but not unprecedented—throughout the ages, clerical lovers have resorted to intimidating their mistresses with such terrifying and hypocritical warnings. Rodrigo's desperate need to possess Giulia overrode his judgment and his pride. His furious accusations about Giulia's clandestine sojourns to Bassenello may have been true. Certainly Romans gossiped that Laura's biological father was none other than her legal one: Orsino Orsini.

In 1497, Giovanni, Rodrigo's son with Vanozza, disappeared one night after a dinner party at his mother's. His body was discovered in the river the next day, hands tied and throat slit. The murderer, likely a cuckolded husband, was never identified. Both Vanozza and Giulia tried to comfort Rodrigo, but he was inconsolable and convinced that his beloved son's death was God's punishment for his own sins. He vowed to reform. But after his grief had run its course, Rodrigo Borgia returned to his old ways.

In 1503, after a dinner party, the seventy-two-year-old pope was stricken by "the Roman disease," likely cholera. For twelve days he suffered agonizing symptoms, including grotesque facial deformities he hid under a hood. On August 18, after receiving the last rites, he died. Romans by then reviled him for having defamed the papacy to enrich and empower his family, and very few attended his funeral. An eyewitness described the once grand pope's final decay. His body had blackened. His nose had swelled up, and his tongue was engorged and lolled out of his mouth. When the coffin proved too short and narrow, the carpenters simply rolled his corpse in an old carpet, then beat it down to size.

Giulia recovered quickly. She returned to Bassenello and, two years later, arranged for her adolescent daughter, Laura, to marry a nephew of Rodrigo's bitter enemy and successor, Pope Julius II. During her tenure as mistress to Rome's most powerful man, Giulia had learned the importance of having the right connections.

Vanozza, too, survived long and well. When she passed away in 1518 at seventy-six, a respected and pious old woman devoted to good works, she willed a fortune in real estate to the Church.

Theodora and Marozia Theophylact had chosen pliant men to transform into puppet-popes and to found their dynasties. They would never have chosen the brilliant and canny Rodrigo Borgia, the man who had averted war between the two great powers of Spain and Portugal by drawing a line through the middle of the Atlantic and assigning the west to Spain, the east to Portugal; who had risked the ire of fellow Catholics by refusing to persecute the Jews; and who had enunciated the radical notion that American natives were *not* subhuman, and were quite capable of deciding whether or not to receive the Christian faith. Vanozza and Giulia, on the other hand, were the "creations" of this exceptional man, who had loved each one of them but had also consciously used them as fertile vehicles to fortify the Borgia dynasty.

THE MODERN CLERICAL MISTRESS[12]
Schisms aside, at any given time there is only one pope, but over the centuries there have been millions of humble priests. Unlike the papal favorites Theodora and Marozia, Vanozza and Giulia, these mistresses could expect neither wealth nor privilege. Instead, they faced persecutory laws, social censure and the severe material hardships of the clerical life, which provided only the meanest of livings.

Today, an estimated 20 to 30 percent of all Roman Catholic priests are sexually involved in relatively stable relationships with women; that is, they have mistresses. Much about these unions is astonishing, not least how well they are concealed and how often both Church officials and congregations tolerate them, often to the point of tacit acceptance. A less savory aspect of these forbidden relationships is how exploitative they are on the part of the transgressing priest. As a man unlike and above mere laymen, he may use his exalted position to influence and seduce women, usually Catholics he meets in the course of his duties. Less frequently and just as surprisingly, some women target priests, exploiting their loneliness and vulnerability. But no matter which party initiates the affair, whenever there is trouble, the Church invariably stands by its errant priest, not the suffering Catholic woman.

The modern Church actually encourages and facilitates its priests' sexual relations by ignoring all but the most scandalous breaches of clerical celibacy. Even then, it takes notice only when media exposure forces the issue. This makes good strategic sense. As long as clerical celibacy remains official doctrine, Church officials will have to turn blind eyes to sexual incontinence if they are to stanch the bleeding that has ravaged the priesthood as priests leave to marry or to lead sexual lives. And, to protect the Church's money, they must continue their millennia-long strategy of victimizing the women involved with priests and, by extension, the priests' children.

One churchly ploy is to retreat behind the sophistical definition of celibacy as the state of being unmarried, rather than what is really intended: sexual abstinence. Other, more practical strategies provide ways for sexually active priests to cope.

The most common strategy is to pass off a live-in mistress as the housekeeper. Some bishops still suggest this stratagem to priests struggling with celibacy.[13] And when trouble arises, often in the form of unwanted pregnancy, the Church sets into motion mechanisms to help the frightened priest, *not* his inconvenient mistress with her demands for financial support. The Church will often help him escape on a leave of absence, so he can mull over his situation. Church counselors may hint that abortion, doctrinally abhorrent, is less scandalous than a priest-sired infant. (Ex-priest and scholar Richard Sipe describes the abortions of priest-sired fetuses as one of the American Catholic Church's "most lethal ticking time bombs.")[14] Church lawyers pressure the mistress to sign punishing legal documents that trade paltry support for her silence about her child's paternity. Canonical courts invariably twist the facts to minimize financial claims against the Church, and to avoid publicity.

In his classic *Shattered Vows: Priests Who Leave*, ex-priest David Rice explains how the Church responds to violations of celibacy with a combination of denial and secrecy. Yet denial is "simply an immature response," and keeping secrets, in this case the bad family kind, hobbles efforts to explore and solve the problems that caused them in the first place. "But secrets in this great family, the family bonded by Christ, are particularly destructive . . . and the seeds of Church pathology, disturbance, and discontent grow," Rice concludes.[15]

Living these lies is excruciating. After twenty-five years, Dutch priest Fr. Willem Berger and his mistress, Henriette Rottgering, broke the silence that had shielded them from the consequences of their relationship. Leading priests and laymen in their diocese had been accomplices, pretending that

Henriette was merely Willem's housekeeping secretary. "There was a kind of agreement," he recalled. "They knew, but without speaking about it. A lot of priests came to our home for meals."[16]

A French priest waited too long to speak out. "I am a wretched man," the cancer-stricken man lamented in deathbed repentance.[17] He had abandoned his mistress out of cowardice, frightened of jeopardizing his career. Love affairs with priests hurt women disproportionately, David Rice points out.

Interestingly, in the five years between *A Secret World* (1990) and *Sex, Priests, and Power* (1995), his scholarly studies of priests and celibacy, Richard Sipe has upgraded his estimate of the ratio of priests with mistresses. It used to be about one-fifth. Now it is one-third. Sipe dissects what he calls the Greeley Syndrome, the plotline behind several of best-selling author Father Andrew Greeley's novels. Basically, Greeley's priests believe they must have sex with a woman, experience the anguished spiritual conflict this produces, then renounce both the sex and the woman, recommit to a life of celibacy and strive for a bishopric.

Unfortunately, as Sipe shows, the same scenario is often played out in real life. The woman becomes an instrument for the priest's personal or spiritual development and, hopefully, his salvation. Mutuality and balance between the two partners seldom figure in these relationships. One rejected woman likened herself to a Greeley heroine and confided, "Greeley has yet to address what happens to the women after the priest has cast them off and learned from them."[18]

Today, priests' mistresses are usually Catholics who meet their lovers at church, confession, counseling or parish activities such as Sunday school. They are often married and unpossessive, being in no position to make too many demands. But some of these women are unmarried, and unmarried women have different stakes and expect more. They often expect to be acknowledged for what they are—clerical lovers. They even dare hope and sometimes push for eventual marriage.

By no means are all women passive victims. With clerical celibacy a long-established ideal, priests have become—to themselves as well as to Catholics in general—men of a different sphere of existence. The notion of a virile, untouchable and celibate priest strikes some women as romantic and exciting—in short, a challenge.

Some priests are well aware of their appeal, and they shamelessly employ it to seduce women who expose their vulnerability in confession and counseling sessions, or who, during parish functions, indicate subtly or otherwise that they are available. Other priests, despite their best intentions, are overwhelmed by longing for a beautiful woman, or by their growing affection for a needy and trusty woman they have come to know intimately.

Usually, mistresses have the advantage of considerably more sexual experience. But this provides them no protection from emotional involvement and the pain that follows a rupture. Then these women, too, feel the unbearable weight of the mighty Church, whose disapproval falls primarily on mistresses rather than their priestly partners in sin.

Church authorities usually hold three assumptions about priests' mistresses. First of all, any woman sleeping with a priest has only herself to blame for her situation, because she has wielded her erotic powers to lure him into having sex with her. Second, she is fortunate that she is involved with a godly man, and should express her gratitude through silence. Third, she has the God-given power to save her lover through her love and sacrifices. She should be gratified rather than wretched if he realizes how much his vocation means to him and breaks off their affair.

Annie Murphy

American Annie Murphy is one among legions of women who have loved priests. She first met Eamonn Casey, the bishop of Kerry and a distant relative of her father, when he visited her family in the United States. Then he was twenty-nine, Annie a child of seven. In April 1973, when she was a grown woman, her father sent her over to Ireland, into Eamonn's care, to recuperate from the emotional turmoil of a failed marriage and, he hoped, to regain her lapsed faith.

From the moment Eamonn met Annie at Shannon International Airport, he was bewitched and bewitching. He flirted and held her hand. Within three weeks, they had sex in the rectory that was his home. On the first night, Eamonn stripped off his faded blue pajamas and stood, naked and vulnerable, in front of the twenty-four-year-old American. "There stood the Bishop, my love, without clerical collar or crucifix or ring, without covering of any kind. The great showman had unwrapped himself. Christmas of all Christmases," Annie later recalled. In bed, Eamonn made love urgently and with all the ineptitude of twenty-five years of celibacy. "I witnessed a great hunger," Annie wrote. "This was an Irish Famine of the flesh."[19]

The next morning, as she watched Eamonn drape himself in bishop's robes and go off to sing mass, Annie worried that he might hate her for what had happened. Already, the complexities of loving a priest were revealing themselves. But Eamonn was too intellectually resourceful to give up this delightful foray into fleshly delights, even after his confessor instructed him to. Annie was wounded in body and mind, Eamonn argued. Only a deep love—his—could heal her. "This is a passage in your life and someone must go with you and help you face its dangers," he told Annie as he contentedly sipped brandy. "If God were here, He would approve of what I am doing."[20]

The affair progressed. Eamonn would pray lengthily before arriving at Annie's bedroom. Then they made love and bantered with each other. Eamonn would quote Scripture to justify what he was doing. Soon Annie had fallen in love with the puckish priest. He claimed that he loved her too, but warned her that he was permanently sworn to his vocation.

The relationship deepened, though Annie realized that Eamonn would abandon her at the first hint of trouble. As if she were tempting fate or forcing him to make a choice between her and his vocation, she attended mass and stared at him throughout, frightening and embarrassing him.

On the subject of birth control, which Annie favored, Eamonn was adamantly opposed, at least publicly. "If I deviate once in the slightest from the Catholic position, I will have to leave the priesthood," he explained. "The Church will forgive me, Annie, whatever sins I commit: murder, theft, adultery. But one careless phrase [such as condoning condoms or the Pill, or questioning the Church's ban on them] and all the good work I'm doing would come to an end."[21] (In the United States, Jesuit Terrance Sweeney would also conclude that this was the Church's *modus operandi*.)

One night, in a frenzy of lust, Eamonn took Annie on the floor outside his bedroom, under the first station of the cross: Jesus Is Condemned to Death. He also confessed to her, anxiously, that even during mass he could not stop thinking about her. And then Annie became pregnant. Eamonn's first reaction was that it was a terrible tragedy. He suggested that another man was the father. Then, in a startling *volte-face*, he wanted to make love to her.

Annie reassured her lover that she did not expect him to marry her or to leave the priesthood. When he told people that she had had an affair with a Dublin hotelier, and was now "in trouble," she confirmed the story. She even agreed to Eamonn's urgent demand that she find God in her heart and allow a Catholic family to adopt her baby. This sacrifice, he assured her, would atone for her sins, and for his in having sired the child.

But when she held the infant Peter in her arms, Annie reneged on her agreement. Eamonn, no longer tender and understanding, ordered her to get rid of "it"—she was not, he said, morally fit to be a mother. When Annie resisted,

Eamonn had her transferred to a home for unmarried mothers, where the nuns, on his orders, withheld proper medical treatment when she developed a blood clot and later an infection. All the while, he pressured her to sign Peter's adoption papers.

But Annie refused, and recalled bitterly how even Saint Augustine had proudly acknowledged his illegitimate son and named him Adeodatus, "Given by God." When she decided to leave Ireland and take Peter back to the United States, Eamonn drove her to the airport in his Mercedes and handed her $2,000 with a warning to spend it sparingly, because it was all he had.

Incredibly, their affair did not end there. Six months later, Annie and her parents returned to Dublin, and she and Eamonn resumed sexual relations. Annie suspected that her father was aware of this but had decided to give the couple both time and opportunity to determine their future course. It did not take him long to realize that Eamonn would never choose Annie over his ambition to be known as savior of the third world. That ambition drove him, among other things, to chair a society called Trócaire—Irish for "compassion"—that raised funds for the third-world poor.

Back in Eamonn's bed, Annie refused to concede defeat and remained in Ireland until, like her father, she concluded that he would never leave the Church. Eamonn was furious that she intended to take Peter back to the United States, and translated his anger into parsimonious child support. The twin issues of money, or lack of it, and Eamonn's refusal to acknowledge Peter, whom he had grown to love, were never resolved.

Sixteen years later, when Eamonn was visiting the United States, Peter ambushed him. Eamonn granted his son four minutes of polite conversation—how was he doing? what college did he plan to attend?—then dismissed him. Peter was as devastated as he was angry, and he decided to launch a lawsuit against his father. Meanwhile, Annie demanded—and received—a final settlement of $125,000. She and Eamonn spent one last surreptitious night together, though she was living with another man. Later, Annie sued Eamonn on Peter's behalf, in Ireland. The lawsuit destroyed Eamonn's reputation and career. In 1992, he resigned as bishop, and issued a statement recognizing Peter as his son and regretting the harm he had done to him and his mother, Annie Murphy. Eamonn also admitted that, to placate and silence Annie, he had stolen her $125,000 settlement money from Trócaire, from funds designated for the poor of the third world. Wealthy parishioners swiftly came to his aid and repaid the money.

Eamonn retired to St. Joseph's Church in Redhill, Surrey, effectively exiled from Ireland. Annie Murphy wrote a book revealing, in salacious detail, the progress of their affair and its unsavory aftermath. In 1999, however, she expressed regret that she had said too much: "Eamonn was such a triumphant spirit and I feel now he is a man without a country," she said.[22]

The Eamonn Casey scandal reminded people of revelations that other bishops and other priests, in Ireland and elsewhere, had also engaged in love affairs, fathered children they had tried to have adopted and—resorting to the Church's time-honored strategy for incorporating women into their lives—introduced their mistresses as housekeepers. Eamonn Casey was not the odd priest out—he had merely been spectacularly "outed."

Father Pat Buckley, a priest in Larne, Northern Ireland, runs a support group for Irish women romantically linked with priests. Buckley's experiences with nearly one hundred of his bereft clients confirm that the Church is myopic in its perspective, and concerned only with its own interests. Silence is more than golden—it is imperative. When love gets out of hand, the bishop (who may be in the same love boat himself) summons his errant priest, and admonishes or transfers him to another parish far away from his mistress. "I've never actually heard of a priest being censured," Buckley reports. "The main interest is to protect the good name of the church."[23]

Buckley's analysis of the troubled priest-mistress issue coincides exactly with others' in Ireland (which Pope John Paul II calls "the rock of the faith") and elsewhere. For example, Irish priest Father Michael Cleary seduced seventeen-year-old Phyllis Hamilton after he had heard her confession. They began an affair that produced two children. After the birth of the first, Cleary forced Phyllis to surrender her child to adoptive parents. Finally, Phyllis left Ireland for a better life in the United States and she took Ross, their second child, with her. Cleary bombarded her with frantic phone calls and letters. He implored her to return to the rectory and promised that Ross could live with them. After some time, Phyllis agreed. Cleary would often point out other priests whose single-mother housekeepers were also their mistresses.

After Cleary's death nearly two decades later, Phyllis approached the Church for guidance. Its stern officials made it clear they had no intention of helping her, and wished only for her and her inconvenient son to disappear.

Worldwide, hundreds of thousands of priests have mistresses, either live-in "housekeepers," married or single parishioners or, occasionally, nuns encountered in the course of priestly service. Each love is unique, but the context is not.

For the married mistress, the affair is often less traumatic. She understands that she can expect nothing more than she has. She is also taking less of a risk, because Catholic husbands have proven astonishingly resilient about sharing their wives with their priests. This is a reflection of their empathy for men forced to swear off sex, of their deep reverence for even sinful priests or of their relief that their wife's extramarital relationship will not endanger their marriage.

Single, non-resident mistresses expect far more from their clerical lovers than clandestine couplings. They frequently suggest or even demand marriage. For their lovers, this can be dangerous and frightening territory. It implies that they should break their vows and abandon not merely their profession, but also the institutional family that has disciplined and nurtured them.

The spiritual issues are just as burning for the priests, and thrust compulsory celibacy into the forefront of their thinking, since this is, above all, what constrains their relationships. Why is it essential? healthy? morally superior? spiritually fulfilling? Questions that have dogged Roman Catholic theology for millennia take on a personal urgency.

When a woman is both a nun and mistress to a priest, she and her partner agonize together over such questions. Both lovers face the same moral dilemma, the same vocational demise, the same social and institutional contempt and shame and, above all, the same spiritual suffering and sorrow. However, the considerable number of ex-nuns now married to ex-priests is proof that, in the end, the prospect of love blessed by the sacrament of marriage is often the most convincing answer.

The burden of loving a priest falls hardest on the resident mistress, the ubiquitous "priest's housekeeper." This woman has no other life than his, no other home, few activities apart from parish life. She is his sin incarnate, the constant and visible source of his shame, a perpetual reproach to his vows of celibacy and obedience. She has the lowly status of a char, and no marital rights at all, though in all other ways she is wifely.

But the housekeeper's bleak situation has consolations. Assuming that she loves her lover (not always the case), this woman has the privilege of living with him on the most intimate terms, knowing most of what there is to know about him, including his colleagues and friends, habits and tastes, vices and virtues, his tenderness as he lies limp and depleted beside her, his anxiety that someone will discover his secret, his remorse that he is wicked and weak, his fear that he is unworthy of the vocation he lies and schemes to preserve.

Paradoxically, though his housekeeping mistress is the mortal most intimately acquainted with his human frailties, the priest may nonetheless bully and intimidate her through the force of his moral authority. What moral authority? That which he holds because he is an ordained priest, privy to the great Christian truths and mysteries. Perversely, many priests wield this authority like a club, especially with mistresses—witness Pope Alexander VI's threatening to excommunicate his beloved Giulia if she persisted in visiting her husband, and Bishop Eamonn Casey's hectoring Annie Murphy to give up her baby as punishment for the sin of loving him.

Even nuns feel something of this moral sledgehammer; though they are also pledged to God, they are mere women, unfit for ordination. Then, too, when a nun commits carnal sin, she usually finds her superiors less tolerant, less willing to attribute her sinfulness to overpowering nature, less prepared to blame her partner.

Louise Iushewitz [24]

Some women in covert relationships with clerics reject the label of "mistress." They believe it denigrates the nature of their relationship, and they reject the validity of the compulsory celibacy that denies them the comfort of the sacrament of marriage. "Michael was my husband and I was his wife," insists fifty-four-year-old American Louise Iushewitz, who in 1994 lost her longtime Jesuit partner to an assassin's bullet in Belfast.

Louise was a few weeks shy of her sixteenth birthday when Michael walked into her life as the teaching assistant for her sophomore philosophy course at the University of Chicago. "He was gorgeous," she recalls, "six foot one, with a chunky build. He had these amazing blue eyes, strange eyes like blue satin that crunched up when he smiled, and a wonderful laugh."

The precocious Louise was more intrigued than smitten with the thirty-two-year-old TA who seemed to have a defensive wall around him. "I bet you can get him," a friend remarked. On the strength of this dare, Louise bet five dollars that she could indeed "get" Michael, and began to pursue him. They began to date casually, but Louise claims that until she was eighteen, she had no idea he was a Jesuit or even a priest.

One day just before his thirty-fourth birthday, Michael sat her down and said, "I'm going to tell you what I do for a living." Louise was so shocked that for two weeks, she refused to speak to him. "I was scared of going to hell," she recalls. Soon, however, she reconciled herself to life as a Jesuit's girlfriend.

When Louise was nineteen, she and Michael began to live together in a Hyde Park apartment, and it was there that they had their first sexual encounter. Michael, who had already had other lovers, set their slow pace. Only when he intuited that Louise was ready for it did he initiate sex. She prepared herself for this new adventure by reading a sex manual. "It was green and had no cover," she says. "I fell off the couch laughing as I read it, but that night, we had sex for the first time."

Their sex life was complicated by Michael's guilt. At first, his excessive drinking dulled his sensibilities. But when Louise was twenty-one, Michael's Jesuit Provincial summoned him and presented him with an ultimatum: You have twenty minutes to decide to either give up the bottle or give up the Jesuits. Michael chose sobriety and spent the next three months in a Minnesota rehabilitation center. Afterward, he attended Alcoholics Anonymous.

But cold sober, he was uncomfortable with the spiritual and vocational implications of his erotic life, and Louise remembers their sex life then as "really terrible." Even fidelity was lacking. After Michael cheated on her with another woman, Louise retaliated with another man, who impregnated her. As a devout Catholic, she would not consider abortion, and in 1969, she gave birth to a son, Jay, whom she gave up for adoption.

Louise's fertility became an urgent issue. She wanted Michael's baby. Michael didn't. Finally, in 1970, Louise broke off their relationship and warned him, "I want to have a child. I'm going to marry the first man who asks me."

That man was very handsome but difficult. Her marriage, Louise came to believe, was God's way of punishing her for having slept with a priest. Ten miserable years and three children later, she left him. Two weeks after this, in August 1980, she and Michael moved into an apartment together.

The final fourteen years of their union were markedly better than the first six. They had both matured, and Louise was no longer "an adoring little thing" who worshipped Michael. She was now the mother of three children who called Michael "Daddy," and their life together consisted of the usual realities: cooking and shopping, arguing and making love, caring for the children.

Nonetheless, their lifestyle was unusual. Almost all their friends were priests and their lovers. Michael's family was sharply divided about Louise: his father condemned her as a Jezebel and a whore, while his mother insisted that Louise was the only thing that kept Michael sane. In retrospect, Louise realizes, their life revolved around lying and teaching the children to lie. Louise abhorred this aspect of her existence. "I don't like lying, living a lie, having my whole life dedicated to lying," she says now with some bitterness.

Quite apart from the mechanics of maintaining their duplicitous life, they faced other obstacles. For one thing, Michael was stationed in Milwaukee and only commuted back to Louise and the children in Chicago on Thursday, to leave again on Sunday. For another, he was actively involved in gathering intelligence for the Irish Republican Army, an activity that ultimately cost him his life. Louise accompanied him on some of his trips to Ireland, and she smuggled in outlawed condoms and birth control pills.

At the core of their long relationship, however, was Michael's vocation. "Half my friends are priests who run parishes and they're better off because someone loves and supports them," Louise declares. She is convinced Jesuit officials knew all about her. They did nothing, however, as long as Michael's ministry was unaffected and his love life did not provoke a public scandal.

Michael himself was seldom conflicted, and conveniently—and ironi-cally—redefined his vows. Celibacy was a gift of God, and therefore not a way of life to be imposed on priests. Chastity meant fidelity to one person—Louise. Poverty was an irrelevancy to American Jesuits, whom he observed all living very well. Obedience was to the Provincial General, and not to the pope, especially John Paul II, whom he despised as "the Anti-Christ." As for sex, Michael believed that experiencing a powerful orgasm was "as close as you can get to understanding the intensity of God's love."

Only once, in 1992, was Michael seized by doubts and remorse. Then he telephoned Louise to announce that he would make her an honest woman by marrying her. "I told him I didn't want to be honest," Louise laughs. "I think Michael was just scared that I'd run off with one of our friends, even though the man in question is gay." Louise's decision was easy. She knew all too well that Michael would be lost if he was not a Jesuit. She knew, too, that leaving the order was an ordeal for Jesuits, and that those who left emerged into the lay world embittered, humiliated and rejected.

At Michael's "stuffy Jesuit funeral," Louise sat with his family. But she and her children were barred from the reception and the wake. Like millions of mistresses, she had no claim on her dead lover.

Six years after Michael's death, Louise was still grieving. Above all, she missed his companionship. "I am an intellectual being," she said, "and my pride and joy is my analytical ability. Michael met all my needs."

Louise has been forced to become more independent. Michael left her only five thousand dollars, and she has had to earn her own living again. Much worse, the insecurity of her new life as a single woman has been "horrible, an emotional wrench."

Louise has continued to feel her own call to the priesthood. "I've even said mass, and the walls didn't fall down," she recalled. "And at the end of the day, I'm very gratified that I had Michael in my life."

Pamela Shoop

Some clerical mistresses are happy in their covert relationships. A few finally marry their lover, after he renounces his vows and returns to "the world." The experience of one Jesuit who fell in love but waited until his wedding night to consummate his relationship illustrates just how the Church, in this case the Society of Jesus, deals with these illicit affairs of the heart.

Father Terrance Sweeney had been a Jesuit for twenty-three years when he met actress Pamela Shoop, a Christian Scientist seeking spiritual solace through conversion to Roman Catholicism. Terry and Pamela see themselves as archetypes of couples whose romantic love has, for centuries, run aground on the rocks of celibacy. "Behind each tortured priest . . . [is] a woman alone . . . in the shadows," they write. That woman has little control over what happens. He, not she, has taken vows, and so she is forced to wait, isolated and lonely, frightened for her future, for her priest's decision.

Pamela and Terry met and fell in love when both were struggling with personal crises. He was particularly troubled about the results of his examination of the origins and history of clerical celibacy, an institution he began to suspect was unethical and unchristian. The Church scorned lovelorn priests more than child molesters. "Why didn't our seminary teachers tell us that married priests and their wives who refused to follow mandatory abstinence were forced out of the priesthood, were beaten, imprisoned, and sometimes even murdered?" he demanded of his spiritual adviser.[25]

But Terry loved the Church, the Jesuits and his vocation. "It's as if I love you with a divided heart, Pam," he confided. He finally decided to leave the Jesuits, but delayed taking the final steps. Then the Jesuits suddenly ordered him to halt his research on celibacy. Terry was so stunned by the unfairness of this decree that after twenty-four years, he freed himself from the Society.

But not from the Church, from which Terry sought incardination, the right to function as a priest. He was letting go, but only in stages.

As Terry dealt with the profoundly difficult transition from Jesuit to ordinary priest, Pamela wrestled different demons. She was lonely, barred from Terry's sparkling social life at dinners, fundraisers and evenings with friends and parishioners. She became jealous and angry, and so sexually frustrated that she still recalls with sadness how Terry's commitment to celibacy kept them from expressing the passionate love they felt for each other. She longed for his entire body but accepted his good-night pecks because she knew that if she slept with him, she would undermine her own personal integrity and Terry's credibility as he spoke out about clerical celibacy.

During the two years she waited for her fate to be decided, Pamela saw herself as merely one in a centuries-long line of despairing priests and their women who had clung "to the desperate hope that somehow, some way, history could be altered, that everything would turn out all right."[26] She remembered Father Franco Trombotto, an Italian priest who spent twenty years in a secret love affair, and could no longer bear either the anguish of living without his mistress or his duplicity in concealing their affair. On January 26, 1985, he hanged himself and explained in his final letter, "I have carried my cross a long way: now I fall under the cross."[27]

Pamela's bitterness poisoned her relationship with Terry. She raged that he was moving with glacial slowness to change his life, and he retorted that after twenty-four years as a Jesuit, he was moving very quickly indeed. Eventually he began to accept Pam's longing for sex. Instead of guilt at his own desire, he felt joy that God had given him this gift of love. One night, he tore off Pam's black lace panties so he could embrace her nakedness though he still could not accept sexual relations outside of marriage.

Pamela's long wait came to an end the next Easter Sunday, when Terry proposed to her. Their wedding was bittersweet. Terry's oldest brother refused to stand as his best man because he had broken his vows and left both the Jesuits and, by then, the priesthood. Many friends shunned Pamela as the seductress who had lured him away from Holy Mother Church. Archbishop Mahoney even banned Terry from Holy Communion for as long as he continued in his "irregular canonical union"—that is, until he divorced his new wife.[28]

Since their marriage, Pamela and Terry have served on the board of advisers of Good Tidings, a nonprofit organization founded in 1983 as a resource for priests and the women they are romantically involved with.[29] Tellingly, Good Tidings was founded after the suicide of a woman whose priest-lover had broken up with her.

Good Tidings, one of a host of such organizations worldwide, takes a matter-of-fact, no-nonsense approach. At the same time, it retains a Catholic perspective and understanding, and defines itself as a ministry. Its mission is to work for spiritual as well as psychological and emotional resolutions, which means that those who seek its help must "discern before God what their relationship is and should be." It may be celibate. It may also be marital.

"A Legal Guide," by Ronald A. Sarno, is Good Tidings' practical handbook for "Mothers or Expectant Mothers of the Children of Roman Catholic Clergy." The "Guide," brutally frank, is designed as a resource to combat the apparatus the Church has designed to crush these shunned mothers into submission. No one reading it should retain any illusions about the primacy of Christian charity in the Church's stance.

Priests or Church officials often give the nod to abortion, though they condemn it in public. "Clergy find it very easy to tell non-clergy what the moral requirement is," Sarno advises, but "they are not always so concise with their own." A woman may find herself bound by a Settlement Agreement or Settlement Order requiring her to withhold from her child his father's identity. As it has for two millennia, the institutional Church discourages priests from assuming any parental responsibility for their offspring.

This forthright disinclination to support children harks back to the Church's original fears that married clergy would allocate Church revenues and property to their families. If the cleric-father is a parish priest or member of an order, his parish or order may be named as codefendant in any legal action against him. This fact, as terrifying to today's Church as to yesteryear's, derives from the legal theory *respondeat superior*, meaning that "the institutional Church, since it supposedly controls the activities of its official members, has a financial responsibility for the harm these officials do."

As for canon law, Sarno writes that "no matter what the canons say in theory, in practice canonical courts and/or canonical inquiries have as their sole purpose the protection of the Church from financial responsibility, and to keep embarrassing facts out of the media. *Canonical courts and/or inquiries are not set up to help women who are bearing the children of Catholic clergy.*"[30]

The Church will employ attorneys against a woman who sues, and their mission is to embarrass her and to keep her financial demands low. These lawyers will also try for a Settlement Order, an agreement not to go to trial. Since the priest and institutional Church desire secrecy almost as much as financial absolution, they will arrange a payment plan in exchange for the mother's promise not to contact the media or continue legal proceedings.

The Church's abhorrence of publicity is the mistress's principal weapon. If negotiations stall, or the priest or his agents offer too small a payment, the threat of media attention often jolts the clerical negotiators into action.

Other heart-wrenching advice for these mothers is to name the Church as a codefendant, "especially if the Church has been directly involved in hiding the birth father from you and from the Court." In fact, "the institutional Church almost always transfers the father out of the State where the mother is." How twisted and sad that the Church, founded on the truths and mysteries of a little boy born in circumstances so awkward that only faith in his miraculous conception saved him from bastardy, has devised so many mechanisms to cripple the attempts of the Virgin Mary's daughters to claim their just deserts.

In the Roman Catholic Church, despite the passage of centuries, little has changed. Priests' mistresses are still one-man harlots, and their children the unsavory fruit of sin. Their lovers remain married to a Church that demands celibacy as well as fidelity and obedience as the price of their vocation to follow in Christ's footsteps and to serve God.

CHAPTER 6

Conquerors
and Their Mistresses

WHEN occupation by a foreign enemy follows or accompanies military conquest, the conquerors often target the conquered people's women for sexual exploitation. Defeated and defenseless, these women have few means to resist their male predators. The sexual use of subjugated women dates back to antiquity and still remains a tragic theme in wartime and its aftermath, when soldiers and their civilian allies extend their victory over enemy civilians.

In the New World, after European conquest brought soldiers and later colonists into contact with native women, sexual relationships soon followed. Coercion was usually present, but sometimes mutual love flowered. Even then, however, the love-struck white men almost never considered marrying their chosen women, and instead relegated them to the lesser status of mistresses.

SPANISH CONQUISTADORS AND NATIVE WOMEN
Malinche [1]

In 1519, Spanish *conquistadors*, under their commander, Hernán Cortés, smashed their way through the vast land now known as Mexico. They destroyed temples, crushed the emperor Moctezuma's soldiers and pulverized the mighty Aztec Empire. Though the *conquistadors* disdained the natives as racially inferior pagans, they relied on some of them as cultural interpreters, laborers and spies. The Spanish also developed relationships with native women, sometimes purely sexual but at other times complex and intimate. Had the women been European, they could have expected marriage.

During the military and cultural devastation of the Spanish Conquest, two natives loomed as large as Hernán Cortés, the Spanish commander, did. They were Moctezuma, the Aztec emperor, and Malinche, Cortés's counselor, diplomatic envoy and mistress.

Malinche was so crucial to Cortés as he waged military and diplomatic war that the natives stopped distinguishing between the two and considered them one indivisible unit. Today, Latin Americans revile Malinche as a treacherous woman who rejected native men in favor of their white conquerors and with Cortés founded the *mestizo* race. The contemptuous label *malinchista*, derived from her name, has come to denote anyone corrupted by foreign influences.

History, too, has painted a harsh portrait of Cortés's young mistress, a misleading and shallow one. When the thirty-four-year-old Spaniard first laid eyes on the teenaged Malinche, he was struck by her intelligence and courage. She spoke several languages and could analyze cultural differences. She was scarred by her past, mature beyond her years and eager to grasp at any opportunities that would serve her personal interests.

The woman whom the Spanish would rename Malinche was born in either 1502 or 1505, in the village of Painalla, in Coatzacualco province in the Yucatan Peninsula. Her father, an immensely wealthy *cacique*, or indigenous nobleman, whose holdings included entire towns and serfs, died when she was still a girl. Her mother married again, and soon Malinche had a half brother.

Her new sibling sealed Malinche's fate. Her mother, probably abetted by her new husband, schemed to get rid of the inconvenient Malinche so her half brother would replace her as heir to her father's fortune.

The plan was a classic of exchanged identities. After a slave's child died, Malinche's mother arranged to bury the corpse. After "mourning" it as her daughter's, she speedily sold the now legally dead Malinche into slavery. By the time she was a teenager, Malinche had become the property of the Mayan *cacique* of Tabasco, who almost certainly used her sexually.

Nobody mistook Malinche for an ordinary slave woman. Her demeanor was aristocratic. She had obviously been educated, as the daughters of nobility often were. During her forced residence in the north, where the Aztec language of Nahuatl prevailed, she became fluent in that language as well as her own native tongue.

But refined and accomplished though she was, Malinche was still a slave. No record remains of her experience, which may or may not have been harsh. At the very least, she must have felt terrible grief and confusion as she was wrenched away from her life as an aristocratic heiress and sold as a slave to foreigners.

In 1519, after several years of servitude, the Mayan chieftain who owned her gave Malinche and nineteen other slave women as a human peace offering to Cortés, newly arrived on his mission of conquest. The Spaniard accepted his gifts, and ordered that they be instructed in Christianity and baptized. This was to become standard procedure for native women bound for sexual service. It gave the Spaniards clearer consciences as they forced themselves on these women. Sometimes these men would take a favorite as a mistress, but not even bachelors would take one as a wife.

Once the women were Christianized, Cortés evaluated them, then distributed them among his officers, though like himself, many of the men were married. Malinche struck him as especially handsome and assertive, a suitable gift for his close friend, Alonso Hernández Puertocarrero. She was christened (and renamed) "Marina," and accorded the title Doña, a mark of respect. Later, in acknowledgment of her influence on Cortés, the Aztecs added the honorific suffix *tzin*. As they pronounced r as l, Doña Marina or Marinatzin became "Malinche."

Malinche's tenure as Puertocarrero's mistress was short, as Cortés soon dispatched him back to Spain to deliver a letter to the Spanish king. Then he appropriated Malinche for himself.

In his campaign of conquest, the odds against Cortés were enormous: hundreds of thousands of native warriors were pitted against six hundred Spanish soldiers and sailors maneuvering in a hostile, foreign land. To combat this, Cortés had only his compulsion to destroy Moctezuma, superior Spanish weaponry and the brilliant advice proffered by his enterprising young mistress.

From the first, Malinche cooperated with the Cortés mission. And why not? Her own safety depended on the efforts of these unfamiliar men, and she felt no loyalty to the people of her birth, who had abandoned her, traded her between them and then offered her as a gift to appease the man they feared. As Cortés's mistress, Malinche was still a slave, but she was so manifestly respected and trusted, privy to her lover's councils of war, his doubts and his fears, and not least to his eager body, that her bondage must have seemed light or even incidental. Her bitter past must have taught her that becoming

Cortés's indispensable liaison with the natives, interpreting their mores and alliances as well as their languages, was her wisest course.

Malinche might also have fallen in love with Cortés. Many women did, attracted by his imperious carriage, his muscular body, his classically sculpted features and the full, carefully pruned mustache that framed his white-streaked beard. And, like her, Cortés likely thrived on challenge and never hesitated to take necessary risks. Their mutual attraction may have prompted Cortés to send Puertocarrero off to Spain so he could have Malinche for himself.

Before Puertocarrero's abrupt departure, Malinche had already begun to collaborate with Cortés, working in tandem with Father Jerónimo de Aguilar. Father de Aguilar had been recently freed from native captivity, during which he had learned a native tongue that Malinche understood. At first, she and de Aguilar communicated in this native language, but very soon Malinche learned Spanish. From then on, she dealt with Cortés directly, and accompanied him and his men everywhere, even on military excursions in the dead of night.

It was bizarre to see a native woman as the Spanish military commander's right hand. But Cortés made no attempt to hide or minimize their relationship, and he even mentioned it in official dispatches.

Translating words, he realized, meant little if it did not reveal the psychology behind the words. So Malinche interpreted and evaluated information, and put it into the context of the complex Aztec politics and diplomacy, where subject peoples allied with and against each other under the omnipotent imperial presence of Moctezuma. Young though she was, she became Cortés's resident ethno-anthropologist and costrategist, and he regarded her advice as vital to his military venture.

Malinche knew that she could not afford to make mistakes. This was war, to the death. One Indian interpreter lost his life when he misjudged Cortés's strength, defected to the Tabascans and urged them to fight rather than negotiate. After Cortés humiliated them in battle and killed eight hundred of their men, the embittered Tabascans sacrificed the interpreter to their gods.

In the final analysis, the Spanish campaign pitted Malinche against Moctezuma. By all rights and probability, the enslaved, disinherited noblewoman should have been no match for the powerful Aztec emperor who was also commander-in-chief of his imperial army. But Malinche had more than cool intelligence and analytic abilities on her side. She had her belief in the Aztec prophecy about Quetzalcóatl, the white, bearded god who, it was believed, would come back and establish himself as ruler over Moctezuma's empire.

Moctezuma, assessing reports about the Spanish invaders, could not decide whether Cortés was one of Quetzalcóatl's demigod acolytes or a dangerous mortal who should be destroyed. But Cortés's immediate problem was not Moctezuma, it was the Tlaxcalans. Cortés admired their orderly cities and their intelligence, and he knew they hated their Aztec oppressors. He was not convinced, however, that they would ally with him instead.

Cortés confided his fears to Malinche, and instructed her to mingle with the people and ferret out whatever information she could. As she wandered purposefully, an older woman, the wife of a *cacique*, stealthily approached her and urged her to desert her foreign companions. Our men are preparing to kill and sacrifice them, she said. Pots full of seasoning tomatoes and peppers are already aboil. Soon Moctezuma's warriors will ambush and kill every last one of the foreigners. Their corpses will be tossed into the waiting pots as sacrifices to the gods, and the priests will eat their seasoned flesh as if it were chili.

Flee while you can, the old woman counseled Malinche. And (coming to the real reason for her intervention) as you are so young and beautiful, you shall become my son's wife, and I will give you refuge.

Malinche considered the offer. If this ambush is such a secret business, how can you possibly know about it? she inquired. The reply was straightforward: The woman had heard it from her husband, a *cacique* whose allegiance Moctezuma had recently purchased.

This must have been Malinche's moment of truth. Cortés's band was in mortal danger, and if she rejected the woman's protection, she, too, would join her lover in the stew pot. The woman had offered her salvation. All she had to do was stay where she was and let Moctezuma's forces pulverize the Spaniards. Afterward, she would be married to a suitably high-ranked man and finally assume her rightful place in Aztec society. She would manage her husband's household, supervising the morning hot chocolate, the pounding of maize, the baking of tortillas, the sweeping and scrubbing of the family compound. Her servitude would be forgotten, her birthright restored. And until other Europeans took up the vanquished Cortés's quest, Moctezuma and the Aztec Empire would flourish.

Yet Malinche chose Cortés, the foreign lover who had taken her measure and valued it, who nourished her intelligence, depended on her advice and put his very life into her safekeeping. She chose, as well, the Christianity she had embraced, proselytizing so fervently that the Spaniards commented on her ardor. She rejected the society that had forsaken and enslaved her. She turned her back on the religion whose gods were voracious carnivores who held out no promises of heaven, either on earth or in the afterlife.

The woman guessed none of this. Thank you! Malinche said to her. I will accept your kind offer, but before I come here to live with you, I must sneak back into the camp and retrieve my clothes and my jewels.

Malinche hastened back to Cortés. After her urgent warning, he captured and interrogated a Cholulan, who divulged more details of the plot. Meanwhile, on the outskirts of the city, Moctezuma's warriors were waiting with their murderous *macanas*—hefty wooden weapons edged with flint or obsidian—to dispatch the hated white men or to take them captive, human fodder for the bloodthirsty gods.

Having seen how the Aztec priests hacked open their prisoners' chests and wrenched out their still-beating hearts as sacrificial offerings, Cortés and his men dreaded capture more than death. Cortés decided to attack, and he launched a surprise offensive. He and his men overwhelmed the overconfident Tlaxcalans and, before the battle ended, slaughtered three thousand.

One of Cortés officers reported home that Malinche "possessed such manly valor that, although she had heard every day how the natives were going to kill us and eat our flesh with chili, and had seen us surrounded in the late battles, and knew that all of us were wounded and sick, yet never allowed us to see any sign of fear in her, only a courage passing that of a woman."[2]

Cortés showed his appreciation by empowering her to conduct the most delicate and difficult negotiations with the natives. The most fraught by far concerned the graceful, pyramidal Aztec temples, which Cortés determined to destroy. To him and his men, they were not places of worship, they were gory abattoirs that stank of human blood.

But the Spaniards' native allies were appalled at this attack on their religion. The indefatigable Malinche set about to convert them. She preached her adopted religion, and she explained why these monuments to lesser, crueler gods had to be eradicated. Then the Spaniards reduced the bloodstained Aztec temples to shards, and Cortés, with Malinche at his side, pushed on to the New World's greatest fortress, the Aztec capital city of Tenochtitlán.

Cortés's victories stunned Moctezuma. In desperation, the emperor invited his Spanish enemies into Tenochtitlán, where he planned to ambush them. At first, both camps maintained the fiction of friendship. But when Cortés discovered that Moctezuma was fomenting rebellion among the Spaniards' native allies, he confronted his host. Malinche intervened and persuaded

Moctezuma that the Spanish soldiers would kill him unless he cooperated. To save his life, the emperor moved to the Spaniards' quarters. There, under a sort of house arrest disguised by his jailers' cynical flattery, he continued to administer his empire.

Convincing Moctezuma to put himself under the protection of Cortés's motley band had taken genius, and only Malinche had the cultural skills and subtlety to achieve it. For six months, Moctezuma personally thwarted every plot that his men concocted to attack his Spanish captors. Moctezuma and Malinche parted company when the bulk of the Spanish contingent departed Tenochtitlán, leaving the emperor guarded by a skeleton military corps. Its panicky commander mistook a religious festival for a revolt and slaughtered the celebrants. The uneasy stalemate between Aztec and Spaniard ended as the Aztecs fought fiercely to avenge the slain civilians. As Moctezuma pleaded with them to put down their weapons, a stone from a slingshot mortally wounded him.

In the ensuing melee, most of Cortés's men died and all the horses were wounded. Malinche survived, clambering over dead Spanish bodies as she fled. As he grasped the extent of his terrible losses, Cortés leaned against a tree and wept.

A year later, Cortés and his allies returned and laid siege to Tenochtitlán, starving its inhabitants and dismantling it stone by stone. On August 13, 1521, the city surrendered. The victorious Cortés then set about to restore what he had destroyed.

Meanwhile, Malinche was pregnant, and in 1522, she delivered their son, Martin, reputedly Mexico's first *mestizo*. This momentous event did not bind Cortés yet closer to his mistress. To the contrary, it marked the beginning of his withdrawal from her, though he preserved their professional relations. The reason for this sudden and unexpected rupture was that Cortés was anticipating elevation to the nobility, and he knew that Malinche could not share his life as a noble. This was not just because he was married. It was also because, whatever Malinche had been to him during his military campaign, she was a dark-skinned native woman whom Spaniards would consider a savage. To avoid his countrymen's derision, Cortés stopped sleeping with her and sent for his Spanish wife, Catalina Suárez Marcayda. Then Catalina died, but her premature death changed nothing, and Cortés acquitted himself of his obligations to Malinche by marrying her off to one of his captains, Juan Jaramillo, a heroic knight. Over a year later, their daughter, Maria Jaramillo, was born.

Malinche's marriage was unhappy. Though Cortés had made her a wealthy woman by granting her vast tracts of land, he had also bound her to a man who—his colleagues afterward alleged—had married her in a drunken stupor. Perhaps he had. Spanish aristocrats did not marry native women, and Jamarillo was an unhappy exception. When Malinche died a few years later, her husband waited only weeks before remarrying.

Latin American historians and tradition have crucified Malinche as a traitor to her people. During her years with Cortés, and later, married to Jamarillo, she must have endured the condemnation of countless native people. We can only guess whether she was pained by or surprised at his refusal to marry her, but it is conceivable she understood how she would have jeopardized his career. Even as his wealthy and respected mistress, the enslaved and disinherited Malinche reinvented herself as a force so powerful that she shares Cortés's glory—and ignominy—for conquering the Aztec Empire.

"COUNTRY WIVES" IN COLONIAL AMERICA[3]

The heroine of one of North America's most romantic stories is Pocahontas, the handsome and spirited daughter of a powerful tribal leader. In May 1607, the twelve-year-old watched her father prepare to execute Captain John Smith, founder and leader of the struggling Chesapeake Bay colony. But Pocahontas, who may have had an adolescent crush on the brusque but charismatic white man, flung herself beside him on the executioner's stone, cradling his bearded head and successfully pleading for his life.

A few years later, the colonists kidnapped Pocahontas as a pawn in their bitter battles with her people. At the same time, they accorded her the respect her father's daughter deserved. They so impressed her that she converted to Christianity and was christened Lady Rebecca. She also fell in love with John Rolphe, one of the settlers. With the consent of her father and the governor of Virginia, she and Rolphe were married.

Pocahontas's story is noble and romantic, and the fact that she died in her early twenties, before Rolphe could tire of her, lends it a tragic finality as well. But thousands of other native women had less idyllic relationships with their white colonial mates, who despite having participated in a ritual of marriage, discarded their "country wives" as if they were only mistresses.

Life on the North American frontier and in the fur-trading hinterland was harsh. Nature, in the form of blinding snowstorms and stone-riddled soil, often seemed inimical. Hunger, like implacable winter, had its seasons. Danger lurked everywhere: in the forestial wilderness where bears and other beasts repelled the invaders and in bleak settlements menaced by hostile native people. Loneliness and fear were endemic; women trapped on isolated farms often sank into madness.

In the uncertain world that was backwoods colonial North America, the fate of fur-trading posts and missions, and of entire settlements, could turn on how local leaders, native and white, dealt with each other. But the displaced native people, ravaged by imported disease and alcohol, and the impatient white men, sure of their racial and moral superiority, could not always find ways to become each other's staunch allies. Often enough, they slipped into bitter enmity.

In the early 17th century of Pocahontas, native societies were still relatively intact, with a strong matrilineal tradition and tribal governments that included powerful women.[4] European newcomers misinterpreted and criticized native cultural mores, in particular those concerning women. European colonists looked askance at a way of life that included equal divorce rights for women. They scorned native matrilinealism as a comment on native women's infidelity: a man could be sure that his blood flowed in the veins of his sister's children, they declared, but he had no such assurance about his wife's.

Some Europeans, however, usually those involved in the fur trade, became intimately acquainted with the native lifestyle, and a few adopted it as their own. Far more simply accommodated to it whenever this suited their interests. Fur traders, for instance, often wed native women in native rituals, and these "country wives" served as their sexual companions, food providers, interpreters and guides as well as as crucial links with their tribe's men.

In the early years, the only women available to most colonists were native and, later, those of mixed blood. White women came out to the colonies in far fewer numbers than the men, and often only after male relatives or prospective spouses had sent for them. Lonely male colonists weighed their options: abstaining until they could provide for a white wife; relying on prostitutes; marrying and remaining married to a native woman; or marrying and later abandoning a native woman if and when a marriageable white woman appeared.

Governing agencies, whether fur-trading companies or military commands, often issued instructions on this issue. The Hudson's Bay Company, for instance, first forbade, then tolerated, intermarriage, while the rival North West Company encouraged it. In reality, though, men from these institutions and other fur traders often deserted their native wives and their mixed-blood children.

To marry or not: for both white men and native women, either option had advantages and disadvantages. Celibacy had the most drawbacks, and put a man's very survival at risk. This was because native women were invaluable partners, crucial to the operation of the fur trade. They knew how to cope in the wilderness. They translated languages and customs, and introduced their husbands to their relatives. They ground and baked corn, the staple food, and made the preserves that held brutal winter at bay. They made clothes, moccasins and snowshoes, a fur trader's essential accoutrements. They warned of treachery brewing.

Native women had much to gain from their white partners. Access to manufactured goods—metal kettles and cotton, for instance—relieved them of such toilsome tasks as boiling water with heated stones and tanning leather. As go-betweens, they garnered influence among both white and native people, and sometimes parlayed this into real power. They enjoyed the trinkets their fur-trading husbands offered them, and abandoned the native custom of eating whatever scraps were left over after their men had eaten.

But unlike their white mates, native women paid high prices for their alliances. When they were confined to forts, they were subject to the regulations and prejudices of an alien white culture, invariably based on uninformed and demeaning views of native civilization. Because white men failed to practice the sexual abstinence that native peoples used to control their birth rates, the women became pregnant much more often than their sisters. This led to more complications and suffering in childbirth, and premature aging. These women were harmed by exposure to unfamiliar diseases and to alcohol. They had to surrender their children to their husbands' control, as European patriarchy (unlike native matriarchy) dictated.

But their worst and most persistent problem was abandonment, and native women lived in dread of their mates' defection. It was no idle fear. All around them, white men threw aside their native wives and took new ones, either native or white. Marriage, in other words, had different meanings to its partners. Native wives expected monogamy, but their white husbands consistently disappointed them by consorting with other women.

Prior to the 19th century, native men approved of these unions as a way of establishing advantageous, even preferential, trading alliances. Some tribes arrogated the collective right to select suitable husbands, while others permitted personal attractions to prevail. But all insisted on formalizing the arrangement called *à la façon du pays*—the custom of the country.

These rituals resembled European rituals. The prospective husband had to call on his intended bride's parents and obtain their consent to the union. Her relatives then set a bride price—one horse was common. Next, the groom smoked a ceremonial pipe with his soon-to-be relatives or their tribal band. The bride's female relatives, meanwhile, prepared her for her new role— cleansing her of bear grease, for instance, and replacing her traditional garb with new, often European-style clothing such as a blouse and short skirt, pet- ticoat and leggings. Finally, the groom—the new "squaw man," the name for a white man married to a native woman—escorted his intended home. From then on, he was her husband, and she was his wife.

Men who ignored or failed to grasp these customs paid high prices. "All nations are the same about these customs," wrote one elderly trader. "There is danger of having one's head broken if one takes a girl from this country with- out her parents' consent."[5]

Perspectives on marriage varied wildly. Prior to the 19th century, many husbands considered themselves legally bound, and English courts tended to agree. If white men's employers tried to force them to get rid of their embar- rassing native wives, many refused and stoutly defended the legitimacy of their marriages.

Serious problems arose when these "squaw men" were company employees rather than independent entrepreneurs. For them, retirement usually also meant a return to the home country, which ended many a marriage. Country wives were not considered "real" wives, and white society circled the wagons to keep them away. Racism played a strong role, and the same people who ingratiated themselves with native people in the hinterland were appalled at the notion of a native woman moving in next door.

Some husbands responded by remaining in native territory. Others resorted to "turning off"—marrying their suddenly burdensome wives to womanless new arrivals. Some simply disappeared into the white world. Left behind, these abandoned wives packed up their mixed-blood children and returned to their tribes, which welcomed them back and stigmatized neither woman nor child. Indeed, the tribes sometimes favored these children as superior, better and bolder hunters, and delighted in initiating them into the tribe.

The first decades of the 19th century saw an infusion of rigidly moralizing missionaries, added to growing numbers of mixed-race adults. This shifting demography and a changing economic situation cast a new and ugly light on marriages consummated by the custom of the country.

The concerted assault on country marriages did not end them. White men came to see native women as sexual objects rather than life mates. Before long, the redefinition of the country wife had drastically altered the situation of thousands of women. This was especially true of mixed-blood people, who lacked the full-blooded native woman's security and sense of self. Humiliated to discover they were seen as mistresses and not spouses, these country wives sometimes even murdered the newborns they felt they could not raise alone.

Sally Fidler, Betsey Sinclair and Margaret Taylor

Sally Fidler, a mixed-blood woman, was a typical 19th-century country wife. In 1818, when the debonair William Williams, governor of the Hudson's Bay Company, sought out her company, Sally rejoiced and quickly entered into a country marriage with him. She was, she believed, his wife. Two children later, when he was transferred to another territory, she learned that she had been deceived. Williams dumped Sally and their children, and sent for his white English wife to join him in his new posting.

George Simpson, Williams's successor, also flung himself into affairs with mixed-blood women. One of the first was Betsey Sinclair, who, like Sally Fidler, assumed that she and Simpson were married. Simpson, however, called her "his article . . . an unnecessary & expensive appendage," and referred to other country wives as "Indian mistresses." Even parenthood did not soften Simpson. Though Betsey gave birth to his daughter, he continued to regard her as merchandise. When he was transferred to another trading post, he transferred her as well—to his friend John G. McTavish. Do with Betsey what you will, he instructed, stipulating only that she not become "a general accommodation shop," by which he presumably meant a sexual outlet for anyone inclined to take her.

Simpson's next liaison (as distinguished from his one-night flings) began just as casually. But as time passed, his feelings for Margaret Taylor intensified and deepened. Margaret had been born in 1805 (1810 according to some sources), to George Taylor, a Hudson's Bay Company employee, and his country wife, a native woman named Jane. Margaret was one of their eight children, all abandoned in 1815 when George retired alone to England, with neither a backward glance nor a financial arrangement.

Jane survived by attaching herself and her large family to the Hudson's Bay post. When Simpson arrived as governor, he hired Margaret's brother Thomas as his personal servant. In 1826, when Margaret was twenty-one, she became the next in the line of Simpson's country wives.

Margaret conceived a child almost immediately. Before she delivered it, Simpson departed for business elsewhere, leaving these brutal instructions to his underling, McTavish: "Pray keep an Eye on the commodity if she bring forth anything in proper time & the right color let them be taken care of but if any thing be amiss let the whole be bundled about their business."[6]

The so-called commodity, however, was an excellent woman and so devoted to him that after he returned, Simpson acknowledged and supported their infant, George. Soon after George Junior's birth, Simpson's relatives intervened, criticizing him for demeaning himself by keeping a native mistress even though she was hidden away, as propriety dictated. But Simpson had become too attached to Margaret to deprive himself of her constant presence. "The commodity has been a great consolation to me," he confided to McTavish.[7]

While Margaret was pregnant with their second son, Simpson returned to England for a holiday. Before he left, he provided for her, George Junior and the child-to-be, and even for her mother, and referred to her brother as his brother-in-law. All these gestures reassured his adoring country wife.

But during Simpson's sojourn in England, his affection for Margaret apparently evaporated, and he fell in love with his cousin, Frances Simpson. Margaret and the children were forgotten. During the Simpson nuptials, no one mentioned the pregnant and loyal Margaret Taylor as a reason that the cousins should not be wed.

Before Simpson arrived back in Canada, Margaret, like everyone else in the settlement, heard that he would be accompanied by his bride. Simpson, however, took pains to keep Margaret and the children out of Frances's way. Presumably he anticipated that Frances would be displeased, even horrified, at his miscegenation, disgusted that he had loved a dark-skinned woman or suspicious that Margaret might continue to command his affection.

We do not know if Frances ever came to know about Margaret and the little boys who were half brothers to her own children. And if she did, she probably did not understand that Margaret, as Simpson's country wife, had expected (or at least hoped) to spend the rest of her days with him.

Yet Simpson did not forget Margaret altogether. After he and Frances were comfortably ensconced, he arranged for Margaret to marry Amable Hogue, one of his former *voyageurs*, an expert fur trader turned stonemason. He also granted Hogue a property on the banks of the Assiniboine River. "The Gov[erno]rs little tit bit Peggy Taylor is also Married to Amable Hogue," remarked one scornful contemporary, "what a downfall is here . . . from a Governess to Sow."[8]

As Mrs. Amable Hogue, Margaret survived another fifty years. Curiously, one of her sons later described her as a Scotswoman, an error that her descendant, Christine Welch, believes Margaret may have initiated. If Welch is correct, her ancestor renounced her native blood to shield her daughters from betrayal at the hands of white men contemptuous of mixed-blood women, men who would treat them as George Simpson had treated her.

Indeed, Simpson's callous behavior marks a turning point for the institution of country marriage. Until then, it was accepted as a form of common-law marriage. But as the social conceits of the 19th century eroded the concept, and more and more white husbands reneged on their obligations to their native wives, the institution of country marriage was transmogrified into a charade in which the men knew what the women feared: that they were mistresses who could be turned out at will. This was how, with Frances at his side, Simpson could dismiss other men's country wives as a "bit of Brown" or a "bit of circulating copper." These were scathing words from the man who had once loved Margaret Taylor.[9]

This racism also victimized Mary, Margaret's beautiful sister. A young white admirer heard that Mary, because she expected a proposal of marriage from him, had spurned another's offer of marriage. Alarmed, he sent a friend to tell her that he would never marry a mixed-blood woman, even one as pretty as she was.

Mary was humiliated once again after she traveled to England to join an elderly white man who had pledged to marry her. Her "fiancé" reneged on his promise but urged her to become his mistress. Mary refused and returned home, where she sank into a deep depression that alarmed her friends. They understood, as she did, how precarious her situation was, and how powerless she and other native women were in the face of importuning white men who seduced and even loved them but could not or would not brave social opprobrium by taking them as wives instead of mistresses.

A bigoted brand of Christianity, by then making serious inroads into North America through the agency of proselytizing missionaries, clergymen and civilian zealots, also targeted native women. Anglican priests scorned country wives, referred to them as commodities and recorded their identity generically (that is, as a nameless native, half-breed or half-caste), as if they were not real people with individual names. One particularly fanatic schoolteacher, John Macallum, ordered his students to ostracize their own mothers if they had not been joined in holy matrimony with their fathers.

White women, increasingly present in North American settlements, also fostered racial prejudice. They denigrated native women as "squaws," though their hostility stemmed from a grudging recognition of the native woman's beauty and from fear that her more relaxed attitude toward sex made her a formidable rival who must, at all costs, be eliminated from the competition for marriageable white men.

A few exceptions were an elite group of mixed-blood girls whose white fathers attempted to ward off the racial discrimination they saw destroying other native women's lives. These men educated their daughters and prepared them for lives in white society, so much so that males of mixed descent could seldom win their hands in marriage.

A few fair-minded judges attempted—unsuccessfully—to force white husbands to marry their country wives and to allot them one-third of their property. Discarded mistresses who belatedly discovered that country wives were not real wives had no recourse but to return to their tribes, which cared for them as best they could.

The concept of country marriage originated as a relationship between native women and the men who were colonizing their people. By creating recognized marital unions and guaranteeing the legitimacy of their offspring, it seemed to satisfy the concerns and needs of both parties and cultures. But the subordinate status of the country wife, as both female and native, eroded the basic goodwill at the heart of the institution. The victims were the women, deceived into believing they were wives when in fact their husbands regarded them as mistresses.

MISTRESSES IN CONQUERED ASIA[10]

In Japan at the turn of the 20th century, Madama Butterfly, Giacomo Puccini's loving but gullible Japanese operatic heroine, tearfully discovered that Pinkerton, her handsome American sailor, would never return for her. Decades later, during and after the war in Vietnam, as thousands of real-life Madama Butterflies waited and hoped for their foreign soldiers to make good on their promises—of marriage, money, visas—a new musical tragedy was adapted to tell their story, and Madama Butterfly became Miss Saigon.

It has always been a sad fact of military occupation that randy young soldiers prey on civilian women. Fear, guilt and homesickness warp their values, and they justify their sexual predations on the grounds that "enemy" women, too, are fair game. But in war zones, voluntary sex with soldiers is perhaps as common as rape. Women offer their bodies for money, expediency or love, or a combination of the three.

Le Ly Hayslip and Dao Thi Mui

The war in Vietnam created thousands of Miss Saigons. Some loved their American men. Others were merely desperate for a new life in the United States. In *When Heaven and Earth Changed Places: A Vietnamese Woman's Journey from War to Peace*, Le Ly Hayslip describes her (unhappy) stints as the mistress of American soldiers before she met and married Ed, the soldier who brought her to the United States.

After the war ravaged Le Ly's rural village, turning it into "broken dikes and battered crops and empty animal pens,"[11] she worked as a maid. Her Vietnamese employer, "a billy goat in a house full of nannies," seduced her, then threw her out when she became pregnant.[12] Le Ly's first American was Big Mike, who pimped her to other GIs for a wad of greenbacks as big as a cabbage, which totaled four hundred dollars. Afterward, she regretted this lucrative lapse into prostitution and found a job in a hospital. She was no virgin or "cherry girl," Le Ly declared, but neither was she a whore.

At the hospital Le Ly met Red, a freckled American medical technician whose buckteeth made him resemble the field mice that pillaged the rice bins. But before long, Le Ly learned to overlook Red's unfortunate appearance because he was kind and respectful—or so she thought.

They began to live together, and at Red's insistence, Le Ly resigned from her hospital job to take up go-go dancing in an American-patronized club. When she rebelled against stripping, Red showed his true colors: "You aren't the only gook girl in the world," he snarled. Le Ly broke off the relationship, but not her dependence on American servicemen.[13]

Le Ly's next lover was Jim, an American helicopter mechanic of Chinese and Irish descent. Their first few months were idyllic, until Jim's heavy drinking fueled violent rages, at home and elsewhere. One day American MPs arrested him. Le Ly moved back with her mother, who was caring for her son.

Paul Rogers, a Texan Air Force officer, came next. He and Le Ly lived together, but he was reserved and made no promises. He's a short-timer, her friends warned, a man about to be shipped back home. Paul denied this and claimed that he had just signed up for an additional six months. Then, one morning, he put on his dress blues, kissed Le Ly lingeringly and marched out of Vietnam, and out of her life. Had sixty-year-old Ed not materialized, and loved and married her, Le Ly would have become another Miss Saigon.

Dao Thi Mui was not so lucky. As a youngster, her life was full of promise. She was the prettiest girl in her village. Her parents arranged her traditional marriage to a policeman. Then came the great exodus from the north, when anybody associated with the French regime fled. Mui's in-laws worked for the Department of the Navy, which sent them to Saigon. There her husband joined the air force, and they had three children.

In 1964, an accident killed Mui's husband and one child. Mui was suddenly her family's sole support. She bought a cart and peddled fruit juice in front of a bar popular with Americans. One of these was forty-one-year-old Henry G. Higgins, a physician who worked in army communications. Henry courted Mui by buying all her juice and distributing it to his companions. After five months, he invited her to live with him. For three years they were lovers, and had two sons, Minh and Thao Patrick Henry.

Thao looked like Henry, but blond, soft-featured Minh did not. Henry treated the boys equally, but refused to acknowledge Minh as his son. After Henry shipped out of Vietnam, he returned briefly to Saigon to teach in a military hospital, then left the country for good. Until 1978, he wrote and sent money for Mui and Thao. By then the Viet Cong had taken over Saigon, and Mui speculates that the ensuing dislocation of society explains why Henry's letters suddenly stopped.

Mui, meanwhile, had managed to send Minh to the United States. through Foster Parents Plan, but she has never again heard from or about him. The new regime conscripted her as an unpaid canal laborer. She rose at 4 A.M. and was bused to Hoc Mon, thirty kilometers out of Saigon. Until 7 P.M., she waded chest deep in water, shoveling earth, sustained only by a lunch of rice and rotten meat. On weekends, she sold gasoline to earn money. After months of this debilitating work, she contracted malaria. She managed to bribe an official with gold she had hoarded, and was finally released from her duties.

Mui's story is a litany of brutish survival through hard work, cunning and a reserve of gold she used only for bribes and for her son Thao's four escape attempts. In 1982, she applied to the Orderly Departure Program for entry to the United States, but a decade elapsed before her application was processed. During this period, a letter dated August 16, 1984, from Miami Shores, Florida, informed Thao that Henry Higgins had died and left him nearly $40,000, and Mui $2,500. Unfortunately, the money could be claimed only in the United States, in person. For years after, despite this substantial inheritance, Mui and her family lived abjectly, focusing only on the day their world would change, when they would finally reach the United States.

Before his death, Henry Higgins had fully intended to continue caring for the child he knew to be his, but he left only a token sum to his former mistress.

Considering his suspicions about Minh, which may or may not have been justified, his behavior in Saigon had been considerate and decent to both Mui and her boys. For as long as he could, he sent them news and money, and he included them in his will. In fact, his remittances may not have ceased until his death. It is quite possible that a corrupt communist postal employee appropriated them as capitalist booty.

Henry never promised to marry Mui. He told her early on that he was married but separated from his wife. Mui, however, always referred to him as her husband. She may have done this to expedite her tortuous passage to freedom, or to erase the stain of illegitimacy from her children's record. Life for Amerasians is difficult enough among the racially purist Vietnamese, and a child branded the bastard of an enemy soldier bears a double burden. As for Mui, if Henry were her husband, she could not be taunted as a whore.

Thousands of American servicemen treated their Vietnamese mistresses as Henry Higgins did, loving them, impregnating them, leaving them, later sending money routinely, sporadically or not at all. Higgins was one of the more responsible, though he did not marry Mui or send for her to join him in the United States. (Nor is it clear from the sources whether Mui succeeded in reaching the United States and claiming the money.)

Wartime mistresses of any conquest face terrible problems. The most obvious is that their country has been invaded, and they are condemned for consorting with the enemy or, in the case of Vietnam, with alien allies. But in destroying economies and warping civil society, war pushes civilians to desperate, sometimes unconscionable, measures.

The fictitious Miss Saigon, a modernized version of Madama Butterfly, is not very different from Le Ly and Mui. She is an innocent country girl named Kim, engaged to be married. In 1975, she arrives in Saigon and meets a modernized version of Pinkerton. He is Chris, a GI disillusioned with the frenetic and cynical eroticism of the city. Their lovemaking ignites powerful emotions in them both. Before the conclusion of their Vietnamese marriage ceremony, Kim's bitter ex-fiancé intervenes and chases them away. When Saigon falls soon after, Kim and Chris are separated and do not see each other again.

By 1978, Chris is back in the United States. He is married to Ellen, but haunted by memories of Kim. She, meanwhile, has given birth to his son, Tam. She supports the child by working as a bar girl in the raucous clubs Chris so disliked when he lived in Saigon. She also dreams of Chris, hoping that one day he will come back and rescue her.

Chris's friend John begins a campaign to reunite Amerasian children with their American fathers. Chris and Ellen join him in Saigon, where Ellen learns about Kim, and Kim learns about Ellen. The reunion torments them all, because Chris realizes he loves both women. Kim evaluates the situation and decides that Tam would be much happier in the United States with his father. Like Madama Butterfly, she commits suicide.

Miss Saigon's fate is more clear-cut than Le Ly's or Mui's, but only because her creator avoided messy plotlines and tedious details, and opted for dramatic climax and resolution. Otherwise she, too, might have limped along and ended up tattered, gray and worn, like Le Ly, Mui and countless other women who are Miss Saigon's less glamorous, real-life versions.

CHAPTER 7

Interracial Sexual Unions Within the "Peculiar Institution"

B LACK African slavery in the Americas was an institution so "peculiar" that even today it casts a dark shadow.[1] From its origins in the 16th century until its abolition in the 19th century, black slavery was governed by tradition and local custom, politics and economic realities, and comprehensive state laws known as "Black Codes." Black Codes regulated slaves (and free and freed blacks) and were constantly revised and refined in response to new situations and issues. For example, the Black Codes outlawed interracial sex, with its "horrific" byproduct of mixed-blood children. When legislation failed to eradicate it, the Black Codes were modified to penalize the offenders and, more particularly and grimly, their offspring. Ultimately, the Black Codes decreed the consequences whenever sexual intercourse crossed racial lines.

New World slavery was based on pseudo-scientific and pseudo-religious notions of race and justified its harshness on the grounds that God had entitled the white race to hold dominion over the black race. Blacks were considered to be childlike in outlook, animalistic in erotic expression and amoral in behavior. The Bible even spelled it out: black Africans, the sons of Ham, shall serve.

In this context, slaves were systematically denied rights, even the right to life itself. This was not just because enraged owners or overseers might torture or lash them to death. In the 18th and 19th centuries, entire plantations in the French and British West Indies, and to a lesser extent in the United States, operated on the principle that the most efficient and productive use of slave labor was to provide slaves with minimal food, shelter and clothing, and to drive them mercilessly to toil in the cane, rice or cotton fields. These exhausted and brutalized men and women died on average seven years after their arrival because it was, on balance, cheaper to replace them with new slaves imported from Africa than to keep them alive longer by providing more tolerable conditions. Harriet Beecher Stowe exposed this school of thought in her novel *Uncle Tom's Cabin*; its vicious antihero, Simon Legree, systematically ill-treated the slaves who toiled under the broiling sun in his Louisiana cotton fields.

Less brutal models of slavery were more common. But nothing guaranteed that a kind master might not resolve an economic reverse by selling off his slaves to the cruelest sort of master. Even the most industrious slave might suddenly find himself "on the auction block, knocked down to the highest bidder, and carried far and forever from those dearer than life, leaving behind a beloved wife and tender and helpless children," a former slave lamented.[2]

This insecurity was fundamental to the form of slavery that targeted a specific race. Even the free or freed black and mixed-race population was subject to Black Code regulations that curtailed its rights and freedoms.

Interracial sexual liaisons were a key area of concern because each relationship posed a potential threat to the status quo. The obvious scenario was white men's targeting of attractive slave women, though some white women also coerced slave men into sexual interludes. The single most dangerous factor in these unions was love. Love could inspire seditious thoughts (and deeds) about the subordinate role of blacks. This happened whenever a white man fell in love with his black mistress and began to treat her as an equal human being, or when he acknowledged his mixed-race children. When loving individuals legitimized what society decreed to be illicit, they shook the very foundations of their slave-owning societies.

Yet as we know from a variety of sources, including many eyewitness accounts, these unlawful intimacies were pervasive. The oft-quoted Mary Boykin Chestnut, the wife of a Charleston, South Carolina, plantation owner, confided this wry observation to her journal:

> [*March 14, 1861*] God forgive us, but ours is a monstrous system, a wrong and an iniquity! Like the patriarchs of old, our men live all in one house with their wives and their concubines; and the mulattos one sees in every family partly resemble the white children. Any lady is ready to

tell you who is the father of all the mulatto children in everybody's household but her own. Those, she seems to think, drop from the clouds. My disgust sometimes is boiling over.[3]

Chestnut's wry comments hint at the sweeping impact this licentiousness must have had: on the slave woman coerced into sexual intercourse with a white man; on the wife of the man who betrayed her with a black woman who was supposed to serve and respect her; on the mixed-race children born of these unions; on the white family members who observed and understood their patriarch's behavior. Consider also the effect of this on the slave husband, brother and father powerless to prevent assaults on a wife, sister or daughter, and equally powerless to prevent her seduction by fear, by ambition and even by pride that the master had singled her out. Privileges such as reduced labor and gifts of money, jewelry or clothes were otherwise unobtainable for a slave. And what about the slave woman who unexpectedly found her heart engaged in this forbidden relationship? Or the master who fell hopelessly in love with the woman he owned or supervised?

To understand the world of slave mistresses, we need to bear in mind slavery-era notions of erotic appeal. White women were elevated onto the proverbial pedestal as chaste and pure beings untouched by erotic longings. White men, on the other hand, were thought to have naturally lusty natures; their drive to satisfy themselves sexually with women other than their virtuous sweethearts and wives was accepted if unacknowledged. Inevitably, this led these men to sexually exploit black women, reputed to be lusty and uninhibited beings who had extraordinary powers of sexuality, and who were legally, socially, physically and economically vulnerable.

Phibbah [4]

The story of Phibbah, enslaved at "Egypt," an 18th-century Jamaican plantation owned by John and Mary Cope, is told entirely by her white lover, Thomas Thistlewood, an overseer who kept remarkably detailed journals. Thistlewood's daily jottings focused on his work on the plantation—indeed, his records are a treasure trove for agricultural historians. He also described, concisely but tellingly, Jamaica's slave rites, celebrations, harsh punishments for slave infractions and—in clipped comments and reflections—the rocky course of his affairs of the heart and the bed.

Thistlewood's journals detail his many sexual encounters with slave women, with Latin abbreviations: *Tup* ("twice"); *Sup. Lect.* ("on the bed"); *Sup. Terr.* ("on the ground"); *In silva* ("in the woods"); *In Mag.* or *In Parv.* ("in the great or small house"); *Illa habet menses* ("she has her period"); and sometimes, notably when his gonorrhea was in an active phase, *Sed non bene* ("but not well").

In 1751, when the thirty-year-old Thistlewood arrived at the Egypt plantation, the Creole-Jamaican slave Phibbah held the important job of managing the cookhouse. It was not love at first sight. Thistlewood was strongly attracted to another slave, Nago Jenny, and brought her to live with him in his quarters for several months. Only when their relationship ended did he take up with the high-spirited, intelligent and ambitious Phibbah.

The relationship was deeply erotic and volatile. They had sex several times a week, including when Phibbah was menstruating. They quarreled, often because Phibbah was jealous about Thomas's infidelities with other slave women. January 4, 1755, was a typical day. After they made love, Phibbah refused to join Thomas in bed and slept instead in a hammock suspended in his hallway. She was "rather too saucy," he noted. Their quarrels were frequent. Phibbah spent days not speaking to Thistlewood, denied him sex, and sometimes stormed off at night to sleep alone in her cabin. Predictably, Thomas followed and fetched her back to his room.

In June 1757, Thomas accepted what was in effect a promotion: a new job at Kendal, another Jamaican estate, whose owner paid one hundred pounds annually plus generous quantities of beef, butter, rum, candles and other supplies. Phibbah took the news hard. "Phibbah grieves very much, and last night I could not sleep, but vastly uneasy, &c.," Thistlewood wrote on June 19.

The lovers continued to suffer at the thought of their impending separation. Thomas attempted to assuage Phibbah's grief with gifts of money, lengths of cloth, mosquito netting and soap. He went to John and Mary Cope, who owned both Egypt and Phibbah, and "begged hard" to either buy or hire his mistress. John Cope was agreeable, but Mary Cope refused. Perhaps she dreaded losing such a capable manager and cook, or she may have disapproved of Phibbah's relationship with the white overseer, which reflected her own husband's affairs with several different slave women under their ownership. Mary's intransigence devastated the lovers. They made love for the last time, and Phibbah gave Thomas a gold ring, provenance unknown, as a keepsake. He said his goodbyes and left for Kendal.

Phibbah, alone at Egypt, was terrified that Thomas would replace her with another woman. Her fears were well grounded. One week after his arrival, Thistlewood relieved his mighty loneliness with Phoebe, the slave cook on the Kendal estate. Knowing nothing of this, Phibbah rode over to Kendal the next day to plead with Thomas to come back to Egypt.

It was not as simple as deciding to return. Thomas had accepted a new job and had contractual obligations. But he was delighted to see his mistress. He escorted her all around the estate and introduced her to the inmates of the "Negro houses." They rose before dawn the next day, and he lent Phibbah his horse so she could make a speedy trip back to Egypt. "I wish they would sell her to me," he complained. "Tonight very lonely and melancholy again . . . and Phibbah's being gone this morning still fresh in my mind."[5]

Phibbah made sure she stayed that way. She sent him a stream of gifts (turtles, crabs) and visited him whenever she could. News that she was ill upset Thistlewood deeply. "Poor girl, I pity her, she is in miserable slavery," he lamented. Their joyous reunions, replete with gift-giving, gossiping and squabbling, continued. Sometimes Thistlewood would send Lincoln, his own teenaged slave, to Egypt with his horse so Phibbah could ride over to Kendal. At other times, he made the journey to Egypt.

Despite his strong affection for Phibbah, Thomas regularly cheated on her with other women, including Aurelia, the loveliest of the Kendal slaves. Phibbah knew and suffered. She implored him to desist and underscored her frustration and pain by withholding sex. In the end, she always relented and forgave him.

When they were apart, Phibbah worked assiduously to maintain their relationship. Her frustration at her inability to leave Egypt and join Thomas at Kendal resonates through his concise reports of what she said to him and how she acted. But was this true love or merely an astute woman's recognition of the many advantages of her status as Thistlewood's mistress? It's impossible to know for sure, but all indications are that Phibbah loved Thomas as deeply as he loved her. Their erotic encounters were frequent and intense. They also shared the homiest details of their lives, even his infidelities, which he either mentioned or admitted to when Phibbah confronted him with well-founded accusations.

Over time, Phibbah evoked in her overseer-lover an anomalous compassion for her servitude, her miserable slavery. Until he met Phibbah, Thistlewood was known for occasional cruelties to the slaves he supervised. His intimacy with Phibbah, however, awakened his sensitivity to the wretchedness of slavery, and he conducted himself more humanely after their relationship began. As Phibbah's feelings became more and more important to him, he began to shape his union with her so she, too, was satisfied.

Phibbah, for her part, used the power of her love and Thomas's desire for her to force him to treat her more respectfully, though he never stopped summoning other slave women to his bed. In the context of 18th-century Jamaican slavery, Phibbah's self-assurance and confidence in Thomas's commitment to her were unusual. Though slavery and gender made their union hopelessly lopsided, Phibbah's forceful character and willingness to demand certain standards of conduct added weight to her position. So did Thistlewood's open acknowledgment that she was his mistress, though Mary Cope and some of the slaves resented her bitterly for this.

At the end of 1757, Cope lured Thistlewood back to work for him, and Thomas was reunited with Phibbah. By this time, Thistlewood was earning more money and had bought several of his own slaves. Phibbah, too, "owned" a slave, in fact if not in law, after a friend, Mrs. Bennett, gave her a woman called Bess.

When Thomas had financial problems, Phibbah willingly helped out. During her pregnancy with Thomas's child, she sold a filly to another slave and gave some of the money to Thistlewood. He accepted it gratefully, and eight months later repaid her. (Thistlewood's 1761 accounts show him indebted to Phibbah for ten pounds, a relatively large sum.) Phibbah's generosity may have been calculated, but it is more likely that she genuinely wanted to help out the man who now referred to her, at least in his journal, as his wife.

On April 28, 1760, Phibbah went into labor. Old Daphne, a midwife, came to assist, and the next day Phibbah gave birth to a son. She recovered slowly. Another slave was sent to care for her, Lucy from the Egypt estate wet-nursed the baby and Mary Cope sent cheering gifts of flour, wine and cinnamon. The infant was named John, later "Mulatto John," though at first Thistlewood referred to him as "Phibbah's child."

After a while, Thistlewood again left the Copes' employ to work on Breadnut Island Pen, a nearby plantation. On the whole, the Copes remained valued friends for Thistlewood, and when Mulatto John was still a toddler, they manumitted him. (Manumission was the formal legal process of emancipating a slave.) Now, when Thistlewood moved away to Breadnut Island Pen, it was like Kendal all over, with constant visiting back and forth.

By 1767, Phibbah was spending almost every night with Thomas, rising early to return home. On November 10, John Cope finally "condescended," in Thistlewood's words, to hire Phibbah out to him for the annual fee of eighteen pounds. Six days later she arrived at Breadnut Island Pen with Mulatto John and her many belongings.

By 1770, Thistlewood had become a respected horticulturist and a member of Jamaica's plantation-owning class. Despite his relatively modest holdings of land and slaves—at his death, his estate listed a mere nineteen slaves—his passion for books and his wide-ranging knowledge gave him personal credibility, and his friendship with the Copes eased his entrance into society. His slave mistress, however, was unwelcome at private dinners and parties. Thistlewood compensated for this by taking her with him to public events, the horse races, for instance.

Life was pleasant for Thomas and Phibbah, though less than perfect. They worried about the specter of slave uprisings. Thomas was anxious, as well, about Mulatto John, an unambitious boy who had not inherited the paternal obsession for reading and who told more than the occasional fib. Thistlewood blamed John's sluggish progress on Phibbah, who spoiled and coddled him. And all of them were prone to illness, with gonorrhea still plaguing Thomas and sometimes rendering him impotent. ("Impots" he noted after one failed interlude.)

In 1786, when he was sixty-six years old, Thistlewood dictated his last will and testament. Five days later, he died. His will speaks volumes about his commitment to and love for Phibbah. He directed that his estate purchase Phibbah from John Cope for a sum not greater than eighty pounds Jamaican, and manumit her. If her manumission was granted, she was to be given two slaves. (As a slave, she could not technically own slaves.) Lastly, he left her one hundred pounds to buy a plot of land of her choosing and to build a house.

Thistlewood also provided for the worst-case scenario—that Phibbah remained a slave. In that case, she would receive fifteen pounds annually for her lifetime. It took five years to validate Thistlewood's will. Then the Copes manumitted Phibbah.

So ends the historical record, though not Phibbah's life. However inadvertently, Thomas Thistlewood was Phibbah's biographer. To flesh out the bones of her life, we have no alternative but to read along and between Thomas's brief lines, extrapolating and conjecturing as soundly as possible. The most sensible interpretation of Phibbah and Thomas is that, with the passage of time, she made a slow transition—at least in his mind—from mistress to wife. Though he was chronically unfaithful, he cherished her company and valued her opinions. He discussed his job with her, his labor problems, the state of the crops and the condition of the farm animals. Phibbah reciprocated with news about the state of affairs at Egypt after he had left the estate. When Phibbah was ill, Thomas monitored her symptoms as closely as if they were his own, a reflection of their unfettered intimacy. Phibbah had confidence in their relationship, set reasonable standards of behavior and offered her assistance when she thought it was required.

Phibbah lost out only on the issue of sexual fidelity, and she had to endure Thomas's unbreakable habit of straying with any slave woman he found attractive, even Phibbah's colleagues or subordinates. But the journals make it clear that she spent her lifetime challenging his promiscuity.

Thistlewood never married. The dearth of white women in Jamaica may have been one reason. A reluctance to give up his intimacy with Phibbah, something a white wife would certainly have demanded, may have been another. But it is tempting to hypothesize that he had no need to marry, because in Phibbah he had everything he could want in a woman, including a mother for his children.

The longevity and intensity of Phibbah's mistressdom, her manumission after her lover's death and Thomas's painstaking care to provide for her until the end of her days paint the picture of a complex and committed relationship. But romantic and sexual unions between a slave woman and a white man were never the stuff of romance. Though they circumvented many of slavery's constraints, Thomas Thistlewood and Phibbah were no Romeo and Juliet. They existed in a cruel and confusing world where interracial sex was illegal, where she was legally subhuman and without rights and he was a superior being entitled—indeed, expected—to buy, sell, exploit and punish men and women who shared her status and her origin. Quite apart from her gender, Phibbah was a slave.

Julia Chinn

In the slave-holding American states, the infamous Black Codes reinforced social standards that condemned interracial sex. Despite the laws, discreet liaisons were usually tolerated. But if a man flaunted his black mistress or acknowledged the children he had sired with her, he paid the price of social opprobrium, if not actual disgrace. If he died leaving a will that manumitted her or named her and any children they had together as beneficiaries of goods, property and money, the likelihood was that his relatives would successfully contest the will. Time and again slaveowning-state courts disallowed manumissions granted in wills and denied the rightful legatees their inheritances.

These strictures against all aspects of overt relationships between white men and their black mistresses were especially true of politicians, whose personal lives were supposed to reflect strong morals and refined values.

Kentuckian statesman Richard M. Johnson (1780–1850) was one such rebel. Johnson was a flamboyant, florid-faced man who favored red vests. In the War of 1812, he fought boldly, rose to the rank of colonel and became known as the slayer of Tecumseh, the native chief. After the war, while continuing to oversee his Kentucky plantation, Johnson entered the civil service in Washington, where he was respected as a capable administrator. At the same time, he rose steadily through the ranks of the Democratic Party.

Many Democrats supported Johnson as a candidate for public office until scandalous details of his personal life became public and what was previously dismissed as "monstrous rumor" was confirmed as fact.[6] Johnson, his horrified colleagues discovered, had never married, but lived in cozy domesticity with Julia Chinn, a free woman of color he introduced as his housekeeper. Julia was his bosom companion, took her meals with him and bore him two daughters. Johnson acknowledged Imogene and Adeline as his children and educated them at good schools. When they were older, he arranged for them to marry reputable white men.

As if this were not shocking enough, Johnson had the gall to lead his two daughters up to the platform with him at a Fourth of July event. His fellow citizens refused to associate with these "quadroon bastards." Johnson was unmoved and angrily declared that if Kentucky law permitted it, he would have married Julia. The news of this admission spread quickly, after which respectable southern Democrats who insisted on high standards of conduct turned against him.

In April 1831, the *Washington Spectator* lamented the possibility that, aided by northern supporters, Johnson would succeed in his campaign for the vice-presidency of the United States: "The colored will have an Esther at the foot of the throne . . . who may not only dictate modes and fashions to the female community, but may deliver her people from civil disabilities, and produce an amalgamation . . . [causing] an African jubilee throughout the country."[7]

The southern, or Dixie, Democrats bitterly opposed Johnson's candidacy, which succeeded only because of strong support from the west. A Kentucky journalist reflected that it was not Johnson's cohabitation with Julia Chinn that created such a furor, but rather his "scorn of secrecy" about it. If only he would pass her off as his servant and deny paternity of her children—as countless other men did—then nobody would think twice about voting for him, certainly not his fellow Southerners.

But Johnson was stubborn and principled. In 1832, he legally conveyed large properties to Imogene and Adeline and their white husbands. The year after this propitious move, Julia contracted cholera and died. Even then, Johnson refused to recant, and to his opponents, he still represented the dangerous principle of amalgamation or mongrelization of the white race. In 1835, after he won the Democratic nomination for vice-president, the Virginian delegates stormed out of the convention in protest.

The little we know about Julia Chinn comes from accounts about sustained political opposition to the fact that Johnson refused to deny that she was his mistress and the mother of his daughters. Julia died before Johnson could test Washington as he had Kentucky. He had already anticipated and tried to mitigate the problems Imogene and Adeline would face after his own death left them vulnerable to merciless courts and disapproving relatives. He knew that what his slave-owning society despised was the transparency of his relationship with Julia and his daughters, which he conducted openly, without the subterfuge that characterized other such unions.

Sally Hemings [8]

Johnson was the first major politician to defy social, legal and racial convention in this way, but only one in a long line of statesmen bound up in intense love affairs with black women. A combination of Jefferson-era gossip, testimony from ex-slaves, family lore and DNA testing has raised the possibility that President Thomas Jefferson was also involved in a long-term affair with a female slave, the now famous Sally Hemings. Hemings is the heroine of the movie *Jefferson in Paris*, and the subject of television documentaries, books, articles and explosive debate, including mean-spirited denials that a beloved president could have dishonored his wife's memory and debased himself by loving this quadroon and siring baby after baby with her. Meanwhile, Sally's descendants, nurtured on family memories, have had their claims partially vindicated by the results of DNA testing, which indicates that at least one of Sally's children, her son Eston, was sired by Jefferson or one of his relatives.

Sally Hemings's mother was Betty Hemings, the mixed-race daughter of an Englishman, Captain Hemings, and a black slave, Betty, the property of wealthy slave owner John Wayles. Wayles took Betty Hemings into his household as a servant. After his wife died, Betty became his mistress and bore six of his children. One of them was Sally, born *circa* 1773. When Wayles died in 1774, his legitimate daughter, Martha Wayles, then married to Thomas Jefferson, inherited his one hundred and thirty-five slaves, including her half sister Sally Hemings.

When her slaves arrived at Monticello, Jefferson's estate, Martha took baby Sally and her other half sisters into the house to train them as domestics. In 1782, after a lengthy and debilitating illness, Martha died. Nine-year-old Sally and her mother were in the room as Martha expressed the tearful wish that her children should never be subjected to a stepmother. "Holding her hand in his," recalled Madison Hemings, Sally's son, "Mr. Jefferson promised her solemnly that he would never marry again. And he never did."[9]

But after a period of terrible mourning, during which he paced incessantly or went on long, melancholy rambles on his horse, Jefferson did fall in love, again and again, with hopelessly unavailable women. These included Betsey Walker, his friend and neighbor's wife, and Maria Cosway, the wife of English painter Richard Cosway.

Meanwhile, Sally Hemings was growing up. By 1787, she was a very light-skinned girl with straight, waist-length hair, and so lovely that the Monticello people called her "Dashing Sally." She was also, according to a contemporary account, sweet-tempered and physically mature.

Sally's arrival in Paris in the summer of 1787 has seduced the popular imagination, as perhaps it did Jefferson himself. This lonely man, sworn to eternal wifelessness and new to France, where the American government had posted him to negotiate commercial treaties and, in 1785, to be its ambassador, spent secret hours penning passionate letters to Maria Cosway. Suddenly, more or less coinciding with the arrival of his daughter Polly and her companion, Sally, he stopped.

Jefferson cared well for Sally. He provided her with extensive tutoring in French, a costly smallpox inoculation and heaps of new dresses. Jefferson may have been indulging Sally because he was falling in love with her, or because he wanted to forestall her joining her brother James, Jefferson's chef, whom he had brought with him to Europe, in demanding her freedom. Sally, who became pregnant in France, did indeed use her status as a free woman in that country to extract a promise from Jefferson to free her children when they reached the age of twenty-one.

Sally's infant son, Tom, was light skinned, and after Jefferson returned to America in 1789, he worried that his political enemies would claim that he had fathered the boy. Jefferson had reason for concern. His cabinet colleague and rival, Alexander Hamilton, was under sustained public attack for his affair with Maria Reynolds, a married woman. A long-term liaison with a female slave, on his own premises, would—and later did—provide ammunition to Jefferson's opponents.

For reasons that remain unclear, from January 1794 to February 1797, Jefferson retired to Monticello. He withdrew from politics, stopped reading newspapers and focused exclusively on his family, his farm and his slaves. These included Sally, who by that time had several more children. But unlike Thomas Thistlewood, who chronicled the minute details of his union with Phibbah, Jefferson documented nothing about a relationship with Sally. The slave lists and the food and supply distribution lists indicate no special favor accorded to her or her children. Jefferson's lifestyle, however, hints at a secret affair. Sally alone was responsible for his bedroom/study, and he permitted nobody else, including his grandchildren, to enter this *sanctum sanctorum*. Another telling fact is that, according to his *Farm Book*, Jefferson was always present nine months before all seven of her (very light-skinned) children's births, and she never conceived when he was absent.

Jefferson's neighbors repeated gossip about Sally's being his mistress. In the spring of 1801, Jefferson's adversary, journalist James Thomson Callender, set about snooping. He discovered that on April 26, Sally delivered a fair-skinned daughter, Harriet, named after a little girl who had died four years earlier. The despicable Callender turned to blackmail. Jefferson responded by giving him fifty dollars, but when he failed to deliver the post office job Callender was angling for, Callender trumpeted the news about Sally in the *Richmond Recorder*: "It is well known that [Jefferson] . . . keeps and for many years has kept, as his concubine, one of his slaves. Her name is SALLY. . . . By this wench Sally, our president has had several children."[10]

Pro-Jefferson journalists countered that Sally's brood had been fathered by another white man. "Is it strange . . . that a servant of Mr. Jefferson's at a house where so many strangers resort, who is daily engaged in the ordinary vocations of the family, like thousands of others, should have a mulatto child? Certainly not."[11] From Jefferson himself—public silence but private denial. There is "not a truth existing which I fear or would wish unknown to the whole world," Jefferson wrote to politician Henry Lee on May 15, 1826, and he repeated this to other friends.[12] However, in the absence of a public disavowal from Jefferson, Callender gloated that "Jefferson before the eyes of his two daughters sent to his kitchen, or perhaps to his pigsty, for this Mahogany coloured charmer, the black wench and her mulatto litter."[13]

A ditty sung to the tune of "Yankee Doodle Dandy" became popular in the anti-Jefferson camp:

> Of all the damsels on the green,
> On mountain, or in valley,
> A lass so luscious ne'er was seen,
> As Monticellian Sally.

> Yankee doodle, who's the noodle?
> What wife were half so handy?
> To breed a flock of slaves for stock,
> A Blackamoor's the dandy.[14]

A vicious ballad called Sally the "false Ethiop." In it she has her throat cut from ear to ear, and her tongue hacked off. Then she is carted off to Hell's blazing inferno. A gentler poem called Sally a "black Aspasia."[15] Another anti-Jefferson editor revealed that Sally had her own room, high status and close personal relations with Jefferson. This was cited as evidence that she was his mistress, though it could also have been a reflection of her status as the half sister of Jefferson's deceased wife, Martha. Either of these hypotheses could explain as well why, at home, Sally's children were privileged slaves, headquartered in the great house, his white family's quarters.

The fact is, somebody fathered each of Sally's children. If it was Jefferson, he did not see fit to provide them with more than a practical education. As teenagers, they were taught a trade. At twenty-one, those light-skinned enough to pass for white disappeared into the free world, not as fugitive or freed slaves, but as white. Jefferson never attempted to find them or, when their whereabouts became known, to reclaim them.

Sally's son Beverly walked away from Monticello, crossed over, so to speak, to the white race and married a white woman. Jefferson paid Harriet's passage to Philadelphia, and she never returned. Her brother Madison (named by Dolly Madison, then visiting Monticello) recalled in his memoirs that Harriet, too, passed as white and married a white man. Louise Mathilda Coolidge, a Jefferson family friend, confirmed that four of Sally's children simply left Monticello and never returned. Madison and another son, Eston, the latter recently identified as a member of the Jefferson family's bloodline, opted for their black heritage. They married black women and settled down in the same black community.

Toward the end of his life, Jefferson specified in his will that five slaves, Sally's sons Madison and Eston and three of her relatives, would be freed at the age of twenty-one. He did not free Sally, or provide for her in his will. If this oversight was motivated by a desire to avoid giving his critics proof that their accusations about his relationship with her were well founded, then he sacrificed Sally to preserve his own reputation. In any case, two years after his death on July 4, 1826, his white daughter Martha freed Sally.[16]

Sally survived for another decade, living in a rented house with Madison and Eston. At her death, they buried her in an African-American cemetery. Her story emerges from biographies of her towering master. But much additional (albeit circumstantial) information may be found in the journals and letters of contemporary journalists, politicians, observers, friends, family and ex-slaves, notably son Madison and the unrelated Israel Jefferson, another Monticello slave. Sally herself left no diaries or letters, only anecdotes preserved in her son's memoirs.

To date, it is impossible to state with absolute certainty that Sally Hemings was Thomas Jefferson's mistress, although Eston's bloodline supports that claim. What is clear, however, is that the viciousness of the charges made by Jefferson's contemporaries underscores the contempt and fear that relationships between slave owners and slave mistresses engendered. If the American president loved an enslaved black woman, he was tacitly denying his society's assumptions about the innate inferiority of black people, assumptions that justified the very existence of the institution of slavery.

Julia Frances Lewis Dickson [17]

Julia Frances Lewis Dickson was a slave mistress whose master-lover's adoration of their mixed-race daughter, Amanda America Dickson, enshrined both mother and child in historical record and lore. So did Julia's own testimony in a nasty court case in which seventy-nine of her deceased master's relatives contested Amanda's enormous inheritance.

Julia was born July 4, 1836, daughter of a slave woman and Joe Lewis, a dark-skinned man of Spanish descent who was, Julia told her grandchildren, "considered white." In February 1849, Julia was a petite twelve-year-old with copper-colored skin, soft wavy hair and lovely teeth. She was owned by Elizabeth Dickson, mother of David Dickson, the richest citizen in Hancock

County, Georgia. Julia was Elizabeth's great pet. She worked as a servant in the main house and had her own room in a little house at the edge of the Dicksons' yard. (Less-favored slaves lived in a large, two-storied dwelling known as the "nigger house.")

The white Dicksons—the widowed Elizabeth Dickson, aged seventy-two, and three of her unmarried children, David, Rutha and Green—all lived together. David, a doting son, had single-handedly built up the family fortune. By 1849, he owned 2,010 acres of land and fifty-three slaves. David had little formal education, but compensated with great curiosity and powers of observation. His peers knew him as a knowledgeable but opinionated man whose word was law and who tolerated no debate.

At noon on a February day, David cantered across a field where Julia was playing. He came, saw and conquered, scooping the little girl up onto his saddle and carrying her off and raping her. (Years later, he admitted that he had "slipped" when he raped her.) He made Julia pregnant, and late in the fall, she delivered the infant to whom David and Elizabeth gave the dramatic name of Amanda America Dickson.

From the beginning, David was obsessed with his fair-skinned daughter. As soon as Julia had weaned her, he took the baby away, and he and his mother raised her as their own. Amanda became Miss Mandy, even to Julia, and spent most of her time in the bedroom she shared with her grandmother. At night, she slept in a specially made trundle bed that, during the day, was pushed under Elizabeth's big one. David lavished affection and luxury on Amanda. He had her bathed in cow's milk, then believed to be a skin lightener. He engaged a tutor to teach her to read and write, something his own sisters had never learned. Amanda read works of literature, had piano lessons and was pampered, protected and privileged.

Nonetheless—the ultimate irony—she remained a slave. Georgia's Black Code prohibited freed slaves from remaining in the state. The only way Elizabeth Dickson and her son could keep their beloved Amanda near them was by foregoing her manumission.

Meanwhile, as she swept the Dicksons' floors, mended their clothes and served them at table, Julia saw her daughter daily. She had to kowtow to her own child and watch her transmogrified into a nearly white, refined and prettily accomplished daddy's girl. According to her descendants, who preserve Julia's reminiscences in their family's oral history, Julia never forgave David for raping her and exacted her revenge by ruling him "with an iron hand."[18]

Julia's "iron hand" (though not her fundamental resentment) may have been more wishful thinking than fact. Evidence from a variety of sources indicates that Julia and David developed a reciprocal affection that ensured her a dominant role in the Dickson household. She had been shunted away from Amanda, but in many other ways David treated her like the wife he never had. He thought nothing of kissing her in front of the other slaves or lifting her down from her horse. Often he and Julia sat together by the fireplace or in his bedroom, discussing domestic concerns and the agricultural ideas and plans that were to make him famous.

As Elizabeth's health declined, the still young Julia and Lucy, another slave, assumed many of her duties, including guarding the keys to the storerooms where sugar, whiskey, meat, clothing and medicine were locked away, and overseeing the all-important kitchen. David also delegated to Julia various financial transactions with tenants and merchants. The picture that emerges is of a strong-minded woman who cooperated in building and operating the Dickson empire, who respected and felt some affection for the man who had fathered Amanda and who carved out her own authoritative role in his life and world.

After her abrupt initiation into sex and motherhood, Julia's growing emotional intimacy with David probably included a sexual relationship. But she was by no means a faithful slave mistress. She openly consorted with Joe Brooken, another Dickson slave, and in 1853, gave birth to Juliana, Brooken's daughter. Thirteen months later, she slept with "Doc" Eubanks, a white acquaintance of the Dicksons. David must have accepted these unions, because he neither reproached nor punished Julia for them, and even granted her more power in his household.

As Julia matured, worked hard and well, and conducted her liaisons with David, Joe and "Doc," David was becoming wealthy and famous for his agricultural innovations. By 1860, he personally owned 150 slaves. Agricultural journals published his radical theories about conserving land through intensive fertilization, crop rotation, shallow planting and varied planting, strategies he claimed would lead to self-sufficiency. Slaves, he believed, should be taught more efficient ways of working, which would simultaneously increase both their pride and their production. "I have in five minutes, learned a hand to pick one hundred pounds more of cotton per day than he has picked on the previous day, and from that point he will continue to improve," David wrote.[19]

David did not always practice what he preached, according to postbellum testimony from some slave "hands." Eula Youngblood, Julia's granddaughter-in-law, recalled that David implemented discipline through slave drivers who had liberal recourse to a whipping post. "When I think of those times I smile to keep from crying," Eula said.[20]

When it came to Amanda, however, David gladly challenged his entire society by sharing his life with his non-white daughter. When guests asked if they were obliged to dine with her, David would roar, "By God, yes, if you eat here!"[21]

To at least one acquaintance, he acknowledged the obvious—that Amanda was his daughter. Another visitor, Dr. E. W. Alfriend, testified in a later court case that because of Amanda's resemblance to David, he had pressed Julia about Amanda's parentage. Reluctantly, Julia told him that Amanda was her daughter. "I told her I supposed it was, but asked if she didn't have any assistance in getting it," Dr. Alfriend recalled. Julia hesitated, and finally admitted "that it was 'Massa David's.'"[22]

In some ways, slavery simplified the dynamics of Julia and David's relationship: no matter how forceful her personality (in any case, his was more forceful), no matter how strong his affection for her, and no matter how ambiguous and conflicted her feelings for him, David was the boss, the owner, the absolute authority. And though Julia grieved when Amanda was taken from her, she strongly approved of how David and Elizabeth raised her child.

Yet what little information we have about Julia's life is confusing and contradictory, and this may well be an accurate reflection of Julia herself. For example, though she was described by everyone who knew her as a black slave, she told her grandchildren that she was Portuguese (by which she surely referred to her father, whom she also described as "Spanish") and had no black blood in her at all.

No record exists of what Julia felt in the period preceding the Civil War, when the possibility that the South would secede became more likely, and the murmurs of agitation among slaves grew louder. She must have been torn between resenting her servitude and her awareness that her security and her daughter's prosperity depended on David Dickson's wealth, which was built on the backs of slaves.

David felt no such conflict of interests. During the Civil War, he supported the Confederates through "almost sacrificial" contributions of cotton, bacon, grain and enormous sums of money. As a consequence, the Dickson family's wealth diminished daily. In 1863, Yankee general William T. Sherman arrived and occupied Hancock County. Though he spared David's house, allegedly because of old Elizabeth Dickson's presence, Sherman's troops carted off hundreds of bales of cotton, stored crops, fifty-five mules and agricultural machinery. David's plantation was ruined, though Julia managed to save the Dickson silver, burying it before the soldiers could steal it.

On August 20, 1865, the Civil War ended. The Dickson slaves, including Julia, were slaves no longer, but Julia chose to stay with the Dicksons. Her desire to stay with Amanda, who would never leave her beloved father, was probably paramount. So, too, must have been her sense that life as a slave had not been bad and might now be better and that, in any case, it was unlikely that she could ever, anywhere, find a job as responsible, prestigious (in its own way) and remunerative (also in its own way) as she had as David's house-keeper. By the time Elizabeth Dickson died on August 6, 1864, Julia had truly become the chatelaine of the ravaged Dickson plantation.

At the age of twenty-nine, Julia was also about to become a grandmother, because Amanda was pregnant by her first cousin, Charles H. Eubanks, David's white nephew. Because of Georgia's strict laws against miscegenation, Amanda and Charles could not marry, but they moved in together on a nearby plantation David may have helped them buy. They named their son Julian, surely after Julia, his grandmother.

David, resolute and resourceful despite his ruin, began to build a second fortune. He applied for pardon from the US government, a necessary formal-ity to recoup his estate, and declared—as he had to—that "slavery is forever gone."[23] At home, he openly regretted this fact because, like all former slave owners, he now faced a devastating labor shortage as black men sought better jobs, black women became their own homemakers and black children gained the right to childhood. Despite these setbacks, he persevered and prospered, manufacturing plows and fabricating "the Dickson Compound," a fertilizer he sold at considerable profit.

Julia's life took another major turn. Soon after Amanda gave birth to her second son, Charles, she suddenly returned home, saying, "I want to live with you, 'Papie.'"[24] David acquiesced, and built a large house for her, Julia and the children, three hundred yards from his own more modest dwelling. He ensured that they were its legal owners through a deed of sale that gave a seven-eighths share to Amanda, the remaining one-eighth to Julia. For the first time since Amanda's infancy, Julia was permitted to live with her elder daughter, while her younger daughter, Juliana, and her family had lodgings close by.

David had another surprise in store, and it must have confounded Julia. At sixty-two, David suddenly got married. His bride, Clara Harris, was only three years older than Amanda. The marriage was unhappy from the beginning, as the accomplished and wealthy Southern belle found herself living in the lesser of two simple homes in a plantation compound, with the finer home housing her new husband's black mistress, daughter and two grandsons, whom he loved to distraction. Clara's brother, Henry Harris, later testified that David had been generous with his sister. He had provided a lovely coach and two fine black horses, and abundant spending money. He had also hired an architect to design a thirty-thousand-dollar mansion, but after sizing up the dynamics of David's rural plantation, Clara was not interested in building anything there, Henry Harris said.

Clara was never happy, but not because David was unkind, Harris continued. Clara and her new husband were simply incompatible, and as a city girl accustomed to a lively social life, she was wretched. In addition, her health was poor. Henry did not add that David's unabashed affection for Julia, Amanda, Julian and Charles was intolerable to Clara and made her a laughing stock.

Julia, too, must have suffered. If she was not jealous, she was certainly anxious about her tenure in the household and her future security, and she must have been wary of this spoiled and demanding intruder. However, years later, she swore under oath before the court conducting a hearing into David's contested will that, by the time of his marriage, David no longer had sex with her. "We separated before he ever married or thought of it, I reckon," Julia said.[25]

The marriage was short-lived, as Clara died of pneumonia before her third wedding anniversary. The period of David's marriage and bereavement was a trying one. Julia turned to the Methodist Cherry Hill Church and devoted herself to its associated school. In 1874, she persuaded David, a non-church-goer, to sell the church three acres of his land—for five dollars. David imposed conditions—if the land was not used for the church and its school, or if the roads fell into disrepair, it would revert back to him. This was hardly a major philanthropic gesture, but it was exactly what Julia had asked for.

In other ways, Julia's life went on as before. She was still David's trusted housekeeper. She still rode into nearby Sparta to buy supplies and sell plantation wares. Her commercial activities frequently brought her to the home of one of David's friends, where she always refused invitations to join the family at meals. She preferred to eat with the servants, in the kitchen. Julia's reputation, understandably, was of a "very quiet, inoffensive woman" who served David's guests and was never forward.[26]

In 1885, David died. Amanda clung to his lifeless body and moaned, "Now I am an orphan; now I am an orphan." There followed the living nightmare of the contested will, because Dickson had died wealthy and had left the bulk of his estate to Amanda. Seventy-nine of his bitter relatives challenged the will, arguing that Julia had exerted undue influence over him and had pressured him into making Amanda his principal beneficiary. Nine months after David's death, Julia was subjected to the hostile questions of her adversaries' scornful lawyers. Episodes from the past, true and fabricated, were bruited in the courtroom. Some have the ring of truth—that when she was a girl, David struck her during a quarrel, and she hit him back; that he treated her like a wife or sweetheart, not a slave; that they had publicly kissed each other. Others—that Julia had threatened to leave David, that he had wept maniacally at hearing this—were likely invented.

For Amanda's lawyers, the difficulty was proving that though Amanda was Julia and David's child, Julia had not been David's mistress at the time he wrote his will. The enemy camp argued the contrary, that she had been his mistress, a position that would have enabled her to put undue pressure on him. Julia's morals and credibility were attacked. "[Juliana was] the child of a black man, wasn't it?" an opposition lawyer inquired. "A dark man," Julia responded. "Wasn't he a nigger?" the lawyer persisted. "I reckon they call him a nigger," Julia replied. The lawyers pressed her, as well, about her three children's different fathers—"You just confined your favors to those three?" "I don't know anything about confining myself; I was not a bad woman," Julia replied with conviction.[27]

Remarkably, the will was upheld, and Amanda became the richest woman of color in Georgia. Despite her grief, she was her father's daughter, and she immediately took charge of her life. She bought a luxurious seven-bedroom house in Augusta and moved into it. And because of the "natural love and affection which she has and bears to her mother," she gave Julia her seven-eighths of their house on the plantation. In another tribute to Julia, Amanda's son Julian and his wife christened their first daughter Julia Frances II. (Two years later, their son David Dickson II was born.)

But more turmoil was in store for Julia's family. Amanda married, without relinquishing any control of her inheritance. Instead, she simply gave her husband, Nathan Toomer, a free man of color, generous gifts. But her frail health, nervous disposition and a family scandal (her second son, Charles, though a married man, became obsessively infatuated with his new stepfather's fourteen-year-old daughter, and tried to kidnap her) debilitated her, and in 1893, in her forty-fourth year, Amanda died.

She died without a will. New legal battles ensued. In 1899, Julia and her friend Mariah Nunn went to Amanda's Augusta house, packed up its contents and shipped them to Sparta, Georgia, where her grandson Julian had bought Julia a splendid house set among pecan trees. Julia won the court case against her and was permitted to keep Amanda's furniture. She told her descendants that she had had David Dickson's body moved to a Sparta cemetery as well, and had erected a monument to him there.

Julia Frances Lewis Dickson's life with David Dickson began with rape, and her sexual liaisons, particularly with Dickson's slave Joe Brooken, may have been her form of defiance. Perhaps she simply fell in love. In either case, she clearly had great confidence in her ability to sustain her relationship with David.

Yet Julia's circumstances were too complex for any decision to be simple. She must have rejoiced that David favored Amanda over anyone else, notably his critical relatives. At the same time, she saw and heard how he treated other slaves, rewarding those who cooperated, using the stick when the carrot proved unappetizing. Julia was one of those who cooperated.

Julia's attitude toward her color and origins is less explicable. Despite what she reportedly told her grandchildren, she could not have believed she had no black blood—why, otherwise, would she have been enslaved? But constant exposure to slavery, even to David and his white visitors, who endlessly and earnestly discussed "the Negro," must have influenced Julia's perceptions. Perhaps she developed a pride in her reddish color and her unkinky hair, perhaps she hoped to distance herself from the degradation of bondage, as if hers had somehow been an error caused by her dark-skinned Latin origins. Perhaps David's unexpected marriage to Clara Harris angered and frightened Julia. Her distress may be glimpsed in her failure to mention David's brief marriage to her grandchildren. Like her black blood, his temporary defection just didn't exist.

The fundamental contradictions at the core of the Dickson world must have bedeviled Julia for most of her life. In her reminiscences, she attempted to make sense of how she had navigated herself through that world, circumventing the dangers and maintaining her self-respect through bravado, intelligence, industry, religious observance and—in old age—the filtering lens of uneasy memory.

Harriet Jacobs [28]

Unlike Phibbah, Julia Chinn and Sally Hemings, ex-slave Harriet Jacobs tells her own story in her book, *Incidents in the Life of a Slave Girl*. Though abolitionist Lydia Maria Child edited and polished the manuscript, Harriet's narrative, published under the pseudonym Linda Brent, allowed her to present her own experience of slavery and of sexual liaisons with a white man.

Harriet's book is a female slave narrative, a literary genre much studied and bitterly debated. Narratives are by definition somewhat suspect, because the slave or ex-slave narrator intended, indeed longed, to reach a wide audience of sympathetic abolitionist readers, and she had to consider those readers' backgrounds and expectations, including their desire for "specific, racialized conventions." As well, the narrator had to contend with an editor who shaped, corrected, altered and excised material in accordance with ideology or personal predilection.

The female slave narrative author had her own sensibilities as well, especially when she had illicit sex with a white man and had been tormented by the shame associated with it. To vindicate herself, to justify her behavior and perhaps the telltale presence of mixed-race children, the slave-mistress-as-narrator had every reason to deny any cooperation or even enjoyment in her relationship. She certainly had no reason to admit to any attraction to or affection for the man who seduced her.

Slave narratives need careful reading. They provide what few other sources can: the slave woman's perspective on her life and world, with details of personality and perception, time and place, and sequence of events. Harriet's narrative in particular has passed the test of time and expert scrutiny.

Harriet Ann Jacobs was a pretty little girl who developed into a pretty woman, a circumstance she later deplored. "If God has bestowed beauty upon her, it will prove her greatest curse," she wrote in *Incidents*. "That which commands admiration in the white woman only hastens the degradation of the female slave."

Harriet was born around 1813 in Edenton, North Carolina, to Elijah, a slave carpenter, and Delilah, who belonged to tavern keepers John and Margaret Horniblow. After Delilah's death in 1819, six-year-old Harriet grew deeply attached to Margaret Horniblow, a kind woman who taught her the elements of reading. Just before Harriet's twelfth birthday, Margaret died. When her will was executed, Harriet found that instead of being manumitted as she had been promised, she had been deeded to Margaret's three-year-old cousin, Mary Mathilda Norcom.

Harriet's little world had crumbled, and her new one soon proved menacing and frightening. Dr. James Norcom, Mary Mathilda's father, was a callous and sadistic man who persecuted the cook and routinely whipped his slaves. In her first week under his roof, Harriet heard "hundreds of blows fall, in succession, on a human being." The victim was a field hand who had (rightly) accused his wife of bearing Dr. Norcom's light-skinned child. In retaliation for the accusation, Norcom whipped the man, then sold both him and his wife, despite the latter's pleas. The new mother had, Harriet noted, "forgotten that it was a crime for a slave to tell who was the father of her child."

By the time Harriet was fifteen, Norcom pursued her without respite, whispering "foul words" into her ear and bullying her. He reminded her that he owned her and therefore had a right to her body. Despite her youth and inexperience, Harriet withstood his campaign to deflower her. His vulgarity shocked her, and the prospect of concubinage horrified her. She was also astute enough to have noticed that as soon as Norcom tired of "his victims," in particular when they gave birth, he sold them away, far from his wife's jealousy and his neighbors' snide speculations. Yet Harriet found it difficult to repel him. Though he did not physically force himself on her, he hounded her relentlessly.

At the same time, Harriet had to deal with Mrs. Norcom, the doctor's much younger second wife, who could not stamp out her husband's passion for her slave. Mrs. Norcom became Harriet's nemesis, and their relationship degenerated into the classically tortured one between a betrayed white wife and a hapless slave who shared her home and was, inadvertently, the agent of her betrayal.

With barely controlled rage, Harriet describes Mrs. Norcom as an enervated hypochondriac who lounged in her easy chair and watched slave women whipped till the blood flowed down their lacerated flesh. If dinner was served late, she spat into the cooking pots so the cook and her children could not scrape out and eat the leavings. She separated the family's cook from her suckling infant. She forced Harriet to trudge barefoot in the snow.

Nothing, Harriet wrote, was more wretched than living in a domestic war zone. "I would rather drudge out my life on a cotton plantation, till the grave opened to give me rest, than to live with an unprincipled master and a jealous mistress," she declared.

Dr. Norcom continued to pursue Harriet. He forced her to stand beside him, brushing away flies, as he slowly sipped tea and spelled out for her the delights she would be throwing away if she continued to defy him. And he threatened her with death if she confided so much as a word to Mrs. Norcom. But Mrs. Norcom was already suspicious. For one thing, the doctor had forbidden her to strike the pretty young slave.

Dr. Norcom stepped up his campaign of seduction. He brought his four-year-old daughter to sleep in his bedroom and insisted that Harriet accompany her. This provoked a raging argument between him and Mrs. Norcom, who afterward came to Harriet with a Bible and directed her to kiss "this holy book and swear before God" to tell the truth. With ringing voice, Harriet denied any wrongdoing. Mrs. Norcom sat her down on a stool, stared directly into her eyes and said, "You have taken God's holy word to testify your innocence. If you have deceived me, beware! . . . Now tell me all that has passed between your master and you."

In an impulsive outpouring, Harriet told her everything. Mrs. Norcom flushed and paled, and groaned with such anguish at this violation of her wedding vows and of her dignity that Harriet was moved. "One word of kindness from her would have brought me to her feet," she recalled.

Mrs. Norcom promised to protect Harriet and managed to put an end to Dr. Norcom's proposed sleeping arrangements. But as she was "not a very refined woman, and had not much control over her passions," Mrs. Norcom was devoured by mistrust and hatred. She took to sneaking into Harriet's room at night and peering down at her. Sometimes she pretended to be Dr. Norcom, whispering into Harriet's ear to see how she would respond. Before long, Harriet began to fear for her life.

During this nightmarish time, Harriet remained silent. She did not confide in her grandmother, Molly Horniblow, a free townswoman, who on several occasions had tried to buy her. (But Dr. Norcom always refused. Harriet was his daughter Mary Mathilda's slave, he said, and so he had no legal right to sell her.) When he got Harriet alone, Dr. Norcom said reproachfully, "Did I not take you into the house, and make you the companion of my own children? Did I ever treat you like a negro? I have never allowed you to be punished, not even to please your mistress. And this is the recompense I get, you ungrateful girl!" Yet if Harriet wept, he would say soothingly, "Poor child! Don't cry! don't cry! . . . Poor, foolish girl! You don't know what is for your own good. I would cherish you. I would make a lady of you. Now go, and think of all I have promised you."

Harriet did think, and her conclusions were sobering: "Southern women often marry a man knowing that he is the father of many little slaves [Dr. Norcom himself had sired eleven]. . . . They regard such children as property, as marketable as the pigs on the plantation; and it is seldom that they do not make them aware of this by passing them into the slavetrader's hands as soon as possible, and thus getting them out of their sight." There were a few "honorable exceptions," when white women forced their husbands to free slaves "towards whom they stood in a 'parental relation.'" Mrs. Norcom, however, was not one of these women. If Harriet became Norcom's mistress, it would be only a matter of time before her babies would be sold away from her, and her existence would become even more wretched.

Harriet's implacable opposition to Norcom did not mean she was immune to other men. She fell in love with a longtime friend, a free-born carpenter who proposed marriage and wanted to buy her. But Harriet knew that the Norcoms would neither agree to sell her nor permit her to be married, except to another slave. When another of their slaves had asked permission to marry a free man of color, Mrs. Norcom had replied, "I will have you peeled and pickled, my lady, if I ever hear you mention that subject again. Do you suppose that I will have you tending *my* children with the children of that nigger?" Nonetheless, and with great trepidation, Harriet asked Dr. Norcom's permission to marry. "Do you love this nigger?" he asked abruptly. Harriet's answer—"Yes, sir,"—provoked an onslaught of abuse, and for the first time, Dr. Norcom struck her and called her "the plague of my life."

For a week after this, Dr. Norcom watched Harriet in hawklike silence. Then he informed her that he was separating from his wife and moving to Louisiana with a few slaves—she could be one of them. After this plan fell through, he caught Harriet on the street talking to her boyfriend, and beat and cursed her. In despair, Harriet urged her beloved to move to a free state, and she and her brother would follow him there.

But flight proved impossible. Harriet was closely guarded, she had no money and her grandmother strongly opposed the idea. Finally, Harriet abandoned her dreams of joining her carpenter and set out on another path entirely.

Her years with the Norcoms had exposed her to sexual innuendo and the raw facts of life, and she was no longer a naive child. "I knew what I did, and I did it with deliberate calculation," she wrote later. What she did was become the mistress of a white man she believed could rescue her from the Norcoms by buying her.

Harriet's lover was Samuel Tredwell Sawyer, an unmarried young lawyer who knew her and her grandmother. Sawyer was increasingly attracted to her, and he often sent her notes. "I was a poor slave girl, only fifteen years old," Harriet reminds her readers. Before long, "a more tender feeling crept into my heart," though affection was mixed with "revenge, and calculations of interest . . . flattered vanity and sincere gratitude for kindness." Furthermore, "to be an object of interest to a man who is not married, and who is not her master, is agreeable to the pride and feelings of a slave, if her miserable situation has left her any pride of sentiment. It seems less degrading to give one's self, than to submit to compulsion."

And so, for this complex of reasons, Harriet began to have sex with Sawyer, though she never mentions when or where this happened. Their affair was not entirely blissful. She worried that her "immorality" would bruise her grandmother Molly's heart, and hoped the old lady would not find out. Then she discovered she was pregnant, which precipitated a new crisis.

Everyone except Dr. Norcom himself (and of course Samuel Sawyer) would assume Dr. Norcom was the father. But Harriet knew that Norcom would punish her because he was not, while Mrs. Norcom would punish her because she would be sure he was. Harriet hoped to find refuge or at least sympathy at her grandmother's. Instead, Molly ripped Harriet's dead mother's wedding ring from her finger, told her she was a disgrace and shouted, "Go away! and never come to my house again." Frightened and ashamed, Harriet fled to a friend's house and confided the whole pitiable story. The unidentified friend intervened with Molly and told her all that Harriet had endured with the Norcoms. Without really forgiving her, Molly took Harriet back home. But she demanded to know why Sawyer, Harriet's co-sinner, had destroyed her "one ewe lamb" when he could have taken another slave woman as his paramour. Sawyer assured Molly that he would care for Harriet and their child. He would even try to buy them, he told her.

Dr. Norcom came to visit and allowed Harriet to remain at her grandmother's only because Mrs. Norcom had banned her from the house. His main concern was to identify Harriet's lover—had it been the carpenter he had forbidden her to marry? Harriet retorted bitterly, "I have sinned against God and myself, but not against you."

"Curse you!" Dr. Norcom muttered. "I could grind your bones to powder! You have thrown yourself away on some worthless rascal. . . . I command you to tell me whether the father of your child is white or black."

Frightened and confused, Harriet hesitated. "Do you love him?" Norcom persisted. "I am thankful that I do not despise him," she retorted. This struck Dr. Norcom hard. He threatened to kill her, then promised that if she broke off all contact with her lover, he would provide for her and her baby. Harriet refused, and Dr. Norcom warned, "Very well, then take the consequences of your wayward course. Never look to me for help. You are my slave, and shall always be my slave. I will never sell you, that you may depend upon."

Baby Joseph was born premature and sickly and, for weeks, teetered between life and death. Harriet, too, had a difficult recovery. Dr. Norcom visited often and reminded her that Joseph was also his slave.

Norcom's sexual jealousy flamed as fiercely as ever. He kept Harriet away from his adult son, and from his plantation overseer. He accused Harriet of wantonness. He pushed her down a staircase and hacked off her lustrous long hair. He continually insulted and humiliated her. Once, vengefully, he jailed her brother. Meanwhile, her secret lover, Samuel Sawyer, slipped over whenever he could, cuddling Joseph and comforting Harriet. But Sawyer could not even name his son, who remained the property of Dr. Norcom's daughter.

Four years passed. Harriet returned to the Norcom home, all the while continuing her clandestine affair. Before she turned nineteen, her daughter, Louise Mathilda, was born. Harriet claimed that her feelings for Sawyer never crystallized into the grand passion she had shared with her first sweetheart, though she felt great affection for and gratitude toward him. There was, as well, she wrote, "something akin to freedom in having a lover who has no control over you, except that which he gains by kindness and attachments."

Harriet's second child was proof that she had remained sexually involved with his unknown white rival. Dr. Norcom was furious. "Slavery is terrible for men; but it is far more terrible for women," Harriet wrote. "Superadded to the burden common to all, *they* have wrongs, and sufferings, and mortifications peculiarly their own." She had to sneak Joseph and Louise Mathilda to their baptismal ceremony when Dr. Norcom, who forbade any baptism at all, was out of town.

In 1835, Norcom sent Harriet to his plantation to punish her for refusing to become his concubine. He also announced his plans to toughen up Joseph so he could be sold. Harriet devised an elaborate scheme to flee. She planned to go alone; then Sawyer would buy the children and free them. Her grandmother objected strenuously: "Nobody respects a mother who forsakes her children," she warned. "If you leave them, you will never have a happy moment."

Harriet disregarded her grandmother's counsel. With the help of Sally, a slave friend who agreed that "When dey finds you is gone, dey won't want de plague ob de chillern," Harriet made her move. She hid at a friend's house, then later, at her grandmother's, in a crawlspace above a storeroom. She was cramped and uncomfortable, but safe from detection, because Dr. Norcom believed she was in the North, and even traveled there to find her and bring her home. Harriet's deception was sophisticated, and included writing him letters she arranged to have posted from various free states.

Meanwhile, with the help of a slave trader, Sawyer tricked Norcom into selling the children, whom the trader immediately resold to him. To authenticate the appearance of the sale, the children were loaded into the trader's wagon alongside other sold slaves, who wailed as they were torn away from their wives, husbands and children. The charade ended for Harriet's family (but not anyone else's) when Joseph and Louise were safely out of town, and Sawyer had them sneaked back to their grandmother's. From her crawlspace upstairs, the incarcerated Harriet often caught glimpses of them, but never dared show herself.

Incredibly, Harriet remained in Molly's attic for seven long years. Meanwhile, Sawyer went on with his life and, in 1837, was elected to Congress as a Democrat. Harriet's "disappearance" had ended their relationship, and with it, apparently, his promise to free Joseph and Louise. They had been living with Molly since Harriet's escape, but were still technically his property. Just before he left for Washington, he came to see Molly about them. Harriet risked her safety by revealing herself—but not her hideout—to him, and implored him to manumit the children. "I want nothing for myself," she said. "All I ask is, that you will free my children, or authorize some friend to do it, before you go." Sawyer readily agreed to her plea and added that he would try to buy her as well.

However, Sawyer failed to do any of this until he married a white woman. In 1840, after his marriage, he sent for Louise, and later arranged for her to live with his cousins in New York. In 1842, Harriet finally left her hideout and escaped to the North, where she contacted her daughter. In 1843, she arranged for Joseph to join her. From then on she supported herself and her children by working as a seamstress. For the next decade, the family lived as fugitives even though they were on free soil, because the Norcoms, including her legal owner, Mary Mathilda, never ceased pursuing Harriet. In 1852, an abolitionist friend, Cornelia Willis, convinced the Norcoms to sell her. Willis paid them three hundred dollars and manumitted Harriet. Free at last, Harriet began to conceive of the narrative that was finally published in 1861 as *Incidents in the Life of a Slave Girl*.

Harriet spent the rest of her life with her daughter, supporting herself in low-paying jobs and working tirelessly for abolitionist causes. After the Civil War, she and Louise returned to the South to do relief work. Later, they returned to the North. In 1897, Harriet died at the age of eighty-four.

Harriet Jacobs's exposé of her life as a slave girl is probably the most explicit and articulate published autobiographical account of a slave mistress's life. Ever since 1861, when it was published, it has generated voluminous and heated debate. In Harriet's time, abolitionists and defenders of slavery fought over the authenticity and veracity of Harriet's account. More recently, a host of historians have engaged in interpreting *Incidents in the Life of a Slave Girl* from a plethora of perspectives. The only agreed-upon conclusion is the staggering importance of Harriet's narrative.

The relentless tension as Norcom stalked her, alternately bullying and cajoling, threatening and promising, is palpable. At the same time, the narrative raises several questions—why did such a ferociously jealous man tolerate his slave's liaison with another man? Why did he not simply force himself on Harriet and rape her? Why did he single her out for such favored treatment when he lashed and sold off other slave women who displeased him?

In fact, the narrative's focus on Norcom, whom Harriet steadfastly resisted, deflects attention from Sawyer, her chosen lover and father of her two children. For the same reason, she concentrated much of her venom on Mrs. Norcom, whose vindictiveness included an unending stream of what today we would identify as psychological abuse. Harriet recognized that Mrs. Norcom was a cuckolded wife trapped in a travesty of a marriage. But even decades later, she could summon up little sympathy for her sometime tormentor. She not only portrayed Mrs. Norcom in the most unflattering terms, she also reproduced, apparently verbatim, reams of the most degrading remarks the white woman had heaped on her youthful head. Again, the extravagance of Mrs. Norcom's cruelties and meannesses diverts readers from wondering how Harriet conducted her duplicitous love life without anyone knowing, or even suspecting.

Harriet's narrative is rich in remembered conversation between herself and the Norcoms. In these exchanges, she is unfailingly courteous but unyielding, a woman inspired by the highest principles of morality and by her abhorrence of Dr. Norcom's sinful propositions. Ironically, she tells us far more about Norcom, her never-was lover, than about Sawyer. From beginning to end, Sawyer remains a shadowy figure, and Harriet couches most references to him in the apologetic tone of a woman confessing to a great sin.

Many slave women were very conflicted about sexual intercourse with their owners or other white men. Harriet's great shame was that Sawyer had not coerced her, though at the same time she believed that giving oneself voluntarily was "less degrading" than being forced into a sexual relationship. She could never admit to loving Sawyer and, even decades after the fact, withheld all the details about their affair. Her main concern was her plea for her readers' understanding.

As Harriet's story shows, not all slave women were subjected to brutality to get them into bed. Some voluntarily entered relationships with white men, and for very good and obvious reasons: protection from the worst abuses of slavery; better and easier work assignments; privileges; revenge over a cruel mistress; material rewards; children who might be freed and enjoy an infinitely better life than any slave; and lastly, affection.

Loving the enemy, however, struck many slaves as unpardonable. Harriet, who had committed this "sin," lacerated herself for it. It was, indeed, a key element in her mistressdom and explains her inability to revel—at least in retrospect—in the erotic pleasures she must have shared with Sawyer, and her refusal to admit to any strong emotional attachment to him.

Then follows the ultimate plea for all slave women sexually involved with white men: "The condition of a slave confuses all principles of morality, and, in fact, renders the practice of them impossible." Using 19th-century Christian morality and social conventions as her guideline, Harriet judges herself, finds herself guilty and then exonerates herself on the grounds that slavery is by definition an amoral condition.

Harriet's narrative focused on her experiences as a slave mistress, but it also suggested the wider consequences of illicit relationships between white men and slave women. Harriet's sexual vulnerability also threatened Mrs. Norcom, who, as a woman, lacked the authority to stop her husband from pursuing slave women. Harriet's love affair with Samuel Sawyer disturbed her grandmother's sense of decency. The older woman worried, as well, that it would skew her carefully orchestrated relations with the white community, which tolerated her as a free black. Like all such liaisons, Harriet's affair with a white man, and the children it produced, called into question the social order that governed life in the slave-owning states.

CHAPTER 8

Sexual Unions
and the Jewish Question

F ROM the early 1930s until World War II ended in 1945, Nazi Germany and Nazi-run Europe enacted laws that defined Jewish women as sexual untouchables for gentiles. At the same time, the powerlessness of Jewish women, in particular those in concentration camps, made them vulnerable to coercion into mistress relationships with gentiles.[1]

In 1924, the publication of Adolf Hitler's *Mein Kampf* (*My Struggle*) proclaimed a fantastical vision of a shiningly blond, tall and superior Aryan "race." The men would be paragons of genetic excellence. Their sisters would be wonderfully suited to the traditional feminine concerns: *Küche, Kirche* and *Kinder* (kitchen, church and children). Hitler had no sympathy for female emancipation, which was, he preached, "only an invention of the Jewish intellect."[2]

Adolf Schicklgruber Hitler, the short, dark-haired Führer of this master race, denounced all non-Aryan races as inferior and dangerously contaminating, but the very worst were the Jews. Like thousands of other Germans, Hitler had read and been influenced by Arthur Dinter's *Die Suende wider das Blut* (*The Sin Against the Blood*). The "sin" referred to was racial pollution—Dinter claimed that one drop of Jewish semen would forever pollute an Aryan woman, and even cause children subsequently conceived with an Aryan mate to display unmistakable Jewishness.

After Hitler assumed the German chancellorship in January 1933, he began to translate his vision into legislation. One of his most important targets was *Rassenschande*—race defilement through interracial sex. Nazi legislation defined *Rassenschande* as racial treason and made it a capital crime.

On September 15, 1935, the Nuremerg Laws stripped everyone of citizenship except Germans and people of "related blood," and the Law for the Protection of German Blood and Honor forbade citizens to marry or engage in sexual intercourse with Jews. In the 1930s, nearly 4,000 Jews and gentiles, both married and unmarried, were convicted of the crime of interracial sex. When the "criminals" were caught, they were severely punished, shamed and brutalized in public parades, or sent to concentration camps. "I am the worst swine; I get involved with Jews," one woman's placard read.[3]

Hitler regarded these anti-Jewish laws—four hundred of them passed between 1933 and 1939—as temporary measures necessary only until he had rid Europe of its Jews. The complex apparatus designed to exterminate Jews and other non-Aryans involved an escalating campaign of terror, ghettoization and finally mass deportation to concentration camps that few inmates survived. Dachau, ten miles outside Hitler's beloved Bavarian city of Munich, was built two months after his installation. As Europe fell to the Nazis, other camps were built elsewhere, notably in Poland.

The ideological sexism at Nazism's core combined with its horror of Jewish procreation to rush Jewish women to destruction. As Auschwitz Kommandant Rudolph Höss recalled in his pre-execution memoirs, "For the women, everything was a thousand times harder, much more depressing and injurious, because the living conditions in the women's camps were incomparably worse. The women were allocated smaller living space, the hygienic and sanitary conditions were greatly inferior."[4]

As the war ended, liberation came in stages. On July 24, 1944, Soviet soldiers liberated Majdanek concentration camp. Six months later, they reached Auschwitz. On May 7, Germany officially surrendered, ending both the war and the Shoah.

The memoirs of thousands of survivors, Nazi officials, employees or close observers; the heaped artifacts and relics of millions of victims; the Germans' meticulous record keeping; and various postwar judicial investigations—all these provide crucial evidence for historians and others dedicated to comprehending the evil that created the Shoah. Since the 1990s, the particular plight of Jewish women, including its sexual dimension, has commanded attention and special study.

These studies, indeed this approach, engender bitter debate centered on controversies about the legitimacy of female-oriented interpretations. Many people believe that because the Shoah destroyed Jewish men and Jewish women equally, introducing a gender-based analytic framework and thereby distinguishing women's ordeals from men's desecrates the living, the memory of the dead, even the Shoah in its incomprehensible enormity.

Other historians assert just as passionately that the Shoah can only be understood, and full weight and honor accorded to its victims, by accepting the reality that the tribulations of men and women were in some respects different. They point out that over and above the merciless brutality and degradation afflicted on men, women suffered what men did not: menstruation and amenorrhea, gynecological experiments, pregnancy, abortion, childbirth, newborns murdered so their mothers might escape execution, and unbearable decisions about staying with children selected for death or leaving them in order to remain alive for other children, or for life itself.

In a book about mistresses, the experiences of Nazi-era Jewish women coerced into sexual relations must be told from their particular perspective. The facts are these: despite the Law for the Protection of German Blood and Honor and their own appalling physical condition, Jewish women were targets for sexual exploitation.[5] The very femininity that put them at risk could, at times, help them. Specifically, some women had the chance, accorded to few men, to wield their sexuality as a tool to stay alive.

CONCENTRATION CAMP LIFE BEFORE DEATH

The "admission" process in Nazi concentration camps was designed to terrorize and humiliate new inmates and reduce them to hopelessness. As soon as their victims stumbled down from the cattle-car transports, Nazi officials began the triage that separated men from women and children, and selected millions for immediate death in the gas chambers.

Jewish women were especially at risk. Their fertility was anathema, representing as it did the perpetuation of their hated race. Everywhere in the Reich, the least sign of pregnancy condemned Jewish women to death.[6] Research also indicates that more women than men were killed immediately upon arrival at extermination camps.

The women selected to live a while longer were mainly young, sturdy and apparently healthy. Survivors recall their disbelief and humiliation at having to disrobe completely, exposed to each other and the enemy guards. The next stage was shaving, as SS men and women denuded them of body hair, including pubic and underarm hair, supposedly to prevent lice. The Nazis employed this public shearing as a weapon to break the women's spirits, and they leered and jeered as they worked. "It was as if one had taken off our skin, as if nothing of our personality was left," recalled one woman. "We weren't any more the girls Helga or Olga or Maria or whomever."[7]

These women also felt they were no longer women, because the subsistence of camp life virtually eliminated menstruation. The few who still menstruated were forced to do so publicly, blood dripping down their legs because they lacked sanitary pads and their only rags were their clothes. The Nazis then punished them for their uncleanness.

Nazi physicians violated every medical vow and sterilized adolescent girls by burning their ovaries with X-rays. Afterward, the screaming young women would writhe on the ground, their pain unendurable. Later, these doctors surgically removed the incinerated ovaries. Dr. Wladislaw Dering was known to rush through so many of these operations that he could finish ten in only two hours.

In women's barracks, rape was a constant threat. SS men dissatisfied with ogling the women sometimes marched into their dormitories and yanked the prettiest from their beds, took them away and raped them. Afterward, the women would return to their dormitory blocks, their shame known to everyone.

Many SS men were afraid of the draconian consequences of having sex with a Jewish woman and preferred to forego its pleasures rather than risk their jobs and safety, perhaps their very lives. But some simply killed their victims after raping them: dead witnesses cannot talk.

In an even more flagrant violation of the Law for the Protection of German Blood and Honor, the SS in many camps—Ravensbrück and Auschwitz, for example—established brothels for their own delectation and sometimes for favored non-Jewish inmates as well. (Auschwitz survivor and writer Ka Tzetnik immortalized these brothels in House of Dolls, a novel based on his fourteen-year-old sister Daniella Preleshnik's diary of her enforced prostitution in a Nazi labor camp.) The brothel women were selected by appearance, in particular the firmness of their breasts, unusual when malnutrition had emaciated so many. (Starved breasts first sagged, then shriveled away until the woman's chest was as flat as a man's.) SS physicians supervised these selections. One was the infamous Dr. Josef Mengele, whose mistress was the SS officer Irma Griese, a bisexual who helped herself to female inmates as well.

Once pressed into brothel service, the women, some of them Jewish, were "auditioned" or gang raped. Then they were set to work, idle most of the day but each forced to submit to about eight men during the two hours the brothel was in operation each evening. Despite anticonception medication, pregnancies occurred. A woman had no control over whether her fetus was aborted or she was killed. The SS often found the latter solution simplest.

To satisfy their sexual cravings, and avoid being punished for the unpardonable crime of *Rassenschande*, many SS men and women simply slept with each other, cheating on spouses with discreet colleagues. But the prisoners, endless streams of desperate women arriving from all over Europe, were too vulnerable and available to ignore. For the captive women, staving off death from day to day, sexual interest was irrelevant. But many soon learned how to use their sexuality as a means to garner tiny rewards that could prolong life, their own or a loved one's.

A still attractive woman, especially one who miraculously retained her womanly roundness, might initially avoid the gas chambers. She might also attract the attention of an SS guard or a more privileged, non-Jewish prisoner who could slip her a slice of sausage or cheese, or a better pair of shoes, items that could literally affect life and death. Some women "gave themselves away for a little bread and butter," but as former inmate Renata Laqueur says, "It was their will to survive, and often also the wish to save their husband and children, that made them take that path."[8] In this surreal world ruled by terror, the real world's rules and conventions about sex ceased to make sense. Yet most people still clung to them, and so even death-camp morality came down harshly on sleeping with the enemy.

This is evident in most Shoah memoirs that touch on this particular experience. More recently, women-oriented interpretations of the Shoah have presented it more sensitively and realistically as *Bett-Politik*—bed politics, usually a female inmate's only weapon.

Sexual blackmailers were not confined to Nazis and SS men. Outside of the extermination camps, in ghettos and work camps, Jewish men, too, demanded sexual favors in exchange for food or other essentials. In partisan hideouts in the forest, so did both Russian and Jewish men.

"S," a Czechoslovakian Jew who survived both Theresienstadt, the so-called model ghetto, and Auschwitz, the extermination camp, recalls that women depended on their brains and their male connections. In the Theresienstadt ghetto, men ran the main offices and the all-important kitchens, positions they used to get what they wanted, including sex. "That was how you survived as a woman," "S" explains, "through the male. . . . in that society, it was the only way you could survive."

The situation, another Theresienstadt survivor reflects, "was similar to that in the outside world except that the valuable commodity was not gold, diamonds, or money but food."⁹ Some men had even more to offer: the life-giving power to prevent the transport of up to thirty relatives and friends to the death camps of the east. Diaries from other ghettos reveal that there, too, certain high-ranked men in the *Judenrat* ("Jewish Council") protected pretty younger women in return for sex.

In forced-labor camps, women discovered that pairing off with a resourceful *kuzyn* ("cousin") could mean the difference between life and death. Many resisted, preferring abstinence to the shame of unmarried sex, and some upper-class women scorned lower-class Yiddish-speakers, even those with lifesaving skills. But women often capitulated to their desperate circumstances, accepted a *kuzyn* and spent their nights together with him behind improvised blinds. Popular ditties mocked these arrangements: "For soup, for soup / For a piece of bread / Girls will spread their ... . / Just between you and me / They'll do it even / When there's no need."¹⁰ The most frightening consequence of *kuzyn* arrangements was pregnancy, for women with swelling bellies were automatically selected for death.

At Auschwitz, with its minimal opportunities for supplementing their meager rations, women whose jobs put them in contact with crematorium workers could sometimes exchange "love," grotesque moments of copulation near the stinking latrine, for a can of food, a pair of shoes or a comb. A Jewish Hungarian physician, Dr. Gisella Perl, desperately needed a piece of string to tie her too-big shoes to her feet. (Shoes were essential to prevent the sores and subsequent infection that could easily cause selection for the gas chamber.) A Polish latrine worker had a piece of string, but would exchange it only for her body, not her bread allocation. "His hand, filthy with the human excrement he was working in, reached out for my womanhood, rudely, insistently." A minute later, Dr. Perl ran away, horrified by what had happened. "How my values had changed. . . . How high the price of a piece of string had soared."¹¹ A woman who in normal life would greet any such proposal with dignified scorn now hesitated, considered, weighed the importance of what was offered and then decided—often no, but sometimes yes.

One woman was Ruth, who in the winter of 1942 arrived at the snowbound Sobibor camp on a transport from Vienna. All we know about Ruth is that she was a dark-eyed, brunette teenager, about sixteen or seventeen years old, so stunning that she caught the eye of Scharführer Paul Groth, a man notorious for his savage treatment of Jewish prisoners. Three of Groth's bizarre stunts:

He forced a Jew to gulp vodka until he was drunk and then, roaring with laughter, urinated into the retching man's mouth. He ordered Jews to clamber up to a roof, and ordered those who fell off to be whipped, then taken to Camp III and shot. He made Jews catch mice and drop them down other men's trousers. When these latter could not stand at attention, he had them whipped.

And then Groth set eyes on Ruth and, to the astonishment of everyone who knew him, fell deeply in love. He assigned her to be his servant, and took her as his mistress. "The love affair became serious," a Sobibor survivor testified, "and Ruth influenced Groth's behavior."[12] The terrifying SS man stopped beating Jews. But the Jews were not the only ones to notice this radical change in Groth's attitude. So did his SS colleagues and superiors, who were shocked at how important Ruth had become to him. SS Obersturmführer Franz Reichleitner, who became Kommandant in August 1942, acted unilaterally. While Groth was away from Sobibor on a three-day leave, two SS men took Ruth to Camp III and shot her. Groth returned to learn that she was dead. Afterward, he resumed his duties and continued to treat the Jews leniently, as he had during the brief period of his illicit love affair. Soon after, the Kommandant had him transferred to Belzec.

How did the very young Ruth feel about Groth, a man who tortured and killed Jews, and who forced her to have sex with him? Quite likely he took her virginity—did she mourn this end of innocence, or was she too aware of the precariousness of her very existence to care? Did she respond to his sudden burst of love, or did she trade her tenderness for his promise to spare her people? Those who knew her during the final days of her life spoke of "love," and the SS Kommandant shared this assessment, at least as far as Groth was concerned. Certainly something happened between him and the Jewish teenager, connecting their emotions. All we know for certain is that Ruth used his unsolicited passion for her in the best way she could, to tame his beastliness and to lessen Jewish pain.

In Auschwitz, Maya was a *Kapo*, a prisoner appointed by the SS to maintain order in the barracks. Maya showed little mercy to her fellow Jews and thrashed anyone who got in her way. Her position earned her a cubicle of her own, and the other inmates believed, though they could not prove it, that every night, one of the SS men came and slept with her there.

The war ended. Maya survived and so did former Auschwitz inmate Lucille E. In 1950 or 1951, Lucille was shopping at Altman's Department Store in New York City, torn between buying a pair of red gloves or black. She noticed a woman standing next to her, a tall woman with short black hair strikingly styled, a smiling woman who was also trying on gloves. Lucille turned to the woman and their eyes met. "Maya," she said. Maya looked at her. "Yes, how do you know?" "Auschwitz," Lucille replied. Maya blanched and began to justify herself, speaking in a rush: she hadn't been that bad, she had been forced to do what she did, she hadn't killed anyone.

What about your husband? Lucille asked, noticing Maya's wedding ring. Surely not the SS man? But yes, Maya's husband was indeed the SS man. After the war, he had followed her from camp to camp. When she emigrated to New York, he had followed her there as well. Finally she decided she might as well marry him. He was, after all, she told Lucille, "quite a decent sort."

Do the two of you have children? Lucille demanded. No, Maya replied, no children. "I hope you never have them," Lucille said, then turned and walked away.[13]

Maya is the mistress who placed her own survival and comfort above other considerations. She may have married the SS man to validate their affair, to justify to herself how truly decent he really was, not like the other SS men. Then, too, she may have shied away from marrying a Jew, who might one day have discovered what Lucille and so many others knew, that his elegant wife was not like most other Auschwitz survivors.

Another Auschwitz affair took place between Dr. Rosenthal, an SS physician, and Gerta Kuernheim, a Jewish prisoner-nurse. During the course of their relationship, Gerta became pregnant, and Dr. Rosenthal aborted the fetus, presumably to save Gerta's life. Gerta's job was to euthanize gravely ill patients. One chilling story about her professional collaboration with her lover speaks volumes about both Auschwitz and Rosenthal, and perhaps about Gerta. Two patients with the same name had been treated, one for typhus, one for a mild abscess. The typhus victim died, and a notice was to be sent to his family. But in error, the notice went to the family of the perfectly healthy abscess patient. When two clerks realized their error, they worked up the courage to inform Dr. Rosenthal so he could contact the grieving family and reassure them. Rosenthal listened to their story. Then he gave an order to Gerta, who returned shortly after and announced, "The error is taken care of. That one is also dead."[14] Expeditious murder had transformed error into truth.

At some point, Dr. Rosenthal and Gerta were reported to higher authorities, not because they had murdered a patient, not because she had had an abortion, but because Rosenthal had committed *Rassenschande*, race defilement. Ultimately, he committed suicide. Gerta's fate is unknown, but she was almost certainly executed.

This might have been a love affair like Maya's. Or perhaps Gerta was unable to extricate herself from the SS doctor who desired her. Her complicity in the case of the confusion between two patients proves nothing—what could she have done if Dr. Rosenthal gave her an order? And given her role in Auschwitz's aggressive euthanasia program, she might have been hardened already to the enormity of her action. In any case, her people were being murdered by the cattle-car load, so a painless death by injection might have seemed innocuous, even merciful. Whatever her feelings and motives, Gerta's affair with Rosenthal probably brought her own life to a premature end.

Jewish doctor Gisella Perl, who traded her body for a lifesaving piece of string, tells the story of Kati, an Auschwitz inmate and the mistress of a German lover she consorted with because, she told Dr. Perl, he helped her to save lives. Kati's heart was "as big as the universe,"[15] and when she found a tiny fifteen-year old whom an SS woman had beaten to a pulp after she was caught scrounging for potato peelings, Kati determined to rescue the girl. She stole as much as she could to help her protégé, but her resources were severely limited. Her *kohana*—lover—was much better placed. He was a German gentile and a prisoner whose green triangle identified him as a common criminal, a thief, perhaps even a murderer. He was physically powerful and respected in the camp, and carried a cane that symbolized his status. He was also well connected with crematorium workers, whose gruesome job sometimes gave them access to food that doomed prisoners arriving directly from city ghettos had to surrender before they entered the gas chambers.

Kati had been on the verge of breaking up with her *kohana*. Her new responsibilities changed her mind. In Dr. Perl's words, "she decided to continue selling her body to the man in exchange for food which she then took back . . . and fed to the little girl." One day Dr. Perl saw Kati, holding tight to the girl's hand, in a cattle car bound for German factories. Dr. Perl was optimistic. "I knew that whatever the cost, Kati would save the life of that little girl."[16] Kati's case was simple. She understood, and confided in Dr. Perl, the nature of her relationship with the German and what it brought her, namely lifesaving food. It must have helped that he was not an SS man but derived his authority primarily from his imposing physique. Auschwitz transformed this criminal into a powerful figure who could offer his Jewish mistress what no one else could: the means to keep another prisoner alive.

In *Return to Auschwitz*, survivor Kitty Hart mentions that the only sexual relationship she was aware of was between an unnamed Hungarian Jew and Wünsch, an Austrian SS man, who was in charge of the stores. Somehow, the woman had kept her good looks, and Wünsch fell terribly in love with her. Hart and other Jewish inmates facilitated the relationship, standing guard as the couple made love behind stacks of supplies. The payoff was that Wünsch, whom they nicknamed "Wiener Schnitzel," treated them "fairly well." After the war, Wünsch's Auschwitz mistress appeared as a witness at his trial at Frankfurt, and testified so eloquently on his behalf that the court acquitted him of war crimes.

This woman's unexpected and dramatic appeal speaks to a wellspring of emotions. Even after the war, with time to reflect and analyze, with the full horror of the Shoah exposed and acknowledged by international courts, this woman's memories of Wünsch (and perhaps even her love) drove her to save his life as, in her view, he had once saved hers. She not only did not blame her SS lover for what had happened, she risked condemnation or at least disapproval from other survivors by defending him.

Eleonore Hodys

For a few people, Auschwitz was paradise. One of these was forty-year-old Rudolph Höss, Kommandant of Auschwitz from May 4, 1940, until December 1943, who with his wife, Hedwig, and his family, lived in a flower-filled oasis amid the prisoners he starved, tortured, gassed and burned. Höss's house was cleaned by specially chosen prisoners, decorated with treasures confiscated from doomed inmates and provisioned with luxury wines and foodstuffs when even German consumption was strictly rationed. "I want to live here until I die," Hedwig Höss declared.[17]

Höss was a strict censor of his SS officers' conduct. He denounced a female SS officer who had "sunk so low as to become intimate with some of the male prisoners," and accused one of his cruelest underlings, Rapportführer Palitsch, of sleeping with a woman imprisoned at Birkenau. Yet he himself was guilty of an affair with an Italian prisoner, Eleonore Hodys, who worked at his house as a domestic and who was widely but erroneously reported to be Jewish.

Several months after Eleonore began working in his home, during which we may suppose Höss had already forced her into sexual relations, he had her transferred, first to a penal colony, later to the notorious Block No. 11. Did Hedwig have anything to do with the transfer? If so, she failed to prevent her husband from seeing Eleonore; he made clandestine nocturnal visits to her cell. But the tight security in Block 11 meant that at least several guards knew about these furtive rendezvous, which even Höss's exalted position could not conceal.

And then Eleonore became pregnant. How, in her rigidly controlled cell-block, could this have happened, unless Höss had fathered the fetus? Though Höss was Kommandant of Auschwitz, he must have been petrified. Other SS men had been executed for *Rassenschande*; if Eleonore was not Jewish, he would, at the very least, be disgraced, demoted and transferred away from the utopia of Auschwitz. And that was to say nothing of the marital discord such a revelation would provoke. And so Eleonore had to go. Höss had her confined to a *Stehbunker*, one of Block 11's four standing cells, which measured a little over half a meter square and were dark, airless and, in winter, cold. Usually these *Stehbunkers* were used to weaken prisoners before they were interrogated. Eleonore was different. The last thing Höss wanted from her was information. To silence her forever, he ordered that she be given no food—before too long, she had starved to death on her feet. Höss was now, he thought, home free.

But Eleonore, intelligent and bitter, had fought her fate with the puny resources at her disposal, namely, by informing on Höss. She had done this by somehow contacting SS officer Maximilian Grabner, head of the political section, who was an enemy of Höss's and under SS investigation at the time. She knew about their enmity: she had overheard conversations during her time as a servant in the Höss household, and Höss may have mentioned it to her as well. But Eleonore's desperate intervention did not save her. At his trial, Grabner used her revelations solely for his own benefit, to discredit Höss.

Eleonore's death, appalling even in death-sated Auschwitz, was far from secret, and rumors about her flew. To this day, she survives in memoirs and the transcripts of Maximilian Grabner's SS trial. When Auschwitz was still in operation, rumor had it that Eleonore had once tried to murder Höss. Had she defended her honor at his house, when he first forced himself on her? Could it have been when she told him (or when he noticed) that she was pregnant, and she realized from his reaction just what danger she was in? Whatever the unknowable truth, the rumor was bracing for those inmates who savored and repeated it. Eleonore Hodys may not have been Jewish, yet Jewish inmates claimed her and took comfort from her courage. To them, she personified the plight of Jewish women trapped in the Nazi nightmare of extermination and slave-labor camps.

In *Schindler's Ark*, later filmed as *Schindler's List*, author Thomas Keneally indirectly affirmed this. Keneally described how Auschwitz's Rudolph Höss, the "star of the camp system," was widely believed to have impregnated a Jewish woman named Eleanor (his spelling) Hodys. Certainly the SS believed it, Keneally wrote, and had even gone so far as to interrogate the wretched woman. Though the SS could not find concrete and irrefutable evidence that Höss had taken a Jewish mistress, the rumors persisted.

Eleonore Hodys's story is one with sex but no love at the core. Yet within the moral and human wasteland of the death camps, love affairs developed and flourished between imprisoned men and women only too aware that each moment brought them closer to certain death. Affection and tender embraces brought a semblance of normality to their hearts, and this was more important than sex, even when they could express their love physically. Most other prisoners honored these relationships with the greatest respect for this defiant assertion of passion.

"PARTISAN" FOREST CAMPS

Out in the forests, where Jewish refugees from the terror met up with non-Jewish, anti-Nazi guerrillas, relationships between warriors and their mistresses were shot through with contempt and usually came about through coercion. In these secret, impermanent camps, the great majority of women, though not of men, were Jewish. As in ghettos or slave-labor and extermination camps, the lives of Jewish men and women who escaped by fleeing into the forests were substantially different.

In 1941, the German assault on Russia brought the Red Army to its cold and hungry knees. Russian soldiers by the thousands evaded the subsequent roundup and took refuge in the Belorussian woods. Later, some of their comrades broke out of POW camps and rejoined their colleagues. These men labeled themselves "partisans"—freedom fighters against Nazism—but in reality most of them formed small thuggish bands called *otriads*, the Russian word for "partisan detachment." The *otriads*, which included Russians, Belorussians, Poles, Ukrainians and sometimes Jews, were devoid of discipline, leadership and weapons and were more interested in survival than in sabotaging the Germans. Over time, however, they managed to arm themselves by overpowering stray German soldiers who, on foot or in trucks, ventured alone into their dangerous territory.

With a few exceptions, these "partisans" usually rejected and sometimes killed Jewish ghetto escapees who attempted to join them. The only Jews the *otriads* welcomed were young males with guns. When Jewish women arrived with children, as so many did, the *otriads* robbed them of anything they had, sometimes raped them, then drove them away or killed them.

Nonetheless, a few attractive Jewish women were admitted and became mistresses of high-ranking Russian leaders. Female physicians, nurses and cooks were welcomed even if they were homely, older or unwilling to have sex. The general rule, however, was that, apart from those with essential skills, *otriad* women were mistresses called "transit wives" who exchanged sex for certain privileges, including more food and preferential treatment. But *otriads* took in so few women that the percentage of females was only 2 to 5 percent, and those who were Jewish were more vulnerable than the gentiles.

The forbidding Belorussian forest, however, had one Jewish *otriad* run by a trio of brothers, Tuvia, Asael and Zus Bielski. These poor and little-educated Jewish peasants were experts in navigating the forest. Under Tuvia, their leader, the nomadic Bielski *otriad* took in any Jew who showed up, including elderly men, helpless women, and intellectuals and professionals whose skills were irrelevant in the woods. As a result, their *otriad* was significantly larger than the others, and the survival of much of its membership depended on younger, fitter and more experienced men.

As much as possible, the Bielskis cooperated with gentile *otriads* to acquire arms and to force farmers to provide food. Later, they jointly blew up bridges, cut telephone wires and derailed trains. The Bielski *otriad* eventually established a settlement, complete with small factories and workshops that also supplied Russian *otriads*. Those without military or artisan training did the lowliest jobs, such as milking cows and chopping firewood. They included most of the women and the elderly, the ailing, and the intelligentsia who lacked practical knowledge. Collectively and contemptuously, these workers were known as *malbushim*.

In the stratified *otriad*, male *malbushim* who aspired to higher status and more and better food could try to upgrade themselves by becoming fighters or scouts. Women, however, could advance only through a protector, by becoming his mistress. The rule of the *otriad* required that an upper-class and formerly privileged woman be paired off with a lower-class and formerly disadvantaged man. The couple simply lived together, and 60 percent of the adults in the Bielski *otriad* were involved in such arrangements.

In prewar society, such unbalanced unions would have been improbable, if not impossible. The young patrician Sulia Rubin hated her life as a *malbush*, and "married" a fighter she would previously have scorned for his ignorance and lack of sophistication. But at his side in the *otriad*, Sulia not only thrived, she could help unluckier friends. Even after the war, she opted to stay with her forest lover. In fact, at war's end the great majority of these women married and remained with their apparently unsuitable mates.[18] They chose to validate their forest life, with its difficult and crucial choices, and transformed once shameful relationships into holy unions on which they founded both their families and their futures.

Like other Jewish women who survived because enamored or lustful men, usually Nazis, traded protection and sustenance for sex, these partisans had to come to terms with their wartime relationships, justifying them and even dignifying them through marriage. But sometimes those women grew to love the men who, at first, coerced them. When a lover was Jewish, his mistress could more easily accept, even welcome, the affection she felt growing between them. When he was a Nazi, that love was shot through with guilt and denial.

But the worst moments, the most shameful, were when a coerced woman responded to her captor and sexual desire for him surged in her. It was inevitable that this would sometimes happen: when women must perform (if not feel) sexually to save their lives, the erotic energy they invoke sometimes escapes the realm of falsehood and invades their own skins. At those moments, these mistresses are the first to label themselves the whores they are not and never have been.

EVA BRAUN:
MISTRESS TO THE AUTHOR OF THE SHOAH[19]

Adolf Hitler's stormy relationship with the German gentile Eva Braun would have been unremarkable had the bachelor dictator not been the architect of the greatest human destruction the world has known. Hitler's strong views on woman's nature and role in society shaped the ideology of National Socialism, and so his conduct in the realm of *Bett-Politik* is a telling glimpse into the core of his thought and the policies derived from it.

Adolf Hitler was born in 1889, the son of Klara Polzl and her cousin Alois Schicklgruber, surnamed Hitler only after his unwed mother married Johann Georg Hiedler, a name that some official registers spelled as Hitler, the variant spelling Adolf's father adopted. Adolf was Klara and Alois's fourth child, but the first to survive. His younger sister, Paula, was developmentally delayed, a fact Hitler both hated and kept hidden.

By the time he met the seventeen-year-old Eva Braun in late 1929, Adolf Hitler was a failed artist turned militant nationalist politician, still battling his way into power. He was unmarried by choice, because (like England's Elizabeth I) he was "married" to his country and could never spare the time a husband should devote to his wife and family. Besides, he did not want children. "I find that the offspring of geniuses usually have it hard in the world. . . . Besides, they are mostly cretins,"[20] he told his housekeeper, a sentiment that probably stemmed from his fear that he might produce another Paula.[21]

But Hitler never lacked for women, who were drawn by the power of his oratory, his charisma and his overwhelming confidence that he could restore Germany to greatness. And so they overlooked his shortness, his shapeless clothes and what Eva Braun called "his funny little mustache," and they flung themselves at him. Some (so the gossip went) even threw themselves under his car so he would stop and comfort them. And Hitler responded with gallantry, kissing their hands, flirting, accepting their adoration as his due.

Hitler saw women as strategists like himself. His theory was that, at first, a woman worked hard to win a man's confidence. Then, her soft fingers on his heartstrings, she began to pull, lightly at first and then harder, until finally she was so firmly in control that she forced the man "to dance according to her desires."[22]

On the whole, Hitler preferred buxom blondes, and enjoyed flirting with actresses and other women who amused or impressed him. He also liked them young, and after his widowed half sister, Angela Raubal, and her teenaged daughter, Angela, or Geli, came to live with him in 1927, he fell in love with Geli. He kept the young woman as a quasi-prisoner in his apartment, forbidding her to go out without his permission and even then only with authorized escorts. Geli stormed and wept, pleaded and threatened, but Hitler was adamant: she would go only where he told her, when he told her, with whom he told her. On September 18, 1931, after a particularly ferocious argument, twenty-one-year-old Geli took Hitler's Walther 6.35-millimeter pistol and shot herself through the heart.

Hitler was shocked and grieved, and also alarmed about the possible political repercussions should the media discover that he was sexually involved with his young niece. His Nazi colleagues, equally concerned, succeeded in "managing" Geli's suicide so well that newspaper accounts of her death merely implied that she was depressed by her failure to become a professional singer. Hitler mourned, briefly. He had an artist render her portrait from a photo and ordered his housekeeper, Anni Winter, to place fresh flowers in Geli's room each week.

Even during his relationship with Geli, the ever-philandering Hitler had been involved with other women. One of these was Eva Braun, who was even younger than Geli. They had met in late 1929, at the studio of his friend, public speaking coach and official photographer, Nazi Heinrich Hoffmann. Hitler entered as Eva was on a ladder shelving stock, a chore that inadvertently showed off her shapely legs. Hitler was pleased to see that her face was equally appealing, and from time to time, in between Geli and his other women friends, he arranged to see her.

After their first introduction, Eva inquired of her employer, "Who is Adolf Hitler?" Who, indeed? Her father, Fritz Braun, dismissed Hitler as a "Jack-of-all-trades, an imbecile who thinks himself omniscient and who wants to reform the world,"[23] while Ilse Braun, Eva's older sister, who worked for and was in love with Dr. Marx, a Jewish laryngologist, despised him.

Hitler was charmed by Eva's total ignorance about him, his party and politics in general. Women, he opined, had a disastrous influence on politics. Look at Lola Montez, who had destroyed Bavaria's King Ludwig I. "I hate political women," Hitler declared. "The girlfriend of a politician must not be smart." From this perspective, Eva was perfect. She banned political discussion in her presence. She never even joined the Nazi Party.

Then what was it about Eva that ultimately set her apart from her many competitors for Hitler's attention? She was very pretty, which counted heavily, a blue-eyed blonde who lightened her hair with peroxide, used makeup to highlight her fine features and dressed with simple elegance in clothes she made herself. She had an excellent figure and was perpetually fit, even after her school days of ice-skating and gymnastics. (In a home movie featuring her and Hitler, Eva vamps and executes an awkward cartwheel.) She was vivacious and friendly, and came from a respectable family. She was reasonably bright but staggeringly uninformed, a devotee of romantic novels such as Margaret Mitchell's *Gone with the Wind* and a fun-loving teenager whose mother hoped she could parlay her good looks into an even better marriage.

At home, Eva shared her bedroom with Ilse and Gretl, their younger sister. Fritz and Franziska were devout Catholics, and Fritz in particular had been very disappointed that Eva's undistinguished career at a convent school ended prematurely because the nuns would tolerate no more of her trouble-making. Fritz tried his best to control her, but Eva was determined and ingenious and, above all, focused on what she wanted in life.

And almost from their first "dates" together, Eva wanted Adolf Hitler. Hitler, however, showed only sporadic interest, and Ilse taunted her younger sister about chasing after an old man. Geli's death eased the situation. Finally Hitler had a safe place to take Eva, his own home. Soon they began to have sex. A favorite location was a long red sofa, its back protected by lace, the same sofa where Mussolini, Chamberlain and Daladier posed for a photograph during the inglorious Munich conference.

Eva was still only one of many women, though she was the first Hitler invited to spend the night. One of her serious rivals was Winifred Wagner, the English widow of composer Richard Wagner's son, Siegfried. But after Winifred weighed Hitler's character and concluded that his smooth public manner was far outweighed by his frightening private beastliness, she discouraged the relationship. Rumor also had it that she was repelled by his sexual demands, namely that she assume the role of his mother and whip him.

Eva either had no such qualms, or else Hitler did not fancy her in the role of dominatrix. They had sex, but this was not her main attraction. Instead, Hitler enjoyed hearing her prattle about actors and actresses, and about the details of parties they attended. His housekeeper judged Eva a not very intelligent but pretty doll, but Hitler found her vacuous chatter a welcome distraction that took his mind off his work as he frog-marched Germany into becoming a blond Nazi monolith.

For long stretches, however, Hitler neglected Eva, and she waited at home, lonely and bored. In 1932, she decided to frighten him into taking her more seriously. On the freezing night of All Saints' Day, just after midnight, she took her father's 6.35-millimeter pistol and turned it on herself. Ilse found her later, lying in pools of blood, a bullet lodged near her neck artery.

Eva had already telephoned a doctor—not Dr. Marx, with whom Ilse was spending the evening, but a man she assumed would notify Hitler. The bullet was easily removed, and Eva was gratified that Hitler, flowers in hand, visited her at the hospital. He even found her failed suicide moving. "She did it for love of me," he supposedly told Heinrich Hoffmann. "Now I must look after her; it mustn't happen again."[24]

But Hitler's main concern was publicity—too many suicidal women in his life would be a serious political liability. Eva lied to her parents about the motives for her suicide attempt, and her life continued as before, except that Hitler paid her more attention and was more appreciative of what he considered her great and disinterested love for him.

Eva—Hitler, too—still had to circumvent the tricky problem of Eva's father, who swore that he crossed to the other side of the street if he saw Hitler approaching. If Fritz Braun had known that his "virginal" daughter was involved with this scoundrel, he would certainly have tried to end the relationship. So Eva resorted to lies—and Hitler never went near her parents' apartment. Instead, he had one of his chauffeured, black Mercedes-Benz limousines pick her up on a street corner. In 1933, a week after he ascended to power, Eva turned twenty-one. To celebrate, Hitler gave her a set of inexpensive tourmaline jewelry that she treasured for the rest of her life. At home, however, she had to hide it. She could wear it only when she was with her lover. Her sisters, Ilse and Gretl, also guarded her dangerous secret. They often overheard her whispered telephone conversations with Hitler, but neither one told on her. Ilse considered tale-telling dishonorable, while Gretl found Eva's secret utterly thrilling.

Nonetheless, Eva's campaign to conquer Hitler's heart produced less than spectacular results. She knew that his colleagues mocked her as "a stupid cow," that he routinely cheated on her and that he had no intention of marrying her. He had also made it clear that she was a "backstreet" girl whom German high society would scorn, and he decreed that no photographs be taken of them together. The still not wholly Nazified public would make a laughingstock of their improbable romance.

Eva knew, as well, that Hitler could be ruthless, and that his solution for troublesome, independent-minded colleagues was execution. On June 30, 1934, after he killed hundreds of his political adversaries, as well as men who had been staunchly loyal to him, Fritz Braun reacted by shouting that Hitler was completely mad. Eva, however, accepted Hitler's explanation: he required absolute loyalty and obedience from his underlings, and he had circumvented the courts of justice because he was himself the "supreme Justicar [sic] of the German people."[25] At the same time, Eva understood that the consequences of defying him could be deadly.

Eva found the "Jewish question" rather more difficult. She had grown up with several Jewish friends, and Ilse was in love with a Jew. But Eva accepted Hitler's verdict that the Jews polluted the nation. She quickly terminated her relations with those she had always known, though she intervened to prevent one Jewish woman from being arrested, sent her a little money and warned her to leave Germany immediately. (Wisely, the terrified woman fled to Italy the next day.) Eva also suggested that Hitler allow Eduard Bloch, the Austrian doctor who had treated his beloved mother during her final days, to emigrate instead of being rounded up. Hitler agreed, though he sent Gestapo men to Dr. Bloch's house to retrieve postcards Hitler had painted and sent the good doctor as a token of his "everlasting thankfulness."

Apart from these interventions, Eva adopted Hitler's poisoned thinking with apparent ease. Ilse, of course, was deadset against Nazism's anti-Jewish racialism. After the Nuremberg Laws were promulgated, her Jewish employer felt obliged to dismiss her, and he later escaped Germany and made his way to the United States. Ilse was brokenhearted, and she and Eva quarreled bitterly over Hitler and the "Jewish question."

Yet despite Hitler's chilling character defects, Eva envisioned herself as his soul mate, his great love, the selfless and noble woman who would live and die for him. A fortune-teller had predicted that one day, all Germany would know her as the lover of a powerful man. Eva believed fervently in the accuracy of this prediction, and worked patiently and skillfully to entice her reluctant lover. "From the time of our first meetings, I promised myself to follow you everywhere, even in death. You know that my whole life is loving you," Eva would remind Hitler in 1944.

By 1934, her parents had finally discovered that she was involved with Hitler. Her father was humiliated to learn that his daughter was Hitler's mistress but, given the Führer's position, could do little to stop it. After Eva's suicide attempt, Hitler tried to call her almost every evening, though he still refused to publicly acknowledge her as his mistress. On the other hand, he was flattered when newspapers published photographs of him dining with famous actresses. Perhaps he was aware that even fervent Nazis in his social circle ridiculed his sexual prowess and suggested that he was impotent. In 1943, a typist was sentenced to two years' imprisonment for reciting this popular ditty: "He who rules in the Russian manner / dresses his hair in the French style / trims his moustache English-fashion / and wasn't born in Germany himself / and teaches us the Roman salute, / asks our wives for lots of children / but can't produce any himself— / he is the leader of Germany."[26]

On February 6, 1935, her twenty-third birthday, Eva began to keep a diary. Her first entry complained that Hitler had sent his adjutant's wife to Hoffmann's studio with so many flowers for Eva that the office smelled like a mortuary, but he had not given her what she longed for, a little dachshund to keep her company during her lonely vigils waiting for her elusive lover. Eva also resented having to continue her job at Hoffmann's to cover up her real vocation—being Hitler's mistress. In this frame of mind, she hinted hard that a place of her own would facilitate their meetings, and Hitler seemed to take the suggestion seriously.

Then Eva made a tactical mistake. She had accepted a ticket to a ball and asked Hitler's permission to use it. He agreed, but after she left him to go dancing, he punished her by ignoring her for weeks. Even when he was in Munich, he did not call. Once, miserable, Eva stood for hours outside a restaurant and watched him attempt to charm another woman. Perhaps, she concluded miserably, his only interest in her had been sexual. But she was also aware that Hitler absolutely had to have his own way, with her, his friends, colleagues and even world leaders. If anyone challenged him, or even stopped him from monopolizing a conversation, he would sulk or throw terrible tantrums. Eva had inadvertently provoked a similar response by trotting off to a dance when she should have insisted on wasting her ticket so she could stay by Hitler's side.

In May 1935, Eva discovered that she had a serious rival, Unity Valkyrie Mitford, the bosomy, thick-legged daughter of England's Lord Redesdale and sister of Diana Mosley, wife of the English Fascist Party leader. Unity was throwing herself at Hitler, and he was responding enthusiastically. Eva was wretched. On May 28, she decided to take action. She wrote Hitler a note giving him a deadline to contact her. When he missed it, she swallowed twenty-four Phanodorm sleeping pills. Again, Ilse found her. She summoned Dr. Marx, who had not yet fled to the United States, and he revived and saved Hitler's distraught mistress.

Eva had calculated well. Suicide attempts caught Hitler's attention and convinced him to take action. In August, he moved Eva into her own small apartment with her sister Gretl as "chaperone," and a Hungarian maid to care for them. Hitler decorated the new love nest with excellent paintings "lent" by German museums or stolen from Jewish art collections. The one Eva cherished, however, was *The Assam Church* by Adolf Hitler himself. Away from her parents' home, fully supported by her increasingly committed lover, Eva was ecstatic. At last she was able to stop working.

But Hitler was still dissatisfied with the arrangement. He was particularly worried that a neighbor might recognize him when he visited. Soon, he moved the sisters into their own house, with a superbly equipped underground bunker, on the outskirts of Munich. He arranged for Eva to have her own private telephone, a Mercedes-Benz with a full-time chauffeur and, the best present of all, two Scottish terriers, Stasi and Negus.

Eva Braun had become Hitler's *maîtresse en titre*, or, as he called her, his *chère amie*. At last she felt secure, and she happily devoted her days to beautifying herself, sunbathing and playing with her Scotties (and later the German Shepherd Dog that Hitler also gave her). Eva confided in and gossiped with Gretl, who dated several SS men before eventually marrying SS Gruppen-führer Hermann Fegelein, liaison officer for Himmler with Hitler. The sisters also shopped, and Eva built up an extensive wardrobe of elegant clothes and shoes, and a jewelry collection. Every afternoon her hairdresser arrived and did her hair. In her one systematic act of defiance, Eva ate carefully and exercised religiously to keep her figure slender and taut rather than soft and fleshy as Hitler preferred. Before they first slept together and he saw her naked body, Eva stuffed her bra with handkerchiefs so that Hitler would think she was bustier than she was. As it was, he complained about her leanness and accused her of being a slave to fashion. Eva, however, was too terrified of becoming fat to gain any weight.

Eva's cousin Gertrude Weisker, whom Eva invited for a visit in 1944 to keep her company when Hitler was away, recalled that Eva changed her clothes at least five times daily, and swam and exercised to fill a "special emptiness in her."²⁷ Eva also suggested that Gertrude listen to the BBC, though doing so was a capital offense. Gertrude listened and took notes, then reported to Eva what she had learned about the progress of the war.

In constructing her busily idle existence, Eva did not neglect the human dimensions. She finally made her peace with her parents, who accepted that their daughter was living in sin with a man twenty-three years her senior. More daringly, she plotted the social demise of those in Hitler's inner circle who still dared treat her contemptuously. The first to go was Hitler's half sister, Angela, Geli's mother, who called Eva a streetwalker. When Hitler heard about this, he angrily ordered Angela out of his house.

Before long, Eva's house had become Hitler's haven. He would arrive each evening by midnight, often depressed and irritable, and leave the next morning refreshed and cheerful, soothed by his mistress's tender ministrations. Eva listened intently to his monologues, including his roiling diatribes against the Jews, his standard dinner-table fare. Despite her liberal upbringing, Eva kept silent, prepared to sacrifice her family's principles on the altar of Hitler's mania. He did not enjoy "political women," and so Eva excised political—and moral—standards from her exchanges with him.

Her sister Ilse, however, had a different agenda. Ilse once attempted to intervene on behalf of Arthur Ernst Rutra, a Jewish writer she admired. But instead of being released, Rutra was shot and killed "while trying to escape." From then on, Ilse refrained from "helping." "I realized," she recalled after the war, "that any further intervention on my part . . . far from assisting the Jews, would have hastened their destruction."²⁸

Eva apparently suffered no such crisis of conscience even as the war progressed, and she must have been aware of what was happening in concentration camps. Heinrich Hoffmann often amused her and Hitler with jokes about nearby Dachau, and in 1944, after an air raid damaged her house, a slave laborer was sent from Dachau to repair it. After Gretl married Hermann Fegelein, Eva visited her new home and probably saw the concentration camp inmates who worked in the Fegelein house. Toward the end of the war, starved Russian prisoners in tattered clothes became a common sight as well. Eva took no notice because she had no interest.

But Eva could exert influence when she cared about an issue. After Heinrich Himmler shut down ladies' hairdressers, Eva lobbied to have the order rescinded. German women needed to look their best for their soldier husbands or lovers, she argued. Eva also had regulations against buying food on the black market repealed—how else could a good German woman feed her fighting husband and children? She persuaded Hitler to order that German soldiers stand up on public transport so women could sit down. Toward the end of the war, Eva learned that a certain general intended to defy orders to execute thirty-five thousand prisoners of war if Hitler could not negotiate a satisfactory truce with the Allies. Somehow, she maneuvered Hitler into entrusting that same general with supervising the POWs, which certainly saved lives. Eva also convinced Hitler to delay an order to flood tunnels to stave off Russian troops. Many German soldiers and civilians had taken refuge there, and she wanted to give them time to escape. About the Jews, however, Eva had nothing to say.

Eva also listened silently when Hitler expounded his rigid and clichéd views about women. He commented about how jealousy could transform the meekest woman into a tiger, and how married women were by nature very demanding. When Fritz Sauckel, the crude and vicious plenipotentiary general for the allocation of labor, reported that 25 percent of the enslaved foreign women were virgins (Sauckel took great pleasure in subjecting them all to vaginal exams), Hitler was unimpressed. Virginity, he declared, was highly overrated, and virgins had nothing special to distinguish them. So much for the gift of Eva's maidenhead.

Hitler and Eva shared only two passions: their conviction that the Führer was not a man like other men, and their love for dogs. Even here Hitler judged some races of dogs, like some races of people, ridiculous and unworthy. He refused to be photographed with Eva's Scottish terriers and never gave her the dachshund she longed for. But he doted on German Shepherd Dogs, praising them for their courage, intelligence and loyalty. He was particularly attached to his bitch Blondie.

Eva's single-minded devotion and doglike love began to pay off. Over the years, she gained status among the Nazi elite and became Hitler's official hostess. As Germany's fortunes of war turned for the worst, Hitler grew more and more dependent on her for solace. But he was adamant that he would never marry her. "The worst feature of marriage is this creating of rights," he would say. "It is wiser to have a mistress. Then there is no burden to carry and everything is simply a beautiful gift." He hastened to add that this aversion to marriage was appropriate only "in the case of exceptional men."[29]

By 1945, Germany's defeat was just a matter of time. Hitler brooded and took solitary walks with Blondie. He suspected his enemies were trying to poison him and, before eating, had someone else taste his food. His physical health degenerated in tandem with his mental deterioration. His ears and head constantly ached. His poor digestion plagued him. His hands shook. Eva fussed over and mothered him, pandering to his illnesses as she had to his hypochondria. "You are the only one who cares," he would whine.[30] This was quite literally true, as a stream of Nazi officials and soldiers began to desert the Führer who had brought Germany to its knees.

By April 1945, the end was in sight. Hitler had moved to a luxurious two-story bunker under the Reich Chancellery in Berlin, and Eva joined him there. She continued to manicure her nails and set her hair, and to change her clothes several times a day. Though everyone else was mired in gloomy depression, she bubbled with forced cheer. She found occasions to celebrate: Franklin D. Roosevelt's death was a particularly jolly one. On April 20, she threw a birthday party for Hitler's fifty-sixth birthday. Most of the top Nazi officials showed up, but their alarm at the physical wreck their Führer had become ruined the festivities, and Hitler left his own party early.

Soon after Hitler's failed birthday party, the Third Reich was defeated. Hitler arranged for the last plane out of Berlin to fly Eva, his secretaries and his cook to safety. Eva refused, took both his hands in hers and said fondly, "But you know that I'll stay with you. I won't let myself be sent away."[31] For the first time ever in public, Hitler kissed his mistress on the lips.

That night at dinner, he handed out vials of cyanide to Eva and the other women, all of whom had also pledged to stay with him. Eva struggled to remain calm. She composed a maudlin letter to Gretl, expressing her contentment that she would die with her Führer, after a perfect life with him. "With the Führer I have had everything. To die, now, beside him, completes my happiness. . . . It is the right end for a German woman."[32] She also left instructions that Ilse should destroy her papers. Eva feared that her dressmaker's bills would fuel accusations that she was too extravagant.

Hitler was making his own final plans. His papers and personal belongings were to be burned. He intended to shoot himself as well as to swallow cyanide. And, at the edge of the abyss, he decided to marry Eva. She was ecstatic. Instead of preparing for premature death, she primped and planned for her wedding. She dressed in Hitler's favorite dress, a black silk with long, narrow sleeves and pink roses at the shoulder. As always, her hair was freshly set. After midnight on April 29, as Allied jets roared overhead and Russian tanks rumbled blocks away, Eva Braun and Adolf Hitler stood side by side in their bunker and vowed to love and honor each other until death did them part. A wedding breakfast followed, with guests and the two chief celebrants indulging in champagne, wine and bonbons, and applauding ludicrous speeches and toasts.

Eva expressed only one concern, that her brother-in-law, Gretl's husband, Hermann Fegelein, by then a general, had not appeared for the ceremony. She discovered the reason for his absence when a guard handed her a note marked as urgent. Fegelein had been imprisoned and condemned to death, and he begged for her help. Eva went to her new husband, who was busily dictating his last will and testament. She reminded him that Gretl was pregnant; surely Fegelein needn't be shot?

"We can't allow family matters to interfere with disciplinary action," Hitler replied. "Fegelein is a traitor."[33] Then he turned back to his analysis of the Third Reich and blamed its disastrous finale on the Jews: "Centuries will pass away, but out of the ruins of our towns and cultural monuments the hatred will ever renew itself against those ultimately responsible whom we have to thank for everything: international Jewry and its helpers."[34]

Eva, usually so cheerfully compliant, wept as she returned to her room. Soon after, on her husband's orders, her brother-in-law was executed. Hitler, meanwhile, was recording for all time his venom against the Jews, and justifying his decision to marry the young woman who, after years of "true friendship," had of her own volition come to Berlin to die at his side. Both she and I, he said, prefer death to the disgrace of defeat or capitulation.

As he and Eva nibbled their first and last breakfast as husband and wife, an aide handed Hitler a Reuters dispatch that reported how Mussolini and Clara Petacci, his mistress, had been captured and killed, then dragged through the streets of Milan and hung head downwards in the public square. Hitler was horrified. He ordered gas brought to the bunker so his body and Eva's could be incinerated rather than defiled. He also handed a vial of cyanide to an aide, with instructions to kill Blondie. Minutes later, Blondie and her five puppies were dead.

The strong scent of gasoline wafted in from the exit to the bunker. Russian troops were one block away. Eva went into her room, washed and set her hair and refreshed her makeup. At teatime, she and Hitler bade everyone farewell and returned alone to their room. Minutes later, a gunshot rang out. Hitler had turned his pistol on himself after taking cyanide. Eva had died instantly.

The bodies were hauled into the Reich Chancellery garden, doused with gasoline and set on fire. Meanwhile, Magda Goebbels murdered each of her six children, then swallowed poison. Her husband, Joseph Goebbels, shot himself. As the Russians moved in to "liberate" the Chancellery, the stench of Eva's and Hitler's burning bodies fouled the air, a fitting olfactory backdrop to the final moments of the Third Reich.

The story of Eva Braun's career as Adolf Hitler's mistress is frightening in its ordinariness. Despite her strict Catholic upbringing, Eva Braun took her life's principles from the steamy pages of her favorite novels, in which true love conquered all and a good woman stood by her man. Her apolitical, gossipy banter amused and consoled the Führer and strengthened him for another day of doing battle. It also reassured him—if he needed reassurance—that he was indeed a genius, and that his vision of Germany had been forged from his white-hot intellect. The daily rituals, the tender nicknames, the abandonment of morality—all this was nothing more than the banality of their love affair, and of the unspeakable evil it was mired in.

JEW AND GENTILE, BEYOND THE CAMPS
Hannah Arendt [35]

In the late autumn of 1924, a precocious teenager walked into a lecture hall to hear one of Germany's preeminent philosophers. Within a very short time, the two entered into a relationship so intense and complicated that it changed their lives and lasted until he died. But theirs was not a beautiful or exemplary love story, because Hannah Arendt, the eighteen-year-old student, was Jewish and Martin Heidegger, her thirty-five-year-old professor, was a German nationalist who later joined the Nazi Party and sabotaged Jewish scholars and colleagues.

Hannah Arendt was the brilliant daughter of assimilated Jews who saw themselves as Germans and never mentioned the word "Jew," yet at the same time cautioned her to challenge any anti-Semitic remarks her classmates might make. "As a child I did not know that I was Jewish," the adult Hannah recalled. Later, she realized that she "looked Jewish . . . looked different" from other children. Sometimes her grandfather took her to a synagogue. That was the extent of her Jewishness.

Hannah was an arresting and stylish presence, a slender girl with delicate features, short hair and brooding dark eyes—"one virtually drowned in them and feared never to come up again," recalled a former boyfriend.[36] Among her peers she "immediately stood out as 'unusual' and 'singular.'" She laid down the law at her interview for admission into a history course—"There must be no anti-Semitic remarks," she said.[37] Like other top students, Hannah had come to the University of Marburg because she had heard that in Heidegger's classroom, "thinking has come to life again; the cultural treasures of the past, believed to be dead, are being made to speak."[38]

The man reputed to make this happen was a self-consciously short man with coal black hair and a dark complexion, a stocky build and small downcast eyes that seldom fixed for long on anyone else's. He was a spellbinding teacher whose nickname was "little magician," and as he elaborated his theory of Being, he both fascinated and confounded.[39] Martin Heidegger dressed folksily, in Black Forest knickerbockers and peasant coat. But with his students, he was the antithesis of folksy and reveled in the European magisterial style, dominating the class, staying aloof, encouraging reverence in his audience. Often his students gathered after class to compare notes and to inquire if any among them had understood a word of his lecture.

When he first laid eyes on Hannah, Heidegger was comfortably married to Elfride Petri, a virulently anti-Semitic Protestant economist whose well-off family had been slow to accept her Catholic husband, a low-paid scholar struggling to rise in the university system. Elfride was an excellent homemaker and mother to their two sons. She assumed the burden of their domestic life so Heidegger could devote himself to intellectual pursuits. And she looked on jealously as his female students clustered adoringly around their charismatic professor.

Heidegger noticed Hannah in his class and summoned her to his office. She arrived swaddled in raincoat and hat, too awed to speak in anything but monosyllables. Within weeks they had raced from polite courting to physical intimacy, and almost certainly Heidegger was Hannah's first lover. He had had affairs before and drew on his experience to orchestrate a complicated system of clandestine meetings, often in Hannah's attic room or on a park bench they thought of as "theirs."

Soon Heidegger was worrying that the relationship was turning his life topsy-turvy, not because Hannah was Jewish, but because he was a married man and her professor. If their affair were to be exposed, his career and his marriage would be destroyed. Though he had no intention of leaving his wife and had often been unfaithful, Hannah was different. She became, he recalled in later years, the passion of his life, and he felt unable to resist her.

After a year, Hannah transferred to Heidelberg University, entirely to facilitate Heidegger, who had too much at stake professionally for her to continue at Marburg. He was not straightforward about asking her to leave. Instead, he implied that, despite being one of Marburg's most outstanding students, she had not "fit in" well and would be better off elsewhere. Hannah neither argued nor protested. But when she moved, she did not give him her new address. Whatever happened next would have to be at his initiative.

Heidegger took that initiative, though it was not easy. He did not dare ask philosophy professor Karl Jaspers, the doctoral supervisor to whom he had recommended her. Eventually, he located her through Guenther Stern, a Jewish student. Heidegger contacted Hannah, and they resumed their affair in all its intensity, with secret codes, flashing lights and passionate letters and poetry. But Heidegger controlled every aspect of it, commanding Hannah to answer his letters only when he requested it, and allowing weeks, sometimes months, of silence to intervene. He found out from Jaspers that Hannah was seeing another student—she was as secretive about this as she was about her relationship with him.

At about the same time, in a calculated career move, Heidegger temporarily broke the affair off. His classic *Being and Time*, which he admitted he could not have written without Hannah, who understood him as completely philosophically as she did personally, had just been published. He had been promoted to replace the retiring Edmund Husserl as a full professor at Freiburg University. He was also flirting with Elisabeth Blochmann, a colleague's (half-Jewish) wife. Hannah was plunged into black despair that she expressed in poetry, sometimes dedicated to him. "I would have lost my right to live had I lost my love for you," she wrote him in desperate passion. "I love you, as I have since the very first day—you know this, and I have always known this."[40]

In September 1929, Hannah married Guenther Stern. Though they would remain lifelong friends, the marriage quickly faded. They soon separated and, in 1937, divorced. Ever loyal to Heidegger, Hannah never told Guenther about her affair. Apparently she also dismissed Guenther's disquieting accounts of their teacher's reactionary politics and strident nationalism, and of his wife's overt anti-Semitism. Instead, Hannah assured Heidegger that "our love became the blessing of my life" and once arranged to secretly watch him board a train. Afterward, she described how she felt "alone, utterly helpless. As always there was nothing I could do but . . . wait wait wait."[41]

While waiting, still married to Guenther and by then deeply concerned about the rise of Nazism and anti-Semitism, Hannah plunged into researching and writing a biography of Rahel Varnhagen, an 18th-century assimilated German Jew whose intellectual salons had been famous. For years Varnhagen struggled to divest herself of Jewishness, but she was ultimately reconciled to her identity. In 1933, Hannah finally acknowledged that Heidegger, recently appointed rector of Freiburg University, had barred Jews from his seminars, snubbed Jewish colleagues and discriminated against Jewish students. She wrote telling him how shocked she was by such behavior.

Heidegger vehemently denied everything and wrote furiously about the ingratitude of his accusers. He had, indeed, intervened to help two Jewish colleagues whom he described as "Jews of the better sort, men of exemplary character," and he arranged a research fellowship in Cambridge, England, for his Jewish research assistant, Werner Brock. He had also forbidden students to post an anti-Semitic poster—"Against the Un-German Spirit"—at the university. But Hannah knew for certain that he had joined the National Socialist Party and had delivered a pro-Hitler speech in his new capacity as rector. In 1933, Heidegger also gave this horrifying answer to Jaspers's question about such a crude man as Hitler ruling Germany: "Culture is of no importance. *Just look at his marvelous hands.*"[42] Meanwhile, Guenther was forced to flee Germany because of his leftist views, and Hannah was imprisoned for eight frightening days at the police headquarters, under interrogation about German Zionists, for whom she had been working. (She had also been harboring persecuted communists, but this had gone unnoticed.)

With her mother, Hannah circumvented Nazi officials by leaving Germany illegally, through a safe house with a front door in Germany and a back door in Czechoslovakia. From there she made her way to Paris, where she devoted herself exclusively to "Jewish work." "When one is attacked as a Jew, one must defend oneself *as a Jew*," she said. Years later, she remarked that during this bleak period, her central concern had been what her friends, not her enemies, were doing.

For seventeen years after this, Hannah had no contact with Heidegger. In January 1940, she remarried, to Heinrich Blücher, a German gentile revolutionary. Their relationship was characterized by intense love and intellectual and political compatibility. In May 1940, Hannah was briefly interned, first in a Paris stadium, then in Gurs, a French concentration camp. Heinrich, too, was imprisoned then released. With Guenther Stern's help, the couple obtained visas to the United States and arrived there in April 1941. At first they endured poverty while they studied English, then Hannah resumed her academic career and writing.

In 1943, Hannah and Heinrich heard about Auschwitz. At first, they refused to believe it—for one thing, it made no sense militarily. (American Supreme Court justice Felix Frankfurter also dismissed a detailed report about Auschwitz, on similar grounds.) Six months later, new and irrefutable evidence surfaced, and "it was as if an abyss had opened," Hannah recalled, because the extermination of the Jews and the apparatus that had facilitated their destruction meant that the unforgivable had happened, something for which no justification could be made and which no punishment expiate. Hannah's shock led to her study *The Origins of Totalitarianism* (written in 1945, published in 1951), in which she identified and indicted "race-thinking" as integrally linked to totalitarianism and imperialism.

In 1946, in an essay in the *Partisan Review*, Hannah specifically castigated Heidegger for having joined the Nazi Party and for banning Husserl, his teacher and friend, from the university. (In fact, Husserl had been banned before Heidegger became rector.) Then, in 1949, on a trip to Germany, she visited Karl and Gertrud Jaspers, who had survived the Nazi regime in Heidelberg. Their greatest bond was the intensity of their feelings for Heidegger, Jaspers as a fellow philosopher, Hannah as Heidegger's former student and mistress. Despite her critical essay, despite unspeakable revelations about the Shoah, despite everything she knew and suspected about him, Hannah had never completely freed herself from the spell of her former lover.

In February 1950, after tremendous vacillation and self-doubt, she decided to see Heidegger. She arrived in Freiburg on February 7 and immediately sent him a note suggesting that he visit her at her hotel. He arrived at 6:30 that evening, unannounced, and once again, Hannah was captivated. "When the waiter announced your name," she told him afterward, "it was as though suddenly time had stopped." Incredibly, she assured him that if she had not communicated with him, it would have been only because of her pride and "pure, plain, crazy stupidity" rather than anything else—in other words, it would not have been due to his Nazi past.

But Heidegger had been a Nazi, and in his important and prestigious position as rector of a major university, he had undermined and sometimes destroyed the careers of Jews and opponents of Nazism, including a devout Roman Catholic. He had not lifted a finger to help Jaspers's Jewish wife when she was in mortal danger from the Nazi regime. On the rare occasions he attempted to intervene on behalf of victimized Jews, he did so on the basis of friendship rather than outrage at Nazi policies. In those early years of the Third Reich, Heidegger had read and clearly understood *Mein Kampf*, in particular its anti-Semitic rancor. Like Hitler, Heidegger believed in an international Jewish conspiracy. As early as 1929, he had written an official letter warning, "We are faced with the choice of either bringing genuine autochthonous forces and educators into our German spiritual life, or finally abandoning it to the growing Judaization in the wider and narrower sense."[43]

How had a love affair developed between this German Nazi and a Jew who had had to flee Germany to avoid being exterminated? Unlike Jewish women who were later violated by Nazis who held them in physical captivity, the young Hannah had been in thrall to Heidegger's soaring intellect and his professorial stature, both of which he used to seduce her and bind her to him. Such was her indifference to what she then regarded as "politics" that she could not believe that he could be a Nazi. Heidegger was clever enough to avoid discussions that might alert her to his passionate nationalism and appreciation of Hitler's terrifying ideas and goals. Given these circumstances, it is difficult to argue that Hannah Arendt knowingly slept with the enemy.

But after the war, Heidegger's Nazi predilections were exposed, and he faced professional and personal disgrace, loss of his teaching position, a ban on his books and reductions in his pension. The basis for these relatively lenient penalties was irrefutable evidence, and Heidegger was forced to defend himself in front of the Freiburg University Verification Commission. For this de-Nazification process, he needed impeccable references. Who better to provide them than his former mistress, the now famous Jewish scholar Hannah Arendt, and his former colleague, Karl Jaspers, whose wife was Jewish?

Such was the attraction of Heidegger's towering intellect that these other two giants caved in, Jaspers less completely than Hannah, and more or less supported Heidegger's indignant version of how the Nazis had persecuted him. They did this though both knew, in Hannah's words, that Heidegger "lies notoriously always and at each opportunity" and that he was a man not so much of bad character as of no character at all. The consequence was that in March 1949, Heidegger was judged "Fellow traveler. No punitive measures."[44]

Afterward, while Jaspers doubted and agonized, Hannah temporized and—against all reason—swallowed Heidegger's prevarications. She even tried to convince others to believe them. Jaspers, however, could not forget Heidegger's callous indifference to Gertrud's suffering and a legion of other wrongs. "He was the only one among my friends . . . who betrayed me," Jaspers wrote.[45] Until he died, unreconciled to Heidegger, Hannah negotiated the difficult path between the two men, praising the former, defending the latter. Once, when Jaspers demanded that she renounce her friendship with Heidegger, she absolutely refused.

Part of the reason was that Heidegger resurrected his relationship with Hannah, except that they no longer had sex. Furthermore, he had by then told Elfride about his long-ago affair—Hannah's version was that "she somehow squeezed the story out of him"[46]—and urged his reluctant wife to welcome his former mistress into their home. Hannah later described their difficult meeting. "The woman is jealous almost to the point of madness," she wrote. "After the years of apparently nursing the hope that he would simply forget me, her jealousy only intensified." Elfride was anti-Semitic, narrow-minded and "reeking with ugly resentment."[47] Elfride rather than Martin was the Nazi, the truly guilty one. "Alas, she is simply stupendously stupid," Hannah told her friends.[48] The nail in the coffin was that Elfride had not typed out ream after ream of Heidegger's great thoughts as, Hannah said, she herself would have.

For the rest of her life, Hannah visited and wrote Heidegger, and peddled his books in the United States. She never concealed this from Heinrich. He considered his wife's "friendship" harmless and was, in any case, awed by Heidegger's genius. Furthermore, Heinrich was in no position to tout fidelity since despite his love for Hannah, he was also sleeping with a younger woman and continued to do so though he knew how painful his affair was to her. (In *Pictures from an Institution*, a *roman à clef* about Hannah and Heinrich, their friend Randall Jarrell used them as models for a couple he called the Rosenbaums. He styled the Rosenbaums' unusual marriage a "Dual Monarchy" of equal, independent but united partners.)

Hannah reverted to her role as Heidegger's admirer. She never mentioned her own books. "Always," she admitted, "I have been virtually lying to him about myself, pretending the books, the name, did not exist, and I couldn't, so to speak, count to three, unless it concerned the interpretations of his works. Then, he would be quite pleased if it turned out that I can count to three and sometimes to four."[49] To maintain her relationship with Heidegger, Hannah had to hide her intellect. "This is the unspoken *conditio sine qua non* of the whole affair," she admitted.[50]

Hannah published *The Human Condition* without a dedication, as a sort of secret dedication to Heidegger. She confided to him in verse: "How could I dedicate it to you, / my trusted friend, / to whom I remain faithful / and unfaithful, / And both in love."[51] Heidegger was furious that Hannah had withheld the dedication, and his fury was no doubt fueled by his resentment at her fame and achievements.

In 1966, when a German magazine attacked Heidegger's Nazi past, Hannah told Jaspers that Heidegger should be left in peace. Jaspers retorted that a man of his stature could not hide his past, which was, in any case, there for all to see and judge. Hannah brushed all this aside. She attributed much of the continued controversy surrounding Heidegger's Nazism to slander. She argued that he had been an innocent academic not attuned to political realities.[52] She denied that he had ever read *Mein Kampf*, which meant he hadn't realized what Hitler really thought. She claimed that Heidegger was pressured into anything he might have done by Elfride, his anti-Semitic ogre of a wife.

But Heidegger *had* read *Mein Kampf*, and in any case, nobody—not Elfride, not Hannah—pushed him into anything. Quite simply, Hannah could not admit the obvious—that Heidegger had been a practicing Nazi—and she worried about the damage to his already battered reputation. Heidegger could not have manufactured a better or more willing ally than Hannah Arendt, a world-renowned Jew who had known him since 1924 and who, in *Eichmann in Jerusalem*, had identified the mechanics of the infrastructure that produced the evil of Nazi Germany.

Hannah's sustained efforts to de-Nazify Heidegger's reputation sprang from deep within her. She had an overriding need to justify her deep love for this man and to make him worthy of her by proving the unprovable.

Heidegger's biographer Rüdiger Safranski describes the intellectual dimension of the relationship between these two great philosophers as complementary: Hannah responded to Heidegger's "running ahead into death . . . with a philosophy of being born; to his existential solipsism of *Jemeinigkeit* (each-one-ness) . . . with a philosophy of plurality; to his critique of *Verfallenheit* (helpless addiction) to the world of *Man* (One/They) . . . by philosophically ennobling the 'public.' "[53]

Hannah retained her admiration for Heidegger's intellect. In his presence, she easily reverted to her role as beloved and favorite student, with none of the arrogance her American colleagues detected. Her contempt for Elfride cleansed her image of Heidegger, and Elfride's jealousy affirmed Hannah's confidence in the depth of his love. For the rest of her life, Hannah and Heidegger remained in touch. When his advanced age induced him to move into a small, single-story house, Hannah sent a housewarming gift of flowers.

Hannah died in 1975, without ever having admitted how Heidegger had betrayed her and lent his authority to pernicious ideas. Heidegger died five months later, having read her books only cursorily and having refused to discuss her work. He likely went to his grave unaware that Hannah had taught the world "the lesson of the fearsome, word-and-thought-denying banality of evil,"[54] the evil committed in the name of the Nazi ideology he had embraced.

CHAPTER 9

Mistresses as Muses

GENIUS may be either a gift or a curse, and those who possess it are seldom ordinary. In every society, creative people, especially men, inspire admiration and a certain respect that, among a small band of fervent devotees, translates into an erotic passion and a desire to simultaneously nurture the genius and live vicariously through him as his muse.

Often enough these women are themselves creators, or they long to be. They even have a name: shadow artists. Writer Rosemary Sullivan describes these women who "have notoriously attached themselves to male artists" as being "in love with art but feeling inadequate and fearful of failure, or simply unable to find their own way."[1] Sometimes the awed respect that binds shadow-artist mistresses to their creative lovers approaches reverence and induces a degree of self-abnegation shocking in its intensity.

Not all mistresses are shadow artists who sacrifice to a lover's creative gift. Some women, as appreciative of self as of genius, demand egalitarian relationships. In rare cases, the couple realize an ideal and become each other's mutually inspiring muses. Even more rarely, an admiring lover devotes himself to a creative woman as her muse. The fact is, some of the most famous mistresses of creators, perhaps a majority of them, have idolized their gifted lovers and judged their interests, needs and value to the world of paramount importance. Because of this, these shadow artists willingly suppress their personal desires and even their rights; of their own volition, they sacrifice themselves on the altar of their lovers' creative genius.

Héloise [2]

In 1115 or 1116, the budding philosopher Héloise was a tall teenager of sixteen or seventeen with a superb figure, a smile illuminated by exceptionally white teeth, and a reputation for erudition second to none. Héloise lived in Paris with her uncle and guardian, Canon Fulbert of Notre-Dame cathedral. (Nothing is known about her mother, Hersindis, or her father, who may have died when she was a child. The family name is unknown.) The childless Fulbert adored Héloise, and provided her with an education fit for a patrician boy but highly unusual for a girl. After sending her to Argenteuil's excellent convent school, Fulbert tutored Héloise in classical philosophy. He also introduced her to the teachings of Peter Abélard, a brilliant philosophy professor who was associated with Notre-Dame.

Abélard was about thirty-seven, an immensely handsome *clericus*, a low-ranked religious who had not been ordained or taken a vow of chastity. Abélard could have married but he preferred bachelorhood; he was ambitious and hoped to rise within the Church to a high position for which only celibates were eligible. Abélard had a reputation as a profound thinker who mesmerized his students but treated his peers with condescending arrogance. Because Abélard and Fulbert inhabited the same rarified world, it was quite natural that the younger man would one day meet Fulbert's niece. What was not natural, or at least not predictable, was that he would fall tonsured head over sandaled heels in love with her. "*Completely alight with love* for this young maiden," Abélard later wrote. "I therefore sought an opportunity to win her confidence."[3]

This proved all too easy. When Abélard proposed that he tutor Héloise in exchange for meals in the canon's house, the unsuspecting Fulbert accepted enthusiastically. After all, did not France's intellectually questing youth flock to Abélard's feet to study there? And so, with every intention of seducing his pupil, Abélard, a self-described "starving wolf" set loose on "a tender lamb," came to stay at Fulbert's house. "I . . . thought I should reach my goal very easily," he confessed afterward. "I had such celebrity at the time and possessed such graces of youth and body that I feared no refusal from any woman I found worthy of my love."

Héloise was not blind to those graces. "When you appeared in public, who did not rush to catch sight of you, or crane his neck and strain his eyes to see you as you departed?" she recalled. "What young girl did not burn for you in your absence or become inflamed by your presence?"[4] And thanks to her trusting uncle, Héloise had Abélard all to herself, for long hours.

Almost at once, Abélard seduced her. She responded joyfully, discovering her own sexuality in their lovemaking sessions. They pretended to study, but "My hands found themselves at her breasts more often than on the book," Abélard admitted.[5] Héloise's sexual inexperience heightened the "burning ardor" with which they surrendered themselves to each other.

Sometimes, to satisfy Fulbert's request that he thrash Héloise if she argued or failed to study, Abélard whipped her. This, too, had an erotic dimension and "surpassed all balms in sweetness," Abélard recalled. "In short, we left no phase of love untried in our passion, and if love-making could find the unusual, we tried this also."[6] Centuries before the notion of sadomasochistic sex was defined, Abélard and Héloise were reveling in it.

Soon Abélard was so hopelessly obsessed with Héloise that he lost interest in philosophy. He lectured so desultorily that his students taunted him. His reputation plummeted. One terrible day, Fulbert caught the lovers in bed together, "like Mars and Venus," making love instead of philosophy. Furiously, he kicked Abélard out of his house.

Then Héloise realized she was pregnant. She managed to notify Abélard, who devised a scheme to steal her away. Héloise disguised herself as a nun, and Abélard brought her to his sister's house in Brittany for the duration of her pregnancy.

Back in Paris, Fulbert was nearly demented with rage and grief, and so bitter that Abélard feared for his own life. With uncharacteristic humility, he went to Fulbert and pleaded for forgiveness, blaming his shameful conduct on "the power of love . . . [and how] since the beginning of the human race, *women had brought down the greatest of men.*"[7] Admittedly, he had sinned, but surely Fulbert could see that it was Héloise's fault?

Abélard proposed this curious solution to the dilemma: he would marry Héloise, but secretly, so his chances of advancement in the Church would not be jeopardized. Fulbert, every bit as cunning as his adversary, agreed.

Abélard was elated. He had, in a single stroke, extricated himself from his predicament and salvaged his career. In this exultant frame of mind he fetched Héloise, newly delivered of their son, Astrolabe, back to Paris to be married. To Abélard's and Fulbert's mutual consternation, Héloise was bitterly opposed to the marriage on the grounds that it would force Abélard to make sacrifices and it would undermine his career. She cited the Bible and the Ancients to prove the incompatibility of marriage and philosophical pursuits, and she argued that a philosopher could not possibly tolerate "the squawlings of infants, the lullabies of nurses,"[8] to say nothing of "the constant uncleanliness of small children."⁹ (She did not even mention Astrolabe, whose inconvenient little person was hidden away with Abélard's relatives.)

Most importantly, the freethinking Héloise declared that her love had been offered freely and unconditionally, in keeping with Cicero's philosophic ideal, and she would much rather remain Abélard's mistress than become his wife. (Years later, still defiant, Héloise swore that even if the emperor Augustus had proposed marriage, she would have chosen to be Abélard's whore rather than Augustus's empress.)

Abélard, however, wanted the chains of marriage to bind Héloise to him forever. "I loved you beyond measure and longed to hold you forever," he admitted years later.¹⁰ He also hoped to placate her powerful uncle, who would help him advance in the Church. In this most unequal of relationships, Abélard's needs eclipsed Héloise's, and so in the summer of 1118, the marriage took place. Héloise wept through the service.

Almost immediately, and as he had always intended to do, Fulbert broke his agreement to keep the marriage a secret. Héloise, obsessed with preserving Abélard's reputation, denied her uncle's words. Fulbert was furious at Héloise's blatant disregard for her own interests, to say nothing of his family's. He turned on her so cruelly that Abélard again abducted her, this time shutting her away in the convent at Argenteuil, disguised as a novice.

Fulbert soon learned what had happened. He wrongly concluded that Abélard had simply wished to be rid of Héloise. In fact, Abélard visited her regularly, and his desire for her was unabated. Once, in the throes of uncontrollable passion, they made love in the refectory that was dedicated to the Virgin Mary.

Back in Paris, Fulbert was plotting his simple and brutal revenge. He bribed Abélard's valet to open the door to Fulbert's henchmen. In the dead of night, these hired assassins attacked Abélard and, in his own words, "in a cruel and shameful manner . . . cut off the organs by which I had committed the deed which they deplored."¹¹

News of the philosopher's castration spread. By morning, a crowd that seemed like "the entire city" gathered outside his house to mourn his mutilation. "The astonishment, the general stupor, the moaning, wailing, and crying"—and above all their pity—tormented him more than his physical pain. "I would be pointed at by everyone, torn apart by all tongues, become a monstrous spectacle," he lamented.¹²

The wounded man fled to the sanctuary of the Benedictine abbey of Saint-Denis in Paris. He never forgave Fulbert and his accomplices, and he hounded them through the law courts until each one was gruesomely punished. His treacherous servant and Fulbert's castrators had their eyes gouged out and their genitals hacked off. All Fulbert's property was confiscated. Abélard even punished Héloise, forcing her to take holy vows though she had neither the vocation nor the inclination to do so.

Héloise's friends and family implored her to refuse to take this drastic step. She was still a teenager and a mother—how could she cut herself off forever from the world? But Héloise was horrified by and angry about her uncle's role in castrating Abélard, and committed to her obsessive love for him. She shocked her family by professing to love Abélard more than God. Then, because Abélard wished her to become a nun, she strode up to the altar and, sobbing dramatically, recited Cornelia's words as she prepares to kill herself after her husband Pompey's death. "My august spouse, so little made for marriage, have I brought this on your noble head? Criminal that I am for having married you and caused your misfortune! Take then in expiation this punishment I now go forth to receive."[13] To atone for the loss of Abélard's genitals and pride, Héloise sacrificed her freedom and her future.

As a eunuch, Abélard ignored Héloise for ten long years. He turned again to teaching and writing philosophy. But once again, this arrogant man ran afoul of clerical enemies and so offended his fellow monks that he had to leave the monastery, though he was still technically subject to its abbot's rule. Abélard settled alone on the banks of the Arduzon, in Champagne, and adopted the ultra-ascetic life of a hermit. But soon admiring scholars sought him out there, and constructed a stone and timber oratory afterward known as the Paraclete, the Comforter.

In 1125, Abélard was appointed abbot of Saint-Gildas monastery in Brittany. When he moved there he discovered a libertine gang of monks who kept concubines and treated their monastery like a fiefdom. The monks despised and terrorized their new abbot, and several times tried to kill him. They poisoned the consecrated wine he sipped during Holy Communion. Then they poisoned his supper, but Abélard's "taster" died on the spot, alerting Abélard to his danger. Ultimately, he survived only because of the armed intervention of a sympathetic local noble.

Over at Argenteuil, Héloise was a reluctant nun who brooded night and day about Abélard. As the years passed, she matured into a compelling presence among her fellow nuns, many as indifferent to the religious way of life as she was. Before she was thirty, Héloise became her convent's abbess.

Héloise's convent was not a model establishment. In 1125, she and her sisters were accused of repeated licentiousness. On orders from the papal legate, the local bishops and the king of France, Héloise and her nuns were expelled from the convent. Suddenly Abélard appeared to salvage her, offering the homeless wanderers a home at the now vacant Paraclete. After ten years of silence, the lovers were reunited.

Héloise still wore her vocation with a heavy heart. Time had stoked rather than cooled her sexual appetite, including her erotic interest in Abélard, castrate though he was. After she was installed there, Abélard began to visit Paraclete as its spiritual adviser. Perhaps Héloise was unable to conceal her passion for her husband, though he displayed only *agape* love for her. Perhaps Abelard's intellectual arrogance enraged his corrupt monks. After several years, they joined other clerics, including a powerful bishop, to make the unlikely charge that castration had not eliminated Abélard's sexual desire. Abélard was so humiliated by the accusation that he stopped visiting Paraclete. Instead, he and Héloise devoted themselves to a tortuous epistolary dissection of their relationship and the nature and meaning of their love.

Héloise, despite being "shut up in a melancholy Place"[14] for a decade, remained a staunch advocate of free love and disdained marriage as a mercenary arrangement that prostitutes women but not their husbands.

Abélard's regret about their love affair tormented her. "I despised the Name of Wife, that I might Live happy with that of Mistress," she declared.[15] He was her Lord, Father, Husband and Brother, and life seemed not worth living without acknowledgment of his love.

Abélard refused to provide this reassurance. To the contrary, he dismissed his former passion as purely physical, and he lauded his castration as a divine gift that had freed him from the raging carnality that had previously consumed them both. Héloise was lucky, he wrote, that he had forced her into a convent, where she had transformed the "curse of Eve into the blessing of Mary."[16] While Héloise gloried in remembering the frenzy of their sexual relations, he wrote, "I gratified in you my wretched desires and this was all that I loved."[17]

Abélard's exhortatory letters fell on deaf ears. But after she suffered a serious illness, Héloise decided she should break off relations with him. "At last, Abélard, you have lost Héloise for ever," she wrote. "I have banished you from my Thoughts, I have forgot you."[18] Then, in language as dramatic as ever, she described her anguish at never again seeing Abélard's sensuous mouth and the majestic body so desirable to women.

After renouncing Abélard, Héloise devoted her considerable energy to her work as abbess. She transformed Paraclete into a model community, richly endowed, productive and a magnet for religious women across France. As its intellectual renown spread, Paraclete also sprouted daughter houses.

Without Héloise to distract or shame him, Abélard attempted to resume his position as a theological philosopher. Once again he provoked enmities that ultimately destroyed his career. In April 1142, at the age of about sixty-three or sixty-four, Peter Abélard died. Héloise returned his corpse to Paraclete, as he had wished, and persuaded Peter the Venerable, a sympathetic bishop, to absolve Abélard of all his sins. She also used the occasion to arrange an ecclesiastical office for her son, Astrolabe, whom Abélard's family had raised.

Héloise died in 1163 or 1164, at about sixty-four. Then she joined Abélard in the grave she had tended since his death. Over the years, a legend arose that as she was interred, his skeletal arms reached out to embrace her. This legend resonates today, with the ever-beautiful Héloise achieving in death what eluded her in life: an eternity in the embrace of the lover for whom she sacrificed so much.

Émilie du Châtelet [19]

Émilie du Châtelet, Voltaire's mistress, was strikingly like Héloise in three respects: she was uncommonly intelligent and uncommonly well educated, and she became the mistress of a celebrated philosopher. But the similarities ended there, because Émilie was the child of an enlightened era, and her lover was a progressive thinker.

Gabrielle Émilie Le Tonnelier de Breteuil was born on December 17, 1706, in Paris, into an aristocratic and book-loving family. Her elderly father, Louis-Nicolas, encouraged his daughter's precociousness by teaching her Latin and Italian, engaging tutors to instruct her in English, mathematics and the sciences, and urging her to immerse herself in his extensive library. In adolescence, Émilie translated Virgil's *Aeneid*. Later, as her formidable intellect matured, she focused on physics, literature, drama, opera and political ideas, including the startling proposition that women and men should have equal rights.

Womanhood transformed Émilie from a gawky, large-footed and large-limbed girl into the striking woman known as "la belle Émilie." She was very tall, with black hair and brows arched over soft sea-green eyes. She was vain and had a tendency to overdress and deck herself in baubles. Her detractors mocked her excessive finery, but Voltaire would find it charming and refer fondly to his mistress as "PomPom."

When Émilie was nineteen, her family arranged her marriage to Florent

Claude du Châtelet, colonel of a regiment, scion of a fine old family and an agreeable man twelve years her senior. The marriage was convenient and amiable, and quickly produced a daughter and a son. Émilie spent much time in Florent's Paris townhouse, and he spent even more on garrison duty. As was quite acceptable among spouses who had already produced heirs and whose marriages were primarily family alliances in which romantic love played little or no part, Émilie took lovers. Her belief that a good wife behaved well and loyally toward her husband by allying herself only with lovers of quality and discretion was typical of her aristocratic social milieu.

When Émilie met the witty and clever Arouet de Voltaire, he was nearly forty and much sought after by women eager for the reflected glory of associating with France's most famous writer and one of the *philosophe* movement's leading lights. The *philosophes* were engaged in reevaluating, in the light of "reason" and "rationality," the entirety of the human experience. Besides ascertaining the truth, their objective was to compile a vast encyclopedia of human knowledge. This enterprise kept them in the public eye, pitting them against the Church and the royal court. Ultimately, it created the moral climate that ushered in the French Revolution. Much of the *philosophes'* interaction took place at certain Parisian salons, where Émilie and Voltaire developed their deepening relationship.

As a child, Émilie had met Voltaire at her father's house. They met again in May 1733, at the opera, soon after Émilie had given birth to her third child, and within three months they were lovers. Voltaire waxed poetic about his new mistress: "This is what Émilie is like," he wrote to a friend. "Beautiful; a good friend, too / Imagination blossoming and true / Her mind is lively, nay, sublime / With too much wit some of the time. / She has a genius that is rare / Worthy of Newton, I do swear."[20]

Voltaire's assessment of Émilie as a dynamo of energy and purpose was correct. She was fascinated by physics and the theories of Leibniz and Newton, and studied them with a discipline that put other scholars, including Voltaire, to shame. She also found time to dine with friends, attend social and artistic events and—alas!—to gamble away small (and sometimes not so small) fortunes at the gaming tables.

When Voltaire fell in love with her, Émilie was equally attracted to the *philosophe* scientist Pierre-Louis Moreau de Maupertuis. Maupertuis admired her beauty and her "sublime knowledge" of matters usually confined to males, and he greatly appreciated the lack of cattiness that (he believed) distinguished her from other women.

Émilie and Voltaire's sexual life was unsatisfying. Voltaire was plagued by chronic digestive problems, including attacks of diarrhea that interfered with his sexual performance and often stopped him from having sex. "It even seems to me that I am not at all made for the passions," he had once lamented to a disappointed mistress.[21] But despite, or perhaps because of, his less than able sexuality, Voltaire could be extremely jealous when he suspected Émilie was, or wished to be, sexually involved with another man.

This was certainly true at the onset of their relationship, when Émilie was still pining for Maupertuis. Voltaire warned her that though his rival was a wonderful scientist, he could never offer her the happiness of committed love. As the months passed and Maupertuis remained emotionally detached from her, Émilie slowly transferred all her love to Voltaire.

Émilie and Voltaire began to travel together, and in 1734 they settled down in Cirey, in her husband's decaying family château. Florent was most cooperative about this arrangement. He would sometimes visit his wife and her lover, but he considerately slept apart from Émilie, and took his meals with his son and the tutor. Above all, he was delighted with the spectacular renovations and redecorating that the lovers undertook with money lent by Voltaire at a low rate of interest.

Voltaire's political problems had prompted this move. The public executioner had orders to publicly burn his revolutionary *Lettres philosophiques*, his publisher had been imprisoned and Voltaire himself was in grave danger. Cirey was an ideal retreat, full of secret hidey-holes and so near the Lorraine border that any time Voltaire was in danger of being arrested, he could escape into Lorraine.

At first, Voltaire lived at Cirey alone because Émilie was reluctant to leave the salons and stimulation of Paris. But she realized that Voltaire would grow increasingly jealous unless she lived with him, and so she arrived at Cirey with hundreds of boxes of luggage and flung herself into renovating. She altered all Voltaire's plans: staircases were installed in place of fireplaces, and windows instead of doors. More importantly, she and Voltaire began a regime of study and literature that came to be known as his Cirey Period (1733–49).

Émilie was now Voltaire's recognized mistress, and she conducted their affair as if it would last a lifetime. But unlike most 18th-century lovers, who resorted to subterfuge in the name of discretion, she and Voltaire cohabited. This took some managing. Whenever she was forced to spend time with her husband, she treated him with affectionate respect. In fact, Florent's very presence belied the fact that she was actually living in sin with Voltaire, and it gave the arrangement a certain legitimacy, something all three of them desired.

Émilie, immensely disciplined and organized, established a regimen of study that focused the more disorganized Voltaire. The day began in Voltaire's quarters, with late morning coffee and discussion. At noon, Émilie and Voltaire sometimes popped in to greet Florent as he lunched with his (and her) son and the tutor, then retreated to their separate studies to work. Sometimes they took a break, snacking and chatting before returning to their books. At nine, they met for dinner, a leisurely and well-provisioned production, and followed it with conversation, dramatic productions in their own tiny theater, and poetry readings. At midnight they dispersed again to their studies, and Émilie worked until about five in the morning. When she retired to her blue and yellow bedroom, so color-coordinated that even her dog's basket had matching blue and yellow lining, she slept for a refreshing four hours. If she had set herself a personal deadline, she would reduce this to one hour and jolt herself awake by plunging her hands into icy water.

Émilie's projects were often linked to Voltaire's. His magnum opus, *Siècle de Louis XIV* (*Century of Louis XIV*) and his *Essai sur les moeurs* (*Essay on Morals*) were largely drafted at Cirey. He also wrote *Alzire, Mérope, Mahomet* and other dramas there, and an opera. Under Émilie's erudite tutelage, Voltaire assimilated (but never mastered) the principles of physics, particularly Leibniz's and Newton's, and incorporated them into the core of his thinking. He generously acknowledged Émilie's influence and dedicated his 1738 *Eléments de la philosophie de Newton* (*Elements of Newton's Philosophy*) to her. He even implied that he had been little more than her amanuensis rather than she his muse.

Émilie, for her part, devoted herself to translating Newton's *Analytic Solution* (*Solution analytique*) and, in 1748, her own *Exposition abrégée du système du monde* (*Abridged Exposition of the World's System*), which experts regard as a more astute reading of Newton than Voltaire's. She translated, with commentary, Bernard Mandeville's *Fable of the Bees*, parts of which Voltaire insinuated verbatim into his *Treatise on Metaphysics*. She also undertook textual analysis of the Book of Genesis and the New Testament, a task made easier by her daily Bible reading with Voltaire. Unlike Voltaire's, most of Émilie's work remained in manuscript form; during her lifetime, only the *Exposition* and a few scientific essays were published. Until just before her premature death, she was immersed in translating and elucidating Newton's *Principia*.

In public as well as private, Voltaire was the first to acknowledge that his mistress was his intellectual and sexual partner and equal. He read aloud what he had written each day and eagerly welcomed her critiques and suggestions. Her keen mind convinced him that women could do everything men could. In a letter to a friend, Voltaire paid Émilie the ultimate compliment: "I [cannot] live without that lady whom I look upon as a great man and as a most solid and respectable friend. She understands Newton; she despises superstition, in short she makes me happy."[22]

Émilie had also reflected deeply on the nature of men and women. Once, she infiltrated a men-only Parisian café disguised as a man. The sole reason that no woman had produced a good tragedy, poem, story, painting or treatise on physics was that women were never trained to think, she lamented. If she were a king, she added, she would right this wrong by encouraging women to participate in all spheres, especially the intellectual. In most ways, Émilie's life as Voltaire's mistress was a lesson in equality.

But parity in their relationship did not eliminate jealousy or emotional insecurity. Both Émilie and Voltaire were jealous, and their infidelities continually shook the relationship. Whenever Voltaire left Cirey, Émilie trembled with terror lest he never return. "The heart loses the habit of loving," she wrote sadly.[23]

Voltaire's return from a five-month visit to Berlin marked a new stage in Émilie's mistressdom—sexual abstinence, at least with Voltaire. He was, he claimed, too old and too unhealthy to indulge, and so instead of being her lover, he would be her dear friend. Émilie acquiesced in this new arrangement but, perhaps to dissipate her anxiety, she gambled even more frenetically and disastrously.

Émilie and Voltaire began to spend more time in Paris, where Voltaire was once again in favor. He had been named royal historiographer, and granted a small apartment in Versailles, albeit a foul-smelling one near the palace's stinkiest latrine. Even the pope graciously accepted Voltaire's proposal to dedicate *Mahomet* to him. Émilie, too, was well regarded. The king authorized publication of her work on Newton years before she finished it. The Italian scientific academy, the Bologna Institute, named her a fellow.

Meanwhile, Voltaire grew enamored of his niece, Louise Denis. "I press a thousand kisses on your round breasts, on your ravishing bottom, on all your person which has made me stiffen so often and plunged me in a flood of delight," he exulted in a letter to her.

At the same time, now that Émilie's breasts and bottom no longer obscured his vision, Voltaire could see her more objectively. Her gambling, intensified after his defection from her bed, horrified him. Voltaire had tried, over the years, to build up a substantial nest egg for her in case of his death. Suddenly he began to erect boundaries between his own finances and his mistress's ruinous gambling debts.

Émilie was devastated by Voltaire's sexual and financial withdrawal. In the course of reflecting on her painful struggle to adjust, and evaluating her own life and the lot of women generally, she produced *Discours sur le bonheur* (*Treatise on Happiness*), a manuscript that attempted to clarify precisely what happiness was, and how a woman could achieve it. Happiness should not depend on another person, she wrote. It should emanate from within, derived from intellectual passions and study. Other components of happiness were freedom from prejudices, particularly religious; a healthy body; definite tastes and preferences; and, of course, passion, despite the painful consequences it often provoked. After all, Émilie argued, the most interesting people are unhappy, and it is their personal plights that are the stuff of drama and tragedy. She ended her treatise with a rationalist conclusion: Our only goal on earth should be to achieve happiness.

But unable to practice what she preached, and desperate to fill Voltaire's place in her life, Émilie turned to other men for intimacy. She fell in love with Jean-François, marquis de Saint-Lambert, the young court poet later notorious for his amatory liaisons. After initial interest, Saint-Lambert distanced himself from the impassioned older woman. Émilie wooed and pursued him, and sometimes he relented. During one tryst at Cirey, Voltaire marched into her bedroom and found Saint-Lambert on top of Émilie, his bare buttocks pumping up and down. Furiously jealous, despite his ongoing affair with Louise, Voltaire raged at them both and threatened to leave Émilie.

The situation was absurd, but Émilie knew how to appease Voltaire. As he stomped out of the room, she went after him. He, not she, had curtailed their sexual intimacy, she reminded him, and she still had urgent desires that, unfulfilled, would undermine her health. Surely satisfying them with a fellow poet, indeed a friend of Voltaire's, would be an ideal solution. Voltaire approved her logic and forgave her. "Ah, madame, you are always right! But since that is the way it is," he added, "you should see to it that it does not occur before my very eyes."[24]

Then, to Émilie's horror, she discovered that at nearly forty-four years of age, she was pregnant. Voltaire helped her concoct and execute a plan. The two of them lured her husband to Cirey and conspired to amuse, flatter and— Émilie's contribution—seduce him. Voltaire outdid himself with witticisms.

Émilie wore her slinkiest gown and most dazzling diamonds. Before dawn, she was in bed with her husband. When she subsequently informed him that they had conceived a child, Florent was ecstatic and never doubted that he was the father. (French courtiers, however, joked that Émilie's sudden urge to see her husband was just one of a pregnant woman's cravings.)

Émilie was reprieved from the shame of bearing an illegitimate child. At the same time, she was overcome by a sense of doom and reiterated time and again that this birth might kill her. She pushed herself even harder to complete her translation of Newton's *Principia*, sleeping only one or two hours each night for months on end. Voltaire remained by her side throughout, yet she could not resist writing to Saint-Lambert that she loved him but not Newton, and that duty, honor and reason alone drove her to finish the translation. Two days before she delivered her daughter, Émilie completed her *Commentary on the Mathematical Principles of Newton* and deposited a copy for registration at the Bibliothèque Nationale.

A few days after the birth, she added that day's date—September 10, 1749—to her manuscript. Hours later, she sunk into unconsciousness. Then, surrounded by Florent, Voltaire and Saint-Lambert, Émilie du Châtelet died. Voltaire was devastated. He lurched outside and, blinded by his tears, fell and smashed his head. When Saint-Lambert rushed to help him, Voltaire shouted accusingly that Saint-Lambert had killed Émilie by impregnating her.

Afterward, Voltaire followed Florent to Cirey so the two men could mourn together. The infant, who had been sent to a wet nurse, died a few days later. A friend suggested that Voltaire prise Émilie's ring from her finger, remove the image of Saint-Lambert hidden inside it and return the ring to Florent. Voltaire did so, adding fatalistically, "Saint-Lambert drove me out. One nail drives out another. That is the way of the world."[25] At Cirey, Voltaire reduced the unpaid loan for the renovations to an interest-free sum representing one quarter of the amount he had provided. Friendship, he told his mistress's grieving husband, was worth more than money.

Émilie du Châtelet's story is an edifying narrative of purpose fulfilled, love reciprocated and passion (usually) requited. The constraints on her—principally the refusal to publish her memoirs, though her translations of men's works were rushed into print—burdened all women. Even at the time, Émilie and her contemporaries knew that her status as Voltaire's mistress rather than her genius guaranteed her a significant place in history.

Émilie's alliance with Voltaire was widely known. Voltaire went out of his way to acknowledge her enormous contributions to his work, and in his private correspondence with Europe's leading thinkers, he reiterated how greatly he was in Émilie's debt. Émilie and Voltaire were the enlightened patrons of an enlightened age, and because they lived in one of history's most socially liberated eras, her association with Voltaire enhanced Émilie's reputation.

Jeanne Hébuterne [26]

Jeanne Hébuterne was a mysterious mistress who destroyed her life for the lover she revered as a great artist. Jeanne was born on April 6, 1898, the gifted only daughter of a comfortable and conservative French Catholic family. Eudoxie, her mother, deferred to Achille, her well-intentioned but traditional and controlling father, who read the classics aloud as she and Eudoxie prepared meals. Jeanne's older brother, André, was a successful landscape artist.

Jeanne met the immensely talented Italian artist Amedeo Modigliani when she was a nineteen-year-old art student in Paris. Modigliani, fourteen years her senior, was a well-known womanizer who had just emerged from a tumultuous love affair with the English poet Beatrice Hastings. The signs of Modigliani's troubled relationships with women were already plain: he had once pushed Beatrice through a closed window.

Jeanne, on the other hand, was both reserved and romantic, and she stood out because of her ethereal beauty and artistic abilities. The dashing Modigliani was so drawn to her that he painted her twenty-five times, immortalizing her as a wistful, stylized face that seems locked in communion with her unseen portraitist. À la Modigliani, Jeanne's face is heart-shaped and elongated, with generous lips clipped and unsmiling, a fragile and pensive woman. A photograph confirms friends' descriptions of the real-life Jeanne's long chestnut hair, blue eyes always smudged by fatigue, sensuous mouth and the milky complexion (her nickname was "Coconut") that added to her aura of frailty.

Modi (Modigliani's nickname, which in French meant maudit, or damned), responded to Jeanne's adoration, to her art, which he encouraged, and to their common love of literature. He also admired her musical ability. She was an uncommonly good violinist and shared his love of Bach. Their attraction was mutual though incomprehensible to Modi's friends, who found Jeanne lovely but dull.

Their friends' reservations did not concern the lovers. Modigliani was as secretive as Jeanne, and they conducted their affair with private passion. After three months, they moved in together.

For Jeanne, this was an act of profound rebellion against her family's values. She had lost her virginity. She was living in sin with a dissolute, drug-taking alcoholic whom former mistresses had named in paternity suits. Modi was also quite literally a starving artist, and an ailing one. As a result of earlier bouts of pleurisy and typhus, the army had rejected him as physically unfit. As if all this were not enough, he was a Jew and, Achille Hébuterne warned his daughter, had no intention of making an honest woman out of the Christian girl he was already sleeping with.

For months Jeanne and Modigliani lived a bohemian existence. They rented a room in a run-down hotel, ate in artists' cafés and visited art exhibits. They also painted, but Jeanne was in such awe of Modi's artistic gift and so desperate to retain his affection that she voluntarily set aside her own work to act as his helpmeet and muse. He often wanted her to model; while he painted, she posed for him, nude or clothed. Other times, she played the violin as Modi labored over his creations. Jeanne the painter was becoming Jeanne the painted.

Jeanne's sacrifices and their life of bare-boned simplicity did nothing to improve her situation. Modi continued to go out with his friends on alcohol and drug-abusing flings, after which he would wait until Jeanne came to support him as he stumbled home. The lovers' financial situation was equally grim, and their hopes for solvency were crushed when rage rather than praise greeted an art show that Modigliani had mounted with considerable optimism. The police shut the show down on the grounds of public indecency because Modigliani's nudes had pubic hair, whereas other painters, as a concession to public sensibility, portrayed nudes with bald pubises. As one potential collector asked querulously, where on earth could he display "those triangles"?

During the final winter of World War I, the temperatures plunged to freezing, food, electricity and coal were rationed, and Germany pounded Paris with bombs. Anyone who could afford to fled to the safer countryside of the south of France. When Jeanne realized that she was pregnant, she and Modigliani decided to join the mass exodus south.

Their party included Jeanne's mother, who was too distressed at Jeanne's plight to renounce her. (The ultra-religious Achille washed his hands of his errant daughter.) But Eudoxie turned into a harridan, urging Jeanne to leave Modigliani and condemning both the man and his art. Finally Modigliani rented a separate hotel room, while Jeanne spent her time refereeing battles between him and her mother. In what little free time they spared her, she sketched and painted.

Jeanne's pregnancy affected Modi deeply, and during this period his loveliest paintings were of children. One interpretation has been that he considered everyone a lost child, including himself and Jeanne. He also documented Jeanne's pregnancy, lovingly and precisely, emphasizing her broadening torso and distended belly. In the words of one art historian, he "stylized his mistress into a Madonna-like creature and, at the same time, envisaged her as a personification of Venus."[27] None of this endeared him to Jeanne's mother.

By the end of her pregnancy, Jeanne's relations with her mother had deteriorated so badly that Eudoxie stormed out and Modigliani moved back in. Soon after, in November 1918, Jeanne delivered her daughter, also named Jeanne Hébuterne, in the Nice Maternity Hospital. Modigliani was ecstatic about Giovanna, as he called her, and on several occasions he announced that he was going to marry Jeanne. But to his mother he wrote only that "The baby is well and so am I." No mention of the baby's mother, by then exhausted and unable to breast-feed her increasingly listless infant, who was sent to an Italian wet nurse. Meanwhile, his own health degenerated and he was severely depressed. In a candid photograph taken in 1919, he was unkempt, his clothes shabby and his shoes scuffed. He was, he confided to a friend, "like the Negro. I just go on."[28] But baby Jeanne, at least, was finally thriving.

During this period of ill health, Modi flung himself into his work, panting and grimacing as he painted. But the product of this grotesque labor in his self-styled "grand style" was graceful and sure, fluid and serene figures in striking and harmonious colors. One image, of a mother and child, required forty sittings. Jeanne was very often his model, and he portrayed her slender body growing heavier and her face drawn and melancholy.

Jeanne had reason for melancholy. By April 1919, she was again pregnant and still unmarried, a fact that tormented her. Her daughter was in the care of a wet nurse, and Modi was ailing. She was emotionally battered by Eudoxie's hostility toward him, her inability to breast-feed her daughter, her lost vocation and, above all, her worries about her lover: his drinking, his roving, his flirtations with other women. In late May, Modigliani returned to Paris, telling Jeanne that he would send for her and the baby as soon as he had found a Parisian wet nurse.

As Jeanne waited in Nice, Modigliani worked, revisited his old haunts and developed an intimate (but apparently nonsexual) relationship with Lunia Czechowska, a petite and appealing Polish woman. He was not happy about the impending birth of his second child and confided to a friend that he found the pregnancy disgusting. After several weeks, Jeanne wired him, demanding money to return to Paris. Modigliani complied, although with a heavy heart, and after mother and baby arrived, he consoled himself with alcohol to relieve his anxiety about his growing familial obligations. He also began to paint a fourteen-year-old student, Paulette Jordain. Jeanne, already anxious about his intimacy with Lunia, was consumed by jealousy at the ease of his camaraderie with young Paulette.

Two weeks after Jeanne arrived in Paris, Modigliani drafted a peculiar document. In it he referred to her as "Jane" and pledged to marry her. But he still spent his evenings with his friends and justified leaving Jeanne to her own resources as "the Italian way." And he made no specific plans to marry her. Meanwhile, baby Jeanne was sent away to a wet nurse in Versailles. Jeanne visited weekly, and Modigliani corresponded with the nurse as frequently as his deteriorating health permitted.

As his health worsened and Jeanne grew heavier, Modigliani's friends rented them a decrepit and shabbily furnished studio apartment. Modigliani was overjoyed. But he was visibly disintegrating, had lost his appetite and had a chronic cough. He refused to see a doctor, probably fearing the diagnosis. Lunia and other friends urged him to return to the healing warmth of the south. But Jeanne, who had been miserable there, refused to accompany him or to hear of his going alone. Instead, she waited for him at home in Paris while he spent every evening in filthy bohemian cafés, drinking and flirting. As his new Swedish acquaintance Thora later recalled, "You only had to look at him to see that he was dangerous." When Thora showed up to pose for Modigliani, she remembered Jeanne as "a delicate and fair little creature who looked at me with horror in her eyes and always treated me with the greatest suspicion."[29]

The situation worsened. Former mistresses surfaced and tried to see Modigliani, to reminisce, to lay claims. Canadian Simone Thiroux alleged that he had fathered her child. Meanwhile, Modigliani grew sicker and sicker and began to cough up blood. At least once, he grabbed Jeanne by the hair and pummeled her in public. Jeanne spent her time in the studio, painting self-portraits in which she depicted herself plunging a knife deep into her breast, a breast once again engorged with milk for an unborn child.

By mid-January, Modigliani was gray-skinned and belligerent. He was admitted to hospital and, before he lost consciousness, his last words were about Jeanne: "I have kissed my wife and we have agreed on eternal happiness."[30] Two days later, he died of tubercular meningitis.

Jeanne, days away from giving birth, was deadly calm. She stared at her lover's corpse, memorizing his face. Then she backed out of the room so she could keep him in view. Achille Hébuterne helped his daughter from the hospital and took her back to the family's apartment. At four o'clock the next morning, Jeanne flung open the window, jumped out and crashed down five stories to her death. She was twenty-one years old.

Jeanne and Modigliani were buried separately, Jeanne in a quiet suburb, Modigliani in Paris, mourned and celebrated by the entire artistic community. Two years later, friends convinced Jeanne's family to exhume and rebury her in the Jewish section of the cemetery where Modigliani was buried. The inscription on her tombstone reads: "Jeanne Hébuterne, Born in Paris 6 April 1898, Died at Paris 25 January 1920, the companion of Amedeo Modigliani Devota fina all'estremo sacrifizio." Little Jeanne Modigliani, who grew up to become an art historian, went to live with her father's family. Her aunt Margherita, who had always disliked Amedeo, adopted her.

Jeanne Hébuterne was as tragic and self-sacrificing as any fictional heroine on the path to self-destruction that ended in a final act of despair. She was astute and knowledgeable enough about art to recognize Modigliani's greatness, but she weighed her own artistic gift against his and decided that, on balance, his art and hence his life were worth more than hers. Yet at the beginning of their relationship Modi had recognized her talent, and other art students considered her exceptional. Jeanne's self-abnegating love for Modi and her need to ensure herself a permanent place in his life outweighed her own artistic goals, and drove her to dedicate her life to playing the role of his anguished muse.

George Eliot [31]

George Eliot is one of the towering names in English literature: *Adam Bede*, *The Mill on the Floss* and the superb *Middlemarch* were her most spectacular creations. George Eliot also created herself, transforming clever, love-prone and homely Mary Ann Evans into the internationally admired novelist who borrowed her *nom de plume* from her lover.

Mary Ann Evans, born November 22, 1819, was the gifted daughter of a rural land agent. After her father's death left her effectively homeless, she moved to London and found work as an editor and book reviewer with the *Westminster Review*, England's leading intellectual journal. Her pay was meager: room and board at publisher John Chapman's home. But her talent and her erudition quickly attracted the attention of the literati, who welcomed this unusual young woman into the world of their salons.

Apart from impecuniousness, Mary Ann (who abbreviated her name to Marian) had another serious social impediment: her homeliness. The few photographs extant (she hated being photographed) show a gaunt woman with piercing eyes, an elongated face dominated by a very large, slightly crooked nose and shaded by one of the incongruously frilly and fashionable Parisian-style bonnets she had hoped might soften her masculine features. Without good looks or money, Marian's marital prospects were unpromising. Nonetheless she yearned for love and fell into it easily and often.

One unreciprocated passion was for a colleague who rebuffed her with the declaration that she was too ugly to love. She had barely recovered when she fell in love with positivist philosopher Herbert Spencer. Spencer praised her as "the most admirable woman, mentally, I ever met," and greatly enjoyed escorting her to the opera, theater and concerts. He cautioned her, however, that he was not in love with her but feared she might be with him. Marian ignored the warning and wrote a letter of abject supplication that must have been frightening to him. "If ever I fall in love thoroughly my whole life must turn upon that feeling," she wrote. "You curse the destiny which has made the feeling concentrate itself on you, but if you will only have patience with me you shall not curse it long. You will find that I can be satisfied with very little, if I am delivered from the dread of losing it."[32]

Fortunately for their friendship, Marian quickly replaced Spencer in the all-enveloping maw of her devotion. Her new man was George Lewes, the author of mediocre novels and several popular works on philosophy, Spanish drama and Auguste Comte, the father of sociology. Lewes was also a versatile journalist and book reviewer who churned out competent work on a wide range of subjects, a contemptible talent to many of his contemporaries, who admired experts rather than generalists. As an editor, Marian had already dismissed him as a writer whose "defective articles" she would use as infrequently as possible.

But George was witty, a mimic who was always funny and never cruel, and a man even more irredeemably ugly than Marian. Spencer described him in 1851, as "about 34 or 35, of middle height, with [wispy] light brown hair, deeply marked with small-pox, and rather worn looking."[33] He also had wet red lips and was known as "hairy Lewes."

And Lewes had Agnes, his very pretty wife and the mother of his three children, who in the spring of 1850 had delivered the first of her two children with Thornton Hunt, her lover and the Leweses' good friend. The Leweses' had been a love match, but after domesticity had eroded the covenant, Lewes granted Agnes her wish to consort with Hunt. He stipulated, however, that they not produce any children. When Agnes produced one baby Hunt and then another, Lewes forgave her and, to spare her (and perhaps his children) the stigma attached to illegitimacy, he registered Hunt's children as his own. An unforeseen consequence of this generous gesture was that by acknowledging the infants as his, Lewes rendered null and void his grounds for divorce. He discovered later, when he hoped to marry Marian, that legally, he was forever bound to Agnes.

When Lewes first met Marian Evans, remarriage was scarcely a consideration. He had engaged in affairs before and was rumored to have fathered an illegitimate child. Marian, on the other hand, longed to be married. But what mattered to her at first was their love, which rooted and grew and was probably consummated in October 1853, after she moved into her own lodgings on Cambridge Street in Hyde Park.

The magnetism and affection between the two Georges held them together until his death. Their union was grounded in intellect and sustained by their mutual devotion to ideas and literary creation. Both were exceptionally intelligent and liberal freethinkers with shared interests. Marian quickly revised her opinion of Lewes's scholarship and instead praised his efforts to popularize difficult subjects. And because he was such a charming man-about-town, she could, through him, taste the exciting worlds of theater and literary gossip hitherto closed to her.

The key to Lewes's commitment to Marian was his awed recognition of her genius and his generosity of spirit that spurred him to encourage and nurture her both as a writer and as an individual. Assuming quotidian custody of Marian's fragile ego, chronic depression and giant talent required endless patience. No matter how deeply or how often she sank into the black gloom of hopelessness, Lewes rallied her. Despite his exhaustion, he neither complained nor faltered—"to know her was to love her," he confided to his journal.[34]

Lewes's devotion to Marian was fed by the joys of intellectual stimulation and professional collaboration with her. Much like Voltaire, who was most productive during his years with the compulsively disciplined and brilliant Émilie du Châtelet, Lewes's work was enriched by Marian's vision; the dynamics of mutually fulfilling union made them each other's muses. Each drew on the other's strengths, and their complementarity forged a lifelong bond between them.

At first, Lewes's acquaintances often questioned his faith in Marian, but his confidence overrode their doubts just as it did Marian's. When she later

credited Lewes with making her success possible, she was referring principally to his emotional nurturing, without which she would have been too
frozen by her complexes to create her masterpieces.

In July 1854, when their lives were now completely intertwined, they did
the (socially) unthinkable: they traveled to Europe and openly lived there
together. German intellectuals and aristocrats welcomed them—as a couple—into their homes. The composer Franz Liszt, who was living with his
married mistress, Princess Carolyne von Sayn-Wittgenstein, eagerly entertained them. But back home in England, scandalized acquaintances and a
few friends sharpened the stabbing points of their pens. That "blackguard
Lewes has bolted with a —————— and is living in Germany with her," wrote
one. "Lewes has cast away his wife," reported another, as if Agnes, who had
shown her preference for another man already, were a pitiful victim of
Lewes's lechery.[35]

The attacks on Marian were even more virulent and condemned her as the
"other woman," responsible for breaking up her lover's marriage. The
renowned phrenologist George Combe revised his earlier opinion that Marian's brain was simply superb, and pronounced her conduct so aberrant that
it indicated a familial abnormality. "I think that Mr. Lewes was perfectly justified in leaving his own wife, but not in making Miss Evans his mistress,"
Combe added.[36]

Nonetheless, their eight-month European sojourn was productive and,
apart from the blistering meannesses from home, harmonious. This made
their return to England, to separate lodgings, that much more painful. Gossipmongers predicted that Lewes would now dump Marian, but he proved
them wrong. As he had promised, he explained everything to Agnes, including Marian's need for confirmation that their marriage was truly dead. Agnes
was courteous and cooperative. She even expressed delight at the prospect of
Marian and her husband marrying. Alas, England's stringent divorce laws forbade such a happy ending. The best Lewes could do was to formalize financial
arrangements with the wife from whom he was now publicly separated, relatively onerous arrangements thanks to Agnes's insistence that he support her
and all her children. Lewes agreed because he had to. Afterward, Marian
joined him in London and they began to live as man and wife, in intention if
not in law.

This cohabitational union allowed Marian, who longed to be Mrs. Lewes
and felt herself to be Mrs. Lewes, to refer to herself as Mrs. Lewes. As "Mrs.
Lewes" she could fool landladies who would otherwise have turned her away

as a sinner. But literary and society London was not fooled. Its denizens censured her and, to a much lesser extent, Lewes. "Miss Evans, the infidel esprit forte . . . is now G. H. Lewes's concubine," tut-tutted Charles Kingsley. Phrenologist Combe warned Marian's old friend Charles Bray, who himself had a murky sexual history, not to invite such an errant woman into his home. "Pray consider whether you will do justice to your own female domestic circle . . . [if you make] no distinction between those who act thus, and those who preserve their honor unspotted?"[37]

Other people targeted women who wished to remain or become friendly with Marian. Feminist Bessie Parkes's father issued dire warnings. "Mr. Lewes . . . is a man of great powers of mind & capacity for analysis & certain generalisations," he allowed. "But he is & always was *morally a bad man.* Of his domestic relations I know more than you as a woman can know."[38] Though male friends often visited Lewes and Marian, they always left their womenfolk at home and excluded Marian in their return invitations. Lewes accepted them anyway, and then Marian would dine alone while he charmed hostesses who, at least behind his back, condemned her for the sin of being his mistress.

In private, with Lewes, Marian agonized about these unrelenting attacks on her character, and her social ostracism. But to her friends she displayed only courageous defiance. "I have counted the cost of the step that I have taken and am prepared to bear, without irritation or bitterness, renunciation by all my friends. I am not mistaken in the person to whom I have attached myself. He is worthy of the sacrifice I have incurred," she wrote.[39] She noted, as well, how society rewards women who indulge in *clandestine* erotic adventures. "Women who are satisfied with such ties do *not* act as I have done—they obtain what they desire and are still invited to dinner," Marian noted acidly.[40]

These disclaimers notwithstanding, Marian suffered terribly as she sat home alone, waiting for Lewes to return from one of the many events she was barred from attending. Her only defense was to devote hours to refuting the wildest of the accusations against her, and to quiver each time the mail or a conversational innuendo suggested another attack.

In 1855, Lewes's biography of Goethe was published to widespread acclaim. Marian's assistance had been invaluable and Lewes acknowledged it proudly, referring to her in his narrative as "a dear friend of mine, whose criticism is always worthy of attention."[41] He still dined with Marian's naysayers, but in other ways he celebrated her brilliance and her importance to his life.

Almost from the beginning, in Germany, the lovers had established a pattern of life that did not deviate for twenty-four years. They worked steadily until lunch, which they ate together, reading and critiquing their current projects and discussing ideas and everything else in their vast range of interests. In the afternoon, they walked, met with friends and sometimes attended concerts. After dinner they occasionally attended the theater or opera, but usually they stayed at home reading, often aloud. The result was a process of continual learning, and the strengthening of the intellectual bond between them. But until Marian's great success as a novelist, the couple struggled with never-ending debts largely incurred because of Lewes's obligations to his wife. Marian accepted Lewes's financial burden as her own, perhaps as another way of binding him to her.

In 1860, when Lewes's elderly mother finally expressed the wish to meet his clever companion, Marian exacted stringent conditions. The old lady had to cease welcoming Agnes and her children into her home, where they often joined Lewes for dinner or came on their own to visit. Marian got her way, but Mrs. Willim reportedly regretted her promise to the end of her days.

Despite Marian's interdiction against Agnes, the children became deeply attached to their father's "friend." As the boys matured, they came to spend holidays with their father and "Miss Evans" rather than with their mother. Apparently the younger children never realized that Lewes was not their father. Lewes went weekly to see Agnes and her offspring, and he treated them all with affection. He and these children were all the family Marian had, her own family having rejected her as an immoral woman. No wonder that she verged on reclusive, venturing out only with trusted friends into the least risky of circumstances.

It was in this hothouse of protective seclusion that Marian first turned her hand to the fiction that has immeasurably enriched the world's literature. For years, she had dreamed of doing so, but had lacked confidence in her "dramatic power." Finally, Lewes's encouragement coincided with her own sense that she should attempt a novel. As she lay abed one morning, the title "The Sad Fortunes of the Reverend Amos Barton" came into her mind.[42] This proved to be the genesis of Adam Bede.

Adam Bede took the literary world by storm in 1859. Marian's inscription in the manuscript, which she presented to Lewes, expresses her judgment of what she owed him: "To my dear husband, George Henry Lewes, I give this M.S. of a work which could never have been written but for the happiness which his love has conferred on my life." She was more precise in a letter to a Swiss male friend: "Under the influence of the intense happiness I have enjoyed in my married life from thorough moral and intellectual sympathy, I have at last found out my true vocation."[43]

Success did not simplify her life or radically change her social acceptability. More men sought out her acquaintance, but they were as reluctant as ever to subject their wives to her immoral company. Isaac, her own brother, went further. Bolstered by the success of *Adam Bede* and longing for a reconciliation, Marian risked writing him a letter that mentioned her "husband." Isaac responded with a formal request from his solicitor to provide details about her marriage. When she explained that she and Lewes were united by a "sacred" rather than a legal bond, Isaac again rejected her. In *The Mill on the Floss*, Marian would condemn the double standard by which public opinion judged women much more harshly than men.

Marian's stunning literary triumphs alleviated the financial burden that had weighed so heavily on her and Lewes. The couple moved from their rented rooms into a large house, and they found it easier to satisfy Agnes's needs. Lewes paid off his debts and no longer scrambled for every possible assignment just to make ends meet. He also appreciated the opportunity to undertake more significant and prestigious works.

Lewes decided it was time to enlighten his sons about the state of his marriage and the nature of his relations with Marian. They all took the news well, and afterward addressed her as "Mother." (Agnes was "Mamma.") Marian afterward reminded thoughtless friends who referred to her as Miss Evans that she was *Mrs. Lewes*, because she had assumed all the responsibilities of a wife, and even had "a great boy of eighteen at home who calls me 'mother,' as well as two other boys, almost as tall, who write to me under the same name."[44]

Despite her sudden fame, security and the affection of Lewes's sons, Marian continued to suffer bouts of wrenching depression. Lewes attributed this largely to her social status, and he again attempted to regularize their union by seeking a divorce from Agnes. But a foreign divorce proved to be as impossible to obtain as an English one, and Marian was forced to accept that she would never be Mrs. Lewes in the eyes of the law. Though she claimed she did not care, her exclusion from mainstream society made her hypersensitive to rejection. Lewes shielded her from all criticism of her novels and permitted her to see only rave reviews. "The principle is this," he explained, "*never tell her anything that other people say about her books, for good or evil*; unless of course it should be something exceptionally gratifying to her—something you know would please her apart from its being praise."[45]

What truly grounded Marian was Lewes's love and constant, cheerful care. When he fell ill, as he often did, she rallied herself to offer him the same attention she herself accepted so needily and she took over his book review assignments. She also disclosed to Barbara Leigh Smith, one of her few women confidantes, that she had an enviable sexual life and that Lewes was a tender lover. She hinted that they practiced birth control—either rhythm or the unreliable reusable condoms then available—because they had decided against having children.

As the years passed and her fame grew, Marian slowly and tentatively extended her socializing by inviting selected and adoring acquaintances and friends into her home on Sunday afternoons. Privately, Lewes referred to them as "Sunday Services for the People." Here, with Lewes at her side and surrounded by fans, Marian felt safe from insults, and held forth regally. When the German composer Richard Wagner came to England, she invited him as well. She also had the satisfaction of meeting Louise, Queen Victoria's fourth daughter, at the admiring princess's request. After such social successes, even comments about Marian's equine face were softened by modifiers—she resembled a *handsome* horse, a *noble* steed.

Twenty-four years after she fell so crashingly in love with George Lewes, George Eliot's most dreaded nightmare came true. On November 30, 1878, after years of poor health and months of suffering the agonizing symptoms of enteritis and cancer, her sixty-one-year-old lover died. After more than two decades of living "for each other and in such complete independence of the outer world that the world could be nothing for them," her cherished lover had left her alone.[46] Her grief was so terrible that she could not attend his funeral. Instead, she shut herself up in her bedroom and, to the servants' consternation, wailed and wailed.

Marian dedicated the next few months to remembrance. She reread Lewes's multitudinous works. She completed his unfinished book, *Problems of Life and Mind*. She reminisced about him with her closest friends. She visited his grave. She felt his presence near her, in a comforting, ghostly communication. She validated his will—which bequeathed his copyrights to his sons, and everything else to "Mary Ann Evans, Spinster"—in court. She reclaimed her property, which was all in Lewes's name, by changing her name by deed poll to Lewes, the surname she had defiantly borrowed. At the end, she had no regrets, only the anguish of losing her best friend, confidant, adviser, critic and lover.

Six months after Lewes's death, in what amounted to a postscript to their union, Marian fell deeply and impetuously in love with a much younger man, New York banker John Cross, a close friend of hers and Lewes's. Rosemary

Ashton, the biographer of both the Georges, sees the odd couple as Héloïse and Abélard in reverse, with Marian the brilliant intellectual and John the worshipful student to whom her every word was golden. Also like Abélard, Marian wanted urgently to marry, and John-*cum*-Héloïse was entranced enough to agree. In the last year of her life, Marian finally achieved the status that had always eluded her and became a wife.

But it was too late, and John was too young. The gossips gossiped, noting how ludicrous the newlyweds looked, and how anxious sixty-year-old Marian appeared in the presence of rivalrous younger women. One witness recalled that Marian was "slightly irritated and snappish . . . He may forget the twenty years' difference between them, but she never can."[47] Despite wagging tongues, Marian reveled in the social rituals she had formerly scorned. But after seven months of wedded bliss, her health failed, and on December 3, 1880, she died.

In a bizarre way, Marian Evans Lewes's marriage to John Cross was the culmination of her affair with Lewes, the marriage that always eluded her, the key to social respectability, the end (she thought) to simmering, malevolent gossip. Lewes, she assured her friends, would not for an instant have objected to her marriage—more than anyone else, he would have understood and cheered her on. She was probably right. Who, after all, knew better than Lewes how much his mistress, even in the guise of *de facto* wife, had longed to be his real wife? Lewes might, however, have been disgusted when Isaac Evans, Marian's long-estranged brother, broke years of silence to congratulate her on her marriage to John Cross—and Marian was almost abject in her gratitude. Like Jeanne Hébuterne, Marian Evans was a reluctant mistress who longed to be a wife.

But this very love that sustained her also held her hostage to society's censure. Because she believed that she could not live without Lewes (or earlier Spencer, and afterward Cross), Marion committed and confined herself to him and shut out the hurtful external world. Her stability and her intellectual growth depended on him. And the impossibility of marrying Lewes forced her decision not to have children. The prominence of her fictional protagonists' relationships with their children and her own real-life devotion to Lewes's sons, lead to the conclusion that this privation might have been the harshest of all.

Despite the hardships of being Lewes's mistress, Marian judged her life almost perfect, and experienced her brief and apparently happy marriage to Cross as its bittersweet finale, the stamp of approval she had craved during her decades in isolation. Lewes, who had given her decades rich in mutual love, respect and intellectual camaraderie, had failed her in this alone. The two Georges had a magnificently rewarding relationship. He was her muse as much as she was his, and as Marian felt—and continually tested—the force of his love, she deemed it as complete as the true love of her fantasies.

Lillian Hellman [48]

On November 22, 1930, at a party hosted by Hollywood producer Darryl F. Zanuck, twenty-five-year-old Lillian Hellman was struck by a startlingly handsome man, tall and gaunt, with dark eyes, chiseled features and a thatch of prematurely white hair. His suit was an elegant pinstripe, and though drunk, he carried himself insouciantly, a cigarette dangling from his thin lips. "Who's that man?" Lillian demanded. "Dashiell Hammett," one of her table-mates replied. Lillian sprang from her seat and followed the man who would become her on-again, off-again lover and companion until he died. Before Dashiell reached his destination—the men's room—Lillian had grabbed his arm and begun to talk. They spent the evening in the back seat of her car, in a marathon of talking. Perhaps, toward morning, they had sex.

Lillian Hellman was a novice writer employed as a Metro-Goldwyn-Mayer manuscript reader. She was married to scriptwriter Arthur Kober. Dashiell was eleven years older and a writer of stature whose detective novels, especially those about private investigator Sam Spade, set new standards for crime writing. Dashiell was also the husband of Josephine Dolan, a nurse who had cared for him when he was hospitalized for tuberculosis. He had married Jo to spare her the humiliation of bearing the illegitimate child she had conceived with another man; her daughter, Mary, never knew she was not Dashiell's biological child. Dash and Jo lived together briefly and produced Josephine. After he struck out on his own, Dash supported Jo and the children erratically.

On the surface, Lily and Dash seemed unlikely soul mates. Lily was an indulged and ambitious only child whose wealthy relatives highlighted her own struggling parents' failures. She had a curiously exotic background, a Southern-born Jewish girl raised partly in New Orleans, partly in New York City. And she was university educated, though she had dropped out of New York University before she graduated and traveled extensively in Germany and France.

Lily Hellman was also a forceful, needy personality, unrelenting in her quest for romantic love and literary success. Love, she believed, hinged on a beauty that eluded her. Instead of the "blond curls and great blue eyes, tiny nose, rosebud mouth"[49] she longed for, Lily was a large-nosed, heavy-bosomed and flat-bottomed brunette. She deplored her plainness, and battled it with an arsenal of makeup and artifice. She wore hats that detracted attention from her face. She dyed her thick hair red or blond, and styled it to hide her big ears. She maintained her slender figure and garbed herself in stylish clothes that emphasized her trim legs and spoke clearly of a self-confident woman with expensive taste. She undermined the effect she created, however, by chain-smoking and by drinking far too much, far too often.

What seduced men was Lily's vibrant personality, her intelligence and wit, her boisterous laugh and her uninhibited sensuality. Her husband adored her even after she divorced him, and most of her lovers remained her lifelong friends. They simply accepted that Lillian Hellman was an incorrigible liar who could be treacherous and self-serving.

Dash Hammett, for his part, was as hard-boiled as Sam Spade, who articulated many of his creator's cynicisms about the essential evil of life. Dash was Catholic by birth and Marxist by conviction. He was a former Pinkerton operative reborn as a best-selling author. Two of his novels—*The Glass Key* and *Red Harvest*—centered on a father's murder of his son. Dash was alcoholic, tubercular and unhealthily skinny. He was chronically unfaithful and afflicted with gonorrhea. He was a spendthrift. And kind and sensitive though he could be when sober, he was also a mean and violent drunk who bullied and pounded anyone who irritated him. Too often that someone would be Lily Hellman.

A few weeks after their first, magical encounter, they met at a party and quarreled furiously. Dash lashed out at her with his fist and knocked her down. Lily's response was to wisecrack to a horrified onlooker: "You don't know the half of it. I can't bear to be *touched*!"[50] Her exposure to Dash's cruel and vicious streak only heightened his appeal. She quickly learned how to anticipate and, sometimes, to forestall an attack.

Lily cast her relationship with Dash, in his daughter Josephine Hammett Marshall's words, as "the Great Romance."[51] It was not a great romance. Dash repeatedly rejected the possibility of the kind of love she yearned for—erotically charged desire and commitment. What he offered instead was an enduring affection grounded in admiration. But he insisted that Lily accept his sexual infidelities, his "chippies," as he dismissively referred to them, though he knew how his every lapse, even a passing display of interest in another woman, tormented her.

Early on, as Lily and her two men—husband and lover—began to go out together, Arthur quietly grieving, Dash openly eyeing other women, it became clear that Lily's distress would never abate. She agonized about her lack of prettiness and quizzed Dash about her vaginal odor—did she stink? Dash attempted to allay her fears about herself—she was, he said, "better than pretty." But he would not stop seducing other women.

Lily decided to become, in Hammett's own words, a sort of "she-Hammett," a flirtatious, attention-provoking libertine. He and Lily forged an uneasy but indissoluble relationship in which sexual disloyalty was prominent. Lily knew what she was doing, and why. She had devised a strategy to coexist with Hammett so he would give her the only thing she wanted as badly as his love: lessons in how to become the great writer he had shown he could be.

It is difficult, at first, to imagine Lillian Hellman devouring Dashiell Hammett's novels, but easier when you imagine how she must have analyzed Sam Spade for clues about his creator. By the time Lily met him, Dash had already written four of his five novels and was "the hottest thing in Hollywood and New York."[52] His prose was spare and each word mattered. "You're still all twisted up," his private eye tells a Russian woman desperate to seduce him into compliance. "You think I'm a man and you're a woman. That's wrong. I'm a manhunter and you're something that has been running in front of me."[53] Lily wanted this gifted writer to teach her how to write as well as he did.

The miracle is that Dash disregarded his own tragic inability to continue writing and, over the next decades, critiqued, revised and polished Lily's plays until they opened to critical acclaim and public rapture, and catapulted her into the literary spotlight she so craved. The "Faustian bargain" by which she endured the unendurable—Dash's women, Dash's whores, Dash's chippies, Dash's refusal to adore her and his propensity to taunt and hit her, Dash's alcoholism and chain-smoking—paid off. As Lily reminded friends aghast at the nature of her relationship, "he gave me *The Little Foxes*."[54]

The story of Lily's thirty years with Dash is a complicated one. Lily divorced but continued to sleep with her husband. Often she and Dash lived together, in hotels, apartments, city and beach houses, in New York City and state, in Hollywood and later at Lillian's 130-acre Hardscrabble Farm in Pleasantville, New York.

They drank, smoked, socialized, quarreled and discussed fiercely, particularly political issues and their own left-wing convictions. They cheated on each other and worked. Dash dredged his last novel, *The Thin Man*, from his unwilling, alcoholic psyche. Published in 1934, *The Thin Man* immortalized Dash-and-Lily-like Nick and Nora, minus their debilitating fights, as a husband-and-wife detective team, and earned him over a million dollars. Lily wrote, too, much more than Dash, who for the rest of his life struggled with declining creativity. The less the words and ideas flowed, the more he drank and smoked and whored. Emotionally he was fragile, unclear about why he should go on living and occasionally tempted not to.

Dash was also chronically ill. Tuberculosis, the same disease that had killed his mother, and recurrent gonorrhea wracked his frail body. Sometimes his weight plunged to 125 pounds. When this happened when Lily was away, he urged her to return to care for him.

Part of Lily's survival strategy with Dash was to leave him and travel or even live somewhere else. Her absences tormented him, and in letters, he would describe to her a love he neither expressed nor demonstrated, perhaps did not feel, when they were together. The *Selected Letters of Dashiell Hammett 1921–1960* contains scores of such epistles:

March 4, 1931, "The emptiness I thought was hunger for chow mein turned out to be for you, so maybe a cup of beef tea . . ."; May 5, 1932, "Mr. Hammett, when interviewed, said: 'A bed without Lily ain't no bed' "; June 6, 1936, "I'm missing you terribly"; March 13, 1937, "Jesus, do I love you"; March 20, 1939, "Weather: clear and cold. / Mood: missing you. / Feelings: love"; January 27, 1950, "It was nicenicenice hearing your voice on the phone this afternoon: it seemed weeks since we had talked. There's something unbecoming about our not being garrulous. . . . I love you very much, Lilipie."[55]

Lily loved him too, resentfully and intermittently, and she needed him too badly to risk losing him. It was Dash who gave her the idea for *The Children's Hour*, the play that initiated her into literary stardom. He had come across an account of 19th-century schoolmarms destroyed by a vindictive little girl who fabricated a tale about their lesbianism, a lie that ultimately shut down their school. At first Dash thought he could adapt this story for his own next opus, a play. Instead, he offered it to Lily, who was desperate to write but lacked inspiration. She seized gratefully on the basic premise, and *The Children's Hour* was born.

It was a slow birth. For month after month, sequestered with Dash at a fishing camp in the Florida Keys, Lily wrote and Dash critiqued, often until Lily wept and threatened suicide if she could not get it right. At last she did, and *The Children's Hour* remains a classic. Sadly, the burnt-out Dash could not bring himself to attend opening night. Instead, he took a job in Hollywood and urged Lily to follow him there to look after him. Lily instead chose the career that would bring her accolades and a glorious future. But she dedicated

The Children's Hour to Dash, and remained convinced that she needed him to inspire and critique her writing.

In assessing the dynamics of Lily's evolving relationship with Dash, Joan Mellen, their biographer, describes an eerie transfer of creativity, with the disintegrating writer preserving his genius by implanting it into his mistress. "Dashiell Hammett," Mellen writes, "transferred to Lillian Hellman his creative enterprise; her abiding restlessness, which amused and exasperated him, was channeled into her writing. Her energy depleted his own for good. She assumed his voice, and her writing became a surrogate for his."[56] Lillian Hellman transformed herself into a woman so Hammett-like tough that, one interviewer surmised, she could bite off the tops of bottles with her teeth.

By 1935, Lily confided to Arthur Kober, her adoring ex-husband, that she and Dash Hammett were incapable of the great romance she had longed for. He helped her with her writing, but he never attempted to be faithful. Worse, he sometimes inveigled her into joining another, prettier woman for a lesbian-tinged sexual interlude *à trois*. For a woman consumed by sexual jealousy, their "arrangement" was degrading and painful. It was also all Dash was prepared to offer: at least once Lily proposed that he marry her, but he refused.

Lily left, returned, left again, returned. In her guise as she-Hammett, Lily had intense affairs with several men, most of them elegant, well-connected gentiles. A few times she conceived, then aborted, their babies. In 1937, she became pregnant with Dash's child. He hastily arranged to free himself from Jo by obtaining a dubious Mexican divorce, but Lily suddenly aborted the child and hence the need to marry him. Indirectly, Dash was responsible; he had arranged for her to discover him in bed with another woman.

Lily fled to Europe, then back to New York, and ignored Dash. In expiation of his sin, or at least his role in driving her to abort their child, he had given up drinking. When she remained cold and uncommunicative, he chased after her with clever, intimate and loving letters. Then he binged so fiercely on alcohol that friends shipped him off to New York, where he was hospitalized. After his release, he and Lily resumed their tortuous relationship.

Lily felt in desperate need of his help. Her latest play, *Days to Come*, had flopped as spectacularly as *The Children's Hour* had triumphed. Critics and audiences panned it, and after seeing it performed, so did Dash. Lily was terrified of failure and certain that she could recapture her magical dramatic powers only with Dash's help.

Help her he did, critiquing endless drafts of her newest work with such comments as "It will be a good play someday, I hope, but tear it up now and start all over again."[57] She did, and in 1939, *The Little Foxes* restored Lillian Hellman to dramatic glory. It did not, however, restore her relationship with Dash, who, after a trifling incident, took a personal pledge never to have sex with her again, and never did.

With the money from *The Little Foxes*, Lily bought Hardscrabble Farm. Because their finances were as intertwined as their lives, and because Lily lied so blithely and habitually, the truth of who paid for what and who owned what is difficult to ascertain. What is clear is that Hardscrabble Farm was registered in Lily's name; that she bought it with revenue from *The Little Foxes*, which Dash helped her write, perhaps to the extent of coauthorship; and that it was Dash's home as much as hers, though they no longer slept together. Diane Johnson, Hammett's biographer, writes that "it was, after all, Lillian's farm, not his."[58] But more recently, Richard Layman, who edited Dash's letters, wrote that Hardscrabble Farm was a joint investment between them, and they entertained friends—and often lovers—independently there. They recommitted themselves to each other in a relationship as strong as marriage but with a different set of vows. Their lives took separate paths, which intersected at intervals. What they shared was a home base.[59]

Hardscrabble Farm made Lily and Dash happy. She became a serious gentleman farmer, working from dawn to dusk raising poodles, chickens, asparagus and roses, milking cows, cooking turtle soup and gumbos, and picking wild raspberries. She also entertained her friends and lovers. He continued to help her with her work, but kept his resolve about not sleeping with her, even when she crawled into bed with him. He also curtailed her habit of resorting to baby talk, usually to soften or disguise lies. For her part, Lily looked after Dash's physical welfare and promised that, when the time came, she would bury him. They often drank until they were besotted, then quarreled ferociously.

Twice, Lily's life with Dash suffered a major interruption: the first in 1942, when he enlisted in the army, and the second in 1951, when he went to jail. Dash's military interlude was pleasant enough for both him and Lily, though she was devastated when he enlisted and could not have been comforted by Dash's remark that it was the happiest day of his life. The emaciated, coughing, bespectacled forty-eight-year-old was a curiosity to his fellow soldiers. To Lily, he evoked their love in a stream of letters including, on February 23, 1944, "I think . . . it would be better all around if you did not marry anybody, but stuck to me. / I have a warm, if small, heart and it may be assumed that I've sown my wild oats."[60]

Toward the end of his military service, mostly spent in Alaska, Dashiell Hammett was engulfed by the rising wave of concern among communist-phobic politicians. He had been a politically active member of the Communist Party. But his work on an army newspaper was outstanding and he was personally kind and unassuming, though often drunk and occasionally late, so when he was discharged in 1945, he was given a letter of commendation.

In 1947, the House Un-American Activities Committee focused its investigations on Hollywood. The story of its bullying and persecutory tactics is well known. Dashiell Hammett was, in 1951, HUAC's victim. His crime was refusing to identify contributors to a bail fund for people charged under the notorious, freedom-suppressing Smith Act—or rather, refusing to utter the words "I don't know," because he did not know. Lily asked why he didn't simply tell the truth and say that he didn't know. "I hate this damn kind of talk," he told her in a nervous rush, "but maybe I better tell you that if it were more than jail, if it were my life, I would give it for what I think democracy is, and I don't let cops or judges tell me what I think democracy is."[61] Dash served five-and-a-half months in prison, including one stretch in a West Virginia federal penitentiary. He cleaned toilets, talked with other inmates and grew weaker. He walked out of prison "a physically broken man with dwindling resources,"[62] even though he had not touched alcohol since a doctor had warned him, after an episode of hallucinations and delirium tremens, that he had to stop drinking.[63]

Later, Lily lied about her own heroism in the face of Dash's imprisonment. In fact, she deserted him, leaving him to his own sadly restricted devices. She survived his incarceration well and had less to fear from HUAC than Dash. Unlike him, she had quit the Communist Party in 1940, after only two years, and in all other ways had committed herself politically far less than he had.[64]

On May 21, 1952, nauseated with anxiety but wearing a new silk Pierre Balmain dress and glimmering blond hair, Lily appeared before the committee. Was she a Communist Party member, had she ever been, when had she ceased being? she was asked. Lily refused to answer, but she made the following statement: "I cannot and will not cut my conscience to fit this year's fashions even though I long ago came to the conclusion that I was not a political person and could have no political place in any political group."[65] After sixty-seven tense minutes, the committee dismissed her.[66]

Lily was, however, blacklisted from writing movie scripts, and her income plummeted from $140,000 annually to $10,000, most of which the Internal Revenue Department claimed for reasons she failed to understand then or later. She had to sell Hardscrabble Farm, and for years after, she and Dash, who lived apart from her but subsisted from their shared finances, had to economize on even the basics of life. He took from their joint safe, Lily said, "only a miserable amount . . . never buying anything for himself anymore except food and rent."[67]

By 1955, Lily was able to buy another property, a charming old yellow cottage on Martha's Vineyard. She earned money by adapting French plays that garnered mixed reviews. Dash declared about one such production, "I made no contribution to that."[68]

In 1958, after acknowledging that his health was so precarious that he could not live alone, Dash moved into Lily's New York lodgings. For the first time in their twenty-eight-year relationship, he had no other home. Lily cared for him grudgingly, complaining about how tiresome it all was, and mentioning off-handedly to friends that Dash was dying.

But she was writing a new play—*Toys in the Attic*—and she needed this sick old man to critique it. Dash obliged. He pronounced it terrible and told her to rewrite it. At her post-performance opening night celebration, he publicly denounced Lily for having produced such "shit." She heard him out in uncharacteristic silence, perhaps aware that he spoke from the depths of his bitterness that she had become the literary idol he had once been, and that he was dying and was utterly dependent on her.

At the end, Lily wanted more than ever for Dash to acknowledge their love. On the thirtieth anniversary of their meeting, she composed a document of heartbreaking pathos and presented it to him to sign. It read in part,

> The love that started on that day was greater than all the love anywhere, anytime, and all poetry cannot include it.
>
> I did not know what treasure I had, could not, and thus occasionally violated the grandeur of this bond.
>
> For which I regret.
>
> . . . What but an unknown force could have given me, a sinner, this woman?
>
> Praise God.
>
> Signed,
>
> Dashiell Hammett

Dash signed, adding in shaky handwriting, "If this seems incomplete it is probably because I couldn't think of anything else at the time. DH."[69]

Despite Dash's signature on her document, Lily could discern no tenderness or any sign that they had shared a great love, or indeed any love at all. Dash went fearfully toward death, hostile to Lily though trustful enough to will her one-quarter of his estate and to appoint her executor. He died on January 10, 1961, and Lily delivered a moving eulogy that completely ignored Josephine and Mary, Dash's daughters. Even then, she was jealous of those he had loved.

If Lily had not had true love in the flesh, she could trumpet it to the world in fabricated reminiscences: *An Unfinished Woman* (1969), *Pentimento* (1973), *Scoundrel Time* (1976) and *Maybe* (1980). Dash was dead and could not restrain her. Her great and haunting love story came to be her most valuable currency. To highlight it, she excised her many other lovers from her stories, including her devoted ex-husband, Arthur Kober, whom she dismissed with a single line in one of her memoirs.

But Hammett had been too famous for Lily to monopolize. Would-be biographers surfaced, and she hated them. When she read that a biographical sketch of Hammett in the *Encyclopedia of Mystery and Detection* referred to her as his mistress, she was outraged. "I was never his mistress. I object to the word mistress," she informed the publisher. Then what was her relation to him? "It's none of your business," she said unhelpfully.[70] She dictated how respected novelist Diane Johnson must research and cast her 1983 biography of Hammett. He had never truly loved anyone but Lily, and he was "a stylish drunk."[71] To a certain extent Johnson complied, but after Lily died in 1984, the year after *Dashiell Hammett* appeared, Johnson wrote that "control, revenge, hate and money" were as integral to the Hammett-Hellman relationship as love. This addendum defined romantic love, or rather the lack of it, as the central theme in the story of Lillian Hellman's decades-long union with Dashiell Hammett. Lily was the mistress of a man who loved her romantically only in her absence. When they were together, their affection was corroded by his cruelty and, the unkindest cut of all, his sexual betrayal. The Faustian bargain that bound these two literary giants together was the creativity that could find only one outlet at a time. For most of three decades, the once great writer Dash Hammett made Lillian Hellman, his mistress, the vehicle for their shared literary genius. He became Lillian's muse, allowing her to draw his creativity away from him and into her own literary productions.

Catherine Walston [72]

Because our love came savagely, suddenly,
like an act of war,
I cannot conceive a love that rises gently
And subsides without a scar
(*from* "I DO NOT BELIEVE")

English novelist and playwright Graham Greene dedicated "I DO NOT BELIEVE" to Catherine Walston, his mistress, muse and great love. Catherine, too, loved Graham, though like him she had other lovers, even during the raging height of their affair. She would later grow to love one of them, Father Thomas Gilby, a dominating and possessive Dominican priest, besottedly. Several years after that, she lost her priority in Graham's heart when he chose another woman over her: Yvonne Cloetta, the petite Frenchwoman who became his mistress for over thirty years, and who held his hand as he lay dying.

Yet it is not Yvonne but rather the stunning Catherine, a member of one of England's most affluent and influential social circles, who has fascinated writers and Greene scholars. Catherine is all the more intriguing because she and her compliant husband, Harry, are seen as the models for Sarah and Henry in Greene's brilliant novel *The End of the Affair*. Sarah's lover Bendrix, of course, bears more than a passing resemblance to Graham Greene himself.

However, despite its apparently identifiable cast of characters, *The End of the Affair* was not a *roman à clef* with Sarah a pseudonym for Catherine. It is true that Sarah was inspired by Catherine and that certain of the novel's details and plotlines were inspired by events in her life, most obviously her relationship with Graham Greene. But Sarah was as much his creation as the novel was. As Graham wrote to his estranged wife, Vivien, explaining why his manic depression would have made him a bad husband to any woman, "I think, you see, my restlessness, moods, melancholia, even my outside relationships are symptoms of a disease & not the disease itself. . . . Unfortunately the disease is also one's material. Cure the disease & I doubt whether a writer would remain."[73]

By the same token, though Sarah and Henry might never have existed if Graham had not known and loved Catherine, Catherine was his muse much more than she was his subject. Indeed, her crucial influence on his work—*The Heart of the Matter*, *The End of the Affair* and *The Complaisant Lover*—gave her much greater power in the dynamic of their relationship than either her striking good looks or her enviable social position.

When they met in 1946, the forty-three-year-old Graham Greene was already a renowned writer (*Brighton Rock, The Power and the Glory*) whose characters reflected his Catholicism and his struggles to abide by its tenets, and his deep guilt and regret when he could not. Catherine, the American wife of the vastly rich and politically ambitious Harry Walston, telephoned Graham's wife, Vivien, to ask if she would intercede with him to stand as her godfather when she was received into the Catholic Church. She wanted this, Catherine explained, because *The Power and the Glory* had moved her to convert to Catholicism. Catherine's story amused Graham. He sent congratulatory flowers, but suggested that Vivien attend the ceremony in his stead.

Vivien did so, and a photo shows her staring questioningly or perhaps anxiously at her husband's new goddaughter with the Lauren Bacall profile, short, curly, gleaming auburn hair, full, reddened lips and a figure as slim as if she had not borne several children. Vivien later told Norman Sherry, Greene's biographer, "I think she was out to get him and she got him. I think it was quite a straightforward grab."[74] Vivien's suspicions were well founded. Steadily and surely, Catherine drew Graham into her web. She trapped him there after one of her charming Dear Godfather letters included an invitation to lunch at Thriplow Farm, the Walston estate.

At Thriplow, Catherine starred against the backdrop of her husband's world, described by Graham's friend, the writer Evelyn Waugh, as "very rich, Cambridge, Jewish [the surname Walston had been changed from Walstein], socialist, highbrow, scientific, farming . . . Picassos on sliding panels . . . gourmet wines & cigars."[75] It was a stark contrast to the Oxford home Graham shared with Vivien and their two children on weekends, or the London flat where during the week he lived, discreetly but not secretly, with Dorothy Glover, his mistress of seven years.

When it was time to leave, Catherine proposed that Graham fly rather than take the train back to Oxford. She arranged and paid for an air taxi, and accompanied him on the short trip. Alone with him, Catherine intensified her campaign of seduction. One former lover, ex-Anglican priest and Cambridge fellow Brian Wormald, summed up her strategy: "Talk, talk, talk, talk, talk, talk [including an early warning against sexual jealousy] and drink, drink, drink, drink, drink."[76]

High in the air with Graham Greene, Catherine listened with flattering attentiveness and told him forthrightly how very much she liked him. At one point, her hair brushed across his eyes, and Graham was ensnared. "A lock of hair touches one's eyes in a plane with East Anglia under snow and one is in love," he recalled.[77]

In early 1947, Catherine escorted Graham in her old Ford car to Achill Island, where she owned a modest peasant cottage she used as a love nest. In fact, she had purchased it to be near (and with) Ernie O'Malley, the charmingly bohemian and attractive IRA intellectual, poet, author and art collector, who had been jailed during the Irish Civil War, been wounded by seventeen bullets and survived a forty-one-day hunger strike. It took Graham some time to learn that Ernie's protracted stays at all the Walston residences, including Thriplow Farm, were not devoted exclusively to promoting his art, but also to sleeping with and loving Catherine.

Like Graham, Catherine was an unfaithful spouse and lover. At nineteen, she married Harry Walston without loving him, because marriage would liberate her from the boredom of her home in Rye, New York. Within months, their unsatisfactory sex life led them to negotiate an arrangement by which they would condone each other's extramarital affairs and forge a marriage that would last forever.

Harry adored his wife, and Catherine had high regard for her indulgent husband. She also greatly enjoyed his inherited wealth, which permitted her to drape herself in mink and designer clothes, to collect Picasso and Henry Moore, to travel at will, to drink the finest Scotch and to relegate much of the rearing of her children to nannies.

Catherine took full advantage of her marital arrangement. She made no secret of her affairs and enjoyed a wide range of lovers, from Ernie O'Malley to American general Lowell Weicker and several priests, all but one Roman Catholic, whom she particularly enjoyed seducing. Catherine was not drawn to friendship with women, indeed was competitive with them.

In her Achill cottage, where the Atlantic winds blew over the door top, Catherine and Graham drank whiskey and orange juice, made bread and eggs over a turf fire and lit up the night with candles. And they talked and talked, about themselves and about the nature of their new relationship in the context of their Catholic faith. Afterward, they made love. In the mornings Graham also wrote, while Catherine—or Cafryn, his pet name for her—whistled and washed dishes in the next room. By the time their few days of isolated togetherness were over, they had committed themselves to each other—albeit after their own fashion.

One afternoon in late April 1947, Vivien Greene returned from visiting relatives to find Catherine and Graham at the front door, waiting for her. Catherine was exhausted from the long journey from Achill Island, Graham explained. Would Vivien allow her to spend the night in the house? Vivien felt constrained to say yes, though she later recalled, "I was sort of stunned that he should bring his mistress to my house."[78] That night Catherine and Graham slept apart, their consciences at ease because they had been to confession before arriving at the house and intended no sexual impropriety under Vivien's roof. In fact, the next morning Catherine invited herself to join Vivien at mass. There, side by side, Graham Greene's wife and his (favorite) mistress knelt together and prayed.

Unlike Graham, Catherine was not anguished by her adultery. But though she claimed not to be a jealous woman, Catherine saw Graham's wife and other mistress as rivals who must be vanquished. It is likely that she provoked Graham, who was terrified of losing her, to treat Vivien with unaccustomed harshness. In Catherine's presence, for instance, he would humiliate his wife, as if to prove his loyalty to his mistress. She was, one of Graham's friends commented, "a bit of a praying mantis. Somebody that likes to eat its victims."[79]

Catherine also nudged Graham into reevaluating his relationship with fifty-year-old Dorothy Glover, the short, stocky children's book illustrator he had been deeply involved with for seven years. He had survived the London Blitz with Dorothy, and to the end of his days loved her for her courage, her feistiness and the depth of her attachment to him. Even at the risk of upsetting Catherine, he could not renounce Dorothy, whom he referred to as "my girl" or "my girlfriend," or deny that he loved her, though what he felt for her could not compare to his passion for Catherine. Finally, having (he believed) convinced Dorothy that "one can love two people!" he packed her off on a West Africa–bound cargo ship for an extended vacation.[80] Then he moved out of the flat they shared in London, and into the Authors' Club. Later, however, he resumed a relationship with Dorothy, friendly and affectionate though probably nonsexual. When she died at only seventy-two, stooped and unkempt and looking about eighty, in agony after an excruciating burn accident, Greene wept and was "absolutely in despair," Yvonne Cloetta recalled.[81]

At Catherine's urging, Graham also walked permanently out of his marriage. Soon after, at mass, Vivien pulled off her diamond engagement ring and put it in the collection plate. A separation, however, was quite different from divorce. Graham had a Catholic horror of divorce, and he was soon to discover that Catherine had no interest in ending her own comfortable marriage so she could marry a jealous, depressive, bad-tempered writer who even at the height of success had infinitely less money than Harry. Nonetheless, he permitted himself to hope that an annulment would solve his marital and spiritual dilemma, and that he could somehow convince Catherine to leave Harry. Then at least Catherine could live with him or—his preference— marry him. "Your husband, Graham," he often signed his letters, and he fantasized that, one day, Catherine Walston his mistress would be Catherine Greene his wife.

Almost always, Catherine controlled the balance of power with her lover. She loved Graham deeply but not exclusively, and without his frantic neediness and desperation. He rained love letters on her that must have flattered her by their ardor and fluency, proving over and over how one of the world's finest literary figures was emotionally enslaved to her. "I love you wildly, hopelessly, crazily."[82] And with exquisite tenderness and devotion,

My dear, you are infinitely dear to me. . . . I believe in
1. God
2. Christ
3. All the rest.
4. In your goodness, honesty and love.[83]

Yet sometimes Catherine must have been irked by the relentlessness of Graham's pleas that she leave Harry and marry him. Certainly his threats of killing himself if she left him alarmed her. "Graham's misery is as real as an illness," Catherine confided to an intimate. "[He is] melancholic by nature . . . and all I do, really, is to make things worse in the long run by my own fears of abandoning him."[84] She took the sensible step of encouraging Graham to see a psychiatrist, Dr. Eric Strauss, who provided useful and calming talk therapy.

After his stay at the Authors' Club, Graham had found permanent quarters, flat #5 in the building where the Walstons maintained flat #6 as their London digs. Now Catherine could easily slip over to #5 during those periods when Harry barred the lovers from meeting, and when he and Graham were on better terms, Graham could just as easily visit Catherine at #6.

When he and Catherine met, in London, at the Walston house, and in Europe, in particular at Rosaio, the villa Graham purchased in Capri with his earnings from *The Third Man*, Graham was alternately cooperative and inconsolable. They could spend passionate hours in discussing Catholic theology and in making love, but they also engaged in long and terrible battles replete with shouting, vicious accusations (almost always Graham's), slammed doors and tears.

Their bitterest fights centered on Catherine's refusal to leave Harry and to end her other sexual relationships. In the interests of personal transparency between them, she and Graham subjected each other to descriptions of their other affairs. Neither took these revelations well.

No matter where they were, Graham almost always incorporated work on a current writing project into their schedule. Catherine would read his manuscripts, which he took great pleasure in discussing with her. This included *The End of the Affair*, with its many parallels to their own affair, which he dedicated to her. (The UK version was "To C," while in the United States it was "To Catherine.")

Though his work was paramount, when they were traveling or vacationing together Graham devoted most of his free time to Catherine and her pursuits, even squiring her to Paris fashion shows. He pretended to enjoy visiting her children, who were shrewd enough to realize he was tolerating them only to please their mother.

Ironically, Catherine longed to have Graham's baby, though she spent too little time with the brood she already had. Graham, just as neglectful of his own son and daughter, fantasized joyful visits to their mythical child's boarding school. Presumably he hoped that a child would bind him permanently to Catherine. But Catherine's doctors had warned against another pregnancy. With sad reluctance, she followed their counsel.

Two years into their affair, Graham's poem "After Two Years" cast his burning love for her in religious terms: "Did I ever love God before I knew the place / I rest in now, with my hand / Set in stone, never to move? / For this is love, and this I love. / And even my God is here."[85] One of the most anomalous aspects of their affair was how both Catherine and Graham identified sexual and religious experiences. An orgasm was as much a tribute to the God-given nature of their love as it was a physiological sensation. Religious ecstasy reflected its glory onto their love, and was transformed into blessed eroticism.

Graham's obsession with marrying Catherine provoked an incident that altered the course of their affair, making it more difficult to sustain. In the spring of 1950, Graham convinced Catherine to tell Harry that she was leaving him. Afterward, he described the sorry event in a letter to Catherine's sister, Bonté. It began with Catherine's lashing out at Harry. Then she, Harry and Graham sat together discussing her nerves. Finally, at a signal from Catherine,

Graham informed Harry that "she couldn't make up her mind between non-marriage with him & marriage with me. We were all very quiet & civilized, but nobody slept more than an hour or two that night."[86]

Harry did not sleep at all. He wept silently until morning, and Catherine could not bear his pain. Afterward, it was understood that she would never leave him. Things had irrevocably changed. Graham had revealed himself as a dangerous man, not just another of Catherine's lovers. From then on, Harry limited the time Catherine could spend with him. Afterward, she doled herself out to Graham in rationed tidbits—an evening here and a day there between weeks and sometimes even months of separation.

Graham suffered terribly, and his letters to his beloved Cafryn spewed out his anger, jealousy and sense of hopelessness, as well as his love and renewed commitment. He took comfort in their secret codes—"onion sandwiches" meant love or sex, and single letters represented entire words, including "I l y c" and "I w t f y" for "I love you Catherine" and "I want to fuck you." He gave her diaries in which he had inscribed special quotations for every single day.

Graham also devoted considerable time, both alone and in his correspondence with Catherine, to exploring the religious implications of his adulterous love for her. He usually reached comforting conclusions, centering on the divine nature of carnal love. Graham interpreted the fact that because she and Harry did not indulge in such love, they were not truly married in the eyes of the Church. The same was true for him and Vivien. He even projected a kind of saintliness onto his love for Catherine. "Some of us only have a vocation to love a human being," he prayed to Saint Thérèse de Lisieux, his favorite saint. "Please let my vocation not be wasted."[87] More stunningly, he declared that Catherine was *the saint of lovers to whom I pray.*"[88]

Graham devised all sorts of scenarios in which he and Catherine would either marry or live together in unmarried bliss, exonerated from sinning in the eyes of their Church. He vowed eternal love, promised her large and permanent shares in his finances and as much time with her children as she wanted. She could even stray from time to time, because no "tipsy frolic" would make him leave her. But nothing Graham could say or promise could sway Catherine's decision to remain Harry Walston's wife.

Catherine was even more preoccupied with Catholic issues and theology than Graham. Visitors to her home noted how her bedside table was heaped with theological books. She was an exceptionally slow reader, but she devoured them determinedly and, some of her guests felt, ostentatiously. By any measure she was more adept in discussion than with books, and who better to converse with than priests? Indeed, Catherine seemed happiest in the company of priests, and she cultivated their acquaintance and friendship. She also seduced those who were seducible, as many were. Better yet, from Harry's perspective and no doubt hers as well, her priests did not want to uproot her life and marry her.

Catherine also had affairs with laymen. She resumed her relationship with American Lowell Weicker and told Graham about it, prompting a rush of angry and anguished letters. When she and Graham vacationed together, they had increasingly bitter fights about the "temporary poison" of her latest love affair, and Graham's consequent "bitterness & desire to hurt" her.[89] Their idylls at the Villa Rosaio, abbreviated now by Harry's orders, were the closest they came to domesticity. Catherine decorated and Graham wrote, and in their spare time they socialized with local residents and visiting friends.

Graham also encouraged Catherine to write a novel of her own. She accepted the challenge, and in her own way worked hard at it, though no trace of it remains. As it is, we can only surmise that she must have been mystified or disappointed by her failure to succeed, she who was the muse for her brilliant literary lover.[90]

By 1950, the matter of marriage had become a cankerous growth in the love affair. Graham could not accept that Catherine was going to stay with Harry. They quarreled about it, often and bitterly. Harry had bought a fabulous estate, Newton Hall. Graham knew that if Catherine moved into it, she would never be willing to prise herself away from it to live with him. For someone with her materialistic values and love of luxuries, Newton Hall was enchanting: twenty-eight bedrooms, eight bathrooms, six reception rooms, stables, a garage and a cottage. Could Catherine resist its splendors?

She could not, and before she even moved in on December 2, 1950, she plunged delightedly into the expensive process of decorating it. How, she asked Graham self-righteously, could she abandon her family to begin a new life with him? Vicious quarrels ensued, during which Graham made stinging accusations—he hated her, he hated her friends, he hated her values, she was selfish and self-centered, she was a liar. Afterward, consumed by remorse, he repented his behavior, took back his vitriolic words and confided his fear that he was ruining what remained of their love.

At one point, Graham arranged for Catherine to speak to his brother Raymond, a medical doctor who would try to diagnose, with clinical objectivity, the nature of their relationship. Raymond concluded that Catherine would never leave Harry; that she believed her life would be much more peaceful and free of strife if she broke up with Graham, though she felt duty-bound not to; and that she was likely a great liar.

Raymond's observations struck Graham as entirely sound, but his love for Catherine transcended common sense, and he needed her desperately to provide the kind of savage peace that inspired him to write great novels. He could not break off with her, and Catherine lacked the will to break off with him.

Graham tried even harder to keep her. He bought her a Cartier infinity ring and had it inscribed "C and G." Much more dramatically, he engineered a marriage-like ceremony in which he exchanged vows with her during morning mass at Tunbridge Wells. For years afterward Graham evoked this "marriage," and for the rest of her life, Catherine wore her infinity ring.

There is no doubt that their staggering infidelities were fundamental to their affair, part of how they tested each other and pushed each other beyond the limits of endurance. Eventually, they could not sustain the force of their relationship. They never ceased to love each other, but Graham ceased to be Catherine's primary lover, and she ceased to be his. She did not precisely fall out of love with him, she simply diluted her feelings for him by loving other men as well.

Four years into their affair, Catherine and Graham struggled to define their relationship and to recapture some of their past joy. To gain perspective, Graham temporarily exiled himself to Indochina. While there he wrote Catherine his sad poem "After Four Years," which ends, "I have struggled to find the final ruse / For forgetting, and found you everywhere."[91]

The September 1951 publication of *The End of the Affair*, which seemed to parallel so much about Catherine and Graham's affair, provoked a crisis. Harry was furious that Graham had publicly exposed and humiliated him. He was also worried that the book could cost him the lordship he was lobbying for, and he banned Catherine from seeing Graham until April 1952. (This ban did not extend to her other lovers, who did not write books about her or want to marry her.)

For quite different reasons, Catherine decided that she and Graham should no longer have sex. Harry had nothing to do with it, but her latest lover, Father Thomas Gilby, did. Father Thomas was instrumental in persuading Catherine that her years with Graham had been a dream, and that she must now awaken and resume her life as a Catholic wife and mother. She need not cut off all contact with him. She need only withhold sex.

Catherine's sister Bonté visited Newton Hall and reported to her husband that Father Thomas was practically a resident and, Bonté added disapprovingly, when Harry was absent, assumed the role of head of the family.

> Not only does he behave in the most possessive manner with Bobs [Catherine's childhood nickname], but he behaves *sexually* in the most possessive manner, she is entirely absorbed in him to the exclusion of everything else & everybody else. . . . His behavior shows a lack of dignity, coupled with a masked brutality. You feel he owns poor Bobs body & soul, and that he wants you to know it.[92]

Graham Greene had a formidable rival.

But even Father Thomas could not cure or frighten Catherine into monogamy. Her promiscuity was too ingrained, and the sexual conquest of men and the challenge of making them fall in love with her were too powerful to abandon. And in her own way, she still loved Graham.

The restructuring of their affair took years and survived serious competing love affairs, including Catherine's with Father Thomas and Graham's with the widowed Swedish actress Anita Bjork. After 1951, Catherine and Graham saw each other in dollops, a trip here or a sneaked reunion there, a letter, a telegram, a phone call. During a visit to Rome in 1955, she attempted to break off with him, and it took Graham "a long night & a long morning" to convince her not to. In 1956, during one of their infrequent lovemaking sessions, Catherine murmured that "in a way" she would like their affair to end, and that even if Vivien and Harry were to die, she would not marry him.

Yet when Graham initiated breakups, Catherine was wretched. After he returned from a trip with a Vietnamese woman, described by a male friend as a "most exquisite little creature," Catherine told a friend that she would do anything to get Graham back.[93] When he did come back, she lacked both the will and the interest to sustain the fiercely loving relationship he craved, and to keep him from becoming seriously involved with other women. Unlike so many other mistresses, Catherine Walston had no desire to marry this lover who signed himself "Your husband," and who hoped, for over a decade, that one day she would be his wife.

At least that is what he said, in letter after letter, phone call after phone call, even in draft documents in which he promised Catherine a large share of his income and other benefits. But another woman, young Australian painter Jocelyn Rickards, who had a brief affair with Graham in 1953 followed by a lifetime's friendship, suggests that "he was desperately trying to shake himself free from her, first with me and then Anita Bjork."[94] At the same time that he was obsessively pursuing and proposing to Catherine, Graham was also discussing marriage with Jocelyn.

What was it like for Catherine, a woman distinguished mainly by what Brian Wormald, one of her lovers, described as "staggering" beauty, social charisma and her husband's high rank and wealth, to love and be loved by a man of such complexity and genius as Graham Greene? Did his anguished references to her as the soul mate who enabled him to create some of his finest work, and his incessant pleas to marry him, strike her as less compelling than they do the casual reader? The answers are quite clear. Catherine respected Graham's artistic talent and was gratified and flattered that her presence, indeed her existence, assisted him in realizing it. But his moodiness and the angry despair that provoked him to lash out at her also drained her. When he was tender and loving, he could be just as exhausting and demanding, and he jeopardized her marriage like no other lover. In the end, Catherine preferred to keep Graham mostly at arm's length, rejoining him after increasingly lengthy intervals when they would try, often halfheartedly, to recapture the remembered warmth of their once blazing love.

Catherine's growing detachment led to Graham's falling deeply in love with Swedish actress Anita Bjork, after which he divided his time between London and Sweden. Yet even when he was with Anita, whom he adored, Graham wrote Catherine, reminding her of their "marriage" at Tunbridge Wells and imploring her to return to him.

In August 1958, Anita broke off with him. A year later, Graham met the woman with whom he would spend the next thirty-one years, and whom he ultimately chose over Catherine Walston. He and Yvonne Cloetta, whose husband was as complacent as Catherine's, began their affair in June 1960. Their first quarrel came when Graham announced that he had to leave Nice for London to take Catherine, to a Picasso exhibition. Yvonne agreed reluctantly, but warned that he must choose between her and Catherine.

Yvonne waited it out while Graham and Catherine, since 1961 Lady Walston,[95] braked their affair to a shuddering halt. When Catherine learned that Graham had begun to take Yvonne to Rosaio, once her special place with him, she was shaken. Worse, in August 1963, Graham brought Yvonne to London, publicly identifying her as his new mistress. After sixteen extraordinary and exhausting years, Catherine Walston had been permanently replaced. When he suggested to Catherine that she might like to meet his new mistress, Catherine refused.

By the mid-1960s, alcohol and over four decades of drinking and smoking had taken a visible toll on Catherine. She was by then an alcoholic who hid whiskey bottles in her pockets, and her health was poor. Men no longer stared at her when she entered a room, and she was no longer a sexual magnet, though people still repeated the gossip that identified her as the model for the heroine of *The End of the Affair*.

Catherine's decline coincided with the end of her affair with Graham Greene, but it was precipitated by an accident at Dublin Airport, where she fell and broke her hip. Surgery after surgery failed to properly repair it, and she began to suffer chronic pain that she dulled with whiskey. Her body deteriorated until she was confined to a wheelchair.

In May 1978, just months before her death at sixty-two, Catherine wrote Graham an affectionate and somewhat wistful letter. She noted ruefully that he was about to leave for Capri—she did not mention that Yvonne was accompanying him—where she and he had so often gone themselves. "What happy times I had there with you and won't ever forget them from the day we walked through the gate for the first time," she wrote.[96] The rest of her letter invokes other joyful memories—playing Scrabble on the rooftop of Rosaio, swimming underwater, smoking opium. "There has never been anyone else in my life like you and thanks a lot," Catherine concluded. She saw him again, briefly. Not long before she died on September 7, 1978, she gently declined a proposed visit. She was very ill with cancer and wanted him to remember instead how they had been long ago, in the happy times.

After Catherine's death, in a letter to the man who had so longed to marry his wife, Harry Walston wrote, "Who can honestly say that he has gone through life without causing pain? And you gave joy too. . . . But you gave Catherine something (I don't know what) that no one else had given her."[97] The elusive gift that Harry could not define had consisted of many things, including passion and erotic love. But its most enduring feature must have been the satisfaction of having been, in her own person, the muse that had inspired her lover to create some of the finest literature in the English language.

Joyce Maynard [98]

To say the least, the grinning gamine who graced the April 23, 1972, cover of the *New York Times Magazine* did not look at all like someone who would soon become the mistress of a famous fifty-three-year-old author. Her photo showed a skinny, breastless elf in worn bell-bottoms and crewneck sweater, one thin arm clutching her sneakered toes, the other, with its too-large watch, cradling her tilted head. But it was the face that was so striking: long, tangled dark hair, with choppy bangs framing a pert face devoid of makeup, huge eyes smudged with fatigue as they peered directly into the camera with sheepish amusement.

Joyce Maynard's appearance was childlike, but the contents of her essay, "An 18-Year-Old Looks Back on Life," a fluent and breezy analysis of her generation's post-Woodstock, TV-watching, Barbie-toting disaffection, was masterful. The teenaged pundit spoke about civil rights, politics, the Beatles, marijuana, women's liberation, "the embarrassment of virginity" in an era of sexual revolution. She ruefully acknowledged the chunk of her life spent in front of television: "If I had spent at the piano the hours I gave to television . . . I would be an accomplished pianist now. Situation comedies steeped me in American culture. I emerged from years of TV viewing indifferent to the museums of France, the architecture of Italy, the literature of England. . . . Vulgarity and banality fascinate me."[99]

The American media and public was fascinated, in turn, with Joyce Maynard, a first-year Yale student. Magazine editors pounded at her door, assignments poured in and she spewed forth a spate of articles characterized by jaded naivete and boundless energy. Her readership was apparently insatiable. She wrote for mainstream magazines and, most impressive of all, had her own column in the *New York Times*.

Many readers contacted her directly. One letter, from the small New Hampshire town of Cornish, stood out from all the others. It warned of the seductions of hasty publishing and urged Joyce to develop the literary gift that editors would undoubtedly try to exploit. Its author, a writer whose name already carried "cultlike significance," instructed her to keep the contents of his letter private and signed his missive, "J. D. Salinger." No matter that Joyce was one of the few Yalies who had never read *Catcher in the Rye* or indeed anything else by Salinger. She was aware of his famed aversion to publicity and immensely impressed that he had written her.

A correspondence ensued. It sparked an intense nine-month relationship that colored Joyce's life and reverberates today in the literary world thanks to her revelatory 1998 memoir, *At Home in the World*. In its earliest stages, her nearly daily exchange of letters with Jerry, as Salinger had begun signing himself, soon dominated her life. Two writers, both in love with words, began the process of mutual seduction.

What kind of a teenager could successfully lob letters with the literary icon J. D. Salinger? In her *Times Magazine* essay, Joyce Maynard had already proved herself exceptional enough to attract Salinger's attention, while her image stirred his emotions and gonads. She was the younger daughter of immensely talented parents. Fredelle Bruser was the favorite child of Jews who fled Russia's pogroms and settled in Canada, where she won the Governor General's Award as Canada's top high school graduate and followed this coup with university triumphs culminating in a doctorate *summa cum laude* from Radcliffe. (Her dissertation explored the concept of chastity in English literature.) Max Maynard, Fredelle's twenty-years-older gentile husband, taught English literature at the University of New Hampshire, painted and sketched, and frightened (and disgusted) his family with intermittent alcoholic rages.

Fredelle and Max were equally devoted to and fiercely ambitious for their children. Both Joyce and her older sister, Rona, won *Scholastic Magazine* contests and Rona raised the stakes with an award-winning short story. Though Joyce was not a great reader, she wrote daily, recording her life and observations according to her mother's stricture that these were all material. But perhaps because of her complicated family life, her model for a happy family life was television's *Father Knows Best*.

The summer before she entered Yale, then in its third year of coeducation, Joyce was an anorexic weighing eighty-eight pounds who wrote, exercised and worked according to a strict schedule and sustained herself on a daily meal of one apple and one ice-cream cone. When the school year began, she became a student who yearned above all "to find somebody who will rescue me from my alienation."[100] When Salinger intruded into her young life, he seemed the embodiment of her every daydream, "my rescuer, my destination."[101]

Joyce and Jerry were a potent mixture. She was naive, talented and driven by ambition and her mother's view that all life's experiences were grist for her literary mill. Jerry was experienced, twice married and divorced, a brilliant man whose desire for privacy was legendary. Like her, he was half Jewish and, unlike her father, seemed to be an all-American father to his son and daughter. He also (Joyce discovered years later) had a penchant for very young and childlike women, who for brief periods could embody his impossibly accomplished but fictitious Phoebe Caulfield.

Within weeks, Jerry suggested Joyce telephone him, and these calls proliferated like their letters, which he signed off with "Love." Though Joyce had by then secured a book contract and several important magazine assignments, her conversations with Jerry were overridingly important. Jerry invited her to visit him at home. Wasn't this at the very least alarming? Not, Joyce remembers, for her. In 1972, she writes, the older man–younger woman duo—Frank Sinatra and Mia Farrow, Pierre Trudeau and Margaret Sinclair—was unremarkable. But this perception stretches the truth, given how contemporaries questioned even those ill-fated unions. (J. D.'s daughter, Peggy, a mere two years younger than her father's new woman, was also dubious about Joyce's extreme youth. "It was so weird . . . this is what Daddy had been waiting for all this time? . . . this bizarre little sister of sorts?" she wrote in her autobiographical memoir.[102])

Fredelle Maynard, however, rejoiced that her daughter was involved with such a famous man, no matter that he was fifty-three, she herself only forty-nine and Joyce eighteen. Instead of urging caution, voicing suspicion or issuing ultimatums, as many parents would have done, Fredelle embarked on a sewing project, an accomplice to Joyce's plan to arrive at Salinger's looking like an androgenous waif. Salinger, very tall, lean and appealing, responded on cue to his soon-to-be mistress.

Salinger's life was as austere as his appearance. He studied, practiced and preached homeopathy. He ate sparingly, mainly raw fruits, vegetables and nuts, and carefully cooked lamb patties. He abhorred ice cream, to which Joyce was secretly addicted. Within hours, he kissed Joyce, then remarked, "You know too much for your age. Either that, or I just know too little for mine."[103]

After this emotionally charged visit, Joyce returned to her idyllic summer job, writing editorial columns for the *New York Times*, and living as a house-sitter in a luxurious Central Park West brownstone. But instead of concentrating on her job, she wrote obsessively to Jerry, "who has moved into my head."[104] Very soon he drove her back to New Hampshire and installed her in his bed.

Their first attempt at sex was unsuccessful. The fifty-three-year-old Salinger pulled his eighteen-year-old darling's dress over her head, and her cotton panties down her starved body. She wore no bra, having no breasts to fill one. Jerry slipped off his jeans and his underwear. He did not mention birth control, and Joyce did not think of it. What she was thinking was that he was her first naked man.

I love you, Jerry told her. Joyce repeated his words, feeling that she had experienced an epiphany and had been "Saved. Rescued, delivered, enlightened, touched by a divine hand."[105] But the epiphany ended when Jerry attempted to penetrate her, and her clenched vaginal muscles, fortresslike, repelled his advancing penis. Joyce ended up sobbing. Jerry did not force himself in, but instead, he put on his bathrobe, massaged Joyce's pressure points to relieve the headache that had come over her, then offered her steamed squash with tamari sauce and a glass of cold water.

Joyce's joy had turned to shame, but Jerry was kind and reassured her that he would consult his homeopathic literature for a solution to her symptoms. But the next day, when they stripped off their clothes and tried again, the same thing happened. "It's all right," Jerry said. "I'll help you with your problem." And, a few days later, "I couldn't have made up a character of a girl I'd love better than you."[106]

The unconsummated affair heated up. Jerry raved about Joyce's essays and articles, and about *Raisins and Almonds*, her mother's memoir of a Jewish childhood on the un-Jewish Canadian prairies. But when he voiced his deep anxiety about sophomore Joyce's impending return to Yale, she felt and tried to suppress alarm that he might pressure her to abandon the refuge of her little New Haven apartment.

The first hints appeared that Jerry could be as acerbic about Joyce as he was about so many others. He told her repeatedly how much he loved her mind, but when the *Times* published two of her editorials, he said mockingly, "Not bad for a girl who grew up on the wrong side of the tracks in Kalamazoo. I'd hardly even know your first tongue was Lithuanian."[107] He dismissed her journalism as "hysterically amusing ... assassination by typewriter" and warned her against becoming "some kind of goddamn female Truman Capote, hopping from one hollow scene to the next."[108] He accused Doubleday, the publisher of the memoir she was trying to finish, of exploiting her youth. He continued his quest for a simillimum, a homeopathic remedy that would cure Joyce's genital impenetrability and—she concluded later—change her personality.

Joyce, precociously intelligent and ambitious, gnawed by a sense of guilt at the personal failings Jerry had clearly enumerated and deeply in love, chose to succumb to the combined powers of his genius and personality. Back in New Haven for her second year at Yale, the day after her morose lover told her that he was glad she could fit a visit to him into her busy schedule, she capitulated. "Come get me," she said over the phone. "It's about time," Salinger replied.[109]

Now Joyce was a Yale dropout and Salinger's live-in mistress, though no simillimum had yet relaxed her genitals. But the magic she had hoped for from the sacrifice of her Yale education, including forfeited tuition and scholarships, was increasingly elusive. Unlike Phoebe Caulfield, Joyce Maynard was materialistic, could not stifle her desire for New York's glittery literary life, devoured magazines rather than literature, baked banana bread when Jerry abhorred such adulterated food and was a messy contrast to his ordered neatness. From one moment to the next, Jerry found something to criticize.

Despite the deterioration of their relationship, Joyce and Jerry spent every day together. They read, she *Women's Day* and *Family Circle*, he Lao Tse, Vivekananda, Idries Shah. They wrote, he alone in his study, composing pages he never once read to her before locking them into a safe. They practiced yoga and meditated. They gardened the vegetables that, along with frozen Birds Eye peas, were their principal fare. And every day, they watched television sit-coms and often, a movie. On Saturdays, they danced to the stately rhythms of the *Lawrence Welk Show*. Jerry resolved the issue of his sexual frustration by pushing Joyce's head down onto his penis and teaching her how to bring him to orgasm. "Tears are streaming down my cheeks," Joyce recalls. "Still, I don't stop. So long as I keep doing this, I know he will love me."[110]

Joyce was having trouble loving herself. She fulfilled her contractual obligations to Doubleday by producing *Looking Back*, a short book (or a long essay) that purported to tell her life's story but omitted key elements of it: her father's alcoholism, her severe anorexia and the startling fact that she was writing her story as a college dropout living with and trying to please a man thirty-five years her senior, a famous writer who called her "a worldly, greedy, hungry person."[111]

Looking Back's publication intensified Jerry's bitterness. He criticized Joyce harshly for undertaking even minimal publicity to sell her books. Her terror of incurring his displeasure, even more of losing him, triggered binge eating that she fed by sneaking food and fought by self-induced vomiting. She gained weight and hated herself for it.

To readers of *At Home in the World*, early clues to the disintegration of the Joyce-Jerry relationship are all too evident. But Joyce, and probably Jerry, too, mostly ignored them. Their sexual dilemma remained unsolved. At Christmas, they hated each other's gifts. Jerry suddenly trashed Fredelle's *Raisins and Almonds* as "shallow and inauthentic."[112] When a *Time* magazine reporter tracked down his phone number through a friend of Joyce's, Jerry was furious. *"You foolish, foolish little girl. Do you have any idea how weary I have grown of you?"* he demanded.[113] Joyce had begun to cry a lot and realized that, one day, Jerry might even hate her.

The finale to their relationship came in Daytona Beach, where they had gone with Jerry's two children. The trip was not purely for pleasure. Jerry also wanted a respected homeopathic doctor to prescribe medication for Joyce's "sexual problem." Instead, Joyce was humiliated by her first pelvic examination, which revealed nothing amiss physiologically. She was also unresponsive to the acupuncture that followed.

Back at the beach, Jerry pronounced the obituary to their love affair. Coldly, wearily and looking very old, he told Joyce that he was finished with the business of having children. "You'd better go home now," he continued. "You need to clear your things out of my house."[114] As Joyce stumbled into an airport taxi, Jerry reminded her to turn down the heat and lock the door after she left his house. Peggy, whose hotel room Joyce had been sharing, knew nothing about the drama between her father and his young mistress, except that "It was as if she had never been there at all."[115]

Decades later, Joyce's pain at the breakup still reverberates. "I look to him to tell me what to write, what to think, what to wear, to read, to eat," she writes. "He tells me who I am, who I should be. The next day he's gone."[116] She could not accept his decision, so sudden and so final. She called and begged him to reconsider. Every day she wrote him frantic letters. To no avail—it really was finished.

Joyce bought herself a little house in the New Hampshire woods and moved there alone. Her bulimia raged, but she managed to solicit enough assignments to support herself. Once she convinced Jerry to visit, but he came with Matthew and stayed only a few minutes. When eager reporters inquired about her life with Salinger, Joyce refused to say a word, citing the "sacred privacy that genius deserves."[117] She comforted herself with the knowledge that Salinger never would or could love another girl as he had her.

The years passed. A gentle boyfriend deflowered her relatively painlessly. It turned out that, sexually, Joyce Maynard was entirely normal. Her career flourished. She married and had three children. She wrote a novel, *Baby Love*, about a young woman and her much older lover. Joseph Heller and Raymond Carver praised it. Immensely proud of her work, Joyce sent Salinger a copy. He responded instantly, by telephone, and denounced the book as "a tawdry, cheapo-shot piece of perversion," "a piece of junk" that "sickened and disgusted" him.[118] Crushed, Joyce understood that her forlorn dream of spending an afternoon with Jerry at the house in Cornish would never happen.

Joyce divorced, bitterly, and moved to California. At age forty-three, twenty-five years after she had been Salinger's mistress, she announced to her editor that at last, she was prepared to write about him. Later she went further and sold his letters at a Sotheby's auction.

Why did Joyce Maynard abruptly break a quarter century's silence? Her reasons were complex. First, she was shocked to learn that she had not been Salinger's only girlfriend, that he had been attracted to other young women and pursued them with his powerful pen just as he had her. When she discovered that he had married one of these women, she concluded that Salinger had betrayed her and thereby annulled her obligation to protect him.

Another reason was that in middle age, Joyce saw clearly how Salinger had used his craft to manipulate her psychologically and to seduce her with words. It occurred to her that in controlling her to suit his own needs, he had ignored his responsibility to protect her, a young woman only two years older than his own daughter.

With her new understanding, Joyce no longer attributed Salinger's insistence on her silence "as evidence of his purity of character." Instead, "his demand for privacy . . . seemed now like the cloak of a man well aware of the fact that his activities, viewed in the light of day, might not reflect favorably on him."[119] She began to believe not only that she had every right to tell her story but that remaining silent was actually wrong.

Many critics, however, rejected Joyce's explanations about why she had decided to speak out. Journalist Alex Beam, who had been a Yale classmate of hers, interviewed her just after he learned about her decision, and wrote a scathing report of their conversation. "The Salinger story was always Joyce's literary high ground, a museum piece of integrity not included in the ongoing fire sale of her life experiences," he wrote. "Yet when I sought her out for comment shortly before she concocted her sob story . . . Joyce told me she whipped up the Salinger submission to fulfill a contractual obligation to St. Martin's. And she complained about the size of the advance."[120]

Beam's scorn previewed the choleric critical reaction to *At Home in the World*, and also to Joyce's sale of Salinger's letters, whose contents she was legally prevented from reproducing though she owned the actual paper they were written on. Joyce was denounced as a vengeful harpie for having revealed what were described—wrongly—as the banal, meaningless details of her affair with Salinger, for delivering up the hitherto insulated icon for public consumption.

Before the book was published, Joyce confronted Salinger, ostensibly to say a personal goodbye. He received her with bitterness and rage. "You have written empty, meaningless, offensive, putrid gossip," he told her. "You live your life as a pathetic, parasitic gossip." He added, furiously, "I knew you would amount to this. *Nothing*."[121]

As Salinger berated her, he broke the last remnants of the spell he had cast over Joyce so long before. Like him, she had fallen in love with an illusion: she with a wise and kindly father, he with a dazzling little girl. Her love for him had been a kind of reverent self-abnegating passion she saw as a gift and a triumph over wrongful critics. His attraction to her began as an attempt to possess in the flesh someone who initially seemed akin to the fictional characters of his creation and to use Joyce as a resident muse for his mysterious new writing. For a time he compared her, indeed preferred her, to the fictional characters who, if they had magically sprung to life, would have been her peers. With his illusions about her shattered, Salinger wasted no time evicting Joyce from his life. She left obediently, but twenty-five years after the eviction, she still saw him, *in absentia*, as the powerful muse whose approval if not permission she must seek to express herself.

CHAPTER 10

Mistresses of Men
Above the Law

MOBSTER MOLLS

Gangsters come in many forms, from criminals who obey only the laws of the underworld to rulers who impose their own laws. What gangsterism—criminal or governmental—has in common is a code of behavior that pays lip service to social conventions and mores but violates them at will, and similarly pretends to respect women but in fact degrades them by reducing them to sexual objects.

Yet some women are attracted to the gangster's raw power and insolent disregard for the law, to the unearned privileges and wealth that usually accompany them, to the thrill of achieving intimacy with such larger-than-life men. Such women may become gangsters' mistresses and attempt to play out their fantasies in flesh-and-blood real life.

Virginia Hill [1]

Perhaps the most famous gangster's moll was Virginia Hill, mistress to Bugsy Siegel, a highly ranked member of the American Jewish Mafia and best known as the man who introduced big-time gambling casinos to Las Vegas. Virginia Hill inspired decades of young moll wannabes to emulate her tough and—to them—glamorous lifestyle. Hollywood, too, succumbed to Virginia's charms in *Bugsy*, a 1991 blockbuster about Bugsy's catastrophic (but prescient) endeavors to transform the poky town of Las Vegas into a giant gaming and entertainment oasis in the Nevada desert. His turbulent relationship with Virginia was integral to this story.

The real-life Virginia was a sort of twisted Horatio Alger. She was born in 1916 in small-town Alabama, the seventh of ten children whose savagely alcoholic father beat them and drank up most of his earnings. Virginia, nicknamed "Tab" for her cowering, tabby-cat-like demeanor, took the brunt of her father's abuse. But when she was just seven, she rebelled. As her "drunken fucking bum" of a father staggered toward her to attack, she grabbed a skillet and smashed him with it. He retaliated by thrashing her mother, but never again laid a hand on Virginia.

Virginia's mother finally left her husband and took Virginia out of school in grade eight to help her. Virginia held various low-paid jobs, did housework and cared for her younger siblings. Before long, she concluded that selling sex would be a much easier and more lucrative way of earning money. By fourteen, Tab had matured into a confidently sexy and sexually experienced bombshell who chafed at the constraints of life in Depression- and Prohibition-era Alabama and yearned for the glamor of the big city.

She rejected New York, teeming with immigrants and street gangs. Chicago, with its job openings at the Century of Progress International Exhibition (1933–4), seemed friendlier. But what mostly attracted Virginia were the immense possibilities for a stunning woman in the gangster world of Al Capone. Capone had been catapulted into notoriety by the Saint Valentine's Day massacre of 1929, which put him squarely in control of Chicago's underworld.

Seventeen-year-old Virginia arrived in Chicago seeking excitement, money and an easy life. Her father's brutality had hardened her and convinced her that men were untrustworthy, an attitude that armed her for life as a moll.

Virginia's first job in Chicago was waiting tables at the San Carlo Italian Village, a Capone-built complex of expensive restaurants patronized by gangsters. Before a year elapsed she had caught the attention of Joey "Ep" Epstein, who controlled Chicago's racetrack betting. She was very pretty, five foot four inches of voluptuousness with long, thick auburn hair and penetrating gray eyes. Though she wore too much makeup, Epstein admired her self-composure and confidence. So did Mimi Capone, Al's sister-in-law; she befriended Virginia and invited her to parties.

After an all-night mob party on June 12, 1934, Epstein initiated Virginia into his money-laundering operations as a courier and confidante. He instructed her in the intricacies of keeping records and dealing with the Internal Revenue Service. He explained the life-and-death etiquette of gangster society, bought her couturier clothing and set her up in an elegant apartment with a three-thousand-dollar weekly allowance. He financed her lavish parties that attracted wealthy Chicagoites on both sides of the law, and he encouraged her to sleep with other gangsters. He did not have sex with her himself. Epstein was likely a closeted homosexual, and having Virginia as his principal moll gave him considerable status and discouraged gossip about his sexuality.

From her vantage point as Epstein's lieutenant, Virginia observed how other Mafia women were treated, and dismissed them as "dumb fucking dolls." Their husbands often abused and beat them and displayed their mistresses like one more bauble. "I grew up with that crap from my father and got away from it," she told a friend of Epstein's. "Why would I put myself back into it now? Especially when I don't have to?"[2] Nineteen-year-old Virginia Hill would only indulge in sexual affairs as a matter of convenience, never for love.

By her twentieth birthday, Virginia was the intimate of Chicago's most powerful racketeers, and had enough detailed information about their schemes and assassinations to destroy them. She knew, however, that the price of disclosure would be summary execution, and she never talked.

Virginia's reputation for discretion did not, however, extend to sex, which she engaged in with a legion of mobsters. At one infamous Christmas party, she declared that she would put her mouth where the money was and crawled on her knees from man to man, unzipping their trousers and performing fellatio. When one disgusted woman called her a whore, Virginia grabbed her hair, slapped her face and shouted, "I'm the best damn cocksucker in Chicago, and I got the diamonds to prove it. I ain't doing nothing that you haven't done and I don't see any diamonds on you."[3] This incident earned her the title of "Queen of the [Chicago] Mob," and elicited even more respect for her toughness.

Virginia's next conquest was Joey Adonis, a vicious New York mobster who controlled gambling and the numbers racket on the east coast. With the blessing of her Chicago associates, who were negotiating for an alliance with the New York Mafia, she moved to New York and soon became "Joey's girl." Virginia and Joey did everything together, including sex and crime. They quarreled ferociously and made enormous sums of money.

One night in a bar with Adonis, Virginia met Bugsy Siegel, who decided to seduce her as a way of insulting Adonis, whom he despised. Bugsy, another senior gangster, was as handsome as Virginia was beautiful, blue-eyed, dimpled and sleek-haired. Though he was vain and self-absorbed, Bugsy could be charming and was known to be loyal to his friends and allies. He also had a hair-trigger temper and was abusive to his molls and his underworld rivals. Only his wife and childhood sweetheart, Esta Krakower, never felt his fists.

Bugsy Siegel was the first man to dent the sheath protecting Virginia's heart. A day after they met, they spent the night making love and Virginia responded to him with her heart as well as her body. But a few days later, Bugsy was sent to Hollywood to centralize the various gambling operations on the west coast.

Virginia was left alone, and Epstein punished her for her unauthorized and unwelcome affair with Siegel by reducing her allowance and responsibilities. Virginia was furious. Before long, she retreated back to her mother's home in Georgia. This was not the hovel she had fled five years earlier. This was an imposing house purchased with the money she regularly sent her mother from up north.

Virginia rested, reconciled with Epstein, treated her mother to the finest home furnishings, clothes, fine restaurants, meals and jewelry. Then she and her younger brother, Chick, headed to Mexico for a last wild fling before returning to Chicago. Mexicans attracted and fascinated her, and her sexual appetite for them seemed insatiable.

Virginia and Chick returned to Chicago and the rackets. Then, on a brief holiday home, Virginia impetuously married Osgood Griffin, a nineteen-year-old University of Alabama football player. Six months later, during which time Virginia constantly left her husband behind on her frequent "business" trips to Chicago, California and Mexico, the marriage was annulled.

Virginia next married Miguelito Carlos Gonzales Valdez, a Mexican night-club owner, so he could emigrate to the United States. Valdez, apparently unaware of her profession, expected her to be wifely and domestic. Virginia grew to despise him, and before long, they too divorced.

By her mid-twenties, Virginia had established herself as the mob's most powerful and trusted female member, with easy access to Chicago, New York and Los Angeles leaders. She was as influential in the power structure as many male gangsters, and no other mob woman has ever achieved such raw power.

This was her status in the spring of 1939 when she and Bugsy Siegel reconnected at a party at actor George Raft's mansion. Virginia took the initiative, and she and Bugsy spent the rest of the weekend in bed. From then on, the two were as thick as the thieves they were, merging sex and business, mingling with movie stars—Gary Cooper, Clark Gable, Cary Grant—eager to associate with the glamorous and risqué couple with apparently inexhaustible funds.

In fact, Bugsy was so impossibly extravagant that he was always broke.

Before Virginia, his molls had had to pay their own way and often his as well. But she was different and special, the great love of his life. Bugsy bought and renovated an elegant house and gave Virginia one of two gold keys to it. Even in immoderate, larger-than-life Tinseltown, Virginia and Bugsy threw around more money than anyone else in tips and gifts, and on themselves. Their house was exquisitely furnished. Their wardrobes were stunning—Virginia's included over one hundred pairs of shoes, designer gowns, cashmere sweaters and a dozen furs. She always drove a new Cadillac. And she spared hundreds of dollars a month to support her mother.

Despite their closeness, Virginia and "Baby Blue Eyes"—an endearment she loved because he hated it—cheated on each other. Virginia could not resist Mexican boyfriends, old lovers and even George Raft, their mutual friend. Bugsy vowed to kill any man she slept with, but never managed to catch her in the act. Surprisingly, neither did the omnipresent reporters, though they trailed her everywhere and filed breathless stories about Bugsy Siegel's gangster moll.

For five turbulent years, Virginia was Bugsy's moll. They had the most satisfying sex Virginia had ever enjoyed. They fought, and when Bugsy battered her as her father had, Virginia pounded him back. Then she concealed her wounds with heavy makeup, and Bugsy did the same. But his terrifying temper, his jealousy and (justified) suspicions, his endless demands for money he never repaid and his refusal to divorce his wife and marry her slowly eroded Virginia's commitment.

After one vicious battle over his refusal to divorce Esta, Bugsy beat Virginia into unconsciousness, threw her down on their bed and raped her. A while later, he invited her to move with him to Las Vegas. He had corrupted the authorities there and planned to construct a luxury hotel and casino called the Flamingo, his pet name for her. Virginia, who said she could never forgive him for raping her, laughed and flew back to New York, where she resumed an intense sexual relationship with Joey Adonis. She also gave detailed reports about Bugsy's activities to rival mob leaders.

Bugsy persisted in wooing her. Virginia seldom visited Las Vegas, but they met when she was in Los Angeles, where he would regale her with stories about the increasingly out-of-control construction, its soaring costs and his own thefts (about two million dollars) from the money other gangsters had invested in it. Virginia made copious notes of every detail and reported them to Bugsy's worried gangster colleagues.

The Flamingo's opening night was disastrous. Weeks earlier, Virginia had moved in because she saw the hotel as a monument to her. She and Bugsy drank heavily and quarreled violently. Afterward, she withdrew completely from Las Vegas and the Flamingo, and reacted with rage at the mention of either. During a tryst with Bugsy in Los Angeles, she cursed him as a "two-bit loser, a fucking chump who made his friends rich but couldn't keep cab fare in his own pocket."4 In retaliation, Bugsy again beat and raped her.

Meanwhile, though the Flamingo was slowly becoming profitable, Bugsy's associates considered him too unreliable and, in May 1947, decided to eliminate him. Despite Virginia's cooperation with them, she was still closely linked to Bugsy and she often seemed unstable, swallowing sleeping pills in apparent suicide bids. As a result, Bugsy's killers came close to ordering her extermination as well. Only Joey Adonis's intervention saved her.

In mid-June, Epstein phoned Virginia and instructed her to leave Los Angeles. On June 20, days after her departure, as Bugsy Siegel lounged on the chesterfield reading the *Los Angeles Times*, his Mafia "friends" shot him to death. "The insect was killed," Joey Adonis reported back in New York.5

From Paris, where she had taken up with a wealthy twenty-one-year-old Frenchman, Virginia granted an interview to the *Times*. "Ben, that's what I always called him, was so nice," she wept. "I can't imagine who shot him or why."6 Soon after, she swallowed another overdose of sleeping pills and was hospitalized.

After returning to the United States, a traumatized Virginia hid out with her brother in Florida, trying to evade reporters seeking to link her with Bugsy's murder. Once again she attempted suicide, the fourth time in four months. As her depression intensified, so did her drinking, her rages and her instability. Joey Epstein, fearful about her diary, with its sensational secrets about the mob, continued to support her.

In February 1950, Virginia fell in love with and married Austrian ski instructor Hans Hauser, a suspected Nazi sympathizer. Nine months later their son Peter was born. In 1951, she was summoned to testify before the Kefauver Commission on organized crime. She appeared because she had to, but she lied and misled her interrogators, denying that she had ever been involved in organized crime. She protected Joey Epstein and attributed her impressive resources to the gifts of generous boyfriends.

Virginia did not escape scot-free. The Department of the Treasury came after her for tax evasion, forcing her to sell her house, furniture, what jewelry she hadn't smuggled to a friend in Mexico and her clothes, including 144 pairs of shoes. Afterward, she traveled to Mexico on an Austrian passport and vowed never to return to the United States "to be persecuted by those rats in Washington. They are the real gangsters in this world, and it is not in my heart to forgive those who have hurt me."[7]

The "rats in Washington" did not leave her alone. In 1954, when she was living in Europe with Hauser, Virginia was indicted for evading $80,180 in back income taxes. Wanted posters for her were posted everywhere, and even in Europe she was ostracized.

Over the years, Virginia's condition deteriorated. She separated from Hauser and moved with their son, Peter, to a humble rooming house in Salzburg. Reflecting on her former life as a mob mistress, she said bitterly to Dean Jennings, who wrote about Bugsy Siegel, "I know hundreds of women in America who were kept by men. Why don't they pay taxes? If they're going to put me in jail for that why don't they put the rest of them?"[8]

By 1966, poor and miserable in Europe, supported by her fifteen-year-old son, Peter, Virginia tried to negotiate an arrangement to return home and face judicial leniency. She also demanded money from her old gangster associates, threatening that unless they gave it to her she would hand over her incriminating notes about them to the authorities.

Virginia's last days were spent in Naples, where she had gone to pressure Joey Adonis into giving her another large sum of money. Adonis claimed afterward that he acceded to her suggestion that they have sex, and that they spent all night making love. After they breakfasted together, he handed her ten thousand dollars in American one-hundred-dollar bills and kissed her goodbye. The next day two horrified hikers found Virginia's corpse. Local police reported that she had overdosed on poison and had left a suicide note.

In recent years, a biography of Virginia Hill has disputed the apparent facts of her death. Andy Edmonds, who interviewed extensively for his biography, theorizes that she was murdered by two of Adonis's cronies, and that back in New York, Joey Epstein knew about it as well. Her assassins drove her to a rural footpath, forced sleeping pills down her throat and left her unconscious, soon to die. The mob had conspired to get rid of their once mighty moll.

Virginia Hill was too notorious to die in obscurity. Her death titillated the media and the general public, who remembered her as she had once been, glamorous and gorgeously garbed, tough talking and irreverent, a sexual powerhouse and an endless font of cash. Mostly, they recalled how powerful she had been in the savage and dangerous world of the Mafia.

All these memories were accurate, in particular Virginia's unique position as the trusted confidante and colleague of some of America's most vicious and unforgiving criminals. In many ways, she had clawed out a form of independence and cushioned herself in a decadent lifestyle. But her independence was conditional on Joey Epstein and other Mafia bosses, so much so that disobedience could mean death. Virginia understood this and rebelled only on minor issues. She was killed when she forgot and tried to threaten her old colleagues and lovers.

For most of her life, Virginia's happiness at her success alternated with misery, and she tried countless times to commit suicide, or at least to signal her deep distress. She suffered terrible depressions, and it is difficult to see how anyone who lived as precariously as she did could have felt otherwise. Virginia Hill's glamorous and exciting lifestyle was, in fact, little more than a facade.

In later life, Virginia harbored a bitter grudge against Epstein, whom she blamed for introducing her to a life of crime in the first place. Mostly, however, she was furious that he had not advised her correctly about how much tax to pay, a banal plaint from a woman famed for her independence.

Virginia died in poverty, sold out by an old lover she had never loved and probably murdered on the orders of old friends and allies. Such was the woman who inspired so many other young women to seek their fortunes as molls in the criminal underworld.

Arlyne Brickman [9]

Arlyne Weiss was born in 1934 in New York's Lower East Side, and she grew up devouring newspaper stories about the exploits of Virginia Hill, whom one paper dubbed "the most successful woman in America."[10] Arlyne's father was a well-connected racketeer who tried to steer her away from the underworld. But from the age of twelve, Arlyne was determined to be a mob girl like Virginia Hill.

Arlyne's grandmother Ida Blum, who owned a funeral parlor, encouraged this ambition. Arlyne knew what was required: good looks, the brains to keep her mouth shut and the lovemaking skills to keep her special "wiseguy" sexually engaged. The payoff would be gifts, status and respect.

Arlyne matured into a tall, slender young woman with a generous bust. She lost her virginity to a young cousin, secretly and painfully, in her grandmother's funeral parlor. After that she sought out older men to see if sex with them was more agreeable. In the evenings, she and three girlfriends cruised around in a car, picking up likely men.

What little reading Arlyne did was about Virginia Hill. "In my eyes," she told her biographer, Teresa Carpenter, "here was a broad that really made it good." Virginia's most impressive accomplishment, Arlyne believed, was being accepted as one of the boys.

Though Arlyne was Jewish, she preferred Italian mobsters, whom she found more romantic and thrilling. Her first wiseguy was Tony Mirra, an enforcer for the Bonanno crime family. For several discouraging weeks, Tony ignored her. Finally he invited her for a car ride in his black Cadillac with the yellow doors, ran his hands over her thighs and breasts, then pushed her face onto his unzipped crotch. When she resisted, he said accusingly, "You're nuthin' but a cockteaser." With that challenge, Arlyne slid her mouth over his penis and learned how to perform oral sex.

Fourteen-year-old Arlyne became Tony's moll. He gave her money and she couriered envelopes and packages to his associates. Whenever she was "on duty" she dressed elaborately and draped herself in a Virginia Hill–like fox stole. Tony's undesirability to her parents made him even more desirable to Arlyne, who stymied all their efforts to keep her away from him and from other equally disreputable mobsters.

After Tony came Italian fighter Al Pennino, whom she met in the company of the up-and-coming boxer Rocky Graziano. Just before an important boxing match, Arlyne's parents forcibly removed her from Al's hotel room. The incident so upset Al that he lost the match. Arlyne blamed herself and compensated him for his lost winnings with money she stole from her father's wallet. But Al's mother and brothers disliked Arlyne, and Al came to expect her handouts. Before long Arlyne decided she had had enough of him and her visits to his "wop house."

Arlyne's next lover was her father's friend Nathaniel "Natie" Nelson, a clothing manufacturer with ties to the underworld. Natie was three decades older than Arlyne, a flashy dresser who glittered with jewelry and rivaled Bugsy Siegel in his good looks. Until she seduced him in a beachside cabana, Natie ignored her attempts to attract him.

This quick session on a chaise longue led, at least on Natie's part, to a passionate love affair. He showered Arlyne with gifts and money. But his increasing possessiveness and talk of marriage so alarmed her that she broke off with him. Natie won her back with a diamond bracelet and by enlisting her grandmother's support. He also stopped mentioning marriage.

Arlyne dropped out of school to become a clothing showroom model. Often she spent the night in Natie's lavishly decorated apartment. One Saturday morning she passed Jimmy Doyle, a well-known gangster, in Natie's building. Then she found Natie dead in the foyer, a bullet hole in his forehead. Horrified, she ran away and said nothing. Jimmy Doyle summoned her to a meeting. Arlyne dressed herself with Virginia Hillish élan and went to meet her death. But Jimmy only wanted sex, quick and raw. Arlyne obliged him. Afterward, Jimmy lit a cigarette and said, "Get the fuck outta here. I'll call ya."[11]

From then on Jimmy used her like a sex slave and shared her with his associates. Arlyne bore this in silence, afraid to confide in her parents. But she lost so much weight and wept so frequently that they sent her to a psychiatrist, who coaxed out her secret and told her parents. Her father went to see Jimmy. In return for his guarantee that Arlyne would never reveal what she knew about Natie Nelson's death, Jimmy agreed to stop seeing her.

Finally safe, Arlyne recuperated. Soon she met and married Norman Brickman, an attractive older man who had just divorced his wife. In retrospect, Arlyne believes she accepted his proposal just so she could marry before her conservative and successful younger sister. Arlyne's marriage was unhappy. Norman seemed implacably demanding about his clothes, his food and how his house was kept. Despite her best efforts, Arlyne failed to satisfy him. They separated, and she took their little daughter, Leslie, with her. She began to date and sleep with hoodlums, former friends like Tony Mirra and new ones.

Arlyne had expectations about these relationships. "With a mobster who had class, you would go out with 'em a few times. You'd give 'em a blow job in the car. Maybe they'd buy you a piece of jewelry. Maybe they'd give you a few hundred-dollar bills. 'Here, go buy yourself a dress.'"[12]

But her latest man, a big time Mafioso named Joe Colombo, demanded sex and gave her nothing in return. "He's the worst fuck in the world!" Arlyne confided indignantly to a more generous wiseguy.[13]

Over time, Arlyne became the trusted moll for all the important crime families: the Gambinos, Genoveses and Bonannos. Her life with these wiseguys was a crashing roller-coaster course of fear (once three wiseguys raped her in a nightclub office) interspersed with large injections of cash.

For years this was how Arlyne existed. Then she met wiseguy Tommy Luca, who despite his anti-Semitism—he publicly referred to her as a "matzoh-grease bastard"—made her his moll, and set her and Leslie up in an apartment. But life with Tommy was distressingly domestic, with Arlyne pressed into service to cook Italian meals for mobsters who ignored her as they discussed their numbers racket. Tommy showered her with jewelry, but whenever he needed money, which happened regularly, he would take back his gifts and pawn them.

Tommy also beat her, often and increasingly more brutally. Once, as she lay bruised on the floor, he raped her. Later, he reproached her for making him do such terrible things and promised her she could always count on him. An archetypal battered woman, Arlyne interpreted his violence as passion and his subsequent remorse as love. She tried her utmost to please him, even fattening herself up and blackening her hair to make herself look more Italian.

The relationship deteriorated as it intensified. Arlyne was so helpful in Tommy's "business" that she assumed he would be unable to do without her. At the same time, she spied on him for rival mobsters as a sort of misguided insurance policy for herself. When they were both arrested for bookmaking, Tommy ordered her to save him by confessing, because her punishment would be more lenient than his. Arlyne confessed, plea-bargained and received probation and a two-hundred-dollar fine.

The years passed. Arlyne ended up in the clutches of a Mafia moneylender she could not pay. She turned official police informant after learning that her loan shark was planning to kill her. For over a decade, while she ran a bookmaking operation and also joined Tommy Luca in selling heroin, Arlyne wore wired handbags and taped mob conversations. In 1986, during a long and difficult trial, she testified for the prosecution and essentially broke the back of the Colombo mob's operation. Then, under federal protection, she left the east coast for a new life in Florida.

From adolescence, Arlyne Weiss Brickman was inspired by Virginia Hill. By any measure, however, Arlyne fell short of Virginia's achievements. She never enjoyed vast amounts of money or the respect of her mob associates, who were also anti-Semites. Unlike Virginia, who had no children during her active association with the mob, Arlyne subjected her daughter to such a violent home life that Leslie once attacked one of Arlyne's abusive wiseguys with a butcher knife. When Leslie became addicted to heroin, Arlyne refused to stop dealing in it. On the other hand, Arlyne has remained alive, not entirely dissatisfied with her life. But she is spending her latter years with limited security, little money and no respect. In the end, Virginia Hill proved a false model.

Sandy Sadowsky, Georgia Durante and Shirley Ryce [14]

Like Arlyne, Sandy Sadowsky and Georgia Durante were models who dated and ultimately married wiseguys. Sandy, a Las Vegas showgirl in the 1950s, deeply admired Virginia Hill. As an adolescent, she had watched Virginia Hill (on a black-and-white, eight-inch television screen) testify during the Kefauver investigation. "There she was in her low-cut black dress and wide-brimmed black picture hat, in sunglasses with a silver fox jacket draped across her shoulders. Notorious, glamorous, mysterious . . . I thought she was sensational," Sandy recalls.[15]

Both Sandy and Georgia experienced the psychotic life of a mob moll. Their lovers heaped clothes and jewelry on them, then reclaimed it when they ran short of money. Once, as Sandy dined with nightclub owner Bernie Barton, a friend of super-hood Meyer Lansky, a bookmaker joined them. Casually, Bernie handed him a signed paper and his car keys. "You've got cash for a cab, right, baby?" he asked Sandy.[16] He had just signed over their car to acquit a gambling debt.

Shortfalls of cash are the lot of mob mistresses and wives, and financial security is as tenuous as other aspects of their existence. (Bernie had to obtain his parole officer's approval before he could marry Sandy.)

Both Sandy and Georgia witnessed instances of the criminal violence that was integral to their partners' profession. Once Sandy arrived home to find a stranger with a bullet hole in his shoulder, whose blood was drenching her custom-made, trapunto-stitched white bedspread and oozing onto her powder blue carpeting. Bernie ordered Sandy to help him dig out the bullet. Taking the man to the hospital was, he said, out of the question. A shaken Sandy assisted Bernie as he sliced into the shrieking man's flesh with a kitchen knife and excised the bullet that he then flushed down the toilet. Afterward Bernie calmly ate a toasted bagel with cream cheese, tomato and red onion.

Georgia's experiences were worse. Handsome, flashy nightclub owner Joe Lamendola, whom she eventually married, was brutal. Georgia watched as he and his associates kicked a man who lay pleading for his life before they shoved him into a car trunk. When Georgia tearfully asked Joe about the incident, he slapped her repeatedly until she agreed that she had seen nothing and would say nothing. "Don't you ever, *ever* fucking question me! Who the hell are you to question me?" Joe roared.[17]

Like Virginia and Arlyne, Sandy and Georgia were victims of repeated beatings. Georgia became a classic battered wife. Sandy was cursed—"Stupid. Bitch. Cunt. Dumb douche bag"—when her sometimes charming lover tried to eat the first meal she prepared for him: charred steak and half-raw baked potato. He slammed the food and plates against the wall, then pounded the table and walls and hurled insults at her.

Both women were dominated and controlled, down to the tiniest aspect of life, including makeup, hairstyle, apparel, friends, activities. Another problem was pregnancy. As Sandy discovered, wiseguys hate their molls to become pregnant. After secretly trying various ways to rid herself of the fetus, including douching with Lysol, Sandy confessed to Bernie. He blamed her for her stupidity and lamented his bad luck in impregnating every woman he slept with. When Sandy defended herself and retorted that she had used the rhythm method, as the Catholics did, Bernie shouted, "Did you ever notice that Catholics have twenty kids apiece?"[18]

In the 1960s, Canadian Shirley Ryce's experiences echoed many of Sandy's and Georgia's, and by later becoming an informant, Arlyne's. Unlike these other women, Shirley was already married. A young mother and bored wife, she began her "career" late, at twenty-three. Cruising the bars one night in her hometown of Hamilton, an industrial city outside Toronto, she was strongly attracted to Rocco Papalia, a leader of the Papalia crime family. He had sex with her on their third "date," at his brother's apartment. He wanted to keep his own pristine for his fiancée, who often visited.

Sex itself was conservative. Unlike many American mobsters, the Papalias scorned oral sex as kinky and disgusting. When Shirley occasionally took his penis in her mouth, Frank Papalia (Rocco's older brother, whom Rocco farmed her out to after tiring of her) refused to kiss her afterward because that "was just so terrible" and he felt soiled. He could not even bring himself to eat with a woman who had done such a revolting thing. For these Italian gangsters, Shirley concluded, the sexual revolution had never happened.

They were equally traditional about marriage. Shirley deduced that Rocco had gotten married when she noticed he had gained quite a bit of weight, the consequence of his wife's cooking. She knew better than to ask any questions about wives, to ask if Rocco (or later, Frankie) loved her or to show jealousy. She had to accept her status as a moll; she had to be pretty, entertaining and—when Rocco asked her—available for sex with various of his associates. At one meeting, Shirley realized she had slept with eight of the nine mobsters in attendance. Rocco joked, "What's this, a reunion?"[19]

In return for pleasing and serving the Papalia wiseguys, Shirley received gifts, money and—when she left her husband—a job at the Papalias' Gold Key Club. As a hostess, she functioned as a moll elder and mentor. She taught young wannabes that the mob liked their molls tastefully garbed, preferably in dresses. They could not use the "f" word in company, though it was permissible one on one. They should aspire to seem refined, drinking liquor instead of beer, wearing classic jewelry rather than gaudy baubles, and never suggest or expect anything but straight sex. "I had to fantasize to make [sex] interesting," she later recalled. "I never had an orgasm in mob sex; I didn't know what a climax was while I was with them."[20]

Mob mistresses who give interviews or write about their hidden pasts usually acknowledge their essential powerlessness. Shirley Ryce attempts a sort of feminist analysis of her promiscuity, arguing that by doing what powerful men do, she was trying to acquire for herself what she saw as the trappings of power. Georgia now understands that she was a classic victim of the battered woman syndrome—so, of course, were Arlyne and Virginia. Many of these women confuse possessiveness with love, violence with passion, and become trapped in nightmarish relationships, often one after the other.

As a prerequisite to uniting her fortunes with criminal men dedicated to subverting mainstream society, a would-be moll must disregard the law and disrespect social moral standards. She must internalize and abide by the very different values of her underworld associates. It is true that the underworld has certain opportunities less easily available to women in the straight or square world—money and the goods it can buy are at the top of the list, followed by the thrill of danger and violence. But molls pay a high price that includes collapsed self-esteem, destroyed families and ferocious personal insecurity that can endure a lifetime.

KREMLIN DOLLS[21]

Totalitarian governments often assume forms of institutional gangsterism reminiscent of the criminal underworld. This is particularly true when high-ranked officials abuse their power to exert nearly absolute control over women they desire sexually. An egregious example of such a man is Lavrenti Pavlovich Beria, a Georgian peasant who rose through Communist Party ranks to head the Soviet Union's Ministry of Internal Affairs (1938), the secret police. After purging the police, Beria implemented a regime of terror infamous for torture and the Gulag Archipelago of forced-labor camps.

After Stalin died, Beria was tried and later executed. At one point in his trial, a prosecutor referred to nine lists containing sixty-two women's names, and asked if they were his mistresses. Yes, Beria replied, most of them. And did he have syphilis? Yes, but he had had it treated. What about the fourteen-year-old schoolgirl he raped, who later had his baby? It was not rape, Beria insisted. The girl had consented to have sex with him.

One of Beria's mistresses was a young Georgian dentist named Vera. Vera was a solemn woman, tall and slender, with a pale complexion and dark eyes.

She practiced her profession in the Lubyanka prison, where she also lived in a small apartment. Beria visited Vera's apartment whenever he pleased, and he also forced her to be his accomplice in torturing prisoners. A guard would escort the victim to Vera's office, supposedly for a routine dental examination. But once the man opened his mouth, the guard would pin him to the chair and interrogate him while Vera drilled. Until the agonized prisoner nodded in response to questions and agreed to confess immediately, she continued drilling. One anti-Stalinist author endured only fifteen minutes before he pleaded guilty to every charge against him.[22]

Unless the never-smiling Vera was as warped as her lover, her relationship with him must have tortured her as much as she tortured Beria's victims. She may have known at least some of them, perhaps sympathized with their "heresies." Their screams must have haunted her day and night, and her apartment inside Lubyanka could not have afforded her much comfort. Vera could never escape from Beria or from her own memories.

Lavrenti Beria was one of the worst examples of political gangsterism. Because he enjoyed Stalin's trust, he was as dangerous as he was powerful, and he exercised his power to subjugate any woman he desired. He suborned the apparatus of state created with such fervor and after so much bloodshed to guarantee the rights of all citizens and the equality of women; he used it as an instrument to procure women for his personal sexual gratification. Stalinism, which Beria personified, betrayed the gender equality at the ideological core of communist ideals and with it, legions of principled and once hopeful women.

CASTRO'S COMRADES[23]

Nearly two decades later and continents away, Cuban president Fidel Castro implemented a purer form of communism, though early Castroism borrowed Stalinist strategies: neighborhood cadres operating as nationwide spy organisms; students encouraged to inform on heretical parents and teachers; homosexuals targeted for abuse. Human rights were crushed. Anti-Castroites, suspected and real, were subjected to torture and lengthy terms of imprisonment. These loathsome measures sullied Castroism's achievements in the realm of racial and gender equality, housing, education, medicine and social welfare.

The Cuba that Castro liberated from military dictator–president Fulgencio Batista[24] was notoriously corrupt and repressive and had happily coexisted with the small, spoiled elite class of Cubans who set Cuba's social tone. Batista had also invited American gangsters to set up gambling shops in Havana. Meyer Lansky and other Mafia leaders established such spectacular casinos and nightclubs that Cuban nightlife won an international reputation for its exuberance, vitality and hedonism. Cuba's rum was smooth, its tobacco mellow and its dancers dynamic. Its prostitutes, disgorged from the surging underclass of desperate peasants, were sultry and young. Most of Cuba's other employed women—9.8 percent of total workers registered—were domestics or beggars. Otherwise women worked at home as unpaid homemakers or undocumented part-time entrepreneurs.

Castroism has taken great strides in improving this situation because of the egalitarianism at its ideological core, and because Castro personally respects and often trusts women. In 1974, he attended every session of a five-day national women's congress.[25] A year later, on Women's Day, his government adopted the Family Code that outlawed the occupations of female prostitute and domestic, and made all Cuban citizens, male and female, equal in the eyes of the law.[26]

In social terms, Castro is still traditional both in his judgments and in his expectations of women. In his own marriage to Mirta Díaz-Balart, Castro demanded almost feudal loyalty but did not hesitate to sacrifice family life for revolutionary activities. He believes in stable marriages and he condones divorce. Yet since his own divorce from Mirta, he has preferred to take mistresses instead of remarrying.

Naty Revuelta

For the women he has been deeply involved with, to love Castro the man is to love Castro the great leader. From his earliest revolutionary days, he has merged his political and personal life. His best-known mistress, Naty Revuelta, learned this slowly and painfully, after she was already nursing the baby she had hoped would permanently ensnare its father.

Natalia Revuelta Clews was born in 1925, four months before Fidel Castro. Her mother, Natica, was descended from a distinguished and wealthy family with British antecedents. With the confidence of beauty reinforced by desire, Natica defied her father and married the handsome but alcoholic Manolo Revuelta. When Naty was four, her parents divorced. Her father moved to far-off Oriente province and removed himself almost entirely from his daughter's life.

Naty, auburn-haired and tanned, green-eyed and voluptuous, was an even greater beauty than her proud mother. Her education included a Philadelphia prep school and Havana's finest American school. All her acquaintances expected Naty to achieve great social success. "She has more than beauty, she has It," her school yearbook avowed.

Naty's marriage to the respected and much older cardiologist Orlando Fernández Ferrer, who had been smitten when Naty was hospitalized for a dangerously ruptured and gangrenous appendix, was eminently suitable. So was motherhood, which followed a year later with little Natalie, known as Nina.

But despite industrious servants who cared for her gracious house and adorable daughter, despite the exclusive Vedado Tennis Club, the fine shops of Havana and even her interesting job at Esso Standard Oil, Naty was dissatisfied.

This was not just because her hardworking and reserved husband bored her. Unaccountably, this favored daughter of Cuba's aristocracy had developed revolutionary sympathies. In 1952, when General Fulgencio Batista overturned the government, squashed upcoming elections and was rewarded with recognition by the United States, Naty risked the ire of her peers and her family by casting her lot with revolutionary students dedicated to defeating Batista.

Naty was serious and determined. When Castro's struggling movement needed money, she contributed her savings. She joined the League of Women Followers of José Martí, sewing look-alike military costumes Castro needed to disguise his men. Daringly, Naty duplicated the key to her house and sent copies to two opposition politicians and a third, secreted in a linen envelope perfumed with Lanvin's Arpege, to Castro.

The key to Naty's house unlocked her heart as well. Quite some time after he received this token from his spirited, socialite supporter, Castro appeared at her door in a clean and starched guayabera. They talked, or rather Castro did, even after Orlando arrived home. Castro spoke so movingly about his opposition to passive resistance that Orlando emptied his pockets and donated his day's earnings. Naty walked Castro to the door. "If you need me, please count on me," she said earnestly.[27] Naty was unaware, her then unborn daughter Alina wrote later, "that her face, her slender waist, and her high-society status made men's hearts beat faster. . . . [She and Fidel] connected immediately, and the rest of the world ceased to exist."[28]

Already Naty was in love and, after his fashion, so was Castro. Naty's husband was devoted and kind, but he was also unexciting, workaholic and oblivious to his energetic wife's ennui. And no matter how Naty must have tried to avoid comparing him to the tall, handsome and charismatic Castro, Orlando was irredeemably short and eggheaded.

Outwardly, Naty and Fidel assumed the mien of political collaborators. He declined her invitation to the Vedado social club but she accepted his to a protest rally. Responding to the students' frenzy, he navigated his way to the platform and took command. As he fought his way through the crowd, he gripped Naty's hand in his and pulled her after him. It did not matter that she crept in very late that night. Orlando was still at work, and Nina's nanny had lulled the girl into peaceful sleep.

Soon Castro was using Naty's gift of her house key almost daily, transforming her home into his strategic headquarters for planning the assault on the Moncada garrison. Before he left, he told Naty that leaving her was difficult. "I want you to know that I am placing you on an altar inside my heart," he said.[29]

At dawn on the day planned for the attack, Naty distributed Fidel's manifestos to politicos, journalists and publishers. But the radio broadcast the dreadful news that Castro's ragtag army had been defeated. Castro himself had fled to the hills, but half his men were taken prisoner, tortured and executed. Naty was in torment. She dared say nothing, however, and could not protest when Orlando suggested lunch at the Biltmore Country Club and, afterward, the beach.

Fidel was captured and imprisoned. As the only person besides the movement's leaders to have had advance information about the Moncada attack, Naty was so seriously implicated that she feared that at any minute she, too, might be arrested. Her mother, in whom she had confided, was so anxious that her thick hair began to thin. But nobody, certainly not Fidel, exposed Naty's complicity, and she remained free to live if not enjoy her pleasant life.

Fidel was sentenced to fifteen years in prison. For Naty, the twenty months he actually served would be the golden era when his bars kept others away from him. For the first and last time, Fidel was dependent on and unreservedly in love with her.

Naty's new mission was to furnish Fidel with everything he wanted, to make herself indispensable to him and, she hoped, to bind him to her forever. She located and mailed him boxes of books and the foodstuffs he craved. Fidel devoured everything and praised her for her bounty and her intellectual range and depth. As their letters deepened into intimacy and then love, the bored and beautiful housewife vibrated with purpose and rejoiced in the relationship. "Your letters to me provide nourishment for my soul . . . help me to know my feelings . . . and to calm my fears," she confided.[30]

Fidel, as indefatigable as he was brilliant, proposed a joint study project of the world's best literature. Together they read, discussed and analyzed everything from Thackeray's *Vanity Fair* to *Das Kapital* to Somerset Maugham's *The Razor's Edge.* "You have a space on every page, in every phrase, in every word," Fidel enthused. "I want to share with you every pleasure that I find in a book. Doesn't this mean that you are my intimate companion and that I am never alone?"[31] And "the part of you which belongs to me accompanies me always, and it will be so forever."[32] He began to sign his letters, "I love you very much."

As their exchange of letters continued, Fidel attributed to Naty a soaring intellectuality and originality, to which she responded with all her heart. But when she discovered that she was not Fidel's only correspondent, her pen (actually her Smith Corona at the Esso office) dripped poisonous jealousy. "I do not know how to love when I am not loved," she raged. "Who else in the world knows me better than you? Since I started writing, I don't keep any secrets. My soul is open to you."[33]

The more their epistolary passion intensified, the more Naty loathed her duplicitous life. She justified it, however. Her heart was large enough, she declared, to love Fidel, Orlando, Nina and even her difficult, reactionary mother. Fidel needed no such rationalizations. He wrote dutiful letters to his devoted but apolitical wife, Mirta Díaz-Balart, who was struggling to raise young Fidelito alone, without any financial support from her incarcerated husband. From afar, Fidel dictated his son's dietary regime and other domestic details, and kept Mirta updated about his version of Cuban politics. He did not share with Naty (or probably feel) any sense of ambivalence much less guilt about their relationship, and he mentioned Mirta only in passing. When Mirta and his sister Lidia quarreled, for instance, Fidel confided to Naty that he intended to reproach his judges for sentencing him to only fifteen years instead of the serenity of twenty.

Never once did Naty feel threatened by Mirta. In fact, her existence, like Fidel's incarceration, kept him safe from potential rivals unencumbered with husbands and children. Naty went out of her way to communicate with and visit Mirta, then wrote to Fidel about how sweet his wife was. Naty also ingratiated herself with Fidel's mother and brother, Raúl.

Less than a year into their paper-strewn passion, a prison official inadvertently or maliciously switched Fidel's letters, sending Naty's to Mirta and Mirta's to Naty. Naty simply forwarded the missive back to Fidel, but Mirta, outraged and wounded, opened Naty's and discovered that the husband who had already caused her such distress was in love with another woman.[34]

Mirta went after Naty furiously, warning her that she would create a scandal for Fidel if Naty persisted in communicating with him. At first, Naty was incapable of grasping the danger to either herself or Fidel, and instructed him to assuage Mirta's fears and pain. "Don't worry, everything in life has a solution," she wrote.[35]

Fidel's solution was to cease writing to her. Personal matters were of little interest to him, he reminded her. Naty, consumed with love for him, found it difficult to identify herself as a "personal matter." Nor did she understand that in expressing his gratitude for all she had done for him, Fidel was extinguishing their burning love.

But Fidel still needed books and, through his sister Lidia, sent Naty wish lists in impersonal, uncompromising letters. The marital scandal he hoped to avert erupted anyway, but not because of Naty. On July 17, 1954, he heard on the radio that the Interior Ministry had laid Mirta off. This was the first indication that Fidel had had that his wife was working for the despised Batista government. He reacted with furious disbelief. The news report was "a machination against me, the worst, the most cowardly, the most indecent, the vilest and intolerable," he wrote to a friend. "The prestige of my wife and my honor as a revolutionary are at stake."[36]

His sister Lidia soon confirmed that the report was true. Days later, the long-suffering Mirta asked for a divorce. Fidel countered by asking for one too. "You know I have a steel heart and I shall be dignified until the last day of my life," he assured Lidia.[37] Mirta, equally dignified, remarried and left Cuba forever, except for annual visits to Fidelito, whose custody she and Fidel contested bitterly until he finally won it.

Naty, meanwhile, waited tensely for Fidel's release from prison in a general amnesty. "Probably Fidel wasn't even aware yet that Naty's attraction for him depended upon her being a conduit, a courier for him—granted, an exciting, desirable one. Fidel was using her to get the books he wanted; that's what remained of his passion," writes Wendy Gimbel, who spent considerable time with Naty as she researched *Havana Dreams*, her book about the four generations of Naty's family.

Before dawn on the morning of his release, Naty sneaked out of the house in a cinch-waisted red skirt and white peasant blouse, and got into Orlando's green Mercedes-Benz. But the triumphant Fidel, surrounded by his sisters, scarcely noticed her among the throng of adoring admirers.

Before their final rupture, Naty and Fidel had several surreptitious meetings in his cramped apartment and consummated sexually the passion that, for Fidel, had ended back in prison. Naty must have hoped that sex, her sensuous beauty and their remembered love would reclaim him, but Fidel remained courteous and emotionally distant. Almost immediately, Naty became pregnant with his child.

With her own particular version of the age-old fancy that a baby might solidify a disintegrating relationship, Naty dreamed of the son she carried, a little Fidel who would survive although the upcoming revolution might kill his father. Fidel, recently exiled, invited her to join and marry him in Mexico, where he was surviving on eighty US dollars monthly. Naty's instincts for self-preservation saved her. She stayed with her safe doctor husband and their daughter.

However, Naty's relations with her husband had changed quite radically. In a fit of conscience and bravado, she had confessed to him that she loved Fidel. She even tried to be faithful to Fidel by refusing to sleep with Orlando. "Once I had a sexual connection to Fidel, I had no alternative but to retreat from my husband," she told Wendy Gimbel.[38] Orlando reacted calmly and did not suggest separating; perhaps he believed Naty was confusing Fidel with his political dreams, so the man and his mission were indistinguishable. On March 19, 1956, Naty delivered the infant daughter she had hoped would be a replica Fidel. Without hesitation, Orlando gave baby Alina his surname.

Naty sent Fidel a sliver of ribbon from Alina's christening gown, and over in Mexico, the new father toasted his daughter. Later, he sent his sister Lidia to inspect Alina and verify her paternity. Lidia examined the baby carefully. "This baby girl is definitely a Castro,"[39] she announced. Then she distributed Fidel's gifts: embossed silver hoop earrings and bracelet for Naty, and platinum-stud pearl earrings with tiny diamonds for Alina, who later lost this rare gift from her father.

Fidel wrote erratically to enlist Naty's help in reinvigorating his revolutionary movement. He did not pretend that he loved her, and Naty was aware of rumors that he was in love with a young woman named Isabel Custodio. On December 2, 1956, undetected by Batista's patrols, Castro and fifty committed Cubans landed in Oriente province and hunkered in for two years of guerrilla warfare. During this period, Castro shared his life and bed with Celia Sanchez, who dedicated her life to him and his revolution. Naty (who then knew nothing about Celia) continued to furnish Fidel with goodies: money and his favorite French pastries from Havana's famous La Casa Potín. Occasionally, he reciprocated with gifts of spent .75-caliber gun shells.

When Alina was almost three years old, Batista packed his bags and fled. Fidel returned to Havana, a conquering hero in olive green army fatigues with a cigar clamped between his teeth. "Fidel! Fidel! Viva Fidel!" shouted the throngs who lined the streets to cheer him on. Among them was Naty Revuelta, who managed to hand him a white flower as he passed by. "I'll send for you tomorrow," he told her. She was not surprised that he did not.

Other Cubans were. Castro's interpreter Juan Arcocha reminisced about Naty to American journalist and author Georgie Anne Geyer. "Fidel had loved her desperately," Arcocha said, "and on January 1, she was ripe for him. . . . She expected to be married to him. She was magnificent, more beautiful than ever. Everybody was saying Fidel would marry her."[40] But Fidel had long ago ceased to love Naty; in any case, he was already married to his revolution.

By 1959, Castro's name was on all Cuban lips, a curse to those facing nationalization and an end to privilege, a benediction to the multitudes glimpsing liberation. Naty, one of the rare members of elite society who continued to support Fidel's revolution, confessed to Orlando that Alina was Fidel's daughter, not his, and requested a legal separation.

For Orlando, this terrible blow followed on the heels of the revolutionary government's nationalization of his clinic. Bereft of wife and clinic, Orlando quietly joined the exodus of professional Cubans. He took Nina with him, leaving Alina with Naty. Naty had agreed to let Nina go on the understanding that she would return to Cuba within a year. For the first time, Orlando betrayed his wife. He had never intended to surrender his daughter. Nina remained with him in the United States and did not see her mother again for two decades.

On a few occasions afterward, Naty and Fidel met together privately. Alina recalls her mother returning from these trysts "all aglow with a smile coming from within and her eyes lost in mystery."[41] A few times Naty swallowed her pride, armed herself with the weapons of seduction—flattering hairstyle, striking clothes, gentle reminders of past promises—and lined up for an audience with Cuba's premier citizen in his office on the twenty-third floor of the Havana Hilton. When her turn came, Fidel, often clad in striped pajamas, received her with unconcealed indifference, impervious to her attractions, eager to see her go.

Fidel had no interest in Naty other than as Alina's mother. Sometimes he visited his daughter in the dead of night. "She looks like a curly little lamb," he exclaimed once, before giving Alina a baby doll in his own image, bearded and dressed in military fatigues. While Naty watched, Fidel crawled on the floor to play with his child, who remembers that when he put out his cigar, he had a "manly smell" and wore no cologne.

Suddenly, without warning, Fidel stopped coming, probably unnerved or irritated by having to confront the hopelessly adoring Naty. He also refused to give Alina his name—she was, he pointed out, Orlando's legal daughter.

Naty the ex-mistress finally faced the fact that Fidel no longer loved her. As if that were not enough, she lost her job with Esso, which shut down its Cuban operation. Orlando had left her and taken Nina. Without love, family or work, Naty lost thirty-five pounds and withdrew into mourning.

She revived in a proletarianized Cuba whose citizens achieved instant equality through shared privation. Electricity was erratic. Water service was problematic. Staple foods disappeared. Ration books dictated pitifully limited diets, and Naty patriotically refused to resort to the black market. Naty's cook, preparing monotonous meals of unsalted lentils or pureed spinach, lamented, "I don't know how to cook without food."[42] (At one point, on a rare visit, Fidel noticed how debilitated Alina had become. He scolded Naty for neglecting her and sent over a can of fresh milk.)

But Naty, who had flung herself into the revolutionary fervor, was too busy for domestic matters. Too late—in refusing to join Fidel in Mexico, she had lost her last chance with him—she decided to embrace whatever austerities the revolution required. She discarded her extensive and fashionable wardrobe for outfits of blue-green army fatigues and a Spanish beret. In one photo, she poses proudly in a field, with rolled-up sleeves and the top buttons of her shirt fetchingly undone. Her lush hair is tied back under her beret, and in her hands she holds a rifle with graceful fingers, much as one might hold a violin.

Naty also decided that the house she shared with her mother and daughter was unconscionably luxurious, and in Alina's words, "she gave it [fully furnished] to the Revolution."[43] A confused and bitter Natica, who despised Fidel and his revolution, salvaged crystal, bone china and silver remnants of the "good old life" and carted them over to their new lodgings, an apartment by the sea. There, Alina remembers, their maid would place bone china plates and silver bowls on the table. Then, while Naty "gobbled up" the cornmeal mush or other unappetizing fare, Natica instructed Alina on the niceties of elegant dining and made snide remarks about the catastrophe of Castro's Cuba.

According to Alina, the stint in the small apartment was of short duration. Fidel arranged for much finer lodgings and a servant to help Tata, their housekeeper. There was also a garage for the Mercedes-Benz Naty was still driving.

By 1964, because (Wendy Gimbel believes) Fidel longed to be relieved of his irksome ex-mistress and their daughter, he assigned Naty to the Cuban

Embassy in Paris, where she was to study the French chemical industry. "This is Celia's doing," Naty said grimly."[44]

Celia Sanchez was as fervent and knowledgeable a revolutionary as Fidel and, since the planning stages of his invasion from Mexico, had become an invaluable member of his command team. During the long and onerous campaign up in the Sierra, Celia had shared his bed. Back in Havana, she was his indispensable guardian, assistant and adviser. On more than one occasion, she had barred Naty from seeing Fidel, likely on his own instructions. Naty, however, preferred to attribute Celia's actions to jealousy.

Alina is venomous in describing the woman she believed was keeping her from her father. To her mind, Celia was as ridiculous as she was hideous. Her "unruly" hair was scrunched into a ponytail worn to one side of her "egregious" head, her lacy slip always trailed beneath her dress and "for the finishing touches to her skinny legs, she wore a pair of bobby sox with stiletto heels."[45] Alina—and perhaps Naty?—must have wondered how this unfashionable and homely woman had beaten out the lovely Naty.

Exiled—as she saw it—to Paris, Naty plunged into her whirlwind new life, which included the Mercedes-Benz she had had shipped from Havana. She worked at the embassy and attempted to produce the report Castro had assigned her though she knew nothing about chemical industries. To free up time for the project, and also for an intensifying social life, Naty sent the resentful Alina to a school and *pension* ten miles outside Paris.

When rumors began to percolate that she was planning to defect, Naty squelched them by sending Alina, her hostage to fortune, back to Cuba. The night Alina arrived, Fidel came to collect the gifts (a suitcase of French cheese, single-malt whiskey) Naty had sent for him, and to visit Alina.

Five months later, Naty returned to Havana. Fidel waited eight months to drop by to greet her. When he did, she subjected him to a litany of complaints, including her lack of employment—nobody would hire her without Fidel's approval. The next day Fidel appointed her chief of documentation and information at the National Center for Scientific Investigations.

Naty also finally revealed to Alina that Fidel, not the long-fled Orlando Fernández, was her father. She then showed Alina her precious letters from Fidel's Isle of Pines prison, letters he had urged her to keep as important documents of the revolution, and that documented, as well, the flowering of their love affair. Naty explained that the name "Alina" derived from "Lina," Fidel's mother's name. She justified not acting on Fidel's suggestion that she join him in Mexico: she could not leave Nina, and in any case he had been in no position to take on a woman and newborn baby.

At last Alina knew what was already common knowledge in Havana, that Fidel Castro was her father. But he still did not answer her many letters. "I could not distract him . . . and get him to come back to my mother," Alina recalls.[46] In the next two years, he summoned her only twice, but mentioned that her name would be changed to Castro when a certain law was changed. He added, referring to Naty, "Your mom has a problem. She is much too good. Don't be that good to any man."[47]

Naty's reduced status with Fidel was reinforced time and again. Alina—and Naty?—put the blame squarely on Celia Sanchez. According to Alina, Celia harassed Naty and blocked her way for the rest of her lifetime. (Celia died in 1980.) As for the Castros, they had been more respectful of Naty as Fidel's "whore" than they were now that she was merely his ex-mistress.

The teenaged Alina was as beautiful as her mother, as vituperative as her version of Celia, as stubborn as her father and as uncooperative and neurotic as a neglected child can be. From the age of seventeen, Alina married and divorced several times. "In terms of marriage, I'm an annual, not a perennial," she liked to quip.[48]

At first Fidel promised to be a better father if she abandoned this madness. Afterward, he was just disgusted. "I can't believe that you have left an Angolan war hero for a ballet dancer!" he reproached her after divorce number one and before marriage number two. "If he is a dancer, he must be queer."[49]

Naty was no happier about Alina's tumultuous love life than Fidel. When Alina announced that she was pregnant, Naty kicked her out. Motherhood in undersupplied, overregulated Cuba was hellish. Fidel's gift was an outfit for Mumin, Alina's infant daughter, a housecoat for Alina, talcum powder and money for a refrigerator. Alina used every expedient to get enough food, including demanding vegetables from an old man who fondled her breasts. When she married a wealthy Mexican who could have provided a better life for her, Fidel denied her an exit permit. After a while the Mexican simply withdrew from Alina's confined and frozen life.

Alina moved back in with Naty and Natica, who (like Naty and Alina) quarreled constantly. Natica was an unrepentant anti-Castroite who vigorously defended her elitist values, including her hardcore racism. As time passed, Alina acted more outrageously. She criticized her father's regime to foreign journalists. She became a bulimic fashion model. She lashed out at family and friends, spewing her lifetime's anger. Though she could not make her father love her, she knew that because of her status, nothing would ever happen to her. When she was forty, Alina fled Cuba, denounced Castro from abroad, sold the letters he had written to her mother and wrote her memoirs about life as his daughter.

Naty endured, indeed clung to, the same gilded prison from which Alina had absconded. Because Castro had once loved her, trusted her with crucial secrets and impregnated her—and because her (now fading) beauty was legendary and her daughter notorious—Naty lived unlike other Cubans. On the one hand, she enjoyed the luxury of a splendid home and a series of decent jobs. On the other, she suffered the indignities that vengeful colleagues heaped on her; the pain of Fidel's refusal to respond to her letters; the fear that Celia was plotting against her; the grinding reality of Cuba's unrelenting shortages; and the daily torment of life with Natica, who despised everything she believed in and bitterly taunted Naty for every privation and inconvenience the household of wrangling women faced.

Fidel Castro's special relationship with women is as well known as his energetic womanizing. Because he trusts and relies on them, women have played a remarkably important role in his revolutionary struggles. He admires beauty, but it affects him only temporarily. What he values above all else is the intellect, as Castro political intimate Melba Fernandez told *New York Times* correspondent Tad Szulc.

Szulc considers Naty Revuelta as one in "an extraordinary contingent of beautiful and/or highly intelligent women who, in effect, dedicated their lives to him and his cause—and without whom he might not have succeeded."[50] Naty voluntarily joined their ranks and remained there, driven by revolutionary conviction but also a forlorn, lingering hope that somehow she might recapture Fidel's heart or at least revive some of the brief passion they had shared.

Ultimately, Naty's story is more remarkable for her tenacity and sacrifice than for the nature of her relationship with Fidel Castro. He loved her exclusively for only months, from the bowels of solitary confinement, the only time she had no rivals and could employ her ample resources to comfort and impress her suffering lover. In the flesh, in freedom, she was truly his mistress for only two months, an unfaithful wife who sneaked off to clandestine rendezvous and sexual trysts that were her last chance to capture the increasingly elusive Fidel. "I was born just to improve my mother's position with Fidel," Alina has said repeatedly.[51]

And fleetingly, this might have worked, except that Naty was not prepared to accept Fidel as he was, impoverished, frenetically bound up in revolution, a man who permitted himself almost no private life and was surrounded by adoring and committed revolutionary women.

Celia Sanchez

Celia Sanchez Manduley succeeded where her predecessor failed and, until her death in 1980, was the most important person in Castro's life. Celia, born in 1927, one of the five daughters of Dr. Manuel Sanchez Silveira, lived in the southwest of Oriente province where she had long been politically active.

From the first, Celia stood out from other educated and privileged women who offered their services to the movement. She was fiercely intelligent and efficient, focused and disciplined. She was in complete sympathy with the movement's philosophy and its concrete political goals. She also had extensive knowledge of Oriente province, its political structure and personalities and its topography and people. As Castro and his colleagues planned their invasion, Celia became one of their principal strategists. She provided navigational maps, organized a revolutionary peasant underground and urban support groups, and amassed and delivered supplies, from food to arms, for the rebels. By the time Celia and Fidel met in person, she was already a key member of his operation.

Celia first laid eyes on Fidel on February 16, 1957, in a pasture in guerrilla terrain. He was bearded and filthy, clad in tattered clothes and a green cap, and he probably reeked from months of scrabbling in the Sierra. After walking all night through the Sierra to reach the rebels, Celia and her companion encountered Fidel and his men just after 5 A.M. They talked there for hours, briefing each other on developments and planning the next stages of their uprising. At noon they ate in a nearby sugarcane field, then continued their discussions until late into the night.

Celia was in most ways Fidel's ideal woman. Up there in the Sierra, with her brilliant grasp of strategy, her expertise with weapons, her ability to transform people into allies and to supply desperately needed food, bullets and anything else Castro needed—a dentist for his aching teeth, a New York Times correspondent to document his progress—she was the answer to his prayers.

Celia's only flaw was that she lacked the beauty Fidel so admired in other women. Unlike lovely and serious Mirta, sultry and voluptuous Naty or beautiful young Isabel Custodio, whom he had briefly loved in Mexico, Celia could look quite plain. She had a prominent, aquiline nose, a long face, olive skin and springy dark hair she sometimes wore upswept but more often scraped back from her face into a ponytail. Her torso was gaunt, her legs skinny, and she had none of the soft curves for which Naty Revuelta was renowned. At thirty, she was not even very young.[52] But she had a ready smile and a husky, throbbing voice. Best of all, she could listen as well as speak. Alina Fernández's description of Celia's sartorial style is accurate if venomous, but Celia added simple decorations to her no-nonsense garb. Photos show her with studs or dangling earrings. In the Sierra, in the heartland of military insurrection, she wore guerrilla green shirt and pants but always slipped a gold ankle chain over her boots.[53]

From their first encounter, Celia and Fidel were soul mates. Celia came and went, bearing information and goods, receiving instructions and lists. When they were apart, she and Fidel kept in close touch by letter, and their correspondence is a vital record not just of their easy and intimate relationship, but also of the military campaign that soon liberated Cuba from the corrupt and repressive Batista.

As this campaign proceeded, the authorities became aware of Celia's activities. When she learned that they wanted to arrest her, she fled up to the rebel camp. Celia and Fidel became inseparable. She moved into Fidel's small and camouflaged wooden house–*cum*–command post. She shared his bedroom and bed. She took over the other small room for her office while Fidel conducted business on the deck. The couple never stopped working, endlessly talking and planning. By the time Batista fell, the rebels in the Sierra had established primitive hospitals, workshops that produced light arms, bullets and leather equipment, a printing press and an all-important radio station.

On the rare occasions Celia had to leave to oversee events elsewhere, Fidel missed her deeply. "Your absence has left a real vacuum. Even when a woman goes around the mountains with a rifle in hand, she always makes our men tidier, more decent, gentlemanly—and even braver." More personally, "And you, why don't you make a short trip here? Think about it, and do so in the next few days. . . . A big hug." After an erroneous report that Celia had been arrested, Fidel drafted a statement that she and another rebel were "our basic pillars. If you and he are well, all goes well and we are tranquil." Che Guevara credited Celia with being the rebels' "only known and safe contact."[54]

What Celia did not inspire were the romantic (and sometimes jealous) flourishes and yearnings that permeate Fidel's letters to Naty Revuelta. And, intelligent and perceptive as she was, Celia must have guessed that her time with Fidel in the Sierra would not be easily repeated. Years later, reminiscing with Fidel and some American journalists, Celia recalled those extraordinary days. "Ah, but those were the best times, weren't they? We were all so very happy then. *Really*. We will never be so happy again, will we? *Never*."[55]

In January 1959, Celia's improbably idyllic life in the Sierra Maestra ended when the revolutionaries took over the cities and the battered Batista regime collapsed. Now all Cuba claimed Fidel. During his triumphant march into Havana, Naty Revuelta waited in the crowd and so did legions of other cheering women, any number of whom envied the special relationship with Fidel that Celia had carved out for herself.

Celia must have known she could not compete for Fidel's heart, or expect marriage or even fidelity. In the different reality of revolutionary Havana, she would have to reinvent her way of life. She would carve out a relationship with Fidel that would unite them always, so when other women intervened, as they inevitably would, they could never challenge that part of Fidel's life that Celia had staked out for herself.

Celia must have devised her strategy with the calm efficiency and attention to detail that characterized her work during the revolution. In broad outline, she would make herself as indispensable to Fidel as she had been in the Sierra Maestra. It helped that she loved the revolution as much as he did.

From the beginning, Celia established her dominance. She controlled Castro's first headquarters, on the top three penthouse floors of the former Havana Hilton Hotel, where he kept an apartment and offices. Later, her cramped and dingy apartment on Eleventh Street in the residential district of Vedado became his central sphere of operations. Celia was his most trusted assistant and adviser, an indefatigable worker who even prepared his meals in her tiny kitchen and had them delivered to him wherever he might be.

Fidel relied on Celia in every dimension of his existence. She alone could criticize him to his face, pointing out errors and suggesting corrections. To the rest of the world, however, she maintained that "Fidel is always right."[56]

Celia's role as Fidel's confidante and right hand made her Cuba's unofficial "First Lady." She also held powerful official positions and, by the time she died, was a ministerial member of the Council of State and a member of the Communist Party's Central Committee. Her purview extended far and wide, even—as Naty Revuelta discovered—to historic sites and to an oral history of the revolution. Celia designed Lenin Park, a magnificent public park and recreation area. She was passionately interested in environmental issues.

Celia was far too intelligent and capable a woman to sacrifice herself for love. She devoted her life to Fidel because revolutionary principles flowed in her blood as in his. Long before she met him, she had committed herself to the politics of social justice. She believed in Fidel as fervently as he believed in himself: with him, because of him, Cuba would be transformed into utopia.

Celia's hand stretched far and often softened what it touched. In the Sierra, she counseled mercy when every rebel instinct was to avenge young collaborators tortured and killed by Batista's brutal forces. But when Fidel replaced Batista and indulged in his own atrocities, Celia's moderating influence did not seem to have survived the descent from the mountains.

The years passed. Celia was untouchable, and even the most lovestruck woman could not depose or replace her. But still she had to deal with Castro's many women, some mistresses, others soon-forgotten infatuations. In Georgie Anne Geyer's dramatic description, Fidel had "a river of devoted and devouring women . . . flowing like quicksilver through his life. . . . even, in a new revolutionary variation on the old seigniorial tradition, eager to be deflowered by him; meanwhile, Celia stood guard as valiantly as she could, shouting at pretty Cubanas and shooing them out of Castro's bed and bedroom."[57]

Marita Lorenz was only seventeen when she caught Castro's eye. At his invitation, the striking German girl came to live with him in a room near his in the Havana Libre Hotel. For quite a long time she was a fixture on Castro's arm, but finally left Cuba for the United States, where she tried to hawk her memoirs.

Typically, Castro sent birthday flowers to his current favorites and, as a special touch, surprised their mothers with a gift of paella and lobster, extraordinary foodstuffs in food-rationed Cuba. The person in charge of having these goodies delivered? Celia Sanchez, who even in the domain of Fidel's women made her presence felt.

One of Castro's mistresses coexisted with Celia until the latter's death. This was Delia Soto del Valle Jorge, with whom Castro fathered six sons. Castro kept her "on the side," and Delia never achieved any official status other than her reputation as Fidel's mistress.

Celia, who shared and shaped his life more than any other woman, though she bore him no children, whose greatest happiness had been when she and Fidel lived cheek by jowl in the Sierra Maestra, died of lung cancer on January 11, 1980. Fidel honored her in death as he had in life, commissioning commemorative statues and ensuring that she would live forever in Cuban legend.

Celia Sanchez, who never married, united herself in what many have called "a historic friendship" with the man she loved, admired, respected and trusted more than any other. Celia wanted Fidel, and knew on what terms she could permanently have him. She was prepared to accept his inability to desire her erotically or to deny himself other, more appealing women. In return, she demanded—and received—a permanent and powerful place at the center of Cuban government, public acknowledgment, respect and a lifetime at Fidel's side. Unlike his other mistresses and ex-mistresses, Celia had no worries about longevity of tenure or disgrace. She had loved Fidel and taken his measure, then tailored her own needs and demands to accommodate him and to satisfy herself.

CHAPTER 11

Mistresses
as Trophy Dolls

I T is a truism that many powerful men acquire a mistress as a symbol of their success; she is a decorative and sexual object that highlights their elevated status. Beauty, usually associated with youth, is a given. But for the ambitious and restless tycoon, youthful beauty is seldom enough: it should be accompanied by fame. As far back as England's mid-17th-century Restoration, when Charles II permitted women to perform on stages, actresses and singers were the mistresses of choice. With the advent of popular cinema, film stars—glamorized in the media, idolized by adoring fans—have joined their onstage sisters as even more visible, and thus desirable, candidates for fulfilling a mogul's dreams.

Marion Davies [1]

Like Pope Alexander VI, who centuries earlier resolved the bitter enmity of Spain and Portugal by dividing the New World into two spheres, American multimillionaire publisher William Randolph Hearst averted conflicts between his wife, Milly, and his mistress, Marion Davies, by dividing the United States and relegating Milly to the east, Marion to the west. By the time he died in 1951, Marion's relationship with him had evolved into an alliance that, at least in its openness, more closely resembled the European model of mistressdom than the American. The main difference was that Hearst left home to live with Marion, though for reasons of propriety (and hypocrisy), he reserved the right to host important guests—Calvin Coolidge, for example—at the side of his wife rather than his mistress. On these occasions, he either entertained at Milly's house or imported her to St. Simeon, his California castle. Marion had to retreat to one of her own mansions.

In most other ways, Hearst was Marion's loyal partner. He provided financially for her and was unremittingly generous, including with her importuning family. He traveled openly with her. Whenever he felt he would not offend his guests' sensibilities by receiving them with his mistress, he did so: the tolerant Winston Churchill was one such visitor. Essentially, Hearst used the power of his fortune, his social prominence and his strong personality to structure his association with Marion to suit his needs and desires. At the same time, he recognized his own vulnerabilities—notably that he was decades older, often preoccupied or absent and would never marry her—and compensated for them in whatever ways he could.

Marion Cecilia Douras, whose stage name was Davies, was the youngest and prettiest of four daughters of a philandering lawyer and his ambitious wife.[2] Fortunately for Hearst, Marion's mother, Rose, had instilled in her daughters a unique perspective on how they should relate to men. Frustrated in her own marriage, Mama Rose trained her girls to enchant men but to shun romantic love as a trap she had personally fallen into and regretted.

Rose's vision of how to captivate men, preferably wealthy older ones, was unorthodox. She promoted the skills of the music hall and the chorus line over the niceties of early-20th-century parlors, and from early ages, Marion, Ethel, Rose and Reine performed onstage.[3] "It seems evident," concludes Marion's biographer Fred Lawrence Guiles, that Rose and her cooperative though non-resident husband "carefully groomed their four daughters . . . to be kept or married by men of substantial means."[4]

Marion's first taste of public adoration came when, as a ten-year-old, she sneaked onstage after Reine's performance. There, to the delight of the roaring audience, she took bow after undeserved bow as her embarrassed family tried to drag her offstage. Three years later, slender and luminously pretty, with long blond curls and brilliant blue eyes, Marion was signed on in the "pony ballet,"[5] the junior dancers in the troupe Reine danced with as a showgirl. Later she became a Ziegfeld Girl and dropped out of school at the Convent of the Sacred Heart, though she continued to study ballet. Marion loved the frenzied pace and uproar, the smells and greasepaint of the theater and the adoring fans who fawned on her, sent telegrams of congratulation and showered her with trinkets.

One of these stagedoor Johnnies[6] was William Randolph Hearst, known to his intimates as W. R., the immensely wealthy publisher who built up the nation's largest chain of newspapers and perfected sensationalist journalism. W. R. had represented New York City in the US House of Representatives in 1903 and 1905, but lost his 1905 bid for the Democratic Party's presidential nomination. He was defeated in the 1905 and 1909 elections for the mayoralty of New York City, and in the 1906 race for the governorship of New York state. Despite his inability to win electoral votes, his delivery of the news gave him immense influence over the American people.

Inevitably, W. R., known among the chorines as "the wolf," took note of the sparkling and talented eighteen-year-old Marion. In 1903, when he was nearly forty, W. R. had married twenty-two-year-old chorus girl Millicent Willson, whom he had dated since she was sixteen. Milly had borne him three sons and was again pregnant, this time with twin boys, as it turned out. Yet W. R. was uneasy in his marriage, because Milly had transformed herself into the very kind of woman he had hoped to escape, one who dressed her servants in livery and assiduously attended the society parties W. R. detested. "She liked Society with a capital 'S,'" recalled her son Bill.

W. R.'s dalliances with showgirls were frequent and, at least among the Ziegfeld crowd, well known. But until he fell obsessively in love with Marion, he had treated them as nothing more than enjoyable flings he paid for with gifts of Tiffany diamonds and money. Marion's performances in the 1915 revue *Stop! Look! Listen!* mesmerized W. R., and though he knew she already had a wealthy beau, he called on her.

"He had the most penetrating eyes—honest, but penetrating eyes," Marion recalled in her memoir. "He didn't have a harmful bone in his body. He just liked to be by himself and just look at the girls on the stage while they were dancing. I think," she added, "he was a very lonesome man."[7] W. R. wooed the irrepressible teenager with money and extraordinarily expensive gifts—for instance, a diamond-encrusted Tiffany watch that Marion immediately lost in a snow bank and he replaced without comment. He was also kind and understanding, reassuring her that the stammering that plagued her was charming. "I knew your genius would be recognized," he wired her after critics praised one of her films.[8] When Rose died, years later, W. R. consoled Marion by asking, "May I be a mother to you?"[9]

W. R. loved Marion long before she was able to reciprocate. He would say, "I'm in love with you. What am I going to do about it?" The plainspoken Marion would reply, "Well, let it ride. It's all right with me."[10] It was very much all right with Marion's parents. They considered W. R. "honest" and pretended that he and Marion were good friends rather than lovers.

For the better part of two years, Marion seemed ambivalent about their relationship. W. R. was a jealous lover, tormented by her love scenes and by the possibility that, offstage too, she had other men. To control her, he entered the motion picture business and signed her to an astonishing $500 weekly contract, a raise of $425. (Marion accepted it gladly, though not before offering her opinion that she wasn't worth that much.) Then he forbade Marion to play steamy love scenes.

From the beginning, Marion strained at W. R.'s traces. Behind his back, she dated other men. She accepted his shower of gifts as her due, the obligatory largesse of the entertainer's sugar daddy. When he irritated her, she shouted and threw things; she also referred to herself caustically as the "little princess" imprisoned in the tower. Yet W. R.'s publicity campaign on her behalf was gratifying, and his unrelenting courtship began to touch her.

Imbued since childhood with the goal of marrying (or being kept by) a wealthy older man, Marion slowly capitulated to W. R.'s consuming love. Yet despite her contention that "love is not always created at the altar. Love doesn't need a wedding ring,"[11] she longed to be his wife rather than his mistress.

W. R.'s views on this crucial matter are unclear. His son Bill maintains that his father "never asked my mother for a divorce. Not a word. Never."[12] Marion, on the other hand, was certain that "for years he tried . . . and because he couldn't, he was miserable. . . . Not only did he have the detectives working [to catch Milly in a compromising situation], but he tried to put a law through that any married couple who had not lived together for the past ten years was automatically divorced. . . . The Catholic Church barged in and killed that."[13] Marion's biographer believes that early on, W. R. asked Milly for a divorce that she refused. Afterward, she referred to Marion as "the woman."

The truth was that W. R. arranged his life to suit his own needs. He lived separately from Milly, but without the disgrace of a divorce or—just as much to the point—its frightening financial implications. "California community property laws could have become a serious problem for him," son Bill points out euphemistically. "And he didn't want more children, since a second family could complicate his estate."[14] So W. R. continued as a presence in Milly's life and in their five sons' lives, while openly cohabiting with the woman he loved to distraction but would not sacrifice everything to marry. Once, when

Marion challenged him to admit that he could not live without her, he replied calmly that indeed he could, he merely preferred not to.

From time to time, especially in the early years, W. R. would withdraw from Marion, though he never wanted to end their affair. This happened when he was considering reentering the political arena and rival politician Al Smith taunted him for "taking up with blond actresses."[15] His 1924 withdrawal from Marion after he received alarming reports from detectives who had been trailing her was more serious. He felt particularly threatened by Marion's not-so-secret lover Charlie Chaplin, the world's top male actor and a multi-millionaire who could compete with him financially. Marion was furious that W. R. had spied on her, but also deeply alarmed that she might lose him.

They reconciled. Having been tested, neither wished to live without the other. Afterward, they achieved balance and understanding of how they would conduct their relationship. Each had to make difficult compromises. W. R. accepted Marion's need for frenetic socializing, her love affairs and—hardest of all—her increasingly problematic drinking. Marion had to accept that Milly, whom she scathingly referred to as "the Black Widow," would always be his wife.

This was made crystal clear when W. R. once felt obliged to take Milly and the boys to Europe. But in England, surrounded by his family, W. R. suddenly missed Marion so sharply he wired her to join him. She went reluctantly, then spent a wretched time there because he could so seldom slip away to see her. Ironically, that episode sparked a deep emotion in Marion and marked the beginning of what would become her lifelong love for W. R.

Meanwhile, Marion was enjoying enviable professional success. "I'm going to make you a star, Marion," W. R. had promised her, and between her comedic talent and stupendous energy and his publicity efforts to promote her, she rose steadily to the top rank of film stars. She worked hard and well, and her joie de vivre was legendary. Every movie set she graced resounded with the laughter provoked by her pranks: her stomach suddenly bulging in fake pregnancy under a chaste costume or her front tooth blackened to imitate toothlessness.

Marion reveled in her career, but her strong sense of inadequacy and her ingrained conviction that she owed him her professional success reinforced her need for W. R. "I couldn't act," she reiterated in her memoirs. But she could and she did, and soon studio heads recognized that "audiences were responding to Marion as a star, and she was no longer simply a producer's girlfriend who was being forced upon the movie-going public."[16]

Nonetheless, Marion found her status as a mistress galling, and she exacted a price from the man who forced it on her. She called W. R. "Daddy" to his face, but "Droopy Drawers" and "the Old Man" behind his back. Knowing that he would not leave her, she risked his ire by sleeping with many, perhaps almost all, of her leading men. "Operator could not find you. Where were you? Explanations are in order," W. R. demanded in a telegram.[17] Marion, however, had none to provide.

The lovers rode out their first two decades together. They had a fundamental respect for each other. Marion was awed by W. R.'s seemingly encyclopedic knowledge. He recognized that she had an excellent head for both the film and real estate industries. Their professional collaboration was remarkable. W. R. vetted scripts, chose directors, monitored sets and films and sometimes even directed individual scenes. Marion acted, provided star presence, cared and entertained for the man who adored her and helped run Cosmopolitan Pictures. Soon, he named her its president. "I wanted to be Marion Davies, having the great privilege of knowing Mr. William Randolph Hearst," she claimed in her memoir. "That was all I wanted."[18]

But of course, it wasn't all she wanted. In California, which W. R. had decreed should be her half of the world, he was constructing a giant castle he called St. Simeon. For Marion, W. R. bought a lavish white stucco mansion at 1700 Lexington Road in Beverly Hills, on a hilltop just off Sunset Boulevard. He also built Ocean House, her oceanside estate that featured thirty-seven fireplaces and so many bedrooms (plus a room gilded in gold leaf) that Marion never counted them. On the set, he provided her a palatial, fourteen-room "bungalow."

Until he stopped juggling Marion and Milly, vacationing with Milly and their boys while anxiously attempting to ensure that Marion was comfortable—and chaste—during his absence, Marion retaliated by hosting spectacular parties. "The film colony enjoyed an era of Arabian Nights," Charlie Chaplin recalled. "Two or three times a week, Marion gave stupendous dinner parties with as many as a hundred guests, a mélange of actors, actresses [including Chaplin himself, Rudy Valentino, John Barrymore and Mary Pickford], senators, polo players, chorus boys, foreign potentates and Hearst's executives and editorial staff to boot."[19] The after-dinner games often lasted until dawn, but somehow Marion always dragged herself to work, her good cheer and enthusiasm never flagging.

Marion's stream of lovers satisfied her need for revenge and also for the kind of sexual and romantic fulfillment that W. R. could not provide. Marion and the super-rich Charlie Chaplin may have loved each other. Certainly they connived to fool W. R., instructing their prop man to warn them if W. R. appeared so Chaplin could escape through the back door of the set.

Marion was even more enamored of actor Dick Powell. By the time of their affair, she was a mature woman in her thirties who had been intimate with dozens of other men. Powell was nervous about the repercussions of seducing W. R. Hearst's mistress, but Marion pursued him, and in the end he happily succumbed. At her insistence he declared that he loved her, then repeated all the details of their affair to his friends. Marion shrugged off this ungentlemanly snitching, and their friendship continued until her death.

It is likely that Marion occasionally got pregnant. In offhand remarks to friends, she indicated that when that happened, she resorted to an abortionist. Her memoirs express no regret at her childlessness. She was, however, deeply attached to a niece and a nephew, and greatly affected by her niece's 1934 suicide, after which she grew even closer to her nephew.

All but one of W. R.'s sons felt and displayed deep hostility toward this woman who, in their version, had wrecked their mother's marriage by stealing her husband. W. R. introduced them to Marion, but did not explain his relationship with her. Son William (Bill) Randolph Hearst, Jr., describes his own reaction when he finally realized she was his father's mistress: "I wept. . . . Because of the embarrassment to both of us, I never initiated the subject with my mother. . . . I was offended and, at times, deeply hurt by the relationship. That was because my mother, who had given Pop five sons, deserved her husband at her side. And so did my brothers and I."[20]

The great difference between W. R. and other American patricians, including the Vanderbilts and the upstart Joseph P. Kennedy, Bill Hearst wrote, was that they "lived a lie" by keeping their mistresses "on the side . . . [while] my father left our mother and consorted openly with Marion. . . . Nevertheless, the nature of all these relationships was the same."[21] Like those other mistresses, Marion was merely "a pleasant distraction," "an expensive but relaxing ornament," his father's "sex kitten."[22]

Only W. R.'s oldest son, George, a chronically overweight bon vivant whom W. R. judged too irresponsible to take over his publishing empire, was consistently friendly to Marion. In her memoir, Marion expressed her gratitude and affection for his steadfast friendship, which contrasted so starkly with his brothers' muted animosity.

Marion's life as W. R.'s mistress took on familiar patterns. At St. Simeon, she and W. R. hosted dinner parties, poolside parties, masquerades and beach parties. Marion enjoyed them, but over the years dreaded the preparations and protocol as tiresome and boring. W. R. would join their guests to swim and play tennis and to dine, but otherwise spent most of his time overseeing his publishing empire, writing editorials and reading his newspapers.

Marion resented his preoccupation with his business, and could be brutally and publicly discourteous to him because of it. Charlie Chaplin recalled that at one of her parties, a drunk Marion was irritated that W. R. was talking shop with his newspaper executives. "'H-H-Hey, y-y-you!' she shouted. W. R., embarrassed, asked quietly, 'Are you speaking to me?' Marion shouted again, 'Y-Y-Yes! Come here!' Rather than cause even more of a scene, W. R. crossed over to his mistress and asked her what she wanted. 'D-D-Do all that b-b-business stuff downtown—not at my party. My g-g-guests are waiting for drinks. Get them!'" Quietly, W. R. did so.[23]

W. R.'s compliance stemmed from his horror of creating a scene, his awareness that Marion was drunk and his belief that because she did not usually find him an amusing companion, he had to accommodate her. Even when she was sober, Marion was frank and, stuttering aside, plainspoken. Primed by liquor, her quick tongue could become caustic. W. R. simply accepted this.

In a life of prodigality, Hearst's art collections and private zoo stood out over all else. Without the least regard for fiscal responsibility—despite his wealth he overspent so seriously that he would end up nearly bankrupt—he bought art in vast quantities. He also indulged his love for animals by maintaining over three hundred, including antelope, bison, cougars, lions, bobcats, a leopard, a cheetah, bears, a chimpanzee, monkeys, a tapir, sheep, goats, llamas, kangaroos, a wallaby and Marianne, the elephant. He kept dachshunds, and at one time he had over fifty in a kennel. Two others, Marion's beloved Gandhi and his Helen, with her progeny, were their inseparable companions.

Their love for their dachshunds, whom they treated like surrogate children, grew into one of Marion and W. R.'s most important bonds. When Helen and then Gandhi died, they shared each other's deep grief. W. R. published a tribute to Helen, who died in his arms in his bed. "He cried and cried," Marion recalled.[24] W. R. buried his dog under a stone engraved, "Here lies dearest Helen—my devoted friend."[25]

Marion was even more devastated when Gandhi died. Gandhi retrieved balls during tennis games. He slept in Marion's bed and warmed her feet. When he was fifteen, he became deathly ill. Marion took him to bed, where he had diarrhea on her feet. She cleaned the sheets and her feet, trying to hide his condition. She failed, and W. R. arrived with the vet and a nurse. While W. R. restrained her, the nurse gave Gandhi a fatal injection.

Afterward, "I tore the place apart," Marion recalled. "I broke everything I could lay my hands on. I almost killed everybody, I was so furious. If they'd left him to me, I could have taken care of him." Marion buried Gandhi in a full service conducted by an Irish Catholic priest. "I didn't think I'd ever get over it," she wrote. "You feel that not only have you lost your best friend, but part of your life has gone."[26]

W. R.'s and Marion's reverence for animals extended beyond their dachshunds. W. R. bought a car for a peasant woman in Europe whose goose his chauffeur had struck and killed. During a movie shoot, when her Saint Bernard costar killed a cat brought in for him to chase, Marion reported the incident to the SPCA. Both she and W. R. fought against vivisection, and Marion forbade it in the hospital to which she contributed millions.

Europe was also important in the Davies-Hearst way of life. They spent months there, in hotels and at their castle at Saint Donat, in France, often with groups of friends whose expenses W. R. covered entirely. Marion respected W. R.'s love of museums and art galleries, and dutifully accompanied him. But these educational tours "bored [me] stiff. All I wanted was an ice-cream soda or a Coke," she wrote. "That was my impression of Europe. Like when you're hit on the head with a hammer. It feels so good when it stops. I liked coming back and seeing the Statue of Liberty. Home sweet home meant an awful lot."[27]

On the other hand, W. R. was more comfortable displaying her in Europe than in the United States. At the Saint Donat castle, where Milly was never especially welcome, Marion presided at W. R.'s side, hosting such celebrities as George Bernard Shaw, Lloyd George and the Mountbattens. Europe exempted W. R. and Marion from the disapproval with which Americans regarded a man and his mistress. Joseph Kennedy, a very rich American banker who befriended her, sympathized with Marion's situation. His own mistress, Gloria Swanson, the highest-paid film star of all, was also subjected to disapproving gossip. Ironically, given his own cavalier treatment of Gloria Swanson, Kennedy was very helpful about suggesting ways for W. R. to protect Marion's interests in the event of his death.

Into the 1930s, in her mid-thirties, Marion maintained her ranking as one of America's top movie stars. Encouraged by W. R., and despite her own terror of failing, she had survived the transition to talking movies, nightmarish to a lifelong stutterer. She was still very beautiful. W. R. deferred to her professionally, secure in the knowledge that she knew the business and was an excellent executive. She was also Hollywood's wealthiest woman and its greatest philanthropist, her special interest the Children's Hospital in Los Angeles.

By then, Marion's drinking had become a serious problem. W. R. banned liquor from his houses, but Marion hid bottles of gin and scotch in the toilet tanks. Occasionally he would force her to dry out, but these periods of sobriety were of short duration. "What can I do?" W. R. said helplessly to friends.[28]

With a notable lack of success, Marion battled alcoholism for the rest of her life. "Perhaps Pop felt," W. R.'s son Bill suggests, "Marion's heavy drinking may have been his fault because he had not married her. This caused him much soul-searching and grief in his final years."[29] Her marital status almost certainly contributed to the anger and sadness Marion tried to banish with liquor.

Marion's declarations, supposedly to validate her status as a mistress, actually revealed her pain. "It's sound historically, or traditionally, and dramatically, [even] if it *is* wicked—for you to have a Follies girl and blond movie star as your mistress. Look at Louis XIV and Charles II and Herod!" Despite her bravado, Marion's desire for marital legitimacy poisoned her relationship with the man she had allied herself with for life.

Nineteen thirty-seven was a watershed year for both Marion and W. R. After forty-six feature films, many of them smash hits, Marion announced her retirement from filmmaking. It was a shrewd decision. At forty years old, she was still cast in the role of women half her age. She realized that if she continued to act, she would have to begin playing middle-aged women. The risk was (or so she feared) that when the seventy-four-year-old W. R. saw her as she really was rather than as the blond ingenue she had once been, she might lose him.

Marion was also profoundly tired of working. For over two decades, she had flung herself into her work, sometimes making two movies simultaneously, scarcely sleeping but never sacrificing her partying. And though she had managed to overcome her stammering in the new talking medium, she remained uneasy about it. On the set, silence prevailed where once her hired bands had played hit songs. Movies, she said, were becoming a "factory business,"[30] and she wanted out.

Aging, drained and alcoholic, less fit and less confident than she had been, Marion claimed that she wanted to devote herself exclusively to W. R. "I thought the least I could do for a man who had been so wonderful and great, one of the greatest men ever, was to be a companion to him," she said virtuously.[31]

Her devotion was soon put to the test. The fabulously wealthy W. R. Hearst was teetering on insolvency. How could such a thing have happened? The answer is that Hearst's "fiscal dipsomania" had driven him to spend fifteen million dollars yearly on personal expenses and at least one million a year on art and relics. In addition, all his assets were heavily mortgaged. "I guess I'm through," he lamented to Marion.

Marion sprang into action. Within a week she had liquidated enough stock and real estate to hand her lover a certified cheque for one million dollars. At first W. R. refused it. Then he accepted it, but insisted on giving her securities in the form of newspaper holdings. But her gift was not enough. The banks demanded at least another two million to stave off bankruptcy. Now Marion sold off her jewelry, mortgaged her real estate and persuaded a friend, Abby Rockefeller, to provide an enormous loan that rounded out the necessary money. Marion's moral triumph at her astonishing and enterprising generosity was tempered only by her strident criticism of Milly for not having pitched in to help.

W. R.'s business continued to decline. His creditors had taken over his empire, and were selling most of it off. He stopped construction on his California properties. He could no longer host elaborate parties. *Time* magazine reported in 1939 that a chastened and much poorer W. R. hoped only "1) to have some of [his empire] survive him; 2) to keep his job. . . . At age 75, the bad boy of U.S. journalism is just a hired editorial writer who has taken a salary cut."[32]

Marion and W. R.'s newly austere life threw them together without the crush of the constant visitors who had for two decades shared their extravagance and alleviated Marion's boredom. They began each long day together. W. R. cooked breakfast, and she cleaned up afterward, "the closest," opines Marion's biographer, "they ever came to domesticity, to playing at keeping house."[33] W. R. dictated the pace of their new lifestyle and enjoyed it much more than Marion. "I know you are young and wild and want to have a good time," he would say. "But I'm tired of so many people. Why don't you try to quiet down?"[34] She did try, soothing herself with alcohol and food that plumped her up and gave her a slightly matronly look. Where once she had partied till dawn, now she quilted and sewed. "She made all his ties," a friend recalled. "All handmade, gorgeous silk ties."[35]

World War II struck. As Hitler ravaged Europe, W. R. retreated even further from the world he had known. Five years earlier, he had had a personal, five-minute meeting with the Führer, whose views on Germanic superiority—but not on the inferiority of Jews—he shared. At the urging of Metro-Goldwyn-Mayer studio chief Louis B. Mayer, he had attempted, in that brief meeting, to confront Hitler about his persecution of the Jews. Marion had not been included in the meeting. "I got skunked out of that one," she recalled. "I didn't talk to anybody for two days, I was so mad. I just wanted to see the guy."[36]

Hearst, meanwhile, had continued to advocate conciliation with Hitler, even after Kristallnacht in 1938. After the war broke out, he began to acknowledge how terribly he had misjudged both Hitler and the European situation, and to understand, with great sadness, why he was the object of so much public contempt and loathing.

Worse—for him and Marion—was to come. In 1941, the twenty-five-year-old Englishman Orson Welles released *Citizen Kane*, a film so brilliant it has been ranked the best of all time. For Marion Davies, on the other hand, it was a vicious character assassination that destroyed her reputation as a film star and comedienne. In *Citizen Kane*, a Hearst-like antihero props up and subsidizes the career of his talentless, alcoholic and anti-Semitic second wife, Susan Alexander, a parody of the very talented, alcoholic and non-anti-Semitic Marion Davies. Kane also constructs Xanadu, a St. Simeon–like castle. The movie was a sensation.

Hearst's allies were devastated. His columnist Louella Parsons called *Citizen Kane* "a cruel, dishonest caricature." Louis B. Mayer left the screening room weeping and offered to buy the film's negative so he could destroy it. Nonetheless, Orson Welles triumphed, and *Citizen Kane* still dominates lists of the world's great movies. But over two decades later, in expiation for the damage his film had done to her, Welles wrote the preface to Marion's 1975 memoir, *The Times We Had*. With a few exceptions "in *Kane* everything was invented. . . . Susan [Alexander] bears no resemblance at all to Marion Davies," Welles declared.

> The wife [Susan] was a puppet and a prisoner; the mistress [Marion] was never less than a princess. . . . The mistress was never one of Hearst's possessions; he was always her suitor, and she was the precious treasure of his heart for more than thirty years, until his last breath of life. Theirs is truly a love story. Love is not the subject of *Citizen Kane*.[37]

In his zeal to make restitution, Welles overstated the W. R.–Marion Davies story, which, though not devoid of love, was mainly the story of W. R.'s love for Marion. Why, then, did this beautiful, talented and fun-loving woman bind herself for life to the much older, more reserved, married man? Why did she commit herself to him when he was an aging dictator on the verge of losing his empire?

The answers lie in Marion's low evaluation of her talents; her need to validate her life with W. R. by staying with him; her feeling that, by her spontaneous gift of a million dollars in his time of need, she had earned the right to his protection and guidance; and lastly, her need to believe that he could not live without her. And so, in the prime of her life, she settled down into the dullness of being nothing but W. R.'s mistress.

After the war, the couple returned briefly to St. Simeon but, in 1946, left it permanently in the face of W. R.'s failing health, Marion's intense unhappiness and sense of isolation plus the sheer cost of maintaining the grandiose structure. Marion provided their new home, a magnificent Mediterranean villa she purchased in Beverly Hills. W. R. was anguished at leaving his beloved castle, but Marion was ecstatic.

Thanks to Marion, the house was in W. R.'s name. Within six weeks of buying it, she had deeded it over to him so he could finish out his life in his own home. But life there was often bitter. Marion's sisters Ethel and Reine had recently died. Now that she was retired, the vast circle of her "friends" dwindled down to a handful of stalwarts, including "Big Joe" Kennedy, who for the rest of her life visited and made sure she was included in all the notable Kennedy events. Otherwise, she and W. R. were seldom invited out.

After years of desperate interest in life-prolonging medications, Hearst finally understood that he was a very old man living out his last years. Increasingly, he mistrusted his sons and executives, believing—rightly, as it turned out—that they would cut Marion out of his publishing empire. As his health deteriorated over the years, W. R. had often delegated to her the task of communicating with various editors and had been thunderously angry any time someone resisted her interventions. As he lay dying, he sought to protect his beloved mistress from the inevitable wrath of his children, among others.

In his eighty-ninth year, the year he died, W. R. made provisions to guarantee Marion the right to advise the Hearst enterprises as she had done so often during his life. But behind his back, his staff did not make all the arrangements W. R. had ordered.

Marion was by then so terrified of losing him that she had descended into an alcoholic morass that affected her circulation. Her legs often gave way and she, too, required nurses. Three times a day she would visit W. R., sobered up by fresh coffee administered by her concerned staff.

Marion was nearly maddened with fear at W. R.'s impending death, a death his sons were surreptitiously plotting to exclude her from. Bill and Hearst's top executive "met to make plans for the eventual death and burial. They didn't include Marion Davies. We were certainly not going to embarrass my mother by inviting both women."[38] The family claimed to be mortified that their patriarch was dying in his longtime mistress's home.

During the night of the deathwatch, the tension between Marion and the sons was palpable. At one point, when she asked one of them how Hearst was, he snarled, "Why should you care, you whore!"[39] Marion's version of what happened next is that with the sons' connivance, her own doctor jabbed a hypodermic needle into her bottom as she bent down to pick up a telegram. While she slept, W. R. died, alone with his dachshund Helena, Helen's successor. His sons arrived soon after, and swiftly removed the corpse. Marion awoke to find the house empty. "His body was gone, whoosh, like that," Marion said bitterly. "Old W. R. was gone, the boys were gone. I was alone. Do you realize what they did? They stole a possession of mine. He belonged to me. I loved him for thirty-two years and now he's gone. I couldn't even say goodbye."[40]

Marion did not attend the funeral. "Why should I?" she said. "Why should I go through that kind of drama when I had him alive all these years?" She shut herself up in her bedroom, but told a friend to remind Milly Hearst "not to forget to wear her widow's weeds."[41] Suddenly, Marion Davies was *persona non grata* in the Hearst world. Only the jovial George remained a friend.

The will and other testaments were read. W. R. had indeed protected the woman he styled "My loyal friend, Miss Marion Douras, who came to my aid during the great depression with a million dollars of her own money."[42] He had confounded everyone and left Marion in control of the Hearst empire. Bill Hearst expressed it simply. "In death, the old man had left us a dilemma: his concern for Marion, balanced by his responsibility to the company." The family rebelled. Their lawyers and Marion's fought it out. Six weeks later, Marion relinquished her company voting rights but agreed to act as "official consultant and adviser to the Hearst Corporation [including] advice on motion picture and other amusement activities."[43]

W. R.'s wishes were substantially satisfied. The next day, Marion Davies stunned everyone and got married. Her groom was Horace Gates Brown III, a Merchant Marine captain eight years her junior. Horace had been in love with her sister Rose who repeatedly rejected his proposals of marriage. Marion befriended him and soon discovered that his salty stories appealed to her own

unorthodox sense of humor. Her puzzled friends surmised that she thought
he resembled W. R.

The marriage was unhappy, and within months, Marion filed, then withdrew, a petition for divorce. But Horace was attractive and sensual, and Marion enjoyed their sex life. This must have weighed heavily in her decision to
stay with him. So, too, must have been her determination to regularize her
life, and to sample the joys of marital respectability after a lifetime as a mistress, sometimes reviled, never fully accepted.

Marion often managed to stop drinking, which had the side effect of weight
loss; in sobriety, she looked almost as beautiful and youthful as ever. Then the
cycle would begin again. Despite her alcoholism, she made important real
estate deals and generated great wealth, much of which she diverted to philan-
thropy. She enjoyed the weddings of two of "Big Joe" Kennedy's children and
lent JFK and Jackie her house for their honeymoon. Later, she proudly
attended JFK's inauguration.

In 1959, Marion was struck with cancer of the jaw. She refused surgery and
accepted only cobalt treatment. She suffered continual pain that she tried to
alleviate with laudanum. To hide her disfigured jaw, she wore a white scarf.
Joe Kennedy had three cancer specialists flown out to California, and she submitted to surgery. At first she rallied, and then, on September 22, 1961, she
died, with Horace and her few remaining relatives at her bedside. Just before
she sunk into her final coma, she told Horace that she had no regrets.

Marion's funeral was a triumphant occasion she would have celebrated.
Among her pallbearers were her old friend Joe Kennedy, her former costar
Bing Crosby, her long-ago lover Dick Powell and W. R.'s oldest son, George
Hearst. These men represented every dimension of her complicated life:
lovers, friends, colleagues and, in George Hearst, the reality of decades of her
life as W. R. Hearst's mistress.

Marion Davies's life as a mistress was in many ways ideal. She was the beneficiary of W. R.'s almost unimaginable wealth, his lifetime devotion and
posthumous testamentary protection and the social triumph of living with
him. But she was also subject to the insecurity of knowing that her lover
remained married to another woman, and to the contempt accorded to mistresses in her society. She had to settle for dachshunds instead of children. Her
conviction that she owed her impressive professional success to W. R.'s helping hand led her to value his help and protection even though she, more than
almost any other woman of her era, could have succeeded brilliantly on her

own. In consequence, she sacrificed herself as an independent woman to remain W. R.'s mistress. Marion's memoir, *The Times We Had*, resonates with her conviction that the relationship had given her life its meaning.

Gloria Swanson [44]

By 1927, Gloria Swanson was America's most popular film star, a petite, sexy twenty-eight-year-old with shiny dark hair, a gently sloping nose and huge blue eyes. She was married to her third husband,[45] the French marquis Henri de La Falaise de La Coudraye, and was mother to Michelle and an adopted son, Joseph. She was intelligent and ambitious, sexually liberal if not promiscuous, an independent-minded woman who took great personal and professional risks. And, before feminism, she was a feminist who thought of the Almighty as Mrs. God. At the height of her career, Gloria turned down a one-million-dollar contract and left the security of Paramount Pictures to found Gloria Swanson Productions and produce her own movies.

But Gloria also had big troubles. Her husbands were always financial liabilities, and Henri was no different. Troublingly, he had decided to move back to France to try to establish himself in his own right.

More ominously, the astronomically paid Gloria Swanson was nearly broke. She had outrageous personal expenses totalling ten thousand dollars a month. Her house was a two-story, twenty-two-room, five-bathroom mansion in Beverly Hills, with a garage for her Pierce-Arrow and Cadillac. "The public wanted us to live like kings and queens," Gloria explained years later. "So we did. Why not?"[46]

Why not indeed? But Gloria's bank accounts were nearly empty and would only be replenished if her movies earned money in the theaters. The consequence of the choice she had made was that her luxurious livelihood was strictly dependent on her success as a producer. Meanwhile, her debut movie, *The Love of Sunya*, had not recouped the money she had borrowed to make it. Distribution of her much-loved second film, *Sadie Thompson*, Somerset Maugham's controversial story about a prostitute and the clergyman who tries to reform her, in which Gloria herself played a sultry and troubled Sadie, was delayed while Gloria's lawyers battled in court against morality laws and the censors who upheld them. As if this was not enough, the Internal Revenue Service was challenging her income tax returns from 1921 to 1926.

Gloria's financial predicament was the reason her advisers brought Joe Kennedy into her life. "Gloria needs handling, needs being properly financed and having her organization placed in proper hands," her friend Robert Kane, a Paramount executive, wrote to Kennedy.[47] Kennedy responded enthusiastically. Gloria represented everything he admired: fame, talent and beauty. She had done what he continually urged his children to do: "Go for it."

By 1927, Joseph Patrick Kennedy was both a very rich banker and a well-connected movie executive (president and chairman of Film Booking Office, Inc.) who owned a string of movie theaters. The boyish, grinning forty-year-old was married to Rose Fitzgerald, the daughter of John Francis "Honey Fitz" Fitzgerald, possibly the most powerful man in Boston. Joe was well on his way to founding his famous dynasty: by 1927, Rose was pregnant with their seventh child.

Gloria staged their first meeting with all the aplomb of the seasoned star. Joe responded to her commanding presence though he seemed surprised at her tininess and her menu choices: braised celery, string beans and zucchini. Gloria thought Joe looked unbankerly, his suit too bulky and his tie too loose. "With his spectacles and prominent chin, he looked like any average working-class person's uncle," she recalled.

The star and the banker talked about the film business, and Joe asked specific questions about her company's finances. She decided to trust him and authorized complete access to all her business records. After studying them, Joe telephoned Gloria with a grim analysis. Her affairs were chaotic, her advisers, consultants and employees "deadwood." In a nutshell, Gloria Swanson Productions was egregiously mismanaged, and Joe was not interested in taking her on as a client.

Some time later, probably because of his growing attachment to her, Joe changed his mind and offered Gloria what she described as a "whopping single deal."[48] "Let me handle everything," Gloria recalled him proposing. "I'll bring along a few members of my staff and we'll perform some emergency surgery. . . . When we get there, heads will roll."[49]

Joe and his colleagues, whom Gloria nicknamed "the horsemen," entered her life in earnest, poring through her records and spending hours at her house. They were so attentive that "every time I reached for a cigarette I all but went up in flames as two or more of them struck matches to light it."[50] By this time, Gloria was convinced that she could safely entrust her finances to these efficient and no-nonsense men and to Joe Kennedy, the boss they obviously admired.

First, Gloria Swanson Productions was dissolved and a new corporate entity, Gloria Productions, established. Meanwhile, Joe would assist Gloria as she concentrated on her forte, making pictures. With trepidation, but certain that Joe Kennedy knew best, Gloria agreed to trade her rights to her first two movies to the finance company she was heavily indebted to, which would not merely wipe out her debt but also provide some liquid capital. "All I knew," Gloria wrote later, "was that I had made mistakes in the past, whereas so far, in his dealings with me, he had made none. Reluctantly, therefore, I told him he could arrange the deal."[51]

Unfortunately for Gloria, this would prove to be Joe's first mistake, and a tremendously costly one because *Sadie Thompson,* which he disliked and mistrusted—ironically, on moral grounds—went on to become a huge hit that enriched its new owner, while Gloria received nothing for it but professional accolades. That, however, was in the future. At the time, Gloria recalled, "in two months Joseph Kennedy had taken over my entire life."[52]

To some extent, Gloria had also taken over his. Joe was deeply attracted to his high-spirited client-partner, and though Gloria loved her husband, she reciprocated. Sex, unspoken but palpable, began to permeate their relationship. Gloria, however, had many reasons not to indulge in an extramarital love affair. Hollywood was ruled by moralistic regulations that governed both movies and their stars, and Gloria had once before fallen afoul of these restrictive rules governing personal behavior. No matter what, she could not risk even the suspicion that she was morally loose. The other issue was her marriage. Though she felt unable to stay closely connected to him, Gloria loved her handsome and charming husband.

Joe's circumstances were quite different. He and Rose had a marriage rooted in their growing brood—Joe's dynasty—rather than their own relationship, which was courteous and distant. In matters of the heart, it was an emotional wasteland. Rose had set standards Joe had to meet—financial security, religious observance, family obligations—and she also sublimated her anger at Joe's sexual betrayals. Because Joe met her standards and indulged her expensive sartorial tastes, he knew Rose would ask no irksome questions or cause a scandal, so he had far fewer constraints on him than Gloria did.

Taking Gloria to bed was now just a matter of time and a little of the planning he was so good at. Adroitly, and with considerable empathy, Joe arranged to get rid of Henri by offering him what Gloria described as "a marvelous position" as the European director of Pathé Pictures. Henri was elated. So was Gloria, who "flashed Joe Kennedy a subtle smile of deep gratitude." Joe and Henri quickly composed a verbal agreement, had papers drawn up and signed them. "In a few brief sessions, then, we had rearranged the world," Gloria wrote.[53]

The next day, Joe arranged for one of his "horsemen" to take Henri deep-sea fishing, but begged off himself so he could work. Gloria did the same, to buy gifts for her children. When Henri was safely at sea, Joe arrived at Gloria's hotel room and lunged across the room at her. Silently, he put his mouth on hers and they kissed. With one hand he held her head; with the other he caressed her body and pulled at her kimono. In a drawn-out moan he repeated, "No longer, no longer. Now." "He was like a roped horse, rough, arduous, racing to be free," Gloria recounted. "After a hasty climax he lay beside me, stroking my hair."

From then on, Gloria recalled, Joe Kennedy, "the strange man beside me, more than my husband, owned me."[54]

Gloria Swanson was now Joe Kennedy's mistress. Joe installed himself in Beverly Hills, renting a Rodeo Drive house that his wife and children never visited. Instead, whenever he found it convenient, he commuted back to the east coast to see them. His house was no simple *pied-à-terre*. It required two maids, a butler, a gardener and a cook to operate it, and he reciprocated Gloria's hospitality by hosting dinners in his own digs.

These dinners were never intimate. Joe's "horsemen" usually attended, and the conversational fare was business-oriented. Afterward, Gloria and Joe made love, and then a horseman drove her home. In the day, she and Joe saw each other rarely, and never alone.

As always, Joe continued to monitor the most minute details of his children's lives and to keep in close touch with Henri, or "Henry," as he called him. He also pressured Gloria to have her adopted son baptized—the thought of an unbaptized soul unsettled his religious sensibilities.

During his periodic trips back to the United States, Henri showed no signs that he suspected anything. Perhaps, Gloria mused, this was out of gratitude for his job, or "out of a cultivated European good sense to let such affairs run their course, particularly inasmuch as this one could almost certainly never lead to marriage." A likelier reason was that Henri had a mistress in Paris.

Joe Kennedy was more difficult. He blurted out that he had been faithful to Gloria by contriving to avoid sleeping with Rose—there had been no Kennedy baby that year, he told Gloria proudly.[55] But Joe wanted Gloria to have his baby. Gloria spoke bluntly: if he so much as mentioned such a thing again, she would pack up and return to California. "You can't manipulate the public, Joseph. I would be finished tomorrow," she said firmly.[56] As time passed, however, she concluded that film people were aware of their affair and saw them as a "modified version of William Randolph Hearst and Marion

Davies, only unimpeachable because we were both solidly married with children; beyond whispers, therefore, and entirely free of the possibility of louder accusations."[57]

Personally, Joe and Gloria were happy with each other, though sex was perfunctory, with Joe giving little thought to Gloria's desires or satisfaction. But their joint business was floundering. *Queen Kelly*, a movie Joe had effectively forced on Gloria, was an eight-hundred-thousand-dollar flop. Joe was furious and bitter. "I've never had a failure in my life," he raged.[58] Meanwhile, Gloria won an Oscar nomination for *Sadie Thompson*, the movie he had predicted would fail.

For Gloria, *Queen Kelly* was an emotional, physical and financial body blow. When she realized how horrible it was, Gloria was so distraught that she had to be hospitalized. "There is no need to go into the personal reaction of Gloria toward owing me considerable money on the picture but it was far from a pleasant one," Joe wrote to Henri. He mentioned, as well, that in their discussions, he and Gloria had faced a "drastic showdown."[59]

Usually, however, Joe was affectionate and, all too often for Gloria's peace of mind, proprietorial. An ill-advised trip to London was the most extreme example. Joe badgered Gloria into traveling on the same ocean liner as he, Rose and his sister. "Please, Gloria, she [Rose] wants to meet you," he pleaded.[60]

Their trip to Europe was a success,[61] though Gloria was never sure how much Rose knew or guessed. Joe spent all his time with Gloria, yet Rose was invariably kind and motherly to her husband's mistress. Once, when Joe flew into a rage because another traveler gawked at Gloria, Rose piped right up and supported him. "Was she a fool," Gloria wondered, "or a saint?"[62]

Henri joined the party, and Rose raved about Gloria's "mah-velous" husband. Henri was upset by Joe's possessiveness, but refrained from confronting him about it for fear of compromising his highly valued job. "Henri was in Joe's employ and I was literally owned by him," Gloria recalled. "My whole life was in his hands. Never before had I ever trusted another person to the extent I had Joe."[63] Joe also fascinated her, though Henri was the love of her heart.

Back in the United States for the New York premiere of *The Trespasser*, the film she correctly predicted would have the success that Joe's *Queen Kelly* had not, Gloria received a summons to a hotel to meet with an unidentified guest. He turned out to be Cardinal O'Connell of Boston. A Kennedy family friend, O'Connell told her that he wished to discuss her relationship with Joe

Kennedy. Gloria was astonished and angry, and replied that they were business partners. O'Connell knew better. "I am here to ask you to stop seeing Joseph Kennedy," he told her. "Each time you see him, you become an occasion of sin for him. . . . There is no way Joseph Kennedy can be at peace with his faith and continue his relationship with you." Gloria got up to leave. "It's Mr. Kennedy you should be talking to," she said firmly. She discovered later that Joe knew nothing about this unsettling conversation. Had Rose or Kennedy family friends pushed the cardinal to act as he had? Gloria never knew. But his intervention was consistent with how the Catholic Church deals with "inappropriate" relationships, blaming the woman and placing the onus on her.

Joe had rebounded from his despair at the failure of *Queen Kelly* and had bought another screenplay he was convinced would vindicate him as a movie mogul. Gloria had serious reservations, but gamely agreed to star in *What a Widow*. *What a Widow* was given its title by Pulitzer Prize–winning playwright Sidney Howard, and Howard won a Cadillac that Joe Kennedy presented to him.

Just before the actual filming, Henri gently ended his marriage with Gloria. "The fire has burnt the beautiful temple that was our love," he wrote. "Little can be saved out of the burning ashes. But let's try and preserve our sweet friendship, our regard for each other, our decency! . . . The bridges are broken between us—nothing ever can mend them—we both know it." He ended his sad missive, "Good-bye, darling—it's all, all over now."[64] Her affair with Joe Kennedy had cost Gloria Swanson her marriage. Henri soon initiated a divorce so he could marry Constance Bennett, a beautiful blond American movie star.

Not long afterward, *What a Widow* proved to be a fiasco. Joe was humiliated, even more so than he had been after *Queen Kelly*, because *What a Widow* highlighted his name in animated titles.

One day Gloria's accountant reported that Sidney Howard's Cadillac had been charged to Gloria's personal account. Shouldn't it be charged to the movie budget? It certainly should, Gloria replied. During a dinner at Joe's house she mentioned that his office had made a bookkeeping error, and added jocularly, "You gave Sidney Howard the car; I didn't. He thanked you for it, not me. So I think it's only fair that you pay for it."[65]

Shocked, Gloria saw Joe glare wordlessly, then begin to choke on his food. Regaining self-control, he stood up and silently left the dining room. After half an hour, as Gloria waited for him to reappear, one of the horsemen tactfully offered to drive her home.

Days later, after waiting for the apologetic phone call or note that never came, Gloria understood that Joe Kennedy had broken off his affair with her, that she was no longer his mistress. The following month, he formally revoked their business relationship, including the power of attorney she had signed over to him.

Joe Kennedy simply evaporated from Gloria's life. Gossip and newspapers reported that he had earned five million dollars by selling film company assets, and planned to withdraw from the film business to concentrate on politics. "I was completely on my own again," Gloria recalled, "without love and without security."[66]

Gloria discovered, as well, that though she owned a few properties and many possessions, she had very little money. How had this happened? She had trusted Joe with her life, and he had relinquished it bruised and battered. She learned, with shocked bitterness, that besides the Cadillac, Joe had charged a fur coat he had given her and an impressive movie-lot bungalow he had built for her to Gloria Productions. Furthermore, the accounts were muddled, and the Kennedy offices refused to provide any help or clarification.

Amanda Smith, who edited *Hostage to Fortune: The Letters of Joseph P. Kennedy* and has read Gloria's memoirs, offers a slightly different perspective on why Joe charged such apparently personal gifts to Gloria Productions. Kennedy's files contain "desiccated contracts and legal documents . . . signed in Swanson's hand . . . [delineating] her obligations to him and to entities connected to him—a guarantee to repay . . . desperately needed cash infusions (at the current rate of interest), an agreement to remunerate . . . for the lavish dressing room upon it befitting a star of Swanson's magnitude."[67] Apparently Joe was never so besotted with his glamorous mistress that he forgot he was a businessman. He even made her legally liable for his egregious errors of judgment. When he presented her with gifts and accepted her grateful thanks, he never reminded her that she, not he, was paying for them, though it must have been crystal clear that she had not comprehended the nature of the many documents he had gotten her to sign.

The stark and sudden breakup with Joe left Gloria struggling to retain her emotional and financial balance. For a while she retreated into ill health, precipitously losing weight and physically shutting down. But her responsibilities as a single mother with a lavish lifestyle and a career she had to keep afire soon prompted her to get up out of bed and, once again, take on the world.

Gloria married again, badly, and had another child. She divorced, remarried, again badly, divorced. These brief and miserable unions did not prevent her from flinging herself into making movies, but by 1942, she had little money and had to drastically curtail her expenditures and find different ways of earning a living. She tried television, then reverted to film. In 1949, at the age of fifty, she had a smash comeback success in *Sunset Boulevard*, a movie about a younger man romancing an older woman in Hollywood. Resurrected, she continued to act, including on Broadway, until she turned to sculpture, where she was also successful. Her sixth and last marriage, to Bill Dufty, when she was nearly seventy-seven and he was sixty, was happy.

A year and a half after abruptly dumping her, Joe Kennedy telephoned Gloria. He had with him, he said, Franklin D. Roosevelt, the next president of the United States. Furious at his gall in calling her, Gloria slammed down the phone. Subsequently, she allowed herself to be jollied into a casual reconciliation. From then until he died, Joe boasted to people about his connection with her. When he was felled by a stroke, she sent a telegram of condolence signed "Kelly." It is difficult to believe that she chose the name of his greatest cinematic failure without at least a tinge of vindictiveness.

Fifty years after she had been Joe Kennedy's mistress, Gloria wrote her memoirs. Her assessment of their relationship was filtered by the passage of time, her own astonishing professional comebacks, her excellent health, personal happiness and extraordinary and natural beauty—in her seventies, on the *Carol Burnett Show*, she danced in a skimpy outfit and displayed a body that could have belonged to a fit thirty-year-old. And, of course, Joe was not only dead, but he had endured years of diminished life after a severe stroke. Gloria Swanson could afford to be forgiving. Yet a half century could not erase her bitterness at her treatment by the man who had promised to save her but instead left her life in chaos. She had been his willing trophy doll, permitting him to parade her in front of everyone he wished to impress, including his wife. She had been complicit in both his and her own deceptions, an eager participant in strategies to fool their intimates as much as the faceless public that made her the star she was. In the end, Gloria Swanson mostly regretted that she had made a bad bargain.

Maria Callas

"Vissi d'arte, vissi d'amore"—"I lived for art, I lived for love"—lamented soprano Maria Callas in Giacomo Puccini's tragic opera *Tosca*. Her own life lent the tormented Floria Tosca's words chilling conviction. Floria sang her desperate aria as her lover was tortured offstage. Maria, however, grieved for the abrupt end to her passionate and all-consuming love affair with shipping magnate Aristotle Onassis, who had suddenly dismissed her so he could marry Jacqueline Kennedy, the world's most eligible widow.

Maria Callas, the diva who propelled operatic drama to soaring new heights, was born Mary Anna Kalogeropoulos on December 2, 1923, in Manhattan, to Greek immigrants. Her mother "Litsa" (Evangelia) took out her personal bitterness on her obese, myopic, hairy and awkward younger daughter. But when she was only five, Mary partially redeemed herself. As Mary sang along with a radio broadcast, Litsa prayed that her daughter's exquisite voice would deliver her from both the United States and her husband. When Mary was thirteen, Litsa informed her husband that their marriage was over. He crossed himself and exclaimed, "At last, my God, you have pitied me!"[68] Litsa took Mary out of school and set out for Greece, where Jackie, her favored older daughter, was waiting.

In Athens, Mary, now known as Maria, won a scholarship to the National Conservatory, and later gained admittance to the top-ranked Conservatory of Athens. She practiced, rehearsed and studied, uninterested in anything but her music. During the war, in which thirty thousand Athenians starved to death in their dangerous and devastated city, Jackie's wealthy lover lodged the three women in an apartment. Litsa provided some necessities by becoming the mistress of an Italian military officer. She also pushed Maria to consort with enemy soldiers, whom Maria reportedly managed to charm with her stunning voice rather than her sexual favors. On her own, however, she enjoyed intimate and affectionate friendships with much older male admirers. One of them, a doctor who was also a neighbor, may have been the first man Maria slept with.

After the armistice, Maria was banned from the now leftist-run opera. She returned home to the United States, but failed to find employment there either. In 1947, she sailed to Verona with borrowed money for a four-concert engagement that paid only $240. There she met a wealthy Veronese opera aficionado, Battista Meneghini, who had retired from the construction business and was determined to make Maria Callas (the new spelling of her name) his life's work.

Battista was then fifty-three, thirty years older than Maria, and a pudgy, melodramatic man who spoke only Italian. Opera inspired their great common passion, though over time they became devoted to each other. They met in a restaurant. "I was moved to pity," Battista recalled. "Her lower extremities were deformed. Her ankles were swollen to the size of calves. She moved awkwardly and with effort."[69] However, this tall, corpulent and double-chinned woman was a magnificent soprano, and Battista proposed a six-month trial period during which he would take care of all her material needs so she could focus entirely on her music. The trial succeeded, and Maria gratefully married the short and rotund Italian who had recognized her genius and rescued her from indifference and poverty.

Their marriage was happy. Battista adored his diva and her earning power, and Maria adored his adoration and his dedication to opera. Sex, too, was agreeable, though in her eleven years with Battista, she never had an orgasm, a sensation whose absence she would only find remarkable after she had experienced it for the first time.

Professionally, Maria Callas soared. Her voice in all but the highest range was pure and true, and even then, "in the upper reaches—shrill or not—she flashed a swordlike power that is already legend."[70] So was Maria's dramatic flair and her reputation for perfectionism. She memorized her scores in less time than any other singer. She delighted in mastering operas so difficult they were scarcely ever performed. She drove herself, and also her colleagues, mercilessly. Her motto was "I work, therefore I am." Her life and her marriage, opined John Dizikes in *Opera in America*, were "based on Spartan domestic economy, rigorous self-discipline and hard work. For a decade, her ambition, will power, passion for self-improvement were focused on her art. Nothing interfered with it."[71]

This included her obesity. Maria was far too intelligent not to realize how bizarre her portrayal of opera's fragile heroines must appear when her five-foot-nine-inch body was larded with 220 pounds. In 1953, she set out to lose weight. Her strategy was extraordinary. She swallowed a tapeworm that consumed much of what she ate, and the pounds fell away until she expelled it. By early 1954, she had shed 66 pounds. In a few months more, she dieted down to 117 pounds, a sylph hovering on anorexia until she regained a few pounds that lent her a becoming sleekness.

Rid of her massive fleshiness—"It was impossible to tell the difference between the legs of the elephants on the stage and those of Aida sung by Maria Callas," one critic had sniped[72]—Maria displayed a newfound elegance and the confidence of her startling, huge-eyed beauty. She began to dress smartly. She accumulated wardrobes full of clothes. She collected jewelry. And she began to respond to the attentions of international high society, suddenly eager to socialize with the glamorous diva.

Slowly, over the years, Maria's fundamental contentment in her marriage eroded. At first, her friend Nadia Stancioff noted, Maria was irritated by Battista's "professional possessiveness and . . . his obsession with the Callas career as a money machine." Then, when she remarked that she was exhausted by the strenuous schedules he arranged for her, Battista informed her that she could not afford to slow her relentless pace. Despite the enormous sums of money she now commanded, they had no money, he confessed. This, Stancioff believed, precipitated an emotional crisis for Maria. "When she finally understood [that he had squandered her money unwisely], she burst open like a steam valve. . . . What she now saw was her 'Santo Benedetto' without the halo she had created for him: a potbellied, unsophisticated little gargoyle."[73]

Battista himself recorded one of her most telling outbursts against him: "You act like my jailer. . . . You never leave me alone. You control me in everything. You're like some hateful guardian and you've kept me hemmed in all these years. I'm suffocating! . . . you're not adventuresome, you don't know languages, your hair is always uncombed, you can't manage to dress smartly."[74]

By 1959, when Maria became involved with Aristotle Onassis, the founder and owner of a shipping line and an airline—"Shipping is my wife, but aviation is my mistress," he quipped—her marriage was already unraveling. A mutual acquaintance, the Czechoslovakia-born American society hostess and former Shakespearian and comic actress Elsa Maxwell, had already presented Maria to the duke and duchess of Windsor, the Parisian Rothschilds, Prince Aly Khan and other celebrities. In 1957, she introduced Maria and Aristotle, "the two most famous living Greeks in the world," to each other.[75] Their meeting prompted Aristotle to invite Maria, Elsa and Battista to cruise with him and a contingent of British guests, including Sir Winston and Lady Clementine Churchill, on his beloved ship, *Christina*.

The *Christina* was awash in almost unimaginable opulence, if questionable taste: the bar stools were covered in stretched whale foreskin, and Onassis enjoyed shocking female guests by noting that they were sitting on the biggest penis in the world. Onassis presided over a world of designer clothes and fabulous jewels, gourmet dining and palatial homes, and immense amounts of leisure time. It was not these luxuries that fascinated Maria. It was Aristotle Onassis himself, the short, stocky and virile magician who commanded the companionship (if not friendship) of statesmen, artists and international society alike. And Ari, his intimates' name for him, reciprocated her rush of emotion so fervently that everyone aboard the *Christina*, including his wife Tina, knew that something untoward had happened.

Athina "Tina" Livanos Onassis was even younger than Maria and, at seventeen, had married Aristotle in deference to her father's wishes for a union of the two Greek shipping families. Petite, blond, extremely pretty and educated more as a cosmopolitan European than a Greek, Tina had acquitted herself of her childbearing duties and provided her husband his longed-for male heir, Alexander, and a daughter, Christina. By then Tina was no longer in love with Ari, if indeed she ever had been, and she turned to other men for the emotional and sexual satisfaction he failed to give her.

Ari reluctantly accepted the affairs of his "baby doll" and not just because he had himself cheated on her from the earliest days of their marriage. There was also the galling fact that, recently, he had been unable to perform sexually, a failing she confided in some detail to her lovers, especially her latest, twenty-two-year-old Venezuelan playboy Reinaldo Herrera, whom she longed to marry.

This, then, was the state of the Onassis marriage when Ari met Maria: Tina was in love with Reinaldo Herrera, and Ari categorically refused to divorce her and—despite recurrent impotence—continued to sleep with her. Maria's marriage was little better: she was still reeling from the shock of discovering that Titta had carelessly wasted all the money she had earned for them. She had never much enjoyed sex with him and engaged in it because, as she told her American friend Mary Carter, "periodically we have to perform our wifely duties."[76]

But on that fated cruise, Ari aroused such erotic passion in Maria that sex became a revelation rather than a chore. Other than Sir Winston Churchill, none of Ari's guests could stand the humorless and forthright Maria, whom they considered uncouth and self-aggrandizing. "I like travelling with Winston Churchill," she informed them. "It relieves me of some of the burden of my popularity." Another guest recalled, "We all hated her."[77] Onassis, already charmed, noticed nothing.

The affair began with intense conversation, in Greek, as Maria and Ari shared their memories of the war. Both had suffered, Maria much more so, having at one point been forced to scavenge for food. Maria and Ari would stay up late at night, nibbling Greek hors d'oeuvres and pouring out their hearts to each other. From then on, almost until the end of her life, "the only person who existed for her, besides her art, was Onassis," said her friend Amalia Karamanlis. "He made her feel like a woman for the first time."[78]

Even as he was falling in love, Ari told Maria that though Tina had a lover she wanted to marry, he would never divorce her because of the children. Maria was shocked. "I don't understand," she said, "how a Greek woman could pretend to love one man and sleep with another."[79] Virtuous words that were vintage Maria! In one self-righteous sentence she denied her complicity in the unraveling of the Onassis marriage; defended Aristotle from charges of abandoning his loving wife; condemned Tina as a hypocrite and an adulterer; and last, spelled out the end of her own marriage.

As an unloved and exploited child, the religious tenets of Greek Orthodoxy nourished Maria where her family did not. She was devout and rigid in her beliefs (though notably flexible in applying them to her own situation). She invoked God's blessing before every performance and ended each day prayer-fully, on her knees before an icon of the Virgin Mary. To a large extent, Onassis shared her religious convictions, which were part of an appealing Greekness that was so notably absent in the anglicized Tina. Maria's friend Prince Michael of Greece recalled that "it was that sense of destiny, that Greekness that she and Onassis had in common. She was profoundly Greek."[80]

Another part of Maria's Greekness was a fluency and comfort in the Greek language that eluded Tina. In Greek, Ari beguiled and excited Maria with amusing stories about his sexual past. At his favorite brothel in Smyrna, an aging prostitute had told him that "One way or another, sweets, all ladies do it for the money." Ari internalized the remark, and repeated to Maria that money and sex were inextricably linked.

These mutual outpourings—in Greek—drew the lovers together and established the tenor of their relationship. Ari also valued Maria's fame, her strong personality, her capacity for devotion (to him) and the erotic passion he aroused in her, to which she responded so joyously. In Ari's arms, on that fateful (Maria's notion) cruise on the *Christina*, Maria experienced her first orgasm. Ari had transformed sex into a glorious union of two loving bodies and, at the same time, restored his sexual self-esteem. (He probably did not mind that Maria disclosed to at least one female friend that he was a splen-didly endowed and imaginative lover.) Unlike the ungainly Battista, Ari took his time and made sure she was writhing with pleasure before he indulged in his own climax.

Ari's erotic talents and his romantic allure provoked such ferocious emo-tions in Maria that she elevated them—and him—into near-sanctification, a true love that would replace art at the core of her existence. For her, the future was obvious. She and Ari would divorce their respective spouses and marry. Then she would relinquish her art to dedicate her life to him. But the reality was not so clear-cut. Though Tina, too, saw her husband's new love as a way to obtain the divorce he had steadfastly refused her, she did not enjoy being upstaged. In her ladylike way, Tina schemed against the brash interloper. She successfully courted Ari's influential sister, Artemis, to support her against Maria. She referred to Maria as "that whore" and ensured that in the inevitable media frenzy that would greet news of the Callas-Onassis affair, and in the eyes of her two neglected children, she would emerge as the wronged wife.

Early one morning on the cruise, after she and Ari had danced late into the night, Maria returned to her stateroom. There she told the anguished Battista, "It's over. I'm in love with Ari." Battista commented later about the passion that cost him his wife: "It was as if a fire was devouring them both."[81]

The cruise ended. Maria returned to Milan and announced publicly that her marriage had failed. Aristotle pursued her by telephone and in person. He also came to see Battista, to negotiate for his mistress's release from her marital bondage. "How many millions do you want for Maria? Five? Ten?" he demanded.[82]

Maria responded coldly to Battista's tearful pleas. "I was with you for twelve years," she said. "That is enough now." She left and took one of their two toy poodles and their maid, Bruna, with her. Battista waged a press campaign against the lovers, delighting low-brow journalists with his almost daily bon mots: "If everything is split and we have to divide our poodle, Maria will get the front and I will end up with the tail."[83]

Quite apart from Battista's refusal to cooperate, Onassis was unable to arrange his life as he wished, which was to keep Tina as his wife and Maria as his mistress. Tina seized the opportunity to sue for divorce; Aristotle pleaded with her to desist, then howled with frustration and wept with grief when she persisted. Though Maria fully expected him to marry her, Aristotle fought as hard as he could to maintain his empty marriage. To make this palatable to Tina, he even proposed that Reinaldo Herrera live with her in France, and that he would join them for summer holidays. But Tina was determined to liberate herself so she could marry, not cohabit with, Reinaldo. The divorce went through.

Maria's lover was free. She, however, was not. Battista refused to divorce her.[84] Maria was tormented by her "back-street" status as a mistress and ashamed that now she was violating her beliefs about the sanctity of marriage. She longed to be Ari's wife and to devote herself exclusively to him. Ari, however, refused to allow her to abandon her career, and so Maria attempted to serve both her music and her man. But she was tired and seldom rehearsed enough. Her voice in the upper ranges was increasingly treacherous, and she sometimes missed the high notes. The public understood quite well why, in 1960, she suddenly ceased performing so she could rest and recuperate.

In fact, her biographer Nicolas Gage reports, Maria Callas was pregnant. With Battista, she had never succeeded in conceiving the child she believed would improve her voice and her skin. With Aristotle, the miracle happened. During her pregnancy Maria declined to be seen by almost anyone, and on March 30, 1960, she delivered a baby boy who survived only a few hours. But she was a mistress, and so the birth and death of this little being, the product of her sinfulness, had to remain hidden away.[85]

Afterward, Maria entered the happiest period of her nine years as Aristotle's mistress. The magnificent soprano tended to her lover, and he was so touched after years of the unresponsive Tina that he repaid her in kind. He made sure she was not wakened at night and sent her extravagant bouquets of roses. But on occasions when he felt the presence of even so illustrious a mistress might compromise him socially, he sent her packing.

Ari, who joked that opera sounded like Italian chefs belting out risotto recipes, was also incapable of appreciating Maria's musical and dramatic genius. Even when she stunned her audience with her heartrending rendition of Bellini's *Norma*, about a druid priestess who was the secret mistress of a Roman proconsul, he could not force himself to watch an entire performance. Then, at the party he hosted afterward, he clearly considered his guests more important than the woman they were celebrating.

Maria, however, was happy to satisfy her demanding lover and to kowtow to his every whim. She cut her hair and wore contact lenses because he wished it. She indulged herself and rebelled against the rigor of her former operatic discipline. She swam in the *Christina*'s pool, danced and drank, and chatted late into the night with her beloved Aristotle. She accepted fewer engagements (one was to perform at JFK's birthday party, where Marilyn Monroe outshone her by wearing a nearly transparent dress) and seldom practiced, which accelerated the deterioration of her voice.

Despite her self-abnegating love and financial independence—she scorned the idea of taking Ari's money and insisted on buying a good deal of her own jewelry and clothes, as well as paying her own airfare on his Olympic Airlines—Aristotle's family, led by Artemis and Ari's two children, blamed her for his divorce from Tina and hated her. Alexander and Christina mockingly referred to her as "the Ugly One" and "Big Ass."

Other unpleasantnesses surfaced. Lee Radziwill, Jacqueline Kennedy's beautiful younger sister, joined the Churchills on a cruise from which Maria, glowering and resentful, had been excluded. Aristotle was fascinated with Lee's connections to the US president and, Maria was convinced, began to sleep with her. In 1963, Ari exiled Maria to Paris so he could entertain Jackie Kennedy herself on the *Christina*.

Yet despite her pain at being shunted off to the sidelines, Maria continued to devote herself to the business of being Ari's mistress. She gave only limited performances, including the tragic *Tosca*, in which she overwhelmed London audiences with the fury of her passion as she sang "Vissi d'arte, vissi d'amore," her personal story as well as Floria Tosca's.

JFK's assassination in 1963 inaugurated the nightmare of competing with Jackie Kennedy, the world's most eligible widow. Ari's calculated courting of both Lee and Jackie had earned him an invitation to the White House to mourn JFK alongside Bobby and Ted Kennedy and other of the former president's intimates. After this, he was noticeably harsher with Maria. He referred contemptuously to her failing voice as a whistle that no longer worked. Sometimes he slapped her, though she always slapped him back. As the quarrels intensified, Maria confided to friends she was terrified she was losing the first man to make her feel like a woman and to truly make love to her.

In 1966, in the wake of her lover's waning affection, Maria freed herself from Battista by renouncing American citizenship and assuming Greek citizenship instead, because Greece acknowledged only marriages between Greek citizens that had been performed in Greek churches. But though she was at last single and marriageable, and in desperate need of legitimizing the relationship that now felt both sinful and shaky, Ari refused to marry her. However, as if to assuage a certain niggling guilt or, more frighteningly, to make final provisions for her, he bought (and always maintained) an elegant Paris apartment for her. Meanwhile, gossip columnists noted how frequently he was seen in Jacqueline Kennedy's company.

Maria could not compete with "E Hira"—the Widow. In 1968, Ari tricked Maria into disembarking from the *Christina*, ushered Jackie aboard and began the elaborate negotiations that culminated in their incongruous and loveless marriage. The sixty-four-year-old groom wanted the thirty-nine-year-old widow's celebrity and powerful connections; she wanted to shield her children from assassination, and she was prepared to barter herself for the fortune that would make them all invulnerable.

And Maria? Even when she discovered the unsavory truth, she succumbed to Ari's solicitations to join him in between his visits to Jackie. Either he expected Maria to continue to serve and adore him despite his marriage to Jackie or, as many of his intimates believe, he never really intended to marry Jackie, merely to publicly flaunt their intimacy.

As Ari and Jackie haggled and flirted, Maria visited friends and waited for his phone call. When it failed to come, she sank into depression. In an interview granted to John Ardoin, the *Dallas Morning News* music critic, she poured out her misery. She was lonely and unloved. Her family and her lover had betrayed her. For nine years, she had endured a "hidden" and "humiliating" life as a mistress.

Meanwhile, Ari had his own troubles. The more Jackie pressed onward with their marriage, the more he wavered. Panicked, he begged Maria to save him by flaunting herself in Athens, which would infuriate Jackie and send her back to the United States. Maria refused. "You got yourself into this, you get yourself out of it," she said.[86] Maria later learned from newspapers that he had gone ahead with his marriage.

One week after he married Jackie Kennedy, Ari whistled to Maria from outside her apartment window. Initially she ignored him, but within a short time she relented, though she refused to sleep with him. Instead, she devoted herself to reinvigorating her career. Her starring role in the film version of *Medea* earned her rave reviews.

Ari hounded Maria to resume their former relationship. At a dinner party, he squeezed her leg and declared how much he preferred "Maria's big fat thighs" to Jackie's "bag of bones." He and Maria resumed an intense but non-sexual relationship, though they embraced and kissed with abandon. In meetings and lengthy telephone calls, Ari complained to Maria about Jackie. By 1970, he courted Maria publicly, either out of bravado or because he hoped that press accounts of their renewed affair would goad Jackie to divorce him. But Jackie, well aware that he wanted to be rid of her, would not cooperate.

At one point, distraught, unbalanced by a resurgence of despair that Ari might again abandon her, Maria was briefly—and, to her, humiliatingly—hospitalized after she took too many of the sleeping pills she always relied on to sleep.

But Ari had no intention of depriving himself of the only woman, besides his mother and sister, who truly loved him. His marriage was a travesty, but Jackie had given him no cause for divorce under Greek law, and try as he might, he could not divorce her. If his rumored attempts at buying her off are true, they, too, failed.

In 1973, after his beloved only son, Alexander, was killed in a plane crash, Ari was desolate. Days later, in Maria's apartment, he wept with grief and recalled their own infant son. Back at Skorpios, he walked at night with a stray dog to whom he confided his terrible grief. At Alexander's grave, he drank ouzo and talked to his lost child. According to Maria's intimate friends, he also implored her to marry him, but failed to commit himself to marriage in writing.

Maria was always available to console her wounded lover, except sexually. For her own erotic fulfillment, and even more for her flagging self-esteem, Maria embarked on a very public romance with the macho and famous operatic tenor Giuseppe di Stefano. Their relationship was at least as much professional as sexual. Their collaboration was disastrous, a sad, sometimes embarrassing spectacle of failing voices, stormy battles, performances cancelled because Maria had taken too many prescription drugs. Throughout these bitter tours, Ari's employees organized Maria's life, and every day he spent hours on the phone with her, treating her to interminable tirades about Jackie's reckless spending, her "faggotty" friends, her coldness and her soulessness.

Ari's life was unraveling much faster than Maria's. Eternally grief stricken over Alexander's death, and terminally ill (with a debilitating disorder that forced him to tape open his eyelids), Ari spent his remaining time imposing order on his financial empire and training his unstable daughter, Christina, to take her dead brother's place. He wrote a new will designed to protect Christina and to limit Jackie's claims on his estate. He omitted Maria, whose housing expenses he had provided for in perpetuity and whom he knew was financially sound. Propriety played a role—Maria had never been more than his mistress. Nonetheless, he could have acknowledged her, as W. R. Hearst had Marion Davies, as his dear friend, surely worth a token of his immense fortune and holdings.

In early 1975, Ari was flown to a Paris hospital for surgery, a desperate attempt to delay his death. As he lay dying, Maria tried frantically to see him. She called the hospital daily and entreated his friends to arrange something. But Christina, still convinced that Maria had caused her parents' divorce, forbade her to come.

Days before Ari died, Maria left Paris for Palm Beach, Florida. There, on March 15, she heard that her lover had died. She mourned openly, and many well-wishers sent cards and telegrams consoling her. "All of a sudden," Maria commented bitterly, "I am a widow."[87]

Maria could not go to the funeral or watch as Ari was reunited with his son in the family's burial plot on Skorpios. She returned to Paris and lived almost reclusively. As she adjusted to Ari's death, she toyed with schemes to revitalize her career. For a while, she continued her desultory affair with di Stefano because, she said, in the absence of "real men," she had nobody better. When she realized that she no longer needed to prove to Ari that she was a great singer and a desirable woman, she abandoned both opera and di Stefano.

After Ari's death, Maria's life was mostly confined to her apartment, where she watched cowboy movies on television, played cards and talked endlessly with her servants Bruna and Ferrucio, took dangerous amounts of sleeping pills and cuddled her poodles. Much of the time she relived her years with Ari. "He really did love me," she told her friend François Valéry. "You can't lie in bed."[88]

On September 16, 1977, Maria Callas died. The cause of death is unknown, but Nicolas Gage, her biographer, notes that she had just reported that she had lost a great deal of weight, and he suggests that she may well have resorted to drastic measures, which weakened and killed her.

"Callas, dead at 53, blazed through the skies and was burned out very early. But what years those were!" eulogized *New York Times* critic Harold C. Schonberg.[89] Schonberg was marveling at the dramatic musical genius that had permanently changed the standards and expectations of the operatic world. Maria herself had evaluated her life differently. She acknowledged the artistic gift that had dominated and shaped her life. But she gave even greater weight to her role as the mistress of Aristotle Onassis, who she believed had, at the end of his life, come to feel that she was the great love of his life.

Marilyn Monroe

Like Europe's royalty, America's equivalent—its elected presidents, the most powerful men in the world—have often taken mistresses. But elected officials have been held to higher moral standards than royalty. This has obliged them to be discreet, even about glamorous women they might otherwise be proud to flaunt. Until recently, if presidents avoided committing gross improprieties, they could count on immunity from the press and hence from the judgments of the American electorate. Of course, this immunity did not extend to the gossip and tale-telling of political enemies and allies, nor of friends, dissident relatives and dismissed servants. Adulterous presidents knew that, unlike reporters, history would not ignore their sexual peccadilloes.

Bill Clinton's lies about his relationship with White House intern Monica Lewinsky signaled the end of any media complicity about the private lives of elected officials. Ironically, Monica was no trophy doll to boast about but rather a giggly and talkative embarrassment. As a character in Philip Roth's *The Human Stain* comments, "This isn't Deep Throat. This is Big Mouth."[90]

One of Clinton's predecessors, the respected president John F. Kennedy, was a sexual warrior who had taken to heart his father Joe Kennedy's stricture that his sons "should get laid as often as they could." JFK was linked with movie stars, the wives of colleagues, socialites, Democratic Party workers, secretaries, airline hostesses, models, showgirls and prostitutes. In Georgetown, the social and residential heartbeat of Washington, Kennedy's sexual insatiability was legendary. "I can't go to sleep without a lay," he told Clare Booth Luce.[91]

JFK's need "to get laid" was an urge devoid of emotional context, an urgent ejaculation that relieved stress and, momentarily, the chronic back pain that had plagued him since childhood and that forced him to lie flat under his sexual partner. He had no interest in a woman's pleasure and was notoriously "terrible in bed."[92] The actress Angie Dickinson, with whom he was proud to be linked, remarked sardonically that sex with Jack had constituted "the most memorable fifteen seconds of my life."[93]

JFK had come to office at the onset of the sexual revolution, a propitious time for a man of his sexual proclivities. Author Nina Burleigh describes Kennedy's Washington as "a phallocentric world." The condition of testicles provided metaphors and their frame of thought: situations were "nut-cutters" or "castrating," men were "kicked in the balls" and aggressors "grabbed by the balls." In Kennedy's White House and conversation, the words *prick* and *fuck* and *nuts* and *bastard* became standard vocabulary.

In this sex-friendly world, JFK wanted more than orgasms. Like his father, he was obsessed with the sort of celestial glamor that only Tinseltown could provide. JFK wanted nothing less than a mistress as celebrated as Gloria Swanson. In the 1960s, that woman was the magnificently sexy and talented film star Marilyn Monroe.[94]

The coming together of the President and the Goddess was a triumph of desire and bravado over common sense. This man was as determined as this woman to ignore the glaring differences between them. He was the handsome and beloved president. She was the gorgeous and adored film star. If his wife and children posed no problem for him, they certainly posed no problem for her. He had his heart set on the most spectacular Hollywood conquest of all. She, wearing hers on her sleeve, had it set on an attentive and powerful man who could do what no other had: validate her very existence.

A social and financial abyss separated the formative worlds of John Fitzgerald Kennedy and Norma Jean Baker a.k.a. Marilyn Monroe. Norma Jean was born in 1926, near Hollywood, California, to divorcée Gladys Monroe. Gladys delivered Norma Jean into a quagmire of sadness. Stan Gifford, the infant's father, refused to marry her. Discrimination against unwed mothers ran high, and so Gladys boarded Norma Jean with former neighbors for five dollars weekly. She visited every Saturday, but to Marilyn's recollection, never hugged or kissed her, or identified herself as her mother.

Marilyn was, in fact, Gladys's third child. She had conceived the first at fourteen, refused to abort it and, with her mother's connivance, married the baby's father, the much older and very reluctant Jasper Baker. Their son was born and, less than two years later, a daughter.

The marriage was brief and brutal. The adolescent bride was a sloppy housekeeper. The groom was alcoholic and beat her savagely. After their divorce, he kidnapped their children and abused his son as he had once abused Gladys. Gladys tracked him down and tried but failed to regain custody of both children.

Back in California, in Venice Beach, Gladys partied to escape her emotions and fell deeply in love with Stan Gifford. She dreamed of marriage, but the divorced Gifford was so determinedly noncommittal that Gladys left him and soon after married Norwegian laborer Edward Mortensen. The price for the stability she had sought in Mortensen was unendurable dullness. After four months, she left him and resumed her relationship with Gifford. After she became pregnant, Gifford broke up with her. Gladys gave Norma Jean the surname Mortensen to conceal the fact that she was illegitimate.

Years later, and still escaping through partying, Gladys was devastated by the news that her fourteen-year-old son had died an excruciating death at his father's hands. An intimate friend recalled that "the underlying problem that led to the deterioration of Gladys's mental state was guilt and self-recrimination."[95] Gladys had a religious conversion to Christian Science and one day announced to the eight-year-old Norma Jean, who still lived as a boarder, that she would build a nice house for them.

For two months, Norma Jean lived with her pretty mother in their pretty white house. To help pay the mortgage, Gladys rented out the second floor. One day her lodger did something sexual to Norma Jean, something so terrible that she tried to tell her mother. But Gladys angrily silenced her complaints about "the star boarder," and Norma Jean cried herself to sleep and wanted to die. She didn't die, but she began to stutter.

Soon after, Gladys had a massive breakdown and was institutionalized. (Years later, she was diagnosed as a paranoid schizophrenic.) The pretty white house was sold to pay her debts. Norma Jean was taken, screaming and stammering, into the Los Angeles Orphans Home as orphan number 3,463.

Her mother's friend Grace dreamed of convincing her new husband to let

Norma Jean live with them. Until then, the orphanage director recommended that Norma Jean be conditioned by living with a family. Once again she became a boarder. She lived with nine different families, bridged by stints at the orphanage, until she shed her legal status as an orphan.

Norma Jean grew up in grinding poverty. Her foster families were poor folks, fighting the Depression by taking in orphans. Norma Jean was the last to bathe in the weekly bathwater and the first to be blamed when things went wrong. She owned two identical outfits, faded blue skirts and white blouses. She was nicknamed "the mouse," but in her dreams she was so beautiful and resplendent in her scarlet, gold, green and white clothes that people could only stare at her as she walked by.

Finally Grace arranged to take her in, and Norma Jean trusted that she finally had a home. Five months later, the drunkenness of Grace's husband forced her to send Norma Jean away, to her aunt's. Grace's Aunt Ana was poor but loving, and Norma Jean adored her. Life outside the cheerful and religion-filled house, however, was harsher. Other schoolchildren sneered at Norma Jean's two identical orphanage outfits and the boys nicknamed her "Norma Jean the Human Bean."[96] She had few friends and hated school.

At church, Norma Jean wrestled with an unorthodox and startling fantasy—that she would strip off her clothes and stand naked before God and man. This fantasy invoked "no shame or sense of sin. . . . Dreaming of people looking at me made me feel less lonely. . . . I was ashamed of the clothes I wore—the never-changing faded blue dress of poverty. Naked, I was like the other girls."[97]

And then one day, Norma Jean was even *less* like the other girls. Unnoticed under the white blouses, her body was rounding and swelling. She borrowed a sweater from a smaller friend and wore it to school: that was the last day anyone called her the Human Bean. Her body had become "a sort of magic friend," and she decorated it with lipstick and mascara. Everywhere she went people gawked, and she realized she had become someone other than Norma Jean from the orphanage.

Norma Jean's troubles were not over. Aunt Ana could no longer care for her. This meant two more years at the orphanage, until she turned eighteen—unless her boyfriend, twenty-one-year-old Lockheed employee Jimmy Dougherty, would marry her. Grace proposed to Jimmy, who accepted. As Jimmy's wife, Norma Jean adored sex, joyfully initiating it anywhere and any time the urge struck her, which was often. Even "undressing for bed was almost unfailingly erotic and . . . if I took a shower and she opened the door, it was the same thing all over again—instant sex," Jimmy recalled.[98]

Norma Jean also adored having a home and kept it spotless. She made Jimmy's sandwiches, put love notes in his lunch box and tried to cook proper dinners, often peas and carrots because she loved the contrasting colors. She braced her stuffed animals and dolls atop the furniture so they could see what was going on in her happy home. "She had no childhood and it showed," Jimmy said later. "You'd catch glimpses of someone who had been unloved for too long, unwanted too many years."[99]

This was wartime, and one day Jimmy decided to enlist. Norma Jean was frantic, but he went ahead with his plan. She moved in with his mother and got a job in an airplane production factory. In her overalls, working on an assembly line, Norma Jean was "discovered" by Corporal David Conover, a photographer recording life in wartime America. Her dream of being gazed at adoringly began to come true.

Jimmy came home, but when his leave ended, Norma Jean withdrew into melancholy. Then she decided to telephone her never-seen father, whose phone number she had managed to locate. Before hanging up on her, Gifford told her he had nothing to say to her and asked her never to call again. Norma Jean wept for days afterward and was inconsolable.

As a war "widow," Norma Jean embarked on the notable modeling career that would lead to Hollywood movie studios, first as a bit actress and finally as a star—indeed, *the* star. She learned how to dress and paint her face, how to fix her curly masses of light brown hair and how to project her sunny smile and bursting sensuality. She earned the first real money she had ever seen and moved out of her disapproving mother-in-law's home. When Jimmy gave her an ultimatum—modeling or marriage—she chose modeling.

Norma Jean had never ceased longing for her sad, sick mother. She brought Gladys to live with her. Until the mental illness forced Gladys back into an institution, she and Norma Jean tried to build the relationship they had never had.

Norma Jean was also taking charge of her career. She capitulated to pressure to transform herself into a blonde and discovered that blondes get more work. She was signed on as a bit player at Twentieth Century-Fox, earning $125 per week. She cooperated in selecting a more appealing name, and Norma Jean became Marilyn Monroe. She studied acting, sitting silently through classes with her small lapdog, concentrating with all her might to

improve herself. At home, for the same reason, she read books, just as she had
plowed through encyclopedias during her brief period as a stay-at-home
housewife.

Determinedly, Norma Jean grew into and filled up Marilyn. She made several movies and, in 1950, finally attracted serious attention for her role as a
corrupt lawyer's mistress in the 1950 John Huston thriller *The Asphalt Jungle*.
Star status followed in 1952, after Marilyn—for so she had become, even to
herself—sparkled in the Barbara Stanwyck movie *Clash by Night*.

As she rode the crest of her wave of popularity, Marilyn began an ill-advised
romance with baseball giant Joe DiMaggio. Though Joe was obsessively jealous and possessive, and violently opposed to Marilyn's lifestyle, they married
on January 14, 1954. DiMaggio lashed out at her with words and huge fists
when jealousy and frustration overcame him. The marriage, brief and desperately unhappy, ended in divorce, filed on October 3, 1954.

Playwright Arthur Miller, Marilyn's next husband, was as distinguished
and at least as unsuitable as Joe DiMaggio—the wonder is how he quashed his
commonsensical premonitions of doom and, in June 1956, went ahead with
the wedding. But the creator of *Death of a Salesman*'s Willy Loman was mesmerized by Marilyn's sensual beauty. "She's kind of a lodestone that draws
out of the male animal his essential qualities," he marveled.[100] His sister found
Marilyn radiant with joy, and this must have been true. On the back of a wedding portrait she wrote, "Hope, Hope, Hope."

Hope was as fleeting as happiness in the Miller-Monroe union. Before long,
Marilyn discovered that the new husband she called "Pa" or "Poppy" (Jimmy
Dougherty had been "Daddy," Joe DiMaggio, "Pa") was questioning his decision to marry her. He pitied her as a child-woman crushed by her demons, but
her insatiable emotional demands were suffocating his creativity. He referred
to her as a "whore" and told her that he had no easy answer to Laurence
Olivier's comment that she was a troublesome bitch.

Professionally, Marilyn was in top form—if you judged her only by her finished work. Her directors and colleagues found her increasingly erratic,
always late, sometimes not showing up at all, rude, imperious, disoriented,
unable to remember simple lines. Tony Curtis, kept waiting for hours day
after day on the set of *Some Like It Hot*, scowled that by the fortieth take of a
romantic scene, kissing Marilyn was like kissing Hitler.

Marilyn's marital adventure was by then irreparably strained. She had
attempted suicide several times. She miscarried a baby and grieved terribly.
She had not-very-secret affairs with other men, including John F. Kennedy.

Despite psychiatric therapy, she was descending ever further into a morass of drunken and drugged despair. After one botched suicide attempt, when a friend asked how she was, Marilyn replied groggily, "Alive . . . bad luck."[101] On the day of John F. Kennedy's presidential inauguration in 1961, Marilyn flew to Mexico for her divorce.

Marilyn began to focus on JFK, now ensconced in the White House. She had met him in the mid-1950s, through a brother-in-law, actor Peter Lawford, who acted as an amateur pimp between Kennedy and a host of sexy and sexually available actresses. JFK liked "knocking a name," both for the thrill of it and for his father's vicarious enjoyment. "Knocking" Gene Tierney, Angie Dickinson, Jayne Mansfield and Lee Remick was impressive, but with Marilyn Monroe, possibly the most famous woman in the world, JFK had bested his father's conquest of Gloria Swanson.

In some ways, Marilyn and Jack were well paired. They had both climbed to the apex of their professions. They were both risk-takers par excellence. They were glamorous, envied and media darlings. They were unabashedly promiscuous, hoping to find in affairs that resembled relationships emotions and rewards to validate and reassure themselves. They both sought and attracted the spotlight. And in their mutual need to prove themselves through sexual conquest, they reached out for and boasted about each other.

But Marilyn was a sick woman on an impossible quest for a husband and lover who was also a father. Her instability and precarious hold on sanity, and her dependence on prescription drugs, were no secret, least of all to JFK.

In 1960, JFK and his managers were all aware of the danger to his campaign if Marilyn talked publicly about their affair. Not that she was the only potential leak—JFK operated with reckless openness, at the White House, at New York's Carlyle hotel and at his sister Pat and Peter Lawford's home in Santa Monica. The secretary of his cabinet, Fred Dutton, lamented that JFK was "like God, ——ing anybody he wants to anytime he feels like it."[102]

The president counted on the discretion of media culture and the frightened compliance of the waiters, drivers, busboys and other servers whom his agents made understand that "you'll see things but you won't see them. You'll hear things but you won't hear them."[103]

This crucial concealment extended to Marilyn. If she wished to see JFK—and she very much did—she had to travel to their rendezvous, often on Air Force One, disguised as a secretary, a bewigged brunette or redhead in bandana and sunglasses who carried—and used!—a steno pad and pencil, scribbling imaginary notes as Peter Lawford wickedly dictated to her. To telephone her lover at the White House, she was assigned the code name "Miss Green," and her calls were immediately transferred to the man she idolized as "the Prez."

It is difficult to believe that Marilyn expected JFK to divorce Jackie and marry her, as several writers have reported. As deluded as she was about men, and as self-destructive as she was, she must have understood the limits to their relationship. JFK always orchestrated their rendezvous. After socializing with his other guests, they withdrew together for the quick sex he specialized in—"like a rooster in a hen house. Bam, bam, bam. . . . I was constantly reminding him to 'zip up.'"[104]

Whether in the White House, where several visitors saw Marilyn, or the Carlyle hotel or, most frequently, at the Lawfords' house, Marilyn and JFK were with his cronies or colleagues. She was always—in these reports—in her cups, or rather champagne flutes, and headed for oblivion. She would be suggestively garbed, her lack of underwear apparent, her hair tousled, but always sexy and magnificent, the Sex Goddess with her lover, the President.

Astonishingly, JFK continued their affair despite his very justifiable fears that she might blab or had already blabbed. During the years of their liaison, Marilyn was never reticent about it, as many people—friends, journalists, colleagues—have confirmed. During JFK's presidential campaign, controlling Marilyn was very much on his agenda. Once he had taken office, the risks escalated, yet he seemed unprepared to deal with them.

By 1962, during the filming of *Something's Got to Give*, what gave was Marilyn's grip on sanity. She had a number of blows, the heaviest being that Arthur Miller had married the woman she had suspected he was seeing during the final days of their marriage, and that his new wife was already pregnant. That year, Marilyn bought a modest ($35,000) house close to Dr. Ralph Greenson, her controlling, omnipresent psychiatrist. Despite her fame and hard work, she had to borrow the downpayment from Joe DiMaggio.

Filming of *Something's Got to Give* began in April, with cast, crew and Cukor watching tensely to see if Marilyn could or would cooperate, control herself, remember her lines, arrive on time, arrive at all. Their fears were justified. If she showed up, she was late, and she often vomited with terror at the prospect of performing. She gobbled Dr. Greenson's prescription pills to cope with her ravaging depression and seemed confused and unprepared. She took ill, and doctors confirmed that she suffered an infected throat. Sometimes she tried to work but collapsed on the set or left early.

Cukor temporized desperately, shooting around her, waiting with the cast and 104 crew members for the star to appear. On May 14, Marilyn was sufficiently recovered to return to work. The collective relief was tempered by new anxiety in the form of a rumor that Marilyn intended to leave for New York for President Kennedy's May 19 birthday celebrations.

Twentieth Century-Fox's lawyers scrummed and instructed Marilyn to remain on the set. Disobeying this order would constitute breach of her contract, they warned. Marilyn consulted a lawyer, Bobby Kennedy, the US attorney general. Bobby was already worried that top Democrats might look askance at her appearance at the birthday party and urged her to stay away. By then journalists were talking about, though not yet reporting, his brother's ill-concealed affair with her. Bobby, the family intellectual, the decent and reliable brother, saw a perfect opportunity for damage control. But JFK insisted that she come, and Marilyn refused to deprive herself of the opportunity of singing "Happy Birthday" to the president of the United States, in front of fifteen thousand Democrats in Madison Square Garden.[105]

The same Marilyn who could not get out of bed and who flubbed her lines when she did planned for her appearance at her lover's birthday party with meticulous care. She directed her designer, Jean-Louis, to create a spectacular dress of flesh-colored silk gauze decorated with oversized rhinestones, so tightly melded to her it had to be sewn onto her naked body. (It cost twelve thousand dollars and fit into the palm of a hand.) She accessorized it with a white ermine jacket from the Twentieth Century-Fox wardrobe, and had her thick blond hair styled in a smooth bouffant with an engaging flip.

Even for this momentous event, Marilyn was late. When she finally entered, jocularly introduced by Peter Lawford as "the *late* Marilyn Monroe," she floated onstage, a luminous vision of a woman. Photographs taken from behind her show JFK watching her alone, Jackie (who would have clad her long, lean body in a designer gown distinguished by its elegant simplicity) having refused to subject herself to the spectacle of Marilyn serenading her husband. *Time* magazine's Hugh Sidey remembered that "you could just smell lust. I mean, Kennedy went limp, or something. We were all just stunned, to see this woman."[106]

Marilyn got through the specially composed birthday song, and the crowd applauded wildly. JFK came up to stand beside her. "I can now retire from politics, after having had 'Happy Birthday' sung to me in such a sweet, wholesome way," he said.[107] That night Marilyn spent two hours with JFK. She would never see him again.

Marilyn returned to the set of *Something's Got to Give*. She filmed her famous nude swimming-pool scene, which once again catapulted her into public notice. For a few days, she worked well. Then, on a Monday morning, she was so distraught that everyone speculated that something terrible had happened over the weekend.

It had. Jack Kennedy, the lover who had vetoed Bobby's plea to cancel Marilyn's appearance—indeed, had arranged for Peter Lawford to send a helicopter to the set of *Something's Got to Give* to transport her to the airport—had at last been frightened into ending their relationship.

What frightened him was a memorable visit, five days after the birthday gala, from FBI director J. Edgar Hoover. Hoover warned the president that his affairs with Marilyn Monroe and especially with Mafia moll Judith Campbell Exner were jeopardizing the presidency at the height of the Cold War and the Cuban crisis.

That same day, JFK phoned Judith and ended their relationship. He also disconnected the private telephone he used to contact Marilyn and instructed the White House switchboard not to accept her calls. He did not attempt to deal with Marilyn himself. That unpleasant and possibly dangerous chore fell to Peter Lawford.

Marilyn, fresh from her triumph at the gala, confident in the power of her beauty and her incomparable figure, the sinewy long legs, full breasts and curvaceous derriere that JFK particularly admired—"What an ass!" he commented. "What an ass!"—could not understand why she had been dismissed.

Patricia Seaton Lawford, Peter's last wife, reported that Peter decided to be brutally frank. "She was told that she'd never be able to speak to the president again—that she was never going to be the First Lady." When Marilyn broke down into tears, Peter added, "Look, Marilyn, you're just another one of Jack's fucks."[108]

Marilyn spent the weekend drifting in and out of drugged sleep. On Monday, she reported to work though she could barely stand up and looked "shattered," and then worked for nine straight days until June 1, her thirty-sixth birthday. Cukor forbade any celebrations, but the crew defied him and surprised Marilyn with a five-dollar cake and coffee. Her always supportive costar Dean Martin brought champagne. Afterward, Marilyn made a scheduled appearance for a muscular dystrophy benefit at Dodger Stadium.

JFK was now unreachable. He also ignored the letters from Marilyn that Peter Lawford, who obviously read them, described as "rather pathetic." Marilyn complained to Lawford, and probably to JFK, that the Kennedys "use you and then they dispose of you like so much rubbish."[109] That week, she felt too sick to go to work. The studio had had enough and, on June 8, fired Marilyn and sued her for one million dollars in damages. Marilyn, fighting for her sanity and career, contacted influential movie executives and garnered enough support to countersue the studio. In a month-long media blitz, she gave interviews with and provided photo ops for *Vogue, Life, Redbook* and *Cosmopolitan* magazines, countless reporters for the other media, and the crew and cast of *Something's Got to Give.*

During her battle for reinstatement and redress, Marilyn saw a good deal of Bobby, JFK's emissary on the mission to impress on her the urgency of keeping her mouth shut, and to convince her to stop trying to contact Jack. Marilyn and Bobby concluded a deal whereby she probably promised to remain silent about JFK. Bobby, in turn, contacted a studio friend, and sixteen days after firing her, Twentieth Century-Fox reinstated Marilyn with a much higher salary. Sometime after this, however, Bobby stopped returning her calls. Angry and hurt, she tried to track him down. After eight documented calls to the Justice Department, she called him at home. "Bobby was furious with Marilyn for taking this liberty," Peter Lawford's daughter Patricia recalled.[110]

Marilyn, too, was furious, and also deeply wounded. "I might just hold a press conference. I've certainly got a lot to say!" she told her friend Robert Slatzer. "I'm going to blow the lid off this whole damn thing! And it's clear to me now that the Kennedys got what they wanted out of me and then moved on!"[111]

On August 4, before she could talk, Marilyn Monroe died of a massive overdose of barbiturates, administered by hands unknown—perhaps hers, perhaps someone else's. Curiously, much of the evidence surrounding Marilyn Monroe's death has been destroyed or has disappeared, but nothing has dampened the quest for the truth. A plethora of investigative writers and journalists continue to uncover new information and to suggest new hypotheses and interpretations. To date, the weight of their data lends credence to the theory that someone injected Marilyn with a lethal dose of barbiturates, accidentally or deliberately. But without more hard data, it is impossible to be sure exactly what really happened.

Joe DiMaggio handled funeral arrangements, and barred the Lawfords, Frank Sinatra, Sammy Davis, Jr., and others from viewing her remains; he blamed the entertainment world for contributing to Marilyn's death. Arthur Miller, assuming she was a suicide, said that it was inevitable. Only Jacqueline Kennedy uttered the platitude that got it right: "She will go on eternally."

With JFK, Marilyn thought she had finally identified a man noble and powerful enough to satisfy her. It was not easy for her to understand that JFK was using her, that his fundamental contempt for women extended to her and that if his thoroughbred of a wife and the mother of his children could not hold him, then she had never stood a chance. Marilyn was not even his primary "other woman." Days before her death, for the first time, Marilyn saw JFK precisely as he was.

Judith Campbell

Judith Campbell was the only one of JFK's first-string mistresses to survive him. Judy's several charms included lustrous black hair, fine features and a shapely figure. Her resemblance to Elizabeth Taylor was so striking that it may explain why, just after Taylor left him, a grieving Eddie Fisher briefly dated Judy, a slenderer version of his estranged wife.

Judy's second attraction lay in her social circle, a curious mix of mob and movie moguls. She dated Frank Sinatra, worked for Jerry Lewis, was intimate with Sam Giancana and Johnny Roselli, knew Peter and Pat Lawford and had once gone out with Robert Wagner, who introduced her to her first husband, struggling actor Billy Campbell. Judy was friendly with Natalie Wood, Charlton and Lydia Heston, Lloyd and Dottie Bridges, and of course Gary Morton, her sister Jackie's ex-husband, who later married Lucille Ball. Last, through her mother's family, Judy was an Irish Catholic girl from a large and wealthy family.

After marrying at eighteen in 1952 and divorcing six years later, Judy reinvented herself as a bachelor party girl. A grandmother's legacy permitted her to live lavishly without working, and Judy flung herself into a life of partying and traveling between New York, Beverly Hills and Las Vegas, her main destinations. She also took extension courses at UCLA, sketched and painted, and indulged in daily shopping, the activity that most validated her existence.

Judith suffered recurrent depression and fought it with stiff glasses of Jack Daniel's and hour-long soaks in hot bathtubs. In 1959, Frank Sinatra noticed her in an Italian restaurant. They began to date and, for a time, she consorted with the Rat Pack, later the Clan, which included Sinatra, Lewis, Dean Martin, Sammy Davis, Jr., and for a while, Elizabeth Taylor and Eddie Fisher.

On a Sunday evening, February 7, 1960, Peter Lawford introduced Judy to two of his brothers-in-law, JFK and Teddy Kennedy. Both brothers flirted with her, Teddy more persistently, but Judy dismissed him as "the baby brother walking in his older brother's shadow."[112] Jack was different, "so young and virile, so dashing" that Judy accepted a lunch date with him. Other dates followed.

Early in their relationship, Judy mentioned Teddy's persistent advances. "That little rascal," JFK laughed delightedly. When their affair was in full swing, Jack would remark that Teddy would have eaten his heart out had he known that they were in bed together. Judy noticed that JFK never denigrated another Kennedy. This consideration extended to Jackie. The most he volunteered was that he was unhappy in his marriage, which wasn't working as he and his wife had hoped.

Judy understood that she and Jack Kennedy were beginning a long-term romance. She bought and read his two books, *Why England Slept* and *Profiles in Courage*, and every other book she could find about the Kennedys. She devoured magazines and newspapers, watched television news. "I couldn't get him off my mind and I wanted to know everything about him I could possibly learn."[113] Jack established a routine of phoning her almost daily, no matter where he was or how tired he was, and often sent a dozen red roses.

After a month apart, they met in the Plaza hotel in New York City, on the eve of the New Hampshire primary. Jack wanted and expected sex. Judy demurred and was not persuaded by his argument that she had known what this was about, and must have expected it. "I have so looked forward to being close to you, to making love to you, and then to just lie in bed and talk the way two people can talk after making love," he said. Soon, they were in bed making love for the first of scores of times.

As his other women discovered, the sexual act with JFK was perfunctory and one-sided. But Judy's new lover's charm, confidence and good humor far outweighed his inadequate sexual skills. He never shared his anxieties or insecurities, except about how his clothes looked. Judy, on the other hand, vacillated between joy and sadness, and was perpetually anxious.

The tenor of the relationship had been established: routine phone calls, rushed meetings in hotels all over the country, messages conveyed through Evelyn Lincoln, JFK's personal secretary. Judy noticed that Jack was jealous of her association with Frank Sinatra, whom he always inquired about, and that he was fascinated by gossip about Judy's Hollywood friends. When he called and Judy did not answer, he wanted to know where she had been, and with whom. In fact, she was by then absorbed in deepening her relationship with Sam Giancana, whom Sinatra introduced to her as Sam Flood.

Giancana was a Mafia assassin who had worked his way to the top echelons of his crime syndicate. When Judy met him, he oversaw a criminal empire of fifty thousand burglars, fences, murderers and extortionists, and politicians, policemen and judges on the take. Though he had been rejected by the US army as a "constitutional psychopath" with an "inadequate personality and strong anti-social trends,"[114] referred to African Americans as "niggers" and treated service workers with breathtaking contempt, Judy found him sensitive, affectionate and wise. In *My Story*, her self-serving and bowdlerized version of her life, Judy also claimed that she remained unaware of his true profession for years and was astounded when FBI agents confronted her and told her who and what Sam Flood really was. But in a cathartic interview with syndicated columnist Liz Smith in *Vanity Fair* magazine just before her 1999 death from bone and breast cancer, Judy admitted that she had sanitized some parts of *My Story*.

Sam, twenty-six years older than Judy, frequently sent her five dozen yellow roses, and for the duration of her affair with Jack Kennedy, she often received his one dozen red roses and Sam Giancana's five dozen yellow roses on the same day. In her *Vanity Fair* interview, Judy acknowledged that she had been Sam's mistress at the same time as she was Jack's.

One night when Jackie was away, Jack Kennedy invited Judy to his house in Georgetown. She chose a black knit suit and a new black mink coat for the occasion, and was rewarded with Jack's heartfelt compliments. Once inside, she was unimpressed with Jackie's interior decorating, finding it pretty but cluttered. However, she did wrestle—briefly—with her numbed conscience. She had come to Jackie's house to sleep with Jackie's husband, and suddenly this struck her as wrong.

Later, after a lovemaking session on one of Jackie and Jack's pale green twin beds, he whispered, "Do you think you could love me?" "I'm afraid I could," Judy responded. Still, Jackie's presence, indeed Jackie's bedroom, made Judy nervous. She consoled herself with the idea that since Jack and Jackie were unhappily married, her affair with him was less sinful.

The act of sex was forgettable, but Judy greatly enjoyed the postcoital cuddling and pillow talk that followed. Jack would hold her in his arms while she lay, head on his chest, his heart beating under her cheek as they talked for hours.

Several times, Jack fantasized about spending a month alone with her in a tropical paradise if he failed to win the presidential nomination. He insinuated, as well, that should he lose, he and Jackie would end their marriage.

Judy alternated between Jack and Sam, but Jack's frenzied schedule meant that she had much more time to spend with Sam in Chicago. Years later, Judy admitted knowing that Sam courted her because of her relationship with JFK. Yet despite this cynical motive, "I do know that he later fell deeply in love with me," she wrote.[115]

At various times, Judy visited both Sam and Jack in Palm Beach. Ironically, their houses were so similar that she could scarcely distinguish them. Sometimes Judy slept with Sam and Jack within hours of each other. When she had surgery to remove ovarian cysts, Sam's five dozen yellow and Jack's one dozen red roses with a note that read "Get well soon—Friends of Evelyn Lincoln," decorated her hospital room.

At one assignation in his Los Angeles hotel room during the Democratic National Convention, Jack proposed a sexual threesome with himself, Judy and a tall, thin woman he did not introduce. Judy reacted furiously. "I'm really sorry," Jack apologized. "It was a stupid mistake." Judy was not placated. "I would think you had enough on your mind without cooking up something like this." Jack smiled tightly. "It wasn't easy."[116]

Judy forgave him and they resumed their perambulating affair. By this time, however, she was aware that Jack compartmentalized his life, with love in one niche and his wife, children, career and family in others.

Late in 1960, two FBI agents confronted Judy about her intimacy with Sam Giancana. They informed her that he was a mobster, asked if he paid her rent and questioned her about other criminals. (They did not mention that the CIA had contracted with him to kill Fidel Castro, who remained alive only because his would-be Mafia assassins botched attempt after attempt.) Sam was calm about this disturbing visit. The safest way to deal with them was to ignore them and say nothing, he advised Judy.

Days later, Judy's other lover won the presidency of the United States by an infinitesimal majority. "If it wasn't for me," Sam boasted to Judy, "your boyfriend wouldn't even be in the White House,"[117] a reference to how the mob used its political influence to back JFK's campaign in Chicago.

Judy did not attend the inaugural dinner to which Jack invited her, largely because she did not want to inflict her presence on Jackie. But when Jackie was out of Washington, she sometimes visited the president in the White House. Jack always urged her to join him in the swimming pool, now notorious for the number of naked young women who swam there with him. Judy, however, refused out of concern for her hairdo.

Judy paid five White House visits to Jack that summer. During one of them, he asked her if she had spread the story about his attempt to involve her in sex *à trois.* She denied it furiously, but later realized that the FBI must have been bugging telephone calls in which she had confided in various close friends.

The lovers reconciled, and Judy accepted his "conscience medicine," a large diamond-and-ruby brooch set in eighteen-carat gold. Jack told her he seldom gave presents, and that her new jewelry should remind her that despite his occasional gaffes, his heart was in the right place.

The White House rendezvous continued until the spring of 1962. Once Jack visited her apartment, but by then the affair was causing Judy serious doubts and depression. Jack's lovemaking irritated her. "He expected me to come into bed and just perform. . . . The feeling that I was there to service him began to really trouble me."[118]

Judy also sensed subtle changes in Jack's behavior as he became "more impressed that he was the President."[119] His phone calls were more imperious. If she declined a suggested meeting, he would hang up on her. She began to evaluate the relationship and decided that flying all over the country to spend two hours with him was not worth it. Slowly, imperceptibly, she had fallen out of love with him.

Judy strongly denied that J. Edgar Hoover's conversation with JFK about her (and about Marilyn Monroe) ended the relationship. Her version was that it trickled to an end, until one day she and Jack were no longer in contact.

Soon after the affair ended, Judy disclosed in her 1999 *Vanity Fair* interview, she realized she was pregnant with Jack's baby. The Catholic president asked her if she wanted to have the baby, then urged her to confide in Sam Giancana who could arrange an abortion. The abortion was duly performed at Grand Hospital in January 1963. (Judy showed Liz Smith the receipts for it.) "I was . . . in love. Was I supposed to have better sense and more judgment than the president of the United States?" she demanded rhetorically. Why had she not mentioned this in *My Story*? "I was afraid for my life," she said.[120] She had decided to speak about it at last because she believed the Kennedy legend needed demystifying.

The aborted pregnancy was not the only legacy of Judy's presidential affair. Once she was no longer a White House intimate, the FBI inaugurated a campaign against her. "I was followed, hounded, harassed, accosted, spied upon, intimidated, burglarized, embarrassed, humiliated, denigrated and . . . driven to the brink of death by the Federal Bureau of Investigation," she charged in her memoirs.[121] But "someone worked a miracle" and she was exempted from a grand jury into mob activities.

Judy's life continued on a downward spiral. She dated other men, including Eddie Fisher, walked through the "valley of the dolls," the current fad of relying on mood-altering prescription pills, and drank herself to exhausted sleep. She became pregnant and gave her son up for adoption. In 1971, Sam Giancana, whom she was no longer involved with, was murdered days before he was to appear before a grand jury investigating Mafia activities. In 1975, Judy married Dan Exner, a much younger golf pro, and as Judith Campbell Exner, achieved instant notoriety after her appearance before the Senate Committee on Intelligence Operations. For the first time, the media trumpeted the news that over a decade earlier, she had been simultaneously the mistress of US president John F. Kennedy and Mafia kingpin Sam Giancana, and (in a very cautious version of the facts) may have known or discussed with her two lovers the failed attempt to kill Fidel Castro.

Judith Campbell was a larger-than-life version of the mistress as trophy doll, a woman who had little besides beauty and underworld connections to offer. Unlike the internationally famed Marilyn Monroe, Judy led an aimless existence fueled by shopping, liquor and partying with key figures in American entertainment and crime. Jack's fascination with celebrities such as Frank Sinatra, coupled with his disinclination to shun the criminally connected and his need to flaunt beautiful women, made Judy the perfect mistress, especially since she was neither jealous, demanding nor indiscreet.

From Judy's perspective, the president of the United States was immensely seductive. He was powerful and respected, apparently interested in her personal and inner lives (such as they were), and handsome and charming. He was a mediocre sexual partner, but his postcoital confidences and pillow talk were more than adequate compensation. His marriage was unfortunate and he was involved with other women, but that allowed Judy to hop guiltlessly from his bed into Sam Giancana's and confuse his Florida house with Sam's. If Judy was a trophy doll for him, JFK was the Oscar of trophy dolls for Judy.

Vicki Morgan [122]

From its inception, the Alfred Bloomingdale–Vicki Morgan affair was a perverse *Pygmalion* parody. In 1968, when the department store heir met her, Vicki Morgan was the teenaged trophy wife of forty-nine-year-old Earle Lamm, who leased a Mercedes 280-SL for her, provided credit cards for her maniacal shopping, watched her having sex with a black woman, introduced her to orgies and proudly showed off his stunning child bride.

When Vicki was sixteen, she had dropped out of school to give birth to Todd, whom her mother was raising. She married Earle to escape the dreariness of her backwater California hometown, but he quickly bored and disgusted her. When Alfred Bloomingdale noticed her in a Sunset Strip restaurant, Vicki was easily persuaded to abandon her husband.

Vicki was tall and slender, with flowing blond hair, sculpted cheekbones and full, sensuous lips. But other than youth and abundant beauty, she had few accomplishments. Her principal domestic skill was shopping for interior decorations, and she could not cook or even assemble ingredients for meals. Earle, a bisexual, had wanted a trophy wife open to sexual experimentation, especially group sex. As he saw it, Vicki was almost perfect.

Alfred Bloomingdale's requirements were not dissimilar, though he expected kinkier sex and a much higher level of social skills and graces than the barely eighteen-year-old Vicki possessed. Unlike Earle, and despite his complaints about his wife, whom he repeatedly promised to divorce so he could marry her, Alfred never saw Vicki as wife material, only as an extremely pretty mistress he could flaunt as testimony to his virility and wealth.

Vicki's first sexual encounter with Bloomingdale plunged her into his perverse eroticism. It was not just that she was one of three women, but that he stripped her, tied her face down on a bed, then began to spank her on the buttocks. The other women were tightly bound with belts and harshly whipped until welts appeared on their behinds. This violence was Bloomingdale's foreplay, after which he entered Vicki and, while the other two victims watched, pumped himself into a frenzied orgasm.

The two hookers were paid off and dismissed, but Bloomingdale wanted to clinch a more permanent deal with Vicki. When she protested that she was married, he replied impatiently that she would no longer be Earle's wife, but his mistress. Taking a mistress was a tradition of long standing, he elaborated, and offered the woman long-term security. "You can get what you need, whenever you need it. I'm that rich," he promised her.[123]

Bloomingdale was not merely extremely wealthy but also powerful, both financially and politically. He had inherited the Bloomingdale fortune, had cofounded Diner's Club, the world's first major credit card, and was heavily involved in other commercial enterprises. The former New York City treasurer had soared to become the trusted confidant of Ronald Reagan and, after Reagan became president in 1981, a member of his "kitchen cabinet." Betsy Bloomingdale was one of Nancy Reagan's closest friends, a bond that cemented the Bloomingdale-Reagan alliance.

When they met, Vicki had never been to New York or heard of Blooming-dale's. When she explained to her husband that she was going to become Alfred's mistress, Earle warned her that to a man like that, she was just one more pretty girl, and he would soon drop her for another one. "Earle, I'm not just pretty, I'm beautiful," Vicki corrected him. Bloomingdale attempted to pay Earle off, but the tearful husband refused. "I'd never take money for the woman I love," he said pitifully.[124]

Vicki became Bloomingdale's mistress. He rented a house for her, furnished it and hired a cook and a housekeeper. He gave her money to buy the "right" sort of clothes. He ordered her to refine her social skills so he could present her, without embarrassment, to his friends. He phoned her constantly, checking on her. And, three times a week, he forced her to participate in sadistic sexual whipping and bondage orgies in which she had to lash groveling women who called her "Mistress." Over time, he escalated his demands. Vicki had to telephone his hookers and book appointments for these sessions, and haggle with them over the price. He also prostituted her, asking her to sleep with various business associates whenever he believed they either merited or would appreciate such an exciting gesture. "It's part of the job," he would say, and he meant it.

Vicki began to understand that Alfred Bloomingdale exacted a heavy price from his mistress. She had difficulty reconciling the gutter level of his sexual obsessions with his expectations for her in "society." To quell her growing uneasiness, she turned to wine, Valium and "downers." Thus medicated, she endured the long days and slept through the long nights.

Though he often criticized her, Bloomingdale was satisfied enough with his mistress to take her traveling and to introduce her as a wealthy young Republican, though presumably nobody was fooled. She met and charmed his friends, leaders in American industry. She measured herself against their wives and began to nourish an ambition to become one of them, a woman of significance in Los Angeles society.

Above all, she shopped. Every day, she roamed Beverly Hills and devoured merchandise, sucking it up voraciously: clothes, linens, dishes, crystal, wine, food, household supplies. Every night, she waited at home for Alfred's phone call at nine sharp.

Within a year, Vicki was deeply unhappy. She drank, numbed herself with medication, wept uncontrollably and had a few quick and secret affairs. She became pregnant and, though Alfred said he wanted her to have his baby, aborted it. "Look," Vicki explained to her biographer a decade later, "I had money . . . things. I had more than most can ever dream of having. And I'm supposed to be happy. Only I'm not happy. I'm confused as all hell, and I'm so neurotic I don't even know if I'm all that confused. . . . I'm the mistress. I'm shopping, I'm seeing Alfred, I'm the one running wild in the streets with his money."[125]

Yet she thought she loved him. Alfred was powerful, fatherly (and she had been raised fatherless), intelligent, wise, funny, witty—"we were so many things to each other . . . friend, lover, parent, child, and damn near everything else in between."[126] If he loved her, truly loved her, he would buy her a house. They went house hunting, but their expeditions ended in bitter quarrels in front of uneasy Realtors, and no sale.

The security he promised was also shaky. Once, Betsy saw Vicki kissing Alfred in front of a beauty salon, and the Bloomingdale domestic entente was shattered. From a pay phone, Alfred relayed to his mistress the news of his disgrace. Betsy had changed his phone numbers, he could no longer call Vicki and, for the time, their relationship was suspended. After days of no communication, Vicki forced her way into Alfred's office and threatened him with a glass paperweight. They argued, she stormed, he temporized. Finally, Vicki walked out of his office with a check for twenty thousand dollars.

Vicki packed up and left for England but soon returned to Los Angeles. By then, Alfred was less afraid of Betsy than of living without Vicki. He tracked her down and, weeping convulsively, begged for a reconciliation. Vicki accepted. Once again Alfred rented her a house, once again she shopped to furnish and decorate it. To satisfy her sexual frustration while Alfred recovered from triple-bypass heart surgery, she took a lover, a rock musician she told Alfred was gay.

Meanwhile Vicki decided to pursue an acting career and, in preparation, had breast implants. Then, through Alfred, she was accepted into the roster of a talent manager, who suggested a psychiatrist to deal with her paralyzing insecurities at auditions. Vicki also took acting lessons from an aging director, but no matter how much she studied or how hard she rehearsed, she was a hopelessly wooden actress whom nobody would cast.

But her flair for attracting important men was undiminished. Vicki met and was briefly enchanted by the much older actor Cary Grant, then embroiled in a custody suit with his ex-wife, Dyan Cannon, over their young daughter. They began to date, and Vicki often spent the night at his house, but—at his wish—in a separate bedroom. Grant's idea of a date was diametrically opposed to Alfred Bloomingdale's. He and Vicki would stay at home, eating the TV dinners he relished and chatting. Grant forbade her to smoke in the house and urged her to scrub her face clean of all makeup and to wear simpler clothes. He waited a long time before he had sex with her. And he had no idea that she was Alfred Bloomingdale's mistress.

But Alfred knew about Cary Grant, and he and Vicki fought bitterly. She took the opportunity of raising other issues, notably Alfred's sexual perversities. Alfred could not achieve orgasm unless Vicki was at least present at these sessions, and he refused to give them up. For the second time, the couple broke off their affair. The checks stopped, and Alfred had Vicki's Mercedes repossessed.

Vicki launched a lawsuit against Alfred, claiming what she alleged he had promised her. Some time later, steeled by Valium and cocaine, she called him to ask for money. Alfred agreed on condition that she drop her lawsuit.

The fractious couple settled their differences. Vicki dropped her lawsuit and proclaimed herself once again Alfred's mistress. Alfred promised her that she no longer had to participate in or even witness kinky sex as part of her "job," and he reinstated her financially.

By this time, Vicki was ill with unhappiness, spending days in bed and seldom going out. She began to date a movie director and moved in with him. To appease Alfred, she explained—falsely—that her new friend was gay and could help her with movie contacts. When this relationship palled, Vicki decided to marry John David, a serious and struggling actor. She proposed to him suddenly, giving him no time to think about it, and rather than lose this beautiful creature, he accepted and the next day they were married. Within months, Vicki was miserable and longing for the luxuries of life Alfred had provided. The marriage was over, and poor John David was sent packing.

Vicki's life careened from the bizarre (a quasi-abduction to Morocco, where King Hassan made expert love to her; drug-laden lesbian relationships; a return to Alfred Bloomingdale) to the homespun (a real estate developer who wanted to marry her). Vicki's easy lies deceived both men, Alfred, who rented and furnished a new house for her, and Bob Schulman, who wanted to move in with her as her husband. Schulman forced a showdown with Alfred, listening as a trembling Vicki told her lover she was getting married. Bloomingdale was devastated. "Vic, don't do this to me again. Vic, I mean it, I'll die without you."

Vicki and Bob began to plan their wedding, but just before the big day, Vicki was consumed by doubt. Perhaps Bob was too boring? Perhaps she should return to Alfred? She decided that if she could negotiate an acceptable deal to resume her "job" as Alfred's mistress, she would leave Bob. Alfred was eager to talk, but found her demand for one million dollars too high. The ex-lovers haggled, and Alfred capitulated but insisted on a payment schedule. Vicki agreed to half a million right away, the rest in six months.

Vicki was again Alfred's mistress, though she wept when Bob moved out. This time, Alfred attempted to integrate her into his world by providing escorts and having her invited to the social functions he attended with Betsy. Vicki's depression deepened. She often had sex with her paid companions, and she depended on drugs to alleviate her pain.

Vicki's confused thinking reflected her psychological deterioration. She decided that marrying Bob was the best thing after all, and she proposed to him. "I made a mistake by not going through with our wedding," Vicki said. "I hope it's not too late for us."[127] They rushed to Las Vegas, found an all-night chapel and married.

Predictably, Vicki soon regretted this marriage. Leaving her teenaged son, Todd, with Bob, she moved in with Jawajar Bint Saud, known as "J," a drug-addicted Saudi Arabian lesbian princess. The two women, and often their friends and J's hangers-on, lost themselves in heroin and other drugs and liquor, and Vicki and J began to sleep together. Two months later, Vicki checked herself into the Thalians Mental Health Center at Cedars-Sinai Medical Center.

"I am a mistress," she would offer at group therapy sessions. "And what is a mistress? Is she a high-class call girl? A second wife? A friend? For half my life I tried to define it." Just hearing the word *mistress*, she said, made her tremble.[128] Vicki no longer looked or acted like a mistress of any definition. Her behavior was infantile, she stuttered and she had a short attention span. Alfred visited the clinic, posing as her father, and assured her that as soon as she was released, he would buy her a house. He also confided that he had been suffering bad stomach pains, and that he might be dying.

Vicki's therapists urged her to accept her position as a mistress for what it was, with its advantages and disadvantages, rather than lacerating herself as an outcast. Whether she internalized much of this is doubtful, though she reported it to Gordon Basichis, her biographer. Despite months of enforced abstinence from the substances she had abused, Vicki's first thought on leaving the facility was to check into a luxury hotel and to invite a hairdresser she scarcely knew to celebrate her release with champagne and caviar.

After she moved to a house, she brought three women friends to live with her and effectively made one of them, Mary Sangre, her mistress. Vicki had sex with Mary, provided her with large sums of money from Albert's monthly allowance and lent her clothes and a car. When her affair with Mary ended, Alfred expressed regret that Mary was leaving and Vicki would be alone. Finally he explained himself. His stomach pains had become so terrible that he believed he had cancer.

After Alfred escorted Betsy to London to the wedding of Prince Charles and Lady Diana Spencer, he submitted his ravaged body to his doctors. The diagnosis was grim: cancer of the esophagus. Alfred survived for only nine more months, much of them in hospital.

Vicki was terrified. She visited Alfred almost daily, disguised as a nurse. She told Basichis that she actually nursed her dying lover, helping the real nurses to change his bedding and to bathe his decaying body. His pain intensified so that he felt he could not endure it. He lost his hearing and could only communicate by paper and pencil.

Not long after, Alfred's condition had become so precarious that he signed over his power of attorney to Betsy, who stopped Vicki's checks. On July 8, 1982, as Alfred lay dying, Vicki filed a five-million-dollar lawsuit against him. Under the guidance of divorce lawyer Marvin Mitchelson, Vicki alleged that she had sacrificed her personal life to act as Alfred's confidante, traveling companion and business partner in return for lifelong support. Betsy was not intimidated and refused to settle out of court. Six weeks later, Alfred died. Vicki doubled her legal claim to ten million dollars and included Betsy in her action. Two weeks after that, Superior Court judge Christian E. Markey ruled that Vicki had been Alfred's well-paid mistress in a relationship "explicitly founded on meretricious (paid) sexual service. Adulterous, immoral and bordering on the illegal."[129] He accepted only two items in Vicki's plea, contracts Alfred had signed that would be honored after her own death, the money going to her son.

Vicki was nearly broke and was living on the proceeds from the sale of her Mercedes. She decided that her biggest asset would be her memoirs as Alfred's mistress but, despite initial enthusiasm, something frightened off each of the literary agents and publishers she contacted. Finally, she was introduced to Gordon Basichis, a young novelist and scriptwriter who agreed to write her story.

Before many of their grueling interview sessions were over, Basichis and Vicki succumbed to a growing sexual attraction and embarked on an intense affair. Basichis warned her that he had no intention of leaving his wife and infant son. Vicki said she understood, but as time passed, she reacted strongly whenever he had to go home, likening him to Alfred and all the other men who had loved and left her.

During the course of her reminiscences, Vicki invited Marvin Pancoast, whom she had met at the mental clinic, to live with her as a roommate and general factotum. Her clinic physician had cautioned her that in certain moods, Marvin could be dangerous. Vicki disregarded the warning, and Marvin moved in with her.

Basichis observed a sadomasochistic relationship, with Vicki harshly domineering and Marvin abjectly obedient. He cooked, cleaned, laundered, walked the dog and did Vicki's errands, then sought relief in anonymous back-alley sex with other men before creeping back to do Vicki's bidding. But behind her back, he gossiped about her. And one night a while later, he took a baseball bat and cudgeled Vicki Morgan to death. Why? "I was tired of her Queen-of-Sheba attitude," Marvin confessed to police. "I just wanted her to go to sleep."[130]

Vicki Morgan was an extreme example of a mistress as trophy doll. Her short, sad, reckless life was the price she paid for her inability to walk away from Alfred Bloomingdale, his money and his promises, and her own self-loathing, emptiness and fear.

Fallen Women: Mistresses in Literature

MOST genres of literature create worlds that to some degree reflect real life, and many classic novels are devoted to those most familiar and ubiquitous of social institutions, marriage and the mistressdom that so regularly accompanies it. In these invented worlds, fictional lovers often resemble living lovers. Many heroines (or antiheroines) are spinsters seeking a loving marriage, or wives, happily or unhappily married. Others are mistresses enmeshed in illicit relationships forged by love and desire, and occasionally by coercion.

The following are some of the most influential and best-known models of mistressdom to be found in Western literature. Jane Eyre and Countess Ellen Olenska, whose creators forbade them to become mistresses for even the fieriest of loves, are included as well.

These woman's stories have struck such responsive chords in so many readers that almost all have been translated into several languages, adapted for the stage and made into movies. The following discussion does not attempt a literary critique but rather suggests how millions of readers have understood and interpreted these novels, in particular their messages about mistresses and mistressdom.

Jane Eyre [1]
In 1847, Charlotte Brontë, a reserved young parson's daughter, stunned the literary world with *Jane Eyre*, a novel about another reserved young woman

whose love affair remains one of the most powerful ever told. Jane is an unusual heroine, a small and plain orphan. As a resident in a home for genteel but destitute children, Jane is educated to tutor the daughters of the gentry. She becomes expert at the skills these girls will need to impress marriageable young men and their mothers: dancing, painting, fine needlework, speaking French, penmanship. She is also highly principled, independent-minded and morally incorruptible.

Jane is immediately thrust into the real world of illicit love. Her first job is teaching little Adèle, the prattling ward of country gentleman Edward Rochester. Rochester is thirty-five, with a heavy brow, a dark countenance and an irascible nature. With Jane he is alternately stern and distant or teasing and confiding.

In one such intimate moment, Rochester reveals that Adèle is the natural child of his one-time mistress Céline Varens, a deceased French "opera-dancer." He tells Jane that because he believed this "Gallic sylph" adored him despite his unhandsome appearance, he "installed her in a hotel; gave her a complete establishment of servants, a carriage, cashmeres, diamonds, dentelles, etc." One evening Rochester surprised his mistress with another lover, "a brainless and vicious youth." Tortured by jealousy, he stood unobserved, eavesdropping on their coarse and mindless chatter. When Céline mocked him as a man so ugly he was deformed, she cured him instantly of his "grand passion" for her.

The affair ended then and there. Rochester marched into Céline's hotel room and ordered her to vacate it. Then he challenged her lover to a duel and left a bullet "in one of his poor, etiolated arms." But what to do with the infant Adèle, whom Rochester had assumed—wrongly—was his daughter? "I . . . took the poor thing out of the slime and out of Paris," he explained to Jane, "and transplanted it here, to grow up clean in the wholesome soil of an English country garden."

Rochester's story encapsulates his views about mistresses, and Jane shares them. A mistress is a fallen woman of limited intellectuality and morals. She is treacherous and mercenary, unstable and often foreign, and any man who consorts with her does so at his peril.

Although a "quaint, inexperienced" eighteen-year-old governess may not seem to be a suitable confidante for such raunchy revelations, Jane accepts his story as a tribute to her discretion. She is equally discreet about the madwoman hidden in his attic. Before long, Jane realizes that she is deeply in love with Mr. Rochester.

Mr. Rochester, however, ostentatiously courts a rich and snobbish beauty Jane believes he will marry. But he manipulates the situation so Jane cannot restrain herself from declaring her love for him. "Do you think because I am poor, obscure, plain, and little, I am soulless and heartless?" Hearing this, Mr. Rochester proposes marriage. "I offer you my hand, my heart, and a share of all my possessions," he says. "I ask you to pass through life at my side—to be my second self and best earthly companion."

Mr. Rochester reassures her that he has never intended to marry anyone else. Jane is marvelously happy except for a nagging concern about her lack of financial resources. "I will not be your English Céline Varens," she announces. "I shall continue to act as Adèle's governess."

Their wedding day arrives. But as they stand at the altar in front of the priest who is marrying them, a stranger interrupts the ceremony and declares, "Mr. Rochester has a wife now living."

Jane's world is shattered. The woman hidden away in Mr. Rochester's attic is his legal wife, the "mad, bad and embruted" Bertha Mason, the poisonous seed of three generations of madwomen, foreigners to boot. Jane has narrowly avoided making Mr. Rochester a bigamist. Worse, "That man had nearly made me his mistress: I must be ice and rock to him," she vows.

Desperate, Mr. Rochester implores Jane to join him in the south of France, where they will live as man and wife. "Never fear that I wish to lure you into error," he pleads, "to make you my mistress." To convince her of this, Rochester describes the two mistresses who followed Céline Varens, the "unprincipled and violent" Italian, Giacinta, and the "heavy, mindless, unimpressible" German, Clara. "It was a grovelling fashion of existence. Hiring a mistress is the next worse thing to buying a slave: both are often by nature, and always by position, inferior. . . . I now hate the recollection of the time I passed with Céline, Giacinta, and Clara."

To avoid the temptation of becoming Mr. Rochester's English mistress, Jane flees into the countryside. She wanders penniless, frozen and nearly starved, from place to place, and at last stumbles into the hands of two devout sisters and their fanatically religious brother, St. John Rivers. After nursing Jane back to health, the siblings provide her with a modest but honorable living teaching rural children. Sometimes Jane aches for what she has rejected, "living in France, Mr. Rochester's mistress; delirious with his love half my time . . . a slave in a fool's paradise at Marseilles."

Jane's simple life is complicated by a proposal of marriage from St. John, who wishes her to accompany him to India as a missionary. Jane does not love him and knows that he only sees her as a helpmeet. As she wrestles with her decision, she learns that an unknown uncle has died and left her a fortune. Suddenly independent, Jane hastens across the countryside to find Mr. Rochester, whom she can now befriend without becoming his mistress.

Mr. Rochester is a ruined man. His insane wife has burned down their house and lost her life in the conflagration. Mr. Rochester has survived, badly burned and blinded, and as deeply in love with Jane as she still is with him. "Jane, will you marry me?" he asks gently. "Yes, sir," she replies, her heart full of joy and contentment.

Jane's iron will and strength of character, fortified by several improbable plotlines, has rescued her from the ignominy of mistressdom. Only in marriage, Charlotte Brontë tells us, can Jane revel in the magnetic power of her mutual attraction to Mr. Rochester.

Hester Prynne [2]

Ever since she strode into American literature in 1850, the Puritan renegade Hester Prynne has symbolized sexual defiance and adultery. American Nathaniel Hawthorne set *The Scarlet Letter*, his novel of guilt and redemption, in the 17th-century Puritan theocracy of Boston, Massachusetts, where adultery was a crime as well as an unforgivable sin.

The Scarlet Letter introduces Hester as she exits the colonial prison where she has been confined for having committed adultery. Hester is an English immigrant whose husband has not yet joined her in America. Hester's pregnancy and infant daughter's birth prove that she has had an extramarital affair. Worse, she has steadfastly refused to identify her lover.

Hester is described in the book as remarkably beautiful. She is tall and curvaceous, with thick dark hair "so glossy that it threw off the sunshine with a gleam." She is elegant and graceful, a dignified woman who seems uncowed by her predicament. As her disgruntled countrywomen watch, Hester carries her infant daughter, Pearl, up to the scaffold where—in lieu of a death sentence—she has been condemned to stand for three hours in all her shame.

In addition to this public exposure on the pillory, her judges have decreed that for the rest of her life, Hester must wear the letter "A" on her breast, an immutable symbol of her crime. But Hester has confounded them; she now wears a stunning scarlet "A" embroidered so lavishly that it seems to set her apart from the rest of humanity rather than symbolize her shame.

The women spectators are furious and vindictive. "This woman has brought shame upon us all, and ought to die," rages the ugliest and most merciless of the matrons. A cleric, the Reverend Arthur Dimmesdale, beseeches Hester "to speak out the name of thy fellow-sinner and fellow sufferer!" "Never!" Hester cries. "And would that I might endure his agony, as well as mine!" "Wondrous strength and generosity of a woman's heart!" Reverend Dimmesdale exclaims in awe.

After her public ordeal, Hester is returned to prison. When little Pearl falls ill, the authorities summon a physician. He is Roger Chillingworth, the humpbacked man Hester has earlier recognized in the crowd, the unloved husband who has finally followed her out to the New World.

The aptly named Chillingworth reproaches Hester, but also declares his own culpability in her tragedy, for her situation cannot be called anything else. "From the moment when we came down the old church-steps together," he declares, "a married pair, I might have beheld the bale-fire of that scarlet letter blazing at the end of our path!"

Hester interjects, "I was frank with thee. I felt no love, nor feigned any."

Chillingworth agrees, but explains how he has longed to spark in her the passion he feels in himself. Admittedly she has betrayed him with another man, yet "mine was the first wrong, when I betrayed thy budding youth into a false and unnatural relation with my decay. . . . Between thee and me, the scale hangs fairly balanced."

Despite her husband's understanding, Hester refuses his request to name her elusive paramour. Chillingworth vows to ferret him out, presumably to expose him as an adulterer and indict him for it. Meanwhile, Chillingworth swears Hester to silence about his own identity.

After seven years, Hester is released from jail, still unrepentant about her forbidden love. She even dreams of the man "with whom she deemed herself connected in a union." Hester becomes the colony's most sought after seamstress. She also donates food and clothes to paupers and comforts suffering and needy women.

Like most fallen women, Hester's greatest vulnerability is her child. Can a sinner such as she, her puritanical co-citizens debate, be permitted to raise Pearl? Hester launches a frantic appeal to the Reverend Dimmesdale, who intercedes with the colonial authorities on her behalf. Pearl remains with her mother.

Meanwhile, Chillingworth identifies the ailing and now celibate Dimmesdale as Hester's lover. "This man, spiritual as he seems, hath inherited a strong animal nature from his father or his mother," he muses. "Let us dig a little farther in the direction of this vein." With Hester powerless to stop him, Chillingworth pretends concern for Dimmesdale's health and moves in with him to become his resident physician.

One day, Hester encounters Dimmesdale in the forest. He tells her of his despair at his sinfulness and declares that her scarlet letter is a solace, unlike his secret shame. Hester responds that his shame is not entirely secret, for a man who knows that they were once lovers now lives under his very roof. Dimmesdale is horrified. "That old man's revenge has been blacker than my sin," he says bitterly. "He has violated in cold blood, the sanctity of a human heart. Thou and I, Hester, never did so!"

"Never, never!" Hester concurs. "What we did had a consecration of its own. We felt it so! We said so to each other!" After this articulation of the intense sexual bond between them, Hester convinces Dimmesdale to flee with her to Europe and free himself from Roger Chillingworth's villainous vigilance. "The future is yet full of trial and success. There is happiness to be enjoyed! There is good to be done!" In preparation for their new life together, Hester rips off her scarlet letter.

But Chillingworth discovers and foils his wife's desperate scheme, and her sickly coconspirator cannot survive this latest blow. In the novel's grand finale, Dimmesdale mounts the infamous scaffold, and Hester and their daughter, Pearl, join him. By this final and belated surrender to Puritan justice, Dimmesdale has destroyed Chillingworth's hold over him. "Hadst thou sought the whole earth over," the frustrated Chillingworth complains, "there was no place . . . thou couldst have escaped me—save on this very scaffold!"

As the Puritans watch, Dimmesdale kisses his daughter and bids Hester farewell. "Shall we not meet again?" she whispers. "Shall we not spend our immortal life together? Surely, surely, we have ransomed one another, with all this woe!"

Dimmesdale dies, and Chillingworth soon follows him. Hester becomes the colony's wise woman, and she promises women made wretched by "the continually recurring trials of wounded, wasted, wronged, misplaced, or erring and sinful passion" that in a future terrestrial paradise, men and women will revel in relationships grounded in "mutual happiness."

When she is very old, Hester dies and joins Dimmesdale under a single tombstone, though her remains lie slightly apart from his, "as if the dust of the two sleepers had no right to mingle." Even in death, life's rigid rules govern them.

"As a great moral lesson this novel will outweigh in its influence all the sermons that have ever been preached against the sin . . . The Scarlet Letter is written to exhibit," enthused the *Boston Transcript* in March 1850.³ But what did Hawthorne's contemporaries take from his cautionary and best-selling romance? In their time, when romantic love was increasingly valued as a motive for marriage, Hawthorne gave Hester spectacular beauty but burdened her with a deformed and repellent husband who leaves her to her own devices in a hostile and alien land. Even so, when she and a young clergyman succumb to their passion, her punishment is necessarily lifelong.

But surely readers took more than that from Hester's story. Some of them must have admired how Hester endures mortal hardship for the sake of a man she loves and who loves her until death. Romantic and erotic love lasts forever, readers may have mused, and its strength and immutability are measures by which a woman may identify it. Taking a lover, becoming a mistress, is sinful and wrong. At the same time, true love makes its own rules even as society imposes other, harsher ones. Readers tasted, in the pages of *The Scarlet Letter*, the depth and power of Hester and Arthur's ardor, including their physical and erotic bond.

Surprisingly, Hawthorne permits Hester to raise her love child, though for purposes of plot development and authenticity he forces her to plead with authorities who deem her an unfit mother not to take Pearl away. Dimmesdale's timely intervention saves the situation, and Hester is never again in danger of losing her daughter.

And so *The Scarlet Letter* teaches wildly discrepant lessons: that illicit love, no matter how pitiable the circumstances that prompt it, is wrong and must be severely punished; that illicit love can be mightier and more glorious than laws and even marriage; and that virtue and sin are seldom as antithetical as they are usually portrayed, and may each partake of elements of the other. No wonder women sneak over to Hester's cottage for advice about their own affairs of the heart and soul—who better than she to understand and guide them?

Hester Prynne is sexuality incarnate, yet in no way depraved. She gives herself to a man other than her husband because she values love over duty. Despite social censure and severe punishment, she never regrets her decision. As 19th-century critic Anthony Trollope noted, "there has been no taint of foulness in her love, though there has been deep sin."⁴ Hester's adultery is the result of such profound love, and her nobility and fortitude contrast so sharply with the vindictiveness of her close-minded Puritan society, that her role as a mistress becomes morally ambiguous. In the end she loses her lover but not his love, and earns such widespread respect that she becomes the guardian angel of other unhappy women.

Emma Bovary [5]

A few years later, Emma Bovary, heroine of Gustave Flaubert's *Madame Bovary*, published in 1857 and set in Normandy in the 1830s and 1840s, joined Hester Prynne as another literary model for the errant wife-*cum*-mistress. Like Hester, Emma is sensual, so profoundly so that critic Harold Bloom ranks her as possibly "the most persuasively sensual of all fictive beings."[6] After one writing session, Flaubert wrote to Louise Colet, his mistress, that he "was so swept away, was bellowing so loudly and feeling so deeply what my little Bovary was going through . . . [that I feel] like a man who has ———ed too much (forgive me the expression)—a kind of rapturous lassitude."[7]

In the novel, thirteen-year-old Emma Bovary, the daughter of a prosperous farmer, enters a convent that will dramatically shape her views of life. Emma loves the mystery, drama and symbols of the convent. She revels in the splendor of the stained glass, the quasi-erotic metaphors for Christ as the Bridegroom, the incense, the flowers on the altar. She is also deeply affected by an old woman who works as a laundress at the convent, a former aristocrat who has been ruined by the French Revolution. This lady regales the students with 18th-century love songs, gossips about her days at court and lends them forbidden novels about love and love affairs, mistresses and their lovers, "broken hearts, vows, sobs, tears and kisses, skiffs in the moonlight, nightingales in thickets." Emma is particularly struck by the stories' heroic noblemen, "all brave as lions, gentle as lambs, incredibly virtuous, always beautifully dressed, and [who] wept copiously on every occasion." Emma has an equally high regard for the French king Louis XIV and his mistress, Louise de La Vallière, as well as for Héloise, mistress of 12th-century French philosopher Abélard.

Emma leaves the convent several years later, and meets her future husband, Charles Bovary, a doctor, then wretchedly married to an older widow. Charles is entranced by the spirited young woman with deep brown eyes that fearlessly hold his gaze, lustrous wings of black hair and a figure that will later captivate other men as well. In short order, he falls in love with her, his sour and jealous wife dies, and Emma and her father delightedly accept his proposal of marriage.

From the very beginning, marriage disappoints Emma. She has expected romantic love of the sort she has read about, but though Charles adores her, he is far from the man of her dreams. This includes the sexual dimension; though their wedding night fills him with joy, she is unmoved even by the loss of her virginity.

The everyday rural life that charms Charles bores and dismays Emma. If only, she muses, they could travel to some exotic place graced by lemon trees and waterfalls—or snowy mountains, or melancholy moors—then they might ignite the fiery love that burns, she thinks, only in such places. Emma tries reciting love poems by moonlight, but nothing much happens.

Emma's dissatisfaction grows. She buys a map of Paris and daydreams. She longs to travel, to return to the convent, to die, to live in Paris. Emma is so starved for companionship that even "the logs in the fireplace and the pendulum of the clock" seem possible confidants. She pours out her heart to her Italian greyhound.

Finally, in response to Emma's alternating despondency and hysteria, Charles moves the family to another town. There Emma has a daughter, Berthe. After she sends Berthe to live with a wet nurse, Emma begins a chaste flirtation with Léon, a young clerk.

Léon moves away to complete his studies. Soon Emma attracts the admiring attention of Rodolphe Boulanger, a wealthy landowner and an experienced rake who considers her a very pretty woman "gasping for love like a carp on a kitchen table gasping for water." Rodolphe has no doubt he can entice her into bed and make her his mistress. But "how would I get rid of her later?" he asks himself.

Seducing Emma is as easy as Rodolphe has imagined. He brushes aside her moral objections with grand declarations about the banality of convention and contrasts it with the splendor of eternal morality, which he defines as the belief that passion is the most beautiful thing in the world. Before long, "her resistance gone, weeping, hiding her face, with a long shudder she gave herself to him."

Afterward Emma repeats joyously, "I have a lover! I have a lover!" At last she has become a mistress, one of the intriguing figures she has never ceased reading about since her convent days. "Love, so long repressed, was gushing forth in joyful effervescence. She savored it without remorse, without anxiety, without distress."

Yet Emma cannot sustain her initial frenzy of happiness. She takes to dropping in on Rodolphe until one day he warns her that she is risking her reputation. Emma is unmoved. She intensifies the affair and speaks so sentimentally that Rodolphe begins to tire of her.

The loss of her romantic illusions grieves her. In each stage of her life, "as virgin, as wife, as mistress," she has seen her dreams shattered. She tries to revive her marriage by attempting to transform Charles into a famous (and hence rich and respected) doctor. She encourages him to perform an ambitious, tricky operation, straightening a clubfoot. His spectacularly botched surgery enrages Emma and drives her with renewed ardor back into Rodolphe's arms.

In fact, the more she loves Rodolphe, the more she detests Charles. In Emma's view, Rodolphe's body is powerful without coarseness, his judgment cool, his passion fiery. Adoring him, Emma keeps herself elegant and desirable, "a courtesan awaiting a prince."

Increasingly, Emma devotes herself to the Byzantine complications of managing her romance within the confines of her travesty of a marriage. The costs are not merely emotional and moral. She also deals with a treacherous merchant who supplies her every material need—for gorgeous clothing and accessories, for (unwanted) gifts to her lover, for anything that strikes her thirsty fancy—and she begins to accumulate impossible debt. Knowingly, and without qualms, she also squanders Charles's inheritance to satisfy her need for luxury and comfort, acquiring the trappings of happiness she imagines but does not feel.

Four years pass, during which Emma's malaise deepens. Finally she implores Rodolphe to run away with her to another country. "You're my everything," she exclaims. "And I'll be yours. I'll be your family, your country; I'll look after you, I'll love you." Horrified at her neediness and her grandiose expectations for their love affair, Rodolphe pretends to agree to her plan but makes secret arrangements to leave her. "But she certainly made a pretty mistress!" he reminds himself. Rummaging in a box where he stores keepsakes from former mistresses, he can scarcely distinguish one from the other. Then he sits down and writes Emma a letter of farewell. "I'll never forget you," he writes, "but some day sooner or later our passion would have cooled—inevitably—it's the way with everything human." After much reflection he signs it, "Your friend."

Emma's suffering at Rodolphe's defection is terrible, and she must endure it in silence. She finds solace in religion and dreams of becoming a saint. She devotes herself to charitable activities. And then, at a performance of *Lucia di Lammermoor* that Charles hopes might lift her spirits, the Bovarys run into young Léon, who has completed his studies and is now working in an office.

Purpose returns to Emma's life. Léon loves her unreservedly. Emma hurls herself into this affair as she did the previous one. She hounds Charles for weekly piano lessons that serve as her cover to meet Léon in a special hotel room they speak of as their eternal home. He adores her—isn't she refined and elegant, a " 'lady,' and married besides? Everything, in short, that a mistress should be?"

Sometimes Emma worries that Léon will break off with her to marry someone else. Though she is happy, she still dreams of escaping to Paris. Never quite content with what she has, she buys more goods from the merchant and demands more time with Léon, whom she calls away from his office though his employer complains. Léon is still too ensnared to resist her. In fact, "he was becoming her mistress, far more than she was his. Her sweet words and her kisses swept away his soul. Her depravity was so deep and so dissembled as to be almost intangible: where could she have learned it?"

But Emma, like Rodolphe, has trouble staying in love. Dreading its absence, she flings herself even more violently into the relationship. She is sexually rapacious, stripping off her clothes and shuddering as she presses her naked body against Léon's. Her fervor, single-mindedness and possessiveness alarm him. His employer warns him against her. In any case, their love is beginning to drain away. Even Emma now feels adultery to be as banal as marriage.

Meanwhile, the merchant calls in her exorbitant loans. Frantic and furious, Emma tries everywhere to borrow enough money to stave him off. She even urges Léon to embezzle money to save her, but he refuses. When a wealthy notary attempts to trade money for her sexual favors, she angrily rejects him. "I'm to be pitied, but I'm not for sale!" she cries.

Her final plea is to Rodolphe, whom she has not seen for years. He, too, refuses her. Her last hope smashed, she knows that she and Charles are ruined. She swallows arsenic, then endures an agonizing death rather than reveal the name of the poison so Charles can provide an antidote. As she dies, she sees in her husband's eyes "a love such as she had never known." Emma asks for her mirror, gazes at her image and weeps.

What Emma sees is the image of waste: beauty wasted on unworthy lovers; wifehood wasted on an insensitive husband; motherhood wasted on a girl child born to share her own constricted possibilities; a romantic heart incapable of fulfillment; raging emotions with no outlet; ferocious passions out of tune with the provincial backwater she has been fated to live in.

Emma is presented as intelligent, reasonably well educated and aware of her role in society. She is resentfully aware that her gender dooms her to a life confined to home and husband, but she assumes—wrongly—that marriage will be the locus of the romantic love that her books seem to promise will enthrall her forever. When disabused of this fantasy, Emma seeks other means—and other men—to satisfy herself.

But what about morals? Aren't Emma's lies, deceptions and convoluted schemes, her cry of wonderment—"I have a lover!"—expressions of immorality that mark her as a wanton with no regard for her society's principles and her religion's ideals? Isn't her hideous, drawn-out suicide punishment for a sexual sinner? Certainly this is what Flaubert suggests, even as he links Emma's downfall to her financial dereliction. All that she has valued is love, her four years as Rodolphe's mistress and later as Léon's. In that equation, her doting (if dull) husband and blameless daughter, her marriage and her motherhood count for nothing. Flaubert (who during the long composition of this novel broke off with Louise Colet, his own mistress) kills off Emma to redeem himself from the charge of condoning her immorality, of implying that an adulterous mistress has the right to thrive, let alone survive.

This is not supposition. When *Madame Bovary* was first published serially in 1856 in the *Revue de Paris*, Flaubert and the magazine were formally charged with offending public morality. Flaubert triumphed in court by arguing that Emma's death was evidence that his novel upheld moral standards by subjecting her to the consequences of her sin.

But, as Flaubert intended, millions of ordinary readers have taken away more from Emma's story than her unhappy end. They remember the intensity of her passions—for religious ecstasy, for her lovers and, in the negative forms of contempt and loathing, for her husband. They sympathize with her attempts to love the bumbling and kindly Charles, and with her frustration at her condition as a woman trapped by her society's rigid expectations.

French poet Charles Baudelaire justified Emma's constant search for passionate experience, and her impatience with anything extraneous to her affairs of the heart: "This woman is truly great and above all pitiable. All *intellectual* women will be grateful to [Flaubert] for having raised the female to so high a level—so far from the pure animal and so near to the ideal man—and for having made her share in that combination of calculation and reverie which constitutes the perfect being."[8] In Baudelaire's interpretation, it is no wonder that Emma so easily sacrifices her moral values to become Rodolphe's mistress and then rejoices at what she believes this relationship will bring her.

Most readers do not exonerate Emma Bovary as completely as Baudelaire did. They see her both as a metaphor for soulless and greedy bourgeois society and as an authentic portrait of a woman who subverts her society's values, injecting the *force majeure* of passion into her own unfulfilled life by becoming the mistress (or concubine, as she puts it) of the two men she loves but is not married to.

Anna Karenina [9]

Anna Karenina, the title character of Russian writer Leo Tolstoy's 1877 novel, towers as one of literature's most fascinating and tragic fallen women. *Anna Karenina* is set in Saint Petersburg in the 1870s, and its main characters are Russian aristocrats. With his opening sentence, "Happy families are all alike; every unhappy family is unhappy in its own way," Tolstoy thrusts us into the painfully unsettled family life of Stiva, whose wife, Dolly, has just discovered that he has had an affair with the children's French governess. Anna, Stiva's sister and the dutiful wife of Aleksey Aleksandrovich Karenin, a powerful official, hastens to mediate and succeeds in patching up her brother's floundering marriage.

Soon after, the lovely Anna meets Count Alexey Kirilich Vronsky, an unmarried army officer. Suddenly she sees her husband with newly critical eyes—his ears stick out strangely, for instance—and daydreams about the dashing and daring Vronsky.

Vronsky's credo is that "the position of a man pursuing a married woman, and staking his life on drawing her into adultery, has something fine and grand about it." Inevitably, he and Anna succumb to their burning mutual desire. Extramarital affairs were by no means unusual among 19th-century Russian aristocrats, most of whom made marriages of convenience, but Anna and Vronsky reject settling for a pleasurable, safe sexual interlude. Instead, they long for grand passion, commitment, permanence and social acceptance.

Nonetheless, Anna refuses to seek the divorce that would permit the couple to regularize their relationship because the law would automatically award her husband sole custody of her son. At the same time, she cannot control her emotions, and when her suspicious husband questions her, she replies with harsh and singularly unwise frankness that she has a lover. She adds, "I love him, I am his mistress; I can't bear you; I'm afraid of you, and I hate you."

Karenin, assuming Anna will eventually repent, behaves admirably. The marriage will continue, he decides, in form if not substance, and time will heal all wounds. But Anna, desperate not to lose Vronsky, refuses to cooperate. She reminds herself that Karenin "crushed my life for eight years, crushed everything that was living in me. He had not once given thought that I'm a live woman who must have love. . . . Haven't I tried, with all my strength, to find something to give meaning to my life? Haven't I struggled to love him, to love my son when I could not love my husband? . . . God has made me so that I must love and live." Vronsky, just as deeply in love, concurs, especially as Anna has just told him that she is pregnant with his baby.

After a series of complications, Anna abandons her husband and her son, and Vronsky his regiment and career. They travel together around Europe until their daughter is born. Their return to Russia is sobering. Friends and relatives warmly welcome Vronsky, and just as deliberately ostracize Anna. She is devastated. Her first reaction is to force the issue, showing up at social events as if her status has not changed.

Vronsky is both saddened and horrified. To "show yourself at the theater is equivalent not merely to acknowledging your position as a fallen woman," he thinks but dares not tell her, "but is flinging down the gauntlet to society, that is to say, cutting yourself off from it forever." The outing is disastrous. Soon after, she, Vronsky and their little daughter move permanently to his country estate.

For a time, Anna is happy: "Something magical has happened to me," she confides to her sister-in-law, Dolly, one of the few people who still maintain contact with her. "I have lived through the misery, the dread, and now for a long while past, especially since we've been here, I've been so happy!"

Her happiness quickly erodes. She cannot see her son and she is unable to truly love her daughter, who under Russian law is surnamed Karenin and subject to her still undivorced husband's control. Vronsky is worried because as long as they are unmarried, every child they have will be legally Karenin's. He urges Anna to negotiate a divorce, and she reluctantly agrees to do so.

Meanwhile, she reads intensively, and is Vronsky's intellectual companion as well as his mistress. But in her isolation and loneliness, she demands that he devote his entire life to her. The more exacting she becomes, the colder he grows. Terrified at the prospect of losing him, she resorts to subterfuge, hysterical scenes and unfounded accusations. Once, in a moment of blinding clarity, she understands how she is destroying herself. "My love keeps growing more passionate and selfish, while his is dying, and that's why we're drifting apart," she muses.

> He is everything to me, and I want him more and more to give himself up to me entirely. . . . If I could be anything but a mistress, passionately caring for nothing but his caresses; but I can't and I don't care to be

anything else. And by that desire I rouse aversion in him, and he rouses fury in me, and it cannot be different. . . . For a long time now he hasn't loved me. And where love ends, hate begins.

Later the same day, standing at the train station, Anna decides to throw herself under the wheels of the oncoming train to "punish him and escape from everyone and from myself." At the last moment, on her knees on the track, a joyful hope seizes her and she tries to rise. It is too late. Seconds later, the "huge and merciless" metal giant crushes the life out of her. It is, Vronsky's embittered mother believes, "the fitting end for such a woman. Even the death she chose was coarse and vulgar."

In valuing love and desire over marriage and motherhood, Anna Karenina does more than forsake her husband and son. She also defies her social peers, challenges Russian society and scorns the standards that underlie Russia's aristocratic world. In doing all this for the sake of a love she believes will give her empty life its meaning, Anna symbolizes an echelon of privileged 19th-century European women whose intelligence was underrated and creativity stifled, so that what was left to them was the tedium and triviality of life in arranged marriages in which they were both subordinate and vulnerable. Tolstoy originally titled his novel *Two Marriages*, and indeed, the Karenins' marriage is a central theme.

Perhaps to underscore the hopelessness of her situation, Tolstoy does not even give Anna the sort of lover she might have expected. Instead, Anna has Vronsky, unmarried, handsome, wealthy, admired and in many ways admirable, loyal, committed and, until quite near the end, as deeply in love with her as she is with him.

Yet even Vronsky cannot protect Anna from the world. In the eyes of society and almost everyone she has ever known, her mistressdom renders her disgraced and powerless, a pariah who has only herself to blame for her plight. But before Tolstoy condemns this magnificently fallen woman to fall yet again, this time in front of an onrushing train, he grants her a moment of the kind of soaring happiness she yearned for when she became Vronsky's mistress.

Mildred Rogers [10]

British novelist Somerset Maugham's *Of Human Bondage*, published in 1915 and set in late-19th-century London, introduces a very different type of mistress, a working-class woman taken up by a struggling medical student. Philip Carey is Byronically clubfooted, intelligent and orphaned, the beneficiary of a modest legacy. Mildred Rogers, a waitress in a teashop he and other medical students frequent, is tall, reed-thin and anemically pale, but her small, fine features and blue eyes lend her a timeless beauty.

For some time Philip is as indifferent to Mildred as she is to him, and he dismisses her as an "ill-mannered slut." Yet her insolence and hostility intrigue him, and against his better judgment, he begins to pursue her. "You are a stoodent [sic] aren't you?" Mildred asks incuriously at one point, then leaves him to immerse herself in a cheap romance novel.

Despite all Philip's efforts, Mildred ignores him while she flirts with other customers. She accepts his invitation to dinner ungraciously, and only champagne livens her conversation. Philip realizes that they are hopelessly incompatible. Nonetheless, he falls in love with her.

This obsession with her is not the ecstatic experience he has expected. It is, rather, "a hunger of the soul, it was a painful yearning, it was a bitter anguish . . . When she left him it was wretchedness, and when she came to him again it was despair."

No wonder: Mildred makes pointed references to his clubfoot, and lets him know that she much prefers other men. She lies to him about her origins, claiming that her father is well connected and that it is difficult for her "having to mix with them girls in the [tea]shop."

Once, when she cancels a date because a more appealing man has invited her out, Philip admits that he loves her with all his heart and threatens that if she doesn't go out with him that night, she will never see him again. "You seem to think that'll be an awful thing for me," Mildred retorts. "All I say is, good riddance to bad rubbish."

Philip neglects his studies and fails a final exam. Meanwhile, Mildred regrets having rejected him for a man who wants only to seduce her. They reunite, and Philip courts her in earnest. He wines and dines her, gives her gifts he cannot afford, declares his longing for her and disregards every instinct warning him that he is heading for disaster. When she permits Philip to kiss her, he knows that she neither minds nor likes it. Most galling of all, she still dates other men.

In fact, Mildred does not even like Philip. He irks her with questions about her feelings for him, torments her with his obsessive jealousy and generally irritates her. He even spies on her. He is, she makes plain, nothing more than a temporary convenience.

Nonetheless, Philip proposes to her. Mildred is amused and flattered, but rejects him when she (correctly) calculates that his salary as a physician will not provide her a much better living than she currently has. Philip accepts this and continues to see her anyway. One day she initiates a rendezvous and, excitedly, he agrees. Mildred has news, she says—she is getting married. Philip grieves, buys her an expensive present and counts down the days until her wedding.

Philip's pain lessens, and he begins to remember Mildred with hatred for the humiliations she rained on him. He meets and spends delightful days with Norah, a single mother who supports herself by writing trashy romance novels. Then one day, Mildred seeks him out in his room. "What the hell d'you want?" Philip growls.

As soon as he says this, Mildred bursts into hopeless weeping. Her "husband" has not married her for the excellent reason that he already has a wife and children, and after she, too, became pregnant, he reacted furiously and left her without a penny. "If you want me still I'll do anything you like now," she tells Philip humbly.

Philip realizes he is still in love with Mildred and breaks off his relationship with Norah. Eroding the small capital that is his only resource to support his studies, he installs Mildred in pleasant lodgings. Almost from the beginning, Philip is back in her thrall. He protects Mildred by introducing himself to her landlady as her brother.

Mildred's hopes that her child will be stillborn are dashed when she delivers a healthy little girl. She finds her daughter a foster home out in the countryside, then she and Griffiths, a visiting friend of Philip's, fall in love. Philip forces a showdown and Mildred tells him, "I never liked you, not from the beginning, but you forced yourself on me, I always hated it when you kissed me. I wouldn't let you touch me now, not if I was starving."

Griffiths turns out to be fickle and penniless, but her fling with him has made Mildred realize how much Philip revolts her. Griffiths, however, finding her vulgar and tedious, leaves her. Mildred bombards him with letters and telegrams, and stalks him. Once she spends the night sobbing on his doorstep.

The next time Philip sees Mildred, she is soliciting men in central London. She is no gladder to see him than the day she left him, but he persuades her to talk to him in a dismal rented room. Up close, Philip notices that despite her garish makeup, she looks ill and exhausted. She has not contacted him, she says listlessly, because she has assumed he would think she has gotten no more than she deserves. "If I could only get out of it!" she moans. "I hate it so. I'm unfit for the life, I'm not the sort of girl for that. . . . Oh, I wish I was dead."

Philip responds on cue. He urges her to come and live in his spare room, assuming the housekeeping duties he is currently paying for. The trio—he, she and her child—will live almost as cheaply as he is by this time obliged to do. Furthermore, he will expect no sexual payback. He does not tell her that this is because for the first time he feels physical revulsion for her and is overjoyed to think that it must signal the end of his passion for her.

Mildred weeps with gratitude and moves in the next day. She begins to make tentative sexual gestures that Philip rejects. Another time, she informs him sullenly that she has learned to love him. But more and more, Philip realizes that the woman he has loved so frantically for so long is unintelligent, crass mannered and as boring as she is bored.

Mildred, meanwhile, is determined to seduce him, to reestablish her former dominance over him through sexual relations. She will make him love her, she decides. She declares her love for him and plops herself onto his lap. "I'm very sorry, but it's too late," Philip responds.

Mildred's invective stuns him. "I never cared for you, not once, I was making a fool of you always, you bored me, you bored me stiff, and I hated you . . . and it used to make me sick when I had to let you kiss me. . . . Cripple!"

The next day, when Philip is out, Mildred trashes their lodgings, smashing, ripping, shredding, then takes the baby and leaves. Philip moves to much cheaper lodgings, immerses himself in his studies and tries to recoup his financial losses on the stock market. Instead, he loses everything, can find no relatives to loan him money and is forced to abandon medical school.

After months of job-hunting, Philip is homeless and close to starvation. Family friends take him in and find him a low-paying job. He grows fonder and fonder of Sally, his friends' daughter.

Mildred reappears, begging him to see her. Her baby has died; she is again a prostitute and has contracted venereal disease. Philip buys her medicine and makes her promise to stop soliciting and infecting new people. Terrified, Mildred promises, but he soon discovers that she is back out on the streets, her condition temporarily assuaged. "What do I care?" she cries. "Men haven't been so good to me that I need bother my head about them." This is the last time Philip sees her.

Philip's uncle dies, leaving him enough money to resume and finish his medical studies. He graduates, finds work and is happy. He also knows that for the rest of his live, he will never quite lose his "strange, desperate thirst for that vile woman" who is Mildred.

No word of pity for Mildred, the painted and infectious streetwalker who cannot love the one man who loves her. *Of Human Bondage* is written entirely from Philip's perspective, with Mildred merely an appendage to the story of his tribulations and triumphs. Nor is Mildred (as shown, glimpsed or read between the lines) a sympathetic character, a whore with a heart of gold. Maugham portrays her as a relentlessly cold and calculating slattern.

As the novel's central female protagonist, Mildred faces the usual choices of how to live her life. Until her world collapses, her goal is marriage and the respectability and financial security she assumes it will bring her. When she finds herself pregnant and unmarried, she tries to conceal her predicament by calling herself Mrs. Miller, the name of her baby's father.

Mildred also craves the romance she reads about in romance novels. When she thinks she has found it—with Miller, and even more so with Griffiths—she forgoes marriage and becomes a mistress. Indeed, she rejects Philip, who desperately wants to marry her, because she finds him physically repulsive. Throughout their fragmented and torturous relationship, they never sleep together. Mildred only attempts to seduce him when she is destitute and ailing because he can give her more money than she is earning as a prostitute.

As Miller's mistress—Griffiths, who sees her only as a weekend fling, scarcely counts—Mildred is the woman betrayed, promised marriage then tricked into mistressdom. The case is classic, right down to her abandonment when she becomes pregnant. As Philip's quasi-mistress, though sex remains out of the equation, she is equally obliged, bound to this man by his love for her and her poverty rather than, as in Miller's case, her love for him.

Of Human Bondage remains one of the few classic novels about a working-class mistress. Maugham's depiction of a woman who loves only the wrong men and falls into trap after trap on the doomed path of her life's journey is merciless. Mildred seems devoid of redeeming qualities, and Philip, her foil, is a self-absorbed antihero. Yet readers find her story compelling, though many must wonder if the price she pays for her errors of birth and circumstances is excessive, and Maugham's—and Philip's—indifference to her fate disturbing and vindictive.

Ellen Olenska [11]

Edith Wharton's finely wrought novel *The Age of Innocence* is set in New York in the last two decades before World War I and centers on a love story between a woman separated from her husband and her cousin's fiancé and later husband. Their relationship develops and is shaped by the patrician New York society they belong to, in which suitable marriages ally two families, last a lifetime and incorporate the values of their members' social order. The novel also reflects Wharton's personal beliefs, with protagonist Newland Archer expressing many of her reflections and conclusions.

May Welland is the perfect bride for Newland Archer, and their families both rejoice when Newland proposes to her and May accepts. Only one thing about their engagement is less than perfect: its announcement coincides with the return of May's cousin Ellen, Countess Olenska, to her New York family after leaving her unfaithful European husband. But in genteel New York, marriage is forever, and Ellen did not merely leave her husband to seek a divorce, she reportedly "bolted with his secretary." This rumor has endangered Ellen's chances of reentering New York's narrowly judgmental social world.

Newland initially cares only about propriety—how it will look to have his future wife so closely associated with an errant cousin. In person, Ellen, who reminds Newland that they were childhood friends, touches him deeply. Ellen is "thin, worn, a little older-looking than her age [thirty] . . . but there was about her the mysterious authority of beauty, a sureness in the carriage of the head, the movement of the eyes." She is also simpler in manner, less concerned with fashion and more independent in her perspective than any woman Newland knows. Before long, Newland admits to himself that he has fallen deeply in love with her.

Ellen Olenska is not his first passion—he has just recovered from a red-hot affair with a married woman who loved him less than she loved the drama of their clandestine relationship. Nor is he madly in love with May, whom he likes and respects, but with whom he can foresee a marriage like everyone else's, "a dull association of material and social interests held together by ignorance on the one side and hypocrisy on the other."

But his relationships with his ex-mistress and with his fiancée have not in one whit disturbed his "belief in the abysmal distinction between the women one loved and respected and those one enjoyed—and pitied." And like everybody else, in the case of an extramarital affair, Newland deems the man foolish, the woman criminal.

Ellen's arrival puts all these notions into question for Newland. He is enlisted by May's family to convince Ellen not to seek a divorce, which though legally possible is contrary to New York social customs. After Ellen accedes to his arguments, Newland realizes that he has actually endangered her, cutting off any chance of her legalizing a love affair through remarriage and thereby making her vulnerable to men attracted by her glamor and unprotected status. When someone wonders about her fate, Newland wishes he could reply that they had all contributed to ensuring that Ellen will become somebody's "mistress rather than some decent fellow's wife."

Meanwhile, Newland is so terrified by the force of his feelings for Ellen that he launches a campaign to convince May to shorten their engagement so that he can, in marrying her, put Ellen out of his thoughts. At first May demurs. She has, she says, guessed exactly what Newland is trying to hide, that he loves someone inappropriate whom he hopes to forget. But she misidentifies the object of his affection as his former mistress, and he is so relieved that she does not suspect Ellen that he is able to convince her that she is wrong.

When Newland declares his love to Ellen—"you are the woman I would have married if it had been possible for either of us"—she replies furiously that by pressuring her to abandon her suit for a divorce, he has made a marriage between them impossible. "And because my family was going to be your family—for May's sake and for yours—I did what you told me, what you proved to me that I ought to do," she reminds him bitterly. Shocked to the core, Newland decides to confess his feelings to May and break off their engagement so he can be with Ellen.

Too late! A telegram announces that May's family has agreed to expedite the wedding, which is now scheduled mere weeks away. Newland's regard for the values and demands of his social order forces him to honor his engagement and marry May. He endures the wedding by losing himself in a reverie. Afterward, he decides that he cannot "emancipate a wife who had not the dimmest notion that she was not free" and who is before his very eyes turning into her—and his—mother. In consequence, he conducts his marriage precisely as everyone else does.

Newland yearns for Ellen more and more. Her situation has changed. Her husband has implored her to come back to their home as an occasional hostess, not a real wife, in return for which he will restore her dowry to her. Ellen, proud and determined, refuses. When Newland meets her again, he tells her that just as he has shaped her life, so she has shaped his by urging him to marry May rather than cause a rupture in the family. "You gave me my first glimpse of a real life, and at the same moment you asked me to go on with a sham one," he accuses her. "It's beyond human enduring—that's all."

Newland is by now so deeply in love with Ellen that he even considers leaving his wife. He longs for Ellen on any terms, including making her his mistress. The families know how he feels, and to get Ellen away from him, they pressure her to accept Count Olenska's overtures. They even cut off her allowance to starve her into submission.

Despite her much-reduced circumstances, Ellen refuses. Besides, one of the families' matriarchs adores her and restores her allowance. Newland seeks her out and declares his love for her again. *"Each time you happen to me all over again."*

"Is it your idea, then, that I should live with you as your mistress—since I can't be your wife?" she wonders.

Newland's reply is heartfelt. "I want somehow to get away with you into a world where words like that—categories like that—won't exist. Where we shall be simply two human beings who love each other, who are the whole of life to each other; and nothing else on earth will matter." But Ellen knows no such world exists, and that people who think they've found it discover it "wasn't at all different from the old world they'd left, but only rather smaller and dingier and more promiscuous."

Soon after this, Newland has an epiphany. His marriage has deadened him, and he will leave it and follow Ellen to Europe, where they will always be together. But though he confides in no one, his entire "tribe" has divined his secret. Worse, for months they have collectively believed that Ellen is already his mistress. To preserve their world, these people who "dreaded scandal more than disease, who placed decency above courage, and who considered that nothing was more ill-bred than 'scenes'" once again take action.

Their scheme is a simple one. May tells Ellen that she is pregnant to guarantee that Ellen will voluntarily go back to Europe. When May's possible pregnancy is confirmed soon after, Newland is trapped for life, and Ellen will never again permit any intimacy.

The Age of Innocence is not so much about a woman who nearly becomes a mistress as it is about what a mistress is, what sort of woman may be a mistress, how society—specifically, patrician New York society in the late 19th century—perceived and treated mistresses, and how that same society, including men who kept mistresses, rallied around wronged wives because taking mistresses, though condoned on the part of bachelors, was considered wrongful on the part of married men.

Wharton's technique is subtle and convincing. Newland is an agreeable and sympathetic protagonist who often reflects on his society's value system, and how and by whom it is enforced. His analysis does not lead to anything like rebellion, but the depth of his love for Ellen and his terrifying sense that his life with May is a living death give him the impetus to challenge his peers and their values. At first, Newland wants Ellen any way he can get her, and the obvious way is to make her his mistress. Soon this seems too tawdry a framework for such a passionate attachment, and increasingly, he knows he cannot settle for a discreet affair. What he really wants is a relationship of mutual devotion, which can succeed only if neither he nor she remains married. The only possible solution is divorce, for her and for him, or elopement to forgiving and less innocent Europe.

By the book's end, when Newland has ceased to feel grounded in his social world and strains against the traces that hold its members in check, he and Ellen are outmaneuvered by a phalanx of relatives led by his own wife. In return for accepting defeat, he and Ellen are forgiven and welcomed back into the fold. Though its values are in question and its fortifications under siege, the age of innocence—including its rules about mistresses—remains intact.

Lara [12]

The scintillating and agonized love affair between the married Dr. Zhivago, in Boris Pasternak's novel of that name, and his mistress, Larisa, unfolds during the chaos of World War I and the Russian Revolution. Yuri Zhivago is a physician whose diagnosis of Russia's social order gives him great sympathy for the revolutionary crusade. As a student, his path crosses Lara's, though she comes from a very different background and has been raised in poverty and deprivation. When they meet as adults, Yuri is happily married to his childhood sweetheart, Tonia, and has a son. Lara is a nurse who is looking for her husband, Pasha Antipov, a revolutionary military leader who has disappeared.

Lara has a past that torments her and haunts her marriage. When she was sixteen, a beauty with flaxen hair and deep gray eyes, her mother's lover, Komarovsky, seduced her. Flattered that a handsome and wealthy older man had taken such an intense interest in her, and believing herself in any case "a fallen women ... a woman out of a French novel," Lara became Komarovsky's mistress.

Lara's infatuation was short-lived, but depression and horror at her immorality (as she comes to see it) and her betrayal of her mother (as anyone would have seen it) continue to grip her, and all she wants to do is sleep. She believes that Komarovsky is "the curse of her life" and that she has become "his slave for life. How," she asks herself, "has he subjugated her? How does he force her to submit, why does she surrender, why does she gratify his wishes and delight him with her quivering unconcealed shame?"

The first time Yuri Zhivago sees Lara is as a medical student at the bedside of Lara's mother, who has just been saved from suicide. Not long after this, Lara takes the momentous decision of escaping her wretched life, and she becomes the live-in governess to a friend's young sister.

Lara's new life is pleasant. Her employers are kind and generous, and she continues taking courses at the university. She also discovers her life's purpose, "to grasp the meaning of [earth's] wild enchantment and to call each thing by its right name." She decides that she will visit Komarovsky and insist that her years with him entitle her to enough money to leave her job and become independent. She takes her brother's revolver with her, and if Komarovsky refuses her, she plans to shoot him.

Lara locates Komarovsky at a large party and simply walks inside. When Yuri Zhivago, a guest, first sees her, she has just missed Komarovsky and has shot her host, who is stunned but only slightly injured. "This girl again!" Yuri exclaims. "And again in such extraordinary circumstances!"

Komarovsky, furious at the thought of the scandal that could result if Lara is tried by a court of law, uses his influence as a prosecutor to save her from prosecution for his own attempted murder. She still refuses to admit to Pasha, her adoring fiancé, what her connection with Komarovsky is, telling him only that she is a bad woman and unworthy of him.

Nonetheless, she and Pasha marry and move to a provincial town, where they teach school and have a daughter, Katenka. Then, driven by patriotism and confusion about their relationship, Pasha enlists in the army. After several months without news of him, Lara qualifies herself as a nurse, gets assigned to a hospital train and sets out to find her husband. At about the same time, Yuri Zhivago is conscripted as a medical officer into the army.

Yuri and Lara meet again in the army hospital where she has just been informed—erroneously, it turns out—that Pasha has been killed in action. She and Yuri are deeply attracted to each other, though they scrupulously avoid sexual intercourse. Indeed, Yuri strives not to love her. But Lara and the doctor are soul mates, united by a fierce love too strong to resist.

Nonetheless, they separate, and Yuri returns to his wife and son in Moscow. Life there is so penurious that starvation is a real possibility. Finally Yuri gives in to his wife's pleas to seek refuge in a country house where they can grow vegetables and where the war might pass them by.

Coincidentally, the Zhivagos' new lodgings are outside the town where Lara and Pasha live, and to which Lara has returned. She and Yuri first glimpse each other in the library, but weeks elapse before Yuri seeks her out in her house. When he does, he sparks the love affair that has stirred millions in its literary and filmed versions.

By this time Lara has learned that Pasha is not dead at all, but has adopted an assumed name and is a revolutionary leader. In loving and sleeping with Dr. Zhivago, she is betraying her husband just as Yuri is betraying Tonia. Yuri begins to spend nights with Lara, lying to Tonia about his whereabouts. His guilt intensifies in proportion to his obsession. He decides to confess everything to Tonia and make a clean break with Lara. But before he can actually do this, he is captured by Red Army soldiers and forced to serve as their battlefield doctor.

Years later Zhivago escapes and returns to find that Tonia and his family have fled back to Moscow. Lara, however, is still there, and he moves in with her and Katenka. They resume their love affair though thoughts of Tonia torment him. But he suddenly understands what Lara is to him. "You could not communicate with life and existence, but she was their representative, their expression, in her the inarticulate principle of existence became sensitive and capable of speech."

Lara and Yuri's love is great, Pasternak writes. "To them . . . the moments when passion visited their doomed human existence like a breath of eternity were moments of revelation, of continually new discoveries about themselves and life." But Lara still grieves about her past with Komarovsky, though in maturity she is clearer about his role in her seduction. "There's something broken in me," she tries to explain to Yuri, "something broken in my whole life. I discovered life much too early, I was made to discover it, and I was made to see it from the very worst side—a cheap, distorted version of it—through the eyes of a self-assured, elderly parasite, who took advantage of everything and allowed himself whatever he fancied."

Yuri responds with his own anguished declaration of love. "I am jealous of your toilet articles, of the drops of sweat on your skin, of the germs in the air you breathe which could get into your blood and poison you. And I am jealous of Komarovsky, as if he were an infectious disease. . . . I can't say it more clearly. I love you madly, irrationally, infinitely."

One day Yuri receives a letter of farewell from Tonia, who is being deported from Russia to Paris. She loves him with all her heart, she writes sadly, but knows that he does not love her. She much admires and esteems Lara, whom she met when he was away at war. "I must honestly admit that she is a good person," Tonia continues, "but I don't want to be a hypocrite—she is my exact opposite. I was born to make life simple and to look for sensible solutions; she, to complicate it and create confusion."

The war and the engulfing revolution create even more confusion. Lara and Yuri learn they are both at risk of being arrested, and so they flee to the country retreat Tonia abandoned after Yuri's capture. "Our days are really numbered," Yuri declares. "Let us use them up saying goodbye to life, being together for the last time before we are parted. We'll say goodbye to everything we hold dear, to the way we look at things, to the way we've dreamed of living and to what our conscience has taught us, and to our hopes and to each other. . . . It's not for nothing that you stand at the end of my life, my hidden, forbidden angel, under the skies of wars and turmoil."

In stark contrast to the idyllic cinematic version, in which Lara and Yuri enter a wonderland of wintry splendor and gleaming icicles in the old mansion where Yuri writes poetry and Lara keeps the house and shares his creative joy, the lovers in Pasternak's original novel are weighed down by apprehension and fear. Lara suffers because in their love she feels "something childish, unrestrained, irresponsible. It's a willful, destructive element, hostile to domestic happiness, such a love. . . . Don't you see," she adds, throwing her arms around Yuri's neck, "you were given wings to fly above the clouds, but I'm a woman, mine are given me to stay close to the ground and to shelter my young."

On the thirteenth day, Komarovsky struggles through the snow and convinces them that he can save Lara by taking her under his protection. Yuri agrees, adding that he will join them before long. He watches Lara leave, swallowing his pain "as if it were a piece of apple stuck in my throat," then returns to the house and plunges into writing poetry. ("Farewell to years of timelessness. / Let us part now, you who threw / Your woman's gauntlet to an abyss of degradations: / I am the arena of your ordeal.")

More than a decade later, Yuri suffers a heart attack and dies. Lara appears at his funeral, musing sadly and bitterly that both he and Pasha are dead, whereas Komarovsky, "who should have been killed, whom I tried to kill and missed . . . that complete cipher who turned my life into a chain of crimes beyond my knowing [is alive] . . . and not one of those who are near to me and whom I need is left."

Her life after leaving Yuri has been hellish, Lara murmurs to Yuri's coffin, but she gives him no details, because "every time I come to that part of my life my hair stands on end with horror." Days later, Lara is arrested on the street, disappears into a prison camp and never emerges.

The haunted love affair that is the lens through which Pasternak tackles the ideological confusion and social chaos of the early revolutionary years in Russia could—should—have been titled *Yuri and Lara*, for *Dr. Zhivago* is as much Lara's story as Yuri's. And from Lara's earliest days with an incompetent mother dependent on a lover to make ends meet, mistressdom is a crucial fact of life. Her own seduction by that same lover and her initial attraction to him suck her into deceiving her mother, Komarovsky's longtime mistress. It also sullies her own perception of herself. As Yuri's mistress, Lara suffers less guilt, partly because her love for Yuri clarifies her vision of the meaning of her life.

On one level, *Dr. Zhivago* is a political parable. At the same time, the power and sadness of Yuri and Lara's love affair, and the aching poetry that survives it, transcend the bleak setting; the intense physician and his exquisite mistress tower as two of literature's greatest lovers. Their relationship is as tempestuous as it is tender, as dangerous as it is comforting. But the bond between the two never erodes even though they are ultimately separated, and Yuri's poems, searing testaments to his joy and anguish, stand as its monument.

Sarah Miles [13]

The End of the Affair, published in 1951, is set in the mid-1940s in wartime London, where air raids and bomb shelters are everyday facts of life. In Graham Greene's hands, the adulterous love affair between Sarah Miles and Maurice Bendrix, the novel's central characters, can never transcend the torment and guilt of its sinfulness. Remarkably, however, Catholic author Greene also creates, next to Sarah and Maurice's powerful erotic union, a parallel seeking for divine love—something that is revealed to Sarah through her attempts to understand her love for the bitter and agnostic Maurice.

Sarah, the caring wife of Henry, a senior civil servant, first encounters Maurice, a writer, when he is researching the daily habits of public officials. They fall quickly and surely in love and into bed, but soon discover that their passionate feelings for each other are unlike anything they have felt for previous lovers, or—in Sarah's case—for Henry. But unlike his generous mistress, Maurice develops, indeed nurtures, such obsessive jealousy about Sarah that it eventually corrodes their relationship.

In fact, jealousy, which Maurice both confuses and equates with hatred, plays as crucial a role as love in their affair. "I always salute [jealousy] as the mark of true love," remarks the private detective Maurice hires to follow Sarah after she has broken off with him. "It is my profession to imagine, to think in images," Maurice recalls later, "fifty times through the day, and immediately I woke during the night, a curtain would rise and the play would begin: always the same play, Sarah making love, Sarah with X . . . Sarah kissing in her own particular way, arching herself in the act of sex and uttering that cry like pain, Sarah in abandonment." Sarah is aware of his vigilance and suspicions. She confides to her journal, "Sometimes I get so tired of trying to convince him that I love him and shall love him for ever. He pounces on my words like a barrister and twists them."

The affair continues for five years despite Sarah's misgivings and Maurice's perpetual jibes and quarreling. One day in 1944, they are together in Maurice's lodgings when an air raid begins. Maurice rushes toward the basement shelter to see if it is suitable for Sarah to use. Just as he reaches the landing, a bomb shatters the air and Maurice is knocked down unconscious under the front door. Sarah, still naked, finds him there, to all appearances dead.

Terrified and remorseful, she kneels on the floor in unfamiliar prayer. First she asks God to make her believe in him and digs her long fingernails into her palms (replicating Christ's wounds at Gethsemane) so she can feel pain. Then she bargains with God. Restore Maurice, she implores, and I'll give him up forever, that's how much I love him. Soon after, Maurice regains consciousness and struggles back to his room, where he finds Sarah still on her knees. He does not know it then, but this is the end of the affair.

For two years, Sarah suffers and keeps her secret promise to God, a promise she comes to bitterly regret. Then Maurice unexpectedly runs into Henry, who believes Sarah has a lover. Maurice reacts with poisonous jealousy, as if she is betraying him rather than her husband. He engages a private investigator to follow her. Maurice, still angry at Sarah for leaving him, forces Henry to listen as he confesses that he and Sarah were once lovers. "You have a good safe income," he adds maliciously, when Henry asks sadly why Sarah has stayed with him. "You're security. . . . You were her pimp. . . . You pimped with your ignorance. You pimped by never learning how to make love with her, so she had to look elsewhere. . . . You pimped by being a bore and a fool."

One day Maurice follows Sarah to a Roman Catholic church, where she merely sits without praying. He also inveigles his private investigator into acquiring her diary, which, to his surprise, chronicles the depth of her love for him, the sacrifice she has made when she thought he was dead and her arduous struggle to find faith and believe in God.

What she does not mention is her own physical decay. Sarah has caught a savage cold that she refuses to treat. It has become a serious, debilitating illness, and she is at the point of death. Not realizing this, Maurice urges her to resume their relationship, and he soon believes he has convinced her to leave Henry and marry him. Before this can happen, Henry phones Maurice to inform him that "an awful thing" has happened, and that Sarah is dead.

In a bizarre twist of plot, Maurice accepts Henry's invitation to move in with him. Together, Sarah's cuckolded husband and former lover prepare for her funeral. Even then Maurice punishes her for leaving him, pushing Henry to cremate rather than bury her. At the ceremony, Maurice notes from the satisfaction on various women's faces that "the extinction of Sarah had left every wife safer."

Reading her diaries and a letter delivered posthumously, Maurice learns that near the end, Sarah had wavered in her bargain with God. One week before she died she wrote, "I want Maurice. I want ordinary corrupt human love." Maurice, her bitter survivor, jeers and taunts God, and denies that God ever conquered Sarah's spirit. However, Sarah has died in a state of grace. "I hate You, God, I hate You as though You existed," Maurice thinks. And he prays in the novel's last line, "O God, You've done enough, You've robbed me of enough, I'm too tired and old to learn to love, leave me alone for ever."

The End of the Affair never gives the affair a chance to last or to metamorphose into marriage. Greene's sense of Catholic responsibility could not tolerate such an immoral resolution. Marriage, in the Catholic Church, is a sacrament, and therefore indissoluble. However, the great love Sarah finds as Maurice's mistress challenges the foundations of her marriage. It also attains such force that it rivals the love she wants to feel for God. This is why Sarah ultimately has to die: not because she is a fallen woman, but because she loves Maurice too much.

Merrion Palmer [14]

Mistresses are also the stuff of mainstream literature. A popular recent novel is Joanna Trollope's *Marrying the Mistress*, which is what Guy Stockdale, the book's central character, intends to do. Guy, a handsome sixty-one-year-old judge, has just informed his wife, Laura, that he intends to divorce her so he can marry thirty-one-year-old lawyer Merrion Palmer, his mistress of seven years. The term shocks and slightly repels Guy, but Merrion insists that it is accurate. "Mistress it is," she tells him. "We sleep together, you pay for some things for me, I keep myself exclusively for you. That's what they do, mistresses."

After seven years, both Merrion and Guy have had enough of sneaking around, spending holidays apart and keeping each other secret from their loved ones. Marriage, after Guy's divorce, is the obvious solution. But Laura, a stay-at-home wife and obsessive gardener, is bitter and uncooperative, and enlists her lawyer-son Simon to take her side against her husband. However, Simon's wife, Carrie, and his brother, Alan, are less inclined to blame Guy. "I'm sorry for Mum but I'm sorry for Dad, too," Alan says. "Laura is one of the most self-absorbed, self-pitying women I have ever met," opines Carrie. Even Laura's plainspoken friend Wendy risks telling Laura, "It looks as if you'd just grown miles and miles apart. Simple as that."

Except for Laura, Guy's family is curious about Merrion, and Carrie invites her for dinner. Carrie appreciates Merrion's intelligence and loyalty, her daughters, Rachel and Emma, approve her fashion sense and Alan likes her steadiness and rationality. Only Simon tries to remain neutral, both for his mother's sake and because the idea of his father having sex with Merrion appalls him.

But Merrion's only relative, her twice-divorced mother, makes much harsher judgments about Guy when she meets him. "You are ruining my daughter's life," she tells him. Among other things, "if she has a baby, you'll be dead before it's grown up." Guy listens in sad silence, then tries to explain. He and Merrion are each other's ideal companions and share a sense that they belong together. "A knowledge. A recognition."

Merrion feels the same way about Guy, but after seven years of living what Guy calls "this part-life," she finds the dynamics of his complex family almost overwhelming. At the same time, she realizes with a pang that her previous priorities and values have suddenly changed. "What had for seven years seemed thrilling and potent and truly essential had become . . . contrived and furtive and distasteful. . . . Her sheer pride in being Guy's *mistress* turned into something, at a stroke, whose glamour she could scarcely remember." On top of this, Guy's family members descend on him, reclaiming him, reminding him of his obligations to them, changing the parameters of his and Merrion's world. The only way she feels she can regain control is by setting a definite wedding date.

As that date approaches, Merrion begins to have doubts about joining the Stockdale clan. Will she lose her priority as number one in Guy's life? Will she lose her identity, the one she has sustained through seven years as his mistress? Suddenly Merrion is not as certain as she has been about her future with Guy.

More frightening for her, neither is Guy. One sunny afternoon, he takes her for a walk and tells her gently that he cannot marry her, because of his age, not hers. "I can't bear it, I can't stand it, I can't—" Merrion cries. "You can. You will," Guy replies.

Later, Merrion surprises Simon with a visit and tells him that she and Guy have broken up. "We knew," she says, "that what we had, what we felt, might not survive being married. That—that the change would kill it. That we couldn't bear what that—might do to us." And so *Marrying the Mistress* ends, with the mistress unmarried and weeping onto the shoulder of her ex-lover's son.

In her tale of family relationships and dynamics, Trollope is not preaching against mistresses, punishing Merrion by depriving her of Guy. Nowhere does she suggest that Merrion's love for Guy is anything but decent and dignified, despite the subterfuge that sustains it. Nor does she send Guy back to Laura— she has made it clear that they can never be reconciled. Merrion as mistress is about as elegant and accomplished as any woman can be, and Guy is a refined and sincere lover.

But accomplished though she is, Merrion confronts many of the mistress's predicaments. She is consigned to the periphery of her lover's life, while he spends holidays with his wife and family. She is in a constant state of vigilance, for nobody must know about her relationship. She is justifiably insecure about their future together. She must consider sacrificing motherhood, because her married lover already has a family and may not want another one. At the end, even the title *Marrying the Mistress* conveys a slightly ominous warning.

That warning is implicit in all the novels discussed here. Only Jane Eyre, who resists the temptation to become a mistress, is rewarded by a blissfully happy marriage, while Ellen Olenska is reinstated in her family's life. Anna Karenina, Mildred Rogers and Merrion Palmer all fail to marry their lovers as they yearn to; Hester Prynne fails to flee to Europe with her partner; and Emma Bovary fails to maintain her amorous relationship. Sarah Miles, who blames herself for betraying God as much as her husband, fails to survive her illness and go away with her lover.

The reasons for the universal stalemate in these mistresses' situations are made clear. The primary one is that society frowns on a mistress's elevation to the status of her lover's wife, and this holds as true for the unmarried as for the unhappily married mistress. Literary mistresses are held to higher standards than real ones, who sometimes get to marry their lovers. This is because authors, wary of critics who might denounce them for sanctioning immorality and of censors who might pursue them in court, have traditionally been cautious of designing happy endings for their mistresses. Only Emma's painful suicide exonerated Flaubert from this charge, and it is no coincidence that Anna also killed herself. Until modern times, marrying the literary mistress is just what could not happen.

Today's social values and expectations are different, and so is Merrion Palmer's experience of mistressdom. Merrion is not guilty of destroying Guy's marriage, which would be unsalvageable even without her, and so she is free to evaluate her relationship in the context of her own needs and desires. But as she contemplates bridging the chasm between mistressdom and marriage, Merrion realizes that the thrill of her affair stems largely from its illicit status. She decides, as well, that the fury of her love would probably not withstand its legitimation and domestication. A century and a half after Jane Eyre expressed her contempt for mistresses, mistressdom continues to be portrayed as a doubtful proposition.

But many authors deliberately send out contrary messages. They depict mistresses as strong and intelligent and also as beautiful and desirable, give them unappealing husbands and unhappy marriages and permit them the excitement of illicit erotic passion. By later denying these women the continued enjoyment of their sinfulness, their creators protect themselves. But they simultaneously paint dreary pictures of marriage that underscore its interdependence with mistressdom, and they imply that the society that shapes their heroines' lives is every bit as flawed as the women themselves. At the same time that they reinforce unflattering views of mistresses, they also provide justification for becoming one.

CHAPTER 13

The 1960s Transform Marriage and Mistressdom

HE social and ideological revolution of the 1960s was sparked by ideas of liberation and equality that, over the years, were embraced by millions. The sexual revolution inspired challenges to all double standards: those that censured sexually liberal women as sluts while applauding their brothers as studs; those that marginalized blacks and other people of color; those that condemned homosexuals as perverts. Activists took up the cudgel for women's rights, civil rights, gay rights. But it took new legislation to outlaw the prejudices and inequalities that had formerly governed society, and to attempt to inculcate new ways of thinking and acting.

Nonetheless, the 1960s did not revolutionize everyone's thinking or lifestyle. A pervasive conservative Right still invoked the Bible's authority to fiercely oppose female equality and to return women to their rightful place under male "protection." Women content in traditional marriages, many of them unpaid homemakers who chose to focus on their families, resisted adopting the persona of the new woman. So did some younger women who either identified with conservative mothers or rebelled against their liberated ones. Women who might otherwise have remained straight were suddenly galvanized by the prevailing negativity toward men and chose lesbianism as an alternative to any sort of intimate relationships with men. At the same time, many more lesbians dared to identify themselves as such.

Egalitarian women who married also faced a multiplicity of choice. They could become wives or partners. They could adopt their husband's surname or keep their father's. They could negotiate marital arrangements to satisfy their need for strict equality. With the advent of reliable and accessible birth control, notably the Pill, they could practice birth control and family planning. As legislation slowly caught up to ideology, they could co-own, co-owe and, if they divorced, coparent. The form as well as the nature of marriage was elastic: it could be religious, civil or common-law. And, as divorce laws eased, remarriage became much more common.

Definitions, once quite rigid, became as flexible as the relationships they described. In particular, women who would previously have been labeled mistresses because they were in long-term relationships with men who were not their husbands might now be seen as girlfriends, partners or companions. As if this were not confusing enough, many married men and women rejected the possibly derogatory implications of the terms *wife, husband* and *spouse*, and instead described themselves as each other's partners. Much depended on self-perception: women had won the right to decide for themselves what they were and what they should be called.

Inevitably, some women romanticized the receding past, in particular, the institution of mistressdom, and sought out like-minded men prepared to "keep" them. Other women became mistresses by happenstance, after they fell in love with a married man who would neither marry nor do without them.[1]

Two celebrated women who exemplify these very different kinds of relationships are Pamela Harriman and Lillian Ross. Harriman, mistress to a series of ultra-wealthy men, sailed through the 1960s untouched by its brand of feminism and revisionist interpretation of male-female relations. Ross, a well-known writer, was the wifelike lover of a married man who could not bring himself to entirely leave his marriage. Harriman and Ross are notable women, but their stories reflect those of countless ordinary women, rooted in the mores of earlier times, whose extramarital relationships emerged relatively untouched by the 1960s.

The French writer Simone de Beauvoir, on the other hand, extolled personal autonomy and liberation over what she condemned as the hypocrisy and bondage of marriage. The novels and essays in which she explored and analyzed her intense and sometimes bitter unions with fellow intellectual Jean-Paul Sartre and later with American novelist Nelson Algren have influenced generations of women in their own decisions about the nature of their intimate relationships with men.

A trio of modern women, unknown but representative of legions of their contemporaries, completes my discussion of modern mistressdom. All three have been mistresses, but their visions and experiences are as individual as they are. Feminism and new egalitarian standards, however, affect each of them, albeit in different ways.

Pamela Digby Churchill Hayward Harriman [2]

When Pamela Digby Churchill Harriman died in 1997, an obituary in *The Times* of London ranked her as "one of the great courtesans of her age," and the *Daily Mail* called her "the world's expert on rich men's ceilings." The *Mail* added, "When historians look back on the 20th century, they will find traces of Pamela Harriman's lipstick all over it."[3]

Pamela's lipstick smeared the lips of some of the world's most powerful men. There were her three husbands: Randolph Churchill, Sir Winston's son; Leland Hayward, Broadway (*Sound of Music, South Pacific, Gypsy*) and Hollywood producer, and Averell Harriman, former New York governor and diplomat. There was also an impressive roster of lovers who declined to marry her: Italian industrialist Gianni Agnelli, French banker Elie de Rothschild and Edward R. Murrow, the American broadcast journalist who came closest to breaking Pamela's resilient heart.

Pamela Digby's father, the eleventh Baron Digby, raised his family in Minterne Magna, his family's fifty-room, 1,500-acre ancestral mansion, aided by twenty-two live-in servants. But Pamela hankered after vast wealth rather than genteel comfort, and set about finding a husband who could provide it.

Despite her rotund beauty and flaming red hair, Pamela did not attract eligible suitors. "English men didn't like her," a fellow debutante recalled.[4] For the rest of her life, Pam would prefer Americans and Europeans, especially older men who responded to her youthful exuberance and sexual openness by giving her enough money to live considerably above the means that her trusting parents had provided.

Then Pam met Randolph Churchill, Winston Churchill's dissolute and alcoholic only son, who proposed to her on their first date. Randolph, about to depart for service in World War II, believed he might be killed in battle, and felt that he urgently needed a woman to provide him an heir. Pam, healthy and attractive, seemed a good prospect. Though at least eight other women had turned him down, Pam accepted his loveless proposal. Only days after they announced their engagement, she and Randolph were married.

Pam quickly became pregnant, and the birth of her infant, Winston, rooted her forever in the Churchill world. Randolph, who had been in bed with another woman while his bride delivered their son, was now dispensable by her.

So was young Winston, whom Pam entrusted to a nanny at a friend's house. Then, unencumbered by son or husband—the latter by then off to war—she indulged in two kinds of lives, the influential and prestigious official one under the wing of the elder statesman Churchill, and an exciting, private one that included a series of lovers.

One lover was the married and immensely rich William Averell Harriman, on official business in London. Pam was as deeply struck by the gaunt and dignified American as he was by Winston Churchill's daughter-in-law. Averell began to provide her with a lovely apartment and an income, and if he knew that his new mistress had sexual relations with other men, he did not seem to mind.

Then Averell was transferred from London to Moscow. Edward R. Murrow, the radio broadcaster posted in London to inform his fellow Americans about the progress of the war, succeeded him as Pam's principal lover. Pam felt so strongly about Ed Murrow that she overlooked his lack of wealth and focused instead on the power conferred on him by his status as a top-ranked journalist.

Notwithstanding his wife, Janet, Pam considered Ed Murrow marriageable, and remarriage was one of her top priorities. In the fall of 1942, she had managed to separate from Randolph Churchill while retaining her insider status with her ex-father-in-law. Why should divesting Ed of Janet and installing herself as his wife be any more difficult?

Pam's odds seemed excellent. At one point, Janet was bedridden with despair. At another, Ed asked Janet for a divorce. But Ed's boss, William Paley, forcefully counseled Ed against leaving Janet for the woman he called "the greatest courtesan of the century."[5] Soon after, Ed and Janet reconciled and, after a decade of childless marriage, conceived a child.

Pam still imagined she had a chance at winning Ed. A month after Casey Murrow was born, Pam filed for divorce from Randolph and flew to New York to plead with Ed, or perhaps overwhelm him with her charms. But the odds were stacked against her. "Casey wins," Murrow supposedly telegrammed her to finally end their affair.[6] He confided to a friend, "I've never been so in love with anyone in my life as I was with Pam, but it wasn't meant to be."[7]

Perhaps to assuage her pain, Pam rekindled her affair with Averell

Harriman. He had ended the affair when he was appointed Secretary of Commerce in 1946, though he stopped paying her rent only in 1950 and continued her generous annual "salary" for nearly three decades, until he married her. Pam had a mistress's perks without a single obligation.

Jilted but not jaded, Pam fled to the welcoming warmth of Paris. There the Churchill name was magic and Pam's fluent though imperfect French was considered adorable. Rich and well-known lovers quickly materialized, eager and indeed proud to sample Pam's charms.

As a mistress, Pam was an event planner of the highest order. She remembered what a man smoked and drank. She elicited all the latest gossip by any means possible, and proffered it as the small treasure it was. She knew everyone who mattered and arranged introductions and meetings.

Notwithstanding her career as a professional mistress, Pam was not keen on the sexual act *per se*. But she understood the role of sexual relations in attracting and binding a man to her, and so she approached sex as an important, though by no means the most important, strategy.

She also recreated herself with and for each one of her lovers. "She just unconsciously assumed his identity, as if she were putting on a glove," her friend Leonora Hornblow explained. During her tenure as chief mistress to multimillionaire Fiat heir Gianni Agnelli, Pam developed an Italian accent, searched for words in English and converted to Roman Catholicism. With French mogul Baron Elie de Rothschild, who thought of her as a European geisha, she took to answering the phone "Ici Pam." But as biographer Sally Bedell Smith observes, "By becoming a perfect extension of the men who kept her, Pam had done her job too well: no man of wealth and rank would marry her, knowing she functioned so well as a mistress."[8]

Broadway and Hollywood producer Leland Hayward was the first of her lovers to capitulate and marry her. In 1960, Pam Digby Churchill at last achieved her ultimate goal: marriage to a wealthy and important man who would support her in luxury and style. (When Hayward asked his wife for a divorce so that he could marry Pam, she spat back, "Whatever you do, for your own protection, for your own dignity, don't marry her. You don't have to. Nobody *marries* Pam Churchill."[9])

Soon after Leland's death in 1970, Pam reencountered Averell Harriman, now a seventy-nine-year-old widower devastated by his wife's death. She wasted no time. She comforted him and included with her comfort the sex the old man still longed for. Six months later, she and Averell married. The conservative Pam transmogrified into a Democrat's Democrat who raised funds, organized and made herself indispensable to her new, blue-blooded diplomat husband.

Despite her curious and, to some, dubious past, the combined power of her money, personal friendships, political savvy and willingness to devote herself to raising funds for the Democratic Party conquered her naysayers. Pam became a leading hostess whose invitations were coveted, and a political personage in the king-making tradition.

Averell died in 1986 and Pam disposed of his remains in a ceremony that cost $171,082. He had left her an enormous fortune in stock holdings, real estate, art and jewelry. She invested some of this money in cosmetic surgery that contoured her face and subtly highlighted her prettiness, transforming the portly and droopy sixty-six-year-old into a sprightly beauty.

In March 1993, newly elected president Bill Clinton honored the indefatigable Democrat with the title of US ambassador to France. Ambassador Pam performed her duties with élan.

In February 1997, Pamela Harriman died of a massive cerebral hemorrhage soon after being stricken by seizures in the pool of Paris's Hotel Ritz, where she had been swimming laps. Pam was, as her obituaries noted, an extraordinarily successful mistress: in marrying two of her lovers, she succeeded where so many mistresses fail. In her search for financial security, Pam invented her own strategies, Italianizing herself for Gianni Agnelli, Frenchifying herself for Elie de Rothschild, Americanizing herself for Leland Hayward, Democratizing herself for Averell Harriman.

Other strategies might have been lifted from Ovid's instructions to mistresses in his *Ars Amatoria*—focusing exclusively on the man in question, fastidiously grooming herself, displaying herself in flattering clothes, adorning herself with jewels that doubled as financial assets and provided security, and—Pam's specialty—disregarding spouses as disposable inconveniences.

The sexual revolution did not change Pamela Harriman—in the area of sexual freedom she was already as liberated as any Cosmo girl. But the new perceptions of women as men's equals, and attacks on female subjugation to male authority, passed her by; she was too mired in chameleon-like adaptation to her current lover. Her ambassadorship, ironically, was a byproduct of the new official attitudes to women, and Pam was a beneficiary of the long struggle to translate theory into reality in the form of status and high-ranked jobs.

Lillian Ross [10]

In 1945, when managing editor William Shawn hired twenty-something Lillian Ross for *The New Yorker* magazine, replacing the males called to duty in World War II, he worried that a woman might find factual reporting difficult. Fortunately, Lillian was fact-friendly, and her reports for "The Talk of the Town" quickly established her as a fine writer.

Despite her professional ambition, however, Lillian was not an advance-wave feminist. She accepted her father's view that women needed a kindly male protector, and she assumed that she would meet and marry one. For years, Lillian was oblivious to how she and Mr. Shawn, whom she referred to as Bill, were slowly growing closer to each other. Then Bill began to leave love poems on her desk. One night, as they worked late, he shocked her by declaring that he was in love with her.

It was 1950, and Bill Shawn was a married man with children at home. He had no intention of leaving Cecille, his wife of twenty-two years. At the same time, he pursued Lillian until she took a long-term assignment in California. During her year and a half there, Bill phoned her often but, reassuringly, never mentioned love.

Lillian returned to New York in 1951, just before Bill Shawn was named *The New Yorker*'s new editor-in-chief, replacing Harold Ross, who had died. Bill renewed his courting. One morning the couple left the office and took a room at the Plaza hotel, where they stayed until that evening, making love with the ease and familiarity of lovers who had been together for years.

At first, Bill's famed reclusiveness made it easy to keep their affair secret. But he was consumed by guilt at deceiving Cecille, and early on decided to tell her the truth. Cecille was deeply hurt. However, she chose to preserve her marriage, no matter how hollow it had become and how burdensome for Bill.

Though Bill would be perpetually torn and guilt-ridden about Cecille's suffering, he felt he could not bear to lose Lillian. She, too, was tormented—"I couldn't reconcile myself to being a 'mistress,'" Lillian wrote. "I didn't *feel* like one. Bill told me I was his 'wife.' I felt I was."[11] She knew, however, that she was not and that every time he left her apartment, he returned home to Cecille and their children, Wallace and Allen, a few blocks away.

In 1953, Lillian fled once again, this time to Paris. By phone, Bill described how he endured her absence as "a dragging torture," but expressed confidence that their love would overcome every obstacle.[12] Lillian returned to New York, to four decades as a mistress in a relationship that was effectively a parallel marriage in a monogamous society.

"Our life," she and Bill called it, not "having an affair," and certainly not "mistressdom." To Lillian, a mistress connoted "a heavily mascaraed woman in a corny movie, wearing a negligee and sitting around sulking and painting her fingernails."[13] Life with Bill consisted of domesticity in an apartment just blocks away from his other home. Bill decorated, shopped, lived and loved with Lillian, left to spend time with his family, returned, left again. At home in his separate bedroom, Bill phoned Lillian last thing at night. In the morning, he picked her up for work and breakfasted with her. They met again for lunch and then for dinner. At *The New Yorker*'s offices, they were colleagues.

Summers, which Bill spent in cooler suburbia for Cecille's sake, were difficult. Lillian suffered bouts of rage and doubt about the relationship. Bill responded by telling her that without her, he would be literally unable to continue living. Before he met her, he said, he had been living someone else's life. "I'm there but not there," he repeatedly said about his marriage. At one point Lillian consulted a psychiatrist who, after a few sessions, advised her against psychoanalysis. "Remember, all decent people feel guilt," he pointed out.

Bill, enduring a lifetime of guilt and depression, was proof of this. He repeatedly questioned his very existence—"Who am I?" he would ask. "Am I really here?"[14] His marriage stifled and his job crushed him; he battled thoughts of suicide. But with Lillian he was romantic and committed. Their love was "changeless," he said. "We must arrest our love in midflight. And we fix it forever as it is today, a point of pure light that will reach into eternity."[15] He invented sacred pledges about fidelity of body and soul. "Our love has a life of its own," he repeated.[16]

Lillian's belief in the strength of his love and devotion sustained her. She accepted her lover's dual life, Cecille's control over his scheduling and the decision to refrain from mentioning Lillian to Wallace and Allen. Lillian also voluntarily changed her own lifestyle to accommodate his: because he disliked smoking, drinking and speeding, she gave up cigarettes and martinis, and sped only when she was driving alone.

After initial negative reaction from family and friends who talked "at" them about the wrongness of their affair, Lillian and Bill enjoyed social acceptance and made no attempt to conceal their love. They ate, shopped and attended concerts and the theater together, walked hand in hand through the streets of New York and vacationed together in their green Triumph sports car.

The New Yorker, their mutual love, also united them. Though the relentless pace and intensity of his work there overwhelmed Bill, his dedication to the magazine and its "friendly, gentle, free, informal, democratic atmosphere" was absolute.[17] Lillian, his soul mate in this enterprise, believed that their love "enhanced the pleasure that we shared in our work."[18]

By the 1960s, Lillian yearned for a baby and despite the serious consequences of embarking on unwed motherhood, she and Bill seriously considered it. After a necessary hysterectomy ended that dream, they decided to adopt an infant. Erik was born in Norway in 1966, and Lillian went alone to bring him to the United States. Bill, waving and weeping, was waiting at the airport. "The three of us got into a taxi and went home and lived happily ever after," Lillian rejoiced.[19]

Lillian was not a single mother—Bill fathered Erik devotedly and, with writer J. D. Salinger, stood as Erik's godfather. Though both he and Lillian were Jewish, they had Erik baptized in a Christian church, as he would have been in Norway. They took their son with them everywhere, including to *The New Yorker* offices. Lillian also told Erik all about her life with Bill.

Despite the semblance of normalcy, Bill had family obligations that kept him away from Lillian and Erik. Sometimes when he arrived at Lillian's apartment she could see his despair at "the remonstrance, accusations, and guilt he had brought with him from his home."[20]

Thanksgiving and Christmas were Cecille's, but Christmas Eve was Lillian's, and whenever they were apart on New Year's Eve, Bill would phone her at midnight. Bill's now-adult son Allen and his wife, the writer Jamaica Kincaid, invited Lillian to visit and included her in their family life.

In 1987, when he was eighty years old, Bill was forced to retire from *The New Yorker* after it was sold to new owners. Lillian was disgusted at how he was treated, and when he requested her to leave with him, she gladly acquiesced. (She returned in 1993, after his death.)

In joint retirement, Lillian and Bill wrote, and Lillian tried to help him find his creative voice. But he dismissed everything he produced as not being what he wanted to write. For a time Bill also edited books for Farrar, Straus & Giroux.

On Easter Sunday, 1992, Bill contracted a viral infection and was confined to his bedroom at Cecille's. Though he phoned Lillian every morning, she began to discover the cost of not being his legal wife. When he injured himself in a fall and could not call her for several days, Lillian was frantic. She finally contacted Wallace, who kept her informed of his father's condition. Lillian could not celebrate Bill's eighty-fifth birthday with him; he spent it at home with Cecille and his sons. On December 9, Lillian called his private number, and for the first time ever, Cecille answered. "He's gone," she told Lillian. "He died in my arms."[21] Bill's obituary in the *New York Times* ended with a list of his survivors, including Cecille and their children. Lillian Ross, his wifely mistress of over forty years, was not mentioned.

The sexual revolution had little effect on Lillian Ross. Despite her professional aspirations, she was rooted in traditional values, her standard for evaluating relationships. By the 1960s, she was already settled into her unwedded relationship with Bill Shawn, justifying its morality on the grounds of Bill's misery in his marriage, his insistence that he would die without her and that Cecille was his wife in name only. Lillian saw herself as a parallel wife, and had no need of the new liberalism to change or to vindicate her life.

Simone de Beauvoir [22]

As young women, both Pamela Harriman and Lillian Ross expected and indeed very much wanted to marry. Early on, however, France's Simone de Beauvoir, who contributed so much to modern feminism, rejected the institution of marriage as hypocritical and stultifying. So did Jean-Paul Sartre, the fellow philosopher, novelist and essayist with whom she had a relationship so convoluted that almost two decades after their deaths, their biographers continue to analyze and interpret it.

In 1929, in their final exams, philosophy students Sartre and Beauvoir graduated in first and second place respectively, and for the rest of their life together, she voluntarily took second place to him. "Sartre corresponded exactly to the dream-companion I had longed for since I was fifteen," she wrote. "He was the double in whom I found all my burning aspiration raised to the pitch of incandescence."[23]

Graduation brought Simone the teaching position, salary and independence she craved. She and Sartre, as she always referred to him, also agreed to a two-year renewable "pact of freedom" that defined their alliance: they would spend two years in "the closest possible intimacy" and remain faithful to each other. Afterward, they would separate for two or three years, but with the security of knowing that each was the other's "essential" love, though they were free to experience "contingent" loves. They buffered the potential pain of each other's infidelity with the promise of perpetual commitment to each other and with the expectation that, unlike marriage, their relationship would never degenerate into duty or habit.

In the Beauvoir-Sartre model, marriage was an outmoded institution linked to bourgeois respectability and sustained by hypocrisy. They linked their "pact of freedom" to a "pact of openness"—neither would lie to or conceal anything from the other. Simone welcomed this pact as a guarantee that

Sartre would never permit her to fall prey to self-delusion. Sartre, however, would consistently observe their pact in bad faith. He once admitted that he lied to all his women, "*particularly* to the Beaver," his name for Simone.[24]

Yet despite Sartre's flagrant affairs, sexual passion eluded him. Because he was short and stubby, walleyed and homely, he never believed women could truly enjoy his body. Simone, on the other hand, was intensely sensual and driven by physical desire. She was, a friend recalled, "extremely pretty . . . [with] ravishing eyes, a pretty little nose."[25] Men eagerly responded to her combination of unselfconscious beauty and intelligence, and Simone had affairs that left her with "burning pangs" of "tyrannical" and "lurid" desires that struck her "with the force of a thunderbolt." Simone had sex with many men and some women, and her inability to control her physical yearnings tormented her. Worse, she did not dare confide in Sartre, so that she compounded her problems by violating her vow of openness. "My body became a stumbling block rather than a bond of union between us," she wrote, "and I felt a burning resentment against it."[26]

Early on, Simone suffered depressive episodes usually precipitated by alcohol. She would sit silently and drink, then erupt in spasms of weeping. In response to her emotional distress, which he likened to schizophrenia, and to guarantee that they would be offered teaching positions together, Sartre proposed marriage. Simone refused. She was determined to overcome her reliance on Sartre, and set off alone to teach in Marseilles. The couple agreed, however, to alter their original pact, and to postpone separation until they turned thirty.

From Le Havre, over five hundred miles away, Sartre continued to urge Simone not to abandon her ambitions and her quest for philosophical truth. He wrote tender letters—"My dearest, you cannot know how I think of you every minute of the day. . . . The thought of you never leaves me and I carry on little conversations with you in my head."[27] Simone conquered her depression with biweekly marathon hikes that invigorated her intellectually. A year later, after she transferred to Rouen and could spend three days a week with Sartre, she began to write a novel. She also critiqued Sartre's writing projects, with him always accepting her advice.

In the mid-1930s, Sartre sank into depression and a form of madness precipitated by a dose of mescaline. Afterward, he was haunted by hallucinations of a giant lobster that scrambled along after him. His wretchedness stemmed from his failure to achieve the great success he had dreamed of. By then Simone had concluded that he lacked talent as a philosopher. She persuaded him to focus on literature, which would eventually bring him the success he craved.

In 1935, seventeen-year-old Olga Kosakievicz "came to stay" with Simone and Sartre. Olga was the first of a stream of Simone's student protegées who joined the Sartre-Beauvoir "family" as surrogate children. She was also one of the few who did not become Sartre's lover. Sartre, then at "the nadir . . . of my madness," conceived a furious passion for the confused, depressive and rebellious teenager.

Philosophically, Simone believed in intense threesomes as a way for she and Sartre to see each other through an intimate's eyes. But though Olga admired Sartre, she found him physically repulsive and refused to have sex with him. At the same time, she used his obsession with her to pressure him into fulfilling all her wishes. Sartre was so ecstatic about Olga that sometimes Simone wondered "whether the whole of my happiness did not rest upon a gigantic lie."[28] Before long, she felt "frankly terrified" at the thought of a future with Olga still in it.

The next year Sartre complicated the situation by seducing Olga's younger sister, Wanda, then rushing to share his triumph with Simone. Sartre's other women often regaled Simone with details about their affairs with him. Simone was, her biographer Deirdre Bair says, "ashamed, saddened and bewildered by her unwanted complicity in what had come to be his sexual life with others and almost never with her."[29]

Simone sought sexual satisfaction with a series of men and young women. One lover was Jacques-Laurent Bost, Olga's boyfriend, an affair that Simone initiated and described in detail to Sartre, and that must have been prompted by a desire for revenge as well as by affection. Simone also worked out her feelings toward the Olga-Sartre union in her 1943 novel, *L'Invitée* (*She Came to Stay*), in which Xavière is Olga, Pierre is Sartre and Françoise is Simone herself. Françoise accuses Pierre of allowing his love for her to grow old. When he denies it, she tells him that his feelings are "hollow inside . . . like the whited sepulchres of the Bible." Françoise tries to engage Xavière in an intense friendship, which she sees as the only way to save herself. After Xavière refuses her overtures, Françoise kills her and disguises the death as a suicide.

In real life, the Kosakievicz sisters were succeeded by other of Simone's protegées. Sartre always seduced them with Simone's complicity, to the point where she has been accused of pimping for him. She denied such accusations. Sartre invoked her name with her students, she told Deirdre Bair, "to insure that he got exactly what he wanted. . . . Also—and I think this is very important—when couples have been together for a long time they play roles and take on responsibilities for each other within the relationship. . . . You don't mind playing these roles to make things easier for the person you love."[30] In later years, whenever a woman refused Sartre's advances, he and Simone would analyze earlier rejections for tips on how to deal with the situation.

In the summer of 1939, Sartre proposed an alteration to their pact: henceforth, they would always be together because nobody could understand them as they did each other. At first Simone was stunned to hear this. Then, suffused with happiness, she agreed.

Six years later, Sartre destroyed that happiness when he fell profoundly in love with a French actress who lived in the United States. Dolores Vanetti Ehrenreich, once the mistress of surrealist writer André Breton and now separated from her American husband, was vivacious and tiny, even shorter than Sartre, and unlike all his other women, unwilling to share him with Simone. Not for Dolores the role of contingent love: she, too, felt essential. Sartre informed Simone that he loved Dolores and would spend a few months with her each year. Simone brooded about the implications of this arrangement then asked him pointblank whether she or Dolores meant more to him. Sartre's reply was ambiguous. Dolores meant an enormous amount to him, he said, but he was with her, Simone.

Simone was shaken as never before about the durability of her union with Sartre. He went back to New York to live with Dolores, then dedicated an entire issue of *Les Temps Modernes*, the journal he, Simone and their fellow existentialists had founded, to Dolores. Was Simone losing the man to whom she had pledged lifetime allegiance?

In 1947, Simone, too, went to New York and, to please Sartre, met Dolores. The rivals were polite, but Simone informed Sartre that Dolores's heavy drinking was worrisome. Soon after, in Chicago, Simone met Nelson Algren, who had just published the first of his novels about the gritty side of American life. Algren lived in shabby poverty, drank hard and was the first man with whom the very experienced Simone ever had an orgasm. They slept together on the day they met, and fell deeply in love.

Nelson Algren's affair with Simone de Beauvoir confirmed his belief that love is never happy. Though they lived together when she visited the United States, and traveled together, Simone could neither marry him nor settle down with him in Chicago and have his baby, as he wished. Nor could she give up Sartre, as he demanded. Instead, she urged him to take lovers or even marry someone, though she assured him that he (like Sartre) was an essential love who meant the world to her. But to Nelson, as to Dolores, theories about essential and contingent love meant nothing—Simone had to choose.

She chose Sartre, and Sartre chose her. For five years, Simone and Nelson exchanged hundreds of letters, hers aflame with love. She habitually referred to him as "my beloved husband" and to herself as "your wife forever." Yet despite her passion for Algren, Simone could not contemplate leaving Sartre. "If I could give up my life with Sartre, I would be a dirty creature, a treacherous and selfish woman. . . . Sartre needs me. . . . It is not possible to love more than I love you, flesh and heart and soul . . . but Sartre needs me."[31] Eventually Simone's relationship with Nelson Algren disintegrated and he remarried his ex-wife.

Simone's confusion about the nature of her relationships with Sartre and Algren inspired her decision to explore the essence of women's condition so that she could understand her own. The result was *The Second Sex* (1949), the classic examination of women through their biology, their history, myths about them, and the reality of their lives. Her final chapter, "Toward Liberation, The Independent Woman," concludes that "To gain the supreme victory, it is necessary . . . that by and through their natural differentiation men and women unequivocally affirm their brotherhood."[32]

The Second Sex has informed, influenced and inspired millions of women. It has also infuriated. British scholar C. B. Radford criticizes Beauvoir's derivation of the philosophical from the personal, and rates *The Second Sex* as "primarily a middle-class document, so distorted by autobiographical influences that the individual problems of the writer herself may assume an exaggerated importance in her discussion of femininity."[33] Deirdre Bair, however, puts it differently: Beauvoir expanded "the study of herself into the study of all women in many different cultures and situations throughout time."[34]

Simone also relived her love affair with Nelson Algren in her 1954 novel, *The Mandarins*, and again in her 1963 memoir, *The Force of Circumstance*. In *The Force of Circumstance*, Simone dismissed sexual fidelity as "often preached, seldom practiced . . . usually experienced by those who impose it on themselves as a mutilation: they console themselves for it by sublimations or by drink." Many couples had arrangements like hers with Sartre, she added, though the danger of a new love supplanting the old always exists, and then "in place of two free persons, a victim and a torturer confront each other."[35]

Algren responded with a furious review of her book in which he ridiculed her notion of essential and contingent loves: "anybody who can experience love contingently has a mind that has recently snapped. How can love be *con-*

tingent? Contingent upon *what*? The women is speaking as if the capacity to sustain Man's basic relationship—the physical love of woman and man—were a mutilation, while freedom consists of 'maintaining through all deviations a certain fidelity!' . . . it means she is able to live only contingently."[36]

The indirect dialogue between the former lovers posed but by no means answered important questions about the nature of relationships. Algren expressed a belief in marriage founded on love and fostered by commitment and raising children. He assumed as well that spouses should live together and he ridiculed Simone and Sartre's very different sort of union. Simone, Algren added, aggrandized "a casual affection twenty years dead into a passion of classic dimension."[37]

But Simone clung to her decades-old pact. It is difficult to conclude that Simone gained through it the independence and personal autonomy she inspired in so many other women. Her insistence on relegating herself as an intellectual and philosopher to a permanent second place after Sartre, her complicity in managing his stable of women and her readiness to lie to her lovers (including Sartre) and to the media are evidence of a parallel life quite unlike the harmonious union of equals she wrote about.

In the 1960s, when Sartre was in his befogged and ailing fifties, he met Arlette Elkaïm, an eighteen-year-old Algerian Jewish student, and made her his mistress. Arlette's attraction, Simone recalled, was that "she was very young, very pretty, very intelligent. And also . . . she was shorter than he."[38] Over the years, and despite the competition of senior mistresses, Arlette won Sartre over. He adopted her, partly for immigration reasons, and made her his literary executor, a role Beauvoir had earned with her lifetime's service, including cleaning him when illness and medication cost him control of both his bladder and his bowels.

To interest Sartre, because by 1974 near-blindness made him unable to read or write, Simone began a serial interview she transformed into a sort of narrated autobiography, published in 1981 as *Adieux: A Farewell to Sartre.* In yet another violation of their pact of openness, she concealed from him how desperately ill he was with cancer, and justified the deception on the grounds that telling him "would only have darkened his last years without doing any good." When the seventy-four-year-old Sartre died in 1980, fifty thousand people walked behind his hearse to the cemetery. Simone was so distraught and numbed by Valium that she could not stand at his graveside, and had to sit on a chair. Afterward she collapsed and was hospitalized with pneumonia.

"My death will not bring us together," she wrote in conclusion. "That is how things are. It is in itself splendid that we were able to live our lives in harmony for so long."[39] It was another deception for the public, while privately she battled bitterly with Arlette—a contingency become essential—over Sartre's literary remains.

Simone de Beauvoir never wrote another book, and died in 1986, almost six years to the day after Sartre. Her life with him, her sacrifices and, even more, her compromises continue to concern women who seek in her life, as in her works, answers to their questions about their own natures, and how they should live in harmony with men.

Today, women from all walks of life continue to confront these issues. Three of them revealed in personal interviews how they resolved their struggles to shape good lives for themselves given their personal circumstances and the options open to them. Their names and details that could identify them have been altered, but otherwise their experiences are faithfully presented.

Paula

The first of these women is American Paula Birmingham. The sexual revolution shaped Paula and affirmed the feminist beliefs by which she measured herself. Twice divorced, she guarded her independence, earned her own living and supported her three daughters. Her work as a freelance editor and part-time community college English teacher was satisfying and challenging. Yet in 1976, on her thirty-eighth birthday, Paula took stock of her life and was frightened by her tally: two failed marriages, three children and too little money in the bank. She discounted her piercing intellect, erudition and wit, and saw herself as fat and aging in a world of thinner and younger women.

In the four years since her divorce, Paula had not had a single date. Her friends advised her to join Sierra Club outings, arriving early for mountain hikes so she could choose a likely man to sit with on the bus ride, hike with and, later, exchange phone numbers with. "But how do you choose them? What about their brain power and their politics? And how do you know if they're married?" Paula objected.

Her friends laughed. "Who cares? It's all about sex. That's the extent of it."

Paula reflected. She missed the intimacy and stimulation of an intense sexual relationship. "The kind of arrangement that most appealed to me was becoming some intelligent man's intellectual and sexual companion. In other words, I wanted to become a mistress," she recalled. "But before that happened, I thought I needed a one-night stand, and my friends coached me about how I could identify the signals I must have been missing any time that a man was interested in me."

Richard Alexander was the beneficiary of Paula's new awareness. Richard was a professor at University of California at Berkeley, and the keynote speaker at a rally against the Vietnam War. Soon after they were introduced, Richard admired Paula's scarf. "It reminds me of my mother's favorite one," he said. Paula tensed: her friends had said that one telltale indication of a man's interest is when he links you to his mother. Could this be what prompted Richard's remark?

It was, and before the week was out, Richard was sitting in Paula's modest living room guzzling a bottle of Scotch and conversing animatedly. After-ward, he proposed dinner at an elegant restaurant, and did not object when Paula insisted on paying her half of the bill. "I'm going to make a pass at you," Richard announced afterward, and drove to a friend's conveniently vacant apartment. Paula was nervous but determined to achieve the one-night stand that would liberate her. She stripped but kept on her half-slip and pulled it over her breasts. But as they lay in each other's arms in the frenzy of sex, Paula forgot both her nervousness and her nakedness. Afterward, at home in her bed, she hugged herself in self-congratulation. She had just made passionate love to a near stranger, a married man she might never see again. She had finally freed herself from the inhibitions that had anchored her in vague lone-liness and a sense that life was passing her by.

But Richard called again. Before long, Paula was smitten, and Richard seemed taken as well. They began to see each other regularly, but only on week-days, because Richard never missed weekends with his family. The sexual dimension of their relationship seemed perfect, "and of course in those days," Paula recalls, "before AIDS and all today's bleak warnings, we never gave STDs a thought, and as I'd had my tubes tied, even pregnancy wasn't an issue. Sex was worry-free, and we were too careful to even really fear getting caught."

The emotional dimension was not as easy. Both Paula and Richard wrestled with their guilt at deceiving Cindy, Richard's wife. Paula knew that the couple fought bitterly, and that years earlier, Richard had left her for another woman, only to return home after Cindy pretended she was pregnant. Paula believed he would never separate or divorce, but apart from her feminist sense that she was betraying another woman, the arrangement suited her very well. Paula's anxious expression softened and she radiated sexual confidence. Suddenly other men noticed her, or perhaps she was just learning how to interpret the signals. Paula began to see two other men, both professors at San Francisco State University, both married and both sleeping with at least one other woman.

One day at her apartment Richard noticed two vases of cut flowers. He said nothing, but later presented Paula with one of his rare gifts, a superb vase. "Unlike those flowers, this will last forever," he said. Soon after, he told her that he loved her. It was not an uncomplicated declaration. "My children come first and they always will," he told her. "But you are, and will always be, the great love of my life."

Paula stopped seeing other men and reveled in her new life as Richard's mistress, sharing intimacy and sex with an intelligent and compatible man. But she insisted that their relationship remain strictly egalitarian. "I loathe the notion of 'kept' women," Paula explains, her small nose wrinkling with distaste. "I hate the institution of 'kept' women as much as I do traditional marriage, where they are 'kept' down and subservient, forced to ask for money, wheedle it out of their menfolk, use sex as a tool and so on." Richard earned almost three times her salary and had inherited a substantial trust fund, but they split every bill in two, even though this constituted a financial hardship for Paula.

"But we were equal. I was Richard's mistress in exactly the same way he was my lover. Sure it cost me money, but not my self-respect. It wasn't his fault he had more money than I did. History, society, the 'system' were responsible, not Richard."

After a year, Richard was so deeply committed to Paula that he added Sunday to the routine of their rendezvous. Every Sunday after the church service he faithfully attended, Richard would drop Cindy and the children off at home and set off "for the office, to work." Then he drove straight to Paula's, where they ate lunch and spent the afternoon together until just before dinnertime—Richard was scrupulous about eating dinner with his children.

After several years, Richard and Cindy had a particularly fierce fight that culminated in his asking her for a divorce. Cindy agreed. Richard and his son moved out into an apartment.

For Paula, the new arrangement was perfect. She had not caused Richard and Cindy's failed marriage, though she was its catalyst. She could see Richard more often, but not too much. Until her children left home, she reserved most of her free time for them.

Years later, after all the children had grown up and left home, Richard reevaluated his life. He found that living alone felt too tentative and lonesome. Paula was the love of his life and, to her profound shock and surprise, he decided he wanted to marry her.

But Paula was one mistress who did not want to marry. Living alone had given her a taste of independence she had no intention of relinquishing, and she declined Richard's proposal. He persisted and they began to quarrel. Twice they broke up over the issue. Finally, rather than lose the man she loved, Paula agreed to a marriage as egalitarian as their current arrangement.

"I preferred being a mistress," Paula shrugs. "I adored living on my own. But on the whole, the marriage has worked out. I am no more a 'kept' wife than I was a 'kept' woman, and so my self-respect, and hence my respect for Richard, remain intact. We continue to suit each other amazingly well, and on every level. We are still as compatible culturally and politically as we have always been in bed. Even now, after decades, the magic is there." And yet, Paula adds wistfully, "I loved being a mistress. I gave and got all the affection and sex I wanted, but there was no accountability, no sense of being trapped in the routine of cohabitation. If Richard were a less traditional man, I'd still be his mistress."

Rachel

Rachel Goldman came of age during the sexual revolution and absorbed its ideals about gender equality. She went to university and developed a passion for environmental issues; she is now considered an expert "green," and is the author of a textbook on ecological issues. But in her personal life, the Shoah and not the sexual revolution has shaped her hopes and her dreams.

Rachel was born in Montreal to a Polish Jewish mother whose arranged marriage to a Russian immigrant had enabled her to escape Nazi-occupied Poland. In 1941, her pregnant mother received terrible news from Poland. There had been a massacre of Jews, and her mother, father, brothers, sisters, aunts, uncles, cousins, friends and neighbors—her entire community—had been slaughtered. She delivered her firstborn, Rachel, into a world of sadness and loss, a world in which the search for surviving relatives overrode all else.

Rachel absorbed her mother's unending grief. She, too, longed for relatives, and she grew up in a state of chronic loneliness, yearning for connections, dreaming of finding lost bloodlines. "The Holocaust affected me from the day of my first consciousness of it. It drew me to the Diaspora, to New York and especially to Israel, where I would go and search for names. I would have been happy to find even a sixth cousin ten times removed, or even just someone from my mother's village."

Rachel saw marriage and children—hers and her brothers'—as ways of recreating the family that had been cut down in a single day. But her marriage to a pediatrician failed. Her sisters-in-law shunned her as an overly educated feminist whose lifestyle threatened their traditional, stay-at-home lives.

After her divorce, Rachel worked, raised her children and suffered through a poisonous affair with a man who would not tolerate her children. And then, when she was a plump and exhausted forty-seven-year-old, she met Ben, a slightly older Israeli environmental specialist who consulted internationally and was visiting Montreal on business. They had dinner at a restaurant. Rachel could scarcely control the trembling in her limbs as she sat with this stranger, picking at her food and falling deeply in love with him. Ben reciprocated, and the next day they slept together. The experience was transcendent. Ben was a powerful personality in a muscular body, and he expressed his sensuality and *joie de vivre* through tender but uninhibited sex.

"Ben is not conventionally handsome, except for his wonderful blue eyes. But he has an extraordinary vitality, energy and a sense of joy about him," Rachel recalled. "It's like the world was created for him. He loves good food, beautiful scenery, great sex."

The new lovers began to unburden themselves to each other. Rachel was seeking a committed relationship. Ben was in a loveless, sexless marriage and had filed for divorce. They managed to meet every three weeks, in Montreal and New York, and much less frequently, in Israel. Each reunion was as thrilling as the last one, beginning with sex the instant Ben arrived and closed their hotel-room door. Dinner followed, with wine and a sense of specialness. Back in the hotel, they made love again, then slept. Ben wakened before dawn, again reached out for Rachel and made love to her.

One evening at dinner, Ben told Rachel that he had bad news. Rachel listened in silent shock. Ben's wife refused to end their marriage. Divorce would humiliate her, she could not bear to live alone, and if he persisted in going through with it, she would take half of everything they had and everything he would ever earn, including his pension. "So there you have it, my love. I'm not free to marry you and I may never be. This"—gesturing at the candle-lit table laden with heaped plates and an uncorked wine bottle—"is what we can have, today and tonight, and I hope a lot of days and a lot of nights. It's up to you, Rachel. We can stop now, we can be friends, we can be nothing, or we can go on. Your decision. This much I can tell you honestly. You and my wife are the only women in my life, and there will never be more."

Rachel was devastated. She loved Ben passionately. She had expected that, eventually, he would either marry her or at least acknowledge her as his partner. She knew that he would never leave Israel, but she had always dreamed of living there, and his commitment to the Jewish homeland was part of his appeal.

"Your decision," Ben said. Rachel made that decision right there in the restaurant. She could not bear to lose him, and was willing to love him in the only way left to her, as his mistress. "Only I couldn't bear for you to abandon me," she said. "If you ever want to leave me, I'll need notice so I can try to adjust to the pain."

The years passed. Rachel applied her feminist beliefs to her mistressdom and its financial implications. She insisted on buying her own plane tickets although—from necessity—she allowed Ben to pay for other expenses she incurred on her trips. Over the course of twelve years, he gave her only four gifts. He also chose a perfume for her—Opium—and brought her bottles of it from duty free shops around the world.

Several years into the relationship, Rachel was diagnosed with an autoimmune disorder that left her chronically fatigued and in pain. She was laid off from her position with an environmental NGO and soon exhausted her severance pay. She could not keep up her mortgage payments, and the bank seized her house. For a period of about four years, Rachel had nowhere to live. "I was creatively homeless. I stored my belongings here and there, found a home for my cat and made extended 'visits' to friends and to my children." Sometimes she had to turn to her brothers for money for food.

During these years, Rachel accepted plane tickets from Ben but never mentioned her homelessness. "The truth is, I didn't know what Ben would do, and I didn't want to find out." Rather than risk yet another rejection, another loss, she held her tongue. "I thought if I lost Ben, I would become suicidal."

Later, when she had crawled out from under her mountain of debt and was trying to buy a little house, Ben wired her the last five thousand dollars that were beyond her power to raise. This was not easy, because his wife kept a close eye on his accounts.

And then, when Rachel had reestablished herself, Ben fell ill with cancer and, almost simultaneously, suffered a heart attack. He survived and returned to work, then suffered a relapse and was hospitalized. During this period of incapacitation, his wife rifled through his papers. His accounts and his credit card and telephone bills told her what Ben had not: that he had a mistress. Just before Ben was carried away for emergency surgery, his enraged wife pressured him into telling her about Rachel.

When Rachel traveled to Israel, Ben made very little time for her, an hour here, an hour there, no more. It was the only way he could circumvent his wife's vigilance, he explained—he had so many family obligations.

Rachel was grief-stricken. Suddenly—or so she perceived it—her lover had put her last on his list of priorities. During one of their rare rendezvous, she confronted him with her unhappiness. "Before, I used to be equal to your family, and you gave me the time I needed," she told him. "Now I'm getting less and less time, less and less thought. I'm like your cleaning lady or the accountant, just someone who provides you a service, in my case sex." The magic of their relationship had disintegrated into sparks of memory.

The end of the affair has been painful. "I'm sad, but I have my dignity to protect," Rachel said. "And I'm lonely, and I don't want to grow old alone. I'm a TV addict. Television has become my best friend." She still plans to retire to Israel, though she notes that older unattached women abound there, many widowed by the endless war. Having lost Ben, she has likely lost her last chance of finding a mate.

Rachel sits pensively as she considers her life with Ben. Fatigue has etched dark circles under her gray eyes, and her fine brown hair is silvered. Her gaze is sad and sweet. Briefly, a crooked smile transforms her. Rachel draws contradictory conclusions from her decade as Ben's mistress. Her caustic comment that "the promises of a married man are worth nothing at all" coexists with recollections, expressed with a catch in her voice, of the intensity of their love, the marvel of their erotic couplings. She can never forget how she learned "with Ben and from Ben, how much infinity can be captured in a single moment."

Michaela

Michaela Kovaleski was born in 1972 in Toronto, into a sexually revolutionized world where women had equal rights and obligations. Yet Michaela found equality burdensome, and longed to become a kept woman like Pamela Harriman or even Virginia Hill, trading glamor and sex for luxury and financial security. "I had been looking for a sugar daddy for a long time. I always wanted more money, and more easy money. And I have an attraction to the sex trade that I haven't quite figured out."

Michaela's attitude to sex is unorthodox even for her generation. Love, she believes, ought to be kept separate from sex. At eighteen, one of the few virgins in her circle of friends, Michaela orchestrated her defloration with a "computer geek" she felt no attraction to. Her next sexual partner was a much older psychiatrist who approached her as they waited together in an ATM line. With her parents' permission, she began to date him. Almost immediately, he took her to bed. In retrospect, Michaela believes the physician was "a bit exploitative," but she harbors no resentment because she appreciated his gifts, including small sums of money.

After graduating from university with an honors degree in French followed by teachers college, Michaela briefly sought the exoticism of Montreal's nightclubs, where she waitressed and, for a commission, lured men into buying drinks. "I was good at it, and I loved it. But I wanted badly to do some serious modeling, and Toronto had much more work."

Back in her home city, Michaela taught night school and struggled to establish herself as a professional model. During this stressful period, she began to date Justin, an older man whose once successful dot-com company had just gone bankrupt. Justin encouraged Michaela to teach, and with much reluctance, she accepted a full-time position in a high school. She hated teaching so profoundly that she still cannot speak about it without weeping. In the first semester of her second year, Michaela resigned and began full-time supply teaching. For the first time in over a year, she was happy, though she earned much less and had no benefits. To supplement her income, she perused the Men Seeking Women section of the personal ads. After choosing "Sammy," she sent him an old modeling folio in response to his request for photos.

Sammy liked what he saw and invited Michaela to his hometown of Darien, Connecticut. He greeted her at the airport carrying flowers. Though he was short, overweight and homely, he was generous and considerate. He took Michaela shopping, her favorite pastime, and bought her expensive clothes. Her favorite was a suit of black latex and leather that "stuck to my body like sweat." Michaela was ecstatic. "Sammy was a man who loved to shop for a woman, and I am a woman who loves to have things bought for her." Later on, Michaela teased Sammy with a sexual game that led quickly to bed and to real sex. After all the money he had spent on her, she reasoned, he deserved it.

Back in Toronto, Michaela heard from Sammy every two or three days. He complained about his wife, Ida, whom he described as an uneducated but streetwise Italian woman with Mafia ties. Michaela hinted about her own problems, all of them financial. Sammy responded immediately. "It would be easiest for me to deposit money into your bank account every month," he said. "How does five thousand sound?" Michaela countered with three thousand. "I didn't want to scare him off and I was afraid of draining him. I mean, what was he getting out of the deal?"

Michaela was now a full-fledged mistress, a "kept" woman with enough money to support herself and Justin, whose existence she concealed from Sammy. She even stopped supply teaching. But soon her expensive tastes drove her to suggest increased payments. Justin, who benefited from Sammy's money, gave Michaela his subdued approval to continue the affair. Juggling two men added to the thrill as well as the challenge of the situation.

Michaela's next encounter with Sammy was in the Bahamas, where he was vacationing with his wife and adolescent son. He booked Michaela into a five-star luxury resort down the beach from his own and, whenever he could escape from his family obligations, he visited her, took her shopping and even spent three of six nights with her. "I was his escape from his work and his wife, and I was just fine playing that role." Michaela spent most of her six days in the spa. "Sammy paid for everything. You could say that Sammy even paid for my breathing."

Back in Toronto, Michaela's parallel affairs became complicated. Justin was jealous and depressed, and began to drink heavily. Sammy, on the other hand, seemed to be falling in love with her. In Toronto's bleak and cold February, Sammy sent Michaela a ticket to Florida, the first leg of a whirlwind Palm Beach–Las Vegas "business" trip. Justin wept, but these rendezvous were their bread and butter.

In Florida, Sammy shared Michaela's room. She did not welcome this new intimacy and found his constant presence unsettling. It was harder for her to telephone Justin. Despite shopping binges and fine restaurant dinners, Michaela realized that she much preferred Sammy as a mostly absentee lover.

Back in Toronto with her new clothes, Michaela and Justin resolved their relationship problems by announcing their engagement, though not, of course, to Sammy. In March, on Michaela's birthday, Sammy failed to arrive in Toronto as planned. Puzzled, Michaela phoned him at home as she had done before. His wife, Ida, answered and said Sammy was in the shower. Michaela thanked her and declined to leave a message. For the next six days, Michaela tried to contact Sammy, but he never answered or called her back. He also stopped his monthly payments to her.

Ida, however, began to leave "creepy" messages on Michaela's answering machine, frightening reminders that Ida had Mafia connections. Michaela became so anxious that she contacted Ron, one of Sammy's associates, to find out whether she was in danger. Ron explained that Ida had discovered that Michaela was Sammy's mistress and had confronted Sammy about it. The couple had then had one of their famously "dirty" fights, and resolved it by deciding to resume marital relations. Coincidentally, Ron added, Sammy had suffered a business reverse and was in deep financial trouble.

Michaela's tenure as Sammy's mistress was over. She is once again a supply teacher trying to make it as a model. Because she does not associate love with sex, she finds monogamy oppressive. Though she loves him, Justin bores her sexually.

"People express love by giving you money. I want lots and lots of it," Michaela says. Furthermore, exchanging sex for money is very appealing to her and she is always tempted by the personal ads. It would be delightful to slide into the role of mistress to another man like Sammy.

Michaela defends herself as a rebellious child of the sexual revolution, a woman who would willingly sacrifice some of her equal rights and her personal and sexual autonomy in return for large and regular sums of money. "I have this work ethic," she explains. "I believe the man should get back the same value as he gives."

Modern mistresses use modern standards, to which feminism and tradition both contribute, to choose and evaluate their lifestyles. Various factors influence them, including sexual and emotional fulfillment, egalitarianism, financial considerations and their views on marriage. The majority of today's mistresses are pragmatists who would likely not have entered into their relationships had they not fallen in love with a married man, and many would prefer the status of wife rather than mistress to their lover.

On the other hand, some modern women who romanticize and fantasize about historic mistressdom have no hesitation about receiving money. They see financial support as integral to mistressdom, indeed, one of its most attractive features, and often what prompts them to become mistresses in the first place. In their version of mistressdom, feminist egalitarianism takes second place to their lover's desires, and the imbalance between them and their lovers is fundamental to the structure of their relationship.

Conclusion:
Mistresses Met

I UNDERTOOK this exploration of millennia of mistresses seeking to answer a plethora of questions: Throughout the ages and in various cultures, what has a mistress been? How has the nature of her relationship with her lover reflected the status and role of women in her society? How has it affected the institution of marriage to which it is integrally linked? And how have mistresses—women as personally different from each other as the Greek intellectual Aspasia, my long-ago German friend Kati, my Haitian acquaintance Ghislaine, the mobster's moll Virginia Hill or Prince Charles's beloved Camilla Parker-Bowles—felt about and defined their experiences?

Early on in my research, I discovered that an astonishing number of women of my acquaintance actually were or had been mistresses—Iris Nowell, a member of my book club, has even written a book, *Hot Breakfast for Sparrows*, about her life as renowned artist Harold Towne's mistress. Other women also identified themselves as mistresses, though almost always in confidence. "You may use my story," they told me one after the other, "but you have to change names and identifying details." Mistresses, I quickly realized, are ubiquitous even in today's liberated, divorce-prone society, but unlike Iris, a good many, perhaps most, prefer to conceal their relationships, past as well as present.

At first it was difficult to see what connection these modern mistresses could have with their historic forebears, but before long the parallels and similarities emerged. Whether ancient or contemporary, each woman's story is unique, but the sum total of each narrative is the stuff of a much wider history.

Conclusion: Mistresses Met

That history begins with concubinage. Concubinage, in many respects a precursor to mistressdom, developed as an offshoot of marriage and of the almost universal tolerance of male infidelity. Possessing concubines permitted husbands to indulge themselves in sexual relationships that, though extramarital, were legally condoned and socially acceptable. Men could flaunt these "other" women as symbols of prestige and of their wealth. They could also use them for wifelike domestic duties; indeed, concubines often worked alongside their lover-master's wife, subject to her will.

Like Hagar the Egyptian, concubines were often slaves owned by either their lover or his wife. They had limited rights and security. As their societies evolved, most were granted the privilege of bearing their master's children and providing him with heirs he could legitimize; the Japanese term "borrowed womb" is an elegant expression of this important function.

Concubinage also allowed unmarried men to enjoy intimate relationships with lower-ranked women their society deemed unsuitable to be their wives. Like Pericles' Aspasia and Saint Augustine's Dolorosa, such a woman might be a wife in everything but name, sharing her lover's life, living under his roof and bearing his children. Other concubines served as mere sexual outlets for men who showed them neither affection nor esteem.

Concubinage disintegrates as a viable institution as societies modernize and abandon lifestyles their citizens now disdain as embarrassingly outmoded. Newly empowered women reject both the role of concubine and also the role of a wife whose marriage includes a concubine. But marital infidelity continues to exist, and so mistressdom accommodates it. This happened when imperial Rome was at the height of its affluence and its privileged elite disdained the old values that held its women to strict standards of chastity and obedience. Defiant patrician women imitated their husbands and took lovers, becoming the mistresses of lusty bachelors or of other women's unfaithful husbands. And when China recast itself as an egalitarian communist society and outlawed the concubinage that had previously flourished, wealthy men who could no longer acquire concubines began to take mistresses instead. Unlike concubines, these mistresses seldom lived with their lovers as concubines usually had. Indeed, cohabitation is an important feature distinguishing concubines from mistresses; not only do mistresses seldom cohabit, but cohabitation very often got the lovers into the sort of trouble a mere extramarital affair did not. Society tormented Marian Evans for cohabiting with her married lover, George Lewes, and the Church punished Countess Teresa Guiccioli for her brief sojourn under Byron's roof. Even court mistresses were merely lodged conveniently near but not actually with their royal or noble lovers, almost all of whom were married and were required to maintain the appearances of familial relations with their wives.

The near-ban on cohabitation is symptomatic of the less formal nature of mistressdom. Yet mistresses share many characteristics and experiences. Sex is an obvious common denominator. Sex looms large in a mistress's life, and unlike wives required to submit to sexual intercourse but not necessarily to excel in it, mistresses understand the importance of keeping their man through sexual attachment. Those who lack sexual virtuosity are often tortured by the fear that they will lose their lovers.

At the same time, fruitful sex has the same undesirable result, for the pregnant mistress is often dismissed and left to cope alone with her unwanted bastard. Until very recently, when legal reforms introduced more egalitarian and child-centered standards and when the miracles of DNA provided testamentary tools, pregnancy was often a terrifying or tragic consequence of mistressdom.

Love is second only to sex in the lexicon of mistressdom. Historically, men usually chose young and attractive women for their sexual unions, and often fell in love with them. At the same time, for much of history little value was placed on romantic love; indeed, it was scorned or feared as a base emotion unworthy of serious consideration, perhaps even destructive to solid relationships. It has only been legitimized as a desirable factor in marriage within the past two centuries. In consequence, even lovestruck men could easily tire of a mistress who seemed demanding or jealous, or who compared unfavorably to a new rival.

Unlike the lovers who chose them, a great many mistresses never loved their male partners, nor did they expect to. Even today, in a culture that reveres and encourages romantic love, Mafia molls and the throwaway playgirl mistresses of wealthy playboys often despise their lovers; for such women, mistressdom has other rewards. On the other hand, some women are so amorously and erotically attached to their lovers that love dominates their lives. Historically, however, they have been the exception.

Like sex and love, lush and preferably youthful beauty has traditionally been associated with mistresses, though a degree of maturity in a married mistress has also been acceptable. Especially when reinforced by sexual prowess, a mistress's beauty can occasionally so enchant a man that he willingly surrenders something of his male privilege to its possessor: the Turkish sultan Suleiman succumbed to the power of Roxelana's beauty, and the Bavarian

King Ludwig to Lola Montez's. Much more frequently, however, beauty is simply expected, and mistresses understand the importance of maintaining it.

In this context, age is a mistress's implacable foe, eroding the beauty that is often her chief capital. In unhealthier centuries, this was more spectacularly true. Traditionally, mistresses have accepted the urgency of enhancing and, above all, retaining their beauty, hence their almost ritual reliance on grooming, cosmetics, jewelry and clothing.

Because mistressdom, unlike concubinage, is illicit even in the most hedonistic societies, it provokes guilt, rationalization, sacrifice and secrecy. The ubiquitous double standard not only condemns the errant woman more than her male partner-in-sin, it also reinforces her insecurity. So do the social conventions that govern mistressdom; they have always been fairly detailed, and the centuries have not drastically changed them. As a rule, mistresses are invited only to intimate events whose other celebrants will be discreet: certain clubs, short business trips and the homes of understanding friends. Sometimes the only safe house is the mistress's own.

The insecurity, self-loathing and anxiety endemic to their lives have driven many mistresses to shop or gamble compulsively, as much as possible with their lovers' money. Many also numb themselves with alcohol and drugs or other self-destructive activities. Mistresses as disparate as Émilie du Châtelet, Eva Braun, Marilyn Monroe, Virginia Hill and Vicki Morgan attempted suicide, and Jeanne Hébuterne, mistress of the moody, impulsive and impoverished painter Modigliani, succeeded. No wonder that, with notable exceptions such as Héloise and Simone de Beauvoir, mistresses have longed to marry their lovers and enjoy the security and respect society accords wives.

Death underscores a mistress's inferior status. When their lovers die, most mistresses lose whatever status they had managed to acquire from their liaison. They are usually unwelcome at the death and funeral rites, and are often excluded from their lovers' wills. Charles II's long-term mistress Nell Gwynne suffered this fate, and Charles appeared to regret it only on his deathbed, where he mumbled ineffectually, "Don't let poor Nell starve."

Today, mistressdom still prevails everywhere. As always, it is founded on male marital infidelity, and it complements and buttresses marriage. But as marriage changes, so does the nature of mistressdom. Feminism and egalitarianism, the sexual revolution and the Pill, and changing mores and standards, notably the elevation of romantic love to an ideal, have stamped marriage as irrevocably as they have the men and women who become each other's husbands and wives, and they have had a ricochet effect on mistressdom.

Marriage has also been transformed by women's altered position in society, by the recognition of women's need for personal and professional fulfillment, to experience orgasm, to live equally with men. Technological advances permit birth control and family planning, and also offer the likelihood of good health for longer lifespans.

Today's spouses believe as well that romantic love should be at the core of their union, and they grieve when domesticity or familiarity deadens it. They search their hearts to discover if they truly love a potential spouse and to decide whether or not to remain married. Love outside of marriage may seem a betrayal not merely of the marriage but also of the sanctity of love itself; often spouses divorce to marry the beloved one because of the intensity of their love.

All these changes have led to well-documented increases in divorce, but also of remarriage; people continue to seek in new marriages that which previous unions failed to give them. The process of divorce has been greatly eased, and divorce itself no longer carries a stigma. Marriage laws are under continual revision, in particular with regard to property and custody or, in the latest parlance, parenting of children.

Outside the courts, thoughtful men and women debate whether marriage is merely a bourgeois financial arrangement in which men offer protection in return for sex, differing from mistressdom only in that it is legally sanctioned. They challenge the traditional concept of marriage for its sexual and sexist underpinnings, and reject the word *wife* for its connotations of women as chattel. Women refuse to exchange their father's surname for their husband's; in the province of Quebec, such name-changing is not even legally recognized. Many men and women prefer to see their union as a partnership that corresponds to their need for a committed relationship between two consenting adults, a relationship in which sex plays an important but not a central role.

At the same time, traditional marriage exists side by side with new versions of society's core union. The confusion and ambiguity about the nature of the institution has now spilled over from personal and public debate into courts and legislatures, which are currently attempting to redefine its boundaries. Employers have already responded to employees' concerns, and many extend benefits once restricted to legally married spouses to "partners" unmarried or married, of the same or opposite sex.

All of this matters, because women have many more rights than they used to, and these translate into financial and other claims they may legitimately make on lovers. At the same time, many, perhaps most, marriages are recognizably traditional in structure, between men and women who enter them voluntarily. The essential change is in what each spouse expects of the other, now that women are not only entitled to work, but are often required to, and now that both husband and wife expect to deeply love and be loved by each other.

These sea changes in marriage directly affect mistressdom, the parallel institution. For one thing, even the definition of mistressdom is now unclear, and circumstances that once clearly described a mistress may now describe a girlfriend or a common-law wife. Intention is becoming a new standard for deciding such arrangements: what did each person understand by the arrangement? What was said that might constitute a contractual obligation between them? Most importantly, the days are long gone when a man can refuse to acknowledge and support any children he conceives with his mistress—the legal concept of illegitimacy is swiftly disappearing.

The consequence of all this is not that mistressdom is disappearing, but rather that it has absorbed and now reflects the changes in marriage, in legal notions of contractual obligation and in society's propensity to live and let live. A mistress who can establish that she has been a "significant other" in a sexual relationship may have her day in court, though her triumph is by no means assured.

But legal suits and claims are the consequence of soured relationships usually forged on promises (or at least expectations) of love and sex, or sex and love. In fact, legions of modern women become mistresses for reasons quite different from those of their forebears, most notably in the realm of personal choice. Women may choose mistressdom over marriage, permanently or for the short term, because they are consumed by passion for a career or vocation or driven by the need for economic self-sufficiency and personal autonomy. Others, having observed their parents' marriages, may simply shrug off wifedom and choose instead the sexual and affectionate dimensions of mistressdom while rejecting the demands of domesticity. When this happens, these mistresses often achieve a high degree of satisfaction in their relationships.

At the same time, it is depressingly remarkable how the experiences of so many modern mistresses resemble those of mistresses past. Mistressdom remains an extension of marriage, a sanctioned outlet for male sexuality. At the same time, even the most liberated women who fall in love and consort with married men are often stimulated by the forbidden nature of their relationship, by its risks, their complicity in their lover's adultery, their defiance of social niceties. Their love, legitimate in the sense that it is a real feeling, is heightened by its illegitimacy. These days, too, the stakes are seldom as high as in the past. Today, a woman as well as a man may indulge in a passionate attraction for its own sake, as an erotic adventure and a surrender to the senses, a delicious interval with a lover who is not, strictly speaking, available, and whom she usually shares with another woman. Yet despite these liberated and liberating possibilities, too many mistresses still cast themselves in the ancient mold, with all its sacrifices and sadness, measuring themselves against the marital model, and finding themselves wanting.

Endnotes

CHAPTER 1

1   The most important source for this section is the Book of Genesis, chapters 16–21:21 and 25:1–18. I used the *The New Oxford Annotated Bible* (New York: Oxford University Press, 1989), supplemented by the following articles that clarify, illuminate and hypothesize about the relevant section in the Book of Genesis: John Otwell, *And Sarah Laughed: The Status of Women in the Old Testament* (Philadelphia: Westminster Press, 1977); Savina J. Teubal, *Hagar the Egyptian: The Lost Tradition of the Matriarchs* (San Francisco/New York/Grand Rapids: Harper & Row, 1990); Phyllis Trible, *Texts of Terror* (Philadelphia, USA: Fortress Press, 1984); John W. Waters, "Who Was Hagar?" in *Stony the Road We Trod: African American Biblical Interpretation*. The Book of Genesis, 16:1–16, 21:8–21, narrates the dramatic story of Hagar in a very few verses that remain tremendously contentious, as scholars continue to debate their true meaning. This includes rereading of the biblical texts and of legal documents and codes then operative, and rigorous analysis, comparison and deconstruction of the texts. I have read, reflected and—with some trepidation— arrived at my own understanding of this shadowy figure who has cast such a long shadow over the centuries. (Phyllis Ocean Berman's article "Creative Hidrash: Why Hagar Left," *Tikkun* 12, [March–April 1997], 21–25, notes that she and her fellow students in Hebrew school heard "the story of the competition between Sarah and Hagar not just once but twice a year in the Torah reading cycle." No wonder Hagar continues to fascinate and attract such concentrated and sometimes bitter attention.)

2   The main sources for the following section are http://langmuir.physics.uoguelph. ca/~aelius/hetairai.html; Shannon Bell, *Reading, Writing & Rewriting the Prostitute Body* (Bloomington and Indianapolis: Indiana University Press, 1994); Eva Cantarella, tr. by Maureen B. Fant, *Pandora's Daughters: The Role and Status of Women in Greek and Roman Antiquity* (Baltimore: Johns Hopkins University Press, 1987); James N. Davidson, *Courtesans and Fishcakes: The Consuming Passions of*

Classical Athens (London: HarperCollins, 1997); Nancy Demand, *Birth, Death and Motherhood in Classical Greece* (Baltimore: Johns Hopkins University Press, 1994); Robert Flacelieve, *Love in Ancient Greece* (London: Frederick Muller Ltd., 1960); Roger Just, *Women in Athenian Law and Life* (London, New York: Routledge, 1989); Eva C. Keuls, *The Reign of the Phallus: Sexual Politics in Ancient Greece* (New York: Harper & Row, 1985); Jill Kleinman, "The Representation of Prostitutes Versus Respectable Women on Ancient Greek Vases." Available online at http://www. perseus.tufts.edu/classes/JKp.html (1998, Aug. 6); Hans Licht, *Sexual Life in Ancient Greece* (London: George Routledge & Sons, Ltd., 1932); Sarah B. Pomeroy, *Goddesses, Whores, Wives, and Slaves: Women in Classical Antiquity* (New York: Schocken Books, 1975).

3   Bell, 32–38, analyses the meaning of *Menexenus*'s many references to Aspasia as a teacher responsible for numerous political speeches attributed to her pupils, including Pericles.

4   Madeleine Mary Henry *Prisoner of History: Aspasia of Miletus and Her Bibliographical Tradition* (New York: Oxford University Press, 1995), 44, citing Cicero and Quintilian, who both preserved this fragment.

5   The main sources for the following section are Richard A. Bauman, *Women and Politics in Ancient Rome* (New York: Routledge, 1992); Eva Cantarella, tr. by Maureen B. Fant, *Pandora's Daughters: The Role and Status of Women in Greek and Roman Antiquity* (Baltimore: Johns Hopkins University Press, 1987); Jane F. Gardner, *Women in Roman Law and Society* (Bloomington: Indiana University Press, 1986); Ellen Greene, *The Erotics of Domination: Male Desire and the Mistress in Latin Love Poetry* (Baltimore: Johns Hopkins University Press, 1998); Mary R. Lefkowitz and Maureen B. Fant, *Women's Life in Greece and Rome: A Source Book in Translation* (2nd ed.) (Baltimore: Johns Hopkins University Press, 1992); Sara Mack, *Ovid* (New Haven: Yale University Press, 1988); Ovid, tr. and ed. by Peter Green, *The Erotic Poems* (New York: Penguin Books, 1982); Sarah B. Pomeroy, *Goddesses, Whores, Wives, and Slaves: Women in Classical Antiquity* (New York: Schocken Books, 1976); Ronald Syme, *History in Ovid* (Oxford: Clarendon Press, 1978); John C. Thibault, *The Mystery of Ovid's Exile* (Berkeley: University of California Press, 1964); L. P. Wilkinson, *Ovid Recalled* (Cambridge: Cambridge University Press, 1955).

6   Ovid, tr. and ed. by Peter Green, "The Amores: Book 1," in *The Erotic Poems*, 89.

7   Ibid., 89.

8   Ibid., 97.

9   Ovid, "The Amores," III, 7, in Diane J. Rayor and William W. Batshaw (eds.), *Latin Lyric and Elegiac Poetry: An Anthology of New Translations* (New York: Garland Publishing, 1995).

10 The main sources for this section are Antti Arjava, *Women and Law in Late Antiquity* (Oxford: Clarendon Press, 1996); St. Augustine, *Confessions* (London: Penguin Books, 1961); Gerald Bonner, *St. Augustine of Hippo: Life and Controversies* (London: SCM Press Ltd., 1963); William Mallard, *Language and Love: Introducing Augustine's Religious Thought Through the Confessions Story* (University Park: Pennsylvania: Pennsylvania University State Press, 1994); Margaret R. Miles, *Desire and Delight: A New Reading of Augustine's* Confessions (New York: Crossroad Publishing Co., 1992); Kim Power, *Veiled Desire: Augustine on Women* (New York: Continuum Publishing Co., 1996).

11 Like Pericles and Ovid for Aspasia and Corinna, Augustine is our primary source for Dolorosa. Hence the importance of his *Confessions*.

12 Bonner, 54.
13 Power, 98.

CHAPTER 2

1 The main sources for the following section are Jung Chang, *Wild Swans: Three Daughters of China* (New York: Simon & Schuster, 1991); Kang-i Sun Chang, *The Late Ming Poet: Ch'en Tzu-lung,* (New Haven: Yale university Press, 1991); Gail Hershatter, "Courtesans and Streetwalkers: The Changing Discourses on Shanghai Prostitution, 1890–1949," *Journal of the History of Sexuality,* (Oct. 1992), 3, no. 2, 245–269; *Inside Stories of the Forbidden City,* tr. by Zhao Shuhan (Beijing: New World Press, 1986); Maria Jaschok and Suzanne Miers (eds.), *Women in the Chinese Patriarchal System: Submission, Servitude, Escape and Collusion* (London: Zed Books Ltd., 1994); Maria Jaschok, *Concubines and Bondservants* (N.J.: Zed Books, 1989); Keith McMahon, *Misers, Shrews, and Polygamists: Sexuality and Male-Female Relations in 18th Century Chinese Fiction* (Durham: Duke University Press, 1995); Marinus Johan Meijer, *Murder and Adultery in Late Imperial China* (The Netherlands: E.J. Brill, 1991); James A. Millward, "A Uyghur Muslim in Qianlong's Court: The Meanings of the Fragrant Concubine," *Journal of Asian Studies,* 53, no. 2 (May 1994), 427–458; Albert Richard O'Hara, *The Position of Women in Early China* (Taipei: Mei Ya Publications, 1971); Sterling Seagrave, *Dragon Lady: The Life and Legend of the Last Empress of China* (New York: Knopf, 1992); Marina Warner, *The Dragon Empress: Life and Times of Tz'u-hsi: 1835–1908, Empress Dowager of China* (London: Weidenfeld & Nicolson, 1972).
2 Fu Xuan, third century, cited by Seagrave, 29.
3 Denise Chong, *The Concubine's Children* (Toronto: Viking, 1994), 8.
4 The Female Domestic Ordinance of 1923 abolished the *mooi-jai* institution, but traces survived much longer.
5 The source for May-ying is Chong, *The Concubine's Children.*
6 The main sources for the following sections on Japanese concubines and geisha are Liza Crihfield Dalby, "Courtesans and Geisha: The Real Women of the Pleasure Quarter," in Elizabeth de Sabato Swinton (ed.) *Women of the Pleasure Quarter: Japanese Paintings and Prints of the Floating World* (New York: Hudson Hills Press, 1995); Liza Crihfield Dalby, *Geisha* (Berkeley: University of California Press, 1998); Liza Dalby, "Tempest in a Teahouse," *Far Eastern Economic Review,* 27 July 1989, 36–37; Sheldon Garon, *Molding Japanese Minds: The State in Everyday Life* (Princeton: Princeton University Press, 1992); Joy Henry, *Understanding Japanese Society* (New York: Routledge, 1987); Laura Jackson, "Bar Hostess," in Joyce Lebra, Loy Paulson and Elizabeth Powers (eds.), *Women in Changing Japan* (Boulder: Westview Press, 1976); Sumiko Iwano, *The Japanese Woman: Traditional Image and Changing Reality* (Cambridge: Harvard University Press, 1993); Yamakawa Kikue, *Women of the Mito Domain: Recollections of Samurai Family Life* (Tokyo: University of Tokyo Press, 1992); Takie Sugiyama Lebra, *Above the Clouds: Status Culture of the Modern Japanese Nobility* (Berkeley: University of California Press, 1993); Lisa Louis, *Butterflies of the Night: Mama-Sans, Geisha, Strippers, and the Japanese Men They Serve* (New York: Tengu Books, 1992); Lady Nijo, tr. by Wilfrid Whitehouse and Eizo Yanagisawa, *Lady Nijo's Own Story* (Rutland: Charles E. Tuttle Company, 1974); Bill Powell, "The End of the Affair?" *Newsweek,* July 10, 1989, 22–23; Albrecht

Endnotes

Rothacher, *The Japanese Power Elite* (New York: St. Martin's Press, 1993); Sharon L. Sievers, *Flowers in Salt: The Beginnings of Feminist Consciousness in Modern Japan* (Palo Alto: Stanford University Press, 1983); and Elizabeth de Sabato Swinton (ed.), *Women of the Pleasure Quarter: Japanese Paintings and Prints of the Floating World* (New York: Hudson Hills Press, 1995). Arthur Golden's *Memoirs of a Geisha* (Toronto: Vintage Canada, 1999) is a fictionalized account of a geisha's life, all the more intriguing because Mineko Iwaskai, a leading geisha in the decades of the 1960s and 1970s, has launched a lawsuit against the author. Golden has gratefully acknowledged his debt to Mineko, whom he interviewed extensively. Mineko charges that the book is actually based on a distorted version of her own life's story, a charge Golden denies.

7 For centuries Shintoism was a popular religion promulgated by oral tradition. In the 14th century, its Five Books were composed, giving it a philosophical basis as well.

8 Benedict, 504.

9 All references to this section are from Karen Brazell, ed., *The Confessions of Lady Nijo* (London: Arrow Books Ltd., 1975).

10 In *Geisha*, American geisha-in-training Liza Crihfield Dalby describes this procedure.

11 The main sources for the following section are Andre Clot, *Suleiman the Magnificent: The Man, His Life, His Epoch* (London: Al Saqi Books, 1989); Carla Coco, *The Secrets of the Harem* (New York: The Vendome Press, 1997); Zeynep M. Durukan, *The Harem of The Topkapi Palace* (Istanbul: Hilal Matbaacilik Koll, 1973); Jason Goodwin, *Lords of the Horizons: A History of the Ottoman Empire* (London: Chatto & Windus, 1998); Roger Bigelow Merriman, *Suleiman the Magnificent* (New York: Cooper Square Publishers, 1966); Barnette Miller, *Beyond the Sublime Portal: The Grand Seraglio of Stambul* (New York: AMS Press, 1931); N. M. Penzer, *The Harem: An Account of the Institution as It Existed in the Palace of the Turkish Sultans with a History of the Grand Seraglio from Its Foundation to Modern Times* (London: Spring Books, 1936); Yasar Yucel and M. Mehdi Ilhan, *Sultain Suleyman: The Grand Turk* (Ankara: Turk Tarih Kurumu Basimevi, 1991).

12 Miller, 87.

13 Through Ibrahim's marriage to Hatice sultan, Suleiman's royal sister.

14 The main sources for this section are Princess Der Ling, *Two Years in the Forbidden City* (New York: Dodd, Mead and Company, 1929); Charlotte Haldane, *The Last Great Empress of China* (London: Constable, 1965); Sterling Seagrave with Peggy Seagrave, *Dragon Lady: The Life and Legend of the Last Empress of China* (New York: Alfred A. Knopf, 1992); and Marina Warner, *The Dragon Empress: Life & Times of Tz'u-hsi 1835–1908 Empress Dowager of China* (London: Hamish Hamilton, 1984 [first ed., 1972]). Seagrave's biography corrects many factual errors on which previous biographies have been based.

15 Warner, 7.

16 Der Ling, 251.

17 Ibid., 252.

18 Seagrave, 92.

19 Ibid., 126.

20 Ibid., 134.

21 Ibid., 140.

22 Ibid., 146.

23 Ibid., 159.
24 Ibid., 175.

CHAPTER 3

1 King James I, *Works,* Chapter 20. Cited in http://www.Norton.com/college/history/Ralph/workbook/ralprs20.htm
2 The main sources for Nell Gwynne are Clifford Bax, *Pretty, Witty Nell: An Account of Nell Gwyn and her Environment* (New York: Benjamin Blom, Inc., 1969); Nigel Cawthorne, *The Sex Lives of the Kings and Queens of England* (London: Prion, 1994); Arthur I. Dasent, *The Private Life of Charles the Second* (London: Cassell & Company, Ltd., 1927); Christopher Falkus, *The Life and Times of Charles II* (London: Weidenfeld & Nicolson, 1972); Antonia Fraser, *King Charles II* (London: Weidenfeld & Nicolson, 1979); Alan Hardy, *The King's Mistresses* (London: Evans Brothers, 1980); Jane Hoare, "The Death of Nell Gwynne," *History Today,* 1977, 27 no. 6, 396–399; Ronald Hutton, *Charles the Second: King of England, Scotland, and Ireland* (Oxford: Claredon Press, 1989); H. M. Imbert-Terry, *A Misjudged Monarch* (London: William Heinemann, 1917); Roy MacGregor-Hastie, *Nell Gwyn* (London: Robert Hale, 1987); Tony Palmer, *Charles II: Portrait of an Age* (London: Cassell Ltd., 1979).
3 Palmer, 75.
4 Cited by Michael Kesterton, "Life Studies: The Strumpet Who Stole a King's Heart," *Globe and Mail,* Nov. 18, 2000.
5 Ibid.
6 Toward the end of his life, Charles began the process of making Nell a countess but died before any new status for her was confirmed.
7 Bax, 161–162.
8 Palmer, 2.
9 The main sources for the section on Madame de Pompadour are Jeremy Black, "Fit for a King," *History Today,* 37 (April 1987), 3; Susan Conner, "Sexual Politics and Citizenship: Women in Eighteenth-Century France," *Western Society for French History,* 10 (1982), 264–273; Lucienne Ercole, tr. by Gleb Struve and Hamish Miles, *Gay Court Life: France in the Eighteenth Century* (London: Hutchinson & Co., 1932); Mme du Hausset, *Memoirs of Marguerite de Valois Queen of France, Wife of Henri IV of Madame de Pompadour of the Court of Louis XV and of Catherine de Medici Queen of France, Wife of Henri II* (New York: P.F. Collier & Son, 1914); Thomas E. Kaiser, "Madame de Pompadour and the Theaters of Power," *French Historical Studies,* 19, no. 4 (1996), 1025–1044; Jacques Levron, tr. by Claire Eliane Engel, *Pompadour* (London: George Allen and Unwin Ltd., 1963); J. J. Mangan, *The King's Favour* (New York: St. Martin's Press, 1991).
    The main sources for the discussion of the origins of the position *maîtresse en titre,* or official mistress, are Olivier Bernier, *Louis XIV: A Royal Life* (New York: Doubleday, 1987); Vincent Cronin, *Louis XIV* (London: Collins, 1964); Robert B. Douglas, *The Life and Times of Madame Du Barry* (London: Leonard Smithers, 1881); James L. Ford, *The Story of Du Barry* (New York: Frederick A. Stokes Co., 1902); Ragnhild Hatton, *Louis XIV and his World* (London: Thams and Hudson, 1972); W. H. Lewis, *The Splendid Century: Some Aspects of French Life in the Reign of*

Endnotes

Louis XIV (London: Eyre and Spottiswoode, 1953); Louis XIV, tr. by Paul Sonnino, *Mémoires for the Instruction of the Dauphin* (New York and London: The Free Press and Collier-Macmillan Ltd., 1970).

10 Cronin, 176–177.

11 Levron, 121.

12 Ibid., 90.

13 Mangan, 178.

14 The main sources for this section are Olivier Bernier, *Louis the Beloved: The Life of Louis XV* (London: Weidenfeld & Nicolson, 1984); G. P. Gooch, *Louis XV: The Monarchy in Decline* (London: Longman's, Green and Co., 1956); Joan Haslip, *Madame Du Barry: The Wages of Beauty* (London: Weidenfeld & Nicolson, 1991); Philip M. Laskin, *The Trial and Execution of Madame Du Barry* (London: Constable & Co. Ltd., 1969); J. J. Mangan, *The King's Favour* (New York: St. Martin's Press, 1991).

15 Bernier, *Louis the Beloved*, 248.

16 Laskin, 125.

17 Ibid., 203.

18 The sources for the following section are Lola Montez, *Lectures of Lola Montez* (New York: Rudd & Carleton, 1858) and Bruce Seymour, *Lola Montez: A Life* (New Haven and London, Yale University Press, 1996).

19 Seymour, 105.

20 Ibid., 50.

21 Ibid., 108.

22 Ibid., 115.

23 Ibid., 157.

24 Montez, 176–177, 190–191.

25 The main sources for Katharina Schratt are Jean de Bourgoign (ed.), *The Incredible Friendship: The Letters of Emperor Franz Josef to Frau Katharina Schratt* (New York: State University of New York, 1966); Francis Gribble, *The Life and Times of Francis Joseph* (London: Eveleigh Nasz, 1914); Joan Haslip, *The Emperor and the Actress: The Love Story of Emperor Joseph and Katharina Schratt* (London: Weidenfeld & Nicolson, 1982); Joan Haslip, *The Lonely Empress: A Biography of Elizabeth of Austria* (New York: The World Publishing Co., 1965); George K. Marek, *The Eagles Die: Franz Josef, Elizabeth, and Their Austria* (New York: Harper & Row, 1974); Alan Palmer, *Twilight of the Hapsburgs: The Life and Times of Emperor Francis Joseph* (London: Weidenfeld & Nicolson, 1994); Joseph Redlich, *Emperor Francis Joseph of Austria* (Hamden: Archon Books, 1965); Henri Weindel and Philip W. Sargeant, *Behind the Scenes at the Court of Vienna* (Toronto: The Musson Book Co. Ltd., 1979).

26 The main sources for the section on Alice Keppel are Theo Aronson, *The King in Love: Edward VII's Mistresses* (London: John Murray Publishers Ltd., 1988); C. Carlton, *Royal Mistresses* (London: Routledge, 1990); Graham Fisher and Heather Fisher, *Bertie and Alix: Anatomy of a Royal Marriage* (London: Robert Hale & Company, 1974); Christopher Hibbert, *Edward VII: A Portrait* (Thetford: Lowe and Brydome, 1976); Richard Hough, *Edward and Alexandra: Their Private and Public Lives* (London; Hodder and Stoughton, 1992); Philippe Jullian, *Edward and the Edwardians* (New York: Viking Press, 1967); John Phillips, Peter quennell, Lorna Sage, *The Last of the Edwardians: An Illustrated History of Violet Trefusis and Alice Keppel* (Boston: Boston Athenaeum, 1985); George Plumptre, *Edward VII* (Lon-

Endnotes

don: Pavilion Books Ltd., 1995); Diana Souhami, *Mrs. Keppel and Her Daughter* (London: HarperCollins, 1996).

27 Plumptre, 165.

28 Souhami, 91.

29 Ibid., 12, citing Virginia Woolf's diary, March 1932.

30 Caroline Graham, *Camilla: The King's Mistress* (Chicago: Contemporary Books, 1994), 152.

31 The sources for this section are Alice-Leone Moats, *Lupescu* (New York: Henry Holt and Company, 1955); Prince Paul of Hohenzollern-Roumania, *King Carol II: A Life of My Grandfather* (London: Methuen, 1988); Paul D. Quinlan, *The Playboy King: Carol II of Roumania* (Westport and London: Greenwood Press, 1995); D. Quinlan, "Lupescu: Romania's Gray Eminence," *East European Quarterly*, 28, no. 1 (1994), 95–104; M. J. Rooke, "Élena Lupescu and the Court of Carol II," *Contemporary Review*, 232, no. 1345 (1978), 84–89. The following Web site was also used: http://www.heritagefilms.com/ROMANIA.html#Increasing%20Anti-Semitism

32 Prince Paul of Hohenzollern-Roumania, 94.

33 Quinlan, *The Playboy King*, 68.

34 Ibid., 116.

35 Ibid., 119.

36 Ibid., 98.

37 Ibid., 114.

38 Ibid., 123, citing Countess Waldeck.

39 Ibid., 124.

40 Prince Paul of Hohenzollern-Roumania, 160.

41 Quinlan, "Lupescu," 95.

42 Moats, 21.

43 Prince Paul of Hohenzollern-Roumania, 161.

44 Ibid., 192.

45 Ibid., 223.

46 "Jewish History of Romania," http://jewishstudents.net/jewish146/romania.html

47 The main sources for this section are: Jonathan Dinbleby, *The Prince of Wales: A Biography* (London: Warner Books, 1995); Caroline Graham, *Camilla The King's Mistress* (Chicago: Contemporary Books, 1994); Andrew Morton, *Diana: Her True Story – In Her Own Words* (New York: Simon and Schuster, 1997); Sally Bedell Smith, *Diana in Search of Herself: Portrait of a Troubled Princess* (New York: Signet, 2000); and Christopher Wilson, *A Greater Love: Prince Charles's twenty-year affair with Camilla Parker Bowles* (New York : Morrow, 1994); and scores of newspaper and magazine files. An outpouring of (mostly mediocre) books about Charles, Camilla and Diana exists, but on the whole, Morton, Bedell Smith, Dimbleby and Wilson stand out as the most credible and informed.

48 In his official biography of Prince Charles, Jonathan Dimbleby writes that Charles' good friend Lucia Santa Cruz arranged for their meeting, saying Camilla was "just the girl" for Charles. P. 182. Smith, p. 82, writes that Andrew Parker Bowles confirmed this story as "dashed accurate." Smith, p. 82.

49 Graham, pp. 9, 8.

50 *Ibid.*, p. 12.

51 *Ibid.*, p. 21.

52 In a footnote on p. 288, Jonathan Dimbleby implies that this is untrue, because the source of the information had died.

Endnotes

53 Dimbleby, p. 286.
54 Dimbleby, p. 383.
55 *Ibid.*, p. 330.
56 Graham, p. 93.
57 Smith, p. 243.
58 "The Diana Tapes," cited by *People Magazine*, 10/20/1997, p. 107.
59 Graham, p. 106.
60 Graham, p. 159.
61 *Ibid.*, p. 155.
62 *Ibid.*, p. 131.
63 *Ibid.*, p. 165.
64 *Ibid.*, p. 170–1.
65 *Ibid.*, p. 203.
66 Cited in *People*, 03/20/1998, http://bigmouth/pathfinder/com/people/970804/features/camilla.html
67 Smith, p. 19.
68 *Ibid.*, p. 350.
69 A.P., Sept. 5, 1997, quoted in the *Los Angeles Times*.
70 Anne-Marie O'Neil, "Charles & Camilla: Finally, Husband & Wife", *People Magazine*, April 25, 2005, Vol. 63, No. 16.

CHAPTER 4

1 The main sources for this section are Arthur Calder-Marshall, *The Two Duchesses* (London: Hutchinson & Co. Ltd., 1978); Phyllis Deutsch, "The Vortex of Dissipation," in Valerie Frith (ed.), *Women & History: Voices of Early Modern England* (Toronto: Coach House Press, 1995); Amanda Foreman, *Georgiana: Duchess of Devonshire* (London: HarperCollins, 1999); Vere Foster (ed.), *The Two Duchesses: Georgiana, Duchess of Devonshire, Elizabeth Duchess of Devonshire (Correspondence)* (Bath: Cedric Chivers, Ltd., 1978); Iris L. Gower, *The Face Without a Frown: Georgiana, Duchess of Devonshire* (London: Frederick Moller Ltd., 1944); James Lees-Milne, *The Bachelor Duke: A Life of William Spencer Cavendish, 6th Duke of Devonshire, 1790–1858* (London: John Murray Publishers Ltd., 1991); Brian Masters, *Georgiana, Duchess of Devonshire* (London: Hamish Hamilton, 1981); and E. A. Smith, *Lord Grey, 1764–1845* (New York: Oxford University Press, 1990).
2 Foreman, 102.
3 Masters, 135.
4 Ibid., 107.
5 Foreman, 267.
6 The main sources for this section are Phyllis Grosskurth, *Byron: The Flawed Angel* (Toronto: Macfarlane Walter & Ross, 1997); Elizabeth Jenkins, *Lady Caroline Lamb* (London: Sphere Books, 1972); Sean Manchester, *Mad, Bad and Dangerous to Know: The Life of Caroline Lamb* (Highgate, London: Gothic Press, 1992); Peter Quennell, *Byron: The Years of Fame* (London: The Reprint Society, 1943); Margot Strickland, *The Byron Women* (London: Peter Owen, 1974).
7 Manchester, 32.
8 Ibid., 42.
9 Ibid., 80.

10 Ibid., 89.

11 Ibid., 92.

12 Grosskurth, 474.

13 The main sources for this section are Robert Gittings and Jo Manton, *Claire Clairmont and the Shelleys 1798–1879* (New York: Oxford, 1992); Phyllis Grosskurth, *Byron: The Flawed Angel* (Toronto: Macfarlane Walter & Ross, 1997); R. Glynn Grylls, *Claire Clairmont: Mother of Byron's Allegra* (London: John Murray, 1939); N. John Hall, *Salmagundi: Byron and the Trollope Family* (no place of publication: Beta Phi Mu, 1975); Marion K. Stocking (ed.) *The Journals of Claire Clairmont* (Cambridge: Harvard University Press, 1968); Marion K. Stocking (ed.), *The Clairmont Correspondence: Letters of Claire Clairmont, Charles Clairmont and Fanny Imlay Godwin*, Vol. 1, 1808–1834 (Baltimore: Johns Hopkins University Press, 1995).

14 Gittings and Manton, 27.

15 Ibid., 28–29.

16 Ibid., 29.

17 Hall, 7.

18 Ibid., 12.

19 Grylls, 218–219.

20 Ibid., 17.

21 Stocking (ed.), *Journals*, 228.

22 Ibid., 241.

23 Gittings and Manton, 242.

24 Ibid., 244.

25 Ibid., 245.

26 The main sources for this section are Austin K. Gray, *Teresa: The Story of Byron's Last Mistress* (London: George G. Harrap and Company Ltd., 1948); Phyllis Grosskurth, *Byron: The Flawed Angel* (Toronto: Macfarlane Walter & Ross, 1997); Iris Origo, *The Last Attachment: The Story of Byron and Teresa Guiccioli as Told in Their Unpublished Letters and Other Family Papers* (London: Jonathan Cape & John Murray, 1949).

27 Origo, 45.

28 Ibid., 49.

29 Ibid., 81.

30 Grosskurth, 353.

31 Ibid., 355.

32 Authors overcame these same obstacles through the improbable device of marrying off their fictional heroines to their employers—Samuel Richardson's servant Pamela, Charlotte Brontë's Jane Eyre. Claire Clairmont, however, was much truer to life.

CHAPTER 5

1 The main sources for this section are Anne Llewellyn Barston, *Married Priests and the Reforming Papacy: The Eleventh Century Debates* (New York: Edwin Mellen Press, 1982); James Brundage, "Concubinage and Marriage in Medieval Canon Law," *Journal of Medieval History* 1, no. 1 (April 1975), 1–17; Eamon Duffy, *Saints & Sinners: A History of the Popes* (New Haven: Yale University Press, 1997); Otto Feldbauer and David Lederer, *The Concubine: Women, Priests and the Council of Trent*

Endnotes

(unpublished manuscript, August 2002); Robin Lane Fox, *Pagans and Christians* (London: Viking, Penguin Inc., 1986); Hency C. Lea, *The History of Sacerdotal Celibacy in the Christian Church* (New York: Russell and Russell, 1957); and Edward Peters, *Torture* (Oxford: Basil Blackwell Ltd., 1985).

2 Lederer and Otto, draft Introduction, 11–12.

3 Ibid, 64.

4 Feldbauer and Lederer, draft introduction.

5 Peters, 55.

6 Lea, 115.

7 The main sources for this section are E. R. Chamberlin, *The Bad Popes* (New York: The Dial Press, 1969); F. L. Glaser (ed.), *Pope Alexander and His Court* (New York: Nicholas L. Brown, 1921); Horace K. Mann, *The Lives of the Popes in the Early Middle Ages* (London: Kegan Paul, Trench, Trubner, & Co., 1910); Arnold H. Mathew, *The Life and Times of Rodrigo Borgia* (London: Stanley Paul & Co., 1912); Peter Stanford, *The She-Pope: A Quest for the Truth Behind the Mystery of Pope Joan* (London: Heineman, 1998).

8 Chamberlin, 29.

9 Ibid., 37.

10 The main sources for this section are Nicolas L. Brown (ed.), *Pope Alexander and His Court* (New York: Nicholas L. Brown, 1921); E. R. Chamberlin, *The Bad Popes* (New York: The Dial Press, 1969); E. R. Chamberlin, *The Fall of the House of Borgia* (New York: Dial Press, 1974); Orestes Ferrara, *The Borgia Pope: Alexander the VI* (London: Sheed and Ward, 1942); Clemente Fusero, *The Borgias* (London: Pall Mall Press, 1979); Michael Mallett, *The Borgias: The Rise and Fall of a Renaissance Dynasty* (London: The Bodley Head, 1969); and Arnold H. Mathew, *The Life and Times of Rodrigo Borgia* (London: Stanley Paul & Co., 1912).

11 Chamberlin, *The Fall of the House of Borgia*, 42.

12 The main sources for this section are James F. Colaianni, *Married Priests & Married Nuns* (New York: McGraw Hill, 1968); "Good Tidings: Ministry for Women and Priests in Relationships," available at http://www.recovering-catholic.com/goodtide.html; Annie Murphy with Peter de Rosa, *Forbidden Fruit: The True Story of My Secret Love Affair with Ireland's Most Powerful Bishop* (Boston: Little, Brown and Company, 1993); David Rice, *Shattered Vows: Priests Who Leave* (New York: Wm. Morrow and Co., Inc., 1990); A. W. Richard Sipe, *A Secret World* (New York: Brunner/Mazel, 1990); A. W. Richard Sipe, *Sex, Priests, and Power: Anatomy of a Crisis* (New York: Brunner/Mazel, 1995); Terrance A. Sweeney and Pamela Shoop Sweeney, *What God Hath Joined* (New York: Ballantine Books, 1993); as well as newspaper articles about Annie Murphy's affair with Irish bishop Eamonn Casey.

13 Sipe, *A Secret World*, 75.

14 Sipe, *Sex, Priests, and Power*, 124.

15 Rice, 129.

16 Ibid., 118.

17 Ibid., 119.

18 Sipe, *A Secret World*, 233.

19 Murphy, 46.

20 Ibid., 60.

21 Ibid., 135.

22 John Burns, "Casey Calls for Peaceful Retirement," *Sunday Times* (London), Jan. 31, 1999.

Endnotes

23 Bill Wigmore, "The Sins of the Fathers," *New Statesman* (London), Oct. 4, 1996.

24 All information about Louise Iusewicz's relationship with Michael is from e-mail correspondence and personal telephone interviews on Jan. 1, 2001, and in late Jan. 2001.

25 Sweeney and Shoop, 63.

26 Ibid., 223.

27 Ibid., 284.

28 Ibid., 307.

29 All quotations in this section are from the *Good Tidings* Web site, http://www. recovering-catholic.com/goodtide.html

30 Emphasis added.

CHAPTER 6

1 The main sources for this section are Jerome R. Adams, *Liberators and Patriots of Latin America: Biographies of 23 Leaders from Dona Marina (1505–1530) to Bishop Romero (1917–1980)* (Jefferson: McFarland & Company, Inc., 1991); Abel A. Alves, *Brutality and Benevolence: Human Ethnology, Culture, and the Birth of Mexico* (Wesport: Greenwood Press, 1996); Joanne D. Chaison, "Mysterious Malinche: A Case of Mistaken Identity," *Americas*, 32, no. 4 (1976), 514–523; Sandra Cypress Messenger, *La Malinche in Mexican Literature: From History to Myth* (Austin: University of Texas Press, 1991); James D. Henderson and Linda Henderson, *Ten Notable Women of Latin America* (Chicago: Nelson-Hall, 1978); Clara S. Kidwell, "Indian Women as Cultural Mediators," *Ethno History*, 39, no. 2 (1992), 97–104; Salvador de Madariaga, *Hernan Cortes, Conqueror of Mexico* (New York: The Macmillan Company, 1941); James Olson (ed.), *Historical Dictionary of the Spanish Empire, 1402–1975* (New York: Greenwood Press, 1992); Rachel Philips, "Marina/Malinche: Masks and Shadows," in Beth Miller (ed.), *Women in Hispanic Literature: Icons and Fallen Idols* (Berkeley: University of California Press, 1983); and Carl Waldman and Alan Wexler, *Who's Who in World Exploration* (New York: Facts on File Inc., 1992).

2 Adams, 8, citing Bernal Diaz.

3 The main sources for this section are Somer Brodribb, "The Traditional Roles of Native Women in Canada and the Impact of Colonization" *The Canadian Journal of Native Studies*, 41, 85–103; Jennifer S. H. Brown, "Changing Views of Fur Trade Marriage and Domesticity: James Hargreave, His Colleagues, and 'the Sex,'" *The Western Canadian Journal of Anthropology*, 6, no. 3 (1976), 92–105; James Thomas Flexner, *Lord of the Mohawks: A Biography of Sir William Johnson* (Toronto: Little, Brown and Co., 1979); Barbara Graymont, "Konwatsi'tsiaienni (Mary Brant)," in Myra Rutherdale, "Revisiting Colonization Through Gender: Anglican Missionary Women in the Pacific Northwest and the Arctic, 1860–1945," *BC Studies*, no. 104 (Winter 1994), 416–419; Valerie Shirer, "A New Look at the Role of Women in Indian Society." *American Indian Quarterly*, 2, no. 2 (1978), 131–139; Coll-Peter Thrush and Robert J. Keller, Jr. "'I See What I Have Done': The Life and Murder Trial of Xwelas, A S'K-lallam Woman," *Western Historical Quarterly*, 16 (1995), 169–188; Sylvia Van Kirk, *"Many Tender Ties": Women in Fur-Trade Society in Western Canada, 1670–1870* (Winnipeg: Watson & Dwyer Publishing Ltd., 1980); Sylvia Van Kirk, "Women and the Fur Trade," *The Beaver* (Winter 1972), 4–22;

Endnotes

Christine Welch, "Voices of the Grandmothers: Reclaiming a Metis Heritage," *Canadian Literature*, no. 131 (1991), 15–24.

4 Of course, the position of women varied widely among various tribes.

5 Van Kirk, 40.

6 Ibid., 161–163.

7 Ibid., 163.

8 Welch, 22.

9 Van Kirk, 205.

10 The main sources for this section are Thomas A. Bass, *Vietnamerica: The War Comes Home* (New York: Soho Press Inc., 1996); Le Ly Hayslip with Jay Wurts, *When Heaven and Earth Changed Places: A Vietnamese Woman's Journey from War to Peace* (New York: Doubleday, 1989); Steven DeBonis, *Children of the Enemy: Oral Histories of Vietnamese Amerasians and Their Mothers* (Jefferson, North Carolina: McFarland, 1995); Gwen Kirk, "Speaking Out About Militarized Prostitution in South Korea," *Peace and Freedom*, no. 55 (Sept. 1995), 12–14.

11 Hayslip, 199.

12 Ibid., 135.

13 Ibid., 284.

CHAPTER 7

1 The main sources for this section are T. Baker & Julie P. Baker, *The WPA Oklahoma Slave Narratives* (Norman, Oklahoma: University of Oklahoma Press, 1996); John W. Blassingame, *The Slave Community: Plantation Life in the Antebellum South* (New York: Oxford University Press, 1979); Josephine Boyd Bradley and Kent Anderson Leslie, "White Pain Pollen: An Elite Biracial Daughter's Quandary," in Martha Hodes (ed.), *Sex Love Race: Crossing Boundaries in North American History* (New York, London: New York University Press, 1999); Victoria E. Bynum, *The Politics of Social and Sexual Control in the Old South* (Chapel Hill, NC: The University of North Carolina Press, 1992); Catherine Clinton, *The Plantation Mistress: Woman's World in the Old South* (New York: Pantheon Books, 1982); E. Cunningham, *In Pursuit of Reason: The Life of Thomas Jefferson* (Baton Rouge: Louisiana State University Press, 1987); Paul D. Escott, *Slavery Remembered: A Record of Twentieth-Century Slave Narratives* (Chapel Hill: University of North Caroline Press, 1979); Laura T. Fishman, Slave Women, Resistance and Criminality: A Prelude to Future Accommodation, *Women & Criminal Justice*, 7, no. 1 (1995) 35–65; David P. Geggus, "Slave and Free Colored Women in Saint Domingue," in D.B. Gaspar and D.C. Hine, *More than Chattel: Black Women and Slavery in the Americas* (Bloomington, Indiana: Indiana University Press, 1996); Elizabeth Fox Genovese, *Within the Plantation Household: Black and White Women of the Old South* (Chapel Hill, NC: University of North Carolina Press, 1988); Eugene Genovese, *Roll Jordan Roll: The World the Slaves Made* (New York: Pantheon Books, 1974); Herbert G. Gutman, *The Black Family in Slavery and Freedom, 1750–1925* (New York: Pantheon Books, 1976); Minrose C. Gwin, "Green-eyed Monsters of the Slavocracy: Jealous Mistresses in Two Slave Narratives," in D. Clark Hine (ed.), *Black Women in United States History* (New York: Carlson Publishing Inc., 1990); Douglas Hall, *In Miserable Slavery: Thomas Thistlewood in Jamaica, 1750–86* (Hong Kong: The Macmillan Press Ltd., 1989); Darlene Clark

Endnotes

Hine, "Female Slave Resistance: The Economics of Sex," in D. Clark Hine (ed.), *Black Women in United States History* (New York: Carlson Publishing Inc., 1990); Martha Hodes, "Illicit Sex Across the Color Line: White Women and Black Men in the Civil War South," *Critical Matrix* 15 (fall/winter, 1989) 29–64; Thomas N. Ingersoll, *Mammon and Manon in early New Orleans* (Knoxville, TN: University of Tennessee Press, 1999); Harriet A. Jacobs, *Incidents in the Life of a Slave Girl* (Cambridge, Mass.: Harvard University Press, 1987); Thelma Jennings, "'Us Colored Women Had To Go Through A Plenty': Sexual Exploitation of African-American Slave Women," *Journal of Women's History* 1, no. 3 (winter 1990): 45–68; James Hugo Johnston, *Miscengenation in the Ante-Bellum South* (New York: AMS Press Inc., 1972), first written in 1937 for a University of Chicago thesis; James Hugo Johnston, *Race Relations in Virginia and Miscegenation in the South, 1776–1860* (Amherst, Mass.: University of Massachusetts Press, 1970); Winthrope D. Jordan, *White Over Black: American Attitudes Towards the Negro, 1550–1812* (New York: Norton & Com., 1977); James Joy, "Searching for a Tradition: African-American Women Writers, Activists, and Interracial Rape Cases," in K.M. Vaz (ed.), *Black Women in America* (Thousand Oaks, CA: Sage Publications Inc., 1995); Wilma King, "Suffer with them till Death": Slave Women and Their Children in Nineteenth Century America, in D.B. Gaspar and D.C. Hine, *More than Chattel: Black Women and Slavery in the Americas* (Bloomington, Indiana: Indiana University Press, 1996); Herbert S. Klein, *Slavery in the Americas: A Comparative Study of Virginia and Cuba* (Chicago: University of Chicago Press, 1967); Peter Kolchin, *American Slavery, 1619–1877* (New York: Hill and Wang, 1993); Hélène Lecaudey, "Behind the Mask: Ex-Slave Women and Interracial Relations," in P. Morton (ed.), *Discovering the Women in Slavery* (Athens, GA: University of Georgia Press, 1996); John G. Mencke, *Mulattoes and Race Mixture: American Attitudes and Images 1865–1918* (no place given: UMI Research Press, 1979); Marietta Morrissey, *Slave Women in the New World: Gender Stratification in the Caribbean* (Lawrence, Kansas: University Press of Kansas, 1989); Michael Mullin (ed.), *American Negro Slavery: A Documentary History* (Columbia, SC: University of South Carolina Press, 1976); Orlando Patterson, *Slavery and Social Death: A Comparative Study* (Cambridge, Mass.: Harvard University Press, 1982); C.L. Perdue, T.E. Barden and R.K. Phillips (ed.), *Weevils in the Wheat: Interviews with Virginia Ex-Slaves* (Charlottesville, VA: University Press of Virginia, 1976); Edward Byron Reuter, *The Mulatto in the United States* (Boston: The Gorham Press, 1918); C.C. Robertson and Martin A. Klein (ed.), *Women and Slavery in Africa* (Madison, Wisconsin: University of Wisconsin Press, 1983); Willie L. Rose, *A Documentary History of Slavery in North America* (New York: Oxford University Press, 1976); Judith Schafter, "'Open and Notorious Concubinage': The Emancipation of Slave Mistresses by Will and the Supreme Court in Antebellum Louisiana," in D. Clark Hine, *Black Women in United States History* (New York: Carlson Publishing Inc., 1990); Ann A. Shockley, *Afro-American Women Writers 1746–1933: An Anthology and Critical Guide* (New York: Meridian Book Printing, 1989); *Six Women's Slave Narratives* (New York, Oxford: Oxford University Press, 1988); Julia F. Smith, *Slavery and Plantation Growth in Antebellum Florida, 1821–1860* (Gainesville, Florida: University of Florida Press, 1973); Kim M. Vaz, "Organization of the Anthology," in K.M. Vaz (ed.) *Black Women in America* (Thousand Oaks, CA: Sage Publications Inc., 1995); Richard C. Wade, *Slavery in the Cities: the South 1820–1860* (New York: Oxford University Press, 1964); Deborah G. White, *Ain't I A*

Endnotes

Woman? Female Slaves in the Plantation South (New York: W.W. Norton & Co., 1985); and Norman R. Yetman (ed.), *Voices from Slavery* (New York: Holt, Rinehart and Winston, 1970). In addition, to assist in my understanding of slave narratives, I read the following critical sources: David Thomas Bailey, "A Divided Prism: Two Sources of Black Testimony on Slavery, *The Journal of Southern History*, 46, no. 3 (August 1980) 381–404; John W. Blassingame (ed.), *Slave Testimonies: Two Centuries of Letters, Speeches, Interviews, and Autobiographies* (Baton Rouge, Louisiana: Louisiana State University Press, 1977); Catherine Clinton, *The Other Civil War: American Women in the Nineteenth Century* (New York: Hill and Wang, 1984); Jill K. Conway, *The Female Experience in 18th and 19th Century America: A Guide to the History of American Women* (Princeton, NJ: Princeton University Press, 1985); Hazel V. Corby, *Reconstructing Womanhood: The Emergence of the Afro-American Woman Novelist* (New York: Oxford University Press, 1987); Alice A. Deck, "Whose Book Is This? Authorial Versus Editorial Control of Harriet Brent Jacobs' *Incidents in the Life of a Slave Girl: Written By Herself,*" *Women's Studies International Forum*, 10, no. 1 (1987) 33–40; Thomas Doherty, "Harriet Jacobs; Narrative Strategies: Incidents in the Life of a Slave Girl," *Southern Literary Journal*, 19, no. 1 (1986) 79–91; Francis Smith Foster, *Witnessing Slavery: The Development of Ante-Bellum Slave Narratives* 2nd ed. (Madison, Wisconsin: The University of Wisconsin Press, 1994); Deborah M. Garfield and Rafia Zafar (ed.), *Harriet Jacobs and Incidents in the Life of a Slave Girl: New Critical Essays* (New York: Cambridge University Press, 1996); Raymond Hedin, "The American Slave Narrative: The Justification of the Picaro," *American Literature* 53, no. 1 (January 1982) 630–645; Raymond Hedin, "Muffled Voices: The American Slave Narrative," *Clio*, 10, no. 2 (1981): 129–142; Carolyn L. Karcher, "Lydia Maria Child's *A Romance of the Republic*: An Abolitionist Vision of America's Racial Destiny," in Deborah E. McDowell and Arnold Rampersad (eds.), *Slavery and the Literary Imagination* (Baltimore: The Johns Hopkins University Press, 1989); Carolyn L. Karcher, *The First Woman in the Republic: A Cultural Biography of Lydia Maria Child* (Durham: Duke University Press, 1994); Joycelyn K. Moody, "Ripping Away the Veil of Slavery: Literacy, Communal Love, and Self-Esteem in Three Slave Women's Narratives," *Black American Literature Forum*, 24, no. 4 (winter, 1990) 633–648; Winifred Morgan, "Gender-Related Difference in the Slave Narratives of Harriet Jacobs and Frederick Douglass," *American Studies*, 35, no. 2 (1994) 73–94; Charles H. Nichols, "Who Read the Slave Narratives?", *Phylon*, 20, no. 2 (1959) 149–162; Robert F. Sayre, "The Proper Study—Autobiographies in American Studies," *American Quarterly*, 29, no. 3 (1977): 241–262; Laura E. Tanner, "Self-Conscious Representation in the Slave Narrative," *Black American Literature Forum*, 21, no. 4 (winter, 1987) 415–424; Deborah Gray White, *Ain't I a Woman? Female Slaves in the Plantation South* (New York, London: W.W. Norton & Co., 1987); Cynthia Griffin Wolff, "Passing Beyond the Middle Passage: Henry 'Box' Brown's Translations of Slavery," *Massachusetts Review*, 37, no. 1 (1996) 23–44; Jean Fagan Yellin, *Women & Sisters: The Antislavery Feminists in American Culture* (New Haven: Yale University Press, 1989); and Jean Fagan Yellin, "Text and Contexts of Harriet Jacobs' Incidents in the Life of a Slave Girl: Written by Herself," in C.T. Davis and H.L. Gates (ed.), *The Slave's Narrative* (New York: Oxford University Press, 1985).

2 Richard C. Wade, *Slavery in the Cities: The South 1820–1860* (New York: Oxford University Press, 1964), 124.

Endnotes

3 Genovese, *Roll, Jordan, Roll,* 426.

4 All references to Phibbah are taken from Hall, *In Miserable Slavery: Thomas Thistlewood in Jamaica, 1750–1786.*

5 Ibid., 80.

6 Clinton, *The Plantation Mistress,* 216.

7 Ibid., 217.

8 I am indebted to Fawn Brodie, *Thomas Jefferson: An Intimate History* (New York: W. W. Norton & Co. Inc., 1974); and Annette Gordon-Reed *Thomas Jefferson and Sally Hemings: An American Controversy* (Charlottesville: University Press of Virginia, 1997). Both argue forcefully that Sally Hemings was Jefferson's mistress, though to date, DNA tests confirm only a Jefferson blood relationship to Sally's son Eston. I have also read much of the growing literature about this issue. Much of it stems from its authors' collective revulsion at the notion that Jefferson could have fathered mixed-race children. Unfortunately, so little evidence directly documents Sally Hemings's life that it is impossible to be certain who fathered her children, including the Jefferson-related Eston.

9 Brodie, 167.

10 Ibid., 349.

11 Ibid., 350.

12 David N. Mayer, in "The Thomas Jefferson–Sally Hemings Myth and the Politicization of American History," available at http://www.ashbrook.org/articles/mayer-hemings.html#V

13 Brodie, 352.

14 Ibid., 354.

15 In 1853, the first black novelist, runaway slave William Wells Brown, published *Clotel, or the President's Daughter,* a potboiler melodramatic novel about one of Jefferson's disowned black mistresses and her illegitimate and "tragic" mulatto daughters.

16 Jefferson died on July 4, 1826.

17 Kent Anderson Leslie, *Woman of Color, Daughter of Privilege* (Athens: University of Georgia Press, 1999) is the source for this section.

18 Ibid., 57.

19 Ibid., 50.

20 Ibid.

21 Ibid., 138.

22 Ibid., 96.

23 Ibid., 59.

24 Ibid., 64.

25 Ibid., 142.

26 Ibid., 72.

27 Ibid., 144–145.

28 The main source for this section is Harriet A. (Harriet Ann) Jacobs, *Incidents in the Life of a Slave Girl: Written by Herself,* ed. by L. Maria Child, with an introduction by Jean Fagan Yellin (Cambridge: Harvard University Press, 1987). All citations in this section are from this book. Whenever possible, references are to the characters' real names, not the pseudonyms Jacobs employed throughout her book.

Endnotes

CHAPTER 8

1 The main sources for this section are Yitzhak Arad, *Belzec, Sobibor, Treblinka* (Bloomington and Indianapolis: Indiana University Press, 1987); Eugene Aroneanu, tr. by Thomas Whissen, *Inside Concentration Camps* (Westport: Praeger Pub., 1996); Elie A. Cohen, tr. by M. H. Braaksma, *Human Behaviour in the Concentration Camp* (London: Free Association Books, 1988); Erica Fischer, *Aimee & Jaguar: A Love Story* (New York: HarperCollins, 1995); Fania Fénélon, tr. by Judith Landry, *Playing For Time* (New York: Atheneum, 1977); Ida Fink, *A Scrap of Time and Other Stories* (New York: Random House, 1987); Ida Fink, *Traces* (New York: Metropolitan Books, Henry Holt, 1997); Erich Goldhagen, "Nazi Sexual Demonology," *Midstream* (May 1981), 7–15; Kitty Hart, *Return to Auschwitz* (London: Sidgwick & Jackson, 1981); Felicja Karay, tr. by Sara Kitai, *Death Comes in Yellow* (Netherlands: Harwood Academic Publishers, 1996); Höss Broad Kremer, *KL Auschwitz Seen by the SS* (New York: Howard Fertig, 1984); Robert Jay Lifton, *The Nazi Doctors: Medical Killing and the Psychology of Genocide* (New York: Basic Books, 1986); Dalia Ofer and Lenore J. Weitzman (eds.), *Women in the Shoah* (New Haven, London: Yale University Press, 1998); Anna Pawelczynska, tr. by Catherine S. Lech, *Values and Violence in Auschwitz* (Berkeley and Los Angeles: University of California Press, 1979); Gisella Perl, *I Was a Doctor in Auschwitz* (New York: Arno Press, 1979); Carol Rittner and John K. Roth, *Different Voices: Women and the Shoah* (New York: Paragon House, 1993); Roger A. Ritvo and Diane M. Plotkin, *Sisters in Sorrow* (College Station: Texas A&M University Press, 1998); Lore Shelley, tr. and ed., *Auschwitz: The Nazi Civilization* (Maryland: University Press of America, 1992); Sherri Szeman, *The Kommandant's Mistress* (New York: HarperCollins, 1993); Nechama Tec, "Women in the Forest," *Contemporary Jewry*, 17 (1996), http://www.interlog.com/~mighty/forest.htm; Nechama Tec, "Women Among the Forest Partisans," in Dalia Ofer and Lenore J. Weitzman (eds.), *Women in the Shoah* (New Haven, London: Yale University Press, 1998); Germaine Tillion, tr. by Gerald Satterwhite, *Ravensbruck* (Garden City: Anchor Press/Doubleday, 1975); Ka Tzetnik, tr. by Moshe M. Kohn, *House of Dolls* (London: Frederick Muller Ltd., 1956); found on internet sites: Johanna Micaela Jacobsen, "Women's Sexuality in WWII Concentration Camps," http://www.itp.berkley.edu/~hzaid/jojanna/paper2.simpletext.htr; "The Nizkor Project, Operation Reinhard: Command Staff—Sobibor," http://www1.us. nizkor.org/faqs/reinhard/reinhard-faq-18.html; and "Return to Survivor/Witnesses," available at http://remember.org/wit.sur.luctr.html

2 "Vera Laska" in Rittner and Roth, 263.

3 Even German women who succumbed to the charms of non-Jewish French and Polish POW agricultural laborers were first shorn, tarred and feathered, then paraded through their villages to be publicly ridiculed before they were sent off to Ravensbruek.

4 Höss, cited in Ofer and Weitzman, 306–307.

5 Excepting relatively rare instances where secretly gay or bisexual SS men abused men.

6 Sometimes the SS men tortured them first, beating and kicking them, and siccing Doberman attack dogs onto them before tossing them, still living, into the crematoria.

7 Jacobsen, "Women's Sexuality," 2.

Endnotes

8 Ibid., 5.

9 Reminiscences of Ruth Bondy, in Ofer and Weitzman, 320.

10 Reminiscences of Felicja Karay, in Ofer and Weitzman, 296.

11 Perl, 58.

12 Ada Lichtman, cited by Arad, 195.

13 Lucille E., "Return to Survivors/Witnesses" [online].

14 Tillion, 174.

15 Perl, 89.

16 Ibid., 90.

17 Rittner and Roth, 157.

18 Tec, "Women Among the Forest Partisans," 228–229; also Fruma Gulkowitz-Berger's memoir in "Women of Valor" www.interlog.com/~mighty/valor/partisan.htm © Judy Cohen, 2001.

19 The main sources for this section are Hans Peter Bleuel, *Sex and Society in Nazi Germany* (New York: Dorset Press, 1973, 1996); Linda Grant, "My cousin, Eva Braun." *The Guardian*, April 27, 2002, found in http://books.guardian.co.uk/departments/history/story/0,6000,690595,00.html; Nerin E. Gun, *Eva Braun: Hitler's Mistress* (New York: Meredith Press, 1968); Glen Infield, *Eva and Adolph* (New York: Grosset and Dunlap, 1974); and Wulf Schwarzwaller, *The Unknown Hitler: His Private Life and Fortune* (Maryland: National Press Books, 1989).

20 Infield, 211.

21 Timothy W. Ryback, "Hitler's Lost Family," *The New Yorker*, July 17, 2000, 48, quotes a US Army intelligence officer, George Allen, who interviewed Paula in late May 1945. Allen judged her "a lower-middle-class woman of great religion but no intelligence whose misfortune it was to be related to a famous person with whom she had nothing in common."

22 Gun, 69.

23 Ibid., 53.

24 Ibid., 66.

25 Infield, 90.

26 Bleuel, 47.

27 Grant.

28 Gun, 179.

29 Ibid., 7.

30 Infield, 221.

31 Ibid., 234.

32 Ibid., 237.

33 Ibid., 245.

34 Michael R. Marrus in his review of Ian Kershaw, *Hitler 1936–45: Nemesis* (London: Allen Lane, 2000), in *The Globe and Mail*, Dec. 9, 2000.

35 The following are the main sources for this section: Elzbieta Ettinger, *Hannah Arendt–Martin Heidegger* (New Haven: Yale University Press, 1995); Bonnie Honig, *Feminist Interpretations of Hannah Arendt* (Pennsylvania: The Pennsylvania State University Press, 1995); Derwent May, *Hannah Arendt* (Harmondsworth, UK: Penguin, 1986); John McGowan, *Hannah Arendt: An Introduction* (Minneapolis: University of Minnesota Press, 1998); Elisabeth Young-Bruehl, *Hannah Arendt: For Love of the World* (New Haven: Yale University Press, 1982); David Watson, *Arendt* (London: Fontana Press, 1992).

36 Rudiger Safranski, (tr. Ewald Osers), *Martin Heidegger: Between Good and Evil* (Cambridge, Mass.: Harvard Univeristy Press, 1998), 137.

37 Ibid.

38 Honig, 67.

39 Ibid.

40 Ettinger, 30.

41 Ibid., 35.

42 Ibid., 48. Emphasis added.

43 Honig, 70.

44 Safranski, 255.

45 Ibid., 373.

46 Ettinger, 98.

47 Safranski, 377.

48 Ettinger, 72.

49 Ibid., 116.

50 Ibid., 101.

51 Ibid., 114.

52 In a 1971 essay on "Heidegger at Eighty," she painted a picture of a scholarly fumbler who, in a rare sortie from the ivory tower, made unwise and wrong choices and swiftly retreated to the tower when "human affairs" shocked and disappointed him.

53 Safranski, 140.

54 Hannah Arendt, "Understanding and Politics," in Jerome Kohn (ed.), *Essays in Understanding 1930–1954* (New York: Harcourt Brace & Company, 1994), 252. Cited by Bethania Assy, "Eichmann, the Banality of Evil, and Thinking in Arendt's Thought," http://www.bu.edu/wcp/Papers/Cont/ContAssy.htm

CHAPTER 9

1 Rosemary Sullivan, *Labyrinth of Desire: Women, Passion and Romantic Obsession* (Toronto: HarperCollins, 2001).

2 The main sources for this section are Joseph Barry, *French Lovers* (New York: Arbor House, 1987); M. T. Clanchy, *Abelard: A Medieval Life* (Oxford: Blackwell, 1997); Leif Grane, *Peter Abelard: Philosophy and Christianity in the Middle Ages* (London: George Allen and Unwin Ltd., 1970); and Alexander Pope, *Eloïsa to Abelard: With the Letters of Heloïse to Abelard in the Version by John Hughes* (1713) (Miami: University of Miami Press, 1965). Héloise's family name has not survived.

3 Grane, 48.

4 Pope, 7.

5 Ibid., 6.

6 Grane, 49.

7 Barry, 9. Emphasis added.

8 Ibid., 10.

9 Grane, 56.

10 Barry, 11.

11 Pope, 9.

12 Barry, 13.

13 Ibid.

14 Pope, 67.

Endnotes

15 Ibid., 73.
16 Barry, 21.
17 Clanchy, 151.
18 Pope, 97.
19 The main sources for this section are Joseph Barry, *French Lovers* (New York: Arbor House: 1987); Esther Ehrman, *Mme Du Chatelet: Scientist, Philosopher and Feminist of the Enlightenment* (Leamington Spa: Berg, 1986); and Nancy Mitford, *Voltaire in Love* (London: Hamish Hamilton, 1957).
20 Ehrman, 22.
21 Barry, 110.
22 Ibid., 128.
23 Ibid., 133.
24 Ibid., 141.
25 Ehrman, 43.
26 The main sources for this section are Patrice Chaplin, *Into the Darkness Laughing: The Story of Modigliani's Last Mistress, Jeanne Hébuterne* (London: Virago, 1990); Anette Kruszynski, *Amedeo Modigliani: Portraits and Nudes* (Munich: Prestel, 1996); and June Rose, *Modigliani: The Pure Bohemian* (London: Constable, 1990).
27 Kruszynski, 70.
28 Rose, 185.
29 Ibid., 204–205.
30 Ibid., 211.
31 The main sources for the following section are Rosemary Ashton, *G. H. Lewes: A Life* (Oxford: Clarendon Press, 1991); Rosemary Ashton, *George Eliot: A Life* (London: Hamish Hamilton, 1996); Rosemary Bodenheimer, *The Real Life of Mary Ann Evans* (Ithaca: Cornell University Press, 1994); Roland A. Goodman, *Plot Outlines of 100 Famous Novels* (New York: Doubleday, 1962); Kathryn Hughes, *George Eliot: The Last Victorian* (London: Fourth Estate, 1998); Cynthia Ozick, *The Puttermesser Papers* (New York: Alfred A. Knopf, 1997); Thomas Pinney (ed.), *Essays of George Eliot* (London: Routledge and Kegan Paul, 1963); and Ina Taylor, *George Eliot: Woman of Contradictions* (London: Weidenfeld & Nicolson, 1989).
32 Ashton, *George Eliot*, 100.
33 Ibid., 92.
34 Ibid., 143.
35 Ibid., 153–154.
36 Bodenheimer, 91.
37 Ashton, *G. H. Lewes*, 122.
38 Ibid., 158.
39 Bodenheimer, 92.
40 Ibid., 97.
41 Ashton, *George Eliot*, 132.
42 Hughes, 176.
43 Ashton, *G. H. Lewes*, 198.
44 Hughes, 252.
45 Ibid., 248.
46 Ashton, *G. H. Lewes*, 282.
47 Ashton, *George Eliot*, 342.
48 The main sources for this section are Dashiell Hammett, *The Big Knockover: Selected Stories and Short Novels of Dashiell Hammett*, ed. Lillian Hellman (New

York: Random House, 1966); Dashiell Hammett, *The Dain Curse* (New York: Alfred A. Knopf, Inc., 1929); Dashiell Hammett, *The Adventures of Sam Spade* (Cleveland and New York: The World Publishing Company, 1945); Lillian Hellman, *Four Plays* (New York: The Modern Library, 1942); Lillian Hellman, *Maybe* (Boston, Toronto: Little, Brown and Company, 1980); Lillian Hellman, *Pentimento: A Book of Portraits* (Boston, Toronto: Little, Brown and Company, 1973); Lillian Hellman, *Scoundrel Time* (Boston, Toronto: Little, Brown and Company, 1976); Lillian Hellman, *An Unfinished Woman* (Boston, Toronto: Little Brown & Company (Canada) Ltd., 1969); Diane Johnson, *Dashiell Hammett* (New York: Random House, 1983); Richard Layman (ed.) with Julie M. Rivett, *Selected Letters of Dashiell Hammett 1921–1960* (Washington, DC: Counterpoint, 2001); Joan Mellen, *Hellman and Hammet: The Legendary Passion of Lillian Hellman and Dashiell Hammett* (New York: HarperCollins, 1996); William F. Nolan, *Hammett: A Life at the Edge* (New York: Congdon & Weed., Inc., 1983); and William Wright, *Lillian Hellman* (New York: Simon and Schuster, 1986). To familiarize myself with both Hellman and Hammett, I read Hellman's plays as well as her three memoirs, and much of Hammett's fiction. I relied most heavily on Joan Mellen's excellent and authoritative biography of Hellman for both fact and interpretation—Hellman was notoriously inventive about her life, and her memoirs are often suspect and must not be taken at face value, including as records of factual events.

49 Mellen, 7.
50 Ibid., 34.
51 Josephine Hammett Marshall in introduction to Layman (ed.), x.
52 Hellman, *An Unfinished Woman*, 260.
53 Hammett, "The Gutting of Couffignal," in *The Big Knockover*, 29.
54 Mellen, 259.
55 All the quotations in this paragraph taken from Layman (ed.), 65, 80, 103, 119, 151, 533.
56 Mellen, 67.
57 Ibid., 133.
58 Johnson, 256.
59 Layman (ed.), 63.
60 Ibid., 288.
61 From Lillian Hellman's introduction to Dashiell Hammett's *The Big Knockover*, xi.
62 Layman 452.
63 In *Scoundrel Time*, Hellman wrote that he went to prison "sickish" and "came out sicker"; 49. In her introduction to Hammett's *The Big Knockover*, she wrote, "Jail had made a thin man thinner, a sick man sicker"; xi.
64 At the same time, she was a courageous political commentator through her plays. *Watch on the Rhine*, for instance, in 1942, was a deeply moving story about the dangers of fascism, and about how far one must go to combat it.
65 Mellen, 301.
66 Hellman's account is found in *Scoundrel Time*, 108–112.
67 Ibid., 134.
68 Mellen, 319.
69 Ibid., 340.
70 Ibid., 401.
71 Ibid., 411.
72 The main sources for this section are William Cash, *The Third Woman: The Secret*

Endnotes

Passion That Inspired The End of the Affair (London: Little, Brown & Co., 2000); Bob Cullen, "Matter of the Heart," *Smithsonian Magazine,* June 2002, available at http://www.smithsonianmag.si.edu/smithsonian/isueso2/jun/02/presence.html; Graham Greene, *Ways of Escape* (Toronto: Lester & Orpen Dennys, 1980); Shirley Hazzard, *Greene on Capri: A Memoir* (New York: Farrar, Straus & Giroux, 2000); Robert McCrum, "Scrabble and Strife," *The Observer,* Jan. 16, 2000, available at http://books.guardian.co.uk/Print/0,3858,3951133,00.html. Norman Sherry, *The Life of Graham Greene. Volume Two: 1939–1955* (London: Jonathan Cape, 1994); and Paul Theroux, "An Edwardian on the Concorde: Graham Greene as I Knew Him," *New York Times,* 21 April 1991, available at http://www.nytimes.com/books/00/02/20 specials/greene-theroux.html.

73 Sherry, 285.
74 Ibid., 226–227.
75 Cash, 4.
76 Ibid., 82.
77 Sherry, 228.
78 Cash, 103.
79 Cash, 287. Michael Meyer's comment on a BBC *Arena* documentary on Graham Greene.
80 Ibid., 140. Greene to Catherine Walston.
81 Ibid., 303.
82 Ibid., 156.
83 Sherry, 325.
84 Ibid., 317.
85 Ibid., 279.
86 Ibid., 327.
87 Ibid., 329.
88 Ibid., 324.
89 Cash, 185.
90 Some of Catherine's letters and diaries survive, but most information about her comes from letters Graham Greene and others wrote her, reminiscences of friends, again usually his, and those of a few of her family members.
91 Cash, 250.
92 Ibid., 361.
93 Ibid., 256.
94 Ibid., 268.
95 Harry was knighted in 1961.
96 McCrum, citing Catherine Walston to Graham Greene, 18 May 1978.
97 Ibid., citing Sir Harry Walston to Graham Greene, 18 Sept. 1978, written ten days after Catherine's death. Greene did not attend her funeral.
98 The main sources for this section are Joyce Maynard, *At Home in the World: A Memoir* (New York: Picador, 1998); "Joyce Maynard Interviews Joyce Maynard," available at http://www.joycemaynard.com/works/ahitw. html; Margaret A. Salinger, *Dream Catcher: A Memoir* (New York: Washington Square Press, 2000), as well as several Internet sites dealing with Maynard and her relationship with J. D. Salinger, including her former Yale classmate Alex Beam's *Slate* magazine article "The Woman Who Mistook Herself for Something Interesting," available at http://slate.msn.com/Features/Maynard/Maynard.asp
99 Maynard, 360–361.

100 Ibid., 54.
101 Ibid., 81.
102 Salinger, 360.
103 Maynard, 112.
104 Ibid., 116.
105 Maynard, 121.
106 Ibid., 122–123.
107 Ibid., 134.
108 Ibid., 139.
109 Ibid., 146.
110 Ibid., 155.
111 Ibid., 167.
112 Ibid., 190.
113 Ibid., 346.
114 Ibid., 206.
115 Salinger, 362.
116 Maynard, 211.
117 Ibid., 223, in which Maynard cites an *Esquire* magazine article quoting her.
118 Ibid., 258.
119 "Joyce Maynard Interviews Joyce Maynard".
120 Alex Beam's interview in *Slate*.
121 Ibid., 343–344.

CHAPTER 10

1 References to Virginia Hill are taken from Andy Edmonds, *Bugsy's Baby: The Secret Life of Mob Queen Virginia Hill* (Secaucus, N.J.: Birch Lane Press, 1993); Mark Gribben, "Bugsy Siegel," in *The Crime Library*, available at wysiwyg://18/http://www.crimelibrary.com/gangsters/bugsymain.htm.; Dean Jennings, *We Only Kill Each Other: The Life and Bad Times of Bugsy Siegel* (Englewood Cliffs: Prentice-Hall, 1967); Georgia Durante, *The Company She Keeps* (Nashville: Celebrity Books, 1998), provided some general information and analyses of a moll's life.
2 Edmonds, 35.
3 Ibid., 42.
4 Ibid., 138.
5 Ibid., 145.
6 Ibid., 148.
7 Ibid., 242.
8 Jennings, 138.
9 The source for this section on Arlene Brickman is Teresa Carpenter, *Mob Girl: A Woman's Life in the Underworld* (New York: Simon & Schuster, 1992).
10 Carpenter, 13.
11 Ibid., 60.
12 Ibid., 85.
13 Ibid., 86.
14 The source for Sandy Sadowsky is Sandy Sadowsky with H. B. Gilmour, *My Life in the Jewish Mafia* (New York: G. P. Putnam's Sons, 1992). The source for Georgia Durante is Georgia Durante, *The Company She Keeps* (Nashville: Celebrity Books,

Endnotes

1998). The source for Shirley Ryce is James Dubro, *Mob Mistress* (Toronto: Macmillan, 1988).

15 Sandowsky, 33.
16 Ibid., 67.
17 Durante, 124.
18 Sandowsky, 79.
19 Dubro, 63.
20 Ibid., 58.
21 The sources for this section are Larissa Vasilieva, *Kremlin Wives* (New York: Arcade Publishing, 1992); and Thaddeus Wittlin, *Commissar: The Life and Death of Lavrenti Pavlovich Beria* (New York: Macmillan, 1972).
22 Wittlin, 239–240.
23 The sources for this section on Fidel Castro's mistresses are Sebastian Balfour, *Castro* (London: Longman, 1995); Alina Fernandez, *Castro's Daughter: An Exile's Memoir of Cuba* (New York: St. Martin's Press, 1998); Georgie Anne Geyer, *Guerrilla Prince: The Untold Story of Fidel Castro* (Boston: Little Brown, 1991); Wendy Gimbel, *Havana Dreams: A Story of Cuba* (New York: Knopf, 1998); Robert E. Quirk, *Fidel Castro* (New York: Norton, 1993); and Tad Szulc, *Fidel: A Critical Portrait* (New York: Avon Books, 1986).
24 Through a military coup in 1933, Fulgencio Batista became Cuba's military chief of staff and ruled Cuba openly or from behind the scenes until 1944, when Cubans defeated his handpicked candidate in elections. In 1952 Batista again seized power again and held it until Castro's revolutionaries ousted him in 1959. Batista's rule was notorious for its widespread corruption and its intimate association with American gangsters.
25 The Second National Congress of the Federation of Cuban Women.
26 Educationally and professionally, Cuban women are infinitely better off now than they were in 1959.
27 Gimbel, 107.
28 Fernandez, 9–10.
29 Gimbel, 111.
30 Ibid., 47.
31 Ibid., 120.
32 Ibid., 124.
33 Ibid., 124–125.
34 This was how Naty and Fidel's daughter Alina put it.
35 Gimbel, 140.
36 Szulc, 340.
37 Ibid., 340.
38 Gimbel, 148.
39 Fernandez, 15.
40 Geyer, 196.
41 Fernandez, 26.
42 Ibid., 33.
43 Ibid., 30.
44 Ibid., 47.
45 Ibid., 47.
46 Ibid., 73.
47 Ibid., 77.

48 Gimbel, 167.
49 Ibid., 136.
50 Szulc, 233.
51 Gimbel, 165.
52 Geyer gives her age as twenty-nine.
53 Adelaide Béquer, *Célia: La Flor Mas Autóctone de la Revolutión* (La Habana: Editorial de Ciencias Sociales, 1999), which contains many photos of Celia from childhood to the last days of her life.
54 Szulc, 462–463, 467.
55 Geyer, 167.
56 Szulc, 58.
57 Geyer, 216.

CHAPTER 11

1 The sources for this section are Marion Davies, *The Times We Had: Life with William Randolph Hearst* (Indianapolis/New York: The Bobbs-Merrill Co., 1975); Fred Lawrence Guiles, *Marion Davies* (New York: McGraw-Hill, 1972); William Randolph Hearst, Jr., with Jack Casserly, *The Hearsts: Father and Son* (Niwot, Colorado: Roberts Rinehart, 1991); and David Nasaw, *The Chief: The Life of William Randolph Hearst* (Boston and New York: Houghton Mifflin, 2000).
2 Marion, Rose, Ethel and Irene (Reine) had a brother, Charles, who drowned as a young teenager. "I saw my brother Charles only once—in his coffin," Marion wrote in *The Times We Had*, 1.
3 However, she claimed that Marion's first contract, when she was only thirteen, broke her heart.
4 Guiles, 43.
5 The pony girls performed their "toe dances" only during scene changes or in the background.
6 W. R.'s son Bill recalled, "He always was a stage-door Johnny, just always. He always used to take us backstage at the Ziegfeld Follies"; Nasaw, 253.
7 Davies, 10.
8 Ibid., 253.
9 Ibid., 112.
10 Ibid., 20.
11 Ibid., 21.
12 Hearst, 238.
13 Davies, 21.
14 Hearst, 238.
15 Guiles, 69.
16 Ibid., 89.
17 Davies, 253.
18 Ibid., 21.
19 Nasaw, 341.
20 Hearst, 176, 179.
21 Ibid., 180.
22 Ibid., 175–176, 180.
23 Ibid., 178.

Endnotes

24 Davies, 227.
25 Guiles, 325.
26 Davies, 227.
27 Ibid., 43, 133.
28 Guiles, 297.
29 Hearst, 179.
30 Guiles, 288.
31 Davies, 195.
32 Nasaw, 546.
33 Guiles, 304.
34 Davies, 251.
35 Hearst, 562.
36 Davies, 147, 149.
37 Davies, preface by Orson Welles.
38 Nasaw, 249.
39 Guiles, 9.
40 Nasaw, 600.
41 Guiles, 17.
42 Ibid., 336.
43 Hearst, 601.
44 The sources for the sections on Joe and John F. Kennedy are Christopher Ander-son, *Jack and Jackie: Portrait of an American Marriage* (New York: William Morrow and Co., Inc., 1996); Nina Burleigh, *A Very Private Woman: The Life and Unsolved Murder of Presidential Mistress Mary Meyer* (New York: Bantam Books, 1998); Sey-mour M. Hersch, *The Dark Side of Camelot* (Boston and New York: Little, Brown & Co., 1997); Ronald Kessler, *The Sins of the Father: Joseph P. Kennedy and the Dynasty He Founded* (New York: Warner Books, 1996); Axel Madsen, *Gloria and Joe* (Toronto: Fitzhenry & Whiteside, 1988); Richard D. Mahoney, *Sons and Brothers* (New York: Arcade Publishing, Inc., 1999); Ralph G. Martin, *Seeds of Destruction: Joe Kennedy and his Sons* (New York: G.P. Putnam's Sons, 1995); Thomas C. Reeves, *A Question of Character* (New York: The Free Press, 1991); Carl E. Rollyson Jr., *Mar-ilyn Monroe: A Life of the Actress* (Ann Arbor: UMI Research Press, 1986); Amanda Smith (ed.), *Hostage to Fortune: The Letters of Joseph P. Kennedy* (New York: Viking, 2001); Daniel Spoto, *Marilyn Monroe: The Biography* (New York: Harper-Collins, 1993); and Gloria Swanson, *Swanson on Swanson* (New York: Random House, 1980).
45 Her first was actor Wallace Beery, her second Herbert Stronborn, who used his set-tlement from their divorce to open the Brown Derby restaurant, which became wildly popular with the movie crowd, including Beery.
46 Kessler, 69.
47 Smith, 61. Kane became involved after Gloria told him she was selling some real estate to pay for *Sadie Thompson*.
48 The sequence of events leading up to Joe's taking over Gloria's affairs comes from Smith, who had access to all Joe's letters and meticulously analyzed them. This quotation is from Swanson, 354.
49 Swanson, 341.
50 Madsen, 153.
51 Swanson, 355.
52 Ibid., 357.

53 Ibid., 355.

54 Ibid., 357.

55 Axel Madsen suggests that Rose initiated this sexual hiatus.

56 Swanson, 366.

57 Ibid., 383.

58 Ibid., 373.

59 Smith, 82. Joseph P. Kennedy to the Marquis de la Falaise, March 13, 1929.

60 Swanson, 385.

61 Madsen writes that Gloria and Joe traveled on different ships, one week apart, but Gloria Swanson is clear about having traveled together with Joe, Rose, Rose's sister and her own friend Virginia Bowker.

62 Swanson, 387.

63 Ibid., 389.

64 Ibid., 399–400.

65 Ibid., 403.

66 Ibid., 404.

67 Smith, 62.

68 Nicholas Gage, *Greek Fire: The Story of Maria Callas and Aristotle Onassis* (New York: Alfred A. Knopf, 2000), 83.

69 Ibid., 9.

70 Ibid., 10, citing *Time* magazine.

71 Ibid., 39.

72 Ibid., 64.

73 Ibid., 145.

74 Ibid., 157.

75 Ibid., 14.

76 Ibid., 33.

77 Ibid., 70, 77.

78 Ibid., 98.

79 Ibid., 101.

80 Ibid., 145.

81 Ibid., 144–145.

82 Ibid., 166.

83 Ibid., 182.

84 Complicating this was the fact that Italy, where they had married, did not recognize divorce. She and Battista would have had to arrange to divorce elsewhere, for instance in Greece.

85 The circumstances of and evidence about Maria's secret childbirth form the subject of Gage's chapter 14, "The Secret Son," 197–214.

86 Gage, 289.

87 Ibid., 360.

88 Ibid., 369.

89 Ibid., 376.

90 Philip Roth, *The Human Stain* (New York: Vintage Books, 2001), 148.

91 Burleigh, 190.

92 Martin, 54.

93 Ibid., 101.

94 The sources for this section are Christopher Andersen: *Portrait of an American Marriage* (New York: William Morrow, 1996); Nina Burleigh, *A Very Private*

Endnotes

Woman: The Life and Unsolved Murder of Presidential Mistress Mary Meyer (New York: Bantam, 1998); Seymour M. Hersh, *The Dark Side of Camelot* (Boston, New York: Little, Brown and Company, 1997); Axel Madsen, *Gloria and Joe: The Star-Crossed Love Affair of Gloria Swanson and Joe Kennedy* (New York: William Morrow, 1988); Ralph G. Martin, *Seeds of Destruction: Joe Kennedy and his Sons* (New York: G. P. Putnam's Sons, 1995); Gil Troy, *Affairs of State: The Rise and Rejection of the Presidential Couple Since World War II* (New York: The Free Press, 1997); Jane Ellen Wayne, *Marilyn's Men: The Private Life of Marilyn Monroe* (New York: St. Martin's Press, 1992); and Donald H. Wolfe, *The Last Days of Marilyn Monroe* (New York: William Morrow, 1998).

95 Wolfe, 117.
96 Ibid, 136.
97 Ibid.
98 Ibid., 147.
99 Ibid., 146.
100 Wayne, 112.
101 Wolfe, 323.
102 Troy, 126.
103 Andersen, 305.
104 Wayne, 165.
105 JFK's birthday was actually May 29.
106 Martin, 378.
107 Andersen, 308.
108 Wolfe, 415–416.
109 Martin, 382.
110 Ibid., 416.
111 Wolfe, 448.
112 Judith Exner, *My Story: As Told to Ovid Demaris* (New York: Grove Press, 1977), 87.
113 Ibid., 97.
114 Ibid., 118. This information is provided by Ovid Demaris.
115 Ibid., 143.
116 Ibid., 166.
117 Ibid., 194.
118 Ibid., 245.
119 Ibid., 249.
120 Associated Press, 11 Dec. 1996.
121 Exner, p. 272.
122 The main source for this section is Gordon Basichis, *Beautiful Bad Girl: The Vicki Morgan Story* (Lincoln: Backinprint.com, 2000). Originally published in 1985.
123 Basichis, 52.
124 Ibid., 72.
125 Ibid., 84.
126 Ibid., 86.
127 Ibid., 217.
128 Ibid., 236.
129 Ibid., 262.
130 Ibid., 289.

Endnotes

CHAPTER 12

1 All quotations taken from Charlotte Brontë, *Jane Eyre*, found in *Great Novels of the Brontë Sisters* (London: Parragon Books, 2000).
2 All quotations taken from Nathaniel Hawthorne, *The Scarlet Letter*, ed. John Stephen Martin (Peterborough: Broadview Press, 1998). Other sources are Harold Bloom (ed.), *Hester Prynne* (New York and Philadelphia: Chelsea House, 1990); D. B. Kesteron (ed.), *Critical Essays on Hawthorne's* The Scarlet Letter (Boston: G. K. Hall Co., 1988).
3 Martin, ed., 381, citing the *Boston Transcript*.
4 Bloom, 5, citing Trollope in the *North American Review* no. 274 (September 1879), 209–211.
5 All quotations taken from Gustave Flaubert, *Madame Bovary* tr. by Francis Steegmuller (New York: Random House, 1957). Other sources are found in Harold Bloom, *Emma Bovary* (New York: Chelsea House Publishers, 1994).
6 Bloom, *Emma Bovary*, 1.
7 Ibid., 3, citing Flaubert to Colet, Dec. 23, 1853.
8 Ibid., 7, citing Baudelaire.
9 All quotations are taken from Leo Tolstoy, *Anna Karenina*, tr. by Constance Garnett, with revisions by eds. Leonard J. Kent and Nina Berberova (New York: The Modern Library, 2000).
10 All quotations taken from Somerset Maugham, *Of Human Bondage* (London: Vintage Books, 1956).
11 All references to *The Age of Innocence* are taken from Edith Wharton, *The Age of Innocence* (New York: Scribner, 1970).
12 All quotations taken from Boris Pasternak, *Dr. Zhivago* tr. by Max Hayward and Manya Harari, poetry tr. by Bernard Guilbert Guerney (New York: Pantheon Books, 1958).
13 All quotations taken from Graham Greene, *The End of the Affair* (New York: Penguin, 1999, originally published in 1951).
14 All quotations taken from Joanna Trollope, *Marrying the Mistress* (Toronto: McArthur & Co., 2002).

CHAPTER 13

1 Two books on modern mistresses are Victoria Griffin, *The Mistress: Histories, Myths and Interpretations of the "Other Woman"* (London, New York: Bloomsbury, 1999); and Wendy James and Susan Jane Kedgley, *The Mistress* (London: Abelard-Schuman, 1973).
2 The main sources for this section are Rudy Abramson, *Spanning the Century: The Life of W. Averell Harriman, 1891–1986* (New York: William Morrow Co., 1992); Alan Friedman, *Fiat and the Network of Italian Power* (Markham: Nal Bodis, 1988); Anita Leslie, *Cousin Randolph* (London: Hutchinson & Co., 1985); Christopher Ogden, *Life of the Party: The Biography of Pamela Digby Churchill Hayward Harriman* (Boston: Little Brown & Co., 1994); Sally Bedell Smith, *Reflected Glory: The Life of Pam Churchill Harriman* (New York: Simon & Schuster, 1996); and dozens of online articles about Pam Harriman.

Endnotes

3 Smith, pp. 445, 451.
4 Ibid., p. 45.
5 Ibid., p. 124.
6 Ibid., p. 126.
7 Ibid., p. 125.
8 Ibid., pp. 156, 157.
9 Ibid., p. 210.
10 The main sources for this section are Brendan Gill, *Here at* The New Yorker (New York: Random House, 1975); E. J. Kahn Jr., *Year of Change: More About* The New Yorker *and Me* (New York: Viking Penguin Inc., 1988); Thomas Kunkel, *Genius in Disguise: Harold Ross of* The New Yorker (New York: Random House, 1995); Lillian Ross, *Here but Not Here: My Life with William Shawn and* The New Yorker (New York: Random House, 1998); and "Remembering Mr. Shawn," *The New Yorker*, Dec. 28, 1992, 134–145.
11 Ross, p. 110.
12 Ibid., p. 115.
13 Ibid., p. 121.
14 Ibid., p. 129.
15 Ibid., p. 126.
16 Ibid., p. 128.
17 Ibid., p. 146.
18 Ibid., p. 160.
19 Ibid., p. 181.
20 Ibid., p. 197.
21 Ibid., p. 238.
22 The main sources for this section are Lisa Appignanesi, *Simone de Beauvoir* (London: Penguin, 1988); Deirdre Bair, *Simone de Beauvoir: A Biography* (New York: Summit Books, 1990); Hazel E. Barnes, "Beauvoir and Sartre: The Forms of Farewell," in *Philosophy and Literature*, ed. by A. Phillips Griffiths (Cambridge: Cambridge University Press, 1984); Simone de Beauvoir, *Adieux: A Farewell to Sartre*, translated by Patrick O'Brian (London: Deutsch, 1984); Simone de Beauvoir, *She Came to Stay* (1943) tr. by Yvonne Moyse and Roger Senhouse (London: Fontana, 1984); Simone de Beauvoir, *The Second Sex* (1952) tr. and edited by H. M. Parshley (New York: Vintage Books, 1974); Kate Fullbrook and Edward Fullbrook, *Simone de Beauvoir and Sartre: The Remaking of a Twentieth-Century Legend* (New York: Harvester Wheatsheaf, 1993); John Gerassi, *Jean-Paul Sartre: Hated Conscience of His Century*, Vol. 1, *Protestant or Protester?* (Chicago and London: University of Chicago Press, 1987); Vivian Gornick, "*The Second Sex* at Fifty," in *Dissent*, Fall 1999, 69–72; Ronald Hayman, *Sartre: A Life* (New York: Simon and Schuster, 1987); Barbara Klaw, "Desire, Ambiguity, and Contingent Love: Simone de Beauvoir, Sexuality, and Self-Creation, or What Good Is a Man Anyway?" in *Symposium*, Sept. 1997, 110–122; Toril Moi, *Simone de Beauvoir: The Making of an Intellectual Woman* (Oxford: Blackwell, 1994); and Jean-Pierre Saccani, *Nelson et Simone* (Monaco: Éditions du Rocher, 1994).
23 Moi, p. 29.
24 Ibid., p. 223. Emphasis Sartre's.
25 Fullbrook and Fullbrook, 57, citing Henriette Nizan, the wife of Sartre's best friend during university.

Endnotes

26 Ibid., 76.
27 Ibid., 78.
28 Appignanesi, 55.
29 Bair, 211.
30 Ibid., 214–5.
31 De Beauvoir to Algren, 19 July 1948, "Letters from Simone De Beauvoir," in http://www.BBC.co.uk/works/s4/beauvoir/lett.shtml
32 Beauvoir, *The Second Sex*, 796, 814.
33 Bair, 386.
34 Ibid., 386.
35 Appignanesi, 109.
36 Ibid., 111.
37 Bair, 477.
38 Ibid., p. 461.
39 Beauvoir, *Adieux: A Farewell to Sartre*, 127.

Acknowledgments

FINISHING a book gives me the chance to acknowledge publicly those who have shared in its creation.

As always, Yves Pierre-Louis has been the wisest and most devoted of friends.

I am blessed to have Louise, Stephen and Bill Abbott as siblings.

Gabriela Pawlus and Michal Kasprzak have been steadfast friends and have contributed much to this book.

I am grateful to Cecile Farnum, for her insightful work on Byron's mistresses, and to Richard Pope, for his original perspective on "framing charisma."

My special thanks to Marta Karenova for her persistence and also her courage in exploring the literature of the Shoah.

Through Aspasia, Claire Hicks and I have become fast friends.

Leah McLaren's advice was practical and fruitful—thanks, Leah.

David Lederer's out-of-the-blue email about *A History of Celibacy* was manna from heaven. It led to his sending me the draft introduction to his and Otto

Acknowledgments

Feldbauer's upcoming publication, *The Concubine: Women, Priests and the Council of Trent*, granting me permission to quote extensively from it, and also critiquing my chapter on clerical mistresses. Thanks so much for everything, David and also Otto. My book is a better one because of yours.

My deepest gratitude to all the women who told me their stories. Your experiences helped me to understand. Special thanks to Louise Iushewitz for her detailed account of her life as a Jesuit's wife.

My editor, Nicole Langlois, has encouraged me throughout—*A History of Mistresses* is her baby as well as mine.

My agent, Heide Lange, is always a breath of fresh air. She and Esther Sung, her cheerful assistant, have been caring and supportive. Their photo of Esther's "Sweetiepie" still adorns my study wall.

I am overjoyed that my son, Ivan Gibbs, is following me down the writer's path. Thanks also, Ivan, for pitching in so handily during the final stages.

I am grateful to Prof. Tirzah Meacham for advising me about the terminology of the Shoah.

Lastly, I would like to acknowledge my research assistants: Suzanne Hébert, Brent Jewell, Angie Lo, Jaclyn Ray, Kim Reaume and Marc Saurette.

Index

Abélard, Peter, 259–264, 283, 408; castra-
    tion, 261; hermit and abbot, 262; letters
    to Héloise, 263; love for Héloise,
    259–260; marriage to Héloise, 260–261
abortion, 2, 7, 21, 25, 152, 288, 392; of
    fetuses sired by priests, 162, 174
Abraham, 11–13
actresses as mistresses, Gloria Swanson,
    359–366; Katharina Schratt, 91–95;
    Marilyn Monroe, 377–388; Marion
    Davies, 344–359, 362–363; Nell
    Gwynne, 72–77
Adam Bede (Eliot), 280, 281
Adeodatus (Augustine's son), 28, 30–31,
    32, 33, 166
Adieux: A Farewell to Sartre (Beauvoir),
    447
Adonis, Joey, 315, 317, 318, 319
adultery, *see* infidelity
"After Four Years" (Greene), 301
"After Two Years" (Greene), 298
agape love, 137
Agapitus I, Pope, 145
age difference in relationships, Joyce
    Maynard and J.D. Salinger, 305–312;
    Marrying the Mistress, 429–431; W.R.
    Hearst and Marion Davies, 344–359
Age of Innocence, The (Wharton), 419–423

Agnelli, Gianni, 437, 438
Aguilar, Father Jerónimo de, 179
Alberic, 154, 155
"Alexander, Richard," 449–451
Alexander VI, Pope, 156–160, 169, 344
Alexandra, Queen of England, 98
Algren, Nelson, and Simone de Beauvoir,
    434, 445–447
Allegra (Bryon's daughter), 131–132, 133,
    138, 141
amico, 137, 141, 142
Amores (Ovid), 19, 22–26
Anna Karenina (Tolstoy), 413–415
anti-Semitism, Eva Braun and, 242–243,
    245–246, 249; in Nazi Germany, 225–257,
    355; in Romania, 99, 102, 103, 104
Arcocha, Juan, 334
Ardoin, John, 375
Arendt, Hannah, 249–257; defends Hei-
    degger, 254–255, 256; meets Heideg-
    ger's wife, 255
Aristophanes, 18
arranged marriages, a cause of mistress-
    dom, 5–6, 136–137, 265; economic rea-
    sons for, 5–6, 31–32; love not
    considered, 5–6, 45, 71, 115; royal mar-
    riages, 71, 77, 108; wives in, 28, 137, 143
Ars Amatoria (Ovid), 26–28, 438

artists, *see* Modigliani, Amedeo
Ashton, Rosemary, 282–283
Aspasia, 6, 13–19, 459
Asphalt Jungle, The (film), 382
At Home in the World (Joyce Maynard),
    305, 309, 311
Athens, 13–19
Augustine, Saint, 6, 11, 166; and
    "Dolorosa," 28–33; tormented by
    lust, 29, 30, 33
Augustus, Emperor of Rome, 19–20, 22,
    28
Auschwitz concentration camp, 230, 253

Baby Love (Joyce Maynard), 310
Bair, Deirdre, 444, 446
barrenness *see* infertility
Barton, Bernie, 324
Basichis, Gordon, 398, 399–400
bastards *see* illegitimate children
Batista, Fulgencio, 327, 329, 333, 340
battered women, 285, 323, 324, 326, 379,
    382
Baudelaire, Charles, 412
Beam, Alex, 311
beauty routine in ancient Rome, 22
Beauvais, Madame de, 77
Beauvoir, Simone de, 434, 442–448, 461
Being and Time (Heidegger), 251
Bennett, Constance, 364
Benson, Carolyn, 107
Berger, Father Willem, 162–163
Beria, Lavrenti, 326–327
Bett-Politik, 229, 238
Bible, concubines in, 10; Hagar, 11–13,
    459; opposition to female equality, 433
Bielski *otriad*, 237
"Birmingham, Paula," 448–451
birth control, 7, 8, 21, 30, 31, 185, 282;
    advent of Pill in 1960s, 434; for mis-
    tresses of priests, 165, 171
Bjork, Anita, 302, 303
"Black Codes," 195, 196, 202, 209
Bloch, Eduard, 242
Blochmann, Elisabeth, 251
Blondie (Hitler's dog), 246, 247, 248
Bloom, Harold, 408
Bloomingdale, Alfred, and Vicki Morgan,
    3, 393–399, 400

Bloomingdale, Betsy, 394, 396, 399
Blücher, Heinrich, 252–253, 255
Boissy, Marquis de, 142
Bolland, Mark, 114
Bonté (sister of Catherine Walston),
    301–302
Bora, Katerina von, 146–147
boredom, in Eastern harems, 6–7, 37;
    marriage seen as liberation from, 295
Borgia, Rodrigo (Pope Alexander VI),
    156–160, 161
"borrowed wombs" *see* surrogate moth-
    ers
Bost, Jacques-Laurent, 444
Bourbon, Marie-Anne de, 78
Bowles, Camilla *see* Parker-Bowles,
    Camilla
Boxer movement in China, 69
Braganza, Catherine of, 73, 74, 76
Braun, Eva, 238–249; avoidance of poli-
    tics, 242, 245; becomes Hitler's mis-
    tress, 244; marriage before suicide,
    248–249; meets Hitler, 239–240; sui-
    cide attempts, 241, 244
Braun, Fritz, 240, 241, 242, 243
Braun, Gretl (Eva's sister), 240, 242, 244,
    246, 247, 248
Braun, Ilse (Eva's sister), 240, 241,
    242–243, 244, 245, 247
Bray, Charles, 279
Brickman, Arlyne, 320–323
Brickman, Norman, 322
Brock, Werner, 252
Brontë, Charlotte, *Jane Eyre*, 401–404
Brown III, Horace Gates, 357–358
Buckley, Father Pat, 167
Buddhism, 35, 44
Burleigh, Nina, 378
Byron, George Gordon, Lord, and Caro-
    line Lamb, 125–127, 128; and Claire
    Clairmont, 131–132, 133, 134; and Teresa
    Guiccioli, 135–143; view of sexual liai-
    son, 139

Callas, Maria, 366–377; husband refuses
    divorce, 372; marriage, 368–372, 374;
    operatic career, 368–369, 372, 373, 377;
    romance with Onassis, 3, 366–367,
    369–377

Callender, James Thomson, 206–207
Campbell, Judith, and JFK, 386, 388–393
Capone, Al, 314
Capone, Mimi, 314
carboneri, 141
Carol II, King of Romania, 99–106; flees Romania, 104–105; and Iron Guard, 102, 103; marries Elena, 105; renounces succession for Elena, 100; return to Romania, 101
Carpenter, Teresa, 320
Casey, Bishop Eamonn, 164–167, 169
caste, 6, 33
Castro, Fidel, 3, 327–343; and Celia Sanchez, see Sanchez, Celia; CIA attempts to kill, 391, 393; and Naty Revuelta, see Revuelta, Naty; numerous female devotees, 342; respect for women, 328, 339; wife (Mirta), 328, 331–332
Castro, Lidia (sister of Fidel), 332, 333
Catholic Church, see Roman Catholic Church
causa mancipii, 21
cavalier servente, 136–137, 141
celibacy, clerical, 7–8, 144–145; attacked in 20th century, 153; economic concerns, 144–145, 152; standard for RC clergy by 16th century, 152, see also papal mistresses; priests' mistresses
Chan Sam, 40–43
Chanel, Coco, 8
Chaplin, Charles, 348, 349–350, 351
Chapman, John, 275
Charles II, King of England, 7, 344, 461; and Nell Gwynne, 72–77
Charles, Prince of Wales, 4, 106–114; "Camillagate," 111–112; goal of marriage with Camilla, 114; marriage to Diana, 108–110; proposal refused by Camilla, 108; public disclosure of relationship, 113
Châteauroux, Madame de, 80
Châtelet, Emilie, Marquise du, 264–271; arranged marriage, 264–265, 266–267, 269–270; becomes Voltaire's mistress, 265–266; gambling, 265, 268–269; influence on Voltaire, 267–268, 270–271, 277; intelligence and disci-

pline, 265, 267, 268; other lovers, 269, 270; writings, 264, 268, 269, 270, 276
Châtelet, Florent Claude, 264–265, 266–267, 269–270
Chestnut, Mary Boykin, 196–197
child support, 4, 7, 117, 131; for children of priests, 166, 174
childbearing, a duty of Eastern concubines, 6, 7, 39, 45, 63; a purpose of marriage, 5–6
children, attitude towards mistresses, 350, 357, 430, 441; illegitimate, see illegitimate children; legitimization, see legitimization of children
Children's Hour, The (Hellmann), 287, 288
China, 6, 459; concubinage in, 34–44; Tz'u-hsi, 59–70
Chinn, Julia, 203–204
choices, in the 1960s, 433–434; Corinna, 28; Malinche, 180–181
Chong, Denise, 39
Chow Guen, 42, 43, 44
Christianity, Augustine tortured by lust, 29, 30, 33; on concubinage, 29, see also Roman Catholic Church
Churchill, Randolph, 435–436
Churchill, Sir Winston, 345, 369, 370
cinq à sept, 5
Citizen Kane (film), 355
Clairmont, Claire, 143; daughter, 131–132, 133; dependence on the Shelleys, 130, 132; later years, 133–134; relations with Byron, 130–134; victim of double standard, 135
Clash by Night (film), 382
class structure, 6, 29, 94
Cleary, Father Michael, 167
clerical mistresses, see priests' mistresses
Clinton, Bill, 4, 377, 438
Cloetta, Yvonne, 293, 296, 303, 304
Codreanu, Corneliu Zelea, 102, 103, 104
cohabitation, 5, 459–460
Colet, Louise, 408, 412
Colombo, Joe, 322
Combe, George, 278, 279
common-law marriages, 5, 8
concentration camps, 226, 227–236
concubinage, in China, 34–44;

distinguished from mistressdom, 34, 459; laws governing, 34, 36; and marriage, 5–6, 11
concubines, in the Bible, 10, 11–13; in China, 34–44, 59–70; divorce, 36; "Dolorosa" and Augustine, 28–33; Eastern, 4–5; geisha mistresses, 48–52; in imperial Rome, 20, 21; in Japan, 44–48; legal protection, 10; marriage of, 10; in Ottoman Empire, 53–59; as property, 10; protection in ancient Rome, 21; provision of heirs by, 11–12; social disapproval, 16–17, 18, 19; and wives, 11–13, 39, 40, 45, 46, 47
condoms, 282
Confessions (Augustine), 28
Confessions of Lady Nijo, The, 46–48
Confucianism, 35
Conover, Corporal David, 381
Constantine (Emperor of Rome), 10
contraception, *see* birth control
Coolidge, Louise Mathilda, 207
Cope, John and Mary, 197, 198, 200–201
Corinna, 19–28
Cortés, Hernán, 176–183
cosmetics, China, 60; Roman women, 22, 27
Council of Nicaea, 145
Council of Trent, 152
country marriages, 183–190
courtesans, 20
Crosby, Bing, 358
Cross, John, 282–283
cultural differences, 4
Curtis, Tony, 382
Custodio, Isabel, 333, 339
Czechowska, Lunia, 273

danna-sans, 50, 51–52
D'Arignano, Vanozza, 156–158
daughters, in ancient China, 35; in imperial Rome, 20–21
David, John, 397
Davies, Ethel (sister of Marion), 356
Davies, Marion, 344–359, 362–363; acting career, 348, 352–353; affairs, 347, 348, 349–350; drinking problems, 348, 351, 353, 358; fear of Hearst's death, 357; financial aid to Hearst, 354; life as a mistress, 358–359; marriage to another man, 357–358; memories of W.R. Hearst, 346, 353, 355; voluntary bondage to Hearst, 355–356
Davies, Reine (sister of Marion), 356
Davies, Rose (mother of Marion), 345, 346
Davies, Rose (sister of Marion), 357
Davis, Moll, 72, 73, 75
definition of *mistress*, 4–5, 434
demands, by mistress, 3, 4, 25, 74–75, 87–88, 89, 90–91, 457; by wife, 278, 280
Denby, Charles, 67
Denis, Louise, 268
dependency, of geisha mistresses, 50, 51–52; of woman on man, 8
Dering, Dr. Wladislaw, 228
Devonshire, Georgiana, Duchess of, 115–122
Devonshire, William, Duke of, 116–122
di Stefano, Giuseppe, 376, 377
Diana: Her True Story (Morton), 112
Diana, Princess of Wales, "Camillagate," 111–112; confronts Camilla, 111; death in auto accident, 113–114; doomed marriage, 108; health problems, 109–110; resentment of Camilla, 108–109, 110, 111; "Squidgey" tape, 112
Diane de Poitiers, 8, 77
Díaz-Balart, Mirta (Castro's wife), 328, 331–332
Dickinson, Angie, 378
Dickson, Amanda America, 208, 209–214
Dickson, David, 208–215
Dickson, Julia Frances Lewis, 208–215
DiMaggio, Joe, 382, 384, 387
Dimbleby, Jonathan, 109
Dinter, Arthur, 225
Discours sur le bonheur (Châtelet), 269
divine right of kings, 71
divorce, 118, 297, 347, 462; of concubine, 36, 42; easing of laws in 1960s, 434; in literature, 420–421, 430; refused by husbands, 3, 8, 372; refused by wives, 298, 299, 300, 439, 452
DNA tests, 204, 460
Dolan, Josephine, 284
"Dolorosa" (Augustine's concubine), 28–33, 459

Index

Don Juan (Byron), 138
Dorchester, Countess of, 72
double standard, 116, 123, 461; challenged in the 1960s, 433; in Japan, 44–45, *see also* male domination
Dougherty, Jimmy, 380–381
Doyle, Jimmy, 321, 322
Dr. Zhivago (Pasternak), 423–427
Drusilla, Livia, 20
du Barry, Count, 84–85
du Barry, Jeanne, 83–88
Duca, Ion, 102
Dumas, Alexandre, 5
Durante, Georgia, 323–325, 326
Dutton, Fred, 383
Duvalier, "Papa Doc," 3

economic basis of marriage, 5, 71
Edmonds, Andy, 319
Edward III, King of England, 98, 106, 112
Edward VII, King of England, 96–98; fascination with Alice Keppel, 97; many mistresses, 96
egalitarianism, 16, 433–434, 457
Ehrenreich, Dolores Vanetti, 445
Eisenhower, Dwight D., 4
Eliot, George, 275–284, 459; devotion to Lewes, 277–282, 283–284; literary success, 280–281; marriage to John Cross, 282–283; novels condemn double standard, 281; social ostracism, 278–279, 281, 283
Elisabeth, Empress of Austria, 92, 94–95
Elizabeth II, Queen of England, 114
Elkaïm, Arlette, 447, 448
employee benefits, 462
End of the Affair, The (Greene), 293, 298, 301, 304, 427–429
Epstein, Joey, 314–315, 316, 318, 319, 320
equality for women, *see* egalitarianism
essential and contingent loves, 442, 445–447
eunuchs, in Chinese harems, 61, 62, 63, 67; in Turkish harems, 54, 55–56
Evans, Isaac (George Eliot's brother), 281, 283
Evans, Mary Anne (or Marian), *see* Eliot, George
Exner, Dan, 393

Farnese, Giulia, 158–161, 169
Federal Bureau of Investigation (FBI), 390, 392
Fegelein, Hermann, 244, 246, 248
Feldbauer, Otto, 146, 153
feminism, 8, 359, 461
Ferdinand I, King of Romania, 100–101
Fernandez, Melba, 338
Ferrer, Alina (Castro's daughter), 333, 334, 335, 336–338
Ferrer, Nina, 329, 334, 335
Ferrer, Orlando Fernández, 329, 330, 333, 334, 335
fertility, *see* infertility; surrogate mothers
fidelity, sexual, dismissed by de Beauvoir, 446, *see also* infidelity
Fidler, Sally, 187
financial demands, *see* demands
Fisher, Eddie, 388, 393
Fitzgerald, John Francis "Honey Fitz," 360
Flaubert, Gustave, *Madame Bovary*, 408–413
focaria, 147
Forbidden City in China, 59
Force of Circumstance, The (de Beauvoir), 446
forest camps, 236–238
Foster, John, 117, 122
Foster, Lady "Bess," 117–123
Fourth Lateran Council, 146
"fragrant concubine," 37–38
Frankfurter, Felix, 253
Franz Josef, Emperor of Austria, 91–95, 97–98
Fu Xuan, 34
Fulbert, Canon, 259, 260, 261
fur traders and "country wives," 183–190

Gabrielle d'Estrées, 77
Gage, Nicolas, 373, 377
gambling, 122
Gang of Eight, 65
gangsters' "molls," 313–326
geisha mistresses, 48–52
gender inequality, *see* double standard; male domination
George II, King of England, 76
George V, King of England, 98

Geyer, Georgie Anne, 334, 342
Giancana, Sam, 389–390, 391, 393
Gifford, Stan, 378, 379
Gilbey, James, 112
Gilby, Father Thomas, 293, 301–302
Gimbel, Wendy, 332, 333, 335
girlfriends and mistresses, 8, 434
Gloria Swanson Productions, 359, 360
Glover, Dorothy, 294, 296
Goebbels, Joseph, 249
Goebbels, Magda, 249
GoFukakusa, 46–48
Gok-leng (Leonard), 43
"Goldman, Rachel," 451–454
Goldsmith, Sir Jimmy, 5
Good Tidings, 173–175
Gordianus, 145
Grabner, Maximilian, 235
Grant, Cary, 396–397
Graziano, Rocky, 321
Greece, Ancient, Pericles and Aspasia, 6,
    13–19
Greeley, Father Andrew, 163
Greene, Graham, and Catherine Walston,
    293–304; joining sex and religion, 298,
    299; love for Catherine, 295, 297, 298,
    299, 301; The End of The Affair,
    427–429
Greene, Raymond (brother of Graham),
    300–301
Greene, Vivien, 293, 294, 295–296
Greenson, Dr. Ralph, 384
Gregory VII, Pope, 146
Grey, Charles, 121, 122
Griese, Irma, 228
Griffin, Osgood, 316
Griggs, Stephen Adelbert, 1
Groth, Paul, 230–231
Guevara, Che, 340
Guiccioli, Count Alessandro, 135, 137–138,
    139–140, 142
Guiccioli, Countess Teresa, 133, 459; love
    affair with Byron, 135–143; written
    memories of Byron, 142–143
Guiles, Fred Lawrence, 345
guilt, 8, 223–224, 404, 427, 439, 440, 441,
    449
Gwynne, Nell, 72–77, 86, 461

Hafsa Hatun, 54, 58
Hagar, 11–13, 459
Hamilton, Alexander, 206
Hamilton, Lady Emma, 8
Hamilton, Phyllis, 167
Hammett, Dashiell, 284–292; critiques of
    Hellman's plays, 286, 287–289, 291,
    292; personal problems, 285, 287, 288;
    relationship with Hellmann, 285–289,
    291–292; Un-American Activities
    Committee, 290
Han period in China, 35
harem concubines, 5, 6, 53–70; eunuchs,
    54, 55–56, 61, 62, 63, 67; in pre-revolu-
    tionary China, 59–70; in Turkish
    Ottoman Empire, 53–59
Harriman, Pamela, 434, 435–438
Harriman, William Averell, 436–437,
    437–438
Harris, Clara, 212
Hart, Kitty, 233
Hart, Sir Robert, 60, 65, 66–67
Hastings, Beatrice, 271
Hauser, Hans, 318, 319
Hawthorne, Nathaniel, The Scarlet Letter,
    404–408
Hayslip, Le Ly, 191
Hayward, Leland, 437, 438
Hearst, Bill (son of W.R.), 346, 347, 350,
    353, 357
Hearst, George (son of W.R.), 350, 357, 358
Hearst, Millicent (Milly) (wife of W.R.),
    344–345, 346, 347, 348, 354, 357
Hearst, William Randolph, 344, 345–359,
    362; falls in love with Marion Davies,
    346–347; marital relationship, 344, 346,
    347; notoriety of Citizen Kane, 355; old
    age and death, 356–357; protects Mar-
    ion in will, 357; St. Simeon castle, 349,
    350–351, 356
Hébuterne, Jeanne, 271–275, 283, 461;
    Modigliani's lover, 271–272; pregnancy
    and daughter, 272–273; suicide follows
    Modigliani's death, 274–275
Heidegger, Martin, 249–257; Nazi sympa-
    thies, 249, 253, 254; trial, 249, 254–255
heirs, a duty of concubines, 6, 7, 39, 45,
    63; a duty of royal couples, 71; a duty of
    wives, 116, 121, 137

Helen, princess of Greece, 99, 104
Hellmann, Lillian, 284–292; character,
    284–285, 286, 288, 289; Hammett's
    writing help, 286, 287–289, 291, 292;
    relationship with Hammett, 285–289,
    291–292; Un-American Activities
    Committee, 290–291
Héloise, 259–264, 283, 408, 461; legends,
    264; love for Abélard, 260–261, 263;
    nun and abbess, 262–264
Hemings, Sally, 204–208
Henry II, King of France, 77
Henry IV, King of France, 77
Hermippus, 17
Herrera, Reinaldo, 370
Hetaerae, 14, 15, 16–17
Higgins, Henry G., 192, 193
Highgrove, 109, 110
Hill, Virginia, 313–320
Himmler, Heinrich, 246
Hing (Winnie), 40, 41, 42, 43, 44
Hitler, Adolf, 225, 252, 354–355; marriage,
    248; "racial pollution" dread, 225–226;
    relationship with Eva Braun, 238–249;
    views about women, 246
Hodys, Eleonore, 234–236
Hoffmann, Heinrich, 239–240, 241, 243, 245
Hollywood, actresses as mistresses, see
    Davies, Marion; Monroe, Marilyn;
    Swanson, Gloria; mistresses of male
    stars, 348, 349–350, 358, 396–397
Holocaust, see Shoah (Holocaust)
Hoover, J. Edgar, 386, 392
Hornblow, Leonora, 437
Höss, Rudolph, 226, 234–236
Hot Breakfast for Sparrows (Nowell), 458
House of Dolls, 228
"housekeepers" of priests, 8, 147, 153, 162,
    167, 168–169
Howard, Sidney, 364
Hsienfeng, Emperor of China, 61, 64
Huangbo, 40, 41
Human Condition, The (Arendt), 255
Human Stain, The (Roth), 377
Hunt, Thornton, 276, 277
husbands, and lovers, 23–24, 285–286,
    297–299, 301
Husserl, Edmund, 251
Hutton, Barbara, 105

"I DO NOT BELIEVE" (Greene), 293
Ibrahim Pasha, 53, 57–58
illegitimate children, 7, 75, 78, 135, 460;
    Athens, 14, 15, 18; illegitimacy concept
    disappearing, 463; Rome, 21
illusion in love, 312
imbalance between mistress and lover,
    457
impotence, 21, 26, 27
Incidents in the Life of a Slave Girl
    (Jacobs), 215–224
infertility, 10, 11, 39, 45–46; grounds for
    divorce, 45; a reason for concubinage,
    45–46, 49
infidelity, and concubinage, 11, 459; con-
    cubinage, marriage, and mistressdom,
    4–6; definition of adultery in Leges
    Juliae, 22
infidelity, female, 6; mistresses to lovers,
    269, 270, 286, 349–350; social condem-
    nation of, 116
infidelity, male, 6, 459, 461; lovers to mis-
    tresses, 286; social tolerance of, 10–11,
    116, 459
inheritance, 21, see also wills
Innocent III, Pope, 146
Innocent VIII, Pope, 145, 159
interracial unions, see country marriages;
    Jewish women; slave mistresses; Span-
    ish conquistadors and native women
interrogation of priests' mistresses,
    147–152
Iron Guard in Romania, 102, 103, 104, 105
Isaac and Ishmael, 12–13
Iushewitz, Louise, 169–172

Jackson, Reverend Jesse, 4
Jacobs, Harriet, 215–224
James I, King of England, 71
Jane Eyre (Charlotte Brontë), 401–404, 431
Japan, concubines and wives, 45; concu-
    bines in, 44–48; male domination in,
    50, 51, 53; Pleasure Quarters, 48; pow-
    erful women in early culture, 44;
    women's rights degraded, 44–45
Jarrell, Randall, 255
Jaspers, Gertrud, 253
Jaspers, Karl, 251, 253, 254–255; opinions
    of Heidegger, 254–255, 256

jealousy, among rival lovers, 94, 300, 347, 348, 349, 427–428; among rival mistresses, 72, 75–76, 244, 288, 444, 445; of husband by lover, 23–24; of lover by husband, 42; of mistress by wife, 12, 98, 108–111, 294, 295–296; of wife by mistress, 51–52, 296, 454
Jefferson, Thomas, 204–208
Jennings, Dean, 319
Jerome, Saint, 144
Jeudi, Ghislaine, 2–3
Jewish women, in concentration camps, 226–236; in forest camps, 236–238; Hannah Arendt, see Arendt, Hannah; Hitler's "racial pollution" dread, 225–226
Jito, 45
John Paul II, Pope, 167, 171
John XIII, Pope, 145
Johnson, Diane, 289, 292
Johnson, Richard M., 203–204
Jordain, Paulette, 274
Judenrat, 230
Julia, 22, 23, 28
"Julian Laws" (Leges Juliae), 20, 22
Julius II, Pope, 161

Kane, Robert, 360
Katerina (Kati), 1–2
"Kati" (Auschwitz inmate), 233
Kay, Richard, 113
Keneally, Thomas, 235
Kennedy, Bobby, 385, 387
Kennedy, Jacqueline ("Jackie"), 367, 374, 385, 387, 388, 390, 391
Kennedy, John F., 4, 358; intrigue with Marilyn Monroe, 378, 383–386; relationship with Judith Campbell, 388–393; sexual insatiability, 377–378, 388
Kennedy, Joseph P., 350, 352, 356, 358, 378; romance with Gloria Swanson, 361–365; takeover of Gloria's finances, 359–361
Kennedy, Rose Fitzgerald, 360, 361, 363
Kennedy, Teddy, 388, 389
Keppel, Alice, 96–98, 106, 107, 114; disliked by Royal Family, 98; marriage to George Keppel, 96, 97, 98; personality, 97

"kept" women, 2, 434, 436–437, 450, 454–457
Kéroualle, Louise de, 75, 76
Kingsley, Charles, 279
Ko-ken, Empress of Japan, 44
Ko-myo, Empress of Japan, 44
Kober, Arthur, 284, 286, 288, 292
Kosakievicz, Olga, 444
"Kovaleski, Michaela," 454–457
Krakower, Esta, 316, 317
Kremlin dolls, 326–327
Kuang Hsu, Emperor of China, 66, 67, 68, 69, 70
Kuernheim, Gerta, 232–233
Kuralt, Charles, 4

La Coudraye, Marquis de, 359, 361, 363, 364
La Vallière, Louise, 78, 408
Lamartine, Alphonse de, 142
Lamb, Lady Caroline, 123–130, 143; affair with Byron, 125–127, 128; attacks Byron in novel, 128–129; instability, 123, 124, 127, 128, 129, 130; marriage, 124–125
Lamb, William, 124, 125, 126, 127, 128–129
Lamendola, Joe, 324
Lamm, Earle, 393, 394, 395
Lang Yu, 67
Langley, Minnie, 1
Langtry, Lillie, 96, 97
Lansky, Meyer, 328
Laqueur, Renata, 229
Lastman, Mel, 4
Lawford, Patricia (Peter's daughter), 387
Lawford, Patricia Seaton, 386
Lawford, Peter, 383, 385, 386, 388
laws, recent revisions, 7, 462, 463; Roman Empire, 10, 20, 22
Layman, Richard, 289
Lea, Henry, 152–153
lead poisoning and impotence, 21, 26
Lectures of Lola Montez, 91
Lederer, David, 146, 153
Leges Juliae, 20, 22
legitimate children, see heirs
legitimization of children, 7, 10, 18, 34, 117, 459
Leigh, Augusta, 128
lesbianism, 433

Lewes, Agnes, 276–277, 278, 280
Lewes, George, 276–282, 283–284, 459; commitment to George Eliot, 277–282, 283–284; impossibility of divorce, 277, 278, 281
Lewinsky, Monica, 4, 377
Li Fei, 62, 63
Liszt, Franz, 88, 278
Little Foxes, The (Hellmann), 286, 289
Looking Back (Joyce Maynard), 309
Lorenz, Marita, 342
Louie, Grace, 4
Louis XIV, King of France, 77–79, 408
Louis XV, King of France, 79–86
Louis XVI, King of France, 85, 86, 87
Louise, Princess (England), 282
love, with an illusion, 312; essential and contingent loves, 442, 445–447; in interracial unions, 196, 197–202; irrelevant in arranged marriages, 5–6, 45, 71, 115; romantic love an ideal today, 8, 461, 462; sex vs., 93–94, 454–455, 457, 460
lovers, and husbands, 23–24, 285–286, 297–299, 301
lovers, famous, Callas and Onassis, 369–377; Camilla and Charles, 106–114; Castro and Sanchez, 339–343; de Beauvoir and Sartre, 442–448; George Eliot and George Lewes, 275–284; Héloise and Abélard, 259–264; Ovid and Corinna, 19–28
lovers in literature, Anna Karenina and Vronsky, 413–415; Ellen Olenska and Newland Archer, 419–423; Hester Prynne and Arthur Dimmesdale, 404–408; Jane Eyre and Mr. Rochester, 401–404; Lara and Dr. Zhivago, 423–427; Sarah Miles and Maurice Bendrix, 427–429
Luca, Tommy, 322–323
"Lucille E" (Auschwitz inmate), 231–232
Ludwig I, King of Bavaria, 88–91, 240, 461
Lupescu, Elena, 99–100; begins relationship with Carol, 99; enemies, 103–104; influence in Romania, 101–102, 103; life in France with Carol, 100; marriage to Carol, 105
Luther, Martin, 146
Lysicles, 18

Macallum, John, 189
Madame Bovary (Flaubert), 408–413
Mafia, American, 313–320, 328
maîtresses en titre, 77–78, 79
makeup, see cosmetics
malbushim, 237–238
male domination, in ancient China, 34–35; in ancient Greece, 14, 17; in ancient Rome, 20–21; in Japan, 50, 51, 53, see also double standard; patriarchy
male infidelity, arranged marriages foster, 5–6, 136–137; foundation of mistressdom, 461; tolerance by society, 10–11, 116, 459
Malinche, 176–183
Manae Kubota, 52
Mancini, Hortense, Duchesse de Mazarin, 76
Mandarins, The (Beauvoir), 446
Manichaeism, 30, 31
manumission (freeing a slave), 200, 201, 202
Maria Theresa, Queen of France, 77
Marie-Antoinette, Queen of France, 85, 86, 87
Marie, Queen of Romania, 100, 101–102
marriage, in the 1960s, 433–434; Algren's belief in, 447; in ancient Greece, 14; arranged, see arranged marriages; Beauvoir-Sartre view, 442; economic basis of, 5, 71; hope of many mistresses, 8, 347, 353, 457, 461; in imperial Rome, 21; and mistressdom, 4, 5, 430, 462, 463–464; mistressdom preferred by a few, 442, 451, 461, 463; to mistresses, 5, 31, 248, 429–432, 437, 451; production of heirs, 5–6, 71, 116, 121, 137; royal marriages, 71, 77, 108; social class, 6, 29, 94, see also divorce; remarriage
Marrying the Mistress (Joanna Trollope), 429–432
Marshall, Josephine Hammett, 285
Martin, Dean, 386
Marx, Dr. (lover of Ilse Braun), 240, 242–243, 244
Mary, Virgin, 175
Maugham, Somerset, Of Human Bondage, 415–419

Index

Maupertuis, Pierre-Louis Moreau de, 265
Maximilian I, 149
Maxwell, Elsa, 369
May-ying (a Chinese concubine), 39–44
Maya (Auschwitz prisoner), 231–232
Mayer, Louis B., 355
Maynard, Fredelle, 306, 307, 308
Maynard, Joyce, 304–312; affair with
   Salinger, 305–310, 311–312; diet and sex
   problems, 306, 307–308, 309; early
   writing, 304–305; normalcy in mar-
   riage and career, 310; writes about
   Salinger, 310–311
Maynard, Max, 306
Mein Kampf (Hitler), 225, 256
mékaké, 46
Mellen, Joan, 288
Meneghini, Battista, 367–369, 372, 373, 374
Mengele, Dr. Josef, 228
menstruation, collective cycle in harem,
   55; defeated in concentration camps,
   228
Michael, King of Romania, 99, 100–101,
   104, 105
Michael, Prince of Greece, 371
Milbanke, Annabella, 127, 128
Mill on the Floss, The (Eliot), 281
Miller, Arthur, 382, 384, 387
Mirra, Tony, 321, 322
misogyny, 44–45
"Miss Saigon," 190–194
missionaries, foes of country wives, 186,
   189
mistressdom, attractions for distressed
   women, 118; children, *see* illegitimate
   children; definitions, 4–5, 463; distinguished from concubinage, 5, 34, 459;
   guilt, 8, 461; in literature, *see* lovers in
   literature; many facets, 9; and marriage, 4, 5, 430, 439–442, 462, 463–464;
   Ovid's advice, 26–27, 438; result of
   arranged marriages, 5–6, 136–137;
   secrecy, 8, 52, 458; social disapproval,
   see social disapproval
mistresses, "kept" women, 2, 434,
   436–437, 450, 454–457
Mitchelson, Marvin, 399
Mitford, Unity Valkyrie, 244
Mitterand, François, 4

mixed-blood children, 195, 196, 197
mizu-age, 49
mobster molls, 313–326
Moctezuma, 177, 179–182
models as mistresses, 271–275
Modigliani, Amedeo, 271–275, 461
money and mistresses, *see* demands;
   dependency
Monica (mother of Augustine), 28–32
Monroe, Gladys (Marilyn's mother),
   378–379, 381
Monroe, Marilyn, 4, 373, 377–388, 393;
   career develops, 381–382; death, 387;
   instability, 382–383, 384–385; and JFK,
   383–386, 388; marriages to DiMaggio
   and Miller, 382; miserable childhood,
   378–380
Montespan, Marquise de, 78–79
Montespan, Monsieur de, 78–79
Montez, Lola, 88–91, 240, 461
mooi-jais, 36–37
morality, 8, 10–11, 79, 224
morals, Roman empire, 19, 20, 22
Morgan, Vicki, 3, 393–399, 400
Mosley, Diana, 244
motherhood, 441
Mountbatten, Lord Louis, 107, 108
Mui, Dao Thi, 191–193
Murphy, Annie, 164–167, 169; pregnancy
   and childbirth, 165–166
Murrow, Edward R., 436
Mussolini, Benito, 248
Mustafa, 53, 57, 58–59
My Story (Campbell), 390

Nakanishi, Mitsuko, 52
names, wife's exchanged for husband's,
   462
Nape, 23, 25, 27
native women, and foreign soldiers in
   Vietnam, 190–194; and fur traders in
   North America, 183–190; and Spanish
   invaders of Aztec land, 176–183
Nelson, Nathaniel "Natie," 321–322
Nijo, Lady (a Japanese concubine), 46–48
Norcom, Dr. James, 216–223
novels, marriage in, 401–432; mistress-
   dom in, 401–432
Nowell, Iris, 458

nuns, attitude of superiors to carnal sin, 169; ex-nuns married to ex-priests, 168; as mistresses to priests, 168
Nuremberg Laws, 226, 242

O'Connell, Cardinal, 363–364
Of Human Bondage (Maugham), 415–419
O'Malley, Ernie, 295
Onassis, Aristotle, marriage to Jacqueline Kennedy, 374–375; romance with Maria Callas, 3, 366–367, 369–377
Onassis, Artemis (Ari's sister), 372
Onassis, Christina (daughter of Ari), 376
Onassis, Tina, 369–370, 371–372
Opium War, 64
orgasm, 27
Orsini, Orsino, 158, 159, 160
otriads, 236–238
Ovid, advice to lovers and mistresses, 27, 438; Corinna's lover, 19, 22–28
Oxford, Lady Jane, 127

Paley, William, 436
Palmer, Barbara (later Lady Castle-maine), 75
Pancoast, Marvin, 400
papal mistresses, 145, 153–161
Papalia crime family, 325
Paraclete oratory, 262, 263, 264
"parallel marriage," 439–442
Parc aux Cerfs whorehouse, 82–83
Parker-Bowles, Andrew, 107–108, 113
Parker-Bowles, Camilla, 4, 106–114;
Charles discloses relationship, 113;
Charles re-establishes relationship, 112–113; divorce from Andrew, 113; first meeting with Charles, 106–107; marriage to Andrew, 108; media image improves, 114; refuses Charles's proposal, 108; marriage to Charles, 113
Pasternak, Boris, *Dr. Zhivago*, 423–427
paterfamilias, 20–21
patria potesta, 20
patriarchy, American slave system, 196–197; Roman Empire, 20–21, *see also* double standard; male domination
Paul III, Pope, 159
Pennino, Al, 321

Pericles and Aspasia, 6, 13–19
Perl, Dr. Gisella, 230, 233
Petacci, Clara, 248
Petri, Elfride, 250, 255, 256
Phibbah, 197–202
philosophes, 265
plantation mistresses, *see* slave mistresses
Plato, 15
Pocahontas, 183
political gangsters, 326–327
Pompadour, Madame de, 79–83
popes, *see* papal mistresses
Powell, Dick, 350, 358
Power and the Glory, The (Greene), 294
power of mistresses, 70, 297, 457
powerlessness of mob mistresses, 326
pregnancies, 2, 11–12, 269–270, 373, 392, 459; of a concubine in China, 38–39, 62–63; abortion *see* abortion
Preleshnik, Daniella, 228
presidents of the U.S., *see* Clinton, Bill; Eisenhower, Dwight D.; Jefferson, Thomas; Kennedy, John F.
priests' mistresses, abortion, 162; assumptions of Church authorities, 164; birth control now, 165, 171; children of priests, 145, 148, 149, 151; Church's property concerns, 144–145, 152; estimates on number today, 161, 163, 167; Good Tidings, 173–175; as housekeepers, 8, 153, 162, 167, 168–169; interrogations by medieval Church, 147–152; married parishioners, 167–168; persecution by Church, 145–152, 162, 167, 173–175; seduction of priests, 163, 295, 300; single, non-resident mistresses, 168, *see also* celibacy, clerical; papal mistresses
prostitutes, 14, 20; Japan's Pleasure Quarters, 48
Protestant Reformation, 146

Queen Kelly (film), 363, 364

"racial pollution," 225
racism, against "country wives," 186–189; against slave mistresses, 195–197, 201, 202–204, 208
Radford, C.B., 446
Radziwill, Lee, 373–374

Raft, George, 316, 317
Raisins and Almonds (Fredelle Maynard), 308, 309
rape, 228
"Rassenschande," 226, 229, 232, 235
Raubal, Angela (Geli), 239, 245
Reformation challenge to clerical celibacy, 148
Reichleitner, Franz, 231
religion and love, for Greene, 298, 299
reproduction, *see* children; pregnancies
reputation, 116, 119
Return to Auschwitz (Hart), 233
Revuelta, Manolo, 328
Revuelta, Natica (mother of Naty), 328, 335, 337, 338
Revuelta, Naty, 328–339, 341; assigned jobs by Fidel, 335–336, 338; and Castro's daughter Alina, 333, 334, 335, 336–338; helps Castro in prison, 330–332; loss of Fidel, 334–335; political support for Castro, 329, 330; shared love with Castro, 330–331; upbringing and marriage, 328–329
Reynolds, Maria, 206
Rice, David, 162, 163
Richmond, Duke of, 121
Rickards, Jocelyn, 302–303
Rockefeller, Abby, 354
Roman Catholic Church, celibacy, 7–8, 144–145, 152, 153; and clerical mistresses, *see* priests' mistresses; in Restoration England, 73, 76
Roman literature, *see* Ovid
romance, *see* love
Rome, imperial, 19–28; *Leges Juliae* (Julian laws), 20, 22; moral decadence, 19, 20; Ovid and Corinna, 22–28
Roosevelt, Franklin D., 366
Rosenthal, Dr., 232–233
Ross, Lillian, 434, 439–442
Rothschild, Elie de, Baron, 437, 438
Rottgering, Henriette, 162–163
Roxelana, 53–59, 68, 460
royal marriages, 71, 77, 108
Rubin, Sulia, 237
Rudolf, Crown Prince of Austria, 92, 94
"Ruth" (inmate of Sobibor Camp), 230–231

Rutra, Arthur Ernst, 245
Ryce, Shirley, 325–326

Sachreuter, Father Adam, 150–151
Sadie Thompson (film), 359, 361, 363
Sadowsky, Sandy, 323–325
Safranski, Rüdiger, 256
Saint Ambrose, 31
Saint Lambert, Jean-François, Marquis de, 269, 270
Salinger, J.D., 441; and Joyce Maynard, 305–310, 312
Salinger, Peggy, 307, 310
salons in ancient Greece, 15
"Sam Spade," 285
Sanchez, Celia, 3, 333, 336, 337, 339–343; importance to Castro's revolution, 339, 340, 341, 343; relationship with Castro, 339–343
Sand, George, 8
Sarah, 11–13
Sarno, Ronald A., 174
Sartre, Jean-Paul, 434, 442–448
Sauckel, Fritz, 246
Saud, Jawajar Bint, 398
Sawyer, Samuel Tredwell, 219–220, 221, 222, 223–224
Scarlet Letter, The (Hawthorne), 404–408
Scherer, Father Georg, 151–152
Schindler's Ark (filmed as *Schindler's List*), 235
Schonberg, Harold C., 377
Schratt, Katharina, 91–95, 97–98; as actress, 92, 94; life as mistress, 93–94, 95
Schulman, Bob, 397, 398
Seagrave, Sterling, 65
Second Sex, The (de Beauvoir), 446
secrecy, 8, 52, 458
selim, 59
separation, 117, 296–297
Sergius III, Pope, 154, 155
Seven Years' War, 83
sex, importance in keeping lover, 437, 460; vs. love, 93–94, 454–455, 457, 460
sexual equality, 16, 457
sexual revolution of 1960s, 378, 433–457
shadow artists, 258
Shand, Major Bruce, 112

Index

Shannon, Patricia, 4

Shattered Vows: Priests Who Leave (Rice), 162, 163

Shawn, Cecille, 439–442

Shawn, William, and Lillian Ross, 439–442

Shelley, Mary, 130, 131, 132, 133, 134

Shelley, Percy, 130, 131, 132, 134

Sherman, William T., 211–212

Sherry, Norman, 294

Shinto goddesses, 44

Shoah (Holocaust), 226–238, 253, 451–452; Adolf Hitler and Eva Braun, 238–249; concentration camps, 226, 227–236; "partisan" forest camps, 236–238

Shoop, Pamela, 172–173

Sidey, Hugh, 385

Siegel, Bugsy, 313, 315–318

Silvestrini, Fanny, 136

Simpson, Frances, 188

Simpson, George, 187–189

Simpson, Wallis, 98, 106, 112

Sinatra, Frank, 388, 389, 393

Sinclair, Betsey, 187

Sino-Japanese War, 67–68

Sipe, Richard, 162, 163

Slatzer, Robert, 387

slave mistresses, 7, 10, 195–224; brutal treatment of slaves, 195–196; Harriet Jacobs, 215–224; Julia Chinn and Richard Johnson, 202–204; Julia Frances Lewis Dickson, 208–215; love, 196, 197, 198–200, 208–215; mixed-race children, 195, 196, 197, 203, 204, 205–208; Phibbah, and Thomas Thistlewood, 197–202; Thomas Jefferson and Sally Hemings, 204–208

Smith Act, 290

Smith, Al, 348

Smith, Amanda, 365

Smith, Barbara Leigh, 282

Smith, Sally Bedell, 437

Soames, Nicholas, 113

Sobibor Camp, 230–231

social class, 6, 29, 94

social disapproval, 8, 352, 463–464; conventions for mistresses, 461; of George Eliot, 278–279, 281, 283; of interracial unions, 195, 196, 197, 202–204, 208, 211, 224; in literature, 404–408, 412–413, 414–415, 419–423, 431–432

Socrates, 15

Solomon, King, 10

Some Like It Hot (film), 382

Something's Got to Give (film), 384–385, 386, 387

Sommersby, Kay, 4

Sosuke Uno, 52

Spanish *conquistadors* and native women, 176–183

Spencer, Charlotte, 116–117

Spencer, Herbert, 276

Stalinism, 327

Stancioff, Nadia, 368–369

Stanford, Karin, 4

Stern, Guenther, 251, 252

Stirbey, Prince Barbu, 102

Stowe, Harriet Beecher, 196

Strauss, Clara, 151

Strauss, Dr. Eric, 297

succession, 63, 76

Suffolk, Lady Henrietta, 76

Suiko, Empress of Japan, 44

Suleiman, 53–54, 57–59, 460

Sullivan, Rosemary, 258

Sunset Boulevard (film), 366

surrogate mothers, 10, 38, 46, 459

Swanson, Gloria, 352, 359–366; financial advice from Joe Kennedy, 359–361; romance with Joe Kennedy, 361–364; termination of affair by Kennedy, 364–365; wounds remembered, 366

Sweeney, Terrance, 165, 172–173

Sylph, The (novel), 115

Synod of Amalfi, 145–146

Synod of Elvira, 145

Synod of Pavia, 145

Szulc, Tad, 338

Taiho Code, 45

Taylor, Elizabeth, 388

Taylor, Margaret, 187–189

Temps Modernes, Les (journal), 445

Thargelia, 16

Theophylact, Marozia, 145, 155–156

Theophylact, Theodora, 145, 153–155

Theresienstadt, 229–230

Thin Man, The (Hammett), 286–287

Index

Third Man, The (Greene), 297
Thiroux, Simone, 274
Thistlewood, Thomas, 197–202
Times We Had, The (Davies), 355, 359
Tolstoy, Leo, *Anna Karenina*, 413–415
Tonton Macoutes, 3
torture used in Church interrogation, 150
Toys in the Attic (Hellmann), 291
Trespasser, The (film), 363
Trollope, Anthony, 407
Trollope, Joanna, 429–432
Trombotto, Father Franco, 173
Tung Chih, 63, 64, 65–66
Turkey, 6
Tzetnik, Ka, 228
Tz'u-an, 65, 66
Tz'u-hsi, 59–70

Ulpian, 150
Un-American Activities Committee, 290–291
Uncle Tom's Cabin, 196

Valdez, Miguelito Carlos Gonzales, 316
Valle Jorge, Delia Soto del, 342
Varnhagen, Rahel, 252
"Vera" (mistress of Lavrenti Beria), 326–327
Victoria, Queen of England, 96
Vietnam War, 190–194
violent relationships, Alfred Bloomingdale and Vicki, 394, 395; Ovid and Corinna, 25; Virginia Hill and Bugsy Siegel, 317–318, *see also* battered women
Virgin Mary, 175
"visitations" by Church officials, 147–149, 153
Voltaire (François Marie Arouet), 80, 81, 82, 83, 265–271; admiration for Émilie, 265, 267–268; influence of Émilie, 267–268, 270–271, 277; withdrawal from Émilie, 268–269; writings, 267

Wagner, Richard, 282
Wagner, Winifred, 241

Walston, Catherine, and Graham Greene, 293–304; influence on Greene, 293–294, 301, 303, 304; other lovers, 293, 295, 298, 300, 301–302; refusal to divorce, 296–297, 298–299, 300; replaced as Greene's mistress, 303
Walston, Harry, 294, 295, 297, 298–299, 300, 304
wartime mistresses, 190–194
Warwick, Daisy, 96, 97, 98
Waugh, Evelyn, 294
Weicker, Lowell, 295, 300
Weisker, Gertrude, 245
Welles, Orson, 355
Wharton, Edith, *The Age of Innocence*, 419–423
What a Widow (film), 364
widowers in ancient Rome, 21
William the Pious, 148–149
Williams, William, 187
Willis, Cornelia, 222
wills, 95, 201, 202, 208, 213–214, 292, 357, 461
wives, and concubines, 39, 40, 45, 46, 47; infertile, 10, 11, 39, 45–46; and mistresses, 1, 4, 5, 76, 294, 347, 437, 449; refusal to leave husband, 298, 299, 300, 439, 452
women, altered position today, 462; in ancient Greece, 14; in ancient Rome, 20–28; Roman Catholic views of, 7–8; in Roman Empire, 20–22
women's rights, 8, 44–45
Woolf, Virgina, 98
Wormald, Brian, 294, 303
Wu, Empress of China, 60
Wünsch (Austrian SS man), 233–234

Xenophon, 15–16
Xiang Fei, 37–38
Xue, General, 38–39

Yang Kuei-fei, 60
Yehenara, Lady, *see* Tz'u-hsi
Yu-Fang (a Chinese concubine), 38–39

ELIZABETH ABBOTT is Dean of Women at Trinity College, University of Toronto. A historian with a doctorate in 19th-century history, she has worked for over a decade as a journalist and writer with a special interest in social history and the environment. She was editor-in-chief of *Chronicle of Canada*, the bestselling illustrated history of Canada, and the author of *Haiti: The Duvaliers and Their Legacy* and *A History of Celibacy*.